ALEXANDER BARCLAY
THE FAMOUS CRONYCLE OF THE WARRE WHICH THE ROMAYNS HAD AGAYNST IUGURTH, USURPER OF THE KYNGDOME OF NUMIDY

SAz

EARLY ENGLISH TEXT SOCIETY
O.S. 344
2014

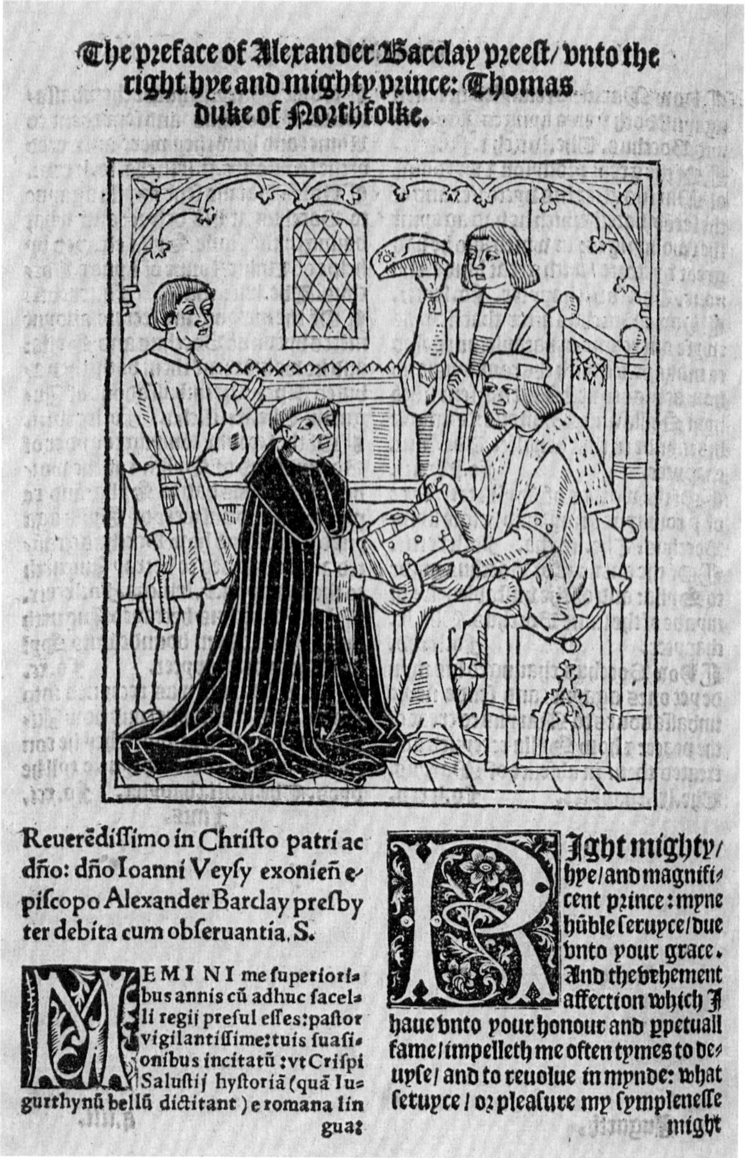

The preface of Alexander Barclay preest/ vnto the right hye and mighty prince: Thomas duke of Northfolke.

Reuerẽdissimo in Christo patri ac dño: dño Ioanni Veysy exonieñ episcopo Alexander Barclay presbyter debita cum obseruantia. S.

MEMINI me superioribus annis cũ adhuc sacelli regij presul esses: pastor vigilantissime: tuis suasionibus incitatũ: vt Crispi Salustij hystoriã (quã Iugurthynũ bellũ dictitant) e romana lingua:

Right mighty/ hye and magnificent prince: myne hũble seruyce/ due vnto your grace. And the vehement affection which I haue vnto your honour and ꝑpetuall fame/ impelleth me often tymes to deuyse/ and to reuolue in mynde: what seruyce/ or pleasure my symplenesse might

Oxford, Bodleian Library, F 6.10(3) Art., sig. a4v. Barclay presents his translation to Thomas, Duke of Norfolk.

ALEXANDER BARCLAY

THE FAMOUS CRONYCLE OF THE WARRE WHICH THE ROMAYNS HAD AGAYNST IUGURTH, USURPER OF THE KYNGDOME OF NUMIDY

Alexander Barclay's Translation
of Sallust's *Bellum Iugurthinum*

EDITED BY

GREG WAITE

Published for
THE EARLY ENGLISH TEXT SOCIETY
by the
OXFORD UNIVERSITY PRESS
2014

OXFORD
UNIVERSITY PRESS

Great Clarendon Street, Oxford OX2 6DP,
United Kingdom

Oxford University Press is a department of the University of Oxford.
It furthers the University's objective of excellence in research, scholarship,
and education by publishing worldwide. Oxford is a registered trade mark of
Oxford University Press in the UK and in certain other countries

First edition published in 2014
Impression: 1

British Library Cataloguing in Publication Data
Data available

ISBN 978-0-19-968819-7

Typeset by Anne Joshua, Oxford
Printed in Great Britain
on acid-free paper by
TJ International Ltd, Padstow, Cornwall

PREFACE

I prepared an electronic text of Barclay's translation of Sallust's *Iugurtha* some twenty years ago, and a decade later commenced work on a critical edition, comparing the three early print editions and taking into account Barclay's use of the Latin commentaries on Sallust's text available to him.

My thanks are due to those who have assisted and encouraged me over the years. Mary Sullivan, Catherine Waite, and Paul Sorrell participated in the keyboard entry and tagging at the outset. Later on, Jane Hollebon worked as my research assistant, helping with the collation of variant readings in the English text and the investigation of variations in the Latin texts and printed commentaries circulating in the fifty years between the appearance of the *editio princeps* and Barclay's text. Lastly, in 2009–10, Marie Hodgkinson worked for me on a University of Otago Summer Studentship, helping in the preparation of the notes.

In the course of the project I have been greatly assisted by the University of Otago, which has provided me with research funding and sabbatical leave at different times. To my colleagues in the Otago Department of English I am grateful for assistance of various kinds along the way, including questions and comments in the research seminars at which I have presented periodically. Particular thanks go to John Hale, Alistair Fox, and Evelyn Tribble.

Much of my work towards the project has been conducted while on leave in Oxford. Janet Wilson of Northampton University, a former colleague at Otago, has provided me with housing there and shared her expertise and experience in editing early modern texts. Members of the Oxford English Faculty, present and past, have made me welcome and assisted in various ways. I thank Douglas Gray, Eric Stanley, Vincent Gillespie, Malcolm Godden, Jane Griffiths, and especially Helen Spencer, Editorial Secretary of the Early English Text Society, copy-editor Bonnie Blackburn, and typesetter Anne Joshua. Thanks also go to Sarah Couper, for assistance both in Oxford and in Dunedin.

Of the libraries and librarians I have dealt with, the greatest debt of thanks goes to the Bodleian Library and its staff, particularly those working in Duke Humfrey's Library, where I ordered up the bulk of the early printed books that I needed to see and pursued various bibliographical inquiries. I acknowledge also the generosity of the librarians at Wolfson College, Exeter College, Corpus Christi College at Oxford (in particular Joanna Snelling), and Corpus Christi College at Cambridge (in particular Sub-librarian Gill Cannell) for opening their doors to me and answering queries from a distance. Thanks are also due to staff at the British Library, Cambridge University Library, the University Library at Austin, Texas, the Beinecke Library at Yale University and the Yale Centre for British Art (in particular Elisabeth Fairman), the University of Illinois Library at Urbana, the University of California Library at Los Angeles (in particular Carol Sommer), and the Chapin Library at Williams College, Williamstown. Mass. (in particular Wayne G. Hammond). The following repositories on the Continent provided microfilms, scanned images, and other forms of assistance for my work with the Latin Sallust editions, and to them I offer thanks: Bibliothèque Humaniste, Sélestat; Médiathèque de Troyes; Bibliothèque Municipale de Rouen; Sächsische Landesbibliothek: Staats- und Universitätsbibliothek, Dresden; and the Biblioteca Apostolica Vaticana, Vatican City.

G.W.

CONTENTS

LIST OF PLATES

ABBREVIATIONS

Editions of Barclay's Translation of Sallust

A (*BarcA* in notes)	Printed by Richard Pynson, [?1522] *STC* 21626
B (*BarcB* in notes)	Printed by Richard Pynson, [?1525] *STC* 21627
C (*BarcC* in notes)	Printed by John Waley, 1557 *STC* 10752

Early Editions of and Commentaries upon Sallust's *Bellum Jugurthinum*

AscT	Gaius Sallustius Crispus, *Crispus Salustius ab Ascensio familiariter explanatus* (Paris, 1504) [edited by and with commentary of Jodocus Badius Ascensius]. For text cited, where it differs from modern editions.
Asc	The commentary of Jodocus Badius Ascensius in the edition above.
Barc–Pynson	The Latin text of Sallust edited by Ascensius, as printed in *A* and *B* above.
Laet–BritT	Gaius Sallustius Crispus, *Opera* (Brescia, 1495) [edited by Pomponius Laetus, with revisions by Johannes Britannicus, and commentary on the *De bello Jugurthino* by Johannes Chrysostomus Soldus]. For text cited, where it differs from modern editions.
Sal	Sallust
Sold	The commentary of Johannes Chrysostomus Soldus in the 1495 edition above.
	Note: references to other editions of Sallust are given by date in boldface type. The editions in question are listed on pp. xxvi–xxxiv.

Modern Editions of Sallust's *Bellum Jugurthinum*

Comber–Balmaceda	*Sallust: The War against Jugurtha*, ed. and trans. Michael Comber and Catalina Balmaceda (Aris and Phillips Classical Texts; Oxford, 2009)
Kurfess	*Catilina, Iugurtha, Fragmenta Ampliora*, ed. Axel Wilhelm Ahlberg and Alfons Kurfess (Bibliotheca

	Scriptorum Graecorum et Romanorum Teubneriana, 3rd edn.; Leipzig, 1968)
Reynolds	*C. Sallusti Crispi, Catalina, Iugurtha, Historiarum Fragmenta Selecta, Appendix Sallustiana*, ed. L. D. Reynolds (Oxford Classical Authors; Oxford, 1991)
Rolfe	*Sallust with an English Translation*, ed. J. C. Rolfe (Loeb Classical Library, rev. edn.; Cambridge, Mass., 1931)

Other Abbreviations

BL	London, British Library
BnF	Paris, Bibliothèque nationale de France
Cont	Barclay's Table of Contents
CTC	*Catalogus Translationum et Commentariorum: Mediaeval and Renaissance Latin Translations and Commentaries. Annotated Lists and Guides*, vol. 8, ed. Virginia Brown, James Hankins, and Robert A. Kaster (Washington, 2003) [Sallust, pp. 183–326, contributed by Patricia J. Osmond and Robert W. Ulery, Jr.]
DOST	*Dictionary of the Older Scottish Tongue*
EETS	Early English Text Society
Extr	Barclay's Compendious Extract
F	French
Goff	Frederick Richmond Goff and Margaret Bingham Stillwell, *Incunabula in American Libraries: A Third Census of Fifteenth-Century Books Recorded in North American Collections* (New York, 1964)
Hodnett	Edward Hodnett, *English Woodcuts, 1480–1535* (London, 1935; repr. with Additions and Corrections, 1973)
ISTC	*Incunabula Short Title Catalogue*
Jamieson	Alexander Barclay, *The Ship of Fools*, ed. T. H. Jamieson, 2 vols. (Edinburgh, 1874)
Johnston	Stanley Howard Johnston, 'A Study of the Career and Literary Publications of Richard Pynson' (Ph.D. thesis, University of Western Ontario, 1977)
L	Latin
LPref	Barclay's Latin Preface

ME	Middle English
MED	*Middle English Dictionary*
ODNB	*Oxford Dictionary of National Biography* (Oxford, 2004)
OED	*Oxford English Dictionary*
OLD	*Oxford Latin Dictionary*
Paul	G. M. Paul, *A Historical Commentary on Sallust's Bellum Jugurthinum* (Liverpool, 1984)
Pref	Barclay's English Preface
Prol	Sallust's Prologue
Renouard	Philippe Renouard, *Bibliographie des impressions et des oeuvres de Josse Badius Ascensius, imprimeur et humaniste, 1462–1535*, 3 vols. (Paris, 1908; repr. New York, 1967)
Renouard *IP*	Philippe Renouard, *Répertoire des imprimeurs parisiens, libraires, foundeurs de caractères et correcteurs d'imprimerie, depuis l'introduction de l'imprimerie à Paris (1470) jusqu'à la fin du seizième siècle* (Paris, 1965)
STC	*Short-title Catalogue of Books Printed in England, Scotland, & Ireland, and of English Books Printed Abroad, 1475–1640* ed. A. W. Pollard and G. R. Redgrave; 2nd edn. revised and enlarged by W. A. Jackson, F. S. Ferguson, and Katharine F. Pantzer, 3 vols. (London, 1976–91)

INTRODUCTION

1. LIFE AND CAREER OF ALEXANDER BARCLAY

Alexander Barclay stands out as one of the major literary figures of his age, yet many details of his life remain unclear. Most biographers have dated his birth to 1475 or 1476, because in the Prologue to his *Eclogues*, some parts of which were composed in 1513 or 1514, he gives his age as 38. Nicholas Orme, however, has recently suggested that he was born in 1484 or a little earlier, pointing out that the Prologue itself may not have been composed as early as 1513–14, and that Barclay's ordination in 1508 would require his age then only to have been 24 at least.[1] Since the sixteenth century biographers have argued over Barclay's birthplace, England or Scotland, and his early life is obscure.[2] It is not known where he gained his degree: Anthony Wood claimed him for Oriel College, Oxford, and Thomas Warton linked him also with Cambridge, on the evidence of the first *Eclogue* (line 865).[3] He first appears in surviving documents from 1508, when

[1] Nicholas Orme, 'Barclay, Alexander (*c.*1484–1552)', in *ODNB*. See also David Carlson, 'Alexander Barclay (Circa 1475 – June 1552)', in David A. Richardson (ed.), *Sixteenth-Century British Nondramatic Writers: First Series*, Dictionary of Literary Biography, 132 (Detroit, 1993), 36–47. For an expansive treatment of Barclay's life and works see *The Eclogues of Alexander Barclay*, ed. Beatrice White, EETS OS 175 (London, 1928). See also *The Ship of Fools*, ed. T. H. Jamieson, 2 vols. (Edinburgh, 1874); John Richie Schultz, 'The Life of Alexander Barclay', *Journal of English and Germanic Philology*, 18 (1919), 360–8; L. S. Colchester, 'Alexander Barclay', *Modern Language Review*, 37 (1942), 198; William Nelson, 'New Light on Alexander Barclay', *Review of English Studies*, 19 (1943), 59–61; R. J. Lyall, 'Alexander Barclay and the Edwardian Reformation 1548–1552', *Review of English Studies*, NS 20 (1969), 455–61; Nicholas Orme, 'Alexander Barclay, Tudor Educationalist', in *Education and Society in Medieval and Renaissance England* (London, 1989), 259–70.

[2] See *The Eclogues*, ed. White, pp. i–xvi, for details. John Bale's informants were divided over Barclay's nationality: see *Scriptorum illustrium maioris Brytanniæ summarium* (Basel, 1557–9) cent. 9 no. 66 (p. 723). Bale himself resiles from his earlier statement in the *Illustrium Maioris Britanniæ Scriptorum . . .* (Wesel, 1548), f. 254^{v}, where he describes Barclay as 'Scotus, rhetor ac poeta insignis'. Nevertheless, William Bulleyn, who was a native of Ely and may have known Barclay, asserts that 'He was borne beyonde the cold river of Twede' in his *Dialogue . . . against the Fever Pestilence* [London, 1564]. Alistair Fox cites *Collyn Clout*, lines 749–51 as hitherto unnoticed evidence that Skelton regarded Barclay as a Scot. See *Politics and Literature in the Reigns of Henry VII and Henry VIII* (Oxford, 1989), 49. If indeed Skelton was thinking of Barclay in his reference to an Observant Franciscan who is a 'poore Scot', then it may be that Barclay's change of religious order occurred as early as 1521–2.

[3] Anthony Wood, *Athenæ Oxonienses*, 2 vols. (London, 1691–92), i, cols. 205–9. Wood's claim for Oriel is based solely upon the circumstantial evidence that Barclay's patron

in March and April he was ordained subdeacon, deacon, and priest at Exeter Cathedral, having moved from the diocese of Lincoln. Immediately following his ordination, he took employment at the collegiate church of Ottery Saint Mary in Devon, where, as *cappellanus*, he taught and trained the choirboys. Scattered references in his own writings have led scholars to surmise that he spent some years on the Continent prior to his ordination. In his first published work, *The Shyp of Folys* (1509), Barclay claims to have been 'a scoler longe: and that in dyuers scoles'.[4] Some other observations suggest that he was familiar with affairs at Paris, and his command of French is clear. If he in fact resided in Paris before his ordination, it is possible that he became acquainted with Josse Bade (Badius Ascensius), who had moved there from Lyon in 1499 and set up his own press in 1503. Several of Barclay's works, including the *Jugurtha* translation, are based upon editions produced by Bade, and Barclay's interest in translating the work of the Carmelite friar Battista Spagnoli 'Mantuanus' may have been inspired by Bade's promotion of his works. Bade and Barclay seem to have shared an admiration for those Italian humanists who combined classical eloquence with Christian themes, and both were reverent towards traditions evolved in the Middle Ages.[5]

It is remarkable that Barclay's known literary output spans only about fifteen years of his long life. While residing at Ottery Saint Mary he completed *The Shyp of Folys* (1509; *STC* 3545), a translation of Sebastian Brant's *Narrenschiff* (1494), working primarily from the Latin and French translations, but also (or so Barclay claims) from

Thomas Cornish was Provost of the College 1493–1507. Thomas Warton, *The History of English Poetry, from the Close of the Eleventh to the Commencement of the Eighteenth Century* (London, 1774), 240.

[4] *This present boke named the shyp of folys of the worlde* . . . R. Pynson, 1509, *STC* 3545 (sig. a6); Jamieson, 3.

[5] Given the prestige and substantial output of Bade's press, however, it need not be the case that Barclay's choices were based upon personal acquaintance or influence. Both men share common ground as religious conservatives, leaning towards humanism, but in some ways still rooted in late medieval traditions of education. See Mark I. Crane, 'A Conservative Voice in the French Renaissance: Josse Bade (1462–1535)' (Ph.D. thesis, Toronto, 2005). The translation of *The Castle of Labour*, printed about 1503 in Paris by Vérard (*STC* 12379), has also been taken as evidence of Barclay's residence in Paris, but John Bale's attribution of the work to him is doubtful. It is unfortunate that only two imperfect copies, lacking beginning and end, remain of Richard Pynson's 1528(?) reprint (*STC* 12382), for he would surely have named Barclay as author in any colophon, if such were the case, following the success of the *Shyp of Folys* in 1509, even if he had no reason to know the author when publishing his 1505 edition (*STC* 12380).

the original German version. It is unclear when Barclay left Ottery, but it may have been in 1511, when Thomas Cornish, suffragan Bishop of Bath and Wells, who had ordained him, retired as Warden of the College. Neville, however, suggests that he resigned his post at Ottery in 1509 and travelled to London in order to see *The Shyp* through the press.[6]

By 1513 Barclay was a Benedictine monk at the cathedral priory of Ely, where he probably produced the bulk of his literary output, although one other possible title composed before his move to Ely is *The Gardener's Passetaunce Touchyng the Outrage of Fraunce* [1512?] (*STC* 11562.5), which has been attributed to him, and may be the same work as the otherwise unknown *Figure of Our Mother Holy Church Oppressed by the French King* attributed to Barclay in Andrew Maunsell's 1595 *Catalogue of English Printed Books* (*STC* 17669).[7] Barclay's next known work appears to have been *The Tower of Virtue and Honour* (1514?), although this survives only as an insertion into his fourth *Eclogue*, of which the earliest printing to survive is Pynson's edition ([1521?] *STC* 1384b). *The Tower* is an allegory memorializing Edward Howard, who died in a naval battle against the French off Brest in 1513, and it is the first of several works in which Barclay honours Edward's father, Thomas Howard, newly created Duke of Norfolk (1 February 1514), after his victory at Flodden on 9 September 1513.

Barclay may have begun work upon his *Eclogues* as early as 1509, and probably completed an early version by 1514. The first three *Eclogues*, which deal with the miseries of a courtier's life, are translated from or based upon the Latin prose epistle *De curialium miseriis* by Enea Silvio Piccolomini (before his election as Pope Pius II in 1458), addressed to the German humanist Johannes Eich. The fourth eclogue, *The boke of Codrus and Mynalcas*, based upon Mantuan's fifth eclogue, is first attested in Pynson's edition of *c.*1521, but must have appeared considerably earlier, for the fifth eclogue *The cytezen and uplondyshman* (based upon Mantuan's sixth) is found in Wynken de Worde's printing of *c.*1518.[8] We can only conjecture that the first editions of the Eclogues were probably printed earlier by Pynson. Barclay's interest in the writings of

[6] Pamela Ayers Neville, 'Richard Pynson, King's Printer (1506–1529): Printing and Propaganda in Early Tudor England' (Ph.D. thesis, University of London, 1990), 200.

[7] See Carlson, 'Alexander Barclay (Circa 1475 – June 1552)', 42.

[8] *The fyfte eglog of Alexandre Barclay of the cytezen and uplondyshman*, *STC* 1385.

recent Italian humanists is evidenced further in *The Myrrour of Good Maners* (*c.*1518), a translation of Domenico Mancini's *De quattuor virtutibus* (1484).[9]

The Life of Saynt George (completed in August 1515 and probably printed shortly after) is extant in a single copy, and is the sole survivor of a number of saints' lives he appears to have composed.[10] John Bale attributes lives of Etheldreda, Catherine, and Margaret to Barclay.[11] The *Saynt George* is based upon a Latin life by Mantuan, who also produced lives of Catherine and Margaret. The work is dedicated to Thomas Howard, and the first known to carry the woodcut presentation scene depicting Barclay and his patron, which later appears in the *Jugurtha* (see Frontispiece).

The *Introductory to wryte, and to pronounce frenche* (STC 1386) was printed by Robert Copland in March 1521. It bears a dedicatory statement resembling that addressed to Norfolk in the 1515 *Saynt George* and in the 1522 *Jugurtha*, claiming to have been composed 'compendiously at the commaundement of the ryght hye excellent and myghty prynce Thomas duke of Northfolke'. Indeed, it carries on the title page a woodcut nearly identical to that which precedes Barclay's *Jugurtha*, showing the lion (Norfolk) ravaging the armorial lion of Scotland, under which Coplande set his 'ballade' 'R. Coplande to the whyte lyon' (Howard):

> Lyon tresdigne des bestes souuerain
> Reluisant/ et pur/ en couleur dargent
> Ton renom sespand es pais loingtain
> Redoubte est ta fureur rugient
> Monstre tu as ta gloire excellent
> Triumphant victor sus les albanois
> Le lyon vermail a prins diffinement
> Par ta noblesse desoubz la rouge crois
> Duc puissant/ dhonneur magnifique
> Autentique/ en noblesse triumphant
> Tresuaillant/ darmes politique
> Pacifique/ en vertus flourissant

9 *Here begynneth a ryght frutefull treatyse, intituled the myrrour of good maners, conteynyng the .iiii. vertues, R. Pynson, at the instance of Rychard yerle of kent* [1518?], *STC* 17242.

10 *Here begynnyth the lyfe of the gloryous martyr saynt George* [R. Pynson, 1515?], *STC* 22992.1.

11 Jamieson, *The Ship of Fools*, p. cix, following Bliss's note to the 1813 edition of Wood's *Athenæ Oxonienses*, also attributes *The Lyfe of the Blessed Martyr Saynte Thomas* (Pynson, 1520? *STC* 23954) to Barclay. The text, however, is an extract from Caxton's translation of Voragine's *Legenda Aurea* (Caxton, 1483; *STC* 24873).

Lion bruyant/ et bray defendant
De leglise/ & la sainte foy
Chescun te voyant/ te vont appellant
Amy de dieu/ amateur de ton roy.

Pynson's woodcut was probably in existence in 1513.[12] It is therefore puzzling to find Copland printing this work, copying Pynson's woodcut, and using a dedication closely modelled on that found in Pynson's printing of the *Saynt George*. If the *Introductory* had been offered to Pynson but passed over to Copland, it seems plausible that Pynson would have loaned the latter his woodcut. If Barclay had bypassed Pynson for some other reason, it is difficult to understand the circumstances, given that he returned to Pynson for the production of the *Jugurtha* the following year. To Barclay's *Introductory* Copland appended his translation 'out of Frenche' (although no source has been found): *The maner of dauncynge of bace daunces after the vse of Fraunce*. One wonders if this entire concoction (perhaps unauthorized) was based upon a lost edition of Barclay's *Introductory*, and whether this edition or its possible precursor were in some way connected with the Field of Cloth of Gold and Anglo–French diplomatic affairs in 1520.

Barclay's translation of Sallust's *Bellum Jugurthinum* is noteworthy as one of the earliest major translations of a classical author into English, and as a departure by Barclay himself from literary composition in verse.[13] It is not clear when Barclay commenced work upon the translation, and the twin prefaces provide seemingly conflicting accounts of how it originated.[14] In addressing the first dedicatee, John Veysey, Bishop of Exeter from 1519, Barclay states that he began the work at Veysey's own urging 'cum adhuc sacelli regii presul esses', that is perhaps as early as 1515, when Henry VIII appointed Veysey as Dean of St George's Chapel, Windsor.[15] In his dedication to Thomas Howard, however, in the English preface printed in parallel with the Latin, he states that 'I haue reuolued

[12] See p. lxi.

[13] For a survey of translations see H. B. Lathrop, *Translations from the Classics into English from Caxton to Chapman, 1477–1620* (Madison, Wis., 1933); also Stephen Medcalf, 'Classical Authors', in Roger Ellis (ed.), *The Oxford History of Literary Translation in English*, i: *To 1550* (Oxford, 2008), 364–89.

[14] Nelson discusses the seeming oddity of twin dedicatory prefaces in *Jugurtha* and in *St. George* in his edition of the latter, *The Life of St. George*, ed. William Nelson, EETS OS 230 (London, 1955).

[15] On Veysey see Nicholas Orme, 'Veysey [*formerly* Harman], John (*c.*1464–1554), bishop of Exeter', *ODNB*. Barclay's acquaintance with Veysey probably began in 1508.

many and dyuerse volumes/ stodyng of which one: the translatyon: might corespond with your noble estat'. Perhaps the title-page statement that the work was translated 'at commaundement of the right hye and mighty prince: Thomas duke of Northfolke' cannot therefore be taken as a prescription for *Jugurtha* specifically.

It has not been widely noticed that the *Jugurtha* was probably Barclay's last publication. A detail overlooked by some recent writers on Barclay is the *Short Title Catalogue* (second edition) *corrigendum*, revising the printing date of the *Jugurtha* from 1520(?), found in *STC2* volume 1, to 1522(?). The internal evidence of Barclay's prefaces supports the typographical.[16] The revised dating extends Barclay's known literary career and possibly his ambitions for advancement somewhat beyond the time of the meetings of Henry VIII and Francis I at the so-called Field of Cloth of Gold, in May and June of 1520. Cardinal Wolsey's agent Sir Nicholas Vaux wrote from France on 10 April 1520 requesting the attendance of 'Maistre Barkleye, the black monke and poete, to devise histoires and convenient raisons to florisshe the buildings and banquet house withal'.[17] There is no evidence, however, that Barclay went to France, or that his departure from Ely can be connected with these events. It seems probable that he left rather to join the Franciscans, a move that appears linked to the abandonment of his literary career. Whether that was shortly after the printing of the *Jugurtha* around 1522, or after the release of the second edition around 1525, is unclear.[18] The revisions of the second edition are on the whole minor, and need not have involved Barclay himself. It is possible that following the commercial success of the first edition, Pynson instigated a reprinting after Barclay had joined the Observant Franciscans, although documentary evidence of the latter's Franciscan career only dates from 1528. The reprinting may be connected with the death of Thomas Howard in 1524, but there is no change to the prefatory matter to mark his decease.

[16] Lathrop, *Translations*, concluded that the Latin dedication to John Veysey, Bishop of Exeter, 'Ex cellula Hatfeldensis regii, in Idus Nouembris' (the second edition reads 'iij Idus Nouembris') cannot be earlier than Nov. 1520, but Veysey was granted the temporalities of the see on 4 Nov. 1519, and the archbishop of Canterbury consecrated him at Otford, Kent, on the 6th, so it is just possible that the preface might date from 1519. The English preface, dedicated to Thomas Howard, sets the *terminus ante quem*, since he died on 21 May 1524.

[17] *Letters and Papers of the Reign of Henry VIII*, ed. J. S. Brewer and R. H. Brodie, 21 vols. in 37, (London, 1862–1932), iii, no. 737.

[18] See n. 2 above for a possible indicator of the date.

It appears that Barclay's time as a Franciscan was somewhat turbulent. Writing to Cardinal Wolsey from Cologne in October 1528, the informer Hermann Rinck included Barclay in his list of apostates from the Observant Order of Saint Francis who ought to be arrested and punished for their adherence to Lutheran heresy. Rinck, however, may be mistaken in his connection of Barclay with the outspoken anti-papists William Roy and Jerome Barlow; and perhaps Barclay's time in Germany was spent in studying theology for a doctor's degree. The English Observant houses were suppressed in 1534, and in 1535 Barclay is recorded as receiving an annuity of £4 from Launceston Priory, where, Orme suggests, he was possibly employed to provide the preaching and lecturing to religious houses required by the crown.[19] Following the 1536 suppression of the Conventual Houses, into which most Observant Friars had been absorbed, Barclay apparently pursued a course of defiance of Henry's statutes, as a series of events in London, Suffolk, and Cornwall in 1538 demonstrate. He only put off his Friar's cowl at this time under threats of hanging. Nevertheless he appears to have suffered no serious repercussions, for in 1546 he was appointed vicar of Wookey (Somerset) and in January 1549 moved to Great Baddow in Essex to take up the position of vicar there, while retaining his Wookey living. Before he could take up a wealthier living in 1552 as rector of All Hallows, Lombard Street, London, he died early in June, in Croydon, Surrey.

Barclay's Relationship with his Printer, Richard Pynson

As the outline of his publications suggests, Barclay's relationship with Richard Pynson (*c*.1449–1529/30) provides an interesting case of author and publisher sharing a long and fruitful partnership. David Carlson observes that Barclay fulfilled a range of roles in this 'thorough-going, long-lived collaboration' as 'propagandist, poet, translator, [and] technical hack'.[20] Except for the *Introductory*, Pynson may have printed the first editions of all Barclay's extant works, beginning in 1509 with *The Shyp of Folys* and ending with the second edition of *Jugurtha*. A distinctive feature of most of Barclay's books is their bilingualism, with the original Latin texts set alongside Barclay's English translations. In *The Shyp of Folys* the texts are set

[19] Orme, 'Barclay, Alexander (*c*.1484–1552)', *ODNB*.

[20] David Carlson, 'Alexander Barclay and Richard Pynson: A Tudor Printer and his Writer', *Anglia*, 113 (1993), 283–302 at 302.

out 'alternatim' (as Barclay puts it), with each section of Jacob Locher's Latin version followed by Barclay's corresponding English. Although he claims to have 'translated out of Laten, Frenche, and Doche into Englysse' (sig. b4), Barclay worked primarily from Locher's Latin adaptation of Sebastian Brant's *Narrenschiff* of 1494 rather than the original German. He also made some use of Riviere's 1497 French verse paraphrase.[21] Barclay's other books, however, employ parallel columns of English and Latin.[22] He claims to be the instigator of this format (rather than Pynson), referring to its provision 'meo more' ('according to my customary practice') in his preface to the *Jugurtha* (Latin Preface, l. 29). He attributes the original idea to his patron Thomas Cornish in the prefatory letter attached to the *Shyp* in 1509: 'Ut tua consuluerit paternitas, autoris carmina cum meis vulgaribus rithmicis una alternatim coniunxi' (sig. +1^{v}). No doubt the practice appealed to Pynson as a bookseller, since the format would attract two kinds of buyer simultaneously, those who are 'lerned and understande Latyn' on one hand and 'many noble gentylmen which understand nat Latyn tong perfetly' on the other, as Barclay explains in the *Jugurtha* preface (ll. 36–7). Furthermore, the books were skilfully set with the English in Textura and the Latin in Roman type (see Pl. 1). Most are spacious and attractive in their appearance, and provided with at least some illustrations. Pynson used a distinctive woodcut author-portrait exclusively for Barclay, beginning with the 1515 *Lyfe of the Gloryous Martyr Saynt George*, showing a black monk (Barclay) presenting a book to a seated nobleman patron (probably intended to represent Thomas Howard, at whose 'commaundement' both the *Saynt George* and the *Jugurtha* were produced).[23]

[21] See Aurelius Pompen, *The English Version of the Ship of Fools: A Contribution to the History of the Early French Renaissance in England* (London, 1925), 311.

[22] On this phenomenon see further Daniel Wakelin, 'Possibilities for Reading: Classical Translations in Parallel Texts ca. 1520–1558', *Studies in Philology*, 105 (2008), 463–86.

[23] See frontispiece; also Edward Hodnett, *English Woodcuts 1480–1535* (Oxford, 1973), no. 1498, and his reproduction, fig. 147.

¶ What ſorowe and heuynes was at Rome: and how they demeaned thẽſelfe in the cite aft that tidyngẽ herof were broght thyder. The.xxvi.cha.

Whan the Romayns vnderſtode of this at Rome / all the cytie was fylled with drede / ſorowe / lamentacyon / and mournyng. Some bewayled the worſhyppe of thẽpyre as loſt by that ſhamefull composicyon: And other vncuſtomed to ſuche beſyneſſe of batayle and nat knowyng nor conſydringe the varyable mutabylite of chaunces of warre feredde the loſſe of their lybertie / of their cyte / & of all their empyre. They all were wrothe and vtterly dyſpleaſed with Aulus / cauſe of this ſubiection and ſhamefull compoſicion. But namely they which had ben good warryours in their dayes were dyſpleaſed with hym mooſt of all: whan they conſydred that he beyng armed and well apoynted to batayle rather ſought meanes to eſcape from dethe by ſuche ſhamefull and bonde compoſicyon than manly abyding the extremyte of batayle to haue delyuered hymſelfe and his company: or els valyantly to haue dyed with honoure. But the conſull Albynus / hymſelfe dreded ſore for theſe thynges conſydring that for his brothers faute in tyme to cõe he ſhulde nat auoyde the dyſpleſure of the ſenatours and cõmens of Rome. For as he cõiectured all his brothers dedes ſhulde redounde to his dyſhonour and parylI / bycauſe he had lymited hym in Numidy in his ſtede to be captayn of the army in his abſence. Wherfore (theſe thynges duely aduyſed) he went to the ſenatours deſyring them to take coũſell and aduyſement whyther they wolde approbate and allowe the ſayd compoſicion bytwene his brother Aulus and Jugurth: or els nat. But he knewe ryght well before that the ſenatours wolde nat conferme the ſame. Wherfore (in meane tyme whyle they were counſelling) he elect ſoudyours for ſupplement to fulfyll and parforme agayne the army whiche was in Affrike / & ſore demyniſſhed. For many of them were ſlayne by Jugurth and his cõpany. Wherfore Albinus rayſed vp ſocours of ſuche as were ney to ỹ coſtes of Rome / and frendes to thẽpire: as Latinyans & Italyans with other nacyons. Of theſe he rayſed as many as he myght / and aſſẽbled them togyder by all meanes which he coude deuyſe to fornyſſhe and augment his army.

At concluſyon the ſenatours decreed in their counſell that no

¶ Sed vbi ea Romæ cõperta ſunt: metus atque meror ciuitatem inuaſere. Pars dolere pro gloria impij: pars inſoliti bellicarum rerum timere libertati.

Aulo omnes īfeſti: ac maxime qui bello p̄clari ſepe fuerāt ꝙ armatus dedecore potiusq̄ manu ſalutem queſiuerat.

Ob ea conſul Albinus ex delicto fratris inuidiam ac deinde periculum timens ſenatum de fœdere conſulebat: tamen exercitui interim ſupplementum ſcribere.

A ſocijs et nomine latino auxilia accerſere: denique omnibus modis feſtinare.

Senatus (vti par fuerat)

Pl. 1. Oxford, Bodleian Library, F 6.10(3) Art., f. 35r, Barclay's translation. Reproduced by permission of the Bodleian Libraries, University of Oxford

2. SALLUST, HIS *OPERA*, AND THEIR RECEPTION IN THE MIDDLE AGES AND RENAISSANCE

Gaius Sallustius Crispus was born *c.*86 BC at Amiternum, perhaps of plebeian origins.[24] Having entered the Senate at some point prior to 52, he became in that year Tribune of the plebs. Although Sallust was expelled from the Senate in 50, Caesar reappointed him to a quaestorship in 49, and in 48 he commanded a legion in Illyricum, without distinction. His mission in 47 to calm the mutinous legions in Campania nearly led to his death at the hands of the troops, but his expedition the following year, to capture enemy stores on the island of Circina, off the African coast, was successful and strategically important in Caesar's campaign. He was rewarded with the post of proconsular governor of *Africa Nova*. Upon Caesar's death he retired from political life in order to write. The *Bellum Catilinae* appeared around 42, and the *Bellum Jugurthinum* perhaps two years later. At the time of his death in 35 or 34 BC, Sallust had completed five books of his *Historiae*, describing the events of the years 78 to 67 BC. Only fragments of the latter work survive, either as excerpted rhetorical set pieces, or as quotations in the works of later historians.

Sallust was attacked both for his personal conduct when in office, and later for his historiographical method and writing style. Nevertheless, his reputation, and the number of his admirers and imitators grew. Martial wrote of him, 'primus Romana Crispus in historia' (*Epigrammata* 14. 191. 2). The 'monographs', as they have come to be termed, represented a significant innovation in historiography at the time, and are noteworthy for their forceful moral judgements on the parties described and more generally on the Roman state. Tacitus was an admirer, and much in his own method can be traced to Sallust, including the sceptical and critical view of Roman politics. Saint Augustine described Sallust as 'nobilitatae veritatis historicus' (*De civitate Dei* 1. 5) and drew upon his predecessor's work for his own moralistic depiction of corruption and discord as the successors to peace, security, and wealth in the declining pagan Empire.

Sallust forged a distinctive style, drawing on Cato for some archaisms in vocabulary and phrasing, but also striving for novelty along with brevity and compression of expression: that is, saying much in few words. Although standing in stark contrast to Cicero's writings stylistically, his works became important in the school

[24] See Ronald Syme, *Sallust* (Cambridge, 1964).

curriculum, where the fictional speeches of historical figures could be excerpted and studied as rhetorical exercises in their own right. F. R. D. Goodyear sums up his position eloquently:

> By his fierce individualism he won a firmer place in the Roman educational tradition than the temperate and compromising Livy ever attained. He, more than anyone, prevented the style and attitudes of Cicero from becoming canonical for prose-writing in general, he enriched the Latin language at a time when it was most in danger of impoverishment, and he secured the continuation at Rome of the stern and uncompromising tradition of historiography, created by Thucydides, which rhetoricians and romantics alike would happpily have discarded.[25]

Sallust was known and studied in many medieval schools, where interest peaked in the twelfth century, but his work was revived later as part of the humanist curriculum.[26] Perhaps the only surprising aspect of Barclay's undertaking is the fact that he took up the *Bellum Jugurthinum* rather than the *Bellum Catilinae*, for the latter was more widely read, and perhaps more consonant with Barclay's moralizing focus. If, as he claims in his Preface, the work was first begun at John Veysey's urging, Barclay may well have planned or even begun to translate the *Catilina* as well. Nevertheless he was aware of the universal appeal of Sallust, and perhaps was conscious of the fact that the *Jugurtha* would prove more palatable for the secular audience he later envisaged as his readership, consisting of gentlemen and soldiers, with the Duke of Norfolk his patron at their head; for as Barclay observes in the preface addressed to Norfolk, the victor of Flodden had 'proued . . . like vnto mighty Marius', the victor in the Jugurthine War. Furthermore, there seems to have been a particular current interest in sources dealing with military tactics and methods, and as Daniel Wakelin notes, 'English humanists often glossed the military vocabulary in their classical texts, as if it were especially difficult; and the readers of English and French translations of Vegetius, or Frontinus too, did likewise'.[27]

[25] F. R. D. Goodyear, 'Sallust', in E. J. Kenney (ed.) and W. V. Clausen (advisory ed.), *The Cambridge History of Classical Literature*, ii: *Latin Literature* (Cambridge, 1982), 268–80 at 280.

[26] See Beryl Smalley, 'Sallust in the Middle Ages' in R. R. Bolgar (ed.), *Classical Influences on European Culture A.D. 500–1500: Proceedings of an International Conference Held at King's College, Cambridge, April 1969* (Cambridge, 1971), 165–75; Patricia J. Osmond and Robert W. Ulery, 'Sallustius', in *CTC* viii. 183–326.

[27] Daniel Wakelin, *Humanism, Reading, and English Literature, 1430–1530* (Oxford, 2007), 83 n. 62: 'For example, Oxford, Balliol College, MS 121, f. iv$^{r–v}$ (list of Roman

Barclay's formative years undoubtedly included classroom exposure to samples of the surviving writings of Sallust, but probably as mediated through the conservative and traditional framework of education such as had existed since the eleventh century, by which time copies of the two historical monographs were to be found in a number of monastic libraries, following renewed dissemination in the Carolingian period.[28] Beryl Smalley argues that 'the Middle Ages knew three aspects of Sallust . . . [f]irst comes the moralist, second the stylistic model, as studied in the arts course, and third the historian'. The three aspects are nevertheless heavily intertwined, for as Smalley points out, Orosius, the simplifier and popularizer of Augustine's moral history, and Sallust himself were the 'twin keys to medieval historiography', and 'boys learned their history in ancient and medieval classrooms alike in the margin of grammar and rhetoric'. That is, history, like mythology, served to explicate literary texts, and writers like Sallust 'supplied a quarry of *exempla* for the orator to draw upon'.[29]

Throughout the Renaissance Sallust was much read, and his work appealed to a wide variety of readers 'ranging from students and scholars to princes and military captains, political thinkers, and theologians'.[30] His reputation as historian did not diminish, and the emergence of texts hitherto virtually unknown in medieval Europe, such as the works of Tacitus, whose style and historiography were profoundly influenced by Sallust, served only to throw his importance into sharper relief.[31] Furthermore, his prestige as a moralist continued unabated. As a stylist he also remained influential in the school curriculum, although some extreme Ciceronian disciples viewed his influence on pupils as problematic, and suggested that he be reserved for advanced study only.[32] Nevertheless, his popularity

officers of state; Valerius Maximus owned by Richard Bole); Oxford, Balliol College, MS 123, ff. 159^{v}–167^{v} (glossary, with many military words; Sallust, owned by Richard Bole); BL, MS Additional 12028, f. 170^{v} (glossary to Frontinus in French); OMC, MS lat. 30, ff. 35^{v}–36^{r}, f. 45^{r}, f. 47^{r}, f. 54^{r}, f. 56^{v}, and CUL, MS Additional 8706, f. 30^{v}, described in *n.* 29 in Chapter 1 above.'

[28] Over 500 Sallust manuscripts are known. See L. D. Reynolds, 'Sallust, in id. (ed.), *Texts and Transmission: A Survey of the Latin Classics*, corr. repr. (Oxford, 1986), 345.

[29] Smalley, 'Sallust in the Middle Ages', 165 and 168.

[30] Osmond and Ulery, 'Sallustius', 196.

[31] For a survey of the manuscript witnesses to Tacitus and an outline of his rediscovery in the 15th c. see Michael Winterbottom, 'Tacitus', in Reynolds (ed.), *Texts and Transmission*, 406–11.

[32] Robert M. Stein, 'Sallust for his Readers, 410–1550: A Study in the Formation of the Classical Tradition' (Ph.D. diss., Columbia University, 1977).

persisted, and his work was read with growing awareness of and sensitivity to his stylistic idiosyncrasies. Following the publication of the *editio princeps* in 1470, Sallust remained one of the most published of ancient historians into the seventeenth century. As Osmond and Ulery conclude, the ready market for his *Opera* was based in part upon his eminent practical relevance. His monographs stimulated imitation of style and structure by historians, and were frequently excerpted for a myriad of purposes:

> Schoolboys and statesmen alike made collections of Sallustian sententiae and exempla, while speeches and letters, often extracted from his texts, and included in large compendia, served as models for rhetoricians, ambassadors, army commanders, and (as we are told by their political opponents) aspiring rebels.[33]

In England, the leaders of the humanist movement confirmed the place of Sallust in education and higher letters. Erasmus frequently quotes him in his letters and rhetorical works, and considered that his style should be studied to instil *brevitas*, where Cicero's could not.[34] In a letter to William Gonell, tutor to his children, Thomas More reveals how Sallust is a standard part of their curriculum:

> Do you, my learned Gonell, have the kindness to see that my daughters study thoroughly the works of those holy men [Jerome and Augustine]. From them they will learn in particular what end they should propose to themselves in their studies and what is the fruit of their endeavours, namely the witness of God and a good conscience. . . . If you will teach something of this sort, in addition to their lesson in Sallust, to Margaret and Elizabeth, as being more advanced than John and Cecily, you will bind me and them still more to you. And thus you will bring about that my children, who are dear to me by nature, and still more dear by learning and virtue, will become most dear by their advance in knowledge and good conduct.[35]

John Colet's school at St Paul's, which set the pattern for English grammar schools in the sixteenth century, was founded upon Erasmian principles, and its curriculum built from the list of authors given by Erasmus in his *De Ratione Studii*. Among the Latins, he specified Terence for speaking, with the addition of

[33] Osmond and Ulery, 'Sallustius', 196. See also the comparative tables in Patricia J. Osmond, 'Princeps Historiae Romanae: Sallust in Renaissance Political Thought', *Memoirs of the American Academy in Rome*, 40 (1995), 101–43 at 132–8.

[34] Stein, 'Sallust for his Readers', 162–3.

[35] *The Yale Edition of the Works of St. Thomas More*, i (New Haven, 1961), 105–6.

those comedies of Plautus which are not obscene; then Virgil, Horace, Cicero, Caesar, and Sallust, 'atque hos quidem ad utriusque linguae cognitionem satis esse duco'.[36]

Alistair Fox observes, not unfairly, that 'Barclay was the kind of man who was influenced by the practices of humanism without ever understanding its aims or imbibing its spirit'.[37] Be this as it may, it is probable that prior to his work of translation, Barclay would have been familiar with some of the humanist scholarship on Sallust, and his importance in the new learning. Indeed the Benedictine house at Ely that he entered had been the home of predecessors with some interest in humanism, and also in Sallust, whose popularity had flagged somewhat by the fourteenth century. Among the surviving manuscripts of the humanist Richard Bole, at Ely from 1467 until his death in 1477, there is a copy of Sallust's monographs, written in his own humanist hand, and a commentary on the *Catiline* and *Jugurtha* also in his hand.[38] Bole was the assistant of William Gray, Bishop of Ely from 1454, and another scholar with humanist interests. If Barclay had no access to such resources early in his education, he came into contact eventually with the new printed editions with appended commentaries that proliferated from 1490, when Lorenzo Valla's commentary on *Catiline* first appeared in print.

3. SELECTED LIST OF SALLUST EDITIONS TO 1521

Bibliographers from the eighteenth century to the present have recorded over 120 editions of Sallust's *Jugurtha* for the period 1470 to 1521.[39] Listed below are those editions mentioned in the introduc-

[36] Desiderius Erasmus, *Opera Omnia . . .*, i/1, ed. J. C. Margolin (Amsterdam, 1971), 116. On grammar schools in England see T. W. Baldwin, *Willam Shakespere's Small Latine & Lesse Greeke*, 2 vols. (Urbana, Ill., 1944); Nicholas Orme, *Education and Society in Medieval and Renaissance England* (London, 1989).

[37] Alistair Fox, 'Facts and Fallacies: Interpreting English Humanism', in Alistair Fox and John Guy (eds.), *Reassessing the Henrician Age: Humanism, Politics and Reform 1500–1550* (Oxford, 1986), 9–33 at 11.

[38] See further p. xxxvii below.

[39] See F. L. A. Schweiger, *Handbuch der classischen Bibliographie*, 2 vols. in 3 (Leipzig, 1830–4); J.-C. Brunet, *Manuel du libraire et d'amateur de livres*, 8 vols. (Paris, 1860–78); G. W. Panzer, *Annales Typographici*, 11 vols. (Nuremberg, 1793–1803); Friedrich A. Ebert, *Allgemeines bibliographisches Lexikon*, 2 vols. (Leipzig, 1821–30), J. G. Th. Graesse, *Trésor des livres rares et précieux*, 7 vols. in 8 (Dresden, 1859–69); *ISTC* and *CTC*. A. Pettegree and M. Walsby, *French Books III & IV: Books Published in France Before 1601 in Latin and Languages Other than French* (Leiden, 2011).

tion that have a particular bearing upon establishing the source texts that Barclay used, together with some other key editions for the history of the text in the fifteenth and early sixteenth centuries.

Early Editions

1470.1 Venice: Videlinus de Spira [Windelin of Speyer]. The *editio princeps*, containing the *Catilina* and the *Iugurtha*. ISTC is00051000. Goff S51. Copy consulted: Oxford, Bodleian Library Auct. L 5.20.

1470.2 [Italy: Printer of Sallustius *Opera*]. *Opera* [*Cat.* and *Iug.*]. ISTC is00552000. Goff S52. Copy consulted: London, BL G.9127.

1471 [Paris: Ulrich Gering, Martin Crantz, and Michael Friburger.] Probably published in January 1471. *Opera* [*Cat.* and *Iug.*]. ISTC is000553000. Goff S53. Copy consulted: Oxford, Bodleian Arch. G e.46.

1473 [Rome]: A[dam] R[ot], [about 1473.] *Opera* [*Cat.* and *Iug.*]. ISTC is00055000. Goff S55. Copies consulted: Oxford, Bodleian Auct. N 3.26 (imperfect, wanting *Catilina*), digital image of Uppsala, Univ. Bibliotek Ink. 32:83.

1472–4 [Basel: Martin Flach (printer of Basel), about 1474]. *Opera* [*Cat.* and *Iug.*]. ISTC is00058000. Goff S58. Copy consulted: Oxford, Bodleian Auct. O 4.22.

1474–5 [Paris: In vico S. Jacobi (Au Soufflet Vert [Louis Symonel et Socii]), about 1475]. *Opera* [*Cat.* and *Iug.*]. ISTC is00060500. Copy consulted: London, BL IA.39236.

1475 Rome: Arnoldus Pannartz, 25 Sept. *Editio princeps* of the *Orationes et epistula* from the *Historiae*, and the *Epistulae ad Caesarem*. ISTC is00091000. Goff S91. Copy consulted: Oxford, Bodleian Auct. 7 Q 5.16 (4).

1478 Paris: Ulrich Gering. Not after 1478. *Opera* [*Cat.* and *Iug.*], edited by Philippus Beroaldus. ISTC is00065000. Goff S65. Copy consulted: London, BL IA.39187.

1483 Paris: Ulrich Gering. [1483?] *Opera* [*Cat.* and *Iug.* with addition of (Ps.-)Sallust: *In Ciceronem invectiva*. Cicero: *In Catilinam orationes I–IV*. (Ps.-)Cicero: *In Catilinam invectiva V*; *In Sallustium invectiva*. (Ps.-)Catilina: *Oratio in Ciceronem responsiva*], edited by Philippus Beroaldus.

ISTC is00071000. Goff S71. Copies consulted: Oxford, Bodleian Auct. N 5.29, London, BL IA.39195.

Pomponius Laetus's Edition

1490 Rome: Eucharius Silber, 3 April. *Opera* edited by Pomponius Laetus. The first edition to contain all of the following: *De coniuratione Catilinae*; *De bello Jugurthino*; *Orationes et epistolae ex libris Historiarum excerptae*. Also *Vita Sallustii*; *Declamatio contra Catilinam* (spuriously attributed to M. Porcius Latro). ISTC is00075000. Goff S75. Copy consulted: London, BL IA.18913.

1491 Venice: Philippus Pincius, 11 May 1491. Contents as **1490**, with the addition of (Ps.-)Sallust: *Invectiva in Ciceronem*. (Ps.-)Cicero: *Responsio in Sallustium*. ISTC is00076000. Goff S76. Copy consulted: Oxford, Bodleian Auct. P inf. 2.1.

1492 Venice: Theodorus de Ragazonibus, 9 July 1492. Contents as **1491**. ISTC is00077000. Goff S77. Copy consulted: Oxford, Bodleian Auct. O inf. 2.6.

1493 Venice: Johannes Tacuinus, de Tridino, 5 Aug. 1493. Contents as **1490**. ISTC is00078000. Goff S78. Copies consulted: Oxford, Bodleian Auct. P 5.1 (1), London, BL IB.24021.

Johannes Britannicus's Revision of Laetus, with Soldus Chrysostomus's Commentary on Jugurtha

1495.1 Brescia: Bernardinus de Misintis, for Angelus and Jacobus Britannicus, 13 January. *Opera*. *Catilina* (Comm.: Laurentius Valla); *Jugurthinum* (Comm.: Johannes Chrysostomus Soldus). *Declamatio contra Catilinam. Orationes et epistolae ex libris Historiarum excerptae.* Also: *Sallustii vita*. (Ps.-)Sallustius: *Invectiva in Ciceronem*. (Ps.-)Cicero: *Responsio in Sallustium*. (Ps.-)Catilina: *Epistola responsiva in Ciceronem*. The *Declamatio* is spuriously attributed to M. Porcius Latro. The body of the *Jugurthinum* has not been revised systematically to reflect Soldus's assumed or preferred readings in his gloss, and there are discrepancies at many points. Of the six surviving printings in this class, from 1495 to 1502, the

Paris edition of 1497/8 shows the greatest number of departures from the 1495 first edition. A significant number of the revised readings in it make their way into Ascensius's 1504 edition and later reprints. ISTC is00082000. Goff S82. Copy consulted: Oxford, Bodleian Auct. N inf. 2.17.

1495.2 Venice: [Christophorus de Pensis, de Mandello, after 14 November]. Contents as for **1495.1**. ISTC is00082300. Goff S81. Copy consulted: London, BL G.9162.

1497 [Venice: Christophorus de Pensis, de Mandello, *c.*1496–7]. Contents as for **1495.2**. ISTC is00084000. Goff S84. Copies consulted: Oxford, Bodleian Auct. P 3.18(2), Inc.c.I4.2.

1497/8 Paris: André Bocard, for Jean Petit, and Jean Alexandre, and Charles de Bougne at Angers, 13 January. Contents as for **1495.1**, but with some textual revisions distinctive to this edition (see below). ISTC is00083000. Goff S83. Copy consulted: Oxford, Exeter College, Strong Rm 9F 1497.

1498–1500 [Venice: Christophorus de Pensis, *c.*1498–1500]. Contents as for **1495.1**. ISTC is00084000. Goff S84. Copies consulted: Oxford, Bodleian Auct. N 3.23, Auct. N 3.24(1).

1500 Venice: Johannes Tacuinus, de Tridino, 20 July. Contents as for **1495.1**, with addition of commentary by Omnibonus Leonicenus on the *Catilina*. ISTC is00085000. Goff S85. Copy consulted: Oxford, Bodleian Auct. P 3.19.

1502 Venice, Johannes Tacuinus, de Tridino, 1502. Contents as for **1500**. Copy consulted: London, BL 1480.c.14.

1506.1 Venice, Johannes Tacuinus, de Tridino, 1506. Contents as for **1500** according to *CTC* viii. 221. Copy consulted: Bologna, Biblioteca comunale dell'Archiginnasio 5. C. II. 24.

1510.1 Milan: Leonardus de Vegiis. Reported in Schweiger, *Handbuch*, ii. 869; *CTC* viii. 221. No copy is presently known.

1511.1 Venice, Johannes Tacuinus, de Tridino, 1511. Contents as for **1500**. Not recorded in *CTC*. Copy consulted: digital scan of Munich, Bayerische Staatsbibliothek 999/2 Class.55.

Badius Ascensius's Editions with Commentary

1504.1 Paris: Josse Badius for Jean Petit, 30–1 October. *Opera*. The edition of Pomponius Laetus, revised by Johannes Britannicus, and further revised by Jodocus Badius Ascensius, with the addition of his *Familiaris explanatio* to replace the earlier commentaries of Laurentius Valla and Johannes Chrysostomus Soldus. Contents otherwise as for **1500** above, supplemented with Cicero's four *Orationes in Catilinam*; ps.-Cicero *Oratio in Catilinam*; ps.-Catiline *Orationes responsivae due in Ciceronem*, and Philippus Beroaldus the Elder's *Invectarum Ciceronis Commendatio* and *Praefatio Sallustiana*. Reproduces the distinctive textual revisions of Paris **1497/8**. Badius's commentary remained dominant up to the time that Barclay completed his work in 1520–2, and is known in at least thirteen editions up to 1521, with further reprintings up to 1590. Renouard, no. 1, Renouard *IP*, no. 27. Copies consulted: Oxford, Bodleian Rawl. 519, DD 20 Art., Broxb. 79.3.

1506.2 Lyon: Jean de Vingle for Étienne Gueynard, 27 October. Contents as in **1504.1**. Renouard. no. 3. Copy consulted: Oxford, Wolfson College.

1508.1 Paris: Jean Barbier, for Jean Petit, 13 September. Contents as in **1504.1**. Renouard, no. 4, Renouard *IP*, no. 138. Copy consulted: London, BL 294.f.4.

1509.1 Lyon: Claude d'Avost for Simon Vincent, 9 June. Contents as in **1504.1**. Renouard, no. 6. Copy consulted: film of Nîmes, Médiathèque de Nîmes 10588.

1511.2 Lyon: Jacobus Mareschal for Simon Vincent, 17 October. Contents as in **1504.1**. Renouard, no. 7. Copy consulted: London, BL 1481.c.24.

1513.1 Lyon: Jean de Platea for Jean Robion and Jean de Clauso, 7 January. Contents as in **1504.1**. Renouard, no. 8. Copy consulted: Oxford, Corpus Christi College Δ.15.15.

1513.2 Venice: Bartholomeus de Zannis de Portesio, 3 February. Contents as in **1504.1**, but with substantial revision of the *Jugurtha* text, with readings taken from the 1509 Aldine text. Renouard, no. 9. Copy consulted: London, BL 9039.i.25.

1514.1 Lyon: Jean de Platea for Simon Vincent, 15 November. Contents as in **1504.1**. Renouard, no. 12. Copy consulted: film of Troyes, Médiathèque de l'agglomeration troyenne NN 4 1332.

1517 Lyon: Joannes de Jonvelle for Simon Vincent, 4 April. Contents as in **1504.1**. Renouard, no. 13. Copy consulted: London, BL C.60.m.7.

1519 Lyon: Jean Marion, 7 July. Contents as in **1504.1**. Renouard, no. 14. Copy consulted: Oxford, Bodleian DD 68 Art.

Composite editions including the commentaries of Valla, Soldus, and Ascensius

1513.3 Venice: Bernard de Vianis de Lexona. From the evidence of the editions of **1514.2** and **1521**, the contents comprised the *opera*, edited by Pomponius Laetus, with revisions by Jodocus Badius Ascensius, including the *Familiaris explanatio* of Badius on all texts, the *Commentarii* of Lorenzo Valla and Omnibonus Leonicenus on the *Catilina*, and the *Expositio* of Johannes Chrysostomus Soldus on the *Iugurtha*. No copies now traceable. See Panzer, *Annales Typographici*, viii. no. 651; Graesse, *Trésor des livres*, vi. 237; Schweiger, *Handbuch*, ii. 869–70; Renouard, no. 11.

1514.2 Venice: Johannes Tacuinus de Tridino, 8 March. At points where Ascensius's revisions provide a reading different from Laetus's, this composite text takes its readings variously from one or the other. Contents as previous. Schweiger, *Handbuch*, ii. 870. Not recorded by Renouard. Closely resembles **1521** and therefore probably a close copy of **1513.3**. Copy consulted: digital scan of Vatican, Bibl. Apost. Loreto.III.25.

1521 Venice: 1521 Bernard de Vianis de Lexona. The *opera*, edited by Pomponius Laetus, with revisions by Jodocus Badius Ascensius, including the *Familiaris explanatio* of Badius on all texts, including the orations and invectives, etc., as in **1504.1**, the *Commentarii* of Lorenzo Valla and Omnibonus Leonicenus on the *Catilina*, and the *Expositio* of Johannes Chrysostomus Soldus on the *Iugurtha*. Probably a close reproduction of his **1513.3** edition.

Schweiger, *Handbuch*, ii. 871; Renouard, no. 18. Copies consulted: Oxford, Bodleian Bod CC 14(2) Art; own copy.

Octavo Editions of Badius Ascensius, or Others, without Commentary

1504.2 Paris: Badius Ascensius, 20 November. *Caij Crispi Salustii Opera cum plusculis additamentis.* Includes Portius Latro, Cicero, Ps.-Sallust, Ps.-Cicero. Octavo edition in Roman type. Essentially **1504.1** without apparatus. Renouard *IP*, no. 28; Moreau, *Inventaire chronologique*, no. 95.[40] Copy consulted: Sélestat, Bibl. Humaniste K 1064b.[41]

1508.2 Paris: Jean Barbier, Jean Petit, 1 September. *C. Crispi Salustii opera cum plusculis additamentis nouiter & diligentissim e Parisius impressa.* Includes *C. Crispi Sallustii vita*, *Historiae descriptio*; *Historici styli precepta* [Badius Ascensius]; *Portii Latronis in Catilinam declamatio*; P. Beroaldus, *Invectivarum Ciceronis commendatio.* Cicero, *In Catilinam invectivae quinque* . . . M. Æmilius, *Lepidi oratio*; *Oratio Philippi contra Lepidum.* Another edition of **1504.2**. Renouard, no. 5, Renouard *IP*, no. 28. Copy consulted: London, BL 587.b.11.

1509.2 Paris: 'ex officina Nicolaum'. 4° *Caij Crispi Salustij opera cum plusculis additamentis in quibus hec sunt. C. Crispi Salustij vita*, etc. Edited by Badius Ascensius. Includes Ascensius's Twenty Precepts. Copy consulted: Oxford, Bodleian Broxb. 30.8 (first sheet is mutilated, and wanting the final leaf).

1512.1 [Lyon, 1512?] *Textus Sallustij. Caij Crispi Sallustij . . . de coniuratione Catilinæ & de bello Iugurthino liber recognitus. Vna cum annotatiunculis a L. de Bosco nuper additis. Eiusdem oratio* [etc.]. The text derives from the 1509 Aldine edition, with brief side notes added by Ludovicus

[40] Brigitte Moreau and Philippe Renouard, *Inventaire chronologique des éditions parisiennes du XVIe siècle* (Paris, 1972).

[41] This volume survives in the collection of Beatus Rhenanus (1485–1547) in his home town of Sélestat. Antoine Renouard proposes that Badius possibly employed him as a corrector from 1503 to 1507 on the basis of the large number of Badius's editions from these years that are found in Rhenanus's library. See Antoine Aug. Renouard, *Annales de l'imprimerie des Alde*, 3rd edn. (Paris, 1834), 67–8.

de Bosco. Copy consulted: Oxford, Bodleian 8° H 183 Art.

1512.2 Paris: Guilelmus le Rouge for Dionysius Roce. A mixed text, apparently based on Badius, but drawing upon Aldus also. Prefaced by Badius's letter. Schweiger, *Handbuch*, ii. 869; Ebert, no. 19970.

1513.4 Paris: Badius Ascensius, 24 October. Largely a reprint of the **1509.3** Aldine edition. Renouard, no. 10, Renouard *IP*, no. 231. Copy consulted: digital scan of copy in Dresden, Sächsische Landesbibliothek.

Aldine and quasi-Aldine Texts

Prior to the publication of Aldus's own edition of Sallust **1509.3** there appeared three editions emulating his distinctive octavo format and typography. These were competently edited and introduced some good new readings.

1503/4 Florence: Filippo Giunta, 27 January. *Opera* edited by Benedictus Ricardinus. See Renouard, *Annales* xxxiv, Pettas, *Giunti of Florence*, 195; Fletcher, *New Aldine Studies*, 103–4. Copy consulted: Cambridge, University Library F150.d.2.21.

1504.3 [Lyon] *Salustius* [*Works*]. The epistle, signed by the editor T. Murchius, is dated 1504. Shaw, 'The Lyons Counterfeit', believes that the typography dates from 1504. The type is Shaw's group IC, used for Aldine counterfeits. See Baudrier, *Bibliographie lyonnaise*, vii. 21–2. Copies consulted: Oxford, Bodleian Vet. E1 f.32; London, BL 803.c.23.

1504.4 [Lyon]: Bartholomaeus Trot, 5 November. *C. Salustii Crispi Bellum Catilinarium. C. Salustii Crispi Bellum Jugurthum, P. Latronis declamatio contra L. Servium Catilinam. Oratio Lepidi Con. ad Populum ex Liberis* [sic] *Historiarum C. Crispi Salustii. Invectiva C. Salustii in Ciceronem. C. Crispi Salustii vita.* Edited by Balthasar Fidelis. Shaw, 'The Lyons Counterfeit', describes this as an Aldine counterfeit, and dates it to 1504 on typographical grounds. Textually the edition is very close to the other Lyon edition **1504.3**. See Baudrier, *Bibliographie lyonnaise*, vii. 20. Copy consulted: London, BL 833.d.15.

1509.3 Venice, Aldus Manutius & Andreas Asulanus (Torresanus) Socer, April. *C. Crispi Sallustii De coniuratione Catilinae. Eiusdem De bello Iugurthino. Eiusdem oratio contra M. T. Ciceronem* . . . Aldus dedicates the work to Bartolomeo d'Alviano, commander-in-chief of Venetian forces, successful in his alliance with the French in 1508, but defeated by them in 1509. In his dedicatory epistle to d'Alviano Aldus states that Giovanni Giocondo (who edited the work) and Ianus Lascaris had brought him two very old manuscripts from Paris to print.[42] Copy consulted: Oxford, Bodleian Auct. 2 R 5.20.

1510.2 [Lyon: 1510]. Counterfeit of 1509 Aldine. Baudrier, *Bibliographie lyonnaise*, viii. 420. Shaw, 'The Lyons Counterfeit', classifies the type as Group IVA and dates to 1510. Copy consulted: London, BL 803.c.22.

4. BARCLAY'S SOURCES AND HIS USE OF COMMENTARIES

It is not surprising to discover that of the numerous editions of Sallust's *Iugurtha* potentially available to Barclay, he based his translation primarily upon a reprint of Badius Ascensius's edition (**1504.1**), and incorporated much material from its extensive commentary. He also made sustained use of Johannes Britannicus's revised version of Pomponius Laetus's edition, with the commentary of Johannes Soldus Chrysostomus 'Brixianus', written around 1469–70 and published twenty-five years later (**1495.1** or reprint), from which further additional material was woven into the translation.[43] (See Pls. 2 and 3.)

There is little in the translation that cannot be accounted for from one or both of these sources, but it is entirely possible that Barclay had recourse to other materials. The one explicit acknowledgement of

[42] 'C. Crispi Sallustii de coniuratione Catilinae, et de bello Iugurthino, duo antiquiss. exemplaria è Lutetia Parisiorum Ioannes Lascaris, qui superioribus annis egit apud Venetos legatum Regium, et iocundus Veronensis viri bonarum literarum studiosissimi in Italiam attulerunt, mihique . . . excudenda dederunt' (sig. [ai]^{v}).

[43] On the life and work of Badius Ascensius (1462–1535) see Crane, 'A Conservative Voice', Renouard, and *CTC*. For what little is known of the Dominican Soldus's life and his work, see *CTC* viii. 220–1, 292–4. See also Greg Waite, 'Alexander Barclay's Translation of Sallust's Jugurtha: A Note on Sources', *Notes and Queries*, 58 (2011), 196–202.

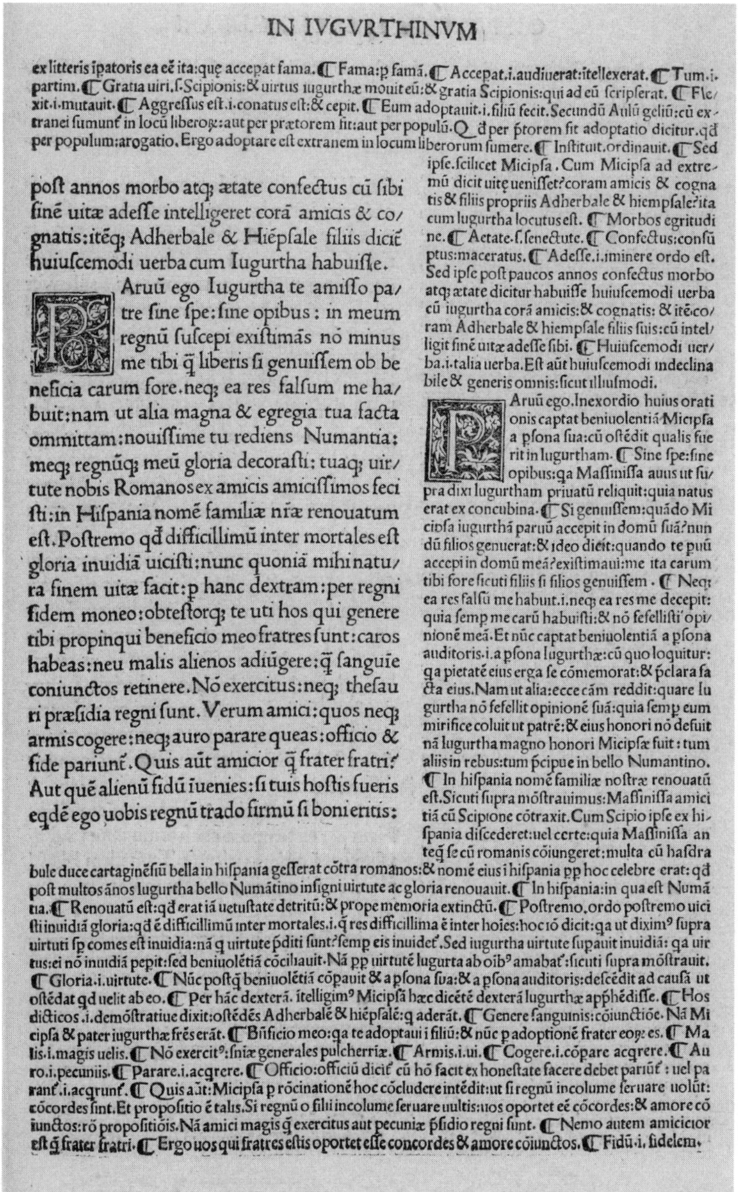

IN IVGVRTHINVM

ex litteris ipatoris ea eẽ ita: quę accepat fama. ¶ Fama: p famã. ¶ Accepat. i. audiuerat: itellexerat. ¶ Tum. i. partim. ¶ Gratia uiri. s. Scipionis: & uirtus iugurthæ mouit eũ: & gratia Scipionis: qui ad eũ scripserat. ¶ Flexit. i. mutauit. ¶ Aggressus est. i. conatus est: & cepit. ¶ Eum adoptauit. i. filiũ fecit. Secundũ Aulũ geliũ: cũ extranei sumunť in locũ liberoꝝ: aut per prætorem fit: aut per populũ. Q đ per ꝑtorem fit adoptatio dicitur. qđ per populum: arogatio. Ergo adoptare est extranem in locum liberorum sumere. ¶ Instituit. ordinauit. ¶ Sed ipse. scilicet Micipsa. Cum Micipsa ad extremũ dicit uitę uenisset? coram amicis & cognatis & filiis propriis Adherbale & hiempsale? ita cum Iugurtha locutus est. ¶ Morbos egritudine. ¶ Aetate. s. senectute. ¶ Confectus: consũptus: maceratus. ¶ Adesse. i. iminere ordo est. Sed ipse post paucos annos confectus morbo atq; ætate dicitur habuisse huiuscemodi uerba cũ iugurtha corã amicis: & cognatis: & itẽ coram Adherbale & hiempsale filiis suis: cũ intelligit finẽ uitæ adesse sibi. ¶ Huiuscemodi uerba. i. talia uerba. Est aũt huiuscemodi indeclinabile & generis omnis: sicut illiusmodi.

post annos morbo atq; ætate confectus cũ sibi finẽ uitæ adesse intelligeret corã amicis & cognatis: itẽq; Adherbale & Hiẽpsale filiis dicit huiuscemodi uerba cum Iugurtha habuisse.

PAruũ ego Iugurtha te amisso patre sine spe: sine opibus: in meum regnũ suscepi existimãs nõ minus me tibi q̃ liberis si genuissem ob beneficia carum fore. neq; ea res falsum me habuit: nam ut alia magna & egregia tua facta ommittam: nouissime tu rediens Numantia: meq; regnũq; meũ gloria decorasti: tuaq; uirtute nobis Romanos ex amicis amicissimos fecisti: in Hispania nomẽ familiæ nr̃æ renouatum est. Postremo qđ difficillimũ inter mortales est gloria inuidiã uicisti: nunc quoniã mihi natura finem uitæ facit: p hanc dextram: per regni fidem moneo: obtestorq; te uti hos qui genere tibi propinqui beneficio meo fratres sunt: caros habeas: neu malis alienos adiũgere: q̃ sanguĩe coniunctos retinere. Nõ exercitus: neq; thesauri præsidia regni sunt. Verum amici: quos neq; armis cogere: neq; auro parare queas: officio & fide pariunť. Quis aũt amicior q̃ frater fratri? Aut quẽ alienũ fidũ iuenies: si tuis hostis fueris eqdẽ ego uobis regnũ trado firmũ si boni eritis:

PAruũ ego. In exordio huius orationis captat beniuolentiã Micipsa a ꝑsona sua: cũ ostẽdit qualis fuerit in Iugurtham. ¶ Sine spe: sine opibus: qa Massinissa auus ut supra dixi Iugurtham priuatũ reliquit: quia natus erat ex concubina. ¶ Si genuissem: quãdo Micipsa iugurthã paruũ accepit in domũ suã? nundũ filios genuerat: & ideo dicit: quando te puũ accepi in domũ meã? existimaui: me ita carum tibi fore sicuti filiis si filios genuissem. ¶ Neq; ea res falsũ me habuit. i. neq; ea res me decepit: quia semꝑ me carũ habuisti: & nõ fefellisti opinionẽ meã. Et nũc captat beniuolentiã a ꝑsona auditoris. i. a ꝑsona Iugurthæ: cũ quo loquitur: qa pietatẽ eius erga se cõmemorat: & ꝓclara facta eius. Nam ut alia: ecce cãm reddit: quare Iugurtha nõ fefellit opinionẽ suã: quia semꝑ eum mirifice coluit ut patrẽ: & eius honori nõ defuit nã Iugurtha magno honori Micipsæ fuit: tum aliis in rebus: tum ꝑcipue in bello Numantino. ¶ In hispania nomẽ familiæ nostræ renouatũ est. Sicuti supra mõstrauimus: Massinissa amicitiã cũ Scipione cõtraxit. Cum Scipio ipse ex hispania discederet: uel certe: quia Massinissa anteq̃ se cũ romanis cõiungeret: multa cũ hasdrabule duce cartaginẽsiũ bella in hispania gesserat cõtra romanos: & nomẽ eius i hispania pp hoc celebre erat: qđ post multos ãnos Iugurtha bello Numãtino insigni uirtute ac gloria renouauit. ¶ In hispania: in qua est Numãtia. ¶ Renouatũ est: qđ erat iã uetustate detritũ: & prope memoria extinctũ. ¶ Postremo. ordo postremo uicisti inuidiã gloria: qđ ẽ difficillimũ inter mortales. i. q̃ res difficillima ẽ inter hoies: hoc iõ dicit: qa ut diximꝰ supra uirtuti sꝑ comes est inuidia: nã q uirtute ꝓditi sunt? semꝑ eis inuideť. Sed iugurtha uirtute supauit inuidiã: qa uirtus: ei nõ inuidiã pepit: sed beniuolẽtiã cõciliauit. Nã pp uirtutẽ Iugurta ab oibꝰ amabať: sicuti supra mõstrauit. ¶ Gloria. i. uirtute. ¶ Nũc postq̃ beniuolẽtiã cõpauit & a ꝑsona sua: & a ꝑsona auditoris: descẽdit ad causã ut ostẽdat qd uelit ab eo. ¶ Per hãc dexterã. itelligimꝰ Micipsã hæc dicẽtẽ dexterã Iugurthæ apphẽdisse. ¶ Hos dicticos. i. demõstratiue dixit: ostẽdẽs Adherbalẽ & hiẽpsalẽ: q aderãt. ¶ Genere sanguinis: cõiunctiõe. Nã Micipsa & pater iugurthæ frẽs erãt. ¶ Bñficio meo: qa te adoptaui i filiũ: & nũc p adoptionẽ frater eoꝝ es. ¶ Malis. i. magis uelis. ¶ Nõ exercitꝰ: sniæ generales pulcherriæ. ¶ Armis. i. ui. ¶ Cogere. i. cõpare acqrere. ¶ Auro. i. pecuniis. ¶ Parare. i. acqrere. ¶ Officio: officiũ diciť cũ hõ facit ex honestate facere debet pariũť: uel parant. i. acqrunť. ¶ Quis aũt: Micipsa p rõcinationẽ hoc cõcludere intẽdit: ut si regnũ incolume seruare uolũt: cõcordes sint. Et propositio ẽ talis. Si regnũ o filii incolume seruare uultis: uos oportet eẽ cõcordes: & amore cõiunctos: rõ propositiõis. Nã amici magis q̃ exercitus aut pecuniæ ꝓsidio regni sunt. ¶ Nemo autem amicicior est q̃ frater fratri. ¶ Ergo uos qui fratres estis oportet esse concordes & amore cõiunctos. ¶ Fidũ. i. fidelem.

Pl. 2. Oxford, Bodleian Library, Auct. N inf. 2.17, Sig. f6r, Laetus's text with Soldus's commentary. Reproduced by permission of the Bodleian Libraries, University of Oxford

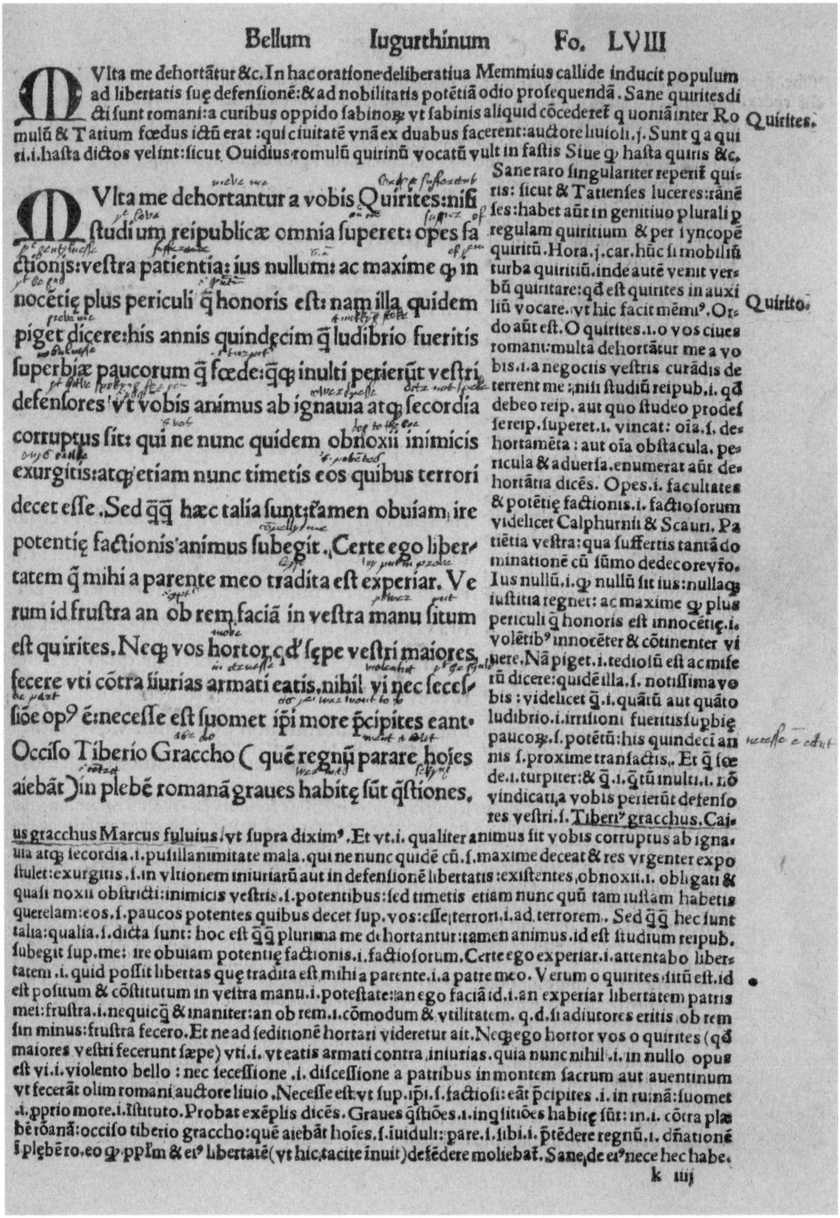

MVlta me dehortātur &c. In hac oratione deliberatiua Memmius callide inducit populum ad libertatis suę defensionē: & ad nobilitatis potētiā odio prosequendā. Sane quirites dicti sunt romani: a curibus oppido sabinoꝝ vt sabinis aliquid cōcederet quoniā inter Romulū & Tatium fœdus ictū erat: qui ciuitatē vnā ex duabus facerent: auctore liuio li. j. Sunt q a quiri. i. hasta dictos velint: sicut Ouidius romulū quirinū vocatū vult in fastis Siue q hasta quiris &c. — Quirites.

MVlta me dehortantur a vobis Quirites: nisi studium reipublicæ omnia superet: opes factionis: vestra patientia: ius nullum: ac maxime q innocetię plus periculi q̄ honoris est: nam illa quidem piget dicere: his annis quindecim q̄ ludibrio fueritis superbiæ paucorum q̄ fœde: q̄q; inulti perierūt vestri defensores: vt vobis animus ab ignauia atq; secordia corruptus sit: qui ne nunc quidem obnoxii inimicis exurgitis: atq; etiam nunc timetis eos quibus terrori decet esse. Sed q̄q̄ hæc talia sunt: tamen obuiam ire potentię factionis animus subegit. Certe ego libertatem q̄ mihi a parente meo tradita est experiar. Verum id frustra an ob rem faciā in vestra manu situm est quirites. Neq; vos hortor q̄d sępe vestri maiores fecere vti cōtra iniurias armati eatis. nihil vi nec secessiōe opꝰ ē: necesse est suomet ipi more pcipites eant. Occiso Tiberio Graccho (quē regnū parare hoīes aiebāt) in plebē romanā graues habitę sūt q̄stiones.

Sane raro singulariter reperit quiris: sicut & Tatienses luceres: rānes: habet aūt in genitiuo plurali p regulam quiritium & per syncopē quiritū. Hora. j. car. hūc si mobiliū turba quiritiū. inde autē venit verbū quiritare: qd̄ est quirites in auxiliū vocare. vt hic facit mēmiꝰ. — Quirito. Ordo aūt est. O quirites. i. o vos ciues romani: multa dehortātur me a vobis. i. a negociis vestris curādis deterrent me: nisi studiū reipub. i. qd̄ debeo reip. aut quo studeo prodesse reip. superet. i. vincat: oīa. s. dehortamēta: aut oīa obstacula. pericula & aduersa. enumerat aūt dehortātia dicēs. Opes. i. facultates & potētię factionis. i. factiosorum videlicet Calphurnii & Scauri. Patiētia vestra: qua suffertis tantā dominationē cū sūmo dedecore vr̄o. Ius nullū. i. q nullū sit ius: nullaq; iustitia regnet: ac maxime q plus periculi q̄ honoris est innocētię. i. volētibꝰ innocēter & cōtinenter viuere. Nā piget. i. tediosū est ac miserū dicere: quidē illa. s. notissima vobis: videlicet q̄. i. quātū aut quāto ludibrio. i. irrisioni fueritis supbię paucoꝝ. s. potētū: his quindeci annis s. proxime transactis. Et q̄ fœde. i. turpiter: & q̄. i. q̄tū inulti. i. nō vindicati, a vobis perierūt defensores vestri. s. Tiberiꝰ gracchus. Caius gracchus Marcus fuluius vt supra diximꝰ. Et vt. i. qualiter animus sit vobis corruptus ab ignauia atq; secordia. i. pusillanimitate mala. qui ne nunc quidē cū. s. maxime deceat & res vrgenter expostulet: exurgitis. s. in vltionem iniuriarū aut in defensionē libertatis: existentes, obnoxii. i. obligati & quasi noxii obstricti: inimicis vestris. s. potentibus: sed timetis etiam nunc quū tam iustam habetis querelam: eos. s. paucos potentes quibus decet sup. vos: esse terrori. i. ad terrorem. Sed q̄q̄ hec sunt talia: qualia. s. dicta sunt: hoc est q̄q̄ plurima me dehortantur: tamen animus. id est studium reipub. subegit sup. me: ire obuiam potentię factionis. i. factiosorum. Certe ego experiar. i. attentabo libertatem. i. quid possit libertas quę tradita est mihi a parente. i. a patre meo. Verum o quirites situ est. id est positum & cōstitutum in vestra manu. i. potestate: an ego faciā id. i. an experiar libertatem patris mei: frustra. i. nequicq̄ & inaniter: an ob rem. i. cōmodum & vtilitatem. q. d. si adiutores eritis ob rem sin minus: frustra fecero. Et ne ad seditionē hortari videretur ait. Neq; ego hortor vos o quirites (qd̄ maiores vestri fecerunt sæpe) vti. i. vt eatis armati contra iniurias. quia nunc nihil. i. in nullo opus est vi. i. violento bello: nec secessione. i. discessione a patribus in montem sacrum aut auentinum vt fecerāt olim romani auctore liuio. Necesse est vt sup. ipi. s. factiosi: eāt pcipites. i. in ruinā: suomet. i. pprio more. i. īstituto. Probat exēplis dicēs. Graues q̄stiōes. i. inq̄sitiōes habitę sūt: in. i. cōtra plæbē roānā: occiso tiberio graccho: quē aiebāt hoīes. s. inuidi: pare. i. sibi. i. ptēdere regnū. i. dn̄ationē ī plębē ro. eo q ppl̄m & eiꝰ libertatē (vt hic tacite innuit) defēdere moliebat. Sane de eiꝰ nece hec habe.

k iiij

Pl. 3. Oxford, Bodleian Library, DD 20 Art., f. 58r, Ascensius's text and commentary. Reproduced by permission of the Bodleian Libraries, University of Oxford

such is the side-note on f. 18^{v}, indicating that he took his information about the foundation of Carthage from Virgil, Servius, and other good authors.[44] At Ely he may have had access to further manuscript or print resources of the kind used by William Gray and Richard Bole, as noted above. By the time Barclay was at Ely, however, their personal libraries had been donated to Balliol College, where Gray had undertaken his early studies. Among the few books that can be identified as Bole's donations to the Balliol collection, MS 258 is a Sallust, completed in February 1461, and MS 123 is a miscellany, probably completed before 1454, including a commentary on the *Catiline* and *Jugurtha* (both are in Bole's own hand).[45] There is nothing to indicate that Barclay consulted Bole's commentary on *Iugurtha*, and there is no firm evidence that any of the other twelve known manuscript commentaries from the Continent were known in England or available to Barclay.[46]

In translating *The Shyp of Folys* Barclay had recourse to Riviere's French translation as well as Locher's Latin text. It seems doubtful, however, that he would have found any such aid as a French translation of the *Jugurtha*, if he had indeed wished for one. The first to appear in print was that by an anonymous author, possibly to be identified as Guillaume Michel, which was published in 1532.[47]

First published in 1504, Ascensius's commentary on Sallust dominated the field in the earlier sixteenth century, and appeared in at least twenty editions (one as late as 1590). It is noteworthy that in most of the editions printed with this commentary, the text of the first edition remains virtually unchanged. This is all the more striking when one considers that Ascensius's own printings without the

[44] '¶Hec tum ex Marone tum ex Servio reliquisque probis auctoribus sunt excepta.' William Nelson, who first noted (in passing) Barclay's use of a commentary when translating the *Jugurtha*, believed that he did not venture to add any information from outside that single source. See *St George*, ed. Nelson, pp. xvii–xviii, and cf. n. 7.

[45] R. A. B. Mynors, *Catalogue of the Manuscripts of Balliol College, Oxford* (Oxford, 1963), pp. xlvi–xlix, 100–1, 279.

[46] In 1495 Filippo Pinzi applied for a privilege to print a commentary on Sallust by Battista Guarini, along with a reprint of Valla's commentary. The edition, if it was produced, has not survived, nor has any manuscript copy of Guarini's commentary. It is not clear from the application whether this was a commentary only on the *Catiline*, like Valla's, or in fact a commentary on the *Iugurtha* to take up where Valla ends. See Rinaldo Fulin, 'Documenti per servire all storia della tipografia veneziana', *Archivio veneto*, 23 (1882), 84–212 at 118, no. 36; Patricia J. Osmond, 'The Valla Commentary on Sallust', in Marianne Pade (ed.), *On Renaissance Commentaries* (Hildesheim, 2005), 29–48 at 34.

[47] J. Chocheyras, 'Les Traductions françaises de Salluste', *Revue de littérature comparée*, 39 (1965), 22–30.

commentary, and most other editions following the Aldine text **1509.3**, introduced improved readings at many points taken from Aldus. Indeed, even prior to Aldus's edition, some editions emerged from Lyon and Paris incorporating better readings, apparently based on manuscripts found in France. For example, the 1509 Aldine reading *obuiam itum* (**5. 1**)[48] first appears in Ascensius's 8° edition **1508.2**. It is found in the three earliest manuscripts (now Paris, BnF lat. 16024, 16025, and Vatican, Pal. lat. 889) and a few others, rather than the more common manuscript reading *obuiatum*. Aldus's preference for *conuenere* rather than *conuenerunt* (**11. 2**) is anticipated in the two Lyon octavos **1504.3** and **1504.4**. The incorrect reading *insolitu metu* (**38. 5**) in Laetus–Britannicus (and retained in Ascensius's **1504.1** text) is corrected to *tumultu insolito* in Murchius's **1504.3** Lyon pseudo-Aldine octavo and in Ascensius's octavo **1508.2** (but not corrected in the quartos with commentary). There is no firm evidence that Barclay availed himself of any of these improved editions.

There are a number of indications within the translation that the **1504.1** Ascensius text (or more precisely, a subsequent reprint of it) was in fact the one Barclay used primarily. Most significant of these are: (1) the method of dividing the work into chapters; (2) the distinctive error 'Tolonia Thercon' in ch. 12 ('colonia Theraeon' **19. 3**); and (3) the extraneous clause 'pro licentia redeundi quam ab eo impetrare nequibat' in ch. 39 (**64. 4**).

Most editions of the *Iugurtha* up to and beyond the time of Barclay's translation employed around twelve large capitals to mark divisions in the text. This is the schema employed in Pomponius Laetus's editions from 1490 (including those revised by Johannes Soldus, and carrying his commentary from **1495.1**), and it is continued in the influential and often-copied edition of Aldus Manutius **1509.3**. By contrast, Badius Ascensius adopted a system of division into sixty-one chapters marked by large capitals. He seems to have based his schema on that found in the Basel edition printed by Martin Flach **1472–4**, in a Paris edition printed by Louis Symonel **1474–5**, and in the Paris editions of **1478** and **1483** (edited by Philippus Beroaldus and printed by Ulrich Gering), which differ from one another in only a few divisions. Barclay adopted Ascensius's sixty-one-chapter schema, but made further divisions, to a total of

[48] Bracketed references in bold figures refer to the standard chapter numeration for modern editions of Sallust. References to Barclay's English text (see below) are given by chapter and line number: for example, 11/62.

sixty-six chapters, and added the summary chapter headings. These are apparently his own creation, but at several points they incorporate additional information from Ascensius's commentary. Those points where Barclay departs from Ascensius's scheme appear to be deliberate rationalizations of it. He omits a division that consists of only two sentences ('Res postulare' **17. 1**), for example, and he adds divisions where Ascensius had set a paragraph mark to indicate a secondary division within a chapter ('¶Dum hæc Romæ' **32. 2**, for example). Barclay appears to have worked from an edition prior to that of 1517, for he does not have a division at **25. 9**, as do editions from 1517 onwards.

On the second point (the error 'Tolonia Thercon'), it transpires that in translating a passage that was often misunderstood, Barclay writes:

The valey of whom I spake before named in Affryke langage Cathabathmon/ deuydeth the countrey of Affrike from Egypt on that syde saue that an arme of the see is bytwene the first cyte or habytacyon of Affrike toward this valey/ [and] is called Cyrene. And nere to the same be other two cites/ the one named Tolonia: the other Thercon.

Sallust (as established by modern editors) states:

Igitur ad Catabathmon, qui locus Ægyptum ab Africa diuidit, secundo mari prima Cyrene est, colonia Theraeon. (**19. 3**)

Comber and Balmaceda, to take one modern example, translate:

Starting at Catabathmos, which divides Egypt from Africa, the first city you come to as you follow the coast [secundo mari] is Cyrene, a colony of Thera [*literally*: of the Theranians].

Ascensius's **1504.1** edition, with its *Familiaris explanatio*, is distinctive in adopting the reading 'Tolonia Thercon', which is apparently taken from Soldus's gloss. Of the six extant printings of Laetus's text accompanied by Soldus's commentary, only the Paris **1497/8** edition takes the erroneous gloss reading into the text. The **1495.1** edition (like all other Laetus editions from 1490) reads 'colonia Thereorum', and this, or 'colonia Theraeon/Thereon', which restores the proper Greek genitive plural (found in most editions between **1470.1** and **1490**), is the reading found in the later editions (Venice **1495.2**, **1497**, **1498–1500**, **1514.2**, **1521**). In his gloss, however, Soldus mistakenly states: 'Tolonia: Tercon: nomina ciuitatum sunt', and Ascensius accordingly adopted the reading 'Tolonia Thercon' in his own text, as did the reviser of the Paris 1497/8 printing. This reading persists in most of the Ascensian editions accompanied by the *Familiaris explanatio* (exceptions are the revised edition Venice 1513.2, and the composite Venice editions of 1514.2, 1521). Nevertheless, already by 1508 or 1509 Ascensius had corrected the error (to 'colonia Thereorum') in his own smaller-format edition of the Jugurtha text without commentary, dedicated to Egidius Quernolignus of Ghent (1509.2), which was several times reprinted thereafter, and also in his edition (1513.4) prepared by Hieronymus Aleander, collated against Aldus Manutius's edition (1509.3) and a very old manuscript made available by Paulus Aemilius. Nevertheless, these octavo editions retain a number of distinctive readings found in 1504.1 such as 'tuti aut honesti' (3. 1), and the 'pro licentia' clause (64. 4)

It might be argued that Barclay derived his translation directly from Soldus's gloss (or the text in the Paris edition 1497/8), rather than Ascensius's text, but Barclay's odd rendering of 'secundo mari' (which Soldus does not gloss) can be traced to the idiosyncratic punctuation in Ascensius's text, where 'qui locus Ægyptum ab Africa dividit secundo mari' is placed in parentheses as a clause unit. (The 1497/8 Paris Soldus does not match Ascensius's punctuation.)

On the third point (the extraneous 'pro licentia' clause) Barclay's translation probably derives from Ascensius's text. This additional phrase admittedly appears in Paris editions from 1474–75, including the 1478 and 1483 editions by Philippus Beroaldus, the 1497/8 edition with Soldus's commentary, and the small Paris editions 1508.2 and 1509.2; but it does not appear in the other printings of Pomponius Laetus's edition (1490, etc.), including those with Soldus's commentary, the Lyon octavo editions (1504.3, 1504.4), or in Italian editions:

This answere of Metellus styredde Marius agaynst hym with greuous yre and wrath/ what for the honour which he desyred: and what for the lycence to depart/ which he coude nat obtayne of him by no prayer nor request at his pleasure. Insomoch that he enraged agaynst Metellus moued by desyre of that office and prouokedde by yre/

Quæ res marium tum pro honore quem affectabat: tum pro licentia redeundi quam ab eo impetrare nequibat contra Metellum vehementer accenderat (1504.1).

Most other editions read:

Quae res Marium cum pro honore quem affectabat tum circa (*some later editions*: contra) Metellum vehementer accenderat. **64. 4**.

Numerous other readings indicate Ascensius as Barclay's principal source, in comparison with the text of Laetus and Britannicus. See, for example: 10/171–2 'our olde ennemis', *nobis* instead of *vobis*; 11/62 'ennemis', *inimicis* instead of *amicis*; 25/40 'he made redy', *preparare* 'prepare' instead of *properare* 'hasten'; 62/5 'coude nat fulfyll his desyre nor parfourme his enterprise', *infecto . . . negotio* instead of *confecto negotio*; 57/45–51 'Howbeit some sayd . . . as equall persones supposed', *quod multi . . . alii quod* where Ascensius supplies *alii*.[49]

Barclay's supplementary use of other editions cannot be discounted entirely, and his use of Laetus–Britannicus–Soldus is certain, based on what he takes occasionally from the text (see, for example, notes to 12/37 ff. *et Libyes* and *humi*, 40/89 *without credence*, 64/11 *father*), and frequently from Soldus's commentary attached to it. Nevertheless, the fact that Ascensius's text was his chief point of reference remains clear. Indeed it is difficult to understand why he preferred to adopt at least three dubious readings that could only have come from the Laetus–Britannicus text, and not from Soldus's commentary attached to it, or from Ascensius:

1. Introduction of the personal name Decius into the translation, based on a textual error *ex Scipione Decio* (instead of *ex Senatus decreto*), which appears in all of the Laetus–Soldus printings from **1495.1** except for the Paris **1497/8** (see note 17/71–3 **28. 3**). This error is apparently based on a misreading of the abbreviated form *ex S. D.*, which appears in the Laetus editions **1490**, **1491**, **1492**, and **1493**). Soldus's gloss to Laetus, like Ascensius, has the correct reading *ex senatus decreto*.

2. The place name Collace, based upon the Laetus–Britannicus reading *ex Collatia* instead of Soldus's gloss and Ascensius's reading and gloss *ex Latio* (see note to 41/80 **69. 4**). The inferior reading is common in later manuscripts, and appears in Laetus's editions from **1490** to **1502**, with the exception of Paris **1497/8**.

3. Introduction of the personal names Quintus Scipio and Marcus Manlius (see note to 67/22–3 **114. 1**). Ascensius is in line with modern editors, giving *Q. Cepione et C. Manlio*, where the Laetus editions read *P. Scipione et M. Manlio* (against which Soldus's gloss: *Qu. Seruilius Cepio consul et M. Manlius proconsul*).

[49] See notes for details.

These readings and a few others (see the notes to 40/87–9 and 64/11, for example) might indicate that Barclay produced some sections of the translation, or perhaps an entire first draft, from a Laetus–Soldus edition, or even an earlier Laetus edition without commentary, before turning to Ascensius, but the evidence is slight; and there are numerous instances where an Ascensian reading is adopted rather than the alternative from Soldus.

It is difficult to pinpoint exactly which edition of Ascensius Barclay might have used, because they differ from one another very little textually, and where an error might find its way into the text, the gloss retains the correct reading, or vice versa. The Venice edition published by Bartholomeus de Zannis (**1513.2**), however, can probably be excluded. It was substantially revised, and takes many readings from the Aldine edition (**1509.3**), including 'colonia Thereon'. It also omits the 'pro licentia' clause as detailed above.

Given Barclay's dependence upon both Soldus's and Ascensius's commentaries, it is reasonable to consider whether he might have used an edition which printed both commentaries. The **1521** Venice edition published by Bernard de Vianis is almost certainly too late to have been Barclay's source, but it is probably a reprinting very similar to the lost edition (**1513.3**) which Bernard published, the existence of which was noted by Panzer and Graesse, but a copy of which neither Renouard nor Osmond and Ulery found.[50] The edition published in Venice by Johannes Tacuinus (**1514.2**), resembling the **1521**, would then appear to be based upon **1513.3**. It includes the woodcut illustrations used in his **1511.1** edition (containing Soldus's commentary, but not Ascensius's). These woodcuts appear to be the model for the set commissioned by Bernard for his lost edition (presumably) and reused in its **1521** reprint. The **1514.2** and **1521** editions provide the commentaries of both Soldus and Ascensius, and have a revised text that proves to be a conflation of Laetus and Britannicus's with Ascensius's. They prefer the reading 'colonia Thereorum' from the former, and omit Ascensius's 'pro licentia' clause. At some other points an Ascensian reading is preferred, but the cumulative evidence, including the fact that the Ascensian chapter divisions are not employed, indicates that

[50] See Panzer, *Annales Typographici*; Graesse, *Trésor des livres rares et précieux*, vi. 237; Philippe Renouard, *Bibliographie des impressions et des oeuvres de Josse Badius Ascensius, imprimeur et humaniste, 1462–1535*, 3 vols. (Paris, 1908; repr. New York, 1967), no. 11; and *CTC*, 221.

Barclay probably did not use the **1513.3**, if indeed it closely resembled the **1521** edition, nor **1514.2**.

The particular edition of Laetus's text with Soldus's commentary that Barclay used is not clear either. The Venice reprints by de Pensis (**1497** and **1498–1500**) are very similar to his first edition (**1495.2**), to the extent that the formes are set up identically, with the same type, and the signatures correspond exactly. The Venice editions of Johannes Tacuinus (**1500** and **1502**) are textually very close to the **1495.1** prototype as well.[51] The distinctive Paris edition of **1497/8** incorporates some revised readings that appear also in the first edition by Ascensius (**1504.1**), and it may well be that Acensius himself had a hand in the revisions for the earlier edition, or possibly the printer had access to a manuscript copy of Ascensius's *Explanatio*, written for teaching purposes in the 1490s. If that is not the case, it appears that this particular edition was influential upon Ascensius's own. Readings such as *ex Scipione Decio* and *ex Collatia* (noted above) are corrected, and it is apparent that Barclay derived them from a Laetus–Britannicus edition other than this one.

Errors or revisions shared between Pynson's printing of the Latin and later reprints of Ascensius's edition (**1506.2**, etc.) suggest that Barclay's parallel text was set using the edition **1514.1** or later. It shares a few unique errors (or variants) with the **1519** edition:

> *fore* instead of *esse* (**14. 18**); *Tum interim* not *Tamen interim* (*Tñ interim* **1514**, **1517**) (**54. 2**); *cœpit* not *cepit* (**71. 2**); *flumine* not *ex flumine* (**75. 6**); *iucultumque* not *incultumque* (**80. 1**); *intentos prælios* not *intentos proelio* (*prelio*, *p̄lio*) (**94. 3**).

Nevertheless, it would be hazardous to claim that these are derived directly from that edition, since at other points Barclay's text agrees with the **1517** and prior editions (and employs the pre-**1517** chapter divisions), where the **1519** has a different reading. They are probably independent setting errors that happen to match errors in **1519**.

It could still be the case that Barclay had himself made use of another, earlier edition of Ascensius's commentary in composing his translation, but as the following example demonstrates, any evidence is equivocal. The translation at 36/58 ('without any thyng brought to

[51] Italian books such as the editions from Venice would also have been readily available in England. See Margaret Lane Ford, 'Importation of Printed Books into England and Scotland', in Lotte Hellinga and J. B. Trapp (eds.), *Cambridge History of the Book in Britain*, iii: *1400–1557* (Cambridge, 2000), 179–201.

ende at Zamam') reflects the correct reading found in the **1504.1–1511.2** copies of Ascensius (*infecto*) where an error occurs in the French editions from **1513.1** to **1519** (*incepto*). Nevertheless, Barclay could in any case have taken the correct reading out of Ascensius's commentary, or from Soldus. (See note to 36/58 for details.)

A few readings, however, suggest Barclay's dependence on a later rather than an earlier edition. For example, in Ascensius's reprinting of Soldus's prefatory summary of Sallust's text, the erroneous reading *a lege* appears instead of *a rege* in the editions from **1504.1** to **1511.2**. This is corrected to *a rege* in the Lyon (**1513.1**) and later editions whence it finds its way into Pynson's edition (see note Extr/154–8). Barclay's translation 'to gete money of [King] Iugurth' is based upon the corrected reading. For a possible isolated instance where Barclay's translation matches a unique error in the **1519** commentary, see note on *condycions* 18/17–8.

The parallel Latin text of the Pynson–Barclay edition appears to corroborate Barclay's prime source, because it is a copy of the Ascensian text, and in the case of the 'compendyous extract', a large section of Ascensius's commentary, itself taken virtually verbatim from Soldus's. It is possible that Pynson independently chose this text from which to set the parallel columns, but it is more likely that he acted on Barclay's instructions or advice. Nevertheless, the Latin is problematic in several respects.

First, it is quite carelessly set and proofed, revealing many errors and omissions that occur in none of the surviving Ascensian texts from France or Italy (*virtus* for *virtutis* **1. 3**, *Sed* for *Sin* **1. 4**, *humanum* for *hominum* **2. 1**, etc.). In virtually every case, Barclay's translation correctly mirrors the Ascensian texts, and not the erroneous Pynson reprint. See, for example:

> Extr/7–9. In the section of Ascensius's commentary set in parallel with Barclay's preliminary 'compendyous extract' a sentence is omitted from the Latin, but is present in the translation: 'Dicit se scripturum esse bellum quod populus romanus gessit cum Iugurtha rege Numidarum' (f. 40^{v}); 'In this . . . is written the batayle whiche the Romayns had with Iugurth vsurper of the kyngdome of Numydy.'
>
> Prol/90–1 (3. 3), where Pynson's text omits 'potentia paucorum', Barclay has translated the phrase.

Similarly 8/48 (**12. 5**) 'ad Iugurtham' is omitted in Pynson, but is present in the translation.

16/49–50 (**25. 9**) Instead of 'exercitu circumdato' the Pynson text has 'exercitu comparato'. Barclay's translation ('he compased the towne rounde about with his army') reflects the correct reading.

27/56–65 (**41. 10**) Pynson omits a sentence ('Nam ubi . . . oriri coepit') that is retained in translation.

There are many errors such as these. Occasionally Pynson's version of the Latin provides a reading from Laetus–Soldus rather than Ascensius. In **93. 1**, for example, Pynson has 'experiretur' where Ascensius, and most editions, read 'opperiretur'. Perhaps Barclay or another reader had taken this reading from a Soldus edition, for it appears in some of them (e.g. **1514.2** and **1521**), but not in others. 12/36 ff. (**18. 1**) appears to have been corrected from Laetus–Soldus where Pynson's text restores 'et Libyes' and 'humi', which are omitted in all but one of the Ascensian editions (the exception is the revised edition from Venice, **1513.2**), and is also omitted in the Paris Soldus (**1497/8**). Yet the compositor omits 'rei' in the previous sentence, although it is present in both Laetus–Britannicus and Ascensius.

At 67/22–3 (**114. 1**) Barclay names the Roman generals 'Quyntus Scipyo/ the other Marcus Manlyus' (*recte* Quintus Caepio and Gnaeus Manlius) following Laetus–Soldus rather than Ascensius. This does not align with Pynson's Latin, where there is a puzzling intervention that involves a confused conflation of the Laetus–Soldus and Ascensian texts (see note 67/22–3 for details).

Pynson's Latin text occasionally improves on Ascensius or Laetus–Britannicus in some cases of punctuation, such as 'Virtute: non malitia' (14/30: **22. 2**).

The reason why these anomalies occur is not clear, but one hypothesis that might be advanced is that Pynson had as his copy-text Barclay's own working copy of Ascensius, somewhat heavily annotated and marked, and perhaps difficult in places to read as a result. One other feature of the Pynson text may support this hypothesis. It is the only surviving version of Ascensius's *Iugurtha* up to **1521** to employ three grades of punctuation (besides parentheses and question mark): the punctus, colon, and virgule. The other editions restrict themselves to punctus and colon (or virgule). It may be that Barclay had marked up his text as an aid to translation, and at many points in the text one sees a resemblance between the Latin and the English punctuation, where the virgule is used mainly to separate noun phrases in apposition, and the colon to separate clause units, or to provide a heavier pause.

Alternative hypotheses cannot be dismissed outright. There may have been a lost edition of the text with commentary (besides the now lost **1513.3**), or Pynson may have set his text from one of the small octavo versions without commentary, but based upon Ascensius. The octavo by Petit (**1508.2**) carries Ascensius's text, but contains errors and idiosyncratic readings not found in Pynson. This edition does, nevertheless, carry a more complex punctuation scheme, employing punctus, colon, and, somewhat haphazardly, virgule and comma. The edition by Nicolaus Depratis (**1509.2**) provides another example of the kind of inferior reprint that might have served Pynson, although this particular reprint clearly was not Pynson's exemplar either. It provides a text very similar to **1504.1** and **1504.2**, but introduces many errors. In common with **1508.2** it retains the 'pro licentia' clause, but has corrected *Tolonia Tercon* to *Colonia Thereorum*.

Pynson did have access to Ascensius's commentary, however, as the transcription of the source for the compendious extract indicates, so it would be odd that he did not simply continue to use this copy for Sallust's text itself. It may be that he, like Barclay, was aware of the potential for an improved punctuation system from editions like the **1502** Venice Laetus–Brittanicus, or the **1514.2** Venice dual-commentary, itself closely resembling Bernard de Vianis's **1521** edition, which probably mirrored his lost **1513.3** first edition.

Dependence on Ascensius's Commentary

As numerous textual notes indicate, the influence of Ascensius's commentary on Barclay's translation is evident at many points either in verbal echoes or in the insertion of information additional to that which Sallust provides. See, for example, the following:

4/4–6 *Publius Scipio captayne . . . Rome.* Barclay adds this sentence (see note).

22/24–31 *And nat withstandyng . . . among the other mo. Sal*: Ac tametsi in ipso magna uis animi erat, confirmatus ab omnibus *etc* (33. 2: see note).

30/29–30 *he made his frende Bomylchar capytayne and gouernour.*

Sal: Elephantis . . . Bomilcarem praefecit (**49. 1**). *Asc*: et praefecit Bomilcharem amicum et propinquum suum (f. 69[r]).

36/68–9 *the Romayns: and specially on them which coursed before the tentes. Sal*: nostros (our Roman soldiers) (**59. 2**). *Asc*: nostros .s. milites Romanos et potissimum equites pro castris agitantes (f. 75[r]).

48/26–7 *but the dyspleasure of his mynde he toke ouer womanly and tenderly to his hert. Sal*: nimis molliter aegritudinem pati (**82. 2**). *Asc*: pati .i. patiebatur: ægretudinem .i. dolorem animi: nimis molliter .i. muliebriter (f. 86[r]).

66/37–8 *And often aduers and contrary to their owne selfe: and with themselfe repugnyng. Sal*: saepe ipsae sibi aduorsae (**113. 1**). *Asc*: ipse .i. ipsemet voluntates regum sunt sæpe aduersæ .i. contrariæ sibi .s. ipsis (f. 106[r]).

Dependence on Soldus's Commentary

Barclay appears also to have had Soldus's commentary constantly at hand when translating, and this means that he also had Laetus and Pomponius's text, as the evidence presented above independently demonstrates. When Soldus's commentary was first printed alongside this text in **1495.1**, many discrepancies between the two were left unresolved, and persisted in later reprintings. A case in point is found in **93. 2** (see note to 54/89–91). The erroneous reading *aliquantum* (or *aliquantulum*) instead of *aquatum* (probably deriving from a misreading of the abbreviation *aq̄tū*) disseminated itself by the 1480s, although the editio princeps (**1471.1**) and early editions such as **1473** carried the correct reading, attested in most manuscripts. The correct reading was restored by Aldus in **1509.3**, and found its way into editions thereafter, but the erroneous reading appeared in Laetus–Pomponius—despite Soldus's accompanying gloss clearly based upon the reading *aquatum*—and persisted in all editions of Ascensius's commentarial editions up to and beyond **1519**, except for the corrected Venice edition (**1513.2**), and the dual-commentary editions (**1514.2** and **1521**). For other examples of alternative readings in Soldus's commentary see notes to 51/31–2 (*adiutus/auctus*) and 62/4–5 (*confecto/infecto*).

In many instances Ascensius's commentary echoes or resembles Soldus's and it is difficult to determine whether Barclay's added content or interpretation is based on one in particular or both. The following examples, however, clearly derive from Soldus in incorporating information not found in Ascensius.

Prol/141–3 Where Sallust observes how certain Romans were inspired by looking upon their ancestral masks, and how memories of great deeds were aroused by the sight (4. 6), Barclay adds a further observation, taken from Soldus: 'Than how moch more ought the clere dyscripcyon of hystores to kyndell vnto boldnes/ and vertu/ the myndes of noble men by redyng of the same.' *Sold*: quia in ipsa imagine quodammodo cernant facta illius: cuius effigiem intuentur: quanto magis hoc facit historia: quæ multo clarius multoque expressius quam statua uel pictura non solum facta sed etiam dicta et consilia et animos uirorum excellentium ante oculos ponat (sig. f1^{v}).

8/6–9 'In which towne he [Hiempsal] had a dwellynge place: than as happened in the same towne was a man of the garde longyng to Iugurth of his lorde ryght derely beloued/ and with hym greatly in fauoure.' Barclay follows Soldus in making Hiempsal owner of the house rather than the 'proxumus lictor', despite Ascensius's correction of Soldus on this point. *Sal*: Sed Hiempsal in oppido Thirmida forte eius domo utebatur qui, proxumus lictor Iugurthae, carus acceptusque ei semper fuerat. *Sold*: ¶Eius domo .s. Hiempsalis . . . ¶Vtebatur: quia hic lictor familiariter uersabatur in domo Hiempsalis (sig. g1^{r}).

45/53 'their lawes/ their apparell and maners'. Barclay's translation of Sallust's 'legum cultusque' (78. 4) follows *Sold*: ¶Cultus: cultus pertinet ad uestitum et ad mores uiuendi (sig. n2^{v}).

65/56–69 '¶Kyng Bocchus I insure and promesse you . . .'. Sallust's summary of Sulla's words is in *oratio obliqua* 'denique regi patefacit, quod polliceatur . . .' (111. 1). Barclay's rendering into direct speech closely follows Soldus: 'O Bocche ego polliceor tibi quod senatus populusque Romanus non erunt ingrati . . .' (sig. q2^{r}).

In some other cases, the clustering of verbal echoes marks Soldus as Barclay's authority:

Prol/146–7 'prodygalyte/ and wastfull expences'. *Sal*: diuitiis et sumptibus (4. 7). *Sold*: prodigalitatem in expendendis. ¶Sumptibus: id est expensis (sig. f2^{r}).

2/62–3 'prone and hedlynge inclyned'. *Sal*: praeceps (6. 3). *Sold*: ¶Et praeceps: id est prona procliuis et inclinata (sig. f4^{v}).

22/35–6 'to haue hym to prison and there to kepe hym in bandes'. *Sal*: in uincula duci (33. 3). *Sold*: ¶In uincula: id est in carcerem (sig. i6^{r}).

29/107–8 'his greattest towne named Vacca/ was alyenate and lost from hym'. *Sal*: urbs maxuma alienata (48. 1). *Sold*: maximam urbem .s. Vaccam . . . ¶Alienata .i. amissa (sig. l1^{v}). *Asc*: Urbs maxima .s. Vacca: alienata a se hoc est ab Iugurtha (f. 68^{v}).

42/107–8 'in abiect and secrete places agaynst the honoure of his estate royall'. *Sal*: loco saepe contra decus regium (72. 2). *Sold*: ¶Contra decus regium: quia in loco humili et abiecto iacebat (sig. m6^{r}).

In a few instances Barclay apparently merges information from both Soldus and Ascensius. See, for example:

29/109–10 'The myndes of his lordes and commens were prouokedde and moued agaynst hym.' Sallust says merely 'animi popularium temptati' ('the loyalty of his subjects had been subverted', 48. 1). Soldus states that 'popularium' means 'hominum uulgarium et infimorum' (sig. l1^{v}) whereas Ascensius glosses 'fautorum utpote legatorum' (f. 68^{v}). Rather than choose one commentator over the other, Barclay combines their disparate explanations.

19/5–6 'Right worthy cetyzins many thynges shuld withdrawe me from defence of you and from charge and medlyng with your besynesses.' *Sal*: Multa me dehortantur a uobis (31. 1). *Sold*: ¶Multa me dehortantur a uobis .i. multa me dehortantur o Quirites a defensione uestri (sig. i1^{r}). *Asc*: a vobis .i. a negociis vestris curandis (f. 58^{r}).

In some instances the commentaries may say the same thing in substance, but Barclay still draws verbal echoes from both, as in his expansion of Sallust's 'probitas' (14. 4) into 'probyte/ honest lyfe/ and innocence' (10/35). He takes 'innocence' from Soldus, 'Ipsa probitas .i. ipsa bonitas ac si diceret. quoniam bonitas mea et innocentia per se tuta esse non potest' (sig. g2^v^), and 'honest lyfe' from Ascensius, 'probitas .i. proba et honesta vita' (f. 47^r^).

Finally, it should be noted that in a few instances Barclay overlooked information in the commentaries that would have improved his understanding and translation. See notes to 16/88 'bothe Numidyans and Italyan marchauntes indyfferently'; 54/15–6 'But in contrari wyse . . . man lyueyng'.

Possible sources in addition to Soldus and Ascensius

Apart from some reasonable conjectures based upon Sallust's own text, and the repetitions and amplifications that clarify Sallust's compressed expression, most additional information in Barclay's translation can be found in one or both of the two main commentaries. There are, nevertheless, a few exceptions. In chapter 7 Sallust states that Micipsa sent forces (Jugurtha among them) to assist the Romans in the war against Numantia. Neither he nor the commentators mention other kings assisting. Barclay, however, states:

> vnto which warre dyuers kynges to them assocyate sent vnto them socours agaynst the same cyte. Amonge whom Micipsa also sent vnto them into socours a fayre company of horsmen and fotemen (2/87–90).

Soldus's gloss on *socios* in the following chapter (8. 1) might account for Barclay's version (see note to 2/123–5); but it may be that he derived his information independently from Livy's summary for Book 57 of *Ab urbe condita*. The contributions of other *socii* are also mentioned in Cicero, *Pro Rege Deiotaro* 19, and Appian's account of the Spanish wars (*Hispania* 84. 365: of which a Latin translation by Petrus Candidus appeared in 1452 and was in print by 1477). As noted above, the sidenote to Barclay's account of Dido (12/123 ff.) indicates that Virgil and Servius are his authorities for details additional to those found in Soldus and Ascensius. In describing Marius's triumph (67/40–56), Barclay adds details such as the four white horses, the golden chariot, and the sacrifice of a bull to Jupiter, which do not appear in Sallust, or in Plutarch's *Life of Marius*, which Ascensius cites. Here Barclay seems to draw on a general knowledge of the Roman triumph taken from other historical sources. Some other minor additions of detail elsewhere in the text are perhaps Barclay's own surmise, such as the addition of wrestling to Jugurtha's catalogue of physical accomplishments (2/45), or the detail (7/26–7) 'by requestes of his brother and of other noble menne of the realme' (see notes and p. lvii below).

5. TRANSLATION METHOD AND STYLE

Barclay must have been aware that in translating Sallust, his was an innovative undertaking, for the *Iugurtha* is one of the earliest English translations direct from the classics, apart from the translations of Boethius by Alfred and Chaucer, the varied uses made of Ovid and Virgil by authors including Chaucer and Gower, and translations of medieval or Renaissance intermediaries such as Skelton's translation of Poggio Bracciolini's Latin version of Diodorus Siculus, the *Bibliotheca Historica* (*c.*1487).[52] Yet in spite of this, Barclay does not articulate particular concerns about translation method such as appear in the prefaces of some other translators. There is no invocation of the classical and patristic trope contrasting 'uerbum ex uerbo' translation with 'sensum e sensu', as we find in Alfred or Trevisa, nor is there any assertion of the fitness or otherwise of English for rendering Latin.[53] By way of contrast, the contemporaneous translators responsible for the parallel-text *Terens in Englysh* proclaim the fitness of English as it had evolved out of the pioneering translation efforts of Chaucer, Gower, and Lydgate:

¶By these men our tong is amplyfyed so
That we therin now translate as well may
As in eny other tongis other can do
Yet the Greke tong and Laten dyuers men say

[52] Some translations made earlier, such as John Tiptoft's 1481 version of Cicero's *De Amicitia*, appear in print later (*c.*1530); Caxton's 1480 translation of Ovid's *Metamorphoses* was not printed, and in any case is based upon Bersuire's moralized version. Caxton's Cato and Aesop are based upon intermediary French versions. For a chronological list of translations from 1477 see Lathrop, *Translations*, 311 ff. On Chaucer's Boethius, and his and Gower's excerptions from Ovid and Virgil see Stephen Medcalf, 'Classical Authors' in Ellis (ed.), *The Oxford History of Literary Translation*, i. 364–89.

[53] On the *sensum pro sensu* formula, and for a survey of medieval translation theory see Rita Copeland, *Rhetoric, Hermeneutics and Translation in the Middle Ages: Academic Traditions and Vernacular Texts* (Cambridge, 1991). Trevisa's letter to Lord Berkeley, prefaced to his translation of the *Polychronicon*, describes his principles: 'I wote that it is your will for to make this translacion clere and playn to be knowen and vnderstonden. In somme place I shall sette word for worde and actyf for actyf and passyf for passyf arowe right as it stondeth withoute chaungynge the ordre of wordes. But in somme place I muste chaunge the ordre of wordes and sette actyf for passyf and ayenward. And in somme place I muste sette a reson for a worde and telle what it meneth. But for al suche chaungyng the menyng shal stande and not be chaunged' (STC 13438: *Cronica Ranulphi Cistrensis Monachi* (Caxton, 1482), f. iii[v]). Caxton also prints Trevisa's *Dialogue between a Lord and a Clerk upon Translation*, which further considers problems for a translator. Modernized texts appear in *Fifteenth-Century Prose and Verse*, ed. A. W. Pollard (Westminster, 1903), 203–10.

Haue many wordys can not be englyshid this day
So lyke wyse in Englysh many wordys do habound
That no Greke nor Laten for them can be found.
¶And the cause that our tong is so plenteouse now
For we kepe our Englysh contynually
And of other tongis many wordis we borow
Which now for Englysh we vse and occupy
These thingis haue gyuen corage gretly
To dyuers and specyally now of late
To them that this comedy haue translate.[54]

Nevertheless, at the conclusion of the work the translators observe that shortcomings may arise from their policy of remaining concise:

The translatours know well it may be amendyd
By theym that be wyse and wold take the payne
It for to rede and to corect agayn
¶Wherfore the translatours now require you this
Yf ought be amys ye wold consyder
The Englysh almost as short as the Latten is
And still to kepe ryme a dyffycult matter
To make the sentence opynly to appere
Which if it had a long expocysyon
Then were it a comment and no translacioun.[55]

In what is Barclay's only declaration of translation policy, in contrast, he states that he will not attempt to imitate the stylistic compression that characterizes Sallust's own manner of writing, and that his text may serve as a commentary upon the Latin as well as a translation in its own right:

such as shall dysdayne to rede my translatyon in Englysshe: may rede this hystorie more compendyouslie and more obscurely written in Latyn. Which hystorie: parauenture shall apere more clere and playne vnto theym in many places by help of this my translation. Which shal nat be to tedyous to such as be ler[n]ed and vnderstande Latyn: but vnto many noble gentylmen which vnderstand nat Latyn tong perfetly I dout nat but that this my labour to them shalbe both pleasure and profet. For by the same they shall haue some help toward the vnderstandyng of Latyn: which at this tyme is almost contemned of gentylmen. And also they shall vnderstande a ryght fruytfull hystorie: both pleasant/ profytable/ and ryght necessary vnto euery degre:

54 *STC* 23894 (*c.*1520, probably from the Paris press of le Noir), sig. A.i^{v}.
55 Sig. D.v^{v}.

but specially to gentylmen/ which coueyt to attayne to clere fame and honour: by glorious dedes of chyualry (Pref/31–44).

Barclay expands Sallust's Latin text of around 21,200 words to over 71,500 words of English (not including the added prefatory matter, chapter headings, or the 'compendyous extract'). A small proportion of this expansion involves the addition of information not found in Sallust (for example, the section on the foundation of Carthage), but most involves amplification, both explicatory and rhetorical, of the substance of Sallust. This is first of all apparent in the heavy use of 'doublets', which are a common feature of late Middle English translations, as for example in John Trevisa's and Caxton's translations.

Doublets

Many of Barclay's doublets are taken directly from the commentaries:

> 10/147 *in dongyons and darknes*. *Sal*: in tenebris (14. 15). *Sold*: ¶In tenebris .i. in carcere (sig. g3^{v}).

> 19/39 *in your handes and power*. *Sal*: in uostra manu (31. 5). *Sold*: ¶In uestra manu .i. uestra potestate (sig. i1^{v}).

> 30/9 *preuented and ouerpassed*. *Sal*: anteuenit (48. 2). *Asc*: anteuenit .i. preuenit (f. 69^{r}).

> 10/35 *probyte/ honest lyfe/ and innocence*. *Sal*: probitas (14. 4). *Sold*: ¶Ipsa probitas .i. ipsa bonitas ac si diceret. quoniam bonitas mea et innocentia per se tuta esse non potest (sig. g2^{v}). *Asc*: probitas .i. proba et honesta vita (f. 47^{r}).

In some instances there is no verbal correspondance, but the commentaries appear to have had an influence:

> 30/19–20 *coueredde and all ouergrowen with wylde olyue trees*. *Sal*: uestitus oleastro (48. 3). *Sold*: ¶Vestitus .i. plenus. Vestire enim significat implere (sig. l2.^{r}). *Asc*: vestitus .i. coopertus (f. 69^{r})

Here Soldus also cites Virgil's *Georgics* 2. 37–8: 'iuuat Ismara Baccho / conserer atque olea magnum uestire Taburnum' ('it is pleasing to plant [even such rugged mountains as] Ismarus with vines, and clothe great Taburnus with olives'), as if to reinforce the picture of lush vegetation in such a wild place.

Elsewhere Barclay provides a doubling where no synonyms or other information are provided by the glossators:

30/31 *and infourmed and taught hym parfitely*. *Sal*: eumque edocet (49. 1).

(In this case, apparently, Barclay adds the adverb *parfitely* so as to make explicit the function of the verbal prefix *e(x)-*.)

30/35 *elect and chosen*. *Sal*: delectis (49. 1).

30/54 *heed and begynnyng*. *Sal*: initium (49. 3).

Repetition and Amplification

In a passage such as the following, Barclay amplifies Sallust through the addition of doublets and some other words for clarification, such as *offyce*, reinforced by its repetition another three times.

Proinde [*v.l.* perinde] quasi praetura et consulatus atque alia omnia huiusce modi per ipsa clara et magnifica sint ac non perinde habeantur, ut eorum qui ea sustinent uirtus est (4. 8).

After suche maner as yf the offyce of a hye Iuge/ of a Tresourer/ a Consull/ a Prouost/ and all such other great offyces were noble and excellent of themselfe. And nat in maner as yf such offyces shulde be counted of worthynes and dygnite: after as the vertue/ and honour is: of such as rule in the same offyces and hy rowmes (Prol/153–8).

In addition, however, he recasts the whole sentence in another form to make its meaning absolutely clear:

But playnly affirmyng the treuth: the man maketh the offyce noble/ and worshypfull: yf his maners shyne by vertue. But yf his conuersacyon be contrary/ no offyce/ nor rowme/ can make hym noble/ nor worshypfull (Prol/158–61).

A similar method is apparent in the following sentence from Adherbal's impassioned plea in the Senate for Roman help against Jugurtha:

Familia nostra cum populo Romano bello Carthaginiensi amicitiam instituit, quo tempore magis fides eius quam fortuna petunda erat.

Our family established friendship with the Roman People during the Carthaginian war, at a time when the good faith of Rome was to be obtained, but not her fortune (14. 5).

Taking up details from Soldus's commentary, Barclay provides a rendering considerably expanded in itself in order to make clear the historical circumstances referred to:

our forefathers and rote of our lynage Massinissa confeterated hymselfe with the peple of Rome in the seconde batayle of Affryke/ or Cartage: what tyme was more faythfulnes to be trusted in them and their good wyll than of welth or riches to be optayned of the Romayns/ beynge at that tyme assayled with warre on euery syde: their ryches and treasours consumed by often batayles (10/48–53).

Barclay then makes a further addition, effectively a repetition and clarification of the preceding sentence.

Thus is it euydent that our auncetry confederat nat themselfe to your felowshyp for their owne defence: in hope of ryches: in hope of domynion: nor for any other pryuate profet: but onely for fauoure and loue whiche they had vnto your empyre (10/53–7).

Some chapters show a more marked use of this technique than others. Instances are clustered quite heavily in Barclay's twenty-second chapter, for example:

Igitur Iugurtha contra decus regium cultu quam maxume miserabili cum Cassio Romam uenit (**33**. 1).

And so at last Iugurth consented to go to Rome with Cassius. Wherfore to enduce the Romayns to the more pyte he arayed hymselfe in rude aparell agaynst his honour royall moche vyle and myserable (22/20–3)

Having replaced 'uenit' by 'consented to go', Barclay then provides another form of words, and in so doing repeats and amplifies what Sallust says, also setting up a progression from planning to executing his show of humility:

and so with Cassius came to Rome nat as a kyng/ but poorly and with a small company (22/23–4).

This may have been inspired by Ascensius's gloss: 'Igitur Iugurtha sic persuasus venit . . .' (f. 60^{v}). Both Soldus and Ascensius take 'cultu' as referring to Iugurtha's garb ('uestitu sordido et abiecto', 'cultu .i. amictu') but in his rephrasing of the sentence Barclay seems to take it more broadly to refer to Iugurtha's habit of travelling with a richly equipped retinue.

In the same chapter we find:

At C. Memmius aduocata contione . . . dignitati quam irae magis consulens sedare motus et animos eorum mollire, postremo confirmare fidem publicam per sese inuiolatam fore (**33. 3**).

Caius Memmius heryng herof called togyder the commenty and alayed the mocyon and wrath of their myndes/ apeasyng their vnauysed rancour. And requirynge them to kepe the fayth and trouth of the cyte (which they [had] promysed to Iugurthe) clere/ inuyolate/ and vndefyled (22/39–43).

This translation is then followed by another, restating and explicating the former:

Thus dyde Memmius exhort them as he which more regarded and set more by the conseruacion of the dygnite of Rome/ than by the parformyng and satysfyeng the wrath and yre of the rude commens (22/43–6).

Another instance appears in the next sentence:

Quibus iuuantibus quibusque ministris ea egerit, quamquam intellegat populus Romanus, tamen uelle manufesta magis ex illo habere (**33. 4**).

And how beit (sayd Memmius) that the Romayns knewe well his supporters yet they wold moost of all that Iugurth shulde openly dyscouer and accuse them hymselfe (22/54–6).

This is followed by a repetition and recapitulation of what had come before.

Wherfore he desyred hym truely to confesse the names of them by whose supportacion he was so bolde to commyt so many imoderate and cruell dedes (22/56–8).

On a number of occasions Barclay inserts a Christian moralist's viewpoint, such as where Sallust makes reference to a sacrifice ('Per idem tempus Vticae C. Mario per hostias dis supplicanti . . .' **63. 1**). Both Soldus and Ascensius describe the process of divination, but in neutral terms, except that Ascensius observes: 'vt cætera superstitiosa: calliditate spirituum malignorum putatur inuenta' (f. 77^{r}). Barclay adds information from the commentators, and his own observation also that such sacrifices and the predictions derived from them were 'a custome damnable . . . among the people at those dayes' (39/7–8). Furthermore, he translates 'dis' as 'ydolles' and refers to the 'blynde errour' of the people (cf. also 'dis immortalibus' translated as 'their ydolles' 34/21). Similar expansions include 'by superfluous habundance of richesse/ voluptuosyte/ and of other worldely delectacyons' (27/7–8: 'atque abundantia earum rerum' **41. 1**); Ascensius: 'et abundantia earum rerum .s. diuitiarum et voluptatum' (f. 65[r]).

It is not often that Barclay adds information that does not appear in one or other of his commentaries, but we might note instances such as the following.

Uti mos gentis illius est, equitare iaculari, cursu cum aequalibus certare . . . (**6. 1**)

but as is the custome and maner of the people of Numidy/ hymselfe he exercysed somtyme in rydinge: somtyme in castynge the dart/ and somtyme in ronnynge and wrestlynge with his companyons of lyke age (2/42–5).

Perhaps Barclay had in mind the English fondness for wrestling (including that of the young Henry VIII) when translating this passage, although if that is the case he probably made this addition before 1520 when Henry suffered a huge embarrassment at the Field of Cloth of Gold, challenging Francis to a wrestling match and being thrown by the lighter French king.

In describing Jugurtha's invasion of Adherbal's part of Numidia, Barclay observes that 'many of thinhabytauntes he murdred' (13/27). Sallust does not say this; only that Jugurtha took many prisoners: 'multos mortalis cum pecore atque alia praeda capit' (**20. 3**). Barclay would have been familiar with Sallust's habitual use of 'mortales' simply to refer to 'people'.

In chapter **40**, Sallust recounts how those in Rome opposed to Gaius Mamilius Limetanus' bill proposing a judicial inquiry operated secretly through their friends from the Latin cities and the Italian allies. Barclay translates:

The princes of these natyons and such other lyke gaue counsell to the senatours which were nat fauty in the premysses/ and also to the commenty: that in suche a troublous/ besy/ and peryllous season no suche examynations shulde be made nor procede forwarde to effect: for drede of many inconuenyences which of the same myght ryse bytwene the noble men and commens (26/89–95).

The Latins and other Italian allies could do little directly to hinder the bill, as they were not franchised until 89 BC. Cf. *Sold*: qui erant ciues Romani. Sed tamen nihil facere potuerunt. Nam rogatio perlata est et iussa (sig. k3[v]). Barclay seems to suggest in his explanatory expansion that they took a conciliatory role. Sallust implies, rather, that those with commercial interests at stake in Numidia were coopted by the nobles to disrupt the proceedings by whatever covert means they could.

In chapter 38 Sallust provides a dramatic account of Jugurtha's surprise night attack upon Aulus's camp:

> The Romayne soudyours which were with Aulus/ thus vnwardly inuaded . . . So that finally it was vncertayne vnto them whether it was better or more sure to fle or abyde to their auenture (25/69–89).

Sallust's fifty-word description of the Roman's perilous situation (38. 4–5) is highly compressed. Barclay expands it to 226 words, imaginatively and vividly reinforcing the reader's consciousness of the soldiers' terror at the situation, and adding the explicit references to death and dying.

Barclay adds a sentence to Sallust 9. 3:

> With these letters of Scipio Iugurth retourned into Numydy vnto his vncle Micipsa: where he was worthely and ioyefully receyued of the commentie (5/3–5).

The statement that he delivers the letter to his uncle as he was directed to do is a reasonable inference; the statement that the commons received him with joy and honour is without foundation, except as an inference from Sallust's earlier statement in chapter 6 that Iugurtha was popular among the Numidians, and that this fact had already deterred Micipsa from having Iugurtha assassinated.

Sallust (23. 1) states that Iugurtha, in addition to applying all the usual stratagems of siege warfare, tried to win over the defenders by bribes or threats, and exhorted his own troops to do their utmost. He does not state, as Barclay does, that Iugurtha employed any new or innovative siege techniques:

> nothyng he omytted wont or possyble to be done in suche a case/ nor no ingen of warre laft he vnprouyded which in those dayes was contryued or founde: but rather besyde all olde inuentyons he ymagined and deuysed newe ingens and ordynaunces of warre nat sene before that tyme: and all for dystruction of the towne of Cyrtha. And of Adherball whom he besyged within the same (15/81–6).

At 28. 7 Sallust states only that Calphurnius took some towns by conquest: 'Igitur Calpurnius initio paratis conmeatibus acriter Numidiam ingressus est, multosque mortalis et urbis aliquot pugnando cepit.' Barclay makes an addition:

suche [townes] as resysted his power he brent them to the grounde to increas fere to their neighbours (17/99–100).

Omissions

Omissions of detail from Sallust are rare, and possibly accidental. Barclay omits Sallust's statement that the Numidians called their boat-shaped huts *mapalia* ('aedificia Numidarum agrestium, quae mapalia [*Laetus–Britannicus* and *Ascensius*: quæ agrestium mapalia] illi uocant' **18. 8**), despite the additional explication provided by Ascensius ('mapalia .i. tuguria' f. 51^{r}). From Sallust's chapter **19. 7** he omits the relative clause 'quos nouissume habuerant'; from **29. 4** 'quoniam deditionis mora indutiae agitabantur'; from **35. 4** 'sicuti multa confecerat' (see notes to 12/168–9, 17/133–5, 23/31–2); and from **40. 1** 'perfugas'. In such instances the corresponding Latin appears in Barclay's source texts and in his Latin side-text. Although in general passages dealing with technical aspects of war are generously treated, with the addition of information from the commentaries, in one instance (29/55 ff.; **46. 7**) Barclay uncharacteristically omits to include any of the commentators' explanations of the Roman hollow square formation, or the equipment belonging to different kinds of soldiers, and furthermore he omits Sallust's phrase 'tribunis legionum et praefectis cohortium'.

6. THE TEXTS OF THE TRANSLATION

The First Edition: STC 21626

STC2 intially assigned a date of '1520?' to Pynson's first edition, later revising this to '1522?' in the *Corrigenda* listed in volume 3. There is no date given in the colophon, and no bibliographical information has come to light subsequently that might provide cause for reconsideration of the estimated date based upon typographical evidence.

Known surviving copies are held as follows: London, British Library; Oxford, Bodleian Library; Cambridge, University Library (imperfect); Manchester, John Rylands Library; Williamstown, Mass., Chapin Library; Urbana, Ill., University of Illinois Library; Austin, University of Texas, Harry Ransom Humanities Research

Center (formerly in the Carl Pforzheimer Library, New York); New Haven, Yale Centre for British Art (formerly in the collection of Paul Mellon).[56]

The size of leaves is 190 × 273 mm; the printed space for the main text measures 151 × 194 mm (exclusive of running head, catchwords, signatures etc.), with the English text-column 107 mm wide and the parallel Latin text-column 40 mm wide. A complete page has 42 lines of English, and 49 lines of Latin. The English appears in Pynson's familiar 95 Textura (black letter), and the Latin in his 80 Roman. Four lines of 114 Roman appear at the end of Barclay's Latin Preface. For title page, chapter headings, headlines, and colophon Pynson employed his usual textura 114 *b*.[57] There is a range of ornamented initials, seen in other books printed by Pynson, for the beginnings of chapters. Most average 32 × 32 mm and occupy the height of seven text lines. A, M, N, P, R, T display the letter against a floral or leafy background. B has two long-necked intertwined beasts, C, a knight fighting a dragon, I, twin unicorns, and O, a winged dragon. Thielman Kerver's alphabet was the model for most of these letters.[58] Some chapters begin with a B, I, K, M, T, or W about 22 × 22 mm, occuping five lines of height. Folio 1 carries a ten-line-high capital I for the beginning of Sallust's Preface in translation, and a three-line-high H for the Latin column.

The composition is as follows: [a.i] a.ii–a.iiii [a.v–a.viii] A.i A.ii A.iii [A.iv–vi] in sixes to Pi–[P.iv] Qi–[Q.vi]. A.i is marked 'Fo. primo', and foliation continues in Roman numerals to [Q.iv] 'Fo. xCii'.

Contents and illustration are as follows:

[a.i] Title: 'Here begynneth the famous cronycle . . .'

Following the title, a woodcut of a shield bearing a lion rampant sinister facing, in fleur-de-lis border like that of the Scottish arms, held, as if attacked, by a lion rampant 'supporter', facing dexter. The woodcut, being heraldic, is not listed in Hodnett.[59] The image of a lion ravaging the Scottish Royal arms reflects the victory of

[56] *STC2* lists a first edition copy at Cambridge, Corpus Christi College, but this is a copy of the second edition, and now correctly catalogued as such.

[57] Type classifications are as given by Frank Isaac, *English & Scottish Printing Types 1501–35, 1508–41* (London, 1930): see fig. 19 for comparison, and preliminary remarks on Pynson's types [unpaginated].

[58] See Oscar Jennings, *Early Woodcut Initials* (London, 1908), 241 for reproductions of Pynson's B and C, and Kerver's C, on which Pynson's was modelled.

[59] For passing comment see Johnston, 488.

Thomas Howard over the Scots at Flodden in 1513. Howard's badge, derived from the Mowbray dukes and earls of Norfolk, was a white lion charged on the shoulder with a blue crescent.[60] It appears that Pynson had the woodcut made in 1513: there survives a late-sixteenth-century manuscript copy (London, BL Add. MS 29506, ff. 1–13) of a lost pamphlet, *Thordre and behavyoure of the right honourabie Erie of Surrey . . . ayonst the kynge of Scottes*, which along with the text reproduces the quire signatures of the lost print-text, the woodcut, and Pynson's colophon: 'Imprynted in fletestrete at the sygne of the George by Richarde Pynson, prynter unto the Kynges noble grace'.[61] On Copland's use of a nearly identical woodcut see above, pp. xvi–xvii. The Norfolk arms (gules, a bend between six cross-crosslets fitchée, argent) are not reproduced, and did not feature a lion until the augmentation of honour after Flodden when Henry VIII granted the addition of 'a demi-lion pierced in the mouth with an arrow, depicted on the colours for the arms of the King of Scotland, which the said James, late King of the Scots, bore'.[62] The crest above the Howard arms was a lion statant with tail extended, or, gorged with a ducal coronet, argent; and the dexter supporter of the arms, a lion, argent.

[a.i^{v}] Full-page woodcut: the arms of Henry VII and Henry VIII (England and France, quartered). A Tudor rose surmounts the crown crest, and is flanked by two angels holding blank scrolls. Below the angels, there is a portcullis badge either side, below which the arms are carried by a gryphon and a greyhound as supporters. Henry's supporters were the same as his father's until later in his reign when he discontinued the greyhound, moved the dragon to the sinister, and introduced one of the lions of England on the dexter. The woodcut does not appear in the second edition. The cut seems first to have been used as the arms of Henry VII in the *Missal* that Pynson published for the King in 1504. It continues to be used during the reign of Henry VIII, lastly in the two parts of Froissart (1523, 1525).[63] The scroll, empty in the 1522 *Jugurtha*, usually carries the motto 'Hec

[60] See Arthur Charles Fox-Davies, *The Art of Heraldry: An Encyclopædia of Armory* (London, 1904), 336.

[61] See Neville, 'Richard Pynson', 111–12, and Nancy Gutierrez and Mary Erler, 'Print into Manuscript: A Flodden Field News Pamphlet Publication', in *Studies in Medieval and Renaissance History*, NS 8 (New York, 1987), 189–230.

[62] Fox-Davies, *Heraldry*, 394.

[63] The cut appears in the following books (in chronological order): *STC* 16179, 16140, 14116, 16190, 5579, 10659, 15724, 9362.6, 9358.5, 16202, 18388, 21626, 11396, 11397.

rosa virtutis de celo missa sereno. Eternum florens regia sceptra feret.'[64]

a.2–a.4^{r} The table of contents, set in two columns.

a.4^{v}–a.8^{r} Barclay's prefaces, Latin and English, set in parallel columns, preceded by a woodcut, depicting a black monk (Benedictine) presenting a book to a nobleman, Hodnett number 1498 (reproduced, fig. 147).[65] It first appears in the 1515(?) edition of *The Life of Saint George* (*STC* 22992.1).

a.8 After the preface, a woodcut image of a monk writing at his desk: Hodnett number 1510 (fig. 142). The cut first appeared in Pynson's 1513 edition of *The Hystorye . . . of Troye* (John Lydgate's translation of Guido delle Colonne; *STC* 5579), and appears in several Pynson editions of clerical authors up to *c.*1529. It does not appear in the second edition.

a.8^{v} Woodcut of an army landing from ships: Hodnett number 1496.[66] The cut is known from only one other edition, the 1516 *Cronycle* of Robert Fabyan (*STC* 10659). It does not appear in the second edition.

A.i –[Q.iv^{v}] The text body.

[Q.v] The colophon.

[Q.v^{v}] Pynson's seventh device (McKerrow no. 44), used in dated works between 1519 and 1526, and probably from 1516 to 1529.[67]

In preparing this edition, three copies of the first edition have been fully collated against one another (the Oxford, Texas, and Illinois copies), with sample collations of other copies. Virtually no variation between copies has been discovered except for a single sheet constituting folios 8 and 11 (with quire mark 'B.ii.').[68] On folio 11, for the chapter opening 'Whan the thre pryncces . . .', the first seven lines are inset for the insertion of a large capital W, but it was not put into the forme. All copies examined except one have an ordinary 95 textura capital W set in the centre of the blank space, as if for a guide letter; this is absent from the Texas copy. In addition, an error on the

[64] See Johnston, Appendix III, 'Coats-of-Arms': COA. 2.

[65] On Pynson's use of this image exclusively in books by Barclay see Carlson, 'Alexander Barclay and Richard Pynson', and Julie A. Smith, 'Woodcut Presentation Scenes in Books Printed by Caxton, De Worde, Pynson', *Gutenberg Jahrbuch*, [61] (1986), 322–43.

[66] See *Additions and Corrections*, 57.

[67] Ronald B. McKerrow, *Printers' & Publishers' Devices in England and Scotland 1485–1640* (London, 1949), p. 16, no. 44.

[68] The original folio numbering is printed in Roman numerals. For convenience references have been converted to Arabic numerals.

verso of f. 11 occurs only in the Texas copy which reads 'Nemydyans', where this is corrected to 'Numidyans' in other, apparently later, copies. A possible explanation for the absent block capital is that it was temporarily unavailable while typesetting was going on, but its return was anticipated in time for printing the sheet. Pynson's other large capital Ws are five lines high, not seven, and one had already been employed in the forme for the facing page (f. 8^{v}). For some reason, the seven-line W remained unavailable, and the five-line one, although out of character with the other seven-line capitals, was then used throughout the remainder of the book. The seven-line W was later available (or a replacement had been made) and was employed for the second edition.[69]

The Second Edition: STC 21627

As for the first edition, there is no date of printing provided in the colophon, but typographical evidence suggests a date around 1525. Known surviving copies are located as follows: London, British Library (two imperfect copies); Cambridge, University Library (two copies, one imperfect); Cambridge, Corpus Christi College Library; Manchester, John Rylands Library; San Marino, Calif., Huntington Library; Los Angeles, University of California Library; Austin, University of Texas, Harry Ransom Humanities Research Center (formerly in the Carl Pforzheimer Library, New York); New Haven, Yale University, Beinecke Library.

The composition is as follows: [a.i] a.ii–a.iiii [a.v–a.vi] A.i A.ii A.iii [A.iv–vi] in sixes to O.1–[O.iv], Pi–[P.iv]. A.i is marked 'Fo. primo', and foliation continues in roman numerals to [P.iv] 'Fo. lxxxvi'.

From the setting of the text proper (from the second quire, with the signature mark 'A') in the 1525 edition, it would appear that Pynson's intention at the outset was to replicate as closely as possible the formes as set up in the first edition. This suggests that only limited revision or correction was planned. Nevertheless the quire preceding 'A', containing the Prefaces and Table of Contents, and given the signature mark 'a', was reset on three sheets (twelve pages) instead of the four (sixteen pages) of the first edition by various expedients, including leaving no blank sides, omitting the woodcuts

[69] The letter W seems to have been particularly vexatious. In Pynson's 1523 edition of Froissart, there are several instances of a guide-letter taking the place of a five-line W (ff. 3^{r}, 5^{r}, 5^{v}) or a three-line W (35^{v}, 195^{v}, 199^{r}, 199^{v}, 210^{r}, 217^{r}). The larger seven-line W does not appear earlier in the book, but is used regularly from f. 74 onwards.

(the arms of Henry VII/VIII, and Hodnett nos. 1510 and 1496), and printing the preface with more lines per page (45 of the textura, against 41 in the first edition). Furthermore, from the beginning of the third quire (signature 'B') the format initially undertaken in signature A was changed. From here on, the text frame contains 45 lines of textura instead of 42. Pages are 185 × 275 mm throughout; the printed frame changes from 151 × 194 mm to 156 × 213 mm, the English column width changing from 106 to 104 mm, and the Latin from 40 to 42 mm. Further small savings of space are achieved by using seven-line woodcut initials less frequently, and five-line ones more so. The second edition then runs to eighty-six numbered folios, with one spare unnumbered folio at the end, whereas the first has ninety-two.

This change in policy may be explained by scrutiny of the changes in the text that occur in the second quire ('A'). There are additions of punctuation to make good some omissions in the first edition, changes in vocabulary, and the removal of some repetitious or redundant words (see below for details). These three kinds of change, given their more or less systematic application throughout the entire text, were most likely entered by hand on the copy-text for the compositors. It seems that after the setting of quire 'A', a decision was made that incorporating these changes took priority over maintaining the exact duplication of formes from the first edition, and a more flexible approach was adopted (with further saving of paper as well).

Differences between Individual Copies of the Second Edition: the Redman Sheet

From full collation of three copies (Cambridge, Texas, and Yale) and sample collation of others, only one variation of significance emerges, and involves the sheet comprising the conjugate folios lxii and lxv. In most surviving copies, these folios appear in a form consistent with the rest of the edition. In the Rylands and Cambridge University Library copies, the top line of f. lxv reads *suhche thynges*, against *suche thynges* in the Texas, Huntington, and Yale copies. In the two BL copies, however, this sheet is missing, and in the Cambridge, Corpus Christi College and UCLA copies the extant sheet displays a completely new printing by Robert Redman, using his 94 Textura for the English, but a 67 Rotunda for the Latin instead of Pynson's 80 Roman, used throughout the rest of the book (as in the first edition). In the reprinted sheet, the heading for Chapter xlix and the running head is in a 114 Textura. This uses a different capital T, similar to that of the rare Pynson 116 found in the title page of *The Articles of our fayth* [1509] (STC 3359) and also in Littleton's *Tenures* [1510?] (*STC* 15723). This type, however, differs slightly, and features the distinctive w^{8} in lower case, while the 94 features the capital w^{8} (1538). At one point on f. lxv^{r}, within the 67 Rotunda text line, Redman's compositor uses his distinctive 66 Roman 'Qu', with the tail of the Q under the u (1536). Both the textura and the rotunda are punctuated with commas rather than virgules. In typography and in format the reprinted single sheet is very similar to Redman's dual-language parallel text of Tyndale's New Testament, printed in 1538 (*STC* 2815).[70]

Redman apparently took over Pynson's shop upon the death of the latter, and seems to have been involved in the sale of the remaining stock of Barclay's book in the 1530s, at which time it was possibly realized that copies had been sold with a sheet missing, as in the BL copies.[71] Either the print run was comparatively large or sales had slowed, if the second edition was still available for sale around 1538, when the first edition had sold out within two or three years of printing around 1522.

1525 Revisions to the Parallel Latin Text

Some errors in the Latin side-text of the first edition were corrected in the second, bringing it into line with Ascensius's text, as it appears in the majority of his commentarial editions (**1504.1**, **1506.2**, etc. to **1519**).

Edition 1	*Edition 2*	
ad gloriam virtus	~ virtuti (recte *virtutis*, as *Asc*)	**1. 3**
Sed captus	Sin captus	**1. 4**
Mumidarum	Numidarum	**5. 4**
raput	caput	**12. 5**
mihi	quod mihi	**14. 4**
sena	seua	**14. 10**
rignum	regnum	**14. 25**
numeribus	muneribus	**20. 1**

[70] For further discussion of the Redman sheet see Greg Waite, 'Alexander Barclay, Robert Pynson, and an Unnoticed Sheet Printed by Robert Redman', *Notes and Queries*, 58 (2011), 193–6. See also the *STC* entry for Pynson's 1523 Froissart (*STC* 11396) for a similar instance of such reprint work by Redman.

[71] On Redman's tempestuous relationships with Pynson prior to taking over some of his stock and equipment, see Alexandra Gillespie, 'Robert Redman', *ODNB*.

Edition 1	*Edition 2*	
Venies	vineas (recte *vineis*, as *Asc*)	21. 3
trepidam . . ciuitatem	trepida . . ciuitate	40. 3
capere	cepere (i.e. coepere)	42. 1
dedicationem	deditionem	46. 1
porcedebant	procedebant	46. 5
incepto	infecto (see note to 36/58)	58. 7
exercitum cogere	exercitum cogeret	96. 1

In numerous other instances, however, the errors of the first edition are repeated in the second:

Editions A and B	*Ascensius (and Laetus–Britannicus)*	
genus humanum	genus hominum	2. 1
omnia	cuncta	2. 3
Nam si quidem	Nam ui quidem	3. 2
q*uam*plures	complures	8. 1
amicitior quam	amicior quam	10. 5
monumento	monumenta	14. 17
omnium	omni	20. 4
comparato	circumdato	25. 9
fedem	caedem/cedem	31. 13
iudicio	indicio	31. 18
cedere	sedere	51. 1
postulabat	poscebat	56. 1
proxima	maxima	61. 1

Numerous omissions in the first edition persist in the second:

Editions A and B	*Ascensius (and Laetus–Britannicus)*	
—	potentiae paucorum	3. 3
ciuitatis	ciuitatis morum	4. 9
tuaque uirtute	tuaque uirtute nobis	10. 2
referunt	ad Iugurtham referunt	12. 5
largiendo	largiendo parare	13. 6
fides eius	fides eius rei	17. 7
[Whole sentence.]	Nam ubi . . . oriri coepit.	41. 10

Changes to Ascensius's word order in the first edition are usually retained in the second:

Editions A and B	*Ascensius*	
has omnes erumnas	omnes has erumnas	14. 23
nobilitatis victoriam	victoriam nobilitatis	16. 2

In a few instances, Pynson's Latin incorporates readings from Laetus–Britannicus. The second edition does not change these back to Ascensius's reading:

Editions A and B	*Ascensius*	*Laetus–Britannicus*	
Getuli et Libyes	Getuli	Getuli et Lybes	18. 1
humi	*om.*	Humi	18. 1
infido	fido (1506–1519)	infido	61. 5

Occasions where the corrector appears to emend a Barclay–Pynson first-edition reading shared with Ascensius (and Laetus–Britannicus) are rare, and their intentionality doubtful. Note, for example, *me nequiuit* (14. 11) changed to *me nequiuerit* (modern editions prefer *nequit*). Several peculiar features of Ascensius's edition are retained from the first to the second edition, including the reading *Tolonia Thercon*, and the additional clause *tum pro licentia . . . nequibat* (discussed above).

In conclusion, it would appear that Pynson was aware of some of the deficiencies of the first-edition Latin text, and some corrections were made, apparently from a copy of Ascensius's commentarial edition—possibly that which originally had served for the first edition. Collation and correction, however, were neither systematic nor complete, and as a result many errors persisted. There is no evidence that reference was made to the Aldine edition (1509.3) or other revised and improved editions like Ascensius's own small format texts (without commentary) that drew upon the Aldine (see, for example, 1513.4).

Revisions to the English of the 1525 Edition

For more detailed discussion of the punctuation in the first and second editions (including the brief but haphazard use of commas in early sheets of the second) see below, pp. lxxv–lxxvii, where the three-grade system is described. This system is carried over into the second edition from the first, but with significant revisions. In particular, over a hundred additional virgules and some twenty colons are supplied for clause or phrase separation. Even so, there remain nearly as many places where one should expect some intermediate punctuation.

It is likely that compositors would smooth out any idiosyncratic spellings in Barclay's fair copy (or perhaps an intermediate scribe's), in line with normal practice. It is interesting then to note some further changes in spelling made to minority forms from the first to the second edition, which may have been relics of the copy-text manuscript orthography, for example: *mayntenars* > *mainterners* (*mainteiners BarcC*) 9/30 (cf. *lengar* > *lenger* 44/120, *tempar* > *temper* 50/61, *leddar* > *ledder* 53/85); *wondes* > *woundes* 37/61, *bonde* > *bounde* 65/14, *asperance* > *esperance* 13/15, *paryls* > *peryls* 2/108, *arragyng* > *enragyng* 42/109.

The past tense of *corrupt* is variously rendered *corrupt* or *corrupted* in *BarcA*. In *BarcB* there is one instance where *corrupt* is changed to *corrupted*. Perhaps such examples indicate that Barclay used *corrupt*, but compositors sometimes imposed the preferred form *corrupted*, if not consistently. Analagous changes are seen in *lette* > *letted* 40/69, *desert* > *deserted* 45/59.

Lexical Changes

Many lexical changes involve the replacement of an idiosyncratic usage or rare word by a more common one, and are therefore likely to be replacements of Barclay's own idiom with another preferred by a corrector or a compositor. The most striking instance is the replacement of *batayle* (in the sense 'war, extended period of conflict') by *war(re)*. The replacement occurs thirteen times and might be described as systematic, except that no change was made to the running head, where 'The batayle of Iugurth' (that is, *Bellum Iugurthinum*) persists on every opening. In one instance within the text, *hoost* replaces *batayle* (29/56) where '*forwarde of the batayle*' refers to the van of a battle formation. Most other changes of one synonym for another are not systematically applied, or involve words that occur once only in the text. For example: of four uses of *newelty*, only one is changed to *nouelty* (the three remaining instances are changed in *BarcC*); *partie* is changed to *part* once in *BarcB*, and two further instances are changed in *BarcC*; *appelynge* is changed to *accusacion* 19/144; *bomen* to *archers* 30/83; *cowarde* (adj.) to *cowardous* 44/38; *endes* to *boundys* 65/41; *gyles* to *trayne* 10/103; *precessour* to *predecessour* 34/19; *confeterated* to *confederated* 10/49; *iest* to *iesture* 37/33. The change of *wawes* to *waues* 45/46 provides a typical instance of a preferred newer form replacing one soon to be obsolete. The formal and semantic overlap of *garnyson* and *garrison* is complex (see *OED*), but the trend towards the former's obsolescence is reflected in sporadic changes to *garrison*, albeit in only three out of thirty instances of *garnyson*.

By contrast, Barclay's use of *worthy* (23/65, 38/96) in *OED* sense 5b 'deserved, merited by default or wrong-doing, condign' (antedating *OED*'s earliest citation) appears to have been a new semantic development that a revisor or compositor thought incorrect, for the latter instance was changed to *condigne*.

In many such examples we probably see Barclay's own usages being phased out in favour of current London usage. Some involve vernacular idiom, but others perhaps reflect a preference for one form of a loanword over another. It may be that some instances occur merely at the whim of the compositor, or possibly to enable the setting of a line of type more easily through the addition or subtraction of letters.

Vnrefrenable 7/56 (changed to *vnresonable* in *BarcC*) appears based upon the obsolete French *irrefrenable*. *OED* cites one example of the latter from 1546 (J. Heywood *Prov.* 45). Similarly, Barclay's knowledge of French may have led to his use of the uncommon *rapynous* 10/146, changed to *rauenous* in *BarcC*. Some other unusual words borrowed from French may be Barclay's own innovation, or at least only appear in the language around his time: for example, *attice* and its derivatives. He is an early user of *barbaric*, and his use of *barbarian* antedates *OED* citations from *c.*1550.

Strypes 9/10 is changed to *strokes* in *BarcB C*, although *strype* 'blow' appears well attested in London English. Barclay appears to have used the term *dysworshyp* habitually (it occurs five times in *Jugurtha*, once in *The Shyp of Foles*, and twice in the *Eclogues*), but it is replaced by the more common *dishonour* in *BarcB C* once at 10/239.

The form *plagge* changed to *place* 51/50 is probably a compositor's attempt to make sense of a misleading spelling form that had already already obscured the less common synonym *plage*.

Scottish Vocabulary

In his 1874 edition of *The Shyp of Folys* Jamieson pointed out certain words in the text that he believed were peculiarly Scottish, and he concluded that their usage indicated Scotland as Barclay's birthplace. The evidence which has since appeared in *OED* and the period dictionaries (*MED* and *DOST*) casts some doubt on Jamieson's conclusion, and indicates that many of the alleged Scotticisms had currency in the North and Midlands of England as well. Furthermore, as Norman Davis has pointed out, certain 'Scottish' or

'Northern' words can be observed entering the language of various members of the East Anglian Paston family in the fifteenth century, and show how regional words might be adopted outside their home locations.[72]

In the *Sallust* also one finds scattered words, forms, or senses of words that appear Scottish or Northern. These tend to be replaced or respelled in the second and third editions. Examples include:

abstinat 13/76, revised to *obstinate* in *BarcC* (cf. *obstinate* in *BarcA* 27/56). *DOST* lists examples of *ab-* forms from sixteenth-century Edinburgh records.

anenst Extr/65, revised to *agaynst BarcB*; *agaynst* Pref/148, changed to *anenst BarcB*; *agaynst* 50/57 in *BarcA* changed to *anenst* in *BarcB*, *ageynste BarcC*. The Scottish, Northern (and perhaps Midland) forms *anent(is)* and *anenst* seem normally to have been changed to *agaynst* by London printers. Three examples of *anenst* appear in *The Shyp of Fools* and five in *The Myrrour of Good Maners*, suggesting that Barclay himself used this form. The change of *agaynst* to *anenst* twice in *BarcB* is something of an oddity, running against the prevailing trends of revision.

orison is used nine times with the sense 'speech, oration', a usage which *OED*, *MED*, and *DOST* note once in Lydgate and once in the Wycliffite Bible, but otherwise only in Scottish texts of the sixteenth century. Barclay also uses *orison* in this sense in the second *Eclogue* 297–8: 'And sometime poetes or oratours ornate / Make orisons before some great estate.' The word is retained in *Barc B* but changed in three instances to *oracion* in *Barc C*.

reaue away 50/217 is changed to *dispoyle* in *BarcB C*; the present participle *reauyng* 27/28 remains unchanged. Once widespread in English, the verb is largely restricted to the North by the sixteenth century.

sherched 63/90 is changed to *serched* in *BarcB* (*searched* C). *sh-*, *sc-* and *sch-* forms are more common in Scots texts, and attested sporadically in English, although disfavoured by printers.

[72] Norman Davis, 'The Language of the Pastons', *Proceedings of the British Academy*, 40 (1954), 119–44 at 133; on the related question of Scotticisms in the language of John Skelton see Greg Waite, 'Approaching the Poet's Language: The Holograph Records of Skelton's English', in David R. Carlson (ed.), *John Skelton and Early Modern Culture: Papers Honoring Robert S. Kinsman* (Tempe, Ariz., 2008), 99–131 at 128.

Barclay's usage perhaps reflects his familiarity with the French precursor *chercher*.

trymbled 67/29 is changed to *trembled* in BarcB C. *i/y* forms were possibly perceived as Northern by the printers at this time.

Stylistic Changes

The revisor sometimes curtails Barclay's habit of expanding Sallust's phrasing. There are numerous instances in the second edition where redundant or repetitive words or phrases have been removed without any change of sense (see, for example, the omission of *he*, *nor*, *purpose*, *which was*, *vnto hym*, all on f. 7v; 2/104 ff.). The rhetorical device of pairing synonyms or doublets, although commonplace in prose of this period, especially frequent in translations, and much used by Barclay, is cut back in at least fifty instances: for example, *dysposed and inclyned* > *inclyned* 2/60–1, *to ouerpasse and omytte* > *to ouerpasse* 6/12, *adnulled and broken* > *adnulled* 7/35.

At other points, the sense is improved by changes to the syntax. See, for example, the change of *nor . . . or* to *and . . . and* Prol/86; the addition of *and* 12/149. The change from *vertues* 17/81 in *BarcA* to *vertuous* in *B* and *C* repairs the syntax, yet *BarcA* seems to echo *Soldus*: Artes .i. uirtutes (sig. h6).

Changes Based upon Reconsideration of the Latin Text

There are a few instances in the second edition where revisions seem to be made upon the authority of the Latin. See, for example, the notes explicating 5/21 *consumed*, 10/84 *our stocke and housolde*, 17/81 *propertis and vertues condycions*, 18/12 *In this prolexite*, 22/18 *Rome that tyme*, 26/111 *causes* changed to *chances*, 28/100–1 *commen and symple soudyours*, 29/25 the change of *mynde* > *purpose*, 38/45 *All they of the towne*, 39/30–1 *ryches and sensualyte*, 40/79–80 *many of them*.

At 56/128 the phrase *with their fete* has been omitted in *BarcB* and *C*, perhaps on the basis of another edition, such as the Aldine (**1509.3**), where the L. *pedibus*, found in *Laet–BritT* and *AscT*, was rejected.

Fewer still are cases where the commentaries seem to have been revisited, but of note are 19/43 *your elders*, and 32/73 *had almost ben made*, where Soldus may have influenced the revision, and the interesting case 32/77 *in stede of their sadnes*, where Priscian's suggested emendation (not noticed by Soldus or Ascensius) seems to have been incorporated (see note).

Other Aspects of Revision

In some instances revision of the English text was probably seen as necessary from context without reference back to the Latin: *kyndled agaynst Iugurth* > *inclyned to Iugurth* 2/73, *your* > *our* 10/84, *ordayned* > *seiourned* 32/95, *dysceyt* > *dysceyuer* 38/20, *to rydde* > *to spede* 41/17.

Yet there are a number of instances where a difficult passage or an error in *BarcA* has not undergone revision in *BarcB*: see *yet Cassius . . . without he wolde* 22/10–2, *the messangers of Iugurth* 16/27, *Nowe iuge and consyder* 50/106–7 (the revision in *BarcC* attempts a remedy), *the first towne . . . yelded to Marius* 35/33–4. Attempts to revise or correct are not always successful: *bothe in peace and in warre* 10/14–5, *hauyng hope of vyctorie . . . place and countrey* 30/5–7, *specially in [two] suche places as were moost conuenyent* 44/122–3.

The Third Edition by Thomas Paynell (1557): STC 10752

Known surviving copies include the following: London, British Library; Oxford, Bodleian Library (two copies); Peterborough, Cathedral Library (held in Cambridge University Library); Cambridge, University Library; Cambridge, Trinity College Library; Edinburgh, University Library; Leeds, Brotherton Library; St Andrews, University Library; Washington DC, Folger Shakespeare Library (two copies); San Marino, Calif., Huntington Library; Cambridge, Mass., Harvard University Library; Urbana, University of Illinois Library; New Haven, Yale University, Elizabethan Club Library. For this edition the copies from London, Cambridge, Oxford, and Illinois have been consulted.

Paynell's combined edition (Barclay's *Jugurtha* and his own translation of Constantius Felicius's *Catiline*) was printed for John Walley by an unidentified printer, who also produced *STC* 22160.5 (formerly 22159) *The seinge of Urynes* [1557?].[73]

The size of leaves is 127 × 177 mm; the printed space measures 98 × 149 mm (exclusive of running head, catch-words, signatures, etc.). The English text stands alone in this edition, and is printed in 92 Textura employing type-forms h^1, s^3, w^5, v^3, y^2. Chapter headings are in 62 textura. A combined title page stands at the front of the book,

[73] Walley employed a variety of printers, and the types in his books vary considerably. See Frank Isaac, *English and Scottish Printing Types 1535–58 & 1552–58* (Oxford, 1932), [appendix].

but the *Jugurtha* as Part 2 is provided with its own title page as well, and an independent colophon. It is signatured and foliated separately also: [i–ii], a.i–[a.iv] in fours to Hh.1–[Hh.iv]. Folios i–cxx run from [a.iv] to [Hh.iv]. Chapters begin with woodcut capital letters set on floriate or leafy backgrounds: the larger ones are 22 × 24 mm (five text-lines in height) and the smaller 15 × 16 mm (three text-lines in height).

Thomas Paynell (d. 1564?) was an Augustinian canon of Merton Priory, Surrey, until its dissolution in 1538, and successively chaplain to Henry VIII, to whom he dedicated his translation of Constantius Felicius's *Historia Coniurationis Catilinariae* (1541), and orator to Queen Mary and Queen Elizabeth.[74] He is known principally as a translator, with links to the circle of Erasmus, whose *De contemptu mundi* and *Complaint of Peace* he translated. Among other works to survive are his translation of Agapetus, *The Preceptes Teachyng a Prynce or a Noble Estate his Duetie* (1529?),[75] an adaptation of Ulrich von Hutten's *De Morbo Gallico* titled *A Muche Profitable Treatise Against the Pestilence* (1533),[76] and *A Compendious and a Moche Fruytefull Treatyse of Well Livynge, containing the Hole Summe and Effect of Al Vertue, wryten by S. Bernard* (*c.*1545).[77]

Paynell claims to have 'perused and corrected' Barclay's translation in order to adjoin it to a new edition of his own 1541 translation of a treatise on the Catiline conspiracy by Constantius Felicius Durantinus (Costanzo Felici of Castel Durante, near Ancona). He did this, he maintains in the preface addressed to his patron Anthony Browne, Viscount Montagu, at the request of 'a friend' (whom H. S. Bennett assumes is Browne himself).[78]

Constanzo Felici completed his *Historia Coniurationis Catilinariae* when only 18 years of age, a year or two before it was first published in Rome in 1518. As Osmond and Ulery note, the work 'was part of a literary endeavor aimed at reasserting Cicero's leading position in the events of his day (particularly in suppressing the conspiracy of Catiline) and at establishing the author's own reputation as a Ciceronian stylist'.[79] As an alternative to Sallust's own *Bellum*

[74] See Geoffrey Eatough, 'Thomas Paynell', *ODNB*.
[75] *STC* 192.
[76] *STC* 14024.
[77] *STC* 1908.
[78] H. S. Bennett, *English Books and Readers 1475 to 1557*, 2nd edn. (Cambridge, 1969), 133.
[79] Patricia J. Osmond and Robert W. Ulery, Jr., 'Constantius Felicius Durantinus and the Renaissance Origins of Anti-Sallustian Criticism', *International Journal of the Classical Tradition*, 1 (1995), 29–56 at 30.

Catilinae, the work probably appealed to Paynell for its Ciceronian style and its synthesis of information about Catiline and his conspiracy from a variety of sources. It further served as a means by which to denounce civil disorder and rebellion in the wake of the 1536 Northern uprisings, and Bigod's rebellion of 1537. In his preface of dedication to Henry VIII, Paynell wrote:

thys Catilines conspiracie . . . I haue translated out of Latine into Englishe, speciallye for this intente, that all that be vnlerned maye se, if God amonge the gentiles, wold not suffer riottous rebelles to ouerrunne rulers and distroye common weales: howe moche lesse then wyll he suffer them to preuayle ageynste a chrysten prynce, his veray image in erthe? (Sig. A.ii^{v})

H. S. Bennett notes in passing how Paynell made very little change to the text of the second Pynson edition of *Jugurtha* which formed his copy-text, despite Paynell's claim to have corrected Barclay's text, because he found it 'here and there (thorough vnlearned correctors) somewhat mangled and corrupted' (Appendix I, 13).[80] Sporadic attempts to revise and correct are found throughout, but most changes are minor. Chiefly, Paynell or his printer made minor stylistic adjustments, no doubt many of them merely updating forms and idioms that seemed antiquated.

Singular and plural are sometimes reversed, for example:

thyng > *thinges* 12/25, *lorde* > *lordes* 12/40, *way* > *waies* 50/97, *mynde* > *mindes* 54/140, *treasours* > *treasure* 8/5, *places* > *place* 12/41, *socours* > *socour* 12/86, 23/58, 36/72, *myndes* > *mind* 27/59, 29/21, 31/16, *handes* > *hande* 31/47, *vytayls* > *vytaile* 33/30, *maners* > *maner* 36/12, *fortunes* > *fortune* 38/46, *priuyleges* > *priuylege* 41/79, *burthens* > *burthen* 44/54, *peoples* > *people* 46/22, *blames* > *blame* 50/4, *occasyons* > *occasion* 50/46, *batayls* > *batayle* 50/300, *maners* > *maner* 55/16, *tymes* > *time* 65/48.

Idioms involving the definite article are changed in some instances: the article is added Prol/78, 13/75, 28/63, 28/90, 29/18, etc., or removed 11/68, 17/157, 19/116, 32/85, etc.

Changes to older words or forms include: *orison* > *oracion* 19/2, *newelties* > *nouelties* 29/22, *in compasse* > *about* 12/135, *nought* > *nothinge* 53/109, *leferre* > *better* 6/31, *vnto* > *to* (ca. 30 occ.), *thyder* > *thither* 11/89, *truys* > *truce* 46/27, *casten* > *cast* 67/60, *eyen* > *eyes* 46/47, *admonest* > *admonishe* 6/25, *nonest* > *nonce* 39/126.

[80] *English Books and Readers*, 133.

Compression by removal of redundant words occurs quite frequently. For example: *that* Prol/81, *so* 6/52, *he* 6/55, *suffreth . . . thanne* 6/57–8, *by* 8/17, *in hope of ryches* 10/55, *our* 10/171, *as* 10/236, *Hierbas* 12/132, *party* 13/69. Yet only a small number of doublings are reduced, compared to the more extensive pruning made for the second edition, for example: *and circuite* 12/135, *robbe/and* 28/48, *brought and* 28/80, *and changes* 40/35, *garde and* 40/42.

As many if not more typographical errors were introduced as were corrected. In cases where the second edition was obviously in error, there appear to be few if any instances where Paynell or the printers referred back to the first edition. The value of collating Paynell's edition thus lies only in the insights that variant readings provide by highlighting aspects of Barclay's language that seem to have been regarded as old-fashioned or non-standard by the late 1550s.

Punctuation in the First and Second Editions

We do not know how Barclay himself punctuated his manuscript copy of the translation, or to what degree the printed version reflects his own policies or those of his printer, Pynson. The print editions employ a three-grade punctuation system—punctus, colon, and virgula (replaced by the comma in the third edition)—supplemented with virgulae convexae (parentheses), and the punctus interrogativus (question mark). This system is used both for the Latin text and the English. In Pynson's second edition some commas appear in the Latin in early quires, in place of virgules or colons, although virgules and colons are still heavily used. This modification seems to have been abandoned as the work progressed, and the system reverts to that found in the first edition. The three-grade system is similarly employed in several of Pynson's books from around the same time: for example, the 1526 black-letter edition of William Bond's *Pylgrimage of Perfection* (*STC* 3277), and the 1519 roman-fount edition of William Horman's *Vulgaria* (*STC* 13811), which also shows the system operating both in Latin and English. As indicated above, all known editions of Ascensius's *Sallust* up to 1519 employed the older system of punctus and one intermediate punctuation mark (either colon or virgule). It appears that Barclay or Pynson made a deliberate decision to revise their exemplar for presentation in the parallel text format.

In relation to the virgule, the colon may mark a heavier intermediate pause, or a clause boundary. The virgule also can mark clause boundaries, but tends to mark lighter divisions within clauses. In addition, it separates words or phrases such as those in apposition in a list, or separated by a preposition. No absolute division can be drawn between the functions of the colon and the virgule, and one finds one or the other in different instances of seemingly identical structures.

Normally the punctus marks the end of a complete sentence, but often it separates a subordinate clause, or other subordinate structures, from the main period. Here too, somewhat confusingly for the modern reader, a capital letter follows. This feature occurs regularly, and is hardly ever changed in the second edition, although other revisions of the punctuation were made. It was clearly an acceptable technique for indicating a heavier pause. It might be observed that in Pynson's work the layout of the Latin is such that the reader of the English text is given a visual clue as to where such punctus marks fall inside the Latin period, which in many cases Barclay follows quite closely. A typical example is the following:

Whiche enuyous maligners: yf they wolde consyder both in what maner seasons and in what ieopardous tymes I haue obtayned offices and rowmes of auctorite and what men wolde gladly/ and yet myght nat obtayne suche rowmes. Moreouer yf they call to mynde what maner of men afterwarde came into the order of senatours. For certayne if my wyllers consyder indifferently these premysses: than shall they thinke that I haue chaunged the purpose of my mynde: more for cause reasonable: and by good aduysement/ than for slouthe and cowardyse and they shall fynde that more profet shall come to the commen wayle by this my study (which they count but ydelnes and tyme mysspent) than of the labour and besynes which other men take upon them fayntly and iniustly admynistryng the commen wele. (Prol/110–21)

Qui si reputauerint et quibus ego temporibus magistratus adeptus sum et quales uiri idem adsequi nequiuerint et postea quae genera hominum in senatum peruenerint, profecto existumabunt me magis merito quam ignauia iudicium animi mei mutauisse maiusque commodum ex otio meo quam ex aliorum negotiis rei publicae uenturum. (4. 4)

End-of-line punctuation is sometimes omitted in early print-texts because the line-end seems sufficient as the 'speech-pause', or because a clause boundary is evident. Such omissions occur occasionally in the text (for example, a colon or full stop seems necessary after *dysplesure* Pref/106, and after *plesures* Prol/21), but they are probably a last resort by the compositor in setting a tight line where no other shortening can occur. For the most part the compositors regularly employ punctuation at the ends of lines.

7. PLAN OF THE PRESENT EDITION

From the preceding discussion it is clear that while the second edition of the *Jugurtha* is in some respects a revised and improved edition, it is also one in which the normalizing tendencies of the printer and his assistants have been brought to bear on the text. It is reasonable to surmise that some aspects of Barclay's own style and some of his linguistic idiosyncracies have been removed in the process. For this reason the first edition has been chosen as the basis for this edition, incorporating where necessary corrections or improvements from the second. As indicated above, substantive variants from the third edition of Paynell are provided, but rather for stylistic interest than to help establish a more reliable text, because this edition derives directly and somewhat inaccurately from the second.

Orthography

The original orthography is retained, with the following exceptions.

Occasional lower-case letters beginning a proper name are silently corrected to upper case.

The looped *r* is transcribed as *re*, and looped *d* as *de* (as in 'where' Extr/196, 'fledde' Extr/80; both sorts are infrequent). Occasional space-saving *es* appears as in 'tydynges' Extr/174.

Contractions and abbreviations have been silently expanded (e.g. nasal (m, n) indicated by macron, ⟨y^{e}⟩ *the*, ⟨w^{t}⟩ *with*, etc.). Tironian *et* and & are expanded to *and* in the English text and *et* in the Latin text.

Word spacing is normalized where necessary: for example, *in to* for *into*; *other syde* for *othersyde*; a few compounds have been left with their variation in word division as it occurs in the copy-text (e.g. *other lyke* beside *otherlyke*; *often tymes* beside *oftentymes*.

Punctuation

In this edition the original punctuation of the first edition has been retained as far as possible. The decision not to modernize punctuation was made because the original has, for the most part, a system and integrity of its own, and complements the syntax and rhetoric of Barclay's prose. Where Pynson's second edition corrects an error in the first edition or adds punctuation in a way that improves the reading, the later version is often adopted. Virgule placement is sometimes improved in *B*, and *B*'s added virgules are supplied to the *A* copy-text, with all such instances noted in the apparatus.

Manifest errors of punctuation shared by the two editions are emended where practicable, and virgules or colons have been supplied in some instances where the meaning of a sentence is otherwise unclear. All such changes to punctuation are indicated in the apparatus.

As noted above, the punctuation employed often involves placement of a punctus and capital letter where modern punctuation requires a comma, because the punctus separates a subordinate clause from its main clause. As an aid to the reader, such 'intermediate' stops are marked by an underlined point (.̱). Clauses beginning 'For' or 'Insomoche that' have been left unmarked.

Question marks appear in the original, but not with complete consistency. They are inserted in place of a punctus in some cases where the sense requires, but other instances are left as apparently intended with punctus (for example, in the Preface).

Original paragraph divisions within chapters reproduce the ¶ marker of the copy-text. Paragraph divisions without such a marker are modern editorial.

Variant Readings

Only substantive lexical variants from the second and third editions are noted, together with variants involving grammatical modification or change of idiom (for example, variations of singular and plural, tense, concord, and the like). Mere spelling variants are recorded only in the few cases where they seem to be of special importance. Manifest errors in *B* (for example, *decycat* where *A* has *dedycate* (Pref/147)) are not recorded, nor are such errors in *C*. Where *A* has been emended the original reading is recorded in the variants.

SELECT BIBLIOGRAPHY

PRIMARY SOURCES

Bale, John, *Illustrium Maioris Britanniæ Scriptorum* . . . (Wesel, 1548).

—— *Scriptorum Illustrium Maioris Brytannie* (Basel, 1557).

—— *Scriptorum Illustrium Maioris Brytanniae Catalogus*, 2 vols. (Farnsworth, 1971).

Barclay, Alexander, 'A Critical Edition of Alexander Barclay's Ship of Fools (1509)', ed. David R. Anderson (Ph.D. diss., Case Western Reserve, 1974).

—— *The Eclogues of Alexander Barclay from the Original Edition by John Cawood*, ed. Beatrice White, EETS OS 175 (London, 1928).

—— *Here begynneth a ryght frutefull treatyse, intituled the myrrour of good maners, conteynyng the .iiii. vertues, R. Pynson, at the instance of Rychard yerle of kent* (London, R. Pynson [1518?]), *STC* 17242.

—— *Here Begynneth the Introductory to Wryte and to Pronounce Frenche* (London, R. Coplande, 1521), *STC* 1386.

—— *Here begynnyth the lyfe of the gloryous martyr saynt George* (London, 1515?), *STC* 22992.1.

—— *The Life of St. George*, ed. William Nelson, EETS OS 230 (London, 1955).

—— *This present boke named the shyp of folys of the worlde* . . . (London: R. Pynson, 1509), *STC* 3545.

—— *The Ship of Fools*, ed. Thomas H. Jamieson, 2 vols. (Edinburgh, 1874).

Bulleyn, William, *Dialogue . . . against the Fever Pestilence* (London: J. Kingston, 1564), *STC* 4036.

The Castle of Labour [Paris, *c.*1503], *STC* 12379; (London: R. Pynson [1505?]), *STC* 12380.

Erasmus, Desiderius, *Opera Omnia* . . ., i/1, ed. J. C. Margolin (Amsterdam, 1971).

Felicius, Constantius, *The Conspiracie of Lucius Catiline* (London, for T. Whalley: 1557), *STC* 10752.

Fifteenth-Century Prose and Verse, ed. A. W. Pollard (Westminster, 1903).

Letters and Papers of the Reign of Henry VIII, ed. J. S. Brewer and R. H. Brodie, 21 vols. in 37 (London, 1862–1932).

More, Thomas, *The Yale Edition of the Works of St. Thomas More*, i (New Haven, 1961).

Reuchlin, Johannes, *Vocabularius Breviloquus* (Basel, 1478), *ISTC* ir00155000.

Sallustius, C. Crispus, *Sallust*, ed. and trans. J. C. Rolfe, Loeb Classical Library 116 (rev. edn., Cambridge, Mass., 1931).

—— *Catilina, Iugurtha, Fragmenta Ampliora*, ed. Wilhelm Ahlberg and Alfons Kurfess (Bibliotheca Scriptorum Graecorum et Romanorum Teubneriana, 3rd edn.; Leipzig, 1968).

—— *C. Sallusti Crispi, Catilina, Iugurtha, Historiarum Fragmenta Selecta, Appendix Sallustiana*, ed. L. D. Reynolds (Oxford, 1991).

—— *Sallust: The War against Jugurtha*, ed. Michael Comber and Catalina Balmaceda (Oxford, 2008).

Skelton, John, *The Bibliotheca Historica of Diodorus Siculus*, ed. F. M. Salter and H. L. R. Edwards, EETS OS 233, 239 (London, 1956, 1957).

Terentius, Publius Afer, *Terens in englysh* [Paris? *c.*1520], *STC* 23894.

Trevisa, John, *Cronica Ranulphi Cistrensis Monachi* [London: Caxton, 1482], *STC* 13438.

SECONDARY SOURCES

Adams, Herbert Mayow, *Catalogue of Books Printed on the Continent of Europe, 1501–1600, in Cambridge Libraries*, 2 vols. (London, 1967).

Axton, Marie, and Carley, James P. (eds.), *'Triumphs of English': Henry Parker, Lord Morley, Translator to the Tudor Court. New Essays in Interpretation* (London, 2000).

Baldwin, T. W., *Willam Shakespere's Small Latine & Lesse Greeke*, 2 vols. (Urbana, Ill., 1944).

Baudrier, Henri Louis, and Baudrier, Julien, *Bibliographie lyonnaise: Recherches sur les imprimeurs, libraires, relieurs, et gondeurs de lettres de Lyon au XVIe siècle*, 12 vols. (Lyon, 1895–1921).

Bell, David N., *The Libraries of the Cistercians, Gilbertines and Premonstratensians*, Corpus of British Medieval Library Catalogues, 3 (London, 1992).

Bennett, H. S., *English Books and Readers 1475–1557*, 2nd edn. (Cambridge, 1969).

Benzing, Josef, and Müller, Jean, *Bibliographie Strasbourgeoise: Bibliographie des ouvrages imprimés à Strasbourg (Bas-Rhin) au XVIe siècle*, 3 vols., Bibliotheca Bibliographica Aureliana, 80, 90, 105 (Baden-Baden, 1981).

Berdan, John Milton, *Early Tudor Poetry, 1485–1547* (New York, 1920).

Bernardo, Aldo S., and Levin, Saul (eds.), *The Classics in the Middle Ages: Papers of the Twentieth Annual Conference of the Center for Medieval and Early Renaissance Studies* (Binghamton, NY, 1990).

Blake, N. F., 'Translation and the History of English', in Matti Rissanen (ed.), *History of Englishes: New Methods and Interpretations in Historical Linguistics* (Berlin, 1992), 3–24.

Bolaffi, E., *Salustio e la sua fortuna nei secoli* (Rome, 1949).
British Museum., Dept. of Printed Books., *et al.*, *Catalogue of Books Printed in the XVth Century Now in the British Museum* 9 vols. (London, 1963).
Burke, Peter, 'A Survey of the Popularity of Ancient Historians, 1450–1700', *History and Theory*, 5 (1966), 135–52.
Byrne, Donal, 'An Early French Humanist and Sallust: Jean Lebègue and the Iconographical Programme for the Catiline and Jugurtha', *Journal of the Warburg and Courtauld Institutes*, 49 (1986), 41–65.
Carley, James P., *The Libraries of Henry VIII*, Corpus of British Medieval Library Catalogues, 7 (London, 2000).
Carlson, David R., 'Alexander Barclay and Richard Pynson: A Tudor Printer and his Writer', *Anglia*, 113 (1995), 283–302.
—— 'Alexander Barclay (Circa 1475 – June 1552)', in David A. Richardson (ed.), *Sixteenth-Century British Nondramatic Writers. First Series*, Dictionary of Literary Biography, 132 (Detroit, 1993), 36–47.
—— *English Humanist Books 1475–1525* (Toronto, 1993).
—— 'The "Grammarians' War" 1519–21, Humanist Careerism in Early Tudor England, and Printing', *Mediaevalia et Humanistica*, NS 18 (1992), 157–81.
—— 'Skelton and Barclay, Medieval and Modern', *Early Modern Literary Studies: A Journal of Sixteenth- and Seventeenth-Century English Literature*, 1 (1995), [e-journal] 17 paragraphs.
Cavallo, Guglielmo, and Chartier, Roger (eds.), *A History of Reading in the West*, trans. Lydia G. Cochrane (Amherst, Mass., 1999).
Chocheyras, J., 'Les Traductions françaises de Salluste', *Revue de littérature comparée*, 39 (1965), 22–30.
Clarke, Peter D., and Lovatt, Roger, *The University and College Libraries of Cambridge*, Corpus of British Medieval Library Catalogues, 10 (London, 2002).
Coates, Alan, *English Medieval Books: The Reading Abbey Collections from Foundation to Dispersal*, Oxford Historical Monographs (Oxford, 1999).
Coates, Alan, *et al.*, *A Catalogue of Books Printed in the Fifteenth Century Now in the Bodleian Library, Oxford* (Oxford, 2005).
Cochrane, Eric, *Historians and Historiography in the Italian Renaissance* (Chicago, 1981).
Colchester, L. S. 'Alexander Barclay', *Modern Language Review*, 37 (1942), 198.
Conley, Carey Herbert, *The First English Translators of the Classics* (New Haven, 1927).
Copeland, Rita, *Rhetoric, Hermeneutics and Translation in the Middle Ages: Academic Traditions and Vernacular Texts* (Cambridge, 1991).
Cosenza, Mario Emilio, *Biographical and Bibliographical Dictionary of the Italian Humanists and of the World of Classical Scholarship in Italy, 1300–1800*, 2nd edn. (Boston, 1962).

Crane, Mark I., 'A Conservative Voice in the French Renaissance: Josse Bade (1462–1535)' (Ph.D. diss., Toronto, 2005).

Davies, Hugh William, *Devices of the Early Printers, 1457–1560: Their History and Development: With a Chapter on Portrait Figures of Printers* (London, 1935).

Davies, Martin (ed.), *Incunabula: Studies in Fifteenth-Century Printed Books Presented to Lotte Hellinga* (London, 1999).

Davis, Norman, 'The Language of the Pastons', *Proceedings of the British Academy*, 40 (1954), 119–44

Devereux, E. J., 'Thomas More and his Printers', in A. A. Macdonald (ed.), *Festschrift for Edgar Ronald Seary: Essays in English Language and Literature Presented by Colleagues and Former Students* (St. John's: Memorial U. of Newfoundland, 1975), 40–57.

Dowding, Geoffrey, *An Introduction to the History of Printing Types: An Illustrated Summary of the Main Stages in the Development of Type Design from 1440 up to the Present Day, an Aid to Type Face Identification* (London, 1961).

Driver, Martha W., *The Image in Print: Book Illustration in Late Medieval England and its Sources* (London, 2004).

DuBruck, Edelgard, 'Barclay's Veritable Source: A Ship of Fools by Pierre Rivière', *Michigan Academician*, 4 (1971), 67–75.

Duff, E. Gordon, *The Printers, Stationers and Book Binders of Westminster and London from 1476 to 1535* (Cambridge, 1906).

Earl, D. C., *The Political Thought of Sallust* (Cambridge, 1961).

Eisenstein, Elizabeth L., *The Printing Press as an Agent of Change: Communications and Cultural Transformations in Early Modern Europe* (Cambridge, 1979).

Ellis, Roger (ed.), *The Oxford History of Literary Translation in English*, i: *To 1550* (Oxford, 2008).

Emden, A. B., *A Biographical Register of the University of Oxford to A.D. 1500* (Oxford, 1957).

Fletcher, III, H. George, *New Aldine Studies: Documentary Essays on the Life and Work of Aldus Manutius* (San Francisco, 1988).

Ford, Margaret Lane, 'Importation of Printed Books into England and Scotland', in Lotte Hellinga and J. B. Trapp (eds.), *The Cambridge History of the Book in Britain*, iii: *1400–1557* (Cambridge, 2000), 179–201.

Fox, Alistair, *The English Renaissance: Identity and Representation in Elizabethan England* (Oxford, 1997).

—— *Politics and Literature in the Reigns of Henry VII and Henry VIII* (Oxford, 1989).

—— and Guy, J. A., *Reassessing the Henrician Age: Humanism, Politics and Reform 1500–1550* (Oxford, 1986).

Fox-Davies, Arthur Charles, *The Art of Heraldry: An Encyclopædia of Armory* (London, 1904).

Friis-Jensen, Karsten, *Peterborough Abbey*, Corpus of British Medieval Library Catalogues, 8 (London, 2001).

Fryde, E. B., *Humanism and Renaissance Historiography* (London, 1983).

Fulin, Rinaldo, 'Documenti per servire alla storia della tipografia veneziana', *Archivio veneto*, 23 (1882), 84–212.

Gillespie, Vincent, *Syon Abbey*, Corpus of British Medieval Library Catalogues, 9 (London, 2001).

Goff, Frederick Richmond, *Incunabula in American Libraries: A Third Census of Fifteenth-Century Books Recorded in North American Collections* (New York, 1964).

—— *Incunabula in American Libraries: A Supplement to the Third Census of Fifteenth-Century Books Recorded in North American Collections (1964)* (New York, 1972).

Graesse, J. G. Th., *Trésor des livres rares et précieux*, 7 vols. in 8 (Dresden, 1859–69).

Grafton, Anthony, *Commerce with the Classics: Ancient Books and Renaissance Readers*, Jerome Lectures, 20 (Ann Arbor, Mich., 1997).

—— 'Renaissance Readers and Ancient Texts: Comments on Some Commentaries', *Renaissance Quarterly*, 38 (1985), 615–49.

Green, Carin Margreta Christensen, 'Barbarian and King: The Character and Historiographical Genesis of Jugurtha in Sallust's "Bellum Jugurthinum"' (Ph.D. diss., University of Virginia, 1991).

Gwosdek, Hedwig, *A Checklist of English Grammatical Manuscripts and Early Printed Grammars c.1400–1540* (Münster, 2000).

Hellinga, Lotte, and Trapp, J. B. (eds.), *The Cambridge History of the Book in Britain*, iii: *1400–1557* (Cambridge, 2000).

Hexter, Ralph J., *Ovid and Medieval Schooling: Studies in Medieval School Commentaries on Ovid's Ars Amatoria, Epistulae Ex Ponto, and Epistulae Heroidum* (Munich, 1986).

Hirsch, Rudolf, 'Christian Allusions and Concerns in Early Printed Vernacular Translations of Classics (1471–1520)', in Wolfgang Milde and Werner Schuder (eds.), *De Captu Lectoris: Wirkungen des Buches im 15. und 16. Jahrhundert dargestellt an ausgewählten Handschriften und Drucken* (Berlin, 1988), 155–66.

—— 'Classics in the Vulgar Tongues Printed during the Initial Fifty Years, 1471–1520', *Papers of the Bibliographical Society of America*, 81 (1987), 249–337.

—— *Printing, Selling and Reading, 1450–1550* (Wiesbaden, 1967).

Hodnett, Edward, *English Woodcuts, 1480–1535* (London, 1935; repr. with Additions and Corrections, 1973).

Humphreys, K. W., *The Friars' Libraries*, Corpus of British Medieval Library Catalogues, 1 (London, 1990).

Isaac, Frank, *English and Scottish Printing Types 1501–35 & 1508–41* (Oxford, 1930).

—— *English and Scottish Printing Types, 1535–58 & 1552–58* (Oxford, 1932).

—— *English Printers' Types of the Sixteenth Century* (London, 1936).

Jiriczek, Otto L., *Specimens of Tudor Translations from the Classics* (Heidelberg, 1923).

Johnston, Stanley Howard, 'A Study of the Career and Literary Publications of Richard Pynson' (Ph.D. thesis, University of Western Ontario, 1977).

Joly, Henri, Baudrier, Henri Louis, and Tricou, Georges, *Bibliographie lyonnaise de Baudrier: Complément a la table des imprimeurs et libraries de Georges Tricou* (Lyon, 1963).

Kenney, E. J., *The Classical Text: Aspects of Editing in the Age of the Printed Book* (Berkeley, 1974).

—— and Clausen, W. V. (eds.), *The Cambridge History of Classical Literature*, ii: *Latin Literature* (Cambridge, 1982).

Ker, N. R., *Medieval Libraries of Great Britain: A List of Surviving Books*, 2nd edn. (London, 1964).

—— *Oxford College Libraries in the Sixteenth Century*, Sandars Lectures 1955 (Oxford, 1959).

King, John N., *English Reformation Literature* (Princeton, 1982).

Kinghorn, Alexander Manson, *The Chorus of History: Literary-Historical Relations in Renaissance Britain: 1485–1558* (London, 1971).

Klotz, Edith L., 'A Subject Analysis of English Imprints for Every Tenth Year from 1480 to 1640', *Huntington Library Quarterly*, 1 (1937–38), 417–19.

Kristeller, P. O., *Latin Manuscript Books before 1600: A List of the Printed Catalogues and Unpublished Inventories of Extant Collections*, 4th edn. (Munich, 1993).

La Perrière, Yvonne de, and Baudrier, Henri Louis, *Supplément provisoire à la Bibliographie lyonnaise du Président Baudrier* (Paris, 1967).

Laing, Arthur Michael Haycock, 'Pastoral Paradox: Studies in Theocritus, Virgil, Barclay, and Spenser' (Ph.D. thesis, University of Toronto, 1979).

Lathrop, H. B., *Translations from the Classics into English from Caxton to Chapman, 1477–1620* (Madison, Wis., 1933).

Lebègue, Jean Albert, *Les Histoires que l'on peut raisonnablement faire sur les livres de Salluste* (Paris, 1962).

Leeman, A. D., *A Systematical Bibliography of Sallust, 1879–1964*, 4th edn. (Leiden, 1965).

Lepreux, Georges, *Gallia typographica: ou, répertoire biographique et chronologique de tous les imprimeurs de France depuis les origines de l'imprimerie jusqu'à la Révolution*, 7 vols. (Paris, 1909–14).

Levin, Richard, 'An Unrecorded Version of the Ship of Fools', *Review of English Studies*, 54 (2003), 464–72.

Levy, Fred Jacob, *Tudor Historical Thought* (San Marino, Calif., 1967).

Lowry, Martin, *The World of Aldus Manutius: Business and Scholarship in Renaissance Venice* (Oxford, 1979).

Lucas, Robert H., 'Mediaeval French Translations of the Latin Classics to 1500', *Speculum*, 45 (1970), 225–53.

Lyall, R. J., 'Alexander Barclay and the Edwardian Reformation 1548–1552', *Review of English Studies*, NS 20 (1969), 455–61.

—— 'Tradition and Innovation in Alexander Barclay's "Towre of Vertue and Honoure" ', *Review of English Studies*, NS 23 (1972), 1–18.

McConica, James, *English Humanists and Reformation Politics under Henry VIII and Edward VI* (Oxford, 1965).

Madrid Castro, Mariano, 'Fuentes para los Comentarios de Jodocus Badius Ascensius', in Jean-Louis Charlet Schnur, Lucia Gualdo Rosa, *et al.* (eds.), *Acta Conventus Neo-Latini Cantabrigiensis* (Tempe, Ariz., 2003), 337–44.

Mazal, Otto, *Die Überlieferung der antiken Literatur im Buchdruck des 15. Jahrhunderts* (Stuttgart, 2003).

Meale, Carol F., 'Wynkyn de Worde's Setting-Copy for Ipomydon', *Studies in Bibliography*, 35 (1982), 156–71.

Massena, Victor (Prince of Essling), *Les Livres à figures vénitiens de la fin du XVe siècle et du commencement du XVIe*, 6 vols. (Venice, 1907–14).

Midzunoe, Yuichi, 'Alexander Barclay and the Ship of Fools', *Renaissance Bulletin*, 12 (1985), 9–12.

Moreau, Brigitte, and Renouard, Philippe, *Inventaire chronologique des éditions parisiennes du XVIe siècle*, 4 vols. (Paris, 1972–92).

Morini, Massimiliano, *Tudor Translation in Theory and Practice* (Aldershot, 2006).

Mueller, Janel M., *The Native Tongue and the Word* (Chicago, 1984).

Mynors, R. A. B., *Catalogue of the Manuscripts of Balliol College, Oxford* (Oxford, 1963).

Nelson, William, 'New Light on Alexander Barclay', *Review of English Studies*, 19 (1943), 59–61.

Neville, Pamela Ayers, 'Richard Pynson, King's Printer (1506–1529): Printing and Propaganda in Early Tudor England' (Ph.D. thesis, University of London, 1990).

Oldham, J. Basil, *Blind Panels of English Binders* (Cambridge, 1958).

Orme, Nicholas, 'Alexander Barclay, Tudor Educationist', *Devon and Cornwall Notes and Queries*, 35 (1984), 84–9 (repr. in Orme, *Education and Society*).

—— *Education and Society in Medieval and Renaissance England* (London, 1989).

Osmond, Patricia J., 'Pomponio Leto's Unpublished Commentary on Sallust: Five Witnesses (and More)', in Bettina Wagner and Marcia Reed (eds.), *Early Printed Books as Material Objects: Proceedings of the Conference Organized by the Ifla Rare Books and Manuscripts Section Munich, 19–21 August 2009* (The Hague, 2010), 135–49.

—— 'Princeps Historiae Romanae: Sallust in Renaissance Political Thought', *Memoirs of the American Academy in Rome*, 40 (1995), 101–43.

—— and Ulery, Jr., Robert W., 'Constantius Felicius Durantinus and the Renaissance Origins of Anti-Sallustian Criticism', *International Journal of the Classical Tradition*, 1 (1995), 29–56.

—— 'Sallustius', in Virginia Brown, James Hankins, and Robert A. Kaster (eds.), *Catalogus Translationum et Commentariorum: Mediaeval and Renaissance Latin Translations and Commentaries. Annotated Lists and Guides*, viii (Washington, DC, 2003), 183–326.

Pade, Marianne, *On Renaissance Commentaries*, Noctes Neolatinae: Neo-Latin Texts and Studies (Hildesheim, 2005).

—— 'Valla's Thucydides: Theory and Practice in a Renaissance Translation', *Classica et Mediaevalia*, 36 (1985), 275–301.

Panzer, G. W., *Annales Typographici*, 11 vols. (Nuremberg, 1793–1803).

Parkes, M. B., *Pause and Effect: An Introduction to the History of Punctuation in the West* (Aldershot, 1992).

Paul, George M., *A Historical Commentary on Sallust's Bellum Jugurthinum* (Liverpool, 1984).

Pettas, William A., *The Giunti of Florence, Merchant Publishers of the Sixteenth Century* (San Francisco, 1980).

Pfeiffer, Rudolf, *History of Classical Scholarship from 1300 to 1850* (Oxford, 1976).

Plomer, Henry R., *English Printers' Ornaments* (London, 1924).

Pollard, Alfred W., and Redgrave, G. R., *A Short-Title Catalogue of Books Printed in England, Scotland, & Ireland and of English Books Printed Abroad, 1475–1640*, 2nd edn. revised and enlarged by W. A. Jackson, F. S. Ferguson, and Katharine F. Pantzer, 3 vols. (London, 1976–91).

Pompen, Aurelius Cornelis Gerard, *The English Versions of the Ship of Fools: A Contribution to the History of the Early French Renaissance in England* (New York, 1967).

Proctor, Robert, *et al.*, *An Index to the Early Printed Books in the British Museum: From the Invention of Printing to the Year 1500: With Notes of Those in the Bodleian Library* (London, 1898; repr. 1960).

Quillet, Bernard, 'Le Narrenschiff de Sebastian Brant, ses traducteurs et ses traductions aux XVe et XVIe siècles', in J. L. Alonso Hernandez *et al.* (eds.), *Culture et marginalités au XVIe siècle* (Paris, 1973), 111–24.

Renouard, Ant. Aug., *Annales de l'imprimerie des Alde, ou histoire des trois Manuce et de leurs éditions*, 3rd ed. (Paris, 1834).

Renouard, Philippe, *Bibliographie des impressions et des oeuvres de Josse Badius Ascensius, imprimeur et humaniste, 1462–1535*, 3 vols. (Paris, 1908; repr. New York, 1967).

—— *Répertoire des imprimeurs parisiens, libraires, foundeurs de caractères et correcteurs d'imprimerie, depuis l'introduction de l'imprimerie à Paris (1470) jusqu'à la fin du seizième siècle* (Paris, 1965).

Reynolds, L. D. (ed.), *Texts and Transmission: A Survey of the Latin Classics* (Oxford, 1983; corr. repr. 1986).

—— and Wilson, Nigel Guy, *Scribes and Scholars: A Guide to the Transmission of Greek and Latin Literature*, 3rd edn. (Oxford, 1991).

Reynolds, Suzanne, '"Let Him Read the *Satires* of Horace": Reading, Literacy and Grammar in the Twelfth Century', in James Raven, Helen Small, and Naomi Tadmor (eds.), *The Practice and Representation of Reading in England* (Cambridge, 1996), 22–40.

Ringler, Jr., William A., *Bibliography and Index of English Verse Printed 1476–1558* (London, 1988).

Rouse, Richard H., *et al.*, *Registrum Anglie de Libris Doctorum et Auctorum Veterum*, Corpus of British Medieval Library Catalogues, 2 (London, 1991).

Rouziès, Étienne, 'Salluste dans les bibliothèques du XVe siècle', in Catherine Volpilhac-Auger (ed.), *D'une antiquité l'autre: La littérature antique classique dans les bibliothèques du XVe au XIXe siècle* (Lyon, 2006), 29–48.

Sayle, Charles, *Early English Printed Books in the University Library, Cambridge (1475–1640)* (Cambridge, 1900).

Schierling, Stephen, 'The Jugurtha Epitaphs: The Texts and Traditions', *Manuscripta*, 39 (1995), 173–85.

Schmidt, Paul Gerhard, 'Jodocus Badius Ascensius als Kommentator', in August Buck and Otto Herding (eds.), *Der Kommentar in der Renaissance* (Boppard, 1975), 63–72.

Schultz, John Richie, 'The Life of Alexander Barclay', *Journal of English and Germanic Philology* 18 (1919), 360–8.

Schweiger, F. L. A., *Handbuch der classischen Bibliographie*, 2 vols. in 3 (Leipzig, 1830–4).

Sharpe, Richard, *English Benedictine Libraries: The Shorter Catalogues*, Corpus of British Medieval Library Catalogues, 4 (London, 1996).

Shaw, David J., 'The Lyons Counterfeit of Aldus's Italic Type: A New Chronology', in Denis V. Reidy (ed.), *The Italian Book 1465–1800: Studies Presented to Dennis E. Rhodes on his 70th Birthday* (London, 1993), 117–33.

Simpson, Percy, *Proof-Reading in the Sixteenth, Seventeenth and Eighteenth Centuries* (London, 1935).

Slights, William W. E., *Managing Readers: Printed Marginalia in English Renaissance Books* (Ann Arbor, 2001).

Smalley, B., 'Sallust in the Middle Ages', in R. R. Bolgar (ed.), *Classical Influences on European Culture A.D. 500–1500: Proceedings of an International Conference Held at King's College, Cambridge, April 1969* (Cambridge, 1971), 165–75.

Smith, Julie A., 'Woodcut Presentation Scenes in Books Printed by Caxton, De Worde, Pynson', *Gutenberg Jahrbuch*, [61] (1986), 322–43.

Stein, R. M., 'Sallust for his Readers, 410–1550' (Ph.D. diss., Columbia University, 1977).

Stoneman, William P., *Dover Priory*, Corpus of British Medieval Library Catalogues, 5 (London, 1999).

Strang, Beth, 'Resignation and Despair in Brant's *Das Narrenschiff* and Barclay's *Shyp of Folys of the Worlde*' (Ph.D. diss., Emory University, 1978).

Syme, Ronald, *Sallust* (Cambridge, 1964).

Trapp, J. B., *Erasmus, Colet and More: The Early Tudor Humanists and their Books* (London, 1991).

Tribble, Evelyn B., *Margins and Marginality: The Printed Page in Early Modern England* (Charlottesville, Va., 1993).

Veneziani, Paolo, *La tipografia a Brescia nel XV secolo* (Florence, 1986).

Volpilhac-Auger, Catherine, and Charon-Parent, Annie, *D'une antiquité l'autre: La littérature antique classique dans les bibliothèques du XVe au XIXe siècle* (Lyon, 2006).

Waite, Greg, 'Alexander Barclay, Robert Pynson, and an Unnoticed Sheet Printed by Robert Redman', *Notes and Queries*, 58 (2011), 193–196.

—— 'Alexander Barclay's Translation of Sallust's *Jugurtha*: A Note on Sources', *Notes and Queries*, *58* (2011), 196–202.

—— 'Approaching the Poet's Language: The Holograph Records of Skelton's English', in David R. Carlson (ed.), *John Skelton and Early Modern Culture: Papers Honoring Robert S. Kinsman* (Tempe, Ariz., 2008), 99–131.

Wakelin, Daniel, *Humanism, Reading, and English Literature, 1430–1530* (Oxford, 2007).

—— 'Possibilities for Reading: Classical Translations in Parallel Texts *c.*1520–1558', *Studies in Philology*, 105 (2008), 463–86.

Warton, Thomas, *The History of English Poetry, from the Close of the Eleventh to the Commencement of the Eighteenth Century* (London, 1774).

Watson, Andrew G., and Ker, N. R., *Medieval Libraries of Great Britain, a List of Surviving Books, Edited by N. R. Ker: Supplement to the Second Edition* (London, 1987).

Weinberg, Bernard, 'Badius Ascensius and the Transmission of Medieval Literary Criticism', *Romance Philology*, 9 (1955), 209–16.

Weiss, Roberto, *Humanism in England during the Fifteenth Century*, 3rd edn. (Oxford, 1967).

—— *The Renaissance Discovery of Classical Antiquity*, 2nd edn. (Oxford, 1988).

Wood, Anthony, *Athenæ Oxonienses: An Exact History of All the Writers and Bishops Who Have Had Their Education in the Most Ancient and Famous University of Oxford, From . . . 1500 to the End Of . . . 1690 . . . To Which Are Added, the Fasti or Annals of the Said University for the Same Time*, 2 vols. (London, 1691–92; new edn. with additions and a continuation by Philip Bliss, London 1813).

¶Here begynneth the famous cronycle of the warre/ which the Romayns had agaynst Iugurth vsurper of the kyngdome of Numidy. Which cronycle is compyled in Latyn by the renowmed Romayne Salust. And translated into Englysshe by syr Alexander Barclay preest/ at commaundement of the right hye and mighty prince: Thomas duke of Northfolke. sig. [a1^{r}]

Title and Contents 1 the^{2}] *om.* C 7 at commaundement . . . Northfolke] And nowe perused and corrected by Thomas Paynell. Newely Imprinted in the yere of oure Lorde God M.D.L vii. C

¶Here foloweth the table of this present hystorie. sig. [a2r]

32 exhorteth] exhorted B

70 Fo.] For. A

92 themselfe] themshelfe A

118 honour] hononr A 121 Numidy] Nnmidy A

159 Iugurth:] *colon from* B   178 .l.] .li. A B

Finis.

The preface of Alexander Barclay preest/ vnto the right hye and mighty prince: Thomas duke of Northfolke. sig. [a4^{v}]

Right mighty/ hye/ and magnificent prince: myne humble seruyce/ due vnto your grace. And the vehement affection which I haue vnto your honour and perpetuall fame/ impelleth me often tymes to deuyse/ and to reuolue in mynde: what seruyce/ or pleasure my symplenesse | might do/ conuenyent and acceptable vnto your (sig. [a5^{r}]) hynesse: therby to testify the honour/ the loue/ and obsequy: which I knowlege myselfe to owe of duety vnto your magnificence. But whan I consyder and compare my symplenesse and impossibylite with your preemynent dygnite: I fynde myselfe greatly insufficyent to parforme or attempt any besynesse or warke which I may condynglie present vnto your honorable presence. Neuertheles after many consyderacions: the gratious regarde of benynge grauyte which I beholde in your countenance: and the euydent signes of humylite which by outwarde signes apereth radicate in your noble hert: reconforteth myne insufficyence and inboldeth my spyrites/ some thyng to write after my custome which I may present into your gratious handes: as a perpetuall remembrance or memoriall. And a[n] euydent testimony of my deuout seruyce/ and amorous affection agaynst your magnifycent hyghnes.

In this consyderation I haue reuolued many and dyuerse volumes/ stodyng of which one: the translatyon: might corespond with your noble estat. But at last I haue remembred that a mercyall matter is moost congruent vnto a mercyall and vyctorious prince. Wherfore I haue attempted to translate into our maternall langage the auncyent cronycle and famous hystorie of the warre: and dyuers batayls which the Romayns dyd agaynst the tyran Iugurth: vsurper of the kyngdome of Numidy. Which hystorie is writen in Latyn by the renowmed Romayne Salust: whose wordes in Latyn I haue al|so added vnto the (sig. [a5^{v}]) marge of this my translation to thyntent that such as shall dysdayne to rede my translatyon in Englysshe: may rede this hystorie more compendyouslie and more obscurely written in Latyn. Which hystorie: parauenture shall apere more clere and playne vnto theym in many places by help of this my translation. Which shal nat be to tedyous to such as be ler[n]ed and vnderstande Latyn: but vnto many noble gentylmen which vnderstand nat Latyn tong perfetly I dout nat

English Preface 6 to] *om.* B 9 of duety] *om.* B 10 impossibylite] impotence B 16 by outwarde signes] outwardly B 18 after] *om.* B 19 remembrance or] *om.* B And an] And a A; an and B 35 to] *om.* B 36 lerned] lerued A

but that this my labour to them shal be both pleasure and profet. For by the same they shall haue some help toward the vnderstandyng of Latyn: which at this tyme is almost contemned of gentylmen. And also they shall vnderstande a ryght fruytfull hystorie: both pleasant/ profytable/ and ryght necessary vnto euery degre: but specially to gentylmen/ which coueyt to attayne to clere fame and honour: by glorious dedes of chyualry.

But I dout nat: but that some calumnyous detractours shall maligne agaynst this my besynes and profitable labour/ sayeng that to a preest and man professed to obseruance of relygion: it is farre contrary and dysagreyng to tangle hymselfe with warfare: or to intermyt with thynges of batayle: outher by dedes/ counsell/ or writyng. But to stoppe the mouthes of such calumnyatours: moost souerayne prince: me semeth right and conuenyent in this place: somwhat to write as well concernyng the commodyties and laudes of hystories: as apertenent vnto myne owne excusation. And first I knowlege it
sig. [a6^{r}] moche more conuenyent: a | preest to arme hymselfe with constaunce/ holy scripture/ purenesse of lyfe/ and radyant vertues: and with suche socours and armour defended: boldely/ and valyantly/ to bydde batayle agaynst vyces: and to pursue the obstynate synners of this worlde. And to contende also against the temptacions of his carnall concupyscences/ agaynst these mundayne blandymentes and delectacyons: and agaynst his gostely ennemies suggestyons. For vnder this maner (as affermeth the holy man Job) mannes lyfe vpon yerth is but a warfare/ and a very mase of myseries: an intrycate circute of varyable: and ineuytable errours. For certayne I deny nat: but that such ought to be the warfare of a man within holy orders: auowed and submyt vnto the holy minysteries and auters of God. But this other temperall warre is permytted vnto worldely lyuers: and may nat be omytted: namely in this worlde oppressed with tyranny of iniuryous and odyous exactours and oppr[e]ssours: whose obstynate presumptyons/ assautes/ and inuasyons can nat otherwyse be repressed: than by vyolence/ armour/ and batayle: by minystracion of good and rightwyse prynces/ defenders and mayntayners of the commen wayle. Than it is laufull: a preest to write such actes for example of our posteryte: for parpetuall remembraunce of the laudes of good princes/ which haue ben here in erth the scourges of God to correct tyrannes and synners.

48 tangle] intermyt B 57 and] *om.* B 66 worldely] wordely B
68 oppressours] opprssours A 70 by^{2}] vnder B 71 prynces/] *virgule suppl.*

Thus: great is the laude and many be the commodyties and vtilyties of hystories and cronycles. An hystore is the recorder of tymes passed: the light of veryte: the maistres of mannes lyueng: the presydent of memorie: the messanger of antyquite. And (as Tytus Lyuius recordeth in his prologue) the knowledge of hystories among other thynges is moost holsome/ necessary/ and profitable. For euery good example whiche in them is written: is set for a | warnyng and monycion vnto sig. [a6v] princes and gouernours therby to rule and order themselfe: and a commen wayle. And euery example of myserable fortune of tyrannes/ is set as a monycion for the same gouernours nat to be of tyrannes behauour/ lest at last they may fall into lyke myserable ruyne: and calamyte. And also (as sayth Cicero) a man to knowe nothing of that which was done before his tyme and remembrance: that is as who sayth alway to be a chylde. But it is a thyng very comely: and necessary before other: to knowe these cronycles and noble actes of auncyent tyme and remembrance to kepe in mynde the order and courses of antyquite: and to haue in mynde the knowledge of examples for euery mater and purpose. For in like wyse as vnto aged men is more credence and auctorite gyuen/ than to yong men: bycause of experyence of many thynges. So such noble and dilygent myndes as delyteth in reding hystories: may haue knowlege nat onely of the dedes of one mannes lyfe: but also of the dedes moost famous of all tymes/ syth creation of the worlde. Wherfore (as sayth Dyoderus) it is a comely and fayre thing/ moch necessary and commendable: a man to refourme and amende his lyfe/ by example of an other mannes fautes. Wherfore Demotreus Phalereus the great phylosopher: after warned and counselled the kyng Ptolomy to exercise himselfe in often redyng of bokes of hystories. For in so doynge: princes shall fynde written in bokes before their eyen right many thinges concernyng their wayle/ honour/ and fame: whiche their frendes dare nat be bolde to tell them for drede of dysplesure: farthermore without the knowlege of hystories neuer man coude become good Oratour. For (as affermeth Quintylian) hystories be of such might and affect that they may norissh the spech of an oratour with soft and swete lycour. These premysses with otherlyke consy|dered moost magnificent prince: me sig. [a7r] thinketh it thing nat inconuenyent to a preest to write of hystories of warre: and also both plesant and profitable to noble men to exercyse

76 Thus] But B   77 and cronycles] *om.* B   101 fautes] fautes and dammages B   after] often B   106 dysplesure:] *colon suppl.* (*end of line*)   108 affect] effect B   111 to[1]] *om.* B   112 also] also methynke B

themselfe in redynge the same. For brefely to speke/ by rightwyse batell: the lawes of God and man be mentayned: vyce and vycious men corrected: vertue/ and good men rewarded and exalted. Our fayth agaynst infydels defended: rebellers and tyrannes subdued: and fynally all thynges dyrected and to due order reduced.

Farthermore the same redyng of hystores semeth to auayle nat a lytell to the knowledge and contempt of this transytorie pleasure mundayne and mysery of this vncertayne lyfe. For whan hystories represent before our syght the valyant and boldeherted knyghtes shyning in armour: and richely aparelled: on comely coursers barded and trapped with golde and syluer: the goodly order and ordynance of a great army of armed men shinyng in harnesse: ferse/ and prepared redy to batell: the trumpettes soundyng: the golden stremers and standerdes blasynge and glystering agaynst the sonne: and brefely all the grounde ouercouerd with men and riches. What els is all this: but a vayne ostentation of yerthly opulence: and caduke glorie prepared besely/ assembled laboriously/ and exposed folisshly and furiously vnto dystruction and to pardycion. But agayne anon after: whan we rede and se in the same hystories the valyaunt mennes bodyes prostrate one the grounde: the carkases of kynges/ dukes/ erles/ knyghtes/ and pages mengled all togyder: all pride and contencyon abated. The bright harnesse dyed with blode: the wounded coursers drawynge after them the deed bodyes of their lordes: the men cryeng: the tentes and townes brennynge. What is all this sight with otherlyke? Forsoth nought els but an euydent spectacle of mannes
sig. [a7v] brutall crudelyte: and an example of | mundayne vanyte: declaryng the immoderat and insacyable desyre of domynion of yerthely princes: and prouyng that vnto man welth is intollerable/ and confounded by his owne folly.

These manyfolde and holsome examples: represented before our sight by redyng of cronycles: hath moued my mynd to translate this present hystorie forth of Latyn into our maternall langage. But among all other noble men of this region: moost hye and mighty prince: ye seme vnto me moost worthy and conuenyent: to whose grace I shuld dedycate this hystore: bothe for myne owne duety to be obserued agaynst your magnifycence: and also for the exellent worthynesse of your merytes and great polycie of chyualry/ which lately haue apered in you: whyle ye nat with lesse wysdome/ than valyantyse haue

113 speke/] *virgule suppl.* 125 soundyng:] *colon from* B 128 yerthly] yertly B
130 to] *om.* B 132 one the grounde] *om.* B 148 agaynst] anenst B

vanquysshed the inuasour and vyolent ennemy of the commen wayle of England. In which noble and glorious act ye haue proued yourselfe like vnto mighty Mari[u]s. But this I omytte: as thyng euydently knowen to euery man: lest I myght seme rather to recount these your strong dedes for adulation: than for true relation. Wherfore most myghtie and magnifycent prynce: pleaseth it your hyghnesse of gratious benyuolence to accept this small present/ translated by your beedman to pleasure and profet of all gentylmen of this our region: but namely of your hyghnes and of the noble men of your progeny and affinyte. But to thyntent that this my small gyft somwhat may be augmented: myselfe/ my seruyce/ and prayer: I offre withall vnto your hyghnes.

Reuerendissimo in Christo patri ac domino: domino Ioanni Veysy Exoniensis episcopo Alexander Barclay presbyter debita cum obseruantia. Salutem. sig. [a4^{v}]

Memini me superioribus annis cum adhuc sacelli regii presul esses: pastor vigilantissime: tuis suasionibus incitatum: vt Crispi Salustij hystoriam (quam Iugurthynum bellum dictitant) e Romana lingua: | in Anglicam compendiose transferrem: quam rem (tametsi ardua videbatur) tamen quantum per exile ingenium/ aliasque (quæ me premunt) curas licuit certum erat capescere: Indignum enim duxi: viri/ bonarum literarum studiosis fauentissimi/ monitis literario in negotio non obtemp[e]rare: Sane quum adieceris/ et tibi/ vniuersisque Anglici nominis proceribus rem gratissimam fore: qui plerunque huiuscemodi labores sponte subeo: a tanto patre admonitus: non potui prouinciam recusare. Huc accedunt illustrissimi principis Thome: borialis gentis duci[s] hortamenta: qui et ipse paulo postquam tua dominatio ad hanc prouinciam me persuaserit non minori impulsu/ eandem ad rem adegit: atque eo: cunctantem animam redegit: vt postridie/ opusculum aggrederet. Cuius quoque magnificentie (vt duci rerum militarium peritissimo/ hystoria bellicis de rebus conscripta: conueniret) libellum non immerito nuncupaui. Atque vt duci strennuissimo/ pontificique doctissimo morem

(sig. [a5^{r}] in margin beside "in Anglicam compendiose transferrem")

153 Marius] Marins A 156 pleaseth it] pleas it B

Latin Preface 6 dictitant] vocant B 7 transferrem] verterem B 9 premunt) curas] premunt curas) A capescere] capessere B 11 obtemperare] obtemporare A adieceris/ et tibi] adiceris/ tibi B 15 ducis] ducie A 16 prouinciam] operam B 18 opusculum] prouinciam B

geram: tentaui ins[i]gnem illam hystoram/ bellumque/ quod cum Iugurtha tyranno regni Numidiæ inuasore: populus Romanus varijs sub consulibus variaque victoria gessit/ ex Latino sermone: in Anglicum (tuis sub auspicijs) traducere. Vt (te authore) habeant Anglici proceres: quod ad rerum magnarum imitationem: digne relegant.

Adhoc/ ipsius Crispi Salustij verba huic nostre translationi ydoneum visum est adijcere: tum vt due linguæ vna in pagina/ per columnas: meo more distincte/ altera alteram magis illustret. Tum vero: vt tetrici illi: qui soli sapere videntur: quique seriosum quicumque aut graue/ vulgarem in sermonem redigi egre ferunt ac pene dedignantur: ha[b]eant etiam quod Latine legant: obscurius tamen: ac hystoriam legant: vix illis forsan/ satis intellectam: ni vel commentariorum aut interpretis alicuius elucidamenta interuenirent. At qui hunc nostrum l[a]borem/ viris literatis: ac Latinæ linguæ eruditis tedio futurum: vix facile crediderim: verum plerisque sig. [a5v] proceribus: quibus est Romana lin|gua vix bene intellecta: non dubium est et delectamento futurum ac commodo nempe eodem ad linguæ Latinæ intellectum aliquantulum [adiumenti] acquirent: hystoriam etiam perutilem intelligent/ nulli mortalium generi non necessariam: potissimumque nobilibus adolescentulis/ qui rei militaris exercitijs clarissimis ad famam gloriamque nituntur.

Verum enim uero: non dubito futuros qui huic labori meo: quantumuis vtili calumnientur: quique forsan oblatrabunt/ homini sacerdoti: sacreque religionis obseruantijs iniciato: longe alienum esse atque absurdum sese militaribus rebus implicare/ aut bellicis sese immiscere tumultibus/ consilio/ factis: scriptisue. Cæterum: quo huiuscemodi obtr[e]ctatorum liuor[e]m compescam: pontifex egregie/ hoc in loco: haud absurdum videtur aliquid inserere: quod tam historiæ commoditates paucis aperiat quam/ quod calumniantium huiuscemodi liuorem compescat. Ac primum quidem fateor/ magis sacerdotem decere/ magisque par esse/ constancia/ sacrarum literarum peritia/ vite sanctimonia/ ac puritate/ cæterisque virtutibus sese armare: atque hijs præsidijs quasi fulgentibus armis munitum: forti

22 geram] gererem B insignem] insegnem A B 23 regni] regi B 25 traducere] vertere B habeant] habeant tandem B 26 relegant] legant B 28 adijcere] in margine annotare B 30 illi] sensores isti B soli] soli sibi B 32 habeant] haheant A 35 laborem] loborem A 37 quibus] *om.* B 39 adiumenti] madiumenti A acquirent] acquirenti acquirent: B 45 esse] *om.* B 47 scriptisue] scriptissue A 47–9 Cæterum . . . inserere] Cæterum hoc in loco: haud absurdum videtur presul eximie aliquid inserere B 48 obtrectatorum liuorem] obtractatorum liuorum A 52 esse/] *virgule from* B 53 peritia/] *virgule from* B

fidentique animo vicijs bellum indicere/ obstinatosque scelerum sectatores persequi. Ad h[æ]c ingenti pectore totisque animi viribus/ carnalibus concupiscentijs: mundi blandimentis: et antiqui hostis suggestionibus reluctari. Nempe hoc modo: Iob attestante: Militia est vita hominis super terram: ac vere miseriarum labarinthus/ inextricabiliumque err[o]rum domus ambigua: neque inficior sane: viri sacris iniciati ac diuinis ministerijs addicti militiam: talem esse debere. Verum altera illa militia seculi amatoribus permittitur: vt scilicet vim vi [repellant]. Neque ab ea abstineri posse arbitror: presertim in orbe tot tyrannicis inuasionibus obruto/ tot odiosis exaccionibus spoliato/ tot raptorum gregibus la[n]iato. Quorum atrox pertinatia: insultusque ferocissimi: non aliter reprimi | possint: sig. [a6^{r}] quam violenti armorum [tumultu] idque auspicijs bonorum principum rei publice fautorum. Neque minus decere existimo: huiuscemodi: modis res gestas/ presbyterum literis mandare: in posteritatis exemplum inque perpetuam bonorum principum memoriam gloriosam: qui ad tyrannorum aliorumque sceleratorum flagitia coercenda: summi Dei optimi maximi: flagella in terris fuere: quam duces illos magnanimos huiuscemodi bella strenue gessisse.

Cæterum quæ ad hystoriæ commoditates attinent: quam breuissime potero absoluam. Nempe ex eiusdem lectione (vt Beroaldus quam disertissime prosequitur) omnium etatum/ omnium gentium: omnium populorum res gestas quasi presentes intueri possimus: quod quanti sit: Cicero declarat dicens. Nihil earum rerum scire: quæ antequam nascereris facte sunt: [hoc est] semper esse puerum. Cumque senibus maior sit experientia fidesque maior propter vnius seculi rerum cognitionem: quanto maior esse debet hystorias lectitanti: ex quibus tot seculorum res geste repetuntur. Est enim hystoria testis temporum: lux veritatis: vite magistra: vetustatis nuntia: quæ et oratori perquam est necessaria. Nam alere potest (vt Quintilianus ait) orationem: molli quodam ac iucundo succo: nec ferme concionem reperies in qua non alicuius rei geste citetur exemplum. Est præterea (vt idem Beroaldus inquit) operi precium in hystoricorum voluminibus omnis exempli documenta velut in illustri monumento posita intueri. Atque (vt Diodorus inquit) | pulchrum est ex aliorum erratis sig. [a6^{v}] vitam nostram in melius instituere: et quid expetendum/ quid

56 hæc] hac A 58 reluctari] reductari B 60 errorum] errarum A
63 repellant] redellat A 65 laniato] lauiato A 67 tumultu] tuum/ tu A; tumultn B
68 existimo] arbitror B 69 modis] *om.* B 71 sceleratorum] sceleratorum hominum B
77 possimus] possumus B 79 hoc est] faciem A 90 melius] mellius A

sectandum: quidue fugie[n]dum sit ex aliorum exemplis posse cognoscere: non ab re: igitur Demetrius Phaler[e]us Ptolomeum regem admonebat: vt libros/ ac præsertim hystoricos: lectitaret quoniam quidem: quæ amici non audent principibus demonstrare: ea omnia in libris scripta: oculis obijciuntur. Hæc Beroaldus Ascencius/ cæterique autores/ de hystoriæ laude scripsere: quibus ex dictis quanti sit hystoria quam ad vitam humanam vtilis accommodat atque nemini non clarescit. Quas res si liuidi oblatratores perpendant (perpenderent autem et saperent pontifex eximie). Haud absurdum ineptum[u]e existimabunt/ sacerdotem hystorias rerum militarium literis commendare nec minus voluntatis accommodi/ egregijs viris in eisdem lectitandis prouenturum. Quippe (vt paucis dicam) iusto bello: diuina humanaque iura aut violata reparantur: aut inviolata conseruantur scelera reprimuntur: flagiciosi coercentur: virtus eminet/ clarescit/ extollitur: boni probique debitis honoribus illustrantur promouentur: Christi fides contra eiusdem sacratissimi nominis hostes protegitur munitur: tyranni legum contemptores alieneque libertatis direptores subijciuntur. Postremo diuina humanaque omnia debitum in ordinem rediguntur stabiliuntur et auges[c]unt.

Præterea eadem rerum gestarum lectio ad rerum terrenarum notitiam: earundemque contemptum ac presentis vite miseriarum sig. [a7r] fastidium: | non modicum videtur conducere. Sane cum hystoriarum lectio ante oculos obijciat: magnanimos duces ac milites: armis fulgentibus decoratos sonipedibus ostro auroque insignibus insidentes: splendidos ordines appar[a]tusque exercituum: feroces ac bello instructos: lituos a rauco clangore aera replentes: vectes vexillosque auro fulgentes ad solemque micantes: cæteraque id genus rei militaris insignia. Quid aliud quæso vniuersa hæc pompa? quam terrene opulentie inanis ostentatio: curiosie conquesita: anxie coaceruata: et ad ruinam perniciemque ingenti mortalium demencia obiecta inque perditionem exposita? At contra: cum paulo post eisdem in hystorijs legamus et quasi ante oculos cernamus: duces comarcos/ satrapas equites veteranos/ gregariosque milites sparsim p[r]ostratos horrida ferocium cadeuera humi strata moribundaque membra solum pulsancia/ occisorum cumulos si[n]e delectu concultata arma san-

91 fugiendum] fugiem dum A 92 Phalereus] Phalerus A; *om.* B 97 quam] quamquam A nemini] nenimini A 99 et] *om.* B pontifex eximie] *om.* B ineptumue] ineptumne A 101 commendare] mandare B 108 direptores] violatores B 109 augescunt] augestunt A 112 videtur] vidētur A videntur B 115 apparatusque] apparotusque A B 116 a] *om.* B 121 inque] et inque AB 122 quasi] *om.* B 123 prostratos] postratos A B 124 cadeuera] cadauera militum B 125 sine] siue A

guine fedata saucios equos moribunda dominorum corpora trahentes/ gemitum morientium: flammam ac fumum castrorum vrbium templorumque ardentium cæteraque belli horrenda spectacula. Quid ea atque huiuscemodi id genus alia? Nempe nihil aliud quam manifesta mortalium belluine seuicie argumenta: terrene vanitatis exempla: humanique exitus miseranda spectacula: quæ principum immoderatam dominandi libidinem declarant: quæque secundas res generi humano intollerabiles probant: ac sui ipsius stulticia: ne dicam dementia in præcipicium | ruentem hominem manifestant. sig. [a7^{v}]

Innumerabilia saluberrimaque huiuscemodi exempla: quæ ex rerum gestarum lectione proueniunt: animum adigerunt vt ex Latino in vulgarem sermonem hanc hystoriam transferrem: atque eo libentius quoniam rem gratam accceptamque tibi futuram intelligo. Equo igitur animo accipias queso: præsul egregie hanc laboris nostri lucubraciunculam. In qua quicquid absurdum ineptum minusque elimatum fuerit: id meæ ignorantiæ ascribi velim. Si vero quid consonum quod legentium audientiumve animos aut aures oblectet obiter occurrat: omnem in te præsul egregie: gratiam transferri volo qui omnium primus ad hunc me impuleris laborem: sopitumque ingeniolum ac studium resuscitaueris. Vale.

Ex cellula Hatfeldensis regii .iii. Idus Nouembris.

Tuus totus si quid est Alexander Barcleus presbyter.

Thus endeth the preface of this present cronycle: by Alexander Barclay preest/ dyrect vnto the right hye and mighty prince Thomas duke of Northfolke. sig. [a8^{r}]

126–7 trahentes/ gemitum] trahentes gemitum/ A 138 libentius] libentius presul eximie B 139 Equo] Ego B præsul egregie] *om.* B 141 Si vero] Sin B 146 iii] in A 147 Tuus . . . presbyter.] *om.* B

sig. A1r
f. 1r

An extract declaryng the boke folowyng.

¶Here begynneth a compendyous extract contayning breffely theffect and processe of this present cronycle compyled in Latyn by the famous Romayn Salust. And translated into Englysshe by Alexander Barcley preest at commaundement of the ryght hygh and myghty prince Thomas duke of Northfolke.

In this present cronycle or hystory of Rome: is written the batayle whiche the Romayns had with Iugurth/ vsurper of the kyngdome of Numydy. The lande of Numydy is part of the countrey of Affryke. In which raygned somtyme a kyng named Massynyssa: felowe and frende to the empyre of Rhome. This Massynissa had thre sonnes thus named/ Micipsa/ Manastaball/ and Galussa. But after the deth of Manastaball and Galussa: the first brother Micipsa obtayned the kyngdome of Numydy alone without any partyner. For after the custome of Numydy/ heritages are wont to be deuyded among brethern by equall porcyons after dyscease of their parentes of whome suche herytage issuyth. This Micipsa so crowned kynge of hole Numidy had two sonnes/ the first called Adherball/ the seconde Hiempsall. But his brother Manastaball which was departed before/ left behynde hym one bastarde sonne named Iugurth: to whom his granfather Massinissa bequethed none heritage/ but left hym priuate without lande or lyuelodde/ for asmoche as he was a bastarde and vnlaufully borne. The kynge Micipsa was moued with pyte and compassyon agaynst this Iugurth: and consyderynge that he was his brothers sonne and without confort he receyued hym into his house/ and cherysshed hym in all thynges as he dyde his owne sonnes.

This Iugurth as he grewe in stature: so grewe he in all gyftes belongyng to nature/ and becam a right strong and hardy knyght/ and also more excellent in wysdome than in courage or myght/ and was moche elder than the two sonnes of Micipsa: named Adherball/ and Hiempsall. What tyme Micipsa consydered the flouryng age/ manlynes/ and wysdome of Iugurth. And on the other part/ whan he remembred the feble yongth and vnexpert of his owne two sonnes/ in this aduysement his mynde was sore troubled with drede: lest after his dethe the same Iugurth myght inuade and vsurpe vnto hymselfe the

An Extract 8 Iugurth/] *virgule from* B 14 any] *om.* B 15 Numydy/] *virgule from* B 21 heritage/] *virgule from* B 22 lyuelodde/] *virgule from* B a bastarde and] *om.* B 25 he] *om.* B 31 age/] *virgule from* B (*end of line* A) 32 part/] *virgule from B* 33 sonnes/] *virgule from* B

kyngdome of Numydy/ his owne two sonnes | beyng nat of power to f. 1v defende themselfe. Micipsa after these thinges consydred: determyned to obiect this Iugurth vnto paryll of batayle and by such menes to assay if it myght fortune hym to be slayne in batell. Therfore what tyme the Romayns hauyng Scipio for their captayne/ beseged the cyte of Numance: this Micipsa sent vnto the Romayns to the same batayle great socours both of horsmen and of fotemen. And made Iugurthe captayn ouer them. This dyde he trustynge that it was possyble and lykely ynough that this Iugurth a knyght yonge/ lusty/ and desyrous of honour myght by some chaunce of fortune be slayne in batayle/ as I sayd before. But at conclusyon it fortuned moche contrary. For the boldnesse and strength of Iugurthe in that batayle was well proued and knowen. For many noble and valyant actes of chyualry dyd he: wherby he wanne moche laude and glory: with great loue and fauour/ nat onely of Scipio the captayne/ but also of all the noblest men of the Romayne army. Insomoche that after this batayle was fynisshed: and the cyte of Numance distroyed/ the captayne Scipio assembled his hole army: and before them all with magnificent and fauorable wordes commended Iugurth with maruelous laudes. This done he rewarded hym with many and ryche gyftes of chyualry. And sent hym agayne to the kyng Micipsa with letters/ wherin also he commended this Iugurth with great laude and praysyng. By instigatyon of which thynges it so befell: that where as the kyng Micipsa nat long before desyred nothyng more than the deth of Iugurth: nowe he coueted nought somoche as conseruatyon of his lyfe and helth. So that nat long after he adopted hym as his sonne/ and ordayned in his testament hym to be one of his heyres and partyner of his kyngdome with his two other naturall sonnes. Which ordynaunce he neuer chaunged/ but at his departyng increased his fauour and benefytes anenst the same Iugurth/ leuynge hym nat onely partyner of his kyngdome: but also of all his treasours. And besyde this decreyd hym to be protectour of his two naturall sonnes/ and of their porcyons of the kyngdome.

Sone after this ordynaunce the kyng Micipsa departed from lyfe. But whan the thre prynces Adherball/ Hiempsall/ and Iugurth determyned among them the tyme whan the treasoure shulde be deuyded and the boundes of the kyngdome lymyted to them eche one

38 batayle] warre B 46 batayle/] *virgule from* B 50 fauour/] *virgule from* B 52 distroyed/] *virgule suppl.* (*end of line* A B) 61 sonne] *virgule from* B 65 anenst] agaynst B Iugurth/] *virgule from* B

his part: at this assemble grewe a dyssencion betwene Hiempsall and Iugurth/ by occacyon wherof Iugurth shortly after slewe Hiempsall by treason and gyle. After this Hiempsall was slayne Iugurthe fixed his mynde to possesse the hole kyngdome of Numydy. Wherfore he |
f. 2r prepared a great and strong army agaynst the other brother Adherball: and at last whan bothe mette in batayle the army of Adherball was ouerthrowen/ and hymselfe put to flyght. Adherbal thus ouercome and spoyled of his kyngdome fledde vnto Rome: and there before the senatours declared the tyrannous cruelte of Iugurth agaynst hym commytted/ and agaynst his brother Hiempsall cruelly murdred: desiryng socours of the same senatours with pytefull wordes and lamentable complayntes. At conclusyon it was decreed of the senatours that .x. noble men of Rome shulde be sent embassadours to Numydy to deuyde the kyngdome betwene Adherball and Iugurth indyfferently.

The same embassadours hasted them to Numydy and dyde the commaundement of the senate to them inioyned: but more to the fauour of Iugurth than of Adherball. Whan the kyngdome was departed and deuyded/ and the sayd embassadours were also departed from Affryke towarde Rome: Iugurth sette his mynde yet ones agayne to inuade and vsurpe the part of the kyngdome which belonged to Adherball by assignement of the embassydours. Wherfore he assembled a newe army. And with the same inuaded his kyngdome: Adherball compelled by necessyte assembled also another army for his part. And proceded forthe and mette with Iugurth. But anone after they ioyned batayle/ Iugurth ouerthrewe the hoost of Adherball and put hym to flyght/ constrayning hym to fle with a fewe horsemen about hym into a walled towne nereby named Cyrtha. Iugurth anone beseged the towne on all partes.

In the meane tyme Adherball by letters certyfied the senatours of Rome in what state Iugurth had brought hym. How he was bereft of his kyngdome by cruelte and ambysion of Iugurth: how he was brought to extremyte by hun[g]er and force of armes/ nat able to abyde the besegynge any lenger: howe it appered euydently that Iugurth set lytell by the decrees and ordynaunce of the senatours/ And at conclusyon of the same letters he humbly besought the senate of ayde and socours in this his extremyte. Whan these letters were

74 Iugurth/] *virgule from* B; *virgule after* Hiempsall *in* A 79 ouerthrowen/] ouerthrowen. A; *virgule from* B flyght.] *no punctuation* A, *punctus in* B 82 commytted] *virgule from* B 89 of[2]] *om.* B 97 batayle/] *virgule from* B 104 hunger] B; hunder A armes/] *virgule from* B

redde before the senatours assembled: many of them were: which iuged it thynge expedyent and conuenyent: to socour Adherball. And anone to sende an army into Affryke agaynst Iugurthe. But his frendes whome he hadde bought for money at Rome: made suche resystence that no suche ordynaunce coude come to effect nor passe forthe agaynst hym. Neuerthelesse newe imbassydours were sent ones agayne to Iugurth: and that men auncyent/ and of great authorite: to compell and commaunde hym in name of the senatours to desyst from his enterprise and cruel|ty in payne of their hye dyspleasure. f. 2v Iugurth blynded these imbassydours with fayre wordes and rewardes/ tyll they were departed agayne from Numydy to Rome/ without any thyng brought to ende. Whan this was knowen at Cyrtha where Adherball lay beseged: they which were with Adherball within the towne counselled hym to yelde vp the towne to Iugurth/ vpon condycion onely to haue his lyfe pardoned vnto hym. Adherball constrayned by famyne and other necessyties condyscended to this counsell. But anone after the towne was yelded/ Iugurth contrary to his fayth and promes which he had made to Adherball: slewe hym with greuous and horryble tourment.

Whan this dede was knowen at Rome: the senatours were sore moued agaynst hym. And toke his demeanoure and dedes inhumayne greuously. Wherfore by commen assent of the senatours and commens of Rome: one named Lucyus Calphurnius that tyme consull of Rome/ was sent with a strong army into Numydy agaynst Iugurth. But within shorte season this Calphurnius corrupted and accloyed with money by Iugurth made a foule bonde of peace with hym to great dyshonoure and shame bothe of hymselfe/ and of all the empyre of Rhome: for which dede the senatours and commens of Rhome were greuously dyspleased. Wherfore Calphurnius was called home agayne to Rome with great dyshonoure and rebuke.

After this Calphurnius/ an other Romayn named Albynus was elect consull and dyrect with newe supplement of warryours into Numydy agaynst Iugurth. But this Iugurth droue him forth vnder hope and coloure as yf he wolde yelde hymselfe to the sayd Albynus: so longe tyll at last the tyme approched of electyon of newe consuls. Wherfore Albynus of necessyte constrayned: and as decrees of the Romayns commaunded: retourned agayne to Rome to be at the sayd electyon (as

118 rewardes/] *virgule from* B 119 Rome/] *virgule from* B 122 Iugurth/] *virgule from* B 123 hym.] *punctus from* B, *no punctuation* A 125 yelded/] *virgule from* B 132 Rome/] *virgule from* B

he was bounde) without any dede laudably done in Numydy. And at his departynge he left behynde hym in Numydy his brother named Aulus: to be capytayne in his stede/ and ruler of his army: and also of the prouynce where the same army soiourned tyll the wynter were ouerpassed. What tyme Albynus was departed towarde Rome: this Aul[u]s blynded by rasshenes/ and foly/ behaued hymselfe right vndyscretely in his rowme. Insomoche that he called the army vnto viage/ and warfare forth of theyr tentes in the moneth of January: in coldest/ and sharpest season of wynter. This dyde he: other bycause he trusted to ende the batayle in his tyme: and so therby to wynne thanke/ and worshyppe: or els to thentent to gete money of Iugurth f. 3r by grauntyng vnto hym peace and rest for his tyme. And | so to constrayne hym to bye his peace. Whan Iugurth perceyued this vnexpertnes and rasshe foly of Aulus: he sent vnto hym embassadours as if he were aferde: by dyssimulatyon to requyre of hym peace. And in the meane tyme the same Iugurth ledde his army amonge hylles and wodes fayning as yf he fledde from Aulus for drede. Aulus vnderstandyng this/ parsued and folowed hym more egarly: and hastely: without aduysment/ order/ or prouycion. Whan Iugurth sawe that he had attysed and drawen the Romayns into a place to fyght for his aduauntage: anone he assayled them and enbatayled with them fyersly: in which batayle he ouercame the Romayns and putte them to flyght. On the next morne after/ Iugurth and Aulus came togyder in communycatyon. And at last trewes was stryken bytwene bothe parties in this maner: and by suche condycions: that all the Romayns shulde passe vnder a spere in signe of subiection/ and that they were ouercome: without more hurt. And afterwarde within ten dayes all shulde depart out of Numydy/ and so was it done. Whan tydynges herof were brought to Rome: all the cyte was troubled with drede and dyspleasure.

After this shamefull trewes of Aulus and dysconfyture: and flyght of the Romayne army/ a noble man named Metellus was creat consull of Rome/ and by commen assent sende vnto Numydy agaynst Iugurth. This Metellus behaued hymselfe as a noble capytayne and valyaunt warryour: and parceyuynge that the resydue of the army which was escaped: was dyssolute and out of order/ by to moche lybertie. And by faute of the captayns which were before/ he first of all reduced the sowdyours to good rule/ and order/ acordyng to the

147 he] *om.* B 151 Aulus] Aulns A 154 wynter. This] *cap.* T *from* B; *punctus suppl.* 168 after/] *virgule from* B

auncient ordynaunces of chyualry: and than in tyme conuenyent: after his army was brought to order/ he assayled Iugurth fyersly. And after certayne sharpe/ and greuous batayles/ he dyminysshed his ryches/ his myght/ and power: and brought hym almost to extremyte.

After this Metellus: one named Marius last of all was creat consull/ and the prouynce and warre of Numydy decreed and commytted to hym. This Marius anone pursued Iugurth in batayle moost sharply and fyersly of all other/ insomoche: that fynally he vtterly brought hym to extremyte: his frendes/ his ryches/ and power/ brought all to nought. And at conclusyon by treason/ and betrayeng of one Bocchus/ kyng of the Mauriens: Iugurth was delyuerd to the same Maryus as prisoner: whom he ledde bo[un]de to Rome with glory and triumphe. At last this Iugurth was throwen into prison/ where at conclusyon he ended his myserable lyfe: in dolors and captyuite.

This is the argument and processe of all this hystory/ | and f. 3v
cronycle: in which the redar: of whatsoeuer condicyon/ and degre he be: shall fynde both profyte/ and pleasure: if he rede it attentyfly and with good aduertens. And moost namely: gentylmen apt to attayne to glorious fame/ and honour/ by fayt of chyualry: shall fynd both plesaunt/ and profytable pastyme/ in redyng this hystory: vnto whose example/ profyte/ and pleasure I chefely haue translated the same.

187 extremyte.] *punctus from* B, *no punctuation* A   195 bounde] bonude A
196 prison/] *virgule from* B; *virgule after* conclusyon *in* A

¶The prologue of this present cronycle compyled in Laten by the famous Romayne Salust: and translated into Englysshe by Alexander Barcley preest.

[1] Mankynde wrongefully complayneth of his naturall dysposicyon: sayeng/ that his feble and frayle lyfe of short contynuaunce of tyme/ is rather ruled by chaunces of fortune: than by prouysion of strength/ or vertu. But yf man well consyder his naturall inclynatyon: contrary to such opynion: he shall fynde that nothyng longynge to mankynde/ may be founde and proued greater/ better/ or more preemynent than his naturall inclynation: and that his owne dylygence and exercyse/ rather feyleth hym/ than other myght or long contynuaunce of lyfe tyme. But in this opynion to iuge indyfferently: let man vnderstande that the mynde is ordaynd/ gyde/ ruler / and captayne of mannes lyfe: which mynde: whan it valyantly intendeth to attayne/ to worshyp/ and dygnyte/ by way of vertu: it is excellent ynough/ myghty/ and clere of itselfe: so that it nedeth nat to force of fortune/ nor to care for her vncertayne gyftes: but to dyspyse her/ as nat able to gyue to any man honesty/ dylygence/ or other good/ and vertuous exercyses: nor able to depryue man agayne of the same gyftes: after he hath obtayned the same. But on the other part if this mynde of man/ taken and blynded with frowarde plesures/ be subdued vnto slouthe and bodely lustes: after it hath exercysed and occupyed such ieoperdous plesure by a lytell season: and after that by cowardous slouth/ both the strength/ the tyme/ and the wyt ar vanysshed away/ and decayed: than anone the infyrmite: and febylnes of nature is accused/ and put in blame. And thus/ all such slouthfull doers transpose and lay away the faute which in themselfe is culpable/ vnto the dyfficulte of such besynesses as they haue omytted by neglygence. But yf it were so: that men had as great cure/ and affectyon of thynges good/ and profytable: as they haue desyre/ and pleasure in sekyng and folowyng thynges contrary vnto f. 4^{r} them and nothyng profitable | ye and also moch perylous and hurtfull: than shulde nat they be more ruled by the chaunces of fortune/ than they shulde rule the sayd chaunces. And thus shulde they attayne/ and procede vnto so great excellence: that where they be mortall of nature they shulde be made immortal by glory and renowmed fame.

[2] For in lyke wyse as man is composed and made of .ii. thynges (that is to say of the body and soule) right so all thynges/ all

Prologue ¶The prologue] C *begins here.* 13 gyde] gyder B C 15–16 it is excellent . . . so that] *om.* C 20 man/] *virgule from* B; *virgule after* taken *in* A 21 plesures/] *virgule suppl.* (*end of line* A B) 23 strength/] *virgule from* B 28 besynesses] besinesse C besynesses/ and exercyses/ to mankynde belongyng/ foloweth some the nature of the body: to decay brefely and to be mortall: as it is some other folowe the nature of the soule/ to be eternall/ and immortall: as it is. Which thing forther to proue by example: we dayly se: that the goodly beauty of the vysage/ and shape of mankynde/ great abundaunce of ryches/ and also the strength of the body/ with all other such thynges/ and semblable/ decayeth and vanyssheth away within short tyme. But contrarely the excellent/ and worthy actes: belongyng to mannes wyt: be immortall and euerlastyng: as the soule is immortall. And finally in lyk wyse as the begynnyng of the gyftes corporall/ or naturall/ and of the gyftes of fortune is caduke/ vayne and vncertayn: ryght so is the ende of the same mutable and transytory. And all thynges which be borne and sprynging: agayne decayeth/ and approcheth to deth: and whan these same be growen and encreased to the hegth of their perfectyon: agayne they begyn to decay and consume by age and debylyte. But the mynde and soule beynge incorrupt/ eternall/ and gouernoure of mankynde/ ruleth and weldeth al thynges: but it selfe can nat be vyolently ruled nor compelled by any thyng erthly/ consyderyng the fre wyll whiche it optayneth of his creatour. For which consyderacion the frowarde iniquyte of them is more to be marueyled: which subdued to the ioyes and pleasures of the body/ passe forthe the tyme of theyr lyfe/ in carnall lustes and ydelnes. But towchyng their wyt (which is the best gyft and grettest treasure graunted to mankynde) that suffre thei to slomber and to slepe without excercyse/ in slouth and ydelnes: whose dulnes surely is so moche more to be reuyled: namely syth so many and dyuers noble exercyses and occupatyons of the mynde be: by whom moost clere nobles/ and fame vndefyled may be optayned.

[3] But of suche dyuers exercyses concernynge the mynde some ar better refused: than procured in troublous tymes and inquyet. And namely in this tyme turbulent/ and season vnquyet: great offyces/ lordshyppes/ rowmes to commaunde and rule: and brefely to speke. All maner cure concernyng the admynystracion of thynges apparteyn-yng to the commen wayle: semeth vnto me nat at all to be couyted or desyred of any wyse man. For neyther is honoure gyuen vnto vertue/ as condygne rewarde and worthy | therto belongyng: nother suche as f. 4^{v}

39–41 some other . . . as it is] *om.* C 44 semblable/] *virgule from* B; *virgule after* decayeth *in* A 52 hegth] high C 55 can nat] cane nat A 56 compelled] *followed by colon* A; *no colon* B 63 reuyled] blamed B C 71 wayle] wele B C 73 belongyng:] *colon suppl.*

haue goten iurysdictyon and honour/ by fraude and vnlaufull meanes (in lyke case) can nat be more sure nor more honest/ by meane of such honour so vnryghtwysly obtayned. For certenly a man to rule his countrey and kynred by myght and vyolence: all if he haue power so to do/ and also though he ryghtwysly correct the crymes of transgressours/ and mysdoers. Neuertheles: so to do it is vnbehouefull and vnexpedyent. And often at conclusyon more perylous and daungerous: than it is sure or profytable/ and that namely/ syth all mutacions of thynges/ and chaunges of gouernours pretend and thretten slaughter of some: of some exyle/ or wylfull flyght/ imprisonment with otherlyke cruelties more longyng to ennemyes of a commen wayle than to defenders of the same. Than forthermore: a man to labour to the vttermast of his power/ and all in vayne. [And] in weryeng hymselfe to gete nought els but euylwyll [and] hatred: it is a poynt of extrem and vtter madnes/ except perchaunce it be suche one which hath a dyshonest/ a foule and perylous pleasure to cast away for nought his owne worshyppe and lybertie for pleasure of a fewe myghty men vsurpers of dominion and lordshyp.

[4] But among all other besynesses which ar exercysed by mannes wyt/ the redyng of hystories and the reducyng of the same to memory: is moche more necessary and profitable to all degrees beryng rule of a commen wele/ but most namely vnto princes. Of power/ profet/ and commodyte wherof: I purpose at this tyme to passe ouer with sylence/ bycause many other authours haue wryten of the same before my tyme. And also that no man shulde suppose my selfe by pride/ or insolence: to bost myne owne study vaynly laudyng the same. But moch contrary I beleue rather that some enuyus malignars shalbe herafter which shall obiect and ascribe a name of slouth and neglygence to this my labour. How great and profitable so euer it be: and that bycause I haue determined to lede my lyfe solytarely: ferre from medlynge with the commen wayle. Certaynly (as I suppose) they onely shall impute and ascrybe such name to me and to this my laboure: whiche thynketh it a moost great and syngular craft or practysed wysdome to wynne benyuolence/ by salutyng the commen people/ and by dyssimulate reuerence done to euery man passyng by them/ or els to gete fauour by festyng and flaterynge the

78 of] of the C   81 that] *om.* C   83 of some:] *om.* B C   84 longyng] belongyng C   86 And] B C; Nor A   87 and] B C; or A   92 besynesses] besinesse B C   93 wyt/] *virgule from* B   101 herafter/] *virgule from* B   104 ferre] fre C

commenty. Whiche enuyous maligners: yf they wolde consyder both in what maner seasons and in what ieopardous tymes I haue obtayned offices and rowmes of auctorite and what men wolde gladly/ and yet myght nat obtayne suche rowmes. Moreouer yf they call to mynde what maner of men afterwarde came into the order of senatours. For certayne if my wyl| lers consyder indifferently these premysses: than f. 5r shall they thinke that I haue chaunged the purpose of my mynde: more for cause reasonable: and by good aduysement/ than for slouthe and cowardyse and they shall fynde that more profet shall come to the commen wayle by this my study (which they count but ydelnes and tyme mysspent) than of the labour and besynes which other men take upon them fayntly and iniustly admynistryng the commen wele. And they shall fynde that my writynge shall proue itselfe more laudable and profytable to the commente: than their vndyscrete gouernaunce.

For often haue I herde of the famous princes Quintus Maximus/ and Publius Scipio/ and besyde these of many other right famous and worthy men of the cytie of Rome: which princes whan they behelde the ymages of their forefathers made of stone/ of waxe/ or of metall/ and erect into hye trownes in a memoriall of the valyaunt and magnifycent actes by them done: for the commen wele: the sayd princes in aduysyng suche ymages were wont to say vnto suche as stode nere by them: that their myndes were gretly kyndeled to vertue and nobles in contemplyng of the same. The case is playne: that suche fygures of metall/ stone/ or wax had nat suche operatyon nor myght within them selfe. But such high courage and flame was kyndeled/ and increase[d] in the hardy hertes of such [n]oble men/ and valyant warryou[r]s/ by remembraunce of the gloryous dedes of their forefathers in their lyfe tyme/ done and represented to their memory by such ymages: in somoche that this flame kyndled in their hertes to vertu coude neuer be slaked nor sacyate in them: tyll tyme that they were equall with their forefathers in vertu/ fame/ and glory. Than how moch more ought the clere dyscripcyon of hystores to kyndell vnto boldnes/ and vertu/ the myndes of noble men by redyng of the same. But moche contrary/ if we aduert the worlde as it is nowe/ among all men whiche lyue/ and conforme themselfe to the maners vsed nowe adayes/ where shall we fynde one: but that dare stryue and contende with their forefathers to ouercome them/ other

126 princes] *om.* B C 128 trownes] trones B C in a memoriall] in memoriall B C 135 increased] B C; increase A noble] B C; uoble A 136 warryours] warryous A; warrious B C 137 tyme/] *virgule from* B 145 dare] wyll B C

in couetyse/ and suparfluous riches/ or els in prodygalyte/ and wastfull expences. And nat in honest and laudable lyfe/ good excercyces/ and dyligence? And moreouer gentylmen of the first heed/ which were wont to preuent auncyent noblemen and ascende vnto vertu/ and nobles/ by vertuous maners: suche laboure now to lordshyp/ honour/ and authorite/ by fraude/ and falshode: rather than by very vertu: or good meanes and laudable. After suche maner as yf the offyce of a hye Iuge/ of a Tresourer/ a Consull/ a Prouost/ and all such other great offyces were noble and excellent of themselfe.
f. 5v And nat in maner as yf such | offyces shulde be counted of worthynes and dygnite: after as the vertue/ and honour is: of such as rule in the same offyces and hy rowmes. But playnly affirmyng the treuth: the man maketh the offyce noble/ and worshypfull: yf his maners shyne by vertue. But yf his conuersacyon be contrary/ no offyce/ nor rowme/ can make hym noble/ nor worshypfull. But this omyttynge I haue proceded in this prologue with ouerferre circumstaunce/ and also with somwhat to moche lybertie of large wordes: more than in a preface is requisite: for that it reweth and pyteth me of these tedyous maners of this oure cytie of Rhome. But nowe wyll I come to my mater purposed and first interpryse begone.

¶Of what mater Salust intendeth to treat in proces of this boke/ and what causes moueth hym of suche mater to write. ¶The fyrst chapter.

[5] In this warke I purpose to wryte of the batayle/ which the Romayns had and executed agaynst the tyranne Iugurth wrongfully vsurpynge the name of a kynge/ ouer the lande of Numydy. Many causes moueth me by writynge to commende this batayle to perpetuall memory. First for that the same was faughten at many tymes with great multytude of men on eyther partie/ with moche cruell murdre/ and varyable victory: the Romayns somtyme/ somtyme the Iugurthyns preuayling in victory. Forthermore bycause that first at this batayle: and from thens forwarde the commen people of Rome matched with the princes and states/ resistynge their pride. For where as before this tyme the noble men of Rome oppressed and subdued the commens with unreasonable rygoure/ the commens elect one named Marius a man of basse byrth to be consull of Rome and

150 heed/] *virgule from* B 158 hy] by C 160 nor] no B C 163 large] *om.* B C 164 reweth and] *om.* B C

Ch. 1 1 this] hys C 3 batayle] warre B C 6 batayle] warre B C 7 that] that in B C 8 partie/] *virgule from* B 12 and states] *om.* B C; *virgule after* princes *in* A

captayne in this batayle: whiche after he had obtayned victory ouer Iugurth with great glory/ triumphe/ and fauour of the comme[n]tie/ he supported them in such wyse agaynst the noble men: that of the same rose a cyuyle batayle and greuous dyscorde bytwene the noble men and commens of Rome: Marius mayntenyng the commens partie/ and Silla susteyning that partie of the noble men. Insomoch that fynally bytwene these two parties and captayns of the same was foughten an vnkynde/ vnnatural/ and cruell batell: to the greuous ruyne of the Romayne empyre and subuercyon of the commen wayle. Which contencion and | varyaunce confounded bothe the lawes of f. 6r
God and man/ and by the same were all good ordynaunces dysordred. And this same furyous debate and foly proceded at last to so vnresonable madnesse and excecate fury that it neuer desysted: nor this varyaunce and dyscencion bytwene the noble men and commens neuer ceased: tyll tyme that cruell and mortall batayle foughten bytwene bothe parties/ and tyll tyme that also dystructyon of the lande of Italy compelled both parties at last to consyder theyr owne blynd foly and cruell furor: and so finally to myttigate and fynisshe their debate and unreasonable dyssencion. But fyrst or I begyn to write of this batell I shall repeat and declare a fewe thinges done before this war began: to thentent that all thynges moost chefe/ worthy and expedient to be knowen may be more euydent/ open/ and clere/ to the reders.

¶How the kyng Massinyssa came into the fauour of the Romayns/ and how the lande of Numydy was commytted vnto hym. The seconde chapter.

[5. 4] The Romayns had thre notable and famous batayls agaynst the Carthaginences/ in which the same Romayns had great dammage. Howbeit in conclusyon of euery batayle they wanne victory of theyr ennemyes: in the seconde of these batayles what tyme Hanyball duke and captayne of the Carthaginences wasted the welth and riches of Italy more than any other ennemy had euer done before/ after the Romayns beganne to haue any great name and to delate their dominion: A famous prince named Massinissa kynge of the lande of Numydy was receyued into frendshyppe and fauour of the Romyns: by one Publius Scipio captayne of the sayd Romayns/ which Scipio afterwarde for his manhode was named Scipio Affrycan/ bycause he

17 comme[n]tie/] commetie A; commontie/ B; commentie, C; *virgule from* B
22 parties] partes C 31 parties/] *virgule from* B

ouercame and subdued the lande of Affrike. This Massinissa so receyued into fauour of the Romayns in the foresayd batayle dyd many noble and famous actes of chyualry: with hygh valyantyse and corage. For which dedes: after the Romayns had ouercome the Carthagynencis and their cyte: and after they had taken prisoner the kyng Sciphar/ which had in Affryke a worthy/ great/ and large impyre: the people of Rome gaue frely vnto the same kynge Massinissa all suche cyties and landes as they had taken and wone in batayle. For which benefites so magnificent and ample Massinissa contynued vnto them in profitable and faythfull frendshyp his life f. 6v induryng: | but at last his lyfe ended: and the welth of his empyre decayed also with hym. This kynge departyng left behynde hym thre sonnes: whose names were/ Micipsa/ Manastaball/ and Galussa: of whome Micipsa succeded his father and alone obtayned the kyngdome: after that his other two brethern Manastaball/ and Galussa were departed frome this lyfe by sickenesse. This Micipsa had two sonnes named Adherball/ and Hiempsall. But Manastaball his brother whiche departed (as sayde is) left behynde hym one sonne nat laufully borne: but a bastarde/ begoten of his concubyne: wherfore departyng he left hym orbate without lande or lyuelode. This consydering Micipsa suffred hym nat to faute nor decay: but forasmoche as he was his brothers sonne: receyued hym into his court/ and hym cherysshed in lyke wyse as he dyde his owne sonnes/ Adherball/ and Hiempsall.

[**6**] This Iugurth after that he was a lytell growen vp to age: was myghty in strength/ comely/ and fayre of face: but moost of all excellent of wyt and wysdome. Nor he gaue nat hymselfe to be corrupt with lust nor incrafty slouthe: but as is the custome and maner of the people of Numidy/ hymselfe he exercysed somtyme in rydinge: somtyme in castynge the dart/ and somtyme in ronnynge and wrestlynge with his companyons of lyke age. And nat withstandynge that in laude and prayse he passed all his perys: yet none inuyed hym/ but he was derely beloued/ cherysshed/ and lauded of all men. Moreouer he passed moche of his tyme in huntyng of wylde bestes which in that lande habounded: he was the first/ or one among the first whiche durst assayle and stryke the lyon/ and other cruell and wylde beestes: he dyde moche: and lytell he sayd or bosted of hymselfe.

Ch. 2 21 impyre:] *colon suppl.* 29 his] this B; the C 40 strength/] *virgule suppl.* (*end of line* A B) 44 dart] dart and iustyng B C 46 hym/] *virgule suppl.* 51 he²] *om.* B C

For suche demeanour his vncle Micipsa at fyrst begynnynge was gladde and ioyefull: supposyng that in tyme to come the manly behauour and strength of Iugurth shuld be glory and honoure to all his kyngdom. But afterwarde in processe of tyme whan he consydred and vnderstode his lyfe approchyng fast to ende/ his naturall sonnes lytell/ yong/ and vnexpert. And this yong man Iugurth in honour and fauour dayly encreasynge more and more: he reuolued many thynges in mynde greatly moued with suche solycitude and besynesse. Forthermore he consydred that all men of kynde be naturally dysposed and inclyned to desyre/ to rule/ and commaunde by lordeshyppe: rather than to be ruled and subiect. And how man is prone and hedlynge inclyned to fulfyll the desyers of his mynde dredyng no daungers: nor suspectyng no peryll/ whyle he is excecate by ambicion and desyre of lordeshyp. Moreouer aduysing the oportunyte of his owne age/ and of the | age of his chyldren which for yongh were nat f. 7r
able to resyst any power or vyolence: which oportunyte is wont to be nat small confort/ audacyte and courage nat onely to bolde hertes/ but also to meane men and cowardes intendyng to conspyre agaynst their princes in hope of pray and promocyons. Such consyderatyons feared sore the mynde of Micipsa/ [and] besyde these his drede and dolour was more augmented: whan he behelde the fauour and hertes of all his subgettes of the lande of Numidy vtterly kyndled agaynst Iugurth: wherfore to put to deth the same Iugurth by any gyle (as his purpose was to do) he drad moost of all: dowtyng lest therof myght succede bytwene hym and his subgettes some insurrexion or batayle.

[7] Micipsa compased about on euery syde with these dyfficulties was sore troubled with the same. And whan he sawe that nother by strength nor begyle he myght dystroy a man so well beloued of the commens as was Iugurth: at last he deuysed an other way to ryd hym: and that without daunger or suspectyon: wherfore aduertyng that he was redy of hande to stryke/ auenterous/ and moche desyrous of honoure/ and laude of chyualry: Micipsa concluded with hymselfe to obiect hym to daunger and peryll of warre: and by that meane to assay the fortune of batayle.

56 ende/] *virgule suppl.* lytell] *om.* B C 58 more:] *colon suppl.* reuolued] reueyled C 61 dysposed and] *om.* B C 66 yongh] youth C 71 and] *om.* A B C 72 more] *om.* C 73 kyndled agaynst] inclyned to B C 77 about] *om.* B C 78 with the same] in mynde B; in mind C 79 begyle] gyle B C 81 suspectyon:] *colon suppl.*; *virgule* B wherfore aduertyng] wherfore Micipsa aduertyng B; wherfore wherfore Micipsa aduertynge C he] Iugurth B C 83 chyualry:] *punctus* A; *virgule* B Micipsa] he B C

¶Nowe at the same season the Romayns warred agaynst a cyte of Hispayne named Numance: vnto which warre dyuers kynges to them assocyate sent vnto them socours agaynst the same cyte. Amonge whom Micipsa also sent vnto them into socours a fayre company of horsmen and fotemen: ouer whom he made Iugurth captayne: and sent hym forth with them into Hispayne/ trustyng that there he lightly shulde be ouerthrowen and slayne in batayle: other in shewyng his manhod and strength/ or els by fyersnes and cruelty of his ennemyes. But this thyng fortuned moche contrary to his opynion. For Iugurth was of mynde and courage valyaunt and bolde/ and of wytte quicke and redy/ so that after he had parceyued the dysposycion and maners of Publius Scipio: whiche at that tyme was captayne of the Romayns/ and whan he had consydred also the maners of his ennemyes/ he behaued hymselfe in suche wyse with moche labour/ besynes/ and cure: in obeyng his captayne with so good maner: and often tymes countryng his ennemyes without drede of peryll. Insomoche that within short tyme he came to so great fame and worshyppe/ that vnto the Romayns he was marueylous dere and well beloued/ and of
f. 7v the Numantynes dradde as deth: and certaynly/ among the che|fyst he was worthy and valyaunt in batayle: and also good of counsell/ of wysdome pregnaunt and circumspect. Which two thynges be moche h[a]rde to be in one man bothe togyder: for wysdome is often wont to make men aferde and to drede many paryls bycause of prouydence. But boldnes and audacyte causeth men to be rasshe and folehardy/ bycause of haut courage. But his wysdome dyrected his strength/ and his strength was obedyent to wysdome. Wherfore Scipio the captayne dyd almost euery ieopardous and weyghty thyng by hand and counsell of Iugurth: hym countyng amonge his chefe frendes and dayly he cherysshed hym more and more and no marueyle/ for there was no counsell/ no interpryse/ nor begon purpose of Iugurth which was frustrate or in vayne/ but all came to good effect. Besyde these gyftes aboue sayd he was curtes of mynd and lyberall / and of his wyt right dyscrete and prudent: by which gyftes he adnexed vnto hym many of the Romayns in familyer frendshyp.

87 them] the commens B C 89 vnto them into socours] *om.* B C 96 redy/] *virgule from* B dysposycion] disposicion/ behauour B; disposision, behauour C 97 whiche] *om.* B C was] *om.* B C 105 counsell/] *virgule from* B 107 harde] herde A; harde B C 108 paryls] peryls B C 110 haut] stout C 112 weyghty] wyghty B whyghty C 113 he] *om.* B C 115 no] nor B C nor] *om.* B C purpose] *om.* B C which was] *om.* B C 117 and[1]] *om.* B C his] *om.* B C 118 adnexed] adioyned B C

[8] At that same season in the army of Rome were ryght many newe gentylmen: and also auncyent gentylmen/ which set more by riches than goodnes or honeste. At home in Rome were they sowers of dyscorde and debatefull/ myghty of fame amonge the frendes of the Romayns. And more famous by worshyppe and rowme/ than by honest conuersatyon. These kyndled the mynde of Iugurth nat a lytell/ promysyng often tymes and sayeng vnto hym to set his courage on fyre: that yf the kyng Micipsa dyscessed the tyme shulde come that Iugurth alone shulde enioye the hole kyngdome of Numidy without any partyner. For in hym (they said) was great vertue/ great manhode/ strength/ and audacyte with wysdome/ able to gouerne suche a kyngdome: and nothynge was so iniust and false but that might be iustyfied at Rome for golde/ and all thynges were there to be solde by couetyse of noble men.

¶How Publyus Scipio counselled Iugurth at his departynge after the cyte of Numance was dystroyed. ¶The thyrde chapter.

[8. 2] Thus contynued Iugurth in the Romayns army in Hispayne with great fauour of the Romayns/ and namely of Scipio the captayne: tyll at last the army of Rome had distroyed the sayd cyte of Numance. Than Publyus Scipio conclu|ded to retourne home agayne to Rome: f. 8r and to congye and lycence suche socours as were sent vnto hym from other kynges: among all other he called Iugurth vnto hym: and before the multytude of all the army assembled: lauded and commended hym magnyficently/ recitynge his glorious actes and manly dedes of chyualry. And than worthely and richely rewarded hym for his labours. This done: he conueyed hym into the captayns tent: and there secretely warned hym that he shulde contynu and worshyppe the frendshyppe of the people of Rome rather hole togyder and commenly/ than priuatly leanyng to any synguler rulers. Moreouer addynge these monycions: that he shulde nat rather rewarde and be lyberall to a fewe priuately: than to a hole commente. For it is a paryllous thynge to bye that: of a fewe persons: which belongeth vnto many in commen. If he wolde parseuer and contynue in so noble condycions as he had begon: he shulde shortly come to great honour/ glory/ and dygnite royall/ more than he wolde desyre. But yf he

121 gentylmen] *om.* B C 123 myghty of] great in B C 124 And] But B C 126 lytell/] *virgule suppl.* vnto hym] *om.* B C

Ch. 3 6 home] *om.* B C 10 magnyficently/] *virgule suppl.* 11 than] after that B C 17 For it is] sayeng that it was B C 18 belongeth] belonge B C

wolde procede and labour to ascende ouer hastely to honour/ than shulde both he and his ryches fall heedlyng to ruyne and decay.

[9] After Scipio had sayd these wordes with such lyke: he lycensed Iugurth to depart/ and sent hym vnto his vncle Micipsa agayne into the lande of Numydy with letters dyrect vnto the same kyng Micipsa: of which letters the tenure and sentence hereafter ensueth: and was suche.

¶The sentence of the letter dyrect from Publius Scipio captayne of the Romayne army in Hispayne vnto Micipsa kynge of Numydy. ¶The fourthe chapter.

[9. 2] Publius Scipio captayne of the Romayns army in Hispayne sendeth helth and salutacyon to Micipsa kynge of Numydy frende and felowe of the empyre of Rome. The vertue/ strength/ and noblenes/ of your neuewe Iugurth whom ye sent vnto our socours hath ben proued in this batayle of Numance/ ferre excellent aboue any other warryour of our retynue/ which thynge I knowe for certayne is to your great pleasure and gladnes. For his worthy merytes he is right
f. 8v dere and well beloued vnto vs. And we shall deuoyr vs to the | best of our power that he may be lyke dere and well beloued of all the senatours and people of Rome. I am surely right ioyefull on your behalfe of this your treasoure Iugurth: thauncyent amyte bytwene you and me: byndeth me to be gladde of this your commodyte. For certaynely lo here haue ye a man of Iugurth worthy to dyscende of suche noble stocke as ye ar and as his granfather Massinissa was in his dayes: whome he foloweth in all poyntes of vertue/ and magnanimyte.

¶Howe the kyng Micipsa adopted Iugurth vnto his sonne. ¶The fyfte chapter.

[9. 3] With these letters of Scipio Iugurth retourned into Numydy vnto his vncle Micipsa: where he was worthely and ioyefully receyued of the commentie. But after that the kynge Micipsa vnderstode by these letters of commendatyon of the captay[n]e Scipio: that the valyaunt and noble actes of Iugurth were trewe: which longe before he had harde by report of the commen fame: than what for the nobles of Iugurth and fauoure bothe of his dedes and commendatyon of Scipio

22 to honour] *om.* B C; *virgule suppl.* 23 decay.] *punctus from* B; *colon* A

Ch. 4 4 romayns] romain B; Romayne C 8 batayle] warre B C 9 retynue/] *virgule from* B

Ch. 5 3 into] unto C

he moued his mynde chaunged from his foresayd purpose/ and nat forther intended to oppres Iugurth by malyce nor enuy. But concluded to attempt to ouercome hym with benefites and kyndenes: to thentent: that he so ouercome shulde nat in tyme to come fynde in his hert for pyte to indammage hym nor his heyres. And soone after this purpose the same Micipsa adopted Iugurthe vnto his sonne: and farthermore decreed and ordayned in his testament that Iugurth shulde be one of his heyres: and partener in possessyon of his kyngdome togyder with his two naturall sonnes/ Adherball and Hiempsall. But a fewe yeres after this ordynaunce Micipsa what by age/ what by sykenesse/ drewe nere vnto his ende of lyfe/ and was consumed [by age and dysease]: wherfore consydring his dethe so fast approchyng it is sayd that he called Iugurth before hym: and than before many of his frendes and kynsmen: also in presence of his two naturall sonnes Adherball and Hiempsall/ he had with the same Iugurth suche wordes as herafter insue and folowe.

¶The exhortacyon which the kynge Micipsa a | lytell before his dethe had to Iugurth. ¶The sixt chapter. f. 9r

[**10**] Mi dere sonne Iugurth/ I knowe it is nat out of your remembraunce: how after that ye hadde lost your father my brother I charytably and louyngly receyued you yong and of tender age into my kyngdome: what tyme ye were without ryches/ without confort: and without any hope of confort or ryches/ but very lykely to haue ben caste away. This dyde I thynkynge that for these my benefytes and kyndnesse I shulde be vnto you nat lesse intyerly beloued thanne of myne owne naturall chyldren with my body begotten. Nor certaynly this my hope and trust hath nat dysceyued me. For why to ouerpasse and omytte your other great/ magnyficent and excellent dedes of you valyauntly done before: specially nowe last of all: ye commynge from the warre of Numance/ haue greatly adourned and inhaunced to honoure and glory bothe of me and of this kyngdome of Numydy. And where as the Romayns in fore tymes were frendes vnto vs: by your vertue/ and manly actes [ye] haue establysshed that amyte: and of frendes made them moche more frendes. So that in

21 by age and dysease] B C; *om.* A 24 Hiempsall/] *virgule from* B with] to B C

Ch. 6 3 Iugurth/] *virgule from* B 6 were] warre C 9 shulde] shulde nat A 11 this my hope and trust] hope and trust *om.* B; this thing C 12 and omytte] *om.* B C great/] *virgule from* B 13 ye] *om.* B C 14 haue] ye B C 15 me] myne owne persone B; mine owne person C 15–16 of this kyngdome of Numydy] this my kyngdome B C 17 ye] B C; *om.* A

Hispayne the name and glory of oure housholde by your manhode is renouate and renewed. Thus finally: ye haue ouercome the enuy of [y]oure ylwyllers onely by your gloryous actes/ and valyaunt interpryses: which is one of the moost hardyest thynges to be done amonge mankynde/ and of moost dyfficultie. Wherfore nowe my sonne Iugurth: sythe it is so: that nature hath nere concluded the ende of my lyfe: I admonest/ charge/ and exhorte you by the fayth of this your ryght hande: and by the fayth and fidelyte whiche ye owe to this my kyngdome I obtest and requyre you/ that ye wyll loue/ mentayne/ and cherysshe these my two sonnes Adherball and Hiempsall: which of kynredde be nere to you/ and by my benefyte and kyndnes are bretherne vnto you. Forthermore I exhorte you that ye counte nat leferre and more pleasure to acquaynt and conioyne vnto you forance or straungers/ thanne to retayne suche as be ioyened
f. 9v to you by naturall blode/ and kynredde. For neyther | is a great army of men nor habundance of treasours: the chefe socoures or defence of a kyngdome: but moche rather trusty and faythefull frendes: whome a manne canne neyther compell by force of armes: nor yet bye with golde nor syluer to parseuer in stedfast amyte: but they be optayned and kept/ by kyndnesse/ good dedes: fydelyte and faythfulnesse. But among all frendes: who canne be more frendly and stedfast in amyte than brother to brother? Certaynely none ought to be more louyng of naturall inclynatyon. Or what straunger shall ye fynde faythfull and trusty to you: if ye shewe your selfe ennemy to your owne kynsmen? For sothe if ye wyll contynue togyder honest/ good/ and louynge in agreable concorde bytwene yourselfe: thanne this kyngdome whiche I commytte and gyue vnto you shall contynue sure and stedfast: as it is nowe. But contrarily if ye be yll and dysagreynge amonge your selfe/ ye shall in shorte season make it right poore/ feble/ and incertayne. For by loue/ peace/ and concorde: small ryches/ small lordshyppes/ and generally all small thynges increase/ and multyplie: by dyscorde the grettest thynges of the worlde decay/ and fall vtterly to ruyne. But you my sonne Iugurthe bycause ye passe these myne other two naturall sonnes in age and wysdome/ therfore it semeth you so moche more than them: to make suche wyse prouycion bothe for your selfe and for them also that nothynge happen otherwyse thanne

21 youre] oure A; your B C 22–3 hardyest . . . moost] *om.* C 25 admonest] admonishe C 26 this] *om.* B C 27 wyll] *om.* B C 31 leferre] better C 32 forance] forayns B C thanne] rather than B C 36 compell] compelled B C 38 kyndnesse/] *virgule from* B 43 wyll] *om.* B C honest/] *virgule suppl.* (*end of line* A B) 45 gyue] gaue B C 46 your selfe/] *virgule from* B 52 so] *om.* C

well. For in euery stryffe and debate: how be it he which is myghtyer and rycher often sufferyth iniury. Neuerthelesse it semeth more that he dothe wronge thanne suffreth: bycause that he is more of power and myght thanne his feble aduersary. But ye my dere sonnes Adherball and Hiempsall se that ye worshyppe and loue this Iugurth your worthy vncle. And beware that ye offende nor dysplease hym nat: but folowe his vertue/ and manly behauour. And do your deuoyr to the best of your power after his example behauynge yourselfe/ so dyscretely/ and so wysely that it be nat hereafter reported by me that I haue takenne vnto me by adoptyon better chyldren thanne I haue begotten. Th[u]s concluded the kyng Micipsa his wordes.

[11] Than howbeit Iugurth well parceyued the kynges wordes but fayned and spoken agaynst his hert: if any other remedy myght haue ben founde: neuertheles he answered benygnely for the tyme/ all | yf (f. 10r) he thought and reuoulued in his mynde moche otherwyse/ and contrary to his humble and mylde answere.

¶How the kynge Micipsa departed frome this lyfe/ and of the first cause of dyscorde betwene Iugurth/ Adherball/ and Hiempsall. ¶The .vii. chapter.

[11. 2] Nat longe after the kyng Micipsa decessed whose dethe was dolourous and sore bewayled of all his subgettes: but most of all to his naturall sonnes it was to be lamented: and nat without great cause as the processe of this hystorie shall afterwarde declare. But after the kynges funerall exequyes were magnificently ended as apertayned to his state royall. The thre prynces that is to say Adherball/ Hiempsall/ and Iugurthe anone assembled them togyder to the intent to commen and treat of besynesses of the kyngdome/ concernynge partycion and separatyon of the same: and all other thynges conuenyent. But whan they shulde sytte downe and take their places in order: Hiempsall yongest of them all was somwhat fyers of nature/ and dysposed to statelynesse. Also in mynde long before this tyme he dysdayned the ignobylite of Iugurth/ for asmoche as he was vnlyke vnto them of byrth towchynge his mothers syde: and a bastarde borne: as is sayde

55 he] *om.* C 57–8 suffreth . . . thanne] *om.* C 60 offende] nat offende B C 61 nat] *om.* B C 65 Thus] This A 66 Than] *om.* B C 68 founde: neuertheles] B; *punctus and cap.* A tyme/] *virgule from* B

Ch. 7 1 this] *om.* B C 2 dyscorde] dissencion and discorde B; dissencion and discord C 10 them togyder] *om.* B C 11 kyngdome/] royalme B C; *virgule from* B 13 downe] *om.* B C 14 them all] the thre B C 15 Also] And B C 16 Iugurth/] *virgule from* B

before. Wherfore he dysdayned that the same Iugurth shulde haue the place of moost honoure amonge them/ whiche were naturall sonnes of a kynge/ and also laufully begotten: and so in contempt of Iugurth he set hym selfe downe on the ryght hande of his brother Adherball: to thintent that Iugurth shulde nat syt in the myddes bytwene them: which rowme the Numydyens count of most honour. And afterwarde howbeit his brother Adherball requyred hym often to gyue place to
f. 10v Iugurth/ bycause of his age: | yet vnnethes coude he with moche payne induce hym therto/ but at laste fatygate by requestes of his brother and of other noble menne of the realme: he chaunged his place and set hym vpon the other syde with countenaunce declaryng his mynde nat contented. And thus at laste satte Iugurth for his age in the myddes bytwene them bothe/ as in place of moost honour.

Whanne the thre prynces were th[u]s sette: and whan they had commyned of many thynges concernynge the admynystracion of the kyngdome: amonge many and dyuers other thynges Iugurth sayde that all the statutes and ordynaunces whiche the kyng Micipsa hadde made fyue yeres before his deth/ ought of congruence to be adnulled and broken as of none effect. For in that season (as sayd he) his wyt what for age/ what for syckenesse was feble/ dull/ and of small valoure. And therfore suche thynges as he had in that space inacted were done without wysdome or reason. Whanne Hiempsall harde Iugurth thus speke: he answered sayeng that it pleased hym right well that it shulde so be done. For within the same thre yeres (sayd he) our father Micipsa hath adopted you to his sonne and in his testament ordayned you to be partyner of his kyngdome: whiche was the worst and moost vnaduised dede that euer he dyd yonge or olde. Wherfore Iugurth accordynge to your owne ordynaunce this must fyrst of all be adnulled and broken/ whiche done/ my brother and I shall nat greatly contende for the remenant. These wordes of Hiempsall pearsedde the hert of Iugurth more profoundely thanne any man there thought or susspected. Wherfore from that tyme forwarde: what for wrathe of these wordes/ and for drede of losse of his porcyon of the kyngdome/ his mynde was in great trouble and anguysshe. Insomoche that from thens forthe: he went aboute/ ymagened/ ordayned/ and onely reuoulued in his mynde: by what gyle or treason Hiempsall myght be caught in his daunger. But whanne his purpose

20 begotten] borne B C   21 of] *om.* C   30 bothe/] *virgule from* B   31 thus] this A   whan they] *om.* B C   36 and broken] *om.* B C   46 broken/] *virgule from* B   done/] *virgule from* B   51 kyngdome/] *virgule from* B

proceded but slowly forwarde/ consydrynge that the frowarde desyre and vnrefrenable appetyte of his mynde coude nat be mytigated nor [pacyfied]: he establysshed and concluded to bryng his enterpryse to effect by any maner meanes: other by preuy treason and gyle: or els by euydent and open vyolence and force of armes.

[**12**] But to retourne agayn where I left: in this firste assemble of the thre prynces of which I spake before: it pleased them all that the tresours of kyng | Micipsa shulde be deuyded among them bycause of f. 11r
this dyssencion. And also that the marches and boundes of eche of their domynions/ seuerally shulde be assygned to eche of them his porcyon. Wherfore the tyme was apoynted and prefixed whanne bothe shulde be done: but the tyme to departe the treasoures was sonner assygned than to deuyde and lymyte the boundes of their domynions. This apoyntment made: the prynces departed company: the mynde of Iugurth nat a lytell inquyeted for the sayde checke of Hiempsall: for whiche cause he awayted his tyme to auenge hym.

¶How Iugurth by treason murdred Hiempsall the yonger sonne of kynge Micipsa. ¶The eyght chapter.

[**12. 2**] Whan the thre prynces were departed in sonder: as I haue sayd before: they soiourned in sundry places/ and that nere to the towre where the treasours lay. Hiempsall drewe hym to a towne named Tyrmyda nat ferre dystant. In which towne he had a dwellynge place: than as happened in the same towne was a man of the garde longyng to Iugurth of his lorde ryght derely beloued/ and with hym greatly in fauoure. This seruaunt of Iugurth was moche conuersaunt and famylyer in the house of Hiempsall[. W]han Iugurth by chaunce remembredde this oportunyte to his myscheuous purpose: he called secretely vnto hym his sayd seruaunt. And after many wordes spoken to serche his mynde: at last by promesse of large rewardes he induced and made hym to consent to go as yf it were to vysyte the house of Hiempsall: as he had often done before tyme: and by some meanes and craft to counterfayte the kayes of the gates and brynge them vnto hym. For the ryght kayes: after the gates were locked: nyghly were delyuerde vnto Hiempsall hymselfe: so myght they nat be vnmyssed

55 forwarde/] *virgule from* B 56 vnrefrenable] A B; vnresonable C 57 pacyfied] parcyfied A; pacyfied B; pacified C establysshed and] *om.* B C 60 left:] *colon suppl.*; *punctus* B 66 sonner] sooner C 70 auenge] reuenge B C

Ch. 8 1 treason] reason C 4 places/] *virgule from* B 5 treasours] treasure C 10 Hiempsall. W] *virgule* A B; *comma* C 14 and made] *om.* B C 17 nyghly] nyghtly C

the space of a nyght. Whan Iugurth had induced the Numydyan to consent to this dede: he promysed hymselfe within shorte tyme after to come to the sayd lodgyng of Hiempsall what tyme the case shulde requyre: with great power of armed men. The Numydyan in shorte tyme perfourmed the commaundement of Iugurth/ in somoche that f. 11v he brought vnto | hym the counterfayted kayes: as he had apoynted. Iugurth hereof was gladde in mynde: and anone prepared secretely a great company of armed men: whome he commaunded to brynge vnto hym the heed of Hiempsall trenched from the body: and in executynge of this dede he commaunded them all to be ruled by the Numydyan whiche had counterfayted the keys. This done the sayd Numydyan conuayed these armed men preuyly by nyght into the house of Hiempsall/ lyke as he was infourmed by Iugurth. Whan this treatoure satellyte was entred with his company and had broken into the inwarde edyfices: dyuers of them serched for the prynce Hiempsall: some murdred his seruauntes as they lay sleypnge in their beddys suspectynge no suche treason: some other awakened with the dynne stert vp and mette their ennemyes defendynge themselfe but all in vayne: for they had no leyser to arme themselfe. And therfore were slayne anone vnarmed of men armed and apoynted to myschefe[. W]han the treatours had longe sought Hiempsall and [coude] nat fynde hym: than serched they more nerely euery hydde corner and secret: close places they brast open: all was full of dynne mengled with noyse and clamour: So moche they sought and so nerely: that at last they founde out Hiempsall/ hydde in the cotage of a pore seruyng woman/ to which place he had fledde at begynnyng of this affray/ as a man astonyed for drede and ignorant of the place. Anone as the Numydyans had founde hym they slewe hym without any mercy. And as they were commaunded cutte of his heed and brought the same to Iugurth.

[13] But shortly after: the fame of this cruell and tyrannous dede was dyuulgate: and ouerspredde all the landes of Affrike: Adherball and all they which were vnder sub[ie]ctyon of Micipsa whyle he lyued: were sore troubled and abasshed with fere for this tyrannous crueltie of Iugurth. The Numydyans anone deuyded themselfe into two parties. The moost part drewe/ and leaned to Adherball/ but suche as were moost manly and best to batayle drewe them to the other partie: and leaned to Iugurth. Wherfore he made redy as great

38 were] were they B C 39 myschefe. Whan] *colon* A B 40 coude] counde A; myght B C 44 woman] *virgule suppl.* 51 subiectyon] subeictyon A; subieccion B C

an army as he myght/ ioynynge vnto hym and bryngyng vnder his subiectyon the townes and cyties of Numidy: some by vyolence/ and some other by theyr owne voluntary wyll. Insomoche that finally he kept vnder his subiection and bondage the hole lande of Numydy. But nat withstandynge that Adherball had sent embassadours to Rome: to certyfy the senatours of the deth of his brother how cowardly he was murdred/ | and also to informe them of his owne myserable fortune f. 12r
and in what case he was: neuerthelesse he made hymselfe redy to fyght with Iugurth as he which had trust and confydence in multytude of his sowdyours assembled redy to batayle.

¶How Iugurth ouercame Adherball in batayl and putte hym to flyght: how Adherball fledde to Rome to complayne to the senatours: and how Iugurthe accloyed with rewardes many of the rulers of Rome: by whose meanes his cruelty was defended. ¶The .ix. chapter.

[13. 4] Now had Iugurth assembled his hoost redy vnto batayle: nat lyke in multytude to the company of Adherball: but as I sayd before moche bolder and better expert and exercysed in warre. On the other partie Adherball had his people redy apoynted: and both the armyes approched togyder. But whan they ioyned togyder: and whan it came to byckerynge: that the mater must be tryed with strypes. Anone Adherball was vanquesshed: and to saue his lyfe fledde forthe of the batayle into a prouynce marchynge on the lande of Numydy: and frome thens with all hast spedde hym vnto Rome to complayne his myserable fortune: and to requyre socours as I shal afterwarde declare. But than Iugurth whan he had all the lande of Numydy at his pleasure: counselled with his frendes of many thynges/ but at conclusyon: whan he consydred by hymselfe that he had slayne Hiempsall and chased Adherball out of his kyngdome: whan he was ydle and at rest: he often secretly reuoulued in mynde his owne crueltie: sore dredynge what punysshement the Romayns wolde ordayne agaynst the same. Nor agaynst the ire and dyspleasu[r]e of the Romayns hadde he none other hope nor confort/ saue in the couetyse of the noble men of Rome: and in thabundaunce of his tresoures: wherwith he trusted to corrupt the rulers of Rome to be

57 myght/] *virgule suppl.* 63 murdred/] *virgule from* B

Ch. 9 4 meanes] fauour B C 6 to] of C 7 and[1]] *om.* B C 9 togyder] batayle B C 10 strypes] strokes B C 11 forthe of] from B C 16 but at] At B C 17 by] *om.* C 18 and] *followed by colon* A; *om.* B 21 dyspleasure] dyspleasue A; displeasure B C 22 confort/] *virgule from* B 24 tresoures] treasours B; treasoure C

fauorable to hym. This consydred within fewe dayes after he sent to Rome embassadours with moche golde and syluer to whom he gaue in commaundement: that fyrst of all they shulde satysfy his olde frendes f. 12v with rewardes and money: and than to | spare no gyftes to gete vnto hym mo newe frendes. And brefely that they shulde nat spare nor tary to procure vnto hym fauourers and mayntenars of his part: and all thynges for his auauntage by gyftes and promysses.

But after these embassadours were come to Rome: acordyng to the commaundement of their kyng: they gaue and sent to his acquayntaunce and frendes/ and to suche as amonge the senatours: at that tyme had moost authorite: large and great rewardes. Insomoche that anone among them was so great a chaunge: that the maruelous enuy/ hatred and euylwyll: which they had agaynst Iugurth was all chaunged into fauour and grace among the noble men. Of whom some were so induced by gyftes receyued: and some other by hope of brybes in tyme to come: that they went about among the senatours from one to one/ labowring and intretyng that at that season nothyng shulde be extremely nor greuously determyned agaynst Iugurth. Thus after the embassadurs of Iugurth had confydence and trust ynough in their mater they laboured to haue a day apoynted to apere in court. The day of apparence was graunted as well to them as to Adherball: to Adherball as playntyfe: and to the embassadours as defendentes for Iugurth[. W]han the day assygned was come both the parties appered in court before the senatours/ than after audyence graunted/ Adherball began to speke vnder forme folowyng for complaynt and declaratyon of his iniuries and oppressyon.

¶Here insueth the oratyon of Adherball: deuysed in forme delyberatyue: in which he exhorteth the senatours to commaunde socours and ayde to be assygned vnto hym/ prouyng the same to be profytable/ honest/ and easy to the Romayns to do: profytable: that he myght contynue a frende vnto the empyre of Rome: honest: for his father and granfather had so deserued: easy to be done: for the Romayns at that tyme had none other warre els where. ¶The .x. chapter.

[14] Moost dyscrete chosen fathers: and noble senatours: Micipsa my father at his hour of deth commaunded me that I shulde thynke nought els of the lande of Numydy to apertayne to me: saue onely the

30 mayntenars] mainterners B; mainteiners C 40 one/] *virgule from* B
44 mater] cause B C 47 Iugurth. Whan] *colon* A B C

Ch. 10 9 his hour of deth] houre of his deth B C

rule and admynystratyon of the same: affirmyng that the tytle of possessyon and empyre of the same | belonged to you and to the f. 13r people of Rome. Moreouer he gaue me in commaundement to do my deuoyr: to be vnto you seruyable aboue all thynges: bothe in peace and in warre. And that I shulde count you vnto me in place and stede of kynsmen: and nerest frendes of alyaunce. Sayeng that yf I shulde so do: than by your amyte and frendshyppe I shulde fynde an army/ ryches/ and defence of the kyngdome of Numydy: and of me and myne in all tymes of nede[. W]hich preceptes of my father: whyle I kest in mynde to obserue: sodaynly Iugurth the moost cruell and cursed of all men whom the grounde susteyneth/ and dothe bere contemnyng and dyspysing your empyre: hath dryuen me from your kyngdome: and from all my other goodes of fortune: nothyng regardyng that I am neuewe of Massinissa and [by] myne auncetry a felowe and frende of the empyre and people of Rome. But certaynly worthy and chosen fathers: syth I am come to that mysery that necessyte constrayneth me to desyre your ayde and socours: I wolde moch rather that I myght call for your helpe: for myne owne merytes agaynst you: than for the merytes of my forefathers: and that by suche meanes of myne owne deseruynge/ your benefytes and socours were due vnto me/ which I wolde God that I neded nat at all: but yf this your ayde myght of you be desyred by my merites and [deseruyng] than shulde I call boldly to you: and vse your socours of duety as myne auncetry haue done in tymes passed. But nowe sithe it is so that probyte/ honest lyfe/ and innocence: in this worlde fyndeth lytell surenesse by themselfe without protectyon of some other. Moreouer syth it was nat in my power to mytygate nor to withstande this tyrannous iniury of Iugurth. Therfore chosen fathers I am nowe fledde vnto you as to my chefe refuge/ coarted of necessyte to requyre your socoures: and constrayned to put you to besynes/ and charge: before or I haue done any pleasure or profet vnto you: which thynge greueth me moost of all/ and is one of my gretest myseries. Ryght worthy senatours other kynges haue ben receyued into your

14 seruyable] seruiable B; seruisable C peace] place B C 15 in] *om.* C and stede] *om.* B C 16–17 shulde so do] so dyd B C 17 an army] socours B; socoure C 19 in] *om.* C nede. Which] *colon* A B; *comma* C 20 kest] caste C sodaynly] *punctus* A; *om.* B 21–2 and dothe bere contemnyng and] *om.* B C 24 by] B C; *om.* A 29 you] you done B; you doone C 31 I[1]] *om.* B C 32 ayde] socours B; socoures C of you] so of you B; soo of you C deseruyng] B; deseruynge C; desiryng A 35 probyte] *om.* B C 39 of] to B C 41 or] *om.* B C 42 greueth] greued B C

frendshyppe and fauour/ after ye haue ouercome them in batayle: or els parceyuyng themselfe in danger and in doutful chaunces of fortune: they haue coueyted and desyred your socyete/ your felawshyppe/ and fauour/ rather for theyr owne wele than for yours. But moch contrarely: our forefathers and rote of our lynage Massinissa confeterated hymselfe with the peple of Rome in the seconde batayle of Affryke/ or Cartage: what tyme was more faythfulnes to be trusted f. 13v in them and their | good wyll than of welth or riches to be optayned of the Romayns/ beynge at that tyme assayled with warre on euery syde: their ryches and treasours consumed by often batayles. Thus is it euydent that our auncetry confederat nat themselfe to your felowshyp for their owne defence: in hope of ryches: in hope of domynion: nor for any other pryuate profet: but onely for fauoure and loue whiche they had vnto your empyre. Wherfore noble senatours suffre nat the progeny and braunches of this stocke to be dystroyed. Suffre nat me whiche am neuewe of your trusty frende Massinissa to aske helpe and socours in vayne.

But prudent fathers: yf it were so that I had none other cause to demaunde socours of you saue onely this myserable fortune wherwith I am oppressed: that I which was lately a kyng by lyneall dyscent: mighty of auncetry: excellent and clere of fame: habundaunt in riches and men of armes. And nowe dysformed by miserable calamyte/ pore and nedy/ am constrayned to seke helpe and socours of other men: yf I had none other mater wherof to complayne/ saue this miserable fortune onely. Neuerthelesse it longeth and is conuenyent to the magesty of the people of Rome/ to prohibyte and to withstande iniury. And nat to suffre the kyngdome or domynion of any man to ryse and increase by falshode and myscheuous tyranny. And the ryght heyres agaynst ryght/ agaynst iustyce/ and agaynst reason/ to be excluded from their true herytage. But verily I am excluded and cast forthe of that countrey which the Romayns in tyme passed gaue vnto my forefathers: out of the which countrey my father and granfather accompanyed with your army and helpe: haue chased the kyng Siphar/ and also the Carthagynences/ bothe moost vyolent enmyes to the empyre of Rome. Your benefites are spoyled fro me: In this myne iniury be ye dyspysed. Wo is m[e] myserable exulate: Alas my

46 your socyete] *om.* B C 49 confeterated] confederated B C 50 Affryke/ or] *om.* B C 53 is it] it is B C 55 in hope of ryches] *om.* C 58 this] his C 59 aske] aske of you B C 65 and] and of B C And] and and C 66 am] so that I am B C 71 And] *om.* C 77 Carthagynences/] *virgule from* B 78 are] be B C 79 me] my A

dere father Micipsa ar your gode dedes and kyndnes agaynst Iugurth come to this poynt and conclusyon: that he before all other shulde namely be dystroyer of your lynage and chyldren: whome ye haue made felowe with your owne sonnes: and also partyner of your kyngdome? alas: than shall [our] stocke and housolde neuer be quyet? Shall we alway be tossed and turned in effusyon of blode/ in batayle/ in exyle/ and in chasyng from our countrey[?

¶W]hyle the Carthagynences raygned in prosperite/ we suffred and that pacyen[t]ly and nat vndeserued all cruelte and vexacion. For then were our ennemies on euery syde of vs: our frendes in whom we shuld haue founde socour at tyme of nede were ferre | dysioyned and (f. 14r) seperate from vs. Thus al our hope: all our trust was in our strength and armour. But nowe after that pestylent dystruction of the Carthaginences is chased and casten out of Affrike we contynued a tyme ioyefull and quyet: demeanyng and passyng our lyfe in peace and tranquylite/ for why we had no ennemy: except paraduenture: for any iniury done agaynst you ye wolde commaunde vs to take your enmy for ours also/ as reson and ryght requyred. But nowe sodaynly and vnwardly to vs: this cruell Iugurth exaltyng hymselfe by his intollerable audacite/ by cruelte/ and pride hath first slayne my brother and his owne nere kynsman Hiempsall: and in augmentynge his myschefe hath vsurped to him as in pray my brothers part and porcion of the kyngdome of Numydy/ and after: seyng that he might nat take me with lyke maner of gyles as he had done my brother/ what tyme I douted nothyng lesse than any violence or batayle in the kyngdome which I holde of you/ he hath chased me (as ye may se) out of your kyngdome/ and hath made me as an abiect outlawe: chased from my countrey: and dwellynge place/ oppressed with pouerty/ and laded with miseres. Insomoche that I may be in more suerty and saue garde in any place of the worlde/ than in my owne natyfe countrey and kyngdome/ which I holde of you.

Forsothe worthy senatours: I haue euer thought in lyke maner as I haue oftentymes herde my father Micipsa openly report with sadnesse: sayeng that they whiche shulde dyligently contynue in your frendshyp by their merytes/ must take great labours at many tymes vpon

80 kyndnes agaynst] kyndnes anenst B; kyndnesses against C 84 kyngdome?] *colon* A B C our] B; oure C; your A housolde neuer] housholde neruer B; houshold neuer C 85 in] and, in C 86–7 countrey? ¶Whyle] *quest. mark suppl.*; *cap. from* B 87 prosperite/] *virgule from* B 88 pacyently] pacyenly A; paciently B C 94 demeanyng and] *om.* B C 98 vnwardly] vnwarely B C cruell] *om.* B C 103 with] *om.* B C gyles] trayne B C 109 my] *om.* C

themselfe in your causes: but of all men they were moost sure from iniury of any man: And sothely all my lynage hath done as moche as in them was at your desyrees: And euer hath ben redy in all batayls and nedes to assyst you. Wherfore if ye folowe the preceptes of gratytude: if ye bere in remembraunce these merytes of myne auncetry/ it is bothe right and honesty that in this myne extreme necessite/ ye ayde and socour me/ and restore me agayne to quyetnes: whyle ye haue none other besynes in hand/ which may be to you impediment in this enterprise. Moost discret fathers: more clerely to declare vnto you my complaynt and my misery: And also to certify your excellence more playnly of myne vnnaturall and vnkynde kynsman Iugurth: and of his cruelty. It is nat vnknowen vnto your mageste: that my father Micipsa after his departyng: left behynde hym vs two brethern his naturall and laufull sonnes: supposynge that by his benefytes and merites Iugurth f. 14v shuld be ioyned with vs/ as thyrde brother. | But alas: moche contrary thone of vs is murdred by this cruell Iugurth/ blynded by insacyable ambycion or desyre of dominyon. And I my selfe the seconde brother skarsly and with great dyfficulte haue escaped his cruell and vnmercyfull handes: what may I do? or whether shall I rathest fle for confort/ vnhappy exulate thus desolate and infortunate as I am? All the socours all the confort/ of my stocke and kynred is extinct by deth[. M]y granfather Massinissa: and my father Micipsa: as necessyte hath constrayned them: haue payed the generall trybute of nature: delyuered from these mundayne vexacions by naturall deth. My nere kynsman Iugurth: moch otherwyse than it became hym to do: hath cursedly bereft my brother of his lyfe by tyranny and myscheuous couetise of domynion: myne other kynsmen by consanguynite and affinyte: withall myne other frendes/ by his cruelty ben also oppressed or put to dethe/ some by one meanes and some by other: some of [them] be taken captyue: some put to shamefull deth of gybet/ galous/ or crosse/ with moost cruell tourment: Some be casten to wylde and rapynous beestes to be deuoured of them. A fewe which ar left with their lyues/ ar closed in dongyons and darknes: passing forth their myserable lyues with mournyng and waylyng more greuous than deth. Thus am I inuyroned with anguysshe on euery syde. But if it were so: that all these socours whiche I haue lost by

122 besynes] busynesses B; businesse C 123 clerely] brefely and clerly B C 124 misery] mysery B; myseries C 131 or] and B; and C 134 confort/] *virgule suppl.* 136 deth. My] *no punct.* A B; *comma* C 142 withall] with C frendes/] *virgule suppl.* 144 them] hym A B; them C 146 rapynous] rapinous B; rauenous C 148 forth] *om.* B C

cruelty of Iugurth: or if all thynges which be turned to me: from prosperyte to aduersyte/ remayned to this hour hole without detriment or dammage lyke as they were in my best estate: yet certaynly noble senatours: yf any yll or mysfortune vnprouyded shulde happen vnto me: I wold be bolde to call vpon your ayde and comfort. Bycause it semeth you to haue cure of right and wronge belongyng to euery man: consydryng the exellent magnitude and gretnes of your empyre/ and to suffre no vertue vnrewarded nor vyce vnpunysshed/ and finally no wretch oppressed to contynue vndefended. But nowe moost of all sithe I am exulate from my natyfe contrey/ from the kyngdome which my father ruled vnder you: and from my owne house and dwellynge place/ also nedy and pore of all thynges belongyng to my estate/ and alone without company or defence: to whom or to what place may I resort: or on whom may I call for ayde or comfort in these my manyfolde myseries? Shall I resort or call for socours of nacyons/ or of kynges adiacent or about the lande of Numidy? alas I shuld lytell preuayle or nought at all. Sith all they for your amyte ioyned with you be mortall ennemies to vs and to our lynage: may | I resort to any f. 15^{r} contrey about vs: but that I shuld fynde there many tokens of crueltie of warre: which my forefathers haue done in their tymes passed in your causes? Whyther shall any of them which haue ben our olde ennemis/ haue mercy or compassyon on vs nowe in this our extremyte? But finally moost noble senatours/ my father Micipsa thus ordred vs at his departyng: and gaue vs in commaundement that we shuld obserue nor mentayne the frendshyp of none other kyng nor peple/ saue onely of the peple of Rome: and that we shulde seke no newe felo[w]shyp/ nor newe confideracyons or bondes of concorde sayeng that in your frendshyp and helpe: we shulde fynde great socours and ayde and that largly. But yf it shulde fortune that the welth of this your empyre shuld fall into ruyne or change from this exellence (which the goddes defende) than: sayd he that we and our kyngdome of necessyte shuld also decay togyder with you.

But nowe lauded be the goddes by whose helpe and fauour/ and by your owne strength and vertue: ye be at this tyme mighty and riche: all thyng to you is prosperous/ and to your commaundement obeyng.

154 vnprouyded] unprouided B; prouided C 155 vnto] to C wold] durst B C vpon] *om.* B C 158 nor] or C 162 my] myne B C 164 on] in B C 165 myseries?] *punctus* A B C 166 or] and B C Numidy?] *colon* A B C 170 forefathers] fathers B C 171 causes? Whyther] *punctus* A B C; Whether C our] *om.* C 172–3 our extremyte?] *punctus* A B C; our *om.* C 177 felowshyp] B; feloshyp A; felowshype C

Wherfore it is somoch more laufull/ easy/ and conuenyent to you to take cure and charge in redressyng thiniures done to your frendes and felowes. I am onely in drede and dout of this one thyng lest the frendshyp and synguler fauour of Iugurth: nat perfetly knowen as he is worthy: do induce the myndes of some to parcialyte agaynst Iustice and right. I here and vnderstand that such labour with all their myght for fauour of Iugurth goyng about from man to man/ prayng and intreatyng with moch solycitude many of you apart by one and one/ desyryng and requiryng you to determyn no thynge agaynst Iugurth whyle he is absent: and the mater and cause nat knowen perfetly: I here such persons corrupt with parcialyte and fauour obiectyng secretly agaynst me and sayeng that I fayne and ymagyn these wordes to acuse Iugurth vnworthely/ and that I fayne to be chased forth of my lande by hym: wher as I might surely ynough haue remayned within the kingdome of Numidy. That wold God I myght se ones the cursed and vnkynde kynsman of myne Iugurth/ by whose vnmercyfull and cruell dedes I am casten in these meseries/ in such case: that he were faynyng the same thynges vnder lyke maner as I fayne them at this tyme: and wold God I myght ones se hym as truely without faynyng dryuen out of the land of Numidy as I am nowe chased from the same by his cruelty: and wolde god that at last other ye or els the immortall goddes wold so care for the besynesses and troubles of vs myserable
f. 15^{v} men in erth: that the same Iugurth | which now bereth himselfe proude of his synful dedes shewing himselfe and countyng him noble onely bycause he escapeth vnpunyssed for his syn and cruelte: might therfore suffre greuous punysshment with all my miseries/ and other myscheues and yls acording to his deseruyng: for his vnmercyfull cruelte shewed agaynst our father Micipsa/ in murdring of my dere brother Hiempsall/ and chasynge me forth of my natyfe countre: thus oppressed with all myseries in extreme necessite.

O my brother/ my brother Hiempsall moost dere to my hart of all creatures: howbeit nowe thy lyfe is bereft the in thy flouryng youth long before thy naturall hour of deth: And that by cruelte of hym whom it semed nat of all men so to haue done: neuertheles me thinketh in my mynde this chaunce of thy deth more to be ioyed of: than to be sorowed. For thou hast nat onely lost thy lyfe and thy kyngdome: but also thou hast escaped this chasyng/ this flyght/ this exyle/ this nede/ this pouerty with all other wretchednesses and myseres/ whiche oppresseth

193 one/] *virgule from* B 198 vnworthely] vndeseruyngly B C 205 of^{1}] *om.* C
220 ioyed] ioyned B

me without comfort or socours. But I vnhappy and myserable exulate th[u]s throwen downe from my fathers kyngdome into so many yls and so great myseries/ may wel be an example and spectacle to all the world of the mutable courses wherin fortune turneth mankynd. O my dere brother vncertayne am I what I do: whyther I thus destitute of socour and ayde: may persecute and reueng thy iniuries and thy deth: or els whether I may prouyde and seke socours for recoueryng of the land of Numidy. I am in that case: that my lyfe and deth dependeth in the socour of other men. Wold God I were deed out of hand: yf deth might be an honest conclusyon of these my miserable misfortunes: rather than to be counted as content and pleased to lyue in rebuke and shame/ as an exulate weryed and ouercome with iniuries: and gyueng place to the iniust cruelty of tyrannous persecucyon/ and as nat able nor bolde to resist the same. Thus now certaynly it is agaynst my wyl that I lyue/ for in my lyfe I haue no lyking nor pleasure/ And yet can I nat dye without dysworshyp.

Wherfore moost prudent fathers and noble senatours: these premysses consydred: I obtest and humbly requyre you: in honour of the goddes immortall: for thauncient amyte bytwene you and my forefathers: for the naturall loue whiche ye haue agaynst your chyldren and parentes/ and by the magesty of the peple of Rome: and this your moost exellent empyre: haue pyte of my manyfold miseris: and socour this my mysery. Resist this tyrannous dealyng and iniury of Iugurth commytted nat onely agaynst my wretched person: but also against you and your empyre. Suffre nat the kyngdome of Numidy: whi| che is (f. 16r) your owne: to decay and be distroyed by cruell tyranny of Iugurth/ and by the effusion of blode and murdre of the linage of Massinissa/ somtyme most faythfull and constant frend of this your empyre.

¶How the embassadours of Iugurth replyed agaynst these wordes of Adherball: and what dyrection was taken for bothe parties of the senatours of Rome. The .xi. chapter.

[15] After that Adherball in forme aboue writen had ended his complaynt: anon the embassadours of Iugurth arose and answerd brefely in fewe wordes: as they which had more trust and confidence in their great gyftes gyuen before to many of the rulers of Rome: than

225 thus] B C; this A 235 shame/] *virgule from* B 236 persecucyon/] *virgule from* B as] *om.* C 237 Thus] But B C 238 lyue/] *virgule from* B 239 dysworshyp] dishonour B; disshonour C 245 miseris] calamitees B; calamites C 249 Iugurth/] *virgule from* B 250 Massinissa/] *virgule from* B

in any right of their cause/ and thus they replyed in effect: sayeng before the senatours that Hiempsall was slayne of the Numidyans for his owne hastines and cruelte/ and nat by knowlege nor consent of Iugurth: and as touching Adherball: he began warre agaynst Iugurth of his owne froward mynd without any occasyon: but after he was ouercome in batayle bycause he was nat able to reueng himselfe/ nor to make his partie gode/ he fled vnto Rome to complayn him to the senatours of Iugurth: where as all the faute was in himselfe/ and in none other concernyng the party of Iugurth: they requyred the senatours in his behalfe in his absence to count hym none other than he was proued and knowen in the warre of Numance: And that they wold nat set more by the wordes of his ennemy: than by his dedes magnificently proued.

[This sayd:] anone after: both parties departed in sunder from the court. Immedyatly the senatours toke counsell what best was to be done in the cause. The fauourers of Iugurth and of his embassadours/ and moreouer a great part of the senatours were corrupt before by parcialyte/ fauour and rewardes of Iugurth: and so deprauat: that they contemned and set at nought the wordes of Adherball/ exalting and commendyng the manhode of Iugurth: with laude/ fauour/ countenaunce/ voyce: and all other signes: And so finally they laboured by all maner of meanes for an others myscheuous vyce and cruell cryme to defende the same: As yf it had ben in defence of their owne honour/ worshyp/ and honeste. But on the other part a fewe other which set more by iustyce and honeste than by fals begoten riches: these counselled to socour Adherball and sharply to punysshe and
f. 16v reuenge the deth of Hiempsall. But among | all other of this opynion: was one named Emilius Scaurus/ a man of noble byrth redy to dysturbe euery besynes/ debateful and besy/ desirous of power/ of authorite/ of honour/ and of riches: but crafty in cloking of these his fautes. After this Emilius Scaurus sawe his gyueng of brybes of Iugurth so shamfully and openly knowen: he fered lest the corruption of the senatours and heed rulers of Rome myght ingender enuy/ debate/ and slaughter bytwene them and the comme[n]s lyke as in such cases often had fortuned in tymes before. Wherfore in this consideration/ he refrayned his mynde at this tyme from his accustomed vnlaufull lustes.

Ch. 11 8 cause/] *virgule suppl.* 10 nor consent] *om.* B C 14 gode/] *virgule from* B 15 senatours of Iugurth:] B; senatours: of Iugurth A where as] where C 20 This sayd] B; This saide C; *om.* A 22 embassadours/] *virgule from* B 26 laude/] *virgule from* B 28 others] other C 30 part] part were B C 31 begoten] goten B C 40 commens] B C; commes A

[16] Neuerthel[e]s among the senatours in this counsell the worst part preuayled: and that part which set more by fauour and rewardes than by ryght and equyte ouercam the other part which laboured to sustayne the right without any fauour or parcialyte. And so the fauourers of Iugurth obtayned their purpose/ And his cruelty had no punysshment. Neuertheles it was concluded and decreed that .x. embassadours shuld be sent into Numidy to deuyde the kyngdome which longed to Micipsa bytwene Iugurth and Adherball. The principall of this imbassade was one named Lucius Opimius a man of noble fame/ of great authorite and power among the senatours in those dayes: what tyme Cayus Gracchus and Marcus Ful[u]ius beyng great fauourers of the commens: were slayne of the noble men of Rome for the same cause: After victory of the noble men agaynst the commens and the same two princes: this Lucius Opimius enraged greuously with rigorous and sharpe inquisycions and examinacyons agaynst the pore commente: And was one of the chefe oppressers of them. What tyme this Lucius Opimius with his company was come to Numidy: Iugurth prepared to attempt his old craftes: And howbeit he had founde the same Lucius for one of his ennemis at Rome/ neuertheles he receyued him worshypfully and with great diligence. And with gyueng and promysing many thynges he brought his purpose so to effect/ that this Lucius at conclusyon preferred the fauour and profet of Iugurth before his owne good name and fydelyte: and brefely: before all thynges belongyng to himselfe. This brought to passe: anone he went in hand with the other of the embassadours after the same way: and many of them he wan and ouercame with gyftes. Very fewe of them were: which set more by their fayth and treuth than by money and rewardes of Iugurth. Wherfore whan i[t] was come to lymitacion and separacyon of the lande of Numidi bytwene Adherball and Iugurth as the said embassadours were commaunded of the senatours: that part of the kyngdom which marched toward Mauritany/ or the lande of the Mau| rians beyng most opulent and f. 17r
plentyfull of fruytfull fyldes and of men/ was gyuen to Iugurth: but the other part which was more plesant than profytable as ornate [with] hauyn townes and fayre edyfices: was commytted to possession of Adherball.

44 Neuertheles] B C; Neuerthels A 46 than] then C 54 Fuluius] B C; Fulnius A beyng] *om.* B C 62 had] than C Rome/] *virgule from* B 65 effect/] *virgule from* B 68 the[1]] *om.* C 70 were] *om.* C 71 than] then C it] B C; is A 76 men/] *virgule from* B 77 with] without A B C

[17] Nowe for asmoch as in this hystory before and moost of all in sequele and processe of the same/ hath and shalbe made mencyon of many places and townes of Affrike: to thintent that thystory may be more clere and euydent/ me thinketh it requisyte and conuenyent brefely to describe the sytuacion of Affrike: and a lytell to touch those peples and contreis which with the Romayns had at any tyme amite or frendshyp/ other peace or warre. But suche places and nations which for heat and wyldernes be lytell frequented of people: or nat inhabyted: of them it is nat easy to dyscribe nor declare the treuth: for by diffyculty of the places fewe or none resorteth theder perfetly to knowe the same. But the other partes frequented of people I shall as brefely declare as can be touched.

¶The descripcion of the habytable partyes of the countrey of Affrike/ namely of suche nacyons as had amyte or warre with the Romayns. ¶The .xii. chapter.

[17. 3] In dyuision of the cyrcle of the worlde the opynion of moost writers is: that it is dyuided into thre partes/ Europe/ Asy/ and Affrike. A fewe other authours hold opynion: that it is deuyded onely into two partes/ that is to say Asy and Europe: so that vnder clymate of the part whiche is called Europe: the thirde part named Affrike is comprehended. But this last opynion is leest alowed. This contrey of Affrike hath his bondes on the see of Italy on the West part/ and on the occean see it abordreth partly on the same syde: on the Est part therof is a declyning and pendant valey ryght ample and large. Thinhabytauntes of this valey call it Cathabathmon in their Affrike langage: that is to say in Englyssh a dependant valey. On this Est syde: the see is outragyous/ c[ru]ell/ perylous/ and without any sure hauen: but the fyldes and soyle on this part ar plentyfull of corne: and for all maner beestes is good pasture/ but the soyle nor grounde is nat apt to trees beryng frute: of water is scarcite/ both of rayne water and of water springyng of the erth. The dyspocityon of the peple is holsome of
f. 17v body/ swyft/ and may well endure labour. Inso| moche that the moost part dye for extreme age/ saue suche as be slayne with wepyn/ or deuoured of wylde beestes. For it is [nat] often sene that corruption of

81 same/] *virgule from* B 83 euydent/] *virgule from* B me thinketh] me thynketh B; I thinke C 84 Affrike:] *colon from* B 86 frendshyp/] *virgule from* B 87 frequented] frequenced C 88 inhabyted:] *colon from* B it] that C treuth:] *colon from* B 89 theder] thyder B; thither C 90 as] *om.* C

Ch. 12 1 Affrike/] *virgule from* B 15 cruell] B; cruel C; curell A 17 nor grounde] *om.* B C 22 nat] *om.* A; nat B; not C

humours ingendring any infyrmite bringeth any to deth. In this countrey be also many rauynous beestes and of dyuers kyndes/ deuouring all thyng whiche they may ouercome. But this omityng I wyll nowe brefely declare what maner of people first of all inhabyted this countrey of Affrike/ and what people thyther resorted to inhabyte next after them. And how the same peples were myngled togider. Howbeit that which I shall write is moche dyuers from the commen fame and opynion of many men: neuertheles I shall folowe the bokes written in Affrike langage which (as it is sayd) belonged to the yonge prince Hiempsall: whom Iugurth murdred[. O]f the same bokes I shall folowe the true interpretacion in this mater/ and lyke as the inhabytauntes of the same countrey afferme to be true. But towchyng the very credence of the treuth of the mater I report that to the authours.

[18] The first peple which inhabyted the countrey of Affryke were named Getulyans/ and Lybeans/ people hard/ sharpe/ and vnmanerd. These lyued on the flesshe of wylde beestes: and fedde vpon the grounde as beestes vnreasonable. And were nat ruled by any maners/ but lyued without lorde or lawes/ as vagabundes and rouers. They had no certayne byding places/ but where as the night toke them: there they rested for the tyme. But after that Hercules dyed in Hispayne: as the Affrycans say: his army which was assembled of dyuers natyons/ whan their captayne and heed was lost: dispersed themselfe abrode anone after his deth and came to dyuers places of the worlde to seke their fortune/ where they might optayne any habytacion or lordshyppe. Of whiche company/ the Medeans/ Perseans/ and Armenyans arryued with their shyppes in that coost of Affryke/ whiche was nerest to the empyre of Rome: and long tyme after occupyed those coostes. But the Persyans inhabyted themselfe more inwarde in the countrey towarde the occean see: and in stede of houses they tourned their shyppes botomes vpwarde and dwelled vnder the same. And no maruayle/ for in the countre about them grewe no tymber nor other stuffe mete to bylding. Nor of the Spanyardes which inhabyted next to them neyther might they bye nor borowe. For the see was so great and tempestous bytwene them: and their langages so dyuers and vnknowen to eyther peple/ that by these two impedymentes they were letted from the cours of marchandyse or exchanges

23 any[2]] *om.* B C 24 kyndes/] *virgule from* B 25 thyng] thinges C 26 of[1]] *om.* B C 32 murdred. Of] *no punct.* A; *colon* B 37 people] people/ A; a people B C 38 on the] of B C 40 lorde] lordes C 41 places] place C 45 themselfe] them C 46 fortune/] *virgule from* B 54 to] for B C 55 neyther might they] neyther myght they B; might they nether C

f. 18r bytwen them. | These Parsyens by meane of mariages by lytell and lytell mengled the Getulyans with them/ and bycause they proued oftentymes the commodyte of their grounde and feldes by often commutacions and chaungynges one with other/ at last they named themselfe Numidyans/ that is to say herdmen deuyded. And to this present day the cotages or tylmens houses/ be made longe with croked sydes or couertures bowyng inwarde as if they were belyes of shippes transposed or turned vpset downe. Towchinge the Medeans and Armenyns they ioyned themselfe with the Libyens. For these Medeans and Armeniens dwelled before more nere to the see of Affrike. The Getulyans inhabyted more nere to the son rysyng: nat farre from the feruent countrey of Inde and this people anone had rowmes and dwelling places: for the see bytwene them and Hispayne was but narowe/ wherfore thei agreed with the Hispaniardes to make exchanges and bartrynges of marchandyse with them. The Libiens corrupted their name by lytell and lytell changyng the same/ and at last in stede of Medyens named themselfe Mauriens by barbarike pronunciatyon of their langage. But the welth and riches of the Persiens in short tyme increased/ and multiplyed. Insomoch that after they had named themselfe Numidyans/ they increased in so great multytude: that theyr first contrey was nat able to norysshe them all: So that afterwarde many of the yong and lusty people departed in sunder from their frendes and laft their countrey/ resortynge to a countrey nere the cyte of Carthage/ vacant at that tyme/ In which countrey they inhabyted themselfe and named it Numidy after their name. Shortely after this both they which remayned styll in theyr first countrey and these which remoued thens/ assysted one another with all maner of helpe and socours. Insomoch that they what by strength and what by fear brought vnder their subiectyon and domynion suche other natyons as marched nere them: so that within shorte tyme they moche inhaunced and augmented their name and glory/ but moost namely they which inhabyted that part of Affryke which is ouer agaynst Italy/ and nere the Italyan see/ these moost increased in welth and honour. For the Lybeans were nat so good men of warre as the Getulyans/ or Numydians. And so all the inwarde part of Affrike was for the moste part in possession of the Numidyans/ and so moch

62 other/] *virgule from* B 66 transposed] transuersed B C 67 these] the C 71 Hispayne] Spaine C 72 Hispaniardes] Spaniards C 73 bartrynges] bartynges B; bargins C 81 countrey/] *virgule from* B 86 of] *om.* C socours] socour C they] *om.* B C 87 brought] they brought B C 89 moost] most B; *om.* C 91 see/] *virgule from* B

dyd they: that all the natyons of them subdued were called Numidyans after the name of ouercomers. Nowe haue we declared howe the Getulians and Libyans were first inhabytauntes of Affrike: and | how f. 18[v] the Perseans/ Medeans/ and Armenyens came afterwarde and ioyned with them. How the Perseans named themselfe Numydyans. And the Medeans and Armenyans by corruptyon of langage were called Mauryans. And nowe consequently I shall declare what other people came afterwarde and inhabyted the same lande of Affryke.

[19] After all these natyons before rehersed: out of the lande of Phenyce came moche people to inhabyte themselfe in Affryke. Some bycause their owne countrey was nat suffycient to sustayne so great a multytude as were of them. And other some great men of byrth and desyrous of lordshyppe raysed vp and assembled the nedy commen people and left their owne countrey: in hope to fynde some other gretter dominion els where/ and in processe of tyme aryued at the lande of Affryke: and there bylded thre cyties vpon the see coost named Hippona/ Adrymentum and Leptis: with other dyuers cyties: but nat so great and famous as these were. These cyties in short tyme were so augmented and increased that some of them were honor/ and some were socoure and ayde to their oryginall countreis. But of the cyte of Cartage which also by them was bylded: and afterwarde became the heed cyte of Affryke: me thynke it better to passe ouer with scylence: than of it to speke a lytell and than to leue the mater in the myddes vnparfet: and also this my besynes procedeth to an other purpose. Neuertheles somwhat shall I touche the first foundatyon of this cyte of Carthage/ nat folowyng myne authour Salust: which wryteth nothyng therof: but folowyng the opynion of Vergyll as he wryteth in the first boke of Eneas.

¶The quene Dydo doughter of Belus kyng of the lande of Cypre and wyfe to Sycheus kynge of Phenyce: fledde with her shyppes laded with golde and other ryches out of her owne countrey: dredyng the cruelty of her brother Pygmalian: which blynded by couetyse and ambycion had slayne her housbande Sicheus by treason. This Dido at last aryued with her shippes and company at the coost of Affryke/ where raygned a kyng named Hierbas: which moued with beaute of Dydo desyred her to wyfe. But she for loue which she had to her first husbande Sycheus wolde nat consent therto by any meanes: but

111 Adrymentum] Adrumentum B; Abrumentum C 112 were] *om.* B C
116 me thynke it] me thynke it is B; I thinke it is C 120 Carthage/] *virgule from* B
130 she[1]] *om.* B C 131 wolde] she wolde B C

desyred to bye of the same kyng Hierbas as moche grounde as she myght compasse about with a hyde of a bull. And after that it was graunted/ she cutte the hyde of a bull so small/ that with the same she compased thre myle of grounde in compasse. In which space and f. 19r circuite she bylded a cyte: which first was named Byr|sa. After in proces of tyme it was called Tyros: and last of all it was called Carthage/ vnder which name by long contynuance soo amply it encreased in fame and welth: that [it] contayned .xxiiii. myles in compasse. But whan it was in moost exellence it was vtterly distroyed by the Romayns/ Publius Scipio Affrycane that tyme beyng captayne of the Romayne army. Touchyng the foundacion of this famous cite of Carthage/ so moch haue I written more than myne authour Salust. But nowe wyll I returne to myne institute and purpose concernyng the dyscriptyon of Affrike/ and brefely bring it to conclusion.

The valey of whom I spake before named in Affryke langage Cathabathmon/ deuydeth the countrey of Affrike from Egypt on that syde saue that an arme of the see is bytwene the first cyte or habytacyon of Affrike toward this valey/ [and] is called Cyrene. And nere to the same be other two cites/ the one named Tolonia: the other Thercon: beyond these thre cytees be two quicksandes/ and bytwene bothe the sandes a cyte named Leptis. Beyond this cyte of Leptis/ is a place named of the Romayns Phylenorum are: in Englysshe: the auters of two brethern called Phylenis/ bycause these two brethern suffred themselfe to be quycke buryed in the same place for the commen wele of their contrey: wherof thystory herafter shalbe written at more oportunyte. This place dyuideth the domynion of Carthage from Egypt on that syde. After this place on the syde costes be other cytees belongyng to the domynion of Punyke. All the places from thens forthe to Mauritany or lande of the Mauriens/ be vnder subiectyon of the Numidyans. The Maurians haue their habytacion nere to Hispayn. But as we rede: the Getulyans haue their habytacion beyond the Numidyans: some in poore lodgys: And some other more vylely without habytacion wandring as vagabundes. Beyond these Getulyans is the lande of Ethyope: and from thens forth be contreis so brent with feruour of the sonne that they be inhabytable. But durynge this batayle bytwene the Romayns and Iugurth: the Romayns had in their

132 Hierbas] *om.* C 132–3 she myght compasse] myght be compassed B C 133 a] *om.* B; the C 134 of a bull] *om.* C small/] *virgule from* B 135 in compasse] about C and circuite] *om.* C 137 it was called] *om.* B C 138 it] B C; *om.* A 141 Romayns/] *virgule suppl.* 147 deuydeth] deuided B C 149 valey/ and] B C; valey A 153 are:] are A B; *om.* C; *colon suppl.* 166 batayle] warre B; war C

possession many townes of Punyke and moche of the costes of thempyre of Carthage: and ruled the same by officers vnder them therto assigned. A great part of Numidy and of the Getulyans vnto a flodde named Mulucham: was vnder domynion of Iugurth. Ouer all the Maurians raygned one king named Bocchus: of whom the Romayns had no knowlege saue of his name onely. And before this batayle: he was nother in peace nor in warre acquaynted: nor knowen of the Romayns. | Of Affrike and of thinhabytauntes of the same: ynough is f. 19v
spoken and as moch as is requysite of necessyte to the processe of this hystory. Now wyll I make regression and prosecute my first purposed mater insuyng myne authour Salust.

¶How Iugurth inuaded the kyngdome of Adherball yet ones agayne: and how Adherball agayne was ouercome in batayle: and put to flyght. ¶The .xiii. chapter.

[**20**] After the embassadours of Rome: of whom I haue spoken before: had dyuided the realme of Numidy bytwene Adherball and Iugurth/ and were departed out of Affrike towarde Rome: anone Iugurth reuoulued in mynde how he escaped vnpunysshed for his cruelty otherwyse than his mynde feared before: And how in stede of punysshment: for his synne: he was rewarded with the better part of the lande of Numidy. Now he consydred in mynde that all was true which his frendes had told hym before whyle he was in Hispayne with the Romayne army in the warre of Numance: that is to say. That nothynge is so false and iniust: but that may be iustifyed at Rome for money/ for althyng might be bought there for money. This consyderation inhaunced his mynde vnto asperance and that nat a lytell. Forthermore he was inflamed with the large promesses of them: whom he had acloyed before with gyftes and rewardes at Rome: Insomoch that agayne of newe he fired his mynde to inuade and vsurpe the kyngdome of Adherball/ and by some poynt of prodycion to take hym in trap as he had done Hiempsall his brother before. This Iugurth was fiers/ sharp[e]/ and apt to warre/ well inured with the same and expert in feates therof: but contrarely Adherball: whom he assayled and pursued: was a me[k]e man and oportune to take iniury/ more ferefull and dredyng other: than to be feared of any man.

171 vnder] vnder the B C

Ch. 13 7 he] he had B C 10 in mynde] *om.* B C 13 is] was B C may] myght B; myghte C 15 asperance] esperance B; esperaunce C 20 before] *om.* B C This] Thus C 21 sharpe] B C; sharpt A warre/] *virgule suppl.* 23 assayled] assaied C meke] mete] A B C 24 feared of any man] drad of other B; dread of other C

Wherfore sodenly: and without any prouision on party of Adherball: Iugurth inuaded the marches of his kyngdom/ with a great power and multytude of men of armes[. M]any of thinhabytauntes he murdred: and many toke he prisoners with beestes and all other maner of prayes/ robbing and spoyling/ euerywhere: as ferre as his army dyspersed/ townes/ castels/ and other edyfices he brent and beat f. 20r downe: and many other | places he assayled and inuaded more inwardly in the contrey by excourses of his horsmen. This done he returned into his countre with all his multytude/ prayes/ and prisoners: supposyng that Adherball moued with angre and dyspleasure wold reuenge these iniures: and that thyng shuld be cause and occasion of open warre bytwene them. But Adherball aduysed hymselfe well: by remembrance of his first batell had with Iugurth that he was nat able to contend with hym in batayle nor in force of armes: and moreouer: he had more confidence and trust in frendshyp of the Romayns than in the inconstant Numidyans/ which leaned more to his ennemy than to hym. These thynges consydred he send embassadours to Iugurth to complayn of these iniures: But these embassadours had nought els of hym but contumelyous/ proude/ and hasty wordes. And dyspised of Iugurth returned agayn to their lorde Adherball[. T]hough suche answers might haue moued any coragious hert: neuertheles Adherball determyned in mynde: to suffre all thynges and to take many i[n]iures in pacience: rather than agayn to begyn batayle with Iugurth. For (as sayd is) the batayle foughten before bytwene them was both to his dishonour/ and also great dammage. But for all this sufferance of Adherball: the mynde of Iugurth was nat more pacified: nor lessed of his cruelte. The pacience of Adherball abated nat the yre of Iugurth: but it augmented: For all redy he had concluded in mynde to inuade the hole kyngdome of Numidy. Therfore he began agayn of newe: nat as before with a company of reuers/ but with a mighty and great army assembled togyder demeanyng open warre/ and chalangyng openly the hole empyre of Numidy/ and with such power proceded into the land of Adherball: wastyng the townes and fyldes on euery syde/ driuyng away with his prayes of catell and other riches: and increasyng corage to his men/ and drede to his ennemis.

27 armes. Many] *punctus suppl.*; *virgule* A B   30 townes/] *virgule from* B   38 in] with B C   40 Numidyans] Numidyan C   44 dyspised] so dispised B; so disposed C   45 Adherball. Though] *colon* A B C   47 iniures] B C; iuiures A   in pacience] paciently B C   49 to his] to B; *om.* C   52 augmented:] *colon from* B   55 reuers] rouers C   59 with his] *om.* B C

[21] Whan Adherball sawe it was come to that point that he moost nedes other abandon and gyue ouer his kyngdome: or els mentayn it with force of armes/ as he which was constrayned by extreme necessite: he assembled and empareyled an army as well as he myght/ and with the same proceded forth to mete Iugurth. At last the two hoostes of Adherball/ and of Iugurth approched and rested nere togyder/ besyde a towne named Cyrtha/ nat ferre dystant from the see coost: And for asmoch as the day drewe nere to nyght: the batayle was nat anone begon: but eyther party remayned in their tentes. Anon after moche of the nyght was ouerpassed: and the starre lyght somwhat dymmed | with obscurite of clowdes. The soudiours f. 20v
of Iugurth raysid by the sounde of trumpets vnwarly and sodenly inuaded and assayled the tentes and felde of Adherball: some they murdredde halfe slepynge: and other some they slewe whyle they were in hand to arme themselfe. On part of Adherball was pytefull [murdre]: and on syde of Iugurth no mercy/ but abstinat persecution and vengeaunce: and so fiersly fought Iugurth and his company that shortly Adherball fled to the towne of Cyrtha/ acompanyed with a fewe horsmen. But Iugurth pursued hym so nerely/ that if the inhabytauntes of the town of Cirtha in hast and with great multytude had nat receyued Adherball: and with force of armes defended the walles/ and kept forth the soudyours of Iugurth which persued Adherball: the batayle bytwen them bothe shuld haue ben begon and ended that one same day/ and that to destruction of Adherball. But Iugurth perceyuing the entre into the town denyed to hym/ anon beseged it on euery syde with all maner ingens inuasyue to his ennemies/ and defensyue to his company: he caused hastely to be framed large pauases and towres of tymbre to be driuen vpon whelis toward the walles of the town. And with these and al maner other ingens went in hand fiersly to assayle the town: and somoch more hastely he sped hym to thintent to bring his purpose to effect/ before or any embassadurs shold come from Rome to resyst his interprise. Forasmoch as before this batayle he had hard that Adherball had send embassadours to Rome to certify the senatours of his myserable state.

61 moost] must B C 69 party] *om.* C 74 other some] some other B C 75 On] On the C 76 murdre] B C; murdred A on syde of Iugurth] on Iugurthes syde C abstinat] obstinate C 83 ben] *om.* B C 84 one] *om.* C 92 or] *om.* B C 93 had] *om.* C

¶How the fauourers of Iugurth at Rome laboured so in this cause/ that thre yong men inexpert and without policy were send embassadours into Affrike to cesse this stryfe bytwene the two kynges: and how these embassadours retourned to Rome without any thyng done. ¶The .xiiii. chapter.

[**21. 4**] But after the senatours of Rome hard tidynges of this batayle/ they send into Affrike thre yong gentylmen in embassade/ commaunding them to go to both the kinges/ and to commaund them in behalfe of the senatours and of the hole peple of Rome to cesse their warre: and to shewe them that the senate and Romayns wylled and vtterly commaunded them so to do. For in so doyng: they shuld do as it semed them: and as of congruence they ought to do both for f. 21r pleasure of the Romayns and for their owne honour and | profet.

[**22**] The embassadours with such commaundment hasted them and came tymely into Affrike/ the senatours had commaunded them to make somoch more expedycion in their iourney/ bycause tydynges were brought to Rome/ whan these embassadours prepared themselfe forward: how the batell was done bytwene Adherball and Iugurth/ and how Iugurth kept Adherbal besegid straytly within the towne of Cyrtha. But this rumour was somwhat alayd and kept vnder by fauourers of Iugurth[. A]fter these embassadours were come to Numidy: they expressed to Iugurth theffect of their embassade in forme as the senatours had commaunded them. Whan Iugurth vnderstode the plesour of the senatours by their wordes and embassade: he answered beningely/ sayng that he counted no erthly thyng more great/ nor exellent/ nor more dere vnto him than the authorite of the senatours and peple of Rome: and that from his yougth to that tyme he had euer so indeuored to order himselfe that euery good and worshypfull man commended and alowed hym for his vertu and manhode/ and nat for malyce nor mysdemea[n]our. And for the same manlynes and nat for malycious dedes/ nor for disordred maners his company and conuersation was accept and plesant vnto the right hygh and worthy captayne Publius Scipio. Moreouer: for the same conuersation and good maners and nat for faute of chyldren naturall/ his vncle Micipsa had adopted hym to son: and made hym

Ch. 14 1 this] his B C cause/] *virgule from* B 6 of] at B C batayle/] *virgule from* B 7 in] *om.* C embassade/] *virgule from* B 11 For in so] And so B C 15 tymely] *om.* B C into] vnto B C 20 vnder] secrete B; *om.* C 21 Iugurth. After] *virgule* A B; *colon* C 25 beningely/] *virgule from* B 30 mysdemeanour] B C; mysdemeauour A 32 plesant] pleasour B; pleasure C 35 to son] for his sonne B C

inheritour of his kyngdom/ partyner with his owne naturall sonnes: and for asmoch as he had demeaned himselfe right well and worthely in executyng of many high and glorious interprises: somoch the lesse coude he suffre iniury done vnto hym vnrevenged. As touching Adherball this Iugurth allegid for himselfe that this Adherball by gile and treason lay in wayt to slee hym: which thyng after he perceyued: he made resystence agaynst the same to the best of his power: as any man was bound to do for sauegard of his own lyfe. And yf the Romayns wold prohybit and deny that vnto hym/ which Iustice permytteth to euery man (that is/ with vyolence to resist and repell vyolence) than shuld they neyther do well nor right wysely in that behalfe. Whan Iugurth had answered the embassadours after this maner: than sayd he for conclusion that shortly after he wold send embassadours to certify the senatours of all other thinges concerning this besynes: and on this poynt Iugurth and the embassadours departed in sonder. Th[u]s Adherball had no confort nor lycence to reply agaynst the wordes of Iugurth/ nor sight or communication with the embassadours: all onely was it graunted vnto hym to appele to the court of Rome/ for of these embassadours coude he haue no iustyce/ nor dyre| ctyon/ in his iniures/ and persecutyon. f. 21v

[23] Whan Iugurth thought that thembassadours were passed out of the lande of Affrike/ towarde Rome: And whan he sawe that with force of armes he coude nat wynne the towne of Cyrtha/ for bycause of naturall situacyon and dyfficulte of the place. Anon he besiged the town agayn of newe/ and all dyfficultes nat withstandyng/ he made a profound and depe trench rounde about the town with sharpe stakes and payles stycked on highest part of the same trenches with sharpe pykes on their vpper endes. This dyde Iugurth for many consideratyons: first to thyntent that the inhabytantes shulde nat breke forth of the towne sodenly at any syde vpon any part of his soudyours which besiged them. Secondly to thintent that on no part any vitayles shuld be brought in to them. Thirdly that the men of warre within the towne shulde nat thrust forth without the town the multytude of poore commens in tyme of famyn and scarcyte of vytayls. And fourthly: that no socours shuld entre in to them to rescue the towne nor to supply their garnyson. Whan this trench was made

40 this[1]] *om.* B C 41 after he] *om.* B C 45 permytteth] permytted B C (that . . . vyolence)] *brackets from* B 51 Thus] B C; This A 56–7 out of the lande] forth B C 58 for] *om.* B C 60 newe/] *virgule suppl.* 62 on] on the C 63 on their] at the C 68 town] *colon* A; *om.* B 71 garnyson] garyson B C

and fynisshed Iugurth moreouer made strong bulwarkes and towres of tymbre without the towne: and strengthed the same with garnyson of wyght and bolde men of armes. Besyde all these ordynaunces he left nothyng vnasayed: nother spared he to attempt euery thyng by strength nor by treson and gyle. Somtyme he proued the watchmen and defenders of the walles with gyftes/ excityng them to betray the towne. Whan his rewardes auayled nought than he thretned them with fiers and sharpe wordes: he inhaunced by exortacions the myndes and courages of his own men to manlynes and audacite. And so he aplyed his besynes that nothyng he omytted wont or possyble to be done in suche a case/ nor no ingen of warre laft he vnprouyded which in those dayes was contryued or founde: but rather besyde all olde inuentyons he ymagined and deuysed newe ingens and ordynaunces of warre nat sene before that tyme: and all for dystruction of the towne of Cyrtha. And of Adherball whom he besyged within the same.

But what tyme Adherball consydred his fortune come to extremyte on all partes/ he kest many thynges in mynde. On the one syde he perceyued his enmy Iugurth vyolent agaynst hym: and no trust of comfort nor of socours. On the other syde he consydred well/ that for penury and want of soudyours and of their thinges necessary he was nat able nother to fyght with his enmy: nor to dryue forth or prolong the batell: and for faute of vytayle he myght nat long defend the
f. 22r towne. These thynges with many mo well reuoulued in mynde/ he | chose forthe two which were moost dilygent and trusty of that company which had fled with hym into Cirtha. To them he wofully bewayled his mysfortune: and made so large promyses of rewardes vnto them: that at last he induced them to go forthe of the towne by nyght priuely/ and if they myght escape their ennemies/ to resort to the next hauyn towne: And from thens to hast them to Rome with letters which he had deuysed and written to be delyuerd to the senatours.

[24] These messangers were trusty and faythfull/ within fewe dayes without any dysturbance: they fulfylled the commaundement of their soueraygne/ and delyuerd the letters of Adherball vnto the senatours. Which letters anone were redde in the counselhous before the senatours and rulers of Rome: of which letters the sentence herafter insueth and was suche.

73 garnyson] garyson B; a garrison C 75 nother] neyther C euery] any C 76 nor] or C 77 gyftes/] *virgule suppl.* 90 nor of] of B; or C 91 of their] other B C 107 and rulers] *om.* C

¶The sentence of the letters sent from Adherball vnto the senatours of Rome: what tyme he lay besyged by Iugurth within the towne of Cirtha. ¶The .xv. chapter.

[**24. 2**] Most worthy fathers it is nat througth my faute that I sende so often to you requiryng your socours/ and complayning myne iniures: but the vyolence and rygour of Iugurth/ compelleth me therto. Whose mynde is fylled with so great a lust and desyre to beraue my life: that neyther hath he in mynd the drede of goddes punysshment/ nor fear of your dyspleasure. My blode he couyteth more than all thinges: In somoch that nowe is the [fift] moneth sith I am kept closed/ and besiged with armed men/ by tyranny of Iugurth. He nothyng regardyng that I am confederate felowe and frende of the peple of Rome. Neyther can preuayle nor helpe the great benifites of my fader Micipsa done to this Iugurth/ nor your authorite nor ordynaunces or decrees. Thus I am vncertayn whyther I am constrayned and oppressed more greuously by force of armes or by hunger/ for both inuoulueth me on all sydes. I wold write vnto you moche more touchyng the tyrannous cruelte of Iugurth/ but my miserable fortune moueth me contrary: and moreouer I haue often perceyued before this tyme: that small credence is gyuen to suche as ar oppressed with mysery: Saue this I per| ceyue clerely that the f. 22v
mynde of Iugurth coueyteth greter thyng than my deth or kyngdom. And if by your sufferance: he shall subdue me and beraue my kyngdom/ at last he shall ryse and rebell agaynst your empyre. Wherfore if ye lyst nat to defende and socour my lyfe: at leest: defend your kyngdom of Numidy/ and preuent the vsurper of your empyre. Suffre nat this tyran to enioye the kyngdom of Numidy/ and your good wyll withall. But truely ye may well perceyue that he loketh nat after your fauoure/ after he shall haue vsurped the realm of Numidy. But whyder he setteth lesse by losse of your frenshyp and fauour/ or of the domynion of Numidy: non is so blynde but that may euydently perceyue the trouth. For his dedes declare: that he counteth lesse greuous to haue your hy displesure/ than to lose his fiers purpose to sle me/ and than to ocupy the hole lande of Numidy. For this hath he proued and made manifest by his vnnaturall and cruell dedes: first of all he hath slayn my brother Hiempsall: which

Ch. 15 1–2 of Rome] *om.* C 6 me] *om.* C 7 beraue] bereue C 10 fift] first A; .v. B C 15 Thus] *om.* B C 17 sydes] *virgule* A B; *colon* C 18 Iugurth/] *virgule suppl.* (*end of line* A B) 22 greter] greater B; a greater C 23 beraue my] beraue me B; bereue me of my C

dede he durst nat haue done if he had feared your dyspleasure: next that: he droue me forth of my contrey and fathers kyngdome. But these iniures for certayne/ were done agaynst my brother and me: and nothyng they longed to you. But nowe he conspyreth hyer: inuadyng/ vsurpyng/ and wastyng the hole land of Numidy with force of armes. And where as ye set me as your lewtenant vnder you to gouern a part of Numidy. This Iugurth now hath dryuen me from my lyberte into the towne of Cyrtha/ and besygeth me with men of armes closed on all sydes with outward drede and inward famyn: So that my peryls may playnly declare how lytell he setteth by the wordes of your embassadours. Certaynly I can se nothyng remayning able to remoue his vyolence/ nor that can socour this my misery/ saue onely your power and vyolence. Forsoth I wold right gladly: that these thinges whiche now I write to you/ and all those thinges which I haue [complayned] before in the counselhouse were but fayned and false/ rather than this my euydent misery shuld proue them true and credyble vnto you. But sith I was borne in that hour/ and my desteny is such that Iugurth moost manifest his cursed cruelte by me/ therfore now my request nor prayr is nat that I may escape the sharpnes and cruelte of miserable deth/ which I behold instant and ineuytable/ but only my prair is that I may escape the long subiection and bondage of my enmy: and prolonged turmentes of my miserable body. But worthy faders: touching the kyngdome of Numidy/ which apertayneth to you: prouide you for the same as it lyketh you/ and if it be your plesure: ryd and delyuer me from the cruell and vnmerciful
f. 23r handes | of Iugurth my mortall enmy for the honour and mageste of your empyre: and for the fidelyte of all frenshyp/ yf any remembraunce of my granfather Massinissa remayneth yet among you.

¶How the senatours sende newe embassadours to Iugurth commaundyng him to desyst from persecution of Adherball: and how they preuayled nothyng: how the town of Cyrtha was yelded to Iugurth: and how he slewe Adherball. ¶The .xvi. chapter.

[25] After these foresayd letters were openly red and recyted before the senatours: many of them were: which counsayled to send an army

40 conspyreth] conspyred C hyer:] *colon suppl.* (*end of line* A) 49 Forsoth] *om.* B C 51 complayned] B C; compyplayned A 54 manifest] manifesteth C 56 miserable] *om.* C 57 ineuytable/] *virgule from* B 63 frenshyp/] *punctus* A; *virgule* B

Ch. 16 2 from] from his C

into Affrike/ and in all hast conuenyent to socour and helpe Adherball. And in the meane tyme they wolde take counsell and aduyse touchyng Iugurth what shulde be done to hym: bycause he had nat obeyed their embassadours. Whan the fauourers of Iugurth hard of this they laboured with all their myght: that no such decre shuld be made nor procede to effect. And thus the commen wayle was ouercome and subdued by priuate profet/ and parciall fauour: as in many other besynesses is dayly wont to happen. Nat withstandyng this parcialyte: at last it was so determyned: that other newe embassadours were sent yet ones agayne into Affrike/ nat yong men and inexpert as before: but well aged men of grauyte and dyscression which were of great dygnite: and had borne great and worshypfull offices in tyme past/ in the cyte of Rome. Amonge which embassadours was one named Marcus Emilius Scaurus/ of whom we haue made mencyon before. This Scaurus was a man by riches and fame counted able to be counsellour of Rome: And also at that tyme a mighty prince and great doer among the senatours/ and in maner ruler of them all.

For asmoch as all men for the moost part were dysplesed with Iugurth and sore murmured agaynst his cruelte and agaynst the parciall fauour shewed to hym at Rome: and also for that the messangers of [Adherbal] besought the embassadours to hast them to Numidy/ therfore the thyrd day after their commyssion they departed from Italy: and toke shypping and in short tyme after aryued in Affrike/ at a cite named Vtica in a prouince subiect to the Romayns. As sone as they were aryued they send letters vnto Iugurth charging hym in all the hast to come to the said prouynce to know the plesure of the senatours of Rome which had send them thyder for the nonys with certen | commaundementes dyrect vnto hym. Whan f. 23v
Iugurth vnderstode that such noble men/ famous/ and of preemynent authourite at Rome were come to prohybit his interprise/ at first begynning he was somwhat troubled with drede/ on the other part his lust was moche kyndled to wyn the towne of Cyrtha/ and to get Adherbal into his handes: and so was his mynde dyuersly dystract with drede and desyre: with drede of the embassadours: and with desyre to bring his purpose to effect. Gretly he feared the angre and dyspleasure of the senatours if he dyd nat obey their embassadours: but his mynde on the other part was vtterly blynded by lust of

16 into] to C 27 Adherbal] Iugurth A B C 28 Numidy/] *virgule from* B 32 the[1]] *om.* B C 33 thyder] ther C 36 interprise/] *virgule from* B 41 Gretly] gretly A; Greatly B C

domynion/ which desyre drewe hym vyolently to performe that he had begon. And so at conclusion in such mynde desirous of lordshyp/ the worst counsell ouercame the best. And couetise excluded fear: and thus he determyned in mynde to wyn the towne (if he myght) before or he wold go to commen with the embassadours. This thyng determyned and fixed in mynde: he compased the towne rounde about with his army: and with great vyolence assayled it contendyng to breke in therto: this dyd he: trustyng that namely: by diuidyng of his army on all sydes of the towne and compellyng his ennemis within [the] towne to breke their hole company for to defende the walles assayled on all partes/ he myght at last by such meanes wyn vyctory ouer them. But after many and sharpe assautes at last whan he sawe his purpose proceded nat to effect/ and that he was nat of power to haue his pleasure of the towne of Adherball before he shuld commen with the embassadours/ he was right pensyue in mynde. And lest his prolonging might angre Scaurus the chefe of the imbassadours whom he greatly dradde: at last he came into the prouince with a small company of horsmen. As sone as he was come the embassadours shewed vnto him many greuous manaces and wordes in name of all the senate: bycause he cessed nat for all their commaundementes from besegyng of the towne of Cyrtha/ but at conclusion after moch communicatyon spent in vayne: the embassadours departed agayn to Rome: without any dyrection or apoyntment made.

[**26**] Whan tidynges herof come to Cyrtha such as defended the towne were moch abasshed/ but Adherball moost of all. At last the Italyans/ of whom many were within the town: and by whose strength the walles were chefely defended/ began to thynke among themselfe that if the town were yelded vp to Iugurth/ he durst nat be so bolde to shewe any vyolence agaynst them for the honour and mageste of the name of Romayns. For asmoch as the same Italyans were counted as
f. 24r Romayns in such dyuises/ they | came to Adherball and hym aduysed to yelde hym selfe and the towne to Iugurth vpon apoynment and condycion/ that the same Iugurth onely wold promyse to graunt hym his lyfe: and as touching all other iniuries which Iugurth had done to hym/ the senatours whan they shuld se tyme oportune and conuenyent wolde se a prouysion and remedy. Adherball heryng this

44 domynion/] *virgule from* B 48 or] *om.* B C 49 rounde] *om.* B C 53 the[1]] B C; to A 57 of] and of B C 62 wordes] wordes of displeasour B; words of displeasure C 74 dyuises/] *virgule suppl.* 79 prouysion] dyreccion B C remedy.] *colon* A B

counsell/ anone considred in his mynde that nothing coude be more vnstable nor more incertayne than was the promysse of Iugurth. Agayne he called to mynde that if he acorded nat to their counsell it was in their power to compell hym therto. And so acordyng to their counsell and aduisment he yelded vp the towne to Iugurth vpon promyse onely to haue his lyfe saued. But anon Iugurth contrary to his promes put Adherball to deth first of all with manyfolde tourmentes. After that he slewe all the yong and lusty men of the towne/ bothe Numidyans and Italyan marchauntes indyfferently: sparyng non namely yf they were founde in harnesse.

¶Howe the senatours certyfied of the cruelty of Iugurth prepared an army agaynst hym: howe the embassadurs of Iugurth were nat receyued into Rome: and how Calphurnius the Romayn captayne was acloyed by bribes of Iugurth. ¶The .xvii. chapter.

[**27**] Whan this cruelty of Iugurth was knowen at Rome the senatours beganne to take counsell what thyng was best to be done in the case. But suche whose fauour Iugurth had bought before sore dystourbed the counsell: And prolonged the tyme with fayre wordes and prayer somtyme: somtyme with fauorable promysses made to other lordes: And other whyle with braulyng and thretnyng couertly. In somoch that by such meanes: at last they alayed the dyspleasure taken agaynst Iugurth and mytigated the cruelty of his dedes. And certaynly all the yll wyll and hatred which was taken agaynst Iugurth shulde vtterly haue ben let fall and quenched by meane of dryuyng forth of the tyme in counsellyng: had nat ben the resystence and repugnaunce of one named Cayus Memmyus: So great was the power of the fauour and treasure of Iugurth. This Memmius | [f. 24v] was elect and assigned to be protectour of the commens for the yere next insuyng and was a man sharpe and fiers of condycions: and agaynst the power of the noble men of Rome with all his myght: and therfore whan he saw this vnresonable fauour and parcialyte among the senatours he informed the commen peple that the senatours were about to pardon the cruelte of Iugurth/ by couetyse and corrupcyon of a fewe debatefull lordes. The commenty vnderstandynge this was sore moued agaynst the senatours and counsell. And the senatours agayne sore feared the commens: bycause of the offences bothe of Iugurth and of them in

84 counsell and] *om.* B C 88 towne/] *virgule from* B Italyan] Italyans B C

Ch. 17 1 the[2]] this B; thys C 4 by] wyth C of Iugurth] *om.* C 7 suche] they B C 9 promysses] promes C 14 meane of] *om.* B C of] *om.* B C

fauouryng hym were openly knowen: therfore they dradde lest all the commens ioyened togyder might make insurrection agaynst them: wherfore they thought it necessary to pacify and alay the commens.

Nowe it was so that long before this tyme a noble man of Rome named Sempronius whyle he was in authorite made a statute and lawe that yf it fortuned at any tyme: that the Romayns [stode] in doute and feare lest any warre or batayle might come vpon them sodenly/ newe consuls than shulde be chosen and assigned for the next yere to come: And send into suche prouynces where the batayle or warre was feared. These consuls were thus newly chosen before the yere of the olde consuls was fully expyred to thintent that in meane tyme they might haue more tyme and layser to make conuenyent prouycion for the warre: And this act so decreed was called the lawe of Sempronius/ bycause he first inacted the same. By this lawe of Sempronius: the two prouynces of Numidy and Italy were decreed to the two Consuls for the yere to come. The prouynce of Italy to be defended and conserued: and the prouynce of Numidy to be recouerd (Scipio Nasica) (and Calphurnius Bestia) were proclamed Consuls for the next yere commyng. The land of Numidy came by lotte to Calphurnius that he shuld do his dyligence to recouer the same. And the countrey of Italy fell to Scipio to defende the same. After this an army was assembled to be sende into Affrike/ and so forth to Numidy: wages/ and vytayls/ for the sowdyours with other thynges nedefull to warre were decreed of the senatours/ and prouyded of the consull Calphurnius.

[28] But whan Iugurth hard tidynges from his frendes of this ordynaunce: and parceyued that the mater went froward other wyse than he trusted it shulde haue done. For his mynde was fyxed that all thyng right and wrong myght be bought and solde at Rome: nowe went he in hand agayne with his olde craftes. And send his sonne with f. 25^{r} other two of his moost familyer and trusty fren| des embassadours vnto the senatours. And lyke as he had commaunded th[o]se embassadours which he send to Rome after he had murdred Hiempsall: right so he commaunded these that they shuld go in hande to stoppe euery mannes mouth with money. For in his great treasour and in couetyse of the rulers of Rome was all his confydence.

32 stode] B C; shulde A 33 sodenly/] *virgule* B; *punctus and cap.* N *in* A 36 newly] *om.* B C 52 tidynges] tidyng C frendes] frendes at Rome B C 53 froward] forward C 58 those] B; these A C 59 which he send] whome he had sende B C

O cursed hunger of golde moost execrable: thou driuest blynde myndes to yls innumerable. Whan these embassadours of Iugurth were come nere to Rome: the consull Calphurnius demaunded aduyse and counsell of the senatours whither it pleased them that the sayd embassadours shuld be receyued within the walles of Rome or nat. But the senatours decreed that except they came to yelde bothe Iugurth and the kyngdom of Numidy vnto the Romayns: vpon a great payne they shuld depart out of the contrey of Italy/ within .x. dayes after. Calphurnius commaunded this ordynance and decre of the senatours to be borne and declared to the Numidyans by one named Decius. And so thembassadours departed home agayne without any thynge done wherfore they came.

In the mean tyme Calphurnius prepared an army: and chose vnto hym noble men/ debatefull/ and hauynge many clyentes and seruantes retayned with them. This dyd he to thintent that yf he dyd any thyng amysse in his vyage: he might trust to be supported by their auctorite. Among whom was one named Scaurus: of whose condycions and behauour I haue spoken before. For in this consull Calphurnius/ were many good propertis and vertues condycions both of mynde and of body: but the cursed vyce of couetyse which was in him: blynded and ouercam all those vertuis: so that he put them nat in execusion[. H]e might well indure labour. His wyt was quicke and pregnant: he was prouydent and ware ynough/ In batayle he was so expert that in grettest paryll he was boldest and strongest agaynst gyles of his ennemies. But to our purpose/ this Calphurnius/ whan he had elect and assembled suche company as hym thought competent for an army/ he deuyded all his hoost into legyons contayning in euery legion .vi.M.vi.C.lx. and six men. And so send forth his men by legions by the c[ou]ntrey of Italy/ to a towne called Regium/ which towne is in the marches bytwene Italy and Cecyle: from this towne of Regium they were conuayed into Cycyle into Affrike/ and there they mustred and were set in aray. And so proceded by lande tyll they attayned vnto Numydy. Anone Calphurnius prepared vytayls and all maner ordy-naunces requysite. And proceded forwarde assaylyng fiersly | the lande f. 25^{v}
of Numidy/ as a hardy captayne pretendyng great valyantyse at the first brunt. Many men toke he prisoners/ and a fewe townes he wanne

65 to] *om.* C 69 the[1]] *om.* C 71 after] next after B C 75 an] his B C vnto] to C 79 one] *om.* B C 80 before.] *no punct.* A B 80 For] But B C 81 vertues] vertuous B C of[2]] *om.* B C 83 execusion. He] *no punct.* A; *colon* B 87 gyles] the gile C purpose/] *virgule from* B 91 countrey] B C; conutrey A 93 Cycyle] Cycile, and so C 98–9 wanne and] *om.* B C

and subdued vnto hym: suche as resysted his power he brent them to the grounde to increas fere to their neighbours.

[**29**] Iugurth aduerting this sharpnes of Calphurnius send embassadours to hym with great plenty of gold to attempt his mynde: And shewed vnto hym the hardnes and difficulte of the batayle which he had begon. Whan Calphurnius felt the weyght and valour of the glystryng golde/ his corrupt and vnstable mynde by contagion of couetyse anone was peruerted to receiue the money: and induced to fauour and assist the part of Iugurth. But Scaurus (of whome I haue spoken before) was receyued vnto them for partyner and fellawe of all their counsels and besynesses. And howbeit at begynnyng this same Scaurus strongly resisted the party of Iugurth: what tyme many other of his sect were corrupt and accloyed with bribes long before this: neuertheles now at last his mynde was abstract lyke other mo from the defence of goodnes and honesty vnto his olde vyce of insacyable and execrable couetyse by meane of habundaunce of golde and great rewardes of Iugurth. But at first begynnyng this Iugurth redemed of Calphurnius/ but onely delayng and deferring of the warre: trustyng that in meane tyme he shulde brynge about somwhat of his purpose at Rome other by price/ prayer/ or fauoure. But nowe after he had wone Scaurus to be partyner of his besynes and fauourer of his cause also with Calphurnius: he was brought into a veray great trust fully to recouer his peace at Rome: and concluded whyle bothe Calphurnius and Scaurus were there present togyder to take aduysement and treat presently with them of all apoyntmentes and thynges necessary to be done for perfourmyng of his purpose. Howbeit he trusted nat Calphurnius so moche that he wolde come to his army/ except some hoostages of the Romayns were left within some strong towne of his: and in warde of his people wherby he myght trust without dammage sauely to be remytted agayn to his army.

Calphurnius to auoyd this dougth of Iugurth and to put hym in more assurance sende the treasourer of the Romayne army named Sextius/ vnto one of the chefe townes belongyng to Iugurth called Vacca/ faynyng among the army that he sent the sayd treasourer thyther for prouysion of whete and other vytayls necessary to his hoost. And the
f. 26r same commaundement to prouyde vytayls the capytayn Calphurni|us

100 neighbours.] *colon* A; *punctus* B 103 batayle] warre B C 104 weyght] wyght B C 105 golde/] *virgule from* B 117 in] in the C 122 there] *om.* C 123 apoyntmentes] apoyntment B; apoyntmente C 125 army/] *virgule from* B 131 Vacca/] *virgule from* B 132 sayd] *om.* C

gaue to his treasourer openly in commen audyence: to thintent that no man shuld susspect his false purpose: sayng to his tresourer that hym neded nat to be in dout of Iugurth/ for asmoche as trues were taken bytwene bothe parties tyll a certayn day prefixed. The tresourer Sextius went to the sayd cyte of Vacca at commaundement of Calphurnius his captayne. Wherfore anone after Iugurth (lyke as he apoynted before) came to the army of Calphurnius. And there in presence of the rulers and counsell of the Romayns/ he spake a lytell of his purgation/ concernyng the dyspleasure/ enuy/ and hateredde/ whiche the senate and commons of Rome had taken agaynst him for his dedes: sayeng that he had nought done but prouoked of his ennemies/ and for his owne defence: with vyolence to resyst vyolence. Howbeit he sayd that he was contented to yelde and submyt himselfe vnto the Romayns clemence and mercy. Somoch spoke he openly before all the chefe counsell of the army. But all the remenaunt he concluded and dyd secretly with Calphurnius and Scaurus at more leasoure/ and thus ended the communycation of this day. On the next day after insuynge the capitayne and the counsell of the army/ and also Iugurth assembled togyder agayne to common of the same mater concernyng peace to be graunted to Iugurth. Now was it so that among the Romayns was decreed an ordynaunce long before this tyme named among the Romayns the Satyre lawe/ whiche lawe commaunded that the captayne of euery army shulde aske aduyse of all the wyse counsell of his hoost whan he went about any weyghty mater concernyng the common wele. Wherfore Calphurnius thought so to order hymselfe that he shulde not be counted a brecarre of this lawe: And desyred counsell and aduyse of all the noble and wyse men of his hoost. This dyd he to thyntent that yf the peace graunted to Iugurth shuld be afterward dysalowed (as it was) he myght auoyde the faut from hymselfe into the common counsell. But at conclusyon/ whan Calphurnius acordyng to the sayd lawe had requyred aduyse of the common counsell: euery man concented that peace shulde be graunted to Iugurth: vpon condycion and couenaunt that he shulde delyuer vnto the Romayns thertie Elyphantes with moche other catell and many horses with a great somme of golde. To which ordynaunce Iugurth acorded and soone after delyuered the same Elyphantes/ cattell/ and

136 hym] he C 137 trues were] truce was C 142 he] *om.* B C a] *om.* C
143 purgation/] *virgule from* B 146 defence:] *colon after* vyolence A
148 clemence] clemencie C 154 among the Romayns] at Rome B C
157 the] *om.* C 163 dysalowed] dysalowed at Rome B C

horses and gold vnto the tresourer of the Romayne hoost. This done f. 26v the consull Calphurnius departed to Rome to requyre the | senatours and other rulers to conferme this peace and concorde which they had made with Iugurth. In meane tyme ouer all Numidy and also in the Romayne army was peace and concorde in abyding the answere of the senate and rulers at Rome.

¶Howe the rulers of Rome for the moost parte were greuously displeased for grauntyng of this peace and disalowed the same. And how Memmius inflamed the commen people agaynst the fauourers of Iugurth. ¶The .xviii. chapter.

[**30**] But after it was knowen at Rhome in what maner the consull behaued hymselfe in Affrike with Iugurth: in euery place about Rome/ and amonge euery company within Rome it was commyned of the dede of Calphurni[u]s. In somoche that among the commenty was raysed greuous hatered and dyspleasure agaynst hym. The senatours were sore troubled and were in doute whyther they myght conferme and alowe this foule and shamefull dede of the consull/ or els abrogate and annull the same. In this prolexite they were longe tyme vncertayne: And moost of all the myght and power of Scaurus (bycause he was a doer and felowe with the consull in the sayed ded) let them frome dyscussing of the ryght. But whyle the senatours in suche wyse prolonged the tyme in this dubytacion: Memmius (of whose condycions/ promptnes of wytte/ and hateredde: which he had agaynst the power of the estates and noblemen we haue written before) at dyuers tymes he assembled the commen people/ exhorting and inflamyng them to reuenge the cruelty of Iugurth/ and parcyalite of his fauourers/ and warnyng them nat to forsake the defence of their commen wayle and lybertie of their cytie. He rehersed vnto them the pride/ the cruelte/ and manyfolde vnlaufull dedes of the senatours and of other estates at many tymes done to disworshyp and oppressyon of the commen wele. And vtterly at conclusyon so he behaued hymselfe that he kyndled the myndes of the vniuersall commentie to resyst the parcialyte of the estates/ and f. 27r to | se the cruelty of Iugurth extremely punysshed. But bycause the eloquence of this Memmius at that season was at Rome notable and moche set by/ dyscrete and of great authorite: I haue intended of so

176 at] of B C

Ch. 18 6 behaued] had behaued B C 8 Calphurnius] B C; Calphurnins A 12 prolexite] perplexite B C 20 people/] *virgule from* B

many exhortacyons as he had to the people: to commyt one to remembraunce by writynge: And specially before all other I wyll write that exhortacyon which after returnynge of Calphurnius from Aphrike he spake before the commen people in fourme folowynge.

¶The orison of Memmius had before the commen people of Rome. In which orison he induceth them to defende their lyberte: And to represse and prosecute with hatered the noble men of Rome. ¶The .xix. chapter.

[31] Right worthy cetyzins many thynges shuld withdrawe me from defence of you and from charge and medlyng with your besynesses were nat the great loue and fauour which I haue to the commen wele: that causeth me to sette asyde all suche impedymentes/ and vtterly to take vpon me the defence of your lyberte agaynst these corrupt estates. More playnly to ascertayne you: the thynges which myght withdrawe me from defence of your cause be these. First the power of them whiche are begynners of this variaunce: that is to say of Calphurnius and Scaurus. Secondly your pacience whiche is easy to be subdued of crueltie: sith ye be dysposed to endure this wronge. And thyrdly the infectyon of Iustice whiche is no where here amonge vs/ but clene exyled from oure cytye. And princypally this letteth me that I se ye ar so innocent/ so feblemynded/ and so symple that in euery place ye ar sure of all the paryll/ of all the laboure/ and of all the payne: but these estates whiche do nought that is commendable haue all the honour/ auantage/ and worshyppe. And sothely: it greueth me | to speke to you f. 27v of the iniury that now of late hath ben done to you: howe moche ye haue ben had in skorne/ derysion/ and in dysdayne: to the power and pride of a fewe estates. And also it greueth me to recount how vngoodly and vnreuenged many of your defenders by them haue shamefully ben put to dethe for your sake within these fyftene yeres. And to se how your myndes be corrupt with cowardyse and neglygence that ye wolde neuer socoure them whiche in your quarell and defence haue subdued themselfe to deth. What intende ye? wyll ye styl be subgette vnto these estates your ennemyes? It is surely tyme at the last to aryse and defende your lybertie[. Y]e do drede them: whom it semeth to dout and

34 he] the sayd Memmius B; the sayde Memmius C

Ch. 19 1 orison] oracion C 2 orison] oracion C 3 represse] expresse C prosecute] persecute B C 5 shuld] shulde B; wolde C 10 you:] *colon from* B 16 that[1]] for that B C 17 ye ar] you B C (ar *om.*) 23 me] *om.* B C vngoodly and] *om.* B C 29 ennemyes?] *punctus* A B C 30 lybertie. Ye] *virgule* A B; *colon* C

to drede you/ consydringe your true querell/ and their vngoodly mysdemeanour. But nat withstandyng that ye be thus dysposed to lose your lyberty and in mysery to passe forthe the resydue of your lyues/ neuertheles the good wyll which I haue to you and to the commen wele causeth and dryueth my mynde to resyst this fals fa[u]oure and parcialyte of these proude and vniust lordes. Certesse I shall assay and proue howe I can defende the lybertie whiche my father left me: but whyther I shall so do to behoue or auauntage or elles in vayne/ that lyeth hole in your handes and power. Surely worthy cytezyns I do nat exhort you to go agaynst or withstande these wronges and oppressions with force of armes as our forefathers haue often done. To resyste and repell this wronge nedeth no vyolence nor deuydynge of you from the senatours as ye haue done before tyme. It must nedes be that these great men confederat in malyce at last shall come to decay by their owne condycions insolent and behauour. Were nat sharpe inquysicyons and greuous examynatyons hadde agaynst the commen people of Rome/ after that Tiberius Graccus was slayne for the defence of the lawes belongynge to the commentie: whom his euylwyllers accused as vsurper of a kyngdome ouer the commen people? And moreouer after that Cayus Graccus and Marcus Fuluius/ were putte to dethe for defendyng of your lyberte/ were nat many of your order and behauoure that is to say of the commentie putte to dethe and murdred in prison? And at both the seasons the estates made none ende of their crueltie agaynst you after the lawe/ but after their immoderate pleasure.

Well forsothe I graunt that it be reputed for treason and vsurpatyon of a kyngdome to defende the lawes and the ryght of the commentie:
f. 28r and I graunt also that what thyng can nat be condygnely punysshed |
without effusyon of blode of many cytesyns: that the same punysshement be executed accordynge to lawe and ryght vpon a fewe suche as were begynners of the trespasse. Within these fewe yeres passed ye dysdayned and murmured secretely and styll amonge your selfe that the sayd lordes spoyled the commen treasoure without your consent: And that kynges and nacyons contrybutory to Rome/ payed their trybutes to a fewe priuate estates/ and nat generall to the vnyuersall cyte in commen: and ye grutched that these estates hadde all the moost dignyte

31 vngoodly] vngodlye C 35 fauoure] B C; fanoure A 38 behoue or] *om.* B C vayne/] *virgule suppl.* 40 go agaynst or] *om.* B C 43 ye] your elders B C 45 insolent and] and insolent B; and insolente C 49 a] *om.* B C people?] *punctus* A B 52 and[2]] or B C 53 prison?] *colon* A B none] no C 54 lawe/] *virgule from* B (*end of line* A) 62 and styll] *om.* B C

and all the rychesse and treasoure/ also in theyr handes. Neuerthelesse they counted but a smalle thynge to escape vnpunysshed for these so great offences. Wherfore nowe are they become so bolde/ so fiers/ and proude: by your sufferaunce that at last they haue betrayed and putte in handes of your ennemyes your lawes/ your dignyte/ your mageste/ with all other thynges bothe humayne and dyuine. So that in pardonyng of these inhumayne and cruell offences of Iugurth they haue polluted and betrayed the lawes bothe of God and man. And howebeit that suche is their demeanoure it nothynge repenteth them: nor they are nought asshamedde therof. But dayly iette before your faces solemly and pompously bostyng them selfe: Some of their dygniteis/ their lordshyppes/ and offyces. And other some crakynge of their tryumphes and vyctories/ as who sayeth that they attayned the same by honoure/ and nat by falsehodde and robberie.

Haue ye nat dayly experyence seyng that symple bondmen bought and solde for money wyll nat suffre nor endure the vniust commaundementes of their lordes or maisters? But contrary wyse ye gentlemen: freborne cytezyns ar contented to suffre with meke myndes this bondage wherin ye are holden subgette by the power of these lordes. But I pray you what maner of men be these whiche thus subdue you: and presume thus longe to occupy the commen wayle at this season? Forsothe they be men moost vycious: with bloddy handes infected/ with the bloode of Innnocentes. Men of immoderate and insaciable couetyse: noysom and greuous to euery good man. Whose pride incredeble no man can comprehende/ whiche for money haue solde and dayly are redy for to sell for lucre their fidelyte/ their worshyppe/ their deuotyon/ and good name: And brefely all thynges honest and dyshonest ar they redy to do for auantage. Wherby it apereth euydently that all their ioye and felycite resteth in couetyse. | f. 28v
Some of them count themselfe more assured bycause they haue slayne the protectours of the commentie to the intent that other may drede them so moche more: And other of them in wrong examynations and inquisicions had agaynst you reioyse and count themselfe hardye and surer therby: And many other thynketh their defence and auauncement in murdringe of you/ bostynge themselfe of the same: and thus howe moche worse that ech of them doth: the more sure he is and more sette by. Insomoch that where they ought to fere you for their

72 dyuine] diuine to your libertie belongynge B C 75 are] be B C 83 maisters?] *punctus* A B C 96 themselfe] hymself C 98 other] other some B C 101 you/] *virgule suppl.*; *comma* C

mysdedes: they transpose that feare vnto you/ and [cause] you by your cowardyse to fear and drede them: whiche are conioyened all togyder agaynst you in one maner desyre of yll/ in one maner couetyse/ in one hateredde of good/ and in one maner fere of your auauncement[. B]ut amonge good men to be all of one mynde vnder this maner one nat withstandyng another it is to be counted for amyte and frendshyppe. Among yll men suche agreyng of maners is but a knotte of dyscorde and causeth sedycion/ varyaunce/ and debate. But verily if ye had so great desyre and care to recouer your lyberte (whiche is lost) as they haue to encrease their lordshyppe: than shulde nat the commen wele be oppressed and wasted as it is nowe: and than shuld the offices/ maistershyppes/ and dygnitees of Rome (whiche ar your benefites to gyue where lyketh you) be in the handes of good and vertuous men/ and nat in the handes of bold bosters and iniust men confyderate in myschefe. The commenty of Rome your forefathers before this tyme haue armed themselfe and forsaken the senatours t[w]o su[n]dry tymes and kept themselfe togyder vpon the hyll of Aduentyne/ onely bycause they wolde haue a lawe decreed and inacted for them: And maisters or officers elect for them which shuld be their protectours agaynst the iniury and [extorcion] of the estates whan nede shulde requyre/ which thynge at last was graunted to them and many other lyberties also. Than shuld nat ye laboure moch more with all your myght for conseruatyon of the same lyberteis which they haue left vnto you as hole as euer they had them? And specially for this cause ought ye to defende your priuileges for that it is more shame and rebuke to lese that priuilege and lybertie which ar goten than neuer to haue obtayned them: And specially what shame is it to you nothynge to augment nor encrease that authorite/ which your elders and forefathers haue left to you: but to suffre the same by your cowardyse by lytell | [f. 29r] and lytell to dekay: and at laste vtterly to be loste and come to nought.

But any of you may than requyre of me: what is your mynde/ what wyll ye that we do? I wyll forsothe and counsel that punysshment be taken vpon them whiche haue betrayed the honour of the commen wele vnto your ennemy Iugurth/ without aduyse of the senatours or

104 cause] B C; bycause A   108 auauncement. But] *colon* A B; *comma* C   116 the] *om.* C   120 two sundry] to sudry A; two sondry B; two sondrye C   kept] kepe B; kepte C   121 Aduentyne/] *virgule in* A *placed after* onely, *not* Aduentyne   12 122 for[1]] of C   123 extorcion] B; extorcyon C; exhortacyon A   124 requyre/] *virgule from* B   127 them?] *colon* A B C   128 specially] speciall C   129 that] the B C   which ar] *om.* B C   135 me:] *colon suppl.*

of the commenty: but this my counsell is nat to punysshe them vyolently with your power in batayle/ for certesse that were more dyshonoure vnto you to do than to them to suffre the same. Nat withstandyng that they be worthy so to be delt with all. But this thyng may be best done by inquysition/ examynation and confession of Iugurth hymselfe/ and by his appelynge of these treatours/ whiche Iugurth surely wyll be obedyent to come hyther to Rome at your commaundement yf it be true that he hath yelded himselfe. But if he dyspice your commaundementes than may ye well thynke and consyder what peace or yeldyng he hath made/ by the whiche yeldynge he is vnpunysshed and pardoned of his detestable and shamefull dedes/ and these estates laded with richesse and treasoure. But oure cytie and welthe of the commenty is come to losse/ dammage/ and vtter shame and dysworshyppe. Thus must ye do/ suche examynations muste ye make/ without ye thynke that these great men haue nat yet sufficyent lordshyppe and power in their handes/ or els without ye shewe outwarde that ye were better pleased and content with that season whan kyngdomes/ prouynces/ iustices/ lawes/ iugementes/ batayle/ peace/ and finally euery thynge both dyuyne and humayne were in handes of a fewe estates. Than ye be nowe pleased with the season and tyme that nowe is whan your lybertie is gyuen to you whiche ye ar able to meyntayn if ye be dysposed. But in that season passed howe beit ye were vnouercome of your ennemies/ maysters/ and emperours/ ouer the moost part of the world: yet had ye ynough to do to defende your owne life from the cruelty of these fewe mighty men. For of you al who was so bolde to withstand their subiectyon and bondage? Wherfore yf ye entend to endure and suffre the destruction of your lyberty as ye begyn/ than truely the tyme which is to come shalbe moch more cruell to you than the tyme passed.

But as for me nat withstandyng that I vnderstande that the great offence and abhomynable of this wycked Iugurth is suffred vnpunysshed: yet wolde I suffre paciently that ye shuld forgyue and pardon the wicked doers of this dede/ men most vngracious bycause they be citezins. If it were nat so/ that such mer| cy and forgyuenes shulde f. 29v
tourne to our dystruction and ruyn of our impyre. For ye may se howe

144 appelynge] accusacion B C 148 made/] *virgule suppl.* (*end of line* A) 153 make/] *virgule suppl.* 155 handes/] *virgule suppl.* 157 and] *om.* C 160 ye be] ye so be B C 165 bondage?] *punctus* A B C 166 begyn/] *virgule suppl.* 169 that[2]] *om.* B C 172 dede/] *virgule suppl.*; dede as C

great oportunyte and sufferaunce they haue in somoch that they count but a small thinge to do vnhappely without punysshment. Wherfore they now dayly encrease their cruelty agaynst you/ if ye do nat herafter take from them the power and authorite therof: And specially contynuall besynes without ende shall remayne vnto you whan ye se playnly that other ye must be seruauntes or bonde men: or els ye must retaygne and defende your lyberte by strength of your handes.

For what hope or trust is there of faithfulnes or of concorde bytwene you and them? None surely. For their mynde is vtterly set to be lordes ouer you: and ye on the other part wyll nedes be fre and at lyberte. They be extremely inclyned and dysposed to do wrong and iniury vnto you. And ye labour to withstande them vtterly. And brefely to speke they take the frendes and felowes of our empyre for enmyes. But our mortall ennemis they take for their felowes and frendes. But ye wolde withstande this cursed and vnkynde behauour. Wherfore can ye suppose that peace/ loue/ or frendshyp can be amonge people so contrary of myndes and dyspocityon? For these consideratyons I warne and exhort you that ye suffre nat so great myschefe to escape vnpunysshed. This offence is nothynge lyke to the robbyng of the common tresour/ nor to the spoyling of money by extorcyon from the felowes and frendes of our empyre. Which dedes (howbeit they be greuous and in maner intollerable) neuertheles by custome and vse of the same they ar reputed for small fautes and for nought. But this dede is moch more greuous and vtterly intollerable. For the authorite of the senate is betrayed to our moost cruell and fyers ennemy Iugurth/ your empyre is falsly betrayed to other mennes handes and possession. The commen wele hath ben put to sale to Iugurth by the senatours bothe at home in our cyte/ and also in our army by Calphurnius the consull. Insomoche that yf examination be nat made herof: and if they be nat punysshed which be culpable and fautie herin. What thyng shall remayn vnto vs but that we must passe our lyfe vnder obeydience and bondage of them which thus haue done/ and vs shall thei kepe in subiection as yf they were kynges? For what thynge longeth to a kynge/ saue to parfourm his wyll and pleasure/ be it good or yll without any resystence or punysshment of any man? Do nat these estates thus without any contradyction/ nat withstandyng that it is in your power to withstand them if ye wyll?

191 dyspocityon?] *punctus* A B C   201 possession.] *punctus* B; *no punct.* A   203 consull.] *colon* A B C   210 man?] *punctus* A B C   thus] *om.* C   211 wyll?] *punctus* A B C

Nor certes worthy | cytesyns I do nat thus exhort you to coueyt rather f. 30r that your cytesyns shulde do yll than well. But I speke to thintent/ that ye shulde nat so fauour and forbere a fewe iniust and yll dysposed men: that the vtter dystruction of all good men shulde procede of suche indyscrete fauour: And also namely in a cyte or a commen wayle it is moche better and more tollerable to forgete the rewarde of good dedes/ than the punysshment of yll dedes. For a good man seyng his goodnes nat rewarded nor set by/ he dothe but onely withdrawe his owne kyndnes: but an yll man nat punysshed/ is the more bolde and cursed: And moreouer if suche as be mysdoers be punysshed/ at the last their nombre shal be abated and decresed/ and yf there be fewe vniust men/ the les wrong is done. And he to whom no wrong is done nedeth nat to call for socoure nor helpe. Thus it is better to leaue a good dede vnrewarded/ than an yll dede vnpunysshed.

¶How Memmius induced the peple of Rome by the sayd orison: so that Cassius was sent for Iugurth to bring hym to Rome to declare and acuse the supporters of his dedes. ¶The .xx. chapter.

[32] Memmius counsellyng and inducynge often tymes by these wordes and other lyke/ at last dyde so moch that Lucius Cassius/ one of the chefe .x. iuges of Rome shuld be sende to Iugurth and assure him of his lyfe/ and to come and returne in saue garde vpon promes and fayth of all the hole commontie of Rome. And vpon this promes to bring him to Rome to thintent that by his owne wordes and confession of the trauth/ the falshode and couetyse of Calphurnius the consull/ of Scaurus and of other which had ben corrupted by hym before by money and rewardes myght be euydently proued and knowen.

¶Of the behauour of the soudyours and other which were laft in Numidy whyle Scaurus the consull was at Rome. ¶The .xxi. chap.

[32. 2] Whyle these thynges were in hand and done at Rome/ in f. 30v meane tyme the chefe of the soudyours/ whiche Calphurnius had left behynde hym in Numidy folowed the maners and beha[u]our of their captayn and dyde many vngoodly and myscheuous dedes. Some of them were so corrupt with golde that they delyuerd agayne to Iugurth the olyphantes/ which he had gyuen to Calphurnius what tyme the peace was graunted and trues/ first taken bytwene them. Some other

219 by/] *virgule suppl.* 224 it is] is it C

Ch. 20 5 lyke/] *virgule suppl.* (*end of line* A B) 7 lyfe/] *virgule from* B

Ch. 21 5 behauour] B; behauoure C; behanour A 6 vngoodly] vngodly C

solde to Iugurth the traytours which had fledde from hym vnto the Romayns army: And other some spoyled and robbed the people of Numidy/ which had all redy peace with the Romayns/ and had submytted themselfe. So great and shamefull was the vyolence of couetyse which had infected their myndes as if it had ben an vniuersall contagion of pestylence. But now wyll I returne to my mater where I left of before concernyng Cassius the iuge and his vyage to Numidy for to bring Iugurth vnto Rome.

¶How Iugurth came to Rome with Cassius and how he behaued hymselfe there. The .xxii. chap.

[32. 5] Cayus Memmius in name of all the commens gaue commaundement to Cassius (accordyng to the ordynaunce inacted) to spede hym towarde Numidy: And to bydde Iugurth come to Rome vnder suerty and condycion before rehersed. Whan the estates which knewe themselfe culpable vnderstode of this they were marueylusly abasshed. But whan Cassius was come to Iugurth/ nat withstandyng that he was ferefull of his part/ and had no confydence in his cause for asmoche as he knewe hymselfe fauty in his owne conscience: yet Cassius aduysed hym and induced hym: bycause he had yelded hymselfe/ to come vnto Rome: without he wolde rather proue the Romayns strength and vyolence than their mercy and pyte: and moreouer the sayd Cassius promysed also his owne fayth and trouth that yf he wolde come to Rome and answere truly to all suche thynges as there shulde be demaunded of hym/ he shuld safely go and come without any impedyment. Cassius had so good a name at
f. 31r Rome that Iugurth had as moch confy| dence in his fayth and promes alone as in the promes or assurance of the hole cytie.

[33] And so at last Iugurth consented to go to Rome with Cassius. Wherfore to enduce the Romayns to the more pyte he arayed hymselfe in rude aparell agaynst his honour royall moche vyle and myserable: and so with Cassius came to Rome nat as a kyng/ but poorly and with a small company. And nat withstandyng that his mynde was moch confermed/ assured/ and bolded: by the confort of them which he had corrupted with rewardes before/ vnder whose defence and supportacyon he had commytted so moche cruelty/ yet he behaued hym so with his gyftes of newe as sone as he was come to

13 submytted] yelded B C 16 of] *om.* B C

Ch. 22 5 towarde] towardes C 7 they] *om.* C 18 Rome] that tyme B C 26 vnder] *om.* C

Rome/ that he induced by great rewardes a lorde of Rome named Cayus Bebius/ one of the protectours of the commenty to be supporter and mayntener of his cause among the other mo. By whose dyshonest and vnmesurable couetise he hoped assuredly to be defended agaynst the lawe from all punysshmentes due vnto his demerites. But the commenty of Rome was vyolent and sore wrathe with Iugurth/ some commaunded to haue hym to prison and there to kepe hym in bandes: And other some wolde that acordyng to the lawe punysshement of dethe shulde be taken of hym as of their mortall ennemy/ yf he wold nat shortly confesse and discouer the felowes/ partiners/ and supporters of his cruell dedes. Caius Memmius heryng herof called togyder the commenty and alayed the mocyon and wrath of their myndes/ apeasyng their vnauysed rancour. And requirynge them to kepe the fayth and trouth of the cyte (which they [had] promysed to Iugurthe) clere/ inuyolate/ and vndefyled. Thus dyde Memmius exhort them as he which more regarded and set more by the conseruacion of the dygnite of Rome/ than by the parformyng and satysfyeng the wrath and yre of the rude commens. But whan sylence was made among all the assemble: anone Iugurth was brought forth before them all. Memmius than began to speke to hym demurely rehersynge and openly recountyng how he had corrupt the estates of Rome with his treasoure/ and cruelly agaynst right had done many abhomynable dedes at Rome/ and also in Numidy agaynst the kyng Micipsa and his sonnes/ as slayne Adherball and Hiempsall/ falsly dysceyued the kyng Micipsa and wasted the kyngdom of Numidy. And how beit (sayd Memmius) that the Romayns knewe well his supporters yet they wold moost of all that Iugurth shulde openly dyscouer and accuse them hymselfe. Wherfore he desyred hym truely to confesse the names of them | by whose supportacion he was so f. 31v
bolde to commyt so many immoderate and cruell dedes. Sayng that if he wolde so do and confesse and dysclose the trouth/ than myght he haue great trust and confydence in the fauour/ clemence/ and mercy of the peple of Rome. But yf he wolde nat so do/ he shulde do no profet by his sylence to the noble men of Rome which had supported him: And also he shulde be dystructyon and vndoyng of hymselfe/ and of his ryches also.

29 he induced by great rewardes] by his great rewardes he induced B; ~ reward ~ C 32 hoped] trusted B C 33 the] *om.* B C 34 vyolent] violently B C 35 with] agaynst B C 37 be] by B hym] them C 41 myndes/] *virgule suppl.* 42 the[2]] *om.* C had] B C; *om.* A 52 Hiempsall/] *virgule suppl.* (*end of line* A B) 59 trouth/] *virgule suppl.* 60 clemence] clemency C

[34] On this poynt Memmius ceassed his wordes and helde hym styll. Anone Iugurth was commaunded of the commenty to make answere. But whan he was reddy to haue spoken/ one Caius Bebius whom he had corrupt before with treasour (as I haue made mencyon before) commaunded hym to holde his pease. In somoche that howbeit the people sore moued with dyspleasure put hym in feare with exclamation agaynst hym with angry countenances/ and often violently rennynge vpon hym/ and with other tokens of yre and dyspleasure. Neuerthelesse for all this the frowarde counsell of Bebius ouercame their thretnyng/ in somoch that Iugurth wolde nothyng speke nor dysclose. And thus the people had in derysion and abused/ departed from the congregation and assemble. Thus the myndes of Iugurth/ of Calphurnius/ and of other their partyners were than inhansed and increased in boldnesse: which were troubled and moche ferefull before/ whan Iugurth was first sende for and brought to be examyned.

¶How Iugurth encreased his crueltie at Rome and renued his murdre in sleayng an other noble man of the stocke of Micipsa by occasion wherof he was constrayned to departe from Rome/ and the batayle renewed agayne of hole. ¶The .xxiii. chapyter.

[35] At the same season was a gentleman at Rome named Massiua/ borne of the countre of Numidy/ which was the sonne of Gulussa/ and neuewe to the good kyng Massinissa. This Massiua was agaynst Iugurth in the stryfe and dyscencion bytwene Adherbal and hym/ whan the towne of Cirtha was yelded/ and Adherball slayne. f. 32r Wherfore he trusted nat Iugurth/ | but to saue hymselfe fledde from Numidy vnto Rome. Now was a lorde at Rome named Albinus/ which was creat consull with an other partyng felawe named Minucius/ the next yere after Calphurnius. This Albinus came to Massiua/ and counsayled hym (bycause he was of the stocke of Massinissa) to greue Iugurth/ asmoch as he coude/ with enuy/ feare/ and dysplesure for his offences and cruelty: And by peticyon to desyre of the senatours the admynistration of the kyngdome of Numidy. Albinus gaue to hym this counsell/ for asmoche as he hymselfe was desyrous of batayle. Wherfore he wold moch rather that euery thynge

67 one] *om.* B C 68 corrupt before] corrupted B C (as I . . . before)] *brackets from* B 76 Thus] So B C

Ch. 23 10 Iugurth/] *virgule from* B 12 partyng] partayninge C 16 offences and cruelty: And] *from* B; offences: and cruelty. And A

were moued with trouble/ than pacified or at rest. Than was it a custome at Rome/ that the consull shulde haue a partyng felawe/ and bytwene them the prouynces belongyng to Rome shulde be deuyded. Thus in departyng of the prouynces/ the contrey of Numidy fell to Albinus/ and the countrey of Macidony to his felawe Minutius. Shortly after Massiua began to moue the mater to the senatours towchyng administratyon of the kyngdom of Numidy. Iugurth hering of this had nat so great trust in his mater nor to his frendes as he had before: For some of them withdrewe their selfe for knowlege of their fautes/ and other some fore fere of yll name and fame/ or rumour of the people. Wherfore Iugurth consydering this required Bomylchar/ one of his most nere and trusty frendes to prouyde and to hyer by gyftes and rewardes a company to sle the sayd Massiua/ and that as priuely as coude be done. But yf it coude nat priuely be done/ than to slee hym openly by one meane or other.

Bomilchar shortly went abo[u]t the commaundement of Iugurth/ and anon prouyded men and hyred suche as were mete for suche a dede: and commaunded them to espy and serche his wayes/ his goynges/ and commynges/ and to wayet a season and place conuenyent to parforme their enterprise. But afterwarde whan he sawe his tyme he prepared to execute this treason. Wherfore one of them which were ordayned and assigned to this murdre/ assayled Massiua rasshely: with small prouysion or auysement/ and slewe hym vnware. But he whiche dyde the dede anone was taken and brought before the iudges. The people in great nombre desyred and at last constrayned hym to tell by whose counsell he dyd that myscheuous dede/ and specially Albinus the consull/ coarted hym therto. The murderer anone confessed the treuthe and declared howe he had done it at the instygation and counsell of Bomylchar: And nat withstandynge that the same Bomylchar came | to Rome/ vnder the sauegarde and f. 32v
assuraunce of the faythe of the commenty as dyde Iugurthe/ yet he was iudged gyltie of the dede/ considerynge that he was counselloure therto: and nat accordynge to the commen lawe/ but after very equite and good conscience. But Iugurth consyderyng hymselfe culpable in the same faute/ yet wolde by no meane confesse nor knowlege hymselfe fawtie/ tyll tyme that he vnderstode and sawe that the enuy and dyspleasure which was taken agaynst this dede passed all

20 it] *om.* B C 23 prouynces/] *virgule from* B 27 nor] not C 29 fame/] *virgule suppl.* 35 about] B C; abont A 43 anone] *no punct.* B; *colon* A 45 dede/] *virgule from* B 49 the[2]] *om.* C

his fauoure and rewardes which he had gyuen at Rome/ so that at last in his gyftes he founde no socoures nor ayde. But howebeit in the first actyon or accusement which was layed agaynst hym/ he had brought in and layd .l. suerties of his frendes for hym and all other of his retynue that he shulde purge hymselfe of euery thyng which was or shulde be layed agaynst him/ yet thought he better to prouyde for the protectyon of his kyngdome than for the helth of his pledges or suerties. And this consydringe he priuely sent Bomylchar away from Rome vnto Numidy/ dredynge that yf condyng and worthy punysshement were taken of Bomylchar at Rome/ than the other commentie of his royalme at home wolde drede to be obedyent to hym. And anone after Bomylchar was departed Iugurth hymselfe fledde also from Rome/ after him commaunded of the senatours to depart from Italy as ennemy to the Romayns/ and their empyre. But whan he was departed a lytell without Rome: it is sayed that he loked often backewarde behynde hym spekyng secretely to hymselfe/ but at the last he spake playnly in audyence that they whiche were assystent myght here hym and sayed. O noble and famous cytie corrupt and accloyed with infect cytezyns/ whose couetyse is so insaciable that they wyll profer the forth to sale/ and shortly thou shuldest be solde and perysshe/ yf thy rulers coude fynde any man that wolde bye the/ and gyue money for the.

¶Howe Albynus consull of Rome renewed the warre agaynst Iugurth/ and at last returned agayne to Rome leauyng his brother Aulus in Numidy/ with the army in his rowme. The .xxiiii. chapter.

f. 33r **[36]** In the mean season Albinus whiche was create consull next after Calphurnius renewed the warre agaynst Iugurth/ and without taryeng: caused vytayls/ wages and all other thynges necessary/ expedyent/ and belongyng to soudyours: to be conueyed spedely into Affrike. And he anon hymselfe in all hast toke his vyage thyderwarde also/ and so forth to Numidy. In which voyage he made more hasty expedycion to thintent to fynisshe the batayle with Iugurth/ other by force of armes/ or els constrayning hym to yelde hymselfe/ or by some other meanes what so euer myght be founde/ namely before the tyme of electyon of newe consuls/ which tyme was

58 socoures] socour C 62 him/ yet] *from* B; him. yet A 62–3 prouyde . . . suerties] prouide for the proteccion for his pledges or suerties C 66 than] lest B C 68 Rome/] *virgule suppl.* 71 hym] *om.* C

Ch. 24 1 agaynst] agayng B; of C 4 after] *om.* C 5 Iugurth/] *virgule suppl.* (*end of line* A B) 6 caused] causeth B C 9 voyage] vyage B C 10 batayle] warre B C 12 founde/] *virgule suppl.*

nat longe thens to come. But contrariwyse Iugurth prolonged euery thing by one cause or other. As fast as Albinus went forwarde/ so fast Iugurth founde impedymentes/ somtyme he promysed to yelde hymselfe/ and somtyme fayned hymselfe afrayed. One whyle he fledde from the army of Albynus whan it was nere hande to him: And anone after lest his men shulde mystrust by dysconfort or dyspayre/ he boldely withstode and defended hymselfe manly. And thus in prolongyng the tyme: somtyme with warre and somtyme with peace/ he abused and mocked the consull/ wherfore some were which suspected that Albynus was nat ignorant of the counsell of Iugurth/ but consentyng to hym by fauoure: And for asmoche as at the begynnynge he was so fyers/ hasty/ and dyligent: it was suspected that he droue forth the tyme nowe rather by falshode and gyle than by cowardyse. But after that the tyme was passed and the day of electyon of newe consules aproched and came fast on. The consull Albynus ordayned his brother named Aulus/ to be in his stede as capytayne/ and ruler in the army: and he hymselfe departed towarde Rome/ to be at electyon of the newe consuls/ as the lawe requyredde.

¶How Aulus and the Romayne army were disconfyted of Iugurth: and how peace was graunted to hym by Aulus: and to what shame the Romayns were put by rasshe foly of the same capytayne Aulus. ¶The .xxv. chapter.

[37] In the same season was the commen wayle moche troubled with f. 33v
varyaunce and debate/ which was betwene the protectours of the commentie. For of them one named Lucullus and an other Annius laboured to contynue and kepe styll their office/ and agaynst the ordynaunce of the lawe to contynue more than one yere. Wherfore the other which were partyng felawes in offyce with them laboured with all theyr myght the contrary to resyst them and to mayntayne the olde constytucion/ ordynaunce and custome. This dyscention and debate letted the electyon of the newe consuls all that yere. Aulus whom Albynus had left with the army in Numidy as his lewtenaunt: herd of this prolonging of the tyme and was brought in great hope to wynne great honour or treasour. Wherfore in the colde moneth of Ianuary he called the souldyours forth of their tentes to execute the batayle with

14 thens] *om.* B C 26 falshode and gyle] craft B C by[2]] *om.* B C 27 that] *om.* B C 29 be] remayne B C

Ch. 25 5 commen wayle] commen wayle at Rome B C 6 which was] *om.* B C 8 office/] *virgule suppl.* 12 constytucion/] *virgule from* B

Iugurth without more delay. Outher dyde he thus shortly to make an ende of the batayle in his tyme/ and therby to wynne honour/ or els with his army to putte Iugurth in feare (so that to haue peace) he shulde redeme the same of Aulus with great treasoure. Aulus concludynge on this purpose: spedde hym so fast with his soudyours makyng dayly great iournayes (nat withstandynge the sharpnesse of wynter) that at last he came to a towne in Numidy/ named Suthull: in which towne the tresours of Iugurth were layed. This towne with walles/ waters/ and mountaygnes of nature was strongly defended: for without the walles buylded on the extreme of a mountaygne broken on the forefronte was a great playne fenne/ or marrayse grounde: all ouercouered with mudde/ and standyng wynter water. In somoche that what for the sharpnesse of the wynter season: and what for naturall defence of the place/ this towne coude by no meanes be well besyged nor taken. Yet this nat withstandyng Aulus to encrease fere to Iugurth/ and for the blynde desyre which he had to wynne the towne/ in maner of dyssimulatyon assayled the same and made pauayses about the walles of sheldes conioyned lyke vynes/ wherunder his men myght fyght with lesse damage or paryll. Than made he a dyche or trenche rounde about the towne with great hepes of erth casten vpon the sydes of the same/ to the entent that no socoures shulde entre into them: nor they escape forth at their pleasurs. And
f. 34r finally he made redy euery thyng which belonged or was | necessary to besygyng of a cyte or towne.

[38] But Iugurth anon perceyuede the vayne and folysshe behauoure of Aulus/ and craftely encreased by polycy the madnes of hym/ sendyng often embassadours vnto hym to requyre in derysion that he wold desyst and leue besyging of the towne/ and intreatyng hym of peace mekely. But in the meane tyme Iugurth himselfe in maner as yf he wolde nat intermell with Aulus/ ledde his army by wodes/ forestes/ by streat passages/ by hyls and dales/ and by backways: causyng Aulus to suspect that he was adradde of hym: And finally he enduced Aulus to truste after some apoyntement. And thus Iugurth with his men fleyng alway into desertes and hydde places gaue confort to Aulus and encreased his corage by suche auoydyng. In somoch that at last Aulus gaue vp the sygyng of the towne of Suthull: And with his hole power hastely pursued Iugurth as fleyng from him for drede into places

19 honour/] *virgule suppl.* 27 extreme] heyght B C 34 towne/] *virgule suppl.* 38 socoures] soucours B; socour C 41 of a cyte or towne] of suche a towne B C 45 towne/] *virgule from* B 48 streat] streyte C backways] bacways B; bywaies C

vnknowen [to hym] and his [men]. Thus was the treason of Iugurth more hydde from Aulus/ wherfore he made the lesse prouysion therfore. In the mean season Iugurth by subtyll messangers attempted the Romayne army day and nyght inducynge them to consent to betray their felawes[. T]he capytayns/ and vndercaptayns: anone for lucre consented to him. Some in tyme of batayle to forsake and betray their owne company and to fight on the part of Iugurth. And other whiche wolde nat graunt to so foule a dede as to fight agaynst their owne company/ he exhorted and induced them whan the trumpettes shulde blowe to batayle to leue their places and array: And depart from their company without stroke on one syde or other.

Whan euery thyng was brought to his purpose and accorded to his requestes: Than about mydnight he stale priuely towarde the tentes of the Romayns: and sodenly with a great company of Numidyans/ compased them about on euery syde and assayled them fiersly. The Romayne soudyours which were with Aulus/ thus vnwardly inuaded: were meruelously abasshed and amased/ for the vnwont and sodayn feare of this treason. Some of the moost noble hertes: with great courage drewe to them their harnes/ and resysted their ennemies valyantly: fully assured and prefixed to dye lyke men: yf fortune shulde graunt them none other meanes to escape that instant danger. Some other as cowardes hydde themselfe in caues and other secrete places/ yf they myght any fynde. The boldest and moost vsed to such chaunces conforted their felawes which were ferefull and vnexpert of such chaunces of warre. Howbeit non of them all was so bold nor so well assured of him| selfe/ but that he was both in great drede and f. 34v danger. And no maruayle/ for in euery place and on all sydes about them they were inuyroned in compase with great vyolence and plentious nombre of their enmys hyd vnder darknes of the nyght and cloudes which vtterly obscured the sterre light. Their paryll was indyfferent and doutfull whyther they fled or abode the batayle. For deth was instant and depended ouer their hedes euery way: and other hope nor esperaunce was none/ saue in dethe ineuytable. So that finally it was vncertayne vnto them whether it was better or more sure to fle or to abyde to their auenture. But of that company which Iugurth had corrupted with rewardes as we haue sayd before/ one

55 to hym and his men] B; ~ him ~ C; and his A 59 felawes. The] *virgule* A B; *comma* C 70 vnwardly] vnwarly B C 81 maruayle/] *virgule from* B 83 vnder] vnder the C 84 sterre] sterres B; starres C 85 whyther] whether C 86–7 other hope nor] either hope or C 87 none/] *virgule from* B in] *om.* B C 89 to^3] *om.* C

bende or cohort of Lomberdes and two turmes that is to say .lx. Thracyens and a fewe rude and commen soudyours betrayed the Romayns and went ouer to Iugurth. Also the centuryon which was assigned to be captayn ouer them which were commytted to fight about the first standard of the thyrd legion drewe him and his company asyde and suffred their enmies to entre into the myddes of the hoost on that syde which they had taken to defend. Thus all the Numidyens brake in on that syde without any resystence. And so at conclusion the Romayns had a foule flight and a shamfull dysconfyture/ insomoch that they trusted more to their fete than to theyr handes or armour: And many of them to ren lighter thrue away fro them their armour and harnes/ and toke the top of an hyll which was nere therby and there taryed. The company of Iugurth/ what for spoyling of the Romayns tentes and derknes of the nyght had les honour of vyctorie and suffred many of the Romayns to escape. On the next day after Iugurth and Aulus came vnto comunycation togyder. Than said Iugurth to Aulus that nat withstandyng that he had hym and his army which were left alyue sure ynough compased and enuyroned with wepen and hunger so that they coude nat escape: and how beit it was in his power to oppres hym and all his. Neuertheles he remembred well ynough the incertayn causes of mannes besynesse and wold nat be to hym cruell nor vncurtes/ so that he wolde make with him a bond of peas and no more contend agaynst hym in batell/ on this condycion that all the soudiours of Aulus shulde do obesance vnto hym/ and passe vnder a spere in token of subiectyon/ and so without more damage depart out of the countre of Numidy within the space of .x. dayes next after. But howbeit this composicyon and condycions were hard/ greuous/ and full of shame and misery: and worthy to be punysshed of the senatours yf Aulus agreed to them. Neuerthelesse their myndes so wauered for drede of deth that at last the composicyon and agrement was concluded and agreed at the wyll and pleasure of Iugurth vpon the sayd condycions.

f. 35r ¶What sorowe and heuynes was at Rome: and how they demeaned themselfe in the cite after that tidynges herof were broght thyder. The .xxvi. cha.

91 .lx.] three score C 98 so] *om.* B C 101 or] and C 101–2 fro them] *om.* B C 102 armour and] *om.* C harnes/ and] B C; harnes. And A 106 vnto] to B C 109 escape] escape hym B C 111 causes] chances B C 112 vncurtes/] *virgule suppl.* 116 subiectyon/] *virgule suppl.* 118 hard] harde, and C

Ch. 26 2 herof] *om.* C

[39] Whan the Romayns vnderstode of this at Rome/ all the cytie was fylled with drede/ sorowe/ lamentacyon/ and mournyng. Some bewayled the worshyppe of thempyre as lost by that shamefull composicyon: And other vncustomed to suche besynesse of batayle and nat knowyng nor consydringe the varyable mutabylite of chaunces of warre feredde the losse of their lybertie/ of their cyte/ and of all their empyre. They all were wrothe and vtterly dyspleased with Aulus/ cause of this subiection and shamefull composicion. But namely they which had ben good warryours in their dayes were dyspleased with hym moost of all: whan they consydred that he beyng armed and well apoynted to batayle rather sought meanes to escape from dethe by suche shamefull and bonde composicyon than manly abyding the extremyte of batayle to haue delyuered hymselfe and his company: or els valyantly to haue dyed with honoure. But the consull Albynus/ hymselfe dreded sore for these thynges consydring that for his brothers faute in tyme to come he shulde nat auoyde the dysplesure of the senatours and commens of Rome. For as he coniectured all his brothers dedes shuld redounde to his dyshonour and paryll/ bycause he had lymited hym in Numidy in his stede to be captayn of the army in his absence. Wherfore (these thynges duely aduysed) he went to the senatours desyring them to take counsell and aduysement whyther they wolde approbate and allowe the sayd composicion bytwene his brother Aulus and Iugurth: or els nat. But he knewe ryght well before that the senatours wolde nat conferme the same. Wherfore (in meane tyme whyle they were counselling) he elect soudyours for supplement to fulfyll and parforme agayne the army whiche was in Affrike/ and sore demynisshed. For many of them were slayne by Iugurth and his company. Wherfore Albinus raysed vp socours of suche as were nere to the costes of Rome/ and frendes to thempire: as Latinyans and Italyans with other nacyons. Of these he raysed as many as he myght/ and assembled them togyder by all meanes which he coude deuyse to fornysshe and augment his army. At conclusyon the senatours decreed in their counsell that no | bonde f. 35^{v}
of peace nor compposityon myght be allowed without their consent and without the aduyse and commaundement of the commen people also: as ryght and reason requyred. And thus was the sayd compposityon of Aulus abrogate/ as thynge presumed without consent or commaundement of the senatours or commens. But whan the consull Albinus had

6 bewayled] bewalyng C 18 these thynges] this thynges B; this thinge C
27 before] *om.* B C 37 allowed] confirmed B C 40 as] as a C

ordayned and prepared supplement of his army (as sayd is) he was prohybet and letted by the protectours of the commenty: Insomoch that he was nat suffred by them to conuey such company as he had raysed into Affrike/ with hym as he intended to repayre and fornysshe the army which there remayned. Wherfore he spedde hymselfe forth into Affrike dysapoynted of his purpose with a small company of men/ of his owne retynue. The army of the Romayns which he before had commytted to Aulus his brother: acordyng to the apoyntment with Iugurth/ was departed forth of Numidy. And to pas forth the wynter/ taryed in a prouynce of Affrike which was subget to thempyre of Rome. Whan Albinus the consull was arryued and come thyder: his mynde ardently was kyndled with desyre to pursue Iugurth/ and to remedy the yl wyll and dyspleasure which the commens at Rome had agaynst Aulus his brother. Neuertheles whan he knewe the maners and yll behauyour of the soudyours: of whom some were fled tretourously to Iugurth (as is sayd before) and some by sufferaunce of their captayne were infected and corrupted with ouermoch pleasure/ dyssolute lyberty/ and voluptuous lyuinge: this consydring he concluded (as the case requyred) to do nothyng for a season: and to attempt no maistry: but to passe forth the wynter with his army without remouyng or puttynge hymselfe in ieopardy or paryll.

[40] ¶In the mean season whyle Albinus and his army soiourned in the prouynce of Affrike tyll the winter were ouerpassed. At Rome was one named Caius Manlius elect and lymited protectour of the commen people whiche anon after he was set in authorite: assembled the commens: and desyred and counsayled them that inquisicyon myght be made of all such by whose supportacyon and counsell Iugurth had dyspysed and set at nought the ordynaunces decreed of the senatours. And agaynst them which had restored agayne to Iugurth the elyphantes which he had delyuerd to Calphurnius at the first composicion and apoyntment which was made with him. And also agaynst them which had receyued any money or other rewardes of Iugurth whyle they were embassadours or captains of armies ayenst
f. 36r h[y]m: send forth by the Romains. And finally | the same inquisicion also was extended agaynst all such as had made any pactions/ apoyntmentes/ or promyses of peace or of warre with ennemies of thempyre without generall consent of the senatours or commens.

69 by] *om.* C 72 he] Iugurth B C 76 hym] þ *used for* y *in* A

¶Whan this inquirie was moued: many of the senatours and noble men of Rome knewe themselfe culpable in the forsayd artycles. And other some douted sore of perels for to come bycause of the yl wyll and malyce which the partie of the commens confederat had agaynst them. Wherfore sith the same noble men myght nat well resyst the examynation of these artycles openly: but of necessyte they must agre therto: other els knowlege themselfe (by their resystence) gylte in the same: therfore they prepared impedyment priuely agaynst such inquisicions by their frendes: but specially by the felawes of thempyre which were confederate with the Romayns/ as Italyans and Latinyans. The princes of these natyons and such other lyke gaue counsell to the senatours which were nat fauty in the premysses/ and also to the commenty: that in suche a troublous/ besy/ and peryllous season no suche examynations shulde be made nor procede forwarde to effect: for drede of many inconuenyences which of the same myght ryse bytwene the noble men and commens. But (this nat withstandyng) it is a merueylous thyng and in maner incredyble to speke of: how besy and dyligent the commens were to haue the same inquysicion to procede/ and to be broght to effect: and that rather for hatered which they had agaynst the noble men (agaynst whom the sayd inquisycion was ordayned) than for any good wyll or care/ which they had to the commen wele. So great pleasure and desyre of varyance was among them. Wherfore whyle the remenant of the noble men were sore troubled with fere and drede. Marcus Scaurus which was before sent into Affrike with Calphurnius (as I haue sayd) prouyded for himselfe in crafty maner as I shall nowe declare. Whyle the commenty was mery and ioyeous of this examynation and many of the company of Scaurus that knew themselfe fauty fledde for fere. And the hole cyte was in moch drede/ Manlius obtayned his peticyon and wyll of the commente. In somoch that anone were orday[n]ed thre noble men commyssioners to examyne the thre artycles before rehersed and here insuyng of whom the first was of them which counselled Iugurth to dyspyce the decreis of the senatours and that toke money or rewardes of hym. The seconde was of them that solde agayne to Iugurth the forsayd elyphantes and the Numidyens that left Iugurth commyng on the Romayns syde. And the | thyrd examynation was of them which f. 36v
had made any apoyntment of peace or warre with the enmis of Rome as was Iugurth. But nat withstandyng that [Scaurus] was culpable in the

95 and] and the B; and the C withstandyng)] *closing bracket om.* A 100 care] fauour B C 107 drede/ Manlius] drede and Manlius A B C 108 ordayned] ordayued A 116 Scaurus] Calphurnius A B C

same asmoch as any other of the noble men. Neuerthelesse he shyfted so for himselfe that he was elect to be one of the examynours or commyssioners to make inquisycion of these thre poyntes rehersed. The inquisycion proceded to effect and was handled and put in execucion with moche vyolence and sharply after the commen rumour and pleasure of the commenty. Thus the peple seyng their pleasure fulfylled/ at that tyme began to be proude and stately therof in likewyse as the estates had ben in foretyme of their power and lordshyp. But here wyll I make a smal dygression fro my purpose and tell wherof this varyance and dyscorde bytwene the commens and noble men first proceded.

¶Wherof the dyscorde and takyng of parties bytwene the noble men and commens of Rome/ had first begynnyng. ¶The .xxvii. chapter.

[41] This maner of deuisyon of the commenty from the estates of Rome. This dyscorde and takyng of parties bytwene them: and this inordynate custom of all other inconuenyences/ began among them but a fewe yeres before this tyme by meane of ouer moche rest and ydlenes: by superfluous habundance of richesse/ voluptuosyte/ and of other worldely delectacyons: which many count and repute for moost chiefe pleasures of this lyfe. For before the dystruction of Carthage/ the senatours and comenty of Rome treated and gouerned the commen wele bytwene them peasably in loue and concorde. So that amonge the cytezyns was no stryfe nor debate/ for laude/ excellence/ for dygnite/ nor for great dominyon. The drede which they had of their ennemies made them ware and kept them in good maners/ causyng them to gouern their cyte with good and vertues instytutes/ without varyance/ without robery/ without oppression/ without slaughter nor other lyke cruell tyrannies. But whan Carthage was ouercome anone was expulsed fere from their myndes: and voluptuosite/ wantonnes/ and pride (which ar greatly loued in welth and prosperite) anone entred their myndes[. S]o that they desyred peace
f. 37r whan they had | warre. But whan the warre was ended: and that they had peace and ydlenes after their owne desyre: their peace and rest was more sharpe/ more bytter/ more intollerable/ and more peryllous to them than the warre was before. For the estates began to tourne their dygnite and worshyppe/ into immoderate affectyon of great lord-

123 that] *om.* C 125 fro] for C

Ch. 27 14 ware] warre B maners/] *virgule suppl.* 20 myndes. So] *colon* A B C 22 desyre:] *colon from* B

shyppe and domynation. And the commen people began to tourne their lybertie into lust and pleasure. Euery man prouyded and drewe to hymselfe/ robbyng and reauynge without measure/ from the commen wele. Thus was the commentie abstract and deuyded from the lordes. So was the cyte deuyded into two partes. And the commen wele which was in the myddes bytwene them on euery syde was pylled/ robbed/ and vtterly wasted of them both: on both sydes.

But the power of the noble men and of their party was more myghtie than the power of the commens. For all the estates were all togyder assembled/ conioyned/ and vnyed. But the commens were dyspersed and spredde abrode into dyuerse places and companyes gettyng their lyueng with labour of their handes and swet of their bodyes. So euery thyng was gouerned both in peace and in warre at pleasure and auyse of a fewe priuate noble men. The commen treasoure/ the prouynces/ maistershyppes/ offices/ trybutes/ worshyppe/ tryumphes/ and all other thynges longyng to honour or auantage were onely in handes and possession of the same fewe noble men. But the symple commen peple was weryed and oppressed with pouerty/ with batayle/ and warfare. Euer in ieopardy/ and neuer in auantage nor lucre. For the captayns with a fewe other noble men pulled such prayes as were taken in batayle onely to their synguler auantage and behofe. But in the mean season the parentes and small chyldren of the soudyours were driuen from their dwellyng places by the sayd noble men: echone of them by that lorde vnto whom they dwelled nerest. And so the might and power of soche noble men conioyned with immoderate couetyse assayled/ defyled/ wasted/ and dystroyed euery thyng without good maner/ without measure or moderatyon: hauyng no respect nor consyderatyon of any thyng belongyng to goodnes or vertue: tyll they had so farforth proceded that at conclusion they were dystroyed and ouerthrowen by theyr owne obstinate pride and tyranny. But at last as sone as euer some of thestates were founde which remembring and consydring themselfe: set more by true and laudable glory/ than by iniust power/ and dygnite. And were moued in myndes by compassion to shewe mercy and | pyte agaynst the commentie and to socour their misery/ than f. 37v
began the cyte to be troubled and moued greuously/ for the courage of the commens was reuyued by supportacyon of such noble men: by

28 hymselfe/] *virgule suppl.* 38 both] *om.* B C at] at the C 42 in] in the C 44 with] *om.* C 48 dwellyng places] dwellyng places and possessions B C 52 maner/] *virgule suppl.* 59 myndes] mind C 61 greuously/] *virgule suppl.*

meanes wherof dyscorde and deuysion began to ryse in the cite/ as it were drye dust of the grounde raysed in a great and tempestyous wynde.

[42] For after that Tyberius Graccus/ and Caius Gracchus (whose progenytours moche encreased the commen wayle in many batayls/ but namely in the batayle of Carthage) began to restore the commentie into their olde lyberty/ and to detect the cruell mysdedes of the fewe iniuryous estates. Than all the lordes confederate: and after maner chafedde with yre assembled their felawes/ as Latynyans and some knyghtes of Rome/ which in hope of promocion left the commens party and helde with the no[b]le men. All these with such as were to them lenyng of other nacyons began to withstande the accusementes of both the sayd Graccus/ which were fauourers of the commenty: and first of all they slewe Tiberius Graccus. And after that within a fewe yeres they slewe the other brother named Caius Graccus/ whyle he was protectour of the commenty: bycause that he acordyng to lawe and ryght deuyded among the poore commente such landes as they had won in batayle of their ennemies. And at the same season the estates put to dethe also a lorde named Marcus Flaccus/ bycause he defended the commens lyberte agaynst their extorcion. But touchyng the two brethern Tyberius/ and Caius Graccus: sothly their myndes were greatly immoderate and vnmesurable in their desyre to ouercome thestates. Neuerthelesse it had be moche better to thestates to haue suffred them in their ryghtwyse tytell/ and somwhat to haue inclyned to their myndes than to haue ouercome them so vyolently and slayne them so iniu[ry]ously/ howbeit that they were ouer hasty and besy. But whan thestates had the victory of them after their desyre and pleasure/ than put they to dethe the commenty without nombre/ and many they exiled and droue out of the cite. Insomoch that from thens forth they rather encreased their crueltie and feare to the commens/ than their owne honoure or power. By which meanes many worthy cytees haue often tymes ben dystroyed whyle the estates and commens contende/ the one to ouercome the other/ by one meane or other. And whyle the party vyctoure wyll punysshe ouergreuously that party which is ouercome. But yf I wolde prepare to write of the besynesse and dedes of both the parties seriatly and

73 noble] B; nobel C; nole A 75 of both . . . fauourers] *om.* C 77 they] the C 87–8 so vyolently and slayne them] *om.* C 88 iniuryously] B; iniuriously C; iniuously A 90 pleasure/] *virgule suppl.* (*end of line* A B) 95 contende/] *virgule from* B; *after* one *in* A

dystincly. And yf I shuld touche | all the maners of the cyte acordyng f. 38r to the gretnesse of the mater and as it requyreth: sothely the tyme shuld fayle me rather than the mater. Wherfore I wyll omyt this superfluous and infenite besynes/ and retourne to my first mater and purpose touchyng this cronycle of this tyranne Iugurth.

¶How Metellus was creat consull and send by the Romayns to warre agaynst Iugurth: and of the wyse and dyscrete behauour of the same Metellus. ¶The .xxviii. chapyter.

[43] After the truse and composicion of Aulus beforesayed made with Iugurth/ and the foule and shamefull flight of the Romayne army: Quintus Metellus/ and Marcus Syllanus/ were creat and proclamed consuls of Rome/ which acordynge to the olde custome parted and deuyded the prouynces belongyng to Rome bytwene them bothe. The countrey of Numidy fell and happened to Metellus. This Metellus was a fierse man and a noble and a worthy warryour. And howbeit he fauoured the party of the noble men and was contrary to the partie of the commens: neuertheles he was of fame vndefyled and vnuyolate/ and counted of good name indyfferently on both parties. Assone as euer this Metellus entred in his office and dygnite/ he thought that euery thyng apartayning to his rowme and charge belonged as well to his partynge felawe as to hymselfe/ saue the warre of Numidy: which onely belonged to hymselfe and to his partyculer charge: Wherfore he commytted all other charges to Syllanus/ and onely sette his mynde to make prouysion for the warre agaynst Iugurth. But bycause he mistrusted the olde army whiche was in Numidy with Albynus and Aulus/ and had no confydence in the myndes of these soudyours corrupted with ydelnes and many other vyces: therfore he elected and assembled newe soudyours. And of all suche as were felawes and frendes confederate to the Romayns/ he called for helpe and socoures. He prepared and made redy armoure/ wepyn/ horse harnes/ and all other ordynaunce expedyent to warfare. And also | he ordayned f. 38v abundaunce of vytayls. And shortly to speke all thynges he ordayned which ar wont to be necessary and profytable to the varyable chaunces and incertayne accydentes/ and ieopardyes of batayle/ whiche requyreth reparacyon of many thynges and chargeable. But suche as were felawes of the empyre of Rome at instaunce and request of the senatours: and by their authorite and by the Latynians/ and many other strange kynges of their owne fre wyll sent socours to Metellus to

Ch. 28 29 batayle] warre B C; *virgule from* B 32 and[3]] *om.* C

auaunce hym in his enterpryse: And shortely to speke the hole cytie laboured with all their myght to socoure and ayde Metellus in his besynesse. Thus at last whan euery thynge was prouyded and sette in order after his pleasure and intent: than toke he his iournay into Numidy/ with great hope of all the cytezins of Rome that for his good maners: and specially for that his mynde was vnouercome with rychesse or couetyse that he shulde do more honoure to the empyre thanne his predecessours had in the warre of Numidy. For before his departynge the welth of Numidy (by couetyse of the officers of Rome) was augmented: but the welth of the Romayns wasted and demynisshedde.

[44] Whan Metellus was come to Affryke/ the army was delyuered vnto hym by Albynus: whiche army was vncrafty/ sluggysshe/ and feble: nouther able to endure paryll nor labour/ of tunge more redy/ fiers/ and hardy than of hande: which was wont to robbe/ and pyll from felawes and frendes of the empyre. But it selfe enduredde by cowardyse to be robbedde and spoyledde of ennemies of the empyre/ as a lawlesse and dysordredde company of men vngouerned and without authorite or maners. Wherfore Metellus the newe capytayne hadde moche more thought and besynesse/ for suche corrupt and vycious maners of a company so farre out of order/ than he hadde helpe or good hope of confort in the multytude of them. Thus howbeit he sawe the tyme of electyon of newe consuls drawe nere. And all yf he also vnderstode that the Romayns dayly loked after some ende of the warre. These causes nat withstandyng yet he concluded/ nat to begyn the warre tyll he hadde excercysed and vsedde the soudyours with besynesse and labour after the instructyon and custome of olde capytayns/ vsed before his tyme. For why Albynus was so astonyed with the aduersyte and myschaunce of his brother Aulus and for murdre of his hoost: that after he purposed nat to depart out of the Romayns prouynce which was in Affrike/ he kept
f. 39r the soudyours alway ydell in theyr tentes as longe as the so| mer season lasted and as long as he was in authorite/ in somoche that they chaunged no place except the corrupt sauoure of the place/ or els necessyte of vytayle constrayned them to remoue. Nor accordynge to the custome and maner of warryours amonge them was no watche: but euery man came and went at his owne pleasure/ and absented

37 into] in C 46 vnto] to C 47 feble:] *colon suppl.* 48 robbe/ and] *om.* C
57 And all yf he also] and also though he C 59 the[1]] *om.* C 63 for] for the C
65–6 the somer season] somer C 66 authorite/] *virgule suppl.*

themselfe from their standardes whan it lykedde them. The scolyons/ and pages wandred day and nyght mengledde among the horsemen and chiefe of the soudyours without any order: And many other as rouers dyspersedde abrode destroyed the countrey/ fyghtynge agaynst the small vyllages/ and nat agaynst cytees nor townes. They caryed away from the sayd vyllages prayes of catell: and the inhabytauntes ledde away also with them as prisoners with other prayes/ stryuinge togyder who myght haue moost/ and than after chaunged the sayd roberies with marchauntes for delycious and strong wynes brought and caryed from other strange countreis/ where better wyne grewe than in that countrey: and for other such delycious thynges. They solde away the whete/ and other vytayles which was delyueredde of their capytayns amonge them in commen/ and dayly they bought their bredde. And finally what euer shame or rebuke longynge to couetyse or lechery: coude outher be sayed/ done/ or ymagynedde of any man: all was vsed in that hoost. And among some: more shamefull dedes than ought to be named.

[45] But Metellus behaued hymselfe as a mighty and wyse man/ nat lesse in this dyffycultie and hardnesse/ than yf it had ben in a batayle foughten agaynst his ennemies as he whiche in myddes of so great couetyse/ voluptuosyte/ and cruelty was singulerly indued with temperaunce: and merueylous good maner vsed he/ in coartynge the same fautes. Wherfore at the first begynnynge he withdrewe and auoyded from the army at his commaundement and ordynaunce: the occasyons whiche styredde the soudyours to suche slouth/ cowardyse/ and voluptuosyte. For he commaunded vnder great payne that no person shulde be so hardy to sell amonge the soudyours nouther bredde nor other vytayle all reddy dressed saue the commen prouicyon: that the pages/ waterlaggers/ and scolyons shuld nat come nere the army/ nor folowe the same. That none of the commen and symple soudyours shulde kepe or mentayne seruaunt nor beest in their tentes nor vyage or army/ whyle they moued fro place to place. These inconuenyences first of all he redressedde and refourmed. After these amended: all other fautes he mesu| red by his wysdome/ craft/ f. 39v
and policy: refourmynge them by lytell and lytell. This done (to haue his soudyours ocupyed) he moued daylie from place to place: and that

76–7 and the . . . them] and led away with them also the inhabitantes C 78 prayes/] *virgule suppl.* 80 brought and] *om.* B C 83 commen/] *virgule suppl.* 84 what euer] what so euer C 89 in[1]] *om.* B 90 in] in the C 91 indued] induced C 92 merueylous good maner vsed he] he vsed meruelouse good maner C 102 or army] *om.* B C

nat in wayes commen and vsed/ but by harde and vnoccupyed wayes. He caused them daylie to cast dychesse and trenches about the army/ to the intent that they shulde nat waxe slouthfull/ nor vycious by ouermoche rest and ydlenesse. He ordayned often watch amonge them euery night: and he hymselfe acompanyed with his vnder captayns and heed officers often serched yf the watches were truely kept/ compasynge about the army on euery syde. Whyle they remoued and chaunged places: somtyme he was in the forwarde and amonge the first/ somtyme in the rerewarde or hynder part/ and anone in the myddes ouerseynge their order to the intent that none shulde passe out of order/ aray/ and place to them assigned. But kepe thicke togyder euery man and company about their owne standerdes: and also he ordayned that among themselfe they shulde conuey and cary their owne vytayls and armoure. And thus in short tyme he confermed and sette the army in good order rather with fayre wordes/ or rebukyng and blamynge their fautes: and prohybitynge their dysorder: than in chastysinge or punysshyng their offences with crueltie.

¶Of the behauour of Iugurth agaynst Metellus: and howe he sende embassadours to Metellus requyring vnfaynedly to yelde vp the kyngdome of Numidy to the empyre of Rome: And howe Metellus behaued hymselfe agaynst the same embassadours. ¶The .xxix. chapyter.

[**46**] In the meane season whan Iugurth vnderstode by messangers and espyes of this behauour of Metellus/ and also whan he remembred that whiche was infourmed to hym at Rome of the integryte and vndefyled name of Metellus/ which wolde nat be corrupt with money nor accloyed with brybes lyke other before: anone he beganne to mystrust his matters and to haue lasse confydence in his cause/
f. 40r thanne euer he had before. In somoche that than he began to laboure | to yelde hymselfe vnfaynedly/ and to make a true composytion with Metellus/ and the Romayns without any fyction/ gyle/ or dysceyt. Wherfore he sende embassadours to Metellus with supplycations and peticyons/ requyring humbly of Metellus to graunt to hym his owne lyfe: and the lyfe of his chyldren onely: and concernynge all other

110 often] ouermuche C 118 standerdes:] *colon from* B; *virgule* A 124 crueltie] rygour or crueltie B; rigour or crueltye C

Ch. 29 10 anone] *om.* B C 15 to Metellus] *om.* B C 16 peticyons/] *virgule from* B; *after* supplycations *in* A

thynges he wolde yelde them into handes of the Romayns. But Metellus knewe well ynough longe before this tyme by often experyence and profe that the Numydians of naturall dyspposityon were vnfaythfull/ mouable/ and vnstable of myndes: newfangledde/ and moche desyrous of newe besynesses and newelties. Wherfore he beganne with the embassadours of Iugurth/ tastyng and prouynge the mynde of eche of them/ by lytell and lytell: and seperately one by one. And whan he knewe that they somwhat inclyned to his mynde: he than promysed to them great gyftes and promocion so that they wolde do some pleasure for hym and for the senatours and people of Rome. Than at last he counsayled and desyred them to delyuer Iugurth to hym alyue specially if it myght be brought about: and yf they coude nat so/ than to delyuer hym outher quicke or deed. But whan he had made this apoyntment secretly with thembassadours deuyded in sonder one by one: than openly (that euery man myght here) he shewed to them all togyder other thynges as his pleasure was that they shuld certyfie their kyng Iugurth concernynge their embassade.

After this within fewe dayes whan he sawe his hoost moost redy and contrary to Iugurth/ he remoued his tentes and so addressed hym with his army redy in aray and went forward into Numidy: where contrary to any simylytude of warre the vyllages and cotages were full of men/ the feldes full of beestes and tylmen: and euery where was moche plenty of people yonge and olde namely rude people and tyllers of the grounde/ which had styll fledde before the army in foretyme for fere/ but at the last whan they sawe no defence nor socoure the kynges lewtenantes and all other left their townes/ vyllages/ and lodges: and went forthe to mete Metellus with all humylite/ honour/ and seruyce submyttinge themselfe to hym/ and redy to gyue to hym whete and other corne suche as they had. And to cary vytayles after his hoost to ease the soudyours and to do and parfourme all other thynges what euer they were commaunded. But for all this: [Metellus] was nat lesse dyligent nor circumspect in orderyng of his hoost/ but proceded forwarde togyder with his army in aray | redy in armoure/ f. 40v
and defended as if their ennemis had ben nere at hande/ serchynge the countrey abrode on euery syde by his espyes/ doutynge treason

18 thynges] thing C into] into the C 20 and profe] *om.* C 21 myndes] minde C 22 besynesses] besynesse B C newelties] nouelties C 25 mynde] purpose B C 26 promocion] promocions C 30 outher] eyther C 33 other thynges] *om.* C 36 Iugurth/] *virgule suppl.* (*end of line* A) 39 was] as C 42 the[1]] *om.* C 47 and[1]] *om.* C 48 Metellus] Metel-tellus *over line break* A 51 hande/] *virgule suppl.* 52 espyes/] *virgule suppl.*

and thynkynge that all these tokens of subiectyon were but for a face or cloke to couer the treason and gyle of Iugurth. And so by suche dysceyt to wayt a tyme to execute his treason. Wherfore Metellus thus mysdemyng kept hymselfe in the forwarde of the batayle with an elect and chosen company of archers/ slyngers/ and other lyke soudyours apoynted in lyght harnes. His vndercaptayne Cayus Marius had rule and charge of the rerewarde among the horsmen/ and on bothe the wynges of his hoost he ordayned horsmen and other soudyours for supplement/ subsidy/ and socours of the forwarde yf nede shulde requyre/ and amonge them to expell their ennemies on what syde so euer they shuld come/ were mengled bowmen and other light harnysed fotemen with dartes/ pykes/ and iauelyns to trouble the horsmen of their ennemies. For in Iugurth was so moch gyle/ so great experience and knowledge of the countrey/ and also so great practyse of chyualrie: that a man coude nat well knowe whether he were more to be douted or more greuous in peace or in warre/ or whyle he was absent or pres[e]nt.

[47] ¶Nat farre from that way which Metellus helde with his army was a towne of the Numydians moche acustomed and frequented of marchantes of Italy and other strange countreis: and the princypall market towne of all the kingdome of Numidy. This towne was named Vacca/ Metellus drewe hym and his army thyder/ and set garnyson into the same towne. This dyd he to proue the myndes of the inhabytantes: for if they had kept forth the garnyson/ than shuld thei euydently haue declared themselfe ennemies of the Romayns. And also he ledde a garnyson thyder to thintent to haue taken the towne by force of armes/ yf the inhabytauntes wolde nat haue admytted the same garnyson. Also he commaunded vytayls/ and all other thynges whiche were necessary or expedyent to warre for to be brought thyder thynkyng (as the case required) that the concours of marchantes resortyng thyder. And his good prouysion of vytayls shuld be great defence and conseruacyon for hym and his army bothe in warre and in peace. But whan the citezins sawe such purueyance as he made of vitels/ considring that he shuld nat hurt nor disprouyde them whyle he had vytell ynough of his owne prouysion: anon they opened the gates and suffred hym to entre with all his garnyson and retynue. But in the mean tyme Iugurth agayn send his embassadours

56 batayle] hoost B C 59 horsemen/] *virgule suppl.* (*end of line* A) 65 gyle/] *virgule suppl.* 69 present] B C; presnt A 75 the myndes of] *om.* C 81 whiche were] *om.* B C 86 vitels/] *virgule suppl.*

to Me|tellus more dyligently and instauntly than he had done before/ f. 41r mekely besechynge and requyringe Metellus of peace: And yeldyng vnto hym e[u]ery thyng/ onely reserued his owne lyfe: and the lyfe of his chyldren. Metellus send these embassadoures home agayne attysedde to the prodycion of their mayster Iugurth as he hadde done to the other embassadours which were sent before. But concernynge the peace which they desyredde in their maisters name: nouther he graunted nor vtterly denyed it. And in this prolongynge of tyme he lokedde alway after parfourmyng of the promesse of the other embassadours/ which before hadde graunted and agreed to the pardicyon and betrayeng of Iugurth.

[48] But whan Iugurth consydredde and pondered togyder the wordes and dedes of Metellus/ and whanne he parceyued in mynde hymselfe assayled with his owne craftes of subtylte: and that Metellus vsedde suche craftes agaynst hym/ as he hymselfe had vsed agaynst other: than was his mynde greuedde moost of all. For Metellus fayned peace/ but in very dedes he shewed sharpe warre. Iugurth thus consydredde also: that his greattest towne named Vacca/ was alyenate and lost from hym: his ennemyes by longe contynuaunce and exercyse knewe the coostes of his countrey of Numidy. The myndes of his lordes and commens were prouokedde and moued agaynst hym. Whanne he aduysedde these dyfficultes with other mo contrary to hym he concludedde and fully determyned at last to resyst and withstande Mettellus in batayle/ and with strength and force of armes and no farther to submytte hymselfe by peticyon.

¶Howe Iugurth prepared and addressed hymselfe agayne to warre: and what ordynaunce and polycy he vsed agaynst the newe consull Metullus. ¶The .xxx. chapyter.

[48. 2] Wherfore Iugurth thus determyninge to assayle hym caused the wayes of Metellus to be espyed hauyng hope of vyctorie by auauncement and auauntage of some place. Where he intended of the place and countrey: and anone pre|pared the greattest army that he f. 41v coude of all sortes of people. This done/ he dyde so moch that by hylles/ narowe passages and bypathes he preuented and ouerpassed the hoost of Metellus.

91 Metellus] hym B; him C 92 vnto] to C euery] B C; enery A 97 nouther] neyther C 100 and agreed] *om.* B C pardicyon and] *om.* B C 106 dedes] dede B C 113 and¹] *om.* B C 114 to submytte] to meke nor submitte B C

Ch. 30 1 agayne] *om.* C 4–5 assayle hym . . . espyed] assayle Metellus cause his wayes to be espyed B; assaile Metellus caused his wayes to be espyed C

¶In that parte of Numidy whiche before in deuysion of the kyngdome was assignedde in possessyon to Adherball: was a flodde named Muthull/ rennyng from the meridyonall part of the countrey. A certayne hyll hy and long was nere to this water/ so that [at] any place the hyll was about .xx. myle from the streme and of equall dystance in length. The grounde of this hyll was of such nature that euer it was barayne/ wherfore it was nat apt to mennes habytacion but desert. About the myddes and pendant of this hyll was an other hyll smaller of quantyte: but of an vnmesurable heght coueredde and all ouergrowen with wylde olyue trees/ with myr trees/ and other sortes of trees wont to growe naturally on dry and sandy grounde. The playne which was by the hylles and the water was desert and vnhabytable for penury and lacke of water: saue such places of the playne as were nere to the flodde of Muthull which part was growen with small trees and occupyed with men and beestes.

[49] Iugurth came to the sayed small hyll which that dyscended from the pendant of the hyll gr[ea]tter ouerthwart the valey. And there toke place with his army nat togyder but dyspersed abrode amonge the trees by companyes and bendes/ he made his frende Bomylchar capytayne and gouernour of his elyphantes/ and of part of his army of fotemen and infourmed and taught hym parfitely how he shulde behaue hymselfe and gouerne them whom he had commytted to hym bothe before the batayle/ and also in the batayle whan it came to the poynt. But he hymselfe drewe nererre to the great hyll with all the horsmen and many of the fotemen which were elect and chosen men. And sette them in ordre and array with moch polycy and wysedome. This done: he hymselfe went about and compasedde euery company/ cohort/ and bende syngulerly: and one by one warnyng and requyryng them to call to their myndes their olde strength/ nobles/ and vyctorie: and thereby to defende themselfe and their countrey of Numidy from the immoderate couetyse of the Romayns/ which were nat content nor satysfied with the possession of the moost part of the worlde/ sayng farthermore that they shuld fight but with such as they before had ouercome and subdued. And howbeit they had chaunged their captayne: the cowardise of their mynde was nat
f. 42r chaun| ged: Also he rehersed and declared to them that he had made

14 hy] *om.* C at] B C; *om.* A 18 this hyll] it B C 22 which was by] bytwene B C 23 penury and] *om.* B C 26 that] *om.* B C 27 hyll greatter] B; greater hyll C; hyll graetter A 31 and taught] *om.* B C 36 and[1]] and in C 43 worlde/] *virgule from* B 45 mynde] hertes B C

all prouycion for them which a captayne myght or ought to make for his army. He declared howe he had taken for them the vpper place: that they were crafty in batayle and many in nombre: and shulde fyght with a fewe vncrafty cowardys. Wherfore he desyredde and exhorted them whan tyme shulde come that than they wolde be redy to assayle the Romayns manly at sounde of the trumpettes/ for that one same day sayd he shulde outher establysshe all their laboures/ vyctories/ and besynesses: or els it shulde be the heed and begynnyng of their most great myschyefe/ and dystruccions. Moreouer [through]out all his army he put them in remembrance man by man of the benefites which he had done to them before for their manly dedes of chyualry: as such as for their worthynes he had rewarded with dygnite/ money/ offyces/ or other worshyp: and shewed such vnto other commen soudyours sayeng that yf they wolde so demeane themselfe manly: so shulde they be promoted and auanced to worshyppe and ryches. And thus he conforted them all euery man after his maners and condycions/ some with giftes/ some with promysses/ some with thretnynges/ and other lyke ways acordyng to the dysposicyon of their mynde and nature.

¶Whyle Iugurth thus exhorted his soudyours Metellus nought knowyng of his ennemies aperyd with his company dyscendynge downe the pendent of the great hyll/ which seyng but fewe men: moche marueyled at first what it myght signyfie/ for he suspected nothyng lesse than batayle: but in beholdynge more intentyfly towarde the toppe of the small hyll afore hym he espyed among the yong trees bothe horse and men which were nat fully hydde/ bycause of the lownesse of the trees. yet was he incertayne what it myght be. For what by secretenes of the place: and what by gyle of Iugurth/ their baners and the moost part of the soudyours were obscured and hydde lyeng downe vpon the grounde. But anone after whan he parceyued this gyle and treason: by lytell and lytell/ he set his army in array procedynge forwarde styll as he dyde before/ faynynge hymselfe ignorant of the treason. But he chaunged the order of his soudyours: and on the ryght wynge which was next to the Numidyens his ennemies/ he ordayned as it were a forwarde enforced with a threfolde subsidy or socoures/ that is to say with thre bendes of proued soudiours to rescue and helpe them whan nede shuld be. The

48 place/] *colon from* B 55 dystruccions] dystruccion B; distruccion C through] throught A 63 promysses] promesse C 64 mynde] myndes B; mindes C 67 hyll/] *virgule suppl.* which] which at first B C 68 at first] *om.* B C 71 horse] horses C 77 before/] *virgule from* B 81 socoures/] *virgule suppl.*; socour C

bomen and such as with slynges shuld cast against their enmis f. 42v plummettes of led and yron/ and all other which were | of light harnes: all these he deuyded among the standerdes of other soudyours as the case requyred: where as after the ryght ordynaunce of batayle/ such soudyours by themselfe deuyded shulde begyn the batayle/ but in this batayle the sytuacion of the place nat so requyred. All the hole company of his horsmen he ordred in the extremytees and cornars of the forefront of the batayle. This done as the breuytc of the tyme suffred he made a short exhortacion vnto his soudyours/ and so proceded forth with his hoost sette in aray in maner beforesayd: but bycause Iugurth was on the small hyll before hym and by that meane on the hyer grounde/ he thought to remedy that i[n]commodyte and led forth his hoost on the syde halfe nat toward Iugurth/ but along on the hyllsyde towarde the flodde of Muthull/ into the playne which was bytwene the hyll and the flodde.

[**50**] But whan he sawe the Numidyans quyet and that they departed nat from the hyll which they had taken: he consydred the hete and faruentnes of the somer season. And lyst his army might perysshe for lacke or scarcite of water: he sent before one of his capytayns named Rutylyus with a company of lyght harnessed soudyours and part of his horsmen vnto the flodde named Muthull for to take vp a place wherin they might sette theyr tentes in tyme of nede: thynkyng that his ennemies wyllyng to contynue longe in that place by often assautes and scarmysshes shuld dysturbe the Romayns whyle they resorted to the water. And for asmoche as the Numidyans trusted nat moch in their strength and armoure. He thought that they purposed and intended to trouble his soudyours with werynes and thurst. Whan Rutylyus was gone towarde the water/ Metellus descended procedyng forth withall by lytell and lytell as the mater and place requyred: he commaunded one named Marius/ with his company to kepe in the rerewarde. But Metellus hymselfe with the horsemen kept hym in the lyft wynge of the forwarde of the batayle/ which alway remoued forward first of all his army.

¶Of the first batayle foughten bytwene Metellus and Iugurth. The .xxxi. chapyter.

f. 43r [**50. 3**] But whan Iugurth sawe that the rerewarde of Metellus was passed his forwarde: he beset the hyll from which Metellus dyscended

83 bomen and] archers B C 94 grounde/] *virgule suppl.* incommodyte] B C; imcommodyte A 96 hyllsyde] hyll B; hill C of] *om.* C 100 lyst] lest C

with two thousande fotemen by which garnyson if Metellus wold agayne take socour of the same hyll/ he shuld be prohibyted and dryuen backeward agayne into the handes of Iugurth. This done: sodenly he dyd the trumpettes to be blowen and anone withall/ inuaded and set vpon the company of Metellus on euery syde. The Numidyens asayled and bete downe the Romayns/ some on the rereward and other some dyd their deuoyre to breke the aray on both sydes: both on the right and lyft wyng/ with all their myght assaylyng the Romayns/ and auaunsyng themselfe on euery syde to breke their array and ordynaunce. And after their power to trouble/ dystourbe/ and deuyde them. The Romayns whiche were moost stable and bolde of myndes in metyng their ennemies were abused and dysceyued with the vncertayne batell. For their ordynaunce and aray was sette and strengthed onely but on one syde. But their ennemies assayled them on euery syde: so that somtyme they were stryken and wounded of their ennemies from farre of/ but by no meanes coude they strike their ennemies agayne nor ioyne with them. For Iugurth had taught his Numidyans on horsebacke before the batayle that whan they shulde begyn to assayle the Romayns: they shulde nat kepe themselfe togyder/ nor nere/ but asmoche dyspersed as they coude/ and in dyuers places: one company here and another there. And where the sowdyours of Iugurth coude nat auoyed nor repell the Romayns which assayled them/ bycause they were mo in nombre: therfore they compased and trapped them behynde or on the sydes/ betyn of and dysioynedde from their company. And where it fortuned any of them to fle/ the Numidyans had more auantage than the Romayns. For where they fledde into the feldes: they assayled the Romayns on the backe halfe or els on both sydes in dyuers companyes. But where thei sawe it was more auayle and expedyent to fle agayne to the hyll where they set first their ordynaunce. They had also auantage therby for their horses were acustomed to mountaynes and combredde wayes/ wherfore they mounted with lesse dyfficultie/ but in contrary wyse the Romayns for the sharpnes of the hylles and lacke of vse coude nat folowe them in their assending without moch dyfficulte/ payne/ and paryll.

[51] But nat withstandynge that Iugurthe and his men had the f. 43v
moost auantage of the countrey and grounde/ yet the batayle on both sydes was varyable/ vncertayne/ vngoodly/ and myserable to

Ch. 31 16 myndes] mynde C 28 betyn of] *colon after* of A B; *no punct.* C
30 fle/] *virgule suppl.* (*end of line* A B) 40 grounde/] *virgule from* B
41 vncertayne/ vngoodly/] vngoodly, vncertein C

beholde: for the best men sonest were slayne and in moost ieopardy. For the courage and valyant myndes and bolde hertes of the Romayns: was worth the gyle and treason of the Iugurthyns: and so on bothe sydes he which was boldest and moost auaunced hymself was sonest ouerthrowen. Some which were deuyded from their owne company and in handes of their ennemies/ gaue place to them and yelded themselfe. And agayne some folowed and chased their ennemies fleyng: where they myght make their party good: there resysted eyther partie manly. None of both parties kept vnder their standerdes: nor folowed nat the order of batayle: nor kept none order nor array/ but euery man resysted and defended hymself there where moost ieopardy and paryll was layed to hym: and endeuoyred hymselfe to withstande the vyolence of his ennemis with hye valyantise. And so the armour defensyfe/ dartes/ men/ horse/ Romayns/ Numidyans/ soudyours/ and pages were all confounded and mengledde togyder: without order or ordynaunce obserued. Nothyng was done with dyscression of the soudyours nor with counsell of the capytayns: vnauysed fortune and chaunce gouerned all the besynesse of that day: so vnstable was the batayle. All was commytted to rule of fortune/ And thus passed forth moch of the day in great murder and slaughter/ yet styll was the ende of the batayle vncertayne and non knewe whyther party shuld haue the vyctorie. At last both parties with labour and heat began to languysshe and become wery. Metellus vnderstandyng that the Numidyans lesse resysted in fyghtyng than they dyde before/ assembled and gathered togyder agayn his soudyours by lytell and lytell/ and without tary restored the aray and set them agayne in order. And .iiii. cohortes taken forth of the legyons he set agaynst the fotemen of his ennemies. But before Metellus had thus assembled his company: a great part of them oppressed with woundes and werynesse/ withdrewe themself to the hyll before named and to the hyer places from the batayle there to refressh and rest themselfe. But whan Metellus (as sayd is) had reasembled them agayne: he began in fewe wordes to pray and exhort them in suche maner.

¶O worthy and trusty soudyours and companyons dyscourage nat yourselfe in this batayle/ nor let nat your olde noblenesse nowe fayle
f. 44r you: suffre nat your ennemies wont to | put their trust in flyght/ nowe to ouercome you by your ferefull myndes. Remembre well: if ye be

47 handes] hande C 49 fleyng:] *colon from* B 54 the] *om.* C 60 fortune/] *virgule from* B 66 before/] *virgule suppl.*

dysposed cowardly to fle: ye haue no tentes/ no cyties/ no townes/ no castels/ nor no maner places of defence: wherto ye may renne for refuge and saue your selfe. Your helth/ your hope/ and defence is onely in your armoure and strength: and specially in your bolde hertes. Wherfore dere frendes remembre your olde worshyp: and suffre nat the hole empyre of Rome to suffre dysworshyp by your temerous and cowarde myndes. Remembre it worthyer to dy in batel lyke men than to fle: and than to be taken and murdred lyke beestes/ or to dye in prison. With these wordes and suche lyke Metellus reconforted the hertes of his soudyours. But in meane tyme Iugurth for his part was nat ydle/ quyet nor lesse prouydent: but compased and went about his men confortyng and exhorting them also and praysing their dedes. He renued the batayle also for his part: and among the myddes of his elect soudyours he fought and proued thextremyte of euery thyng: and assayd all meanes wherby any auantage myght be wonne conforting and socouryng his men with wordes/ dedes and example. He boldely fought and assayled suche of the Romayns as were in fear or dout: and such as he knewe and proued bolde and stedfast/ he kept them of with arowes/ iauelyns/ and dartes that they coude nat approche to their felowes to auaunce them nor to be socoured of them.

[52] Thus two worthy men noble and exellent captayns fought and contended togyder bytwene themselfe. They themselfe lyke in strength/ courage/ wysdome/ and policy: but of thynges longyng to chyualry vnlyke of prouysion. For Metellus had strength of soudyours sufficyently: but the auantage of the countrey and place was moche contrary to hym. But Iugurth had euery thing necessary and expedyent saue company of men of armes which he wanted.

¶At last the Romayns whan they vnderstode that there was no sure place wherto they might fle: and also that they coude fynde no meanes to fyght with their ennemies indyfferently hand to hand. And that the nyght was come vpon them at last: they ascended vpon the toppe of an hyll which was ouer agaynst them lyke as Metellus their captayne commaunded them to do. For the Numidyans had lost that place and were fledde and spredde abrode dyspersed/ but fewe of them were slayne. For they were swyft: and the contrey was nat well knowen to the Romayns to pursue them: wherby many of the Numidyans were defended: and so by flyght escapedde. But Iugurth | with his horsmen f. 44v

84 hertes] hert C 86 cowarde] cowardes B 93 his] *om.* C 95 his] *om.* C

of garde for his body: fled also from the batell whan he had long foughten and sawe none auayle nor auantage.

¶How Bomylchar vndercaptayne of Iugurth and his company were dysconfited by Rutilyus vndercaptayne of Metellus. ¶The .xxxii. chap.

[52. 5] In the mean season Bomylchar/ whom Iugurth had made maister of his elyphantes/ and of a part of the fotemen (as I haue written before) assone as he sawe that Rutilyus (which Metellus had sent vnto the flodde of Muthull to prouyde a place for their tentes) was ouerpassed his company: by lytell and lytell he conuayed and ledde downe his company into a playne. And whyle this Rutilyus hasted hym towarde the fludde as he was commaunded of Metellus. Bomilchar set his company in order and array styll and quietly as the mater and case requyred. And in meane tyme he forgat nat to serche by espyes what Metellus dyd/ and what way Rutilyus toke toward the sayd fludde: and in what maner he behaued himselfe and gyded his army. Wherfore after he vnderstode by his esypyes that Rutilyus with his company had taken their place by the sayd fludde where he wolde abyde: and was voyde of besynes/ quiet/ and doutyng no paryll. And on the other syde whan he vnderstode that the cry of the batayle bytwen Iugurth and Metellus encreased: he fearedde lest Rutilyus (if he vnderstode therof) wold leue his place by the flud: and retourne to the batayle to socour his felowes which were in ieopardy. In this consyderation Bomylchar: where as before he had ordered his army nere togyder by craft and that bycause he mystrusted the courage of his men: and in their boldnesse had no great confidence. Therfore nowe agayne he deuyded them abrode moche larger than they were before: and so proceded towarde the tentes of Rutilyus to thintent to lette hym and his company on euery syde/ if they prepared towarde rescous of Metellus.

[53] Rutilyus and his company suspectynge no paryll sodaynlie of vnware aduysedde/ and behelde a great vyolence of smoke and dust styred vp and raysed by mouyng of the grounde: but what it myght be they coude nat parceyue by any meane bycause of the thicknesse of
f. 45r the yonge trees that grewe on | all the grounde bytwene them which letted their syght. First of all they thought it had proceded of drines of the ground by mouynge of the wynde. But afterwarde whan they sawe

Ch. 32 5 the] hys C 12 in] in the C 30 and behelde a] *om.* B C 33 the[1]] *om.* C 35 the[1]] *om.* C

the same smoke and dust contynue styll after one maner: and that the same approched alway nerer and nererre lykewyse as the company of their ennemies moued and drewe toward them. Than they parceyued and knewe the mater as it was: and in all hast euery man toke to hym his harnesse: and stode redy before the defence of their tentes as their captayne Rutilyus had ordredde and commaunded them euery man redy to defence and in aray. After whan their ennemies approched nerer with an horrible noyse and cry/ they ranne togyder on bothe parties. The Numydians dyd but onely contynue the skirmysshe abydynge and lokyng after [their] elyphantes in helpe of whom was all their trust. But whan they sawe that their elyphantes were stoppedde and lette with thicknesse of the bowes of the treis: and so taryed and kept from their socours by the compasing of the Romayns so that in them was no trust of socours. Than all they toke them to flyght with all their power. But many of them (leuyng their armour behynde them) escaped without wounde by helpe of the hylles which were about the place: which they coude better and quicklyer ascende than the Romayns. And also by socour of the darknesse of the nyght (which than was at hande) many of them escaped hole and sounde and saued themselfe. Foure of the elyphantes were taken and all the remenant (fourty in nombre) were slayne. Whan this was done: the company of Rutilyus/ nat withstandyng that they were fatygate and weryed with great iourneis before/ and also with moche labour in orderyng of their tentes: and with the sayd batayle or skirmysshe. Neuerthelesse whan they sawe that Metellus their chefe captayne taryed langer than they thought he wold haue done yf althyng had happened well with hym/ they ordredde themselfe redy and dyligently went backward agayne to mete hym. For the falshode and gyle of Iugurth and of the Numydyans caused them to be besy/ dilygent/ and circumspect in euery thyng for saueguarde of their lyues: and suffred them to do nothyng slouly nor with delayeng. But whan they were in their iourney in the darkenesse of the nyght the companyes on bothe parties were nat farre in sondre the one from the other: and bothe parties approched togyder nat knowyng eche other as if they had ben ennemies. The one agaynst the other making noyse and clamour/ eche one increasyng feare to other as war| ryours ar wont to do at f. 45v
begynnyng of a batayle. In somoch that a myserable dystruction and murdre had almost ben made bytwene them by their imprudent

42 to] at B C 45 their] B C; *om.* A 70 clamour/] *virgule suppl.* 72 a[1]] *om.* C 73 made] committed B C

neglygence/ yf the espyes and horsmen which were sent bytwene them on bothe sydes had nat with more dilygence and wyselyer espyed the treuth of the mater. But whan the parties knewe ech other/ in stede of their sadnes and fear they were all sodenly fylled with great ioye and gladnesse. The soudyours ioyfully anone mette togyder one salutynge and welcomyng an other. One shewedde to other their actes done on bothe parties: and ioyous they were to here on bothe sydes euery man commendynge and exaltynge their owne dedes/ and also the dedes of other vnto heuen with myrthe and gladnesse. And that as well suche as were worthy men as vnworthy cowardesse ascrybed to themselfe worthynesse: and certes in suche besynesse it often happeneth/ that on that syde which hath the vyctorie: suche as be but cowardes/ rude and vncrafty/ exalteth them/ enioyeth/ and may boost themselfe on other mennes dedes and worthynesse. But in contrari wyse on that partie which is ouercome though many be good warryours/ noble and worthy men: yet ar they reputed for cowardes without policy/ bycause of other mennes cowardyse and aduersyte of fortune. Thus fareth it in skirmysshes of batell.

[**54**] But whan Metellus and Rutilyus (as I haue sayed before) were mette togyder and rehersed their actes one to an other/ Metellus hasted hym with all his army to the fludde of Muthull/ and taryed in the places and tentes which Rutilyus preparedde and ordayned there the space of foure dayes. In this season he was besy in refresshyng and healyng his soudiours which were wounded/ suche as manly had behaued themselfe in the batayle he worthely rewarded them/ he called them togyder all into one company and greatly lauded and commended them: thankyng and moche praysing them for the great dilygence/ payne/ and labours: which they had taken in defence of the honour and dygnite of their empyre with suche wordes.

¶O worthy soudyours ye se nowe that the hardest of our labour is ouerpassed by your boldnesse and manhode: wherfore I exhort you: be ye of lyke courage in the resydue of our besynesse/ which shalbe but light and easy in comparyson of this which is ouerpassedde. The begynnyng and first brunt of euery besynesse is hardest. Which shall be but lyght vnto bolde and circumspect begynners and constant felowes of their enterprises. But this begynnyng ye haue manly

77 in stede . . . great] their sadnes and feare tourned to great B C 79 an] *om.* B C 83 cowardesse] cowardys B; cowardis C 85 the] *om.* C 93 an] *om.* B C other/] *punctus* A, *no punct.* B C 95 Rutilyus] Rutilius had B C ordayned] seiourned B; soiourned C 109 felowes] folowers B C

ouercome by con|stant labour as thyng moost easy. Ynough haue we f. 46r foughten all redy for the glorie of victory: for that haue we optayned in this first conflyct. If we labour or fight any more it shalbe but onely for prayes and robberies of our ennemies: wherby we shalbe enryched in substance: lyke as we nowe be inhaunced with glorie of victory. Wherfore my dere felowes and moost constant frendes of the commen welth nowe I exhort you for complement of all your honorable fame: to remembre your olde and acustomed worthynesse. And suffre nat this exellent honoure and glorie which ye haue nowe obtayned by boldnes: to be quenched and decay agayne by ignomynious cowardyse.

¶With suche wordes and many other lyke Metellus reconforted his company: and marueylously kyndled their courages to the desyre of honour by valyant feates of armes. But in the mean season the knowen gyle of Iugurth went nat from his mynde: and therfore to exclude all danger of treason he sent forth certayne of the Numidyans/ which betraynge Iugurth had forsaken hym and fledde to the Romayns: and also with them he sent forth dyuerse other of his owne company which were expert of the countrey/ and oportune to such besynesse to serche and espy amonge what people or in what place Iugurth helde hymselfe: and wherin he was ocupyed. Whyther he kept hym with a small company: or whyther he had an army reassembled for a newe batayle/ and how he behaued hymselfe and where about he went syth he was ouercome. But Iugurth had conuayed hymselfe into suche places as were full of dychesse/ valeis/ hylles/ treis/ busshes/ and dales defended of nature. And there had he assembled agayne a newe army of men/ mo in nombre than he had before. But they were but vncraftie/ inexpert/ and dull to batell: and coude better tyll the grounde and kepe beestes/ than exercyse the dedes of chiualry. For therto had they neuer ben vsed before: but in the other seruyle ocupatyons and besinesse had they ben ocupyed all their lyftyme without intermyxtion of other ocupatyon. It fortuned that Iugurth had none other soudiours but such rurall people about hym at this tyme namely for this cause. For whan he fledde from the batayle foughten before with Metellus/ none of all his soudyours folowed hym except the horsemen of his garde. For all the other sowdyours departed where it lyked them best. Nor this is nat counted nor reputed for any faute or rebuke amonge the Numidyan soudyours.

110 as] as a C 112 this] the C 117 and] *om.* C 122 courages] courage B C 127 forth] *om.* C 140 besinesse] besynesse B; businesses C

For suche is the custome of the countrey: whan the capytayne fleeth the hoost forsaketh hym.

f. 46v ¶What wast and dystruction Metellus made in the lande of Numidy after this first batell and flight of Iugurth: and of the gyle of Iugurth agaynst Metellus. ¶The .xxxiii. cha.

[54. 5] Whan Metellus vnderstode by his espyes that the mynde of Iugurth contynued yet styll in his olde fyersnesse and cructie thoughe he was lately ouercome in batayle. And whanne Metellus sawe that Iugurth renewed the warre agayne and prepared a newe batayle which coude nat be done but at pleasure of Iugurth/ bycause he had taken suche a place to abyde in that no man coude conuenyently contende with hym for dyfficultie therof. Metellus thus knowyng aduysed hymselfe of many thynges. Namely he consydredde that they were nat indyfferent and egall on bothe parties in executyng therof. For all yf that he had the vpper hande ouer Iugurth and had put hym to flyght: yet lost he mo men and had more dammage in ouercomyng hym/ than Iugurth had which was ouercome. For this consyderation Metellus purposed no more to contende with Iugurth in playne feldes nor in ordered batayle/ but by an other maner to execute the warre with hym from thensforthe. This determyned: Metellus with his hole hoost and ordynaunce went forth into the moost riche and plentyfull places of all Numidy/ and there wasted and dystroyed the feldes and contrey on euery syde. He toke without any resystence castels and townes/ nat strongly defended with walles/ dychesse/ nor garnyson. And brent and bete them downe to the grounde. All suche as came in his way and were able to bere harnesse: full growen of age or apt to batayle: he slewe and rydde out of hande. Thinkyng that the mo he slewe the fewer aduersaries and ennemies shulde he haue to contende agaynst hym. He commaunded his sowdyours to spare no robbery nor prayes: but put althyng to hauocke among his sowdyours.

¶For feare of this crueltie many of the Numidyans yelded themselfe to the Romayns: and gaue vnto them hostages/ vytayls/ soudyours/ and all other thynges necessary abundantly. In some townes which were taken: Metellus sette defence and garnyson where nede required and fortyfied them suffyciently. This besynes troubled the mynde of Iugurth moche more than the batayle that was foughten

Ch. 33 8 at] at the C 10 thus] this C 16 Iugurth] hym B; him C 17 the] *om.* C 18 determyned:] *colon from* B 24 of] to C or] and C 28 put] gaue B C 30 vytayls] vytaile C

before to his great dammage and dysconforte of his menne. For he loost more people by this way thanne by any other meanesse before. | f. 47r
Thus Iugurth which before put all his hope and trust in his flight: was now of necessite compelled to folowe and pursue his ennemies: and he which coude nat defende his owne places whiche styll remayned in hs possession: was constrayned nowe to warre in those coostes/ which Metellus had wonne of hym to recouer them yf fortune wolde suffre hym. Neuertheles of suche poore shyft and counsell as he had he toke the best which coude be taken by his aduyse in suche extreme necessite. He commaunded his army for the moost part to remayne styll in the same place where they were. And he hymselfe with a company of horsmen which were bolde and chosen men ensued Metellus priuely/ makyng his iourneis by night tyme by bywayes and secrete valeis. And at last sodenly of vnwars he fell vpon a part of the Romayns which were dyspersed abrode from the hoost in foragyng and spoylinge. Many of them without armour were slayne: and many taken. Non of them all escaped clene nor fre without dammage/ but outher were slayne or els sore wounded. Whan Iugurth had done this skyrmisshe anone he withdrue hymselfe and his company into the hylles and mountayns next to them: before any socours or rescous shulde come from Metellus to reueng their treason and deth of the Romayns.

¶Of the great ioy which was demeaned at Rome for this worthy behauour of Metellus: and how he gyded hymself and his army to contynue and augment this honour which he had goten. The.xxxiiii. chap.

[55] Whyle Metellus and Iugurth stryued thus togyder: the one with manhode/ wysdome/ and strength: the other with treason/ craft/ and gyle: Tidynges were brought to Rome of this noble behauour of Metellus. Ouer all the cite was demeaned great ioye and gladnesse for that Metellus behaued hymselfe and gyded his army acordyng to the maner and ordynaunce of olde noble capytayns of the Romayns before his days. And howbeit he was in place aduers and contrary to hym yet had he the vpper hande of his ennemies as vyctoure ouer them. And by his strength and manhode he had in possession the contrey of his ennemies: and had driuen them from place to place. | All these f. 47v

36 meanesse] meane B C 47 priuely/] *virgule from* B 51 escaped] scaped C 55 shulde] myght B C

Ch. 34 1 which] that C 12 vyctoure] victorie B C

thinges consydred: they moche reioyced and greatly commended Metellus: namely for that he had caused Iugurth to put his trust of helth onely in fleyng into the mountayns and wyldernesses/ which before was magnificent and proude by the fear and cowardyse of Aulus precessour of Metellus. Wherfore for these fortunat and glorious dedes of Metellus/ the senatours decreed and commaunded ouer all the cyte sacrifyces and suffrages to be done to their ydolles. The citezyns which before were ferefull and sore troubled doutyng the vnsure chaunce and incertayne fortune of the ende of the batayle: demened now among them myrth and gladnesse ouerall. The honoure and fame of Metellus was recounted very noble/ exellent/ and gloryous in euery mannes mouth. Wherfore he somoch was the more dyligent and laboured more besely towarde the vyctore/ laboring and hastyng to finysshe the warre by all meanes and wayes so it myght be to his honour and confusion of Iugurth. But neuertheles he was well ware from puttyng hymselfe in danger of his ennemies: and was ware exchuyng oportunyte of their gyle in euery place where he went. He remembred well and considred that often after laude and glorie foloweth enuy and euylwyll. And therfore howe moche more noble that he was reputed: the more besy and dyligent he was to mentayne his fame and honour/ and in drede to lose this worthy fame whiche he had obtayned. Nor after the foresayd gyle of Iugurth he suffred nat his hoost to deuyde nor to depart themselfe dysparsed one from an other: nor to make excourses to forage or spoyle in dyuers places farre dystant in sondre. But whan thei had nede outher of mannes meate or horsemeat: all the horsemen with great companyes of the fotemen/ went forthe and kept them nere about suche as were sende forthe to make prouysion to defend and socour them: if nede shuld require. Metellus hymselfe deuyded his hoost in two partes: the one part he kept with hymselfe: and the other he commytted to a noble warriour of his hoost named Marius/ bytwene them both they dystroyd and wasted the contrey on euery syde/ but rather with fire than with robbry or prayes. Metellus and Marius set their tentes in two places nat farre dystant in sondre. But whan any perylous or nedy besynesse was to be done with Iugurth or his company which requyred great myght: than anone Metellus and Marius were redy togyder: but they kept themselfe thus in sonder in

17 wyldernesses] wyldernesse B; wildernes C 19 precessour] predecessour B; predecessor C 23 the batayle] this warre B C 27 vyctore/] *virgule suppl.* 36 had] *om.* C 38 an] *om.* B 40 outher] eyther C 48 two] *om.* C

dyuerse places to trouble the Numidyans/ and increase their feare more largly in euery coost: and to make | them fle and auoyde more ferre abrode in compasse for fear. f. 48r

¶At this season Iugurth ensued by the hylles and desert places sekyng and espyeng a conuenyent season or place to make some skyrmysshe with the Romayns (that is to say) if he coude espy any parcell of them sekynge forth fountayns of water for the army of the which was moch penury in those costes. If he myght any such espy than anone wolde [he] breke downe from the hylles vpon them. Somtyme he shewed hymselfe to Metellus/ somtyme to Marius/ somtyme he wolde assemble his company togyder in a bend as if he wold fyght with the Romayns to attempt them/ and anone after wold he retourne agayne vnto the mountaynes. And afterwarde sodenly appere agayne thretnyng nowe the one company of the Romayns/ and nowe the other. Yet wold he neyther auenture batayle nor suffre neyther the Romayns to be ydle or in rest/ nor yet hymselfe. His mynde was onely sette to kepe his ennemies from their begynnyng and purpose of distroyeng of the countrey whiche they intended.

¶Howe Metellus besyeged Saman one of the strongest townes of Numidy: and howe Marius vndercaptayne of Metellus escaped the danger of Iugurth. ¶The .xxxv. chap.

[**56**] Whan Metellus the Romayne captayn sawe hymselfe so fatygate and weryed with the gyles and craftes of Iugurth/ and that by no policy he coude haue faculty or tyme to fight with hym in playne batayle: at last he concluded to besyge and assayle a great towne named Zamam/ which was the most chefe and strongest holde of all the realme of Numidy in that part of the lande where it was buylded. And so spedde hym thyder with all his army and ordynance where the sayd holde was/ thynkyng (as the mater requyred) that Iugurth wold drawe thyder for defence of his chife towne and for socour and relefe of his peple and so shulde the batayle be there foughten bytwene them. But whan Metellus was in his iourney thyderward/ anon were certayn of his army which fled to Iugurth and certified hym of this prouysion and interprise of Metellus. Whan Iugurth herof was certified he hasted him by gret iourneis so that he ouerpassed the company of Metellus and cam to the towne of Zamam before him: | f. 48v

53 more[2]] *om.* B C 60 he] *om.* A 63 anone] *om.* C

Ch. 35 4 the Romayne captayn] *om.* B C 4–5 fatygate and] *om.* B C 11 was/] *virgule suppl.* (as . . . requyred)] *opening bracket before* thynking A B C

and there exhorted the inhabytantes boldely to defende the walles. And farthermore assigned to socour and helpe them all suche as had fledde fro the Romayns/ and had brought hym those tidynges. These treatours were the surest men which Iugurth had. For they coude nat dysceyue hym/ but yf they wolde yeld them agayne to the Romayns whom they had forsaken and betrayed which thing was nat sure to them to do. Whan Iugurth had ioyned these soudyours to the garnyson and socours of the towne and castell/ and had ordred and apoynted all other thinges acordyng to his mynde: than he promysed to be there agayne with them with all his hole army in tyme of nede. This done he departed from the towne into the moost preuy and secret places which he knewe in his countrey therby.

But whan Metellus was in his iourney towarde Zaman/ he sende Marius for prouysion of whete and other corne and vytayle for the army vnto a towne named Sicca/ which was the first towne that forsoke Iugurth and was yelded to Marius after the batayl late foughten with Iugurth to his great damage. Whan Iugurth had knowledge herof he went thyder by night priuely with his elect soudyours/ so that whan Maryus had spedde his matters and was redy to depart forthe of the towne: Iugurth was redy at the gates to assayle the Romayns cruelly cryeng with a hye voyce to them of the towne and exhortynge them to assayle the Romayns also on the backe halfe: sayng that fortune had offred to them the chaunce of a noble act/ of an excellent and glorious dede: so that (yf they wolde folowe his desyre) they shulde restore hym agayne into his kyngdome and themselfe into their lyberte and from thensforth to passe their tyme without paryll/ without daunger: or drede. And certaynely if Marius had nat boldely and strongly broken out of the towne with his standerdes and men of armes through the thickest of his ennemies which were in the gates. All they of the towne for the moost part wolde haue broken their oth and promesse/ which they had made before to Metellus whan they first yelded themself and the cyte to hym. The myndes of the Numidyans be so vnstedfast and mouable. But Iugurth so conforted his soudyours that they resysted the Romayns a lytell season. But whan Marius and his company began to encrease their vyolence agaynst the Iugurthyns and more fiersely to prease vpon them. Anone some were slayne and the residue fledde with their maister Iugurth.

21 fro] from B C   44 to] *om.* B C   48 for] or B C

[57] This daunger ouerpassed: Marius departed thens towarde the towne of Saman/ | and at the last came thyder sa[f]e with all his f. 49r company and besynesse spedde wherfore he was sent.

¶This Samam was a towne bylded in the playne ground without hylles or waters nere it so that it was rather defended by the warke of mannes handes than by nature of the place. In it fayled nothyng necessary to batayle. For it was well garnisshedde bothe with men/ ordynaunce/ vytayls/ and armour. Anone whan Marius was come: Metellus acordyng to the tyme and place made redy all thynges necessary and compased the walles on euery syde with his army: assignyng to euery one of his vndercapytayns a separate place of the towne to assayle and there to do his deuoyre and shewe his manhode. Whan euery thyng was thus ordredde Metellus commaunded to sound to the assaut with trumpettes and claryons. The Romayns immedyatlie assayled the towne on euery syde with horryble noyse and clamoure. The Numidyans therof were nat adradde at all: but abode styll and kept themselfe in sylence as if they had nat ben dyspleasedde nor prouoked to batell: howbeit they kept the walles euery man on the part to him assigned and all were redy to resyst and to assayle the Romayns. Anone the batayle was begone. The Romayns exercysed and occupyed themself euery man with such wepyn as he coude best handell and was moost expert in: some with slynges thrue plummettes of leed/ and some stones from afarre into the cyte/ and at them which defended the walles/ some assayled the towne nerer inuadyng the same/ and couetyng to haue entre and vndermynyng the walles/ some boldly esca[l]ed walles desyring to come so nere that they might fyght hande to hande. On the other syde thinhabytauntes of the towne and garnyson resysted manly. Some rowled downe and ouertourned gret and weyghty stones on suche as were nerest to them/ and that vndermyned the walles. Some pytched downe vpon them dartes/ iauelyns/ pykes/ firebrandes: and also great brennynge polles/ faggottes/ and blockys ouercouered with pytche and bremstone arden[t]ly flamyng. Some boldly ouertourned the scalyng ladders and slewe and ouerthrue such as scaled the walles. But some other which were farther from the towne and for prease coude nat approche nere to the walles in the meane season were nother fearfull nor ydell. For there was no maner instrument of

57 safe] B C; saue A 61–2 so that it was rather defended . . . handes] defended rather by the warke of mannes hande B C 73 abode] stode C 82 escaled] B; scaled the C; escaped A 89 ardently] ardenly A B; ardentlye C

batayle which coude be throwen with hande or with any other ingynne of batayle: but that they thrue it into the towne/ wherwith they
f. 49v wounded and slewe many of the inhabytantes | and of the defenders of the walles. The dartes and crosbowes on bothe parties were nat vnoccupyed. Artellery nor gonnes had they none. For at that tyme was no mencyon of them nor they were nat yet inuent. The Romayns which were farthest of all from the walles escaped nat fre: but with dartes were ouerthrowen in great nombre. How beit their cowardous and fearfull myndes caused them to drawe themselfe a loufe behynd all other for to saue themselfe/ yet coude they nat auoyd the peryll. Thus were the worthy and vnworthy of the Romayns in lyke ieopardy and peryll: but their glory and fame was moch vnlyke.

¶Howe Iugurth assayled and inuaded the tentes of the Romayns in the mean tyme whyle Metellus gaue assaut to the towne of Zammam. ¶The .xxxvi. chapyter.

[58] Whyle the assaut endured and contynued thus at Zammam/ with great murdre and dystructyon on bothe parties: Iugurth sodenly and of vnware stale downe from the mountayns where he was hydde/ and with a great power of men assayled and inuaded the Romayns tentes whyle the soudyours whom Metellus had assygnedde to the warde and defence of them were within the same at their rest: and suspecting nothing lesse than any such assaut. Wherfore Iugurth brake in vpon them vnprouyded. The Romayns were sore abasshed of that soden feare. And euery man prouyded for hymselfe acordyng to his maners and dysposytion. Some which were cowardes fled away with all their myght/ some other valyant and bolde herted men drewe to their harnes and manly withstode their ennemis. Neuerthelesse the moost part of them all were outher wounded or slayne. But among all the company and of all the multytude of them were no mo but .xl. men which abode. These .xl. acompanyed themselfe togyder remembryng the worshyp of the empyre of Rome/ and toke a place a lytell aboue their ennemies: which place they defended so manly that they coude nat be driuen from it by moche vyolence of their ennemies/ agaynst whom they thrue dartes from a farre. And suche dartes as their ennemies thrue at them: they thrue the same agayne. So they beyng but a fewe agaynst so many dyd nothing in vayne. For they coude

99 inuent] inuented C 104 of the] *om.* C

Ch. 36 4 endured and] *om.* B C 12 maners] maner C 13 away] *om.* B C 16 outher] eyther C 17 mo] more B C

throwe no dart/ but that it lyghted among the thic| kest of them. But f. 50[r] so coude nat their ennemies do agaynst them. For they were so fewe: so nere togyder: and on so sure a place that their ennemies myght lytell thyng preuayle agaynst them. But whan the Numidyans approched nerer to them: than specially these .xl. valyant Romayns shewed and bestowed their manhode and strength with moost exellent courage assaylyng their ennemies: ouerthrowyng and chasing them backwarde by very force and strength.

¶In the meane tyme whyle Metellus was moost of all ocupyed and besyed in the forsayd assaut of Zamam: sodenly he herde behynde hym a great clamour and noyse of people. Anone he refrayned his horse: and in tourning backe he parceyued great companyes of men rennyng toward hym: wherby he well knewe that they were of his owne peple and company. But whan he vnderstode all the chaunce which was befallen. Anone in all hast he sent all the hole company of his horsmen vnto his tentes: and soone after he sent thyder also his chife vndercaptayne Caius Marius with his retynue and company to hym assigned. And sore wepyng he obtested/ exhorted/ and besought hym for all loue and frendshyppe: and for honour of the commen wayle/ that he wold nat suffre any disworshyp or contumely remayne in the Romayns that day whiche euer thytherto had ben vyctorious and ouercomars with great laude and honour: and that he wolde nat suffre their ennemy Iugurth and his company to depart away vnreuenged. Marius dyd the commaundement of Metellus and that shortly. But in the m[e]ane season Iugurth parceyued many of the kepars of the tentes fallen into the dyches that were made about the same for defence: so that for hast to ronne away they hurt themselfe more/ than he dyde. Iugurth aduysing their daunger consydred that hymselfe was lyckely to be let vnder the same maner yf he auentured ouer farre. And therfore he departed betyme into the surest places that he coude deuyse nere by/ leauynge many of his men behynde: outher deed or mortally wounded. Th[u]s was Marius frustrat of his labour: for Iugurth was fledde before he came to the tentes. But Metellus (without any thyng brought to ende at Zamam) whan the night drewe nere: retourned with his hoost into his tentes.

[59] On the next morne after/ before he retourned agayne to the assaut of Zaman: he commaunded all the company of his horsmen to course vp and downe before their tentes on that syde where they

36 he] *om.* B C 43 for[2]] for the C 49 meane B C; mane A 50 the[2]] *om.* C
53 let] set C 56 outher] eyther C Thus] B C; This A 60 morne] morowe C

supposed Iugurth wolde come to socour his people. The entres into f. 50v the tentes and places nere to them he commytted and deuy| ded to warde of his vndercapytayns. After that he retourned agayne to the towne and fiersly assaylinge the walles in lyke maner as he had done the day before.

¶In the mean season Iugurth agayne sodenly stale vpon the Romayns: and specially on them which coursed before the tentes. They which were next hym and whom he encountred first of all were a lytell tyme sore troubled and abasshed: but the remanent of the Romayns lightly assembled their socours. And so valyantly behaued themselfe that the Numidyans shuld nat long haue contynued the skirmysshe: if their fotemen myngled with the Romayns horsemen had nat in the mydell commytted great myschefe and dystruction. For the horsemen of Iugurth trustyng to the helpe of these fotemen which were myngled among them: dyd nat first procede forwarde auauncyng themselfe and than retourne backe agayne as the vse is in a batayle of spere men. But they ran in makynge incourses among the thyckest of the Romayns ouerthwart and sydelinges: infoldyng and dowblyng the courses: and contendyng to trouble and dysorder the aray and order of the forwarde and wynges of the Romayne hoost. In somoche that what with the Numidyans on horsebacke and with them on fote it lacked but lytell: but the Romayns were confounded and ouercome in that greuous conflict.

¶But here wyll I leue the horsmen of the Romayns fightyng for their lyues and honour agaynst Iugurth and his speremen. And nowe shall I declare how Metellus the chefe captayn of the Romayns behaued himself with his host in the assaut of Zammam.

¶How Metellus behaued himself for his part and of the great conflyct which the Romayns had agaynst the Numidyans: Metellus with his fotmen assaylinge the towne of Zammam for the one part: and Iugurth fiersly fighting with the Romayns speremen for the other part. The .xxxvii. chap.

[**60**] In the same tyme whyle this skirmysshe contynued bytwene the Romayns horsmen and the Numidyans/ which were with Iugurth: the assaut also agaynst the towne of Zammam induredde with moche strength/ vyolence/ and murder. And specially wher as Metellus had

66 assaylinge] assaylyd B; assayled C 72 socours] socoure C 80 sydelinges] sydlinge C the] theyr B C

Ch. 37 4 for] on C

assigned his vnder| captayns on euery syde of the towne (as I haue sayed before) there contynued the assaut moost sharply. One of them put nat his trust nor hope in another: but euery man in his owne dedes and in hymselfe. Under the same maner dyde the garnyson and inhabytantes of the towne behaue themselfe: they fought manly agayne and also ordayned all thinges conuenyent for their defence in euery place of the towne. Both the parties were redyer and more besye one to stryke and wounde an other than to defende themselfe. The clamoure and noyse was myxt with exhortacion and confort of some/ and the ioye of the quellars and murderers was myngled with the waylinge of them which were quelled and murdredde. The sounde of the armour/ horrious/ and strokes mounted to the ayre. The sky was darkedde with dartes fleyng on eyther syde. And the walles and dychesse were dyed with blode: and fylled with deed corses pytefull to se. But whan the Numidyans were somwhat at layser and whan the Romayns a lytell abated and remytted the assaut: than they which defended the walles of the towne loked out a farre and intentifely behelde the batayle of the horsmen which styll contynued. There might one haue sene them somtyme mery and ioyous/ somtyme full of dolour and heuynesse after as they sawe the case of the part of Iugurth wente forwarde or backward. And as well as they coude be sene and harde of their felowes which were with their kyng Iugurth: some warned them to audacite/ some exhorted them to courage/ outher they gaue them signes with their handes or with the iest of their bodyes and countenances mouynge and excityng them to boldnesse. If they sawe a Romayne stryke a Numidyan: thei moued and withdrue their bodyes auoyding the stroke as yf it had ben themself which had ben stricked. And if they sawe a Numidyan cast a dart agaynst a Romayn: they moued their bodes also as if they had cast it themself. Thus toke they so intentife hede to the batell that they forgate themselfe where they were/ and it semed them that they had ben with their felowes in batayle. f. 51r

Whan Marius which besyged the towne on that syde: vnderstode this maner and behauour of the inhabytauntes and garnyson: he abated his fiersnes for policy and was more slowe in besyeging of the towne than before/ fayning that he had no trust nor confidence to

12 another] other B C 17 an] *om.* B C 21 horrious/ and strokes] horrious and strokes B; and horrious strokes C 33 outher] other B C iest] iesture B C 37 stricked] striken B C 38 bodes] bodyes B; bodies C if] *om.* B C 43 garnyson] garyson B C 45 before/] *virgule suppl.*

wynne it/ and suffred the Numidyans within the towne to beholde the batell of their kyng: for a whyle without any resystence or besynesse. But whan he sawe them moost intentyfely beholdyng the batayle/ and f. 51v moost amased | for the besynes of their felawes and contrey men: than sodenly with all his power he gaue assaut to the walles so that many of the Romayns with ladders and other ingens/ had almoost mounted vnto the highest part of them. Thynhabytantes seing this expelled their amasednes remembryng themself: and ran manly agaynst them with resystence throwyng vpon them stones/ fyre/ and all maner dartes of batayle. The Romayns at begynnyng resysted valyantly/ defendyng themself and auancyng them to the walles. But whan thinhabytantes had first ouerthrowen and broken one ladder/ and than ouertourned an other. They which abode last were maymed or slayne. Anone the remenant departed and gaue ouer the walles vnder the best maner that they coude a fewe or non hole. For a great part of them withdrewe themself transfixed with mortall wondes. Anon after the night fell vpon them which caused both the parties to desist and leue of the batel.

¶How Metellus remoued the siege from Zammam: and how Bomylchar so perswaded Iugurth that he yelded hymselfe/ his kyngdome/ and all other thynges/ to mercy and grace of the Romayns. And howe Iugurth after losse of his men/ treasour/ elephantes/ armour/ and horse: changed his mynde agayne. ¶The .xxxviii. chapyter.

[**61**] But whan Metellus sawe his purpose and labour all in vayne: and that he coude nat wynne the towne. and also that Iugurth dyde nought but begyle and falshode/ nor wolde nat fight but yf it were in places for his profet and great auantage. And also whan he perceyued that the somer was passed: he departed from the siege of Zammam: and in such townes as he had won of Iugurth which were strongly defended with walles and water: he set garnyson and soudyours of his company to defend them. But the remenant of his army he conuayed and ordred in the next prouynce vnto Numidy/ which was subget to the Romayns: to remayne there tyll the sharpnesse of the wynter were passed. Nor in the meane tyme he suffred nat them/ nor hymselfe to be corrupted with superfluous welth/ rest/ nor lechery: after the f. 52r maner of other before hym. But bycause the | warre proceded forwarde but lytell with armour or strength: he began to proue and

46 it/] *virgule suppl.* 55 valyantly/] *virgule from* B 61 wondes] woundes C

Ch. 38 8 begyle] by gyle B C 15 the[2]] *om.* C 16 he] *om.* C

prepare treason agaynst a treatour/ dysceyt agaynst dysceyt: and gyle agaynst gyle of Iugurth: and this thought he to proue by such as were moost chefe frendes of Iugurth/ and moost familyar about him. So that he purposed to vse the falshode and treason of them agaynst their mayster: in stede of armour and batayle. Wherfore first of all he began to proue the mynde of Bomylchar which had ben before at Rome with Iugurth: and (as I haue sayd before) fledde priuely from thens for the deth of Massiua/ leuyng his sureties behynde in danger for his cause. Metellus considred that this Bomylchar (by cause of the great frendshyppe and familyarite which he had with Iugurth) sonest might dysceyue and betray hym. Wherfore (as I haue sayd before) he began and went in hande with hym first of all by promysing of great rewardes. And first of all he dyde somoch: that this Bomylchar came priuely to Metellus and spake with hym. Metellus anon promysed hym on fayth and treuth to do so for hym: that the senatours shulde pardon hym of all thynges past/ and of his lyfe and goodes. So that he wold betray or delyuer vnto hym Iugurth other quycke or deed: lightly he perswaded the Numydan. For anon Bomylchar agreed therto: what for his treaterous and false mynde which he had of nature. And what for that he douted if any peace or composicyon after that shuld be made bytwene Iugurth and the Romayns hymselfe shulde be delyuerd by condycion to the Romayns to be punysshed for the deth of Massyua whom he caused to be slayne at Rome.

[**62**] This Bomylchar whanne he sawe his tyme toke leue of Metellus on this apoyntment: and sone after came to Iugurth whom he founde doutfull/ in care and bewayling his aduers and myserable fortunes with profounde syghes and heuynesse/ and doutynge what way was moost expedyent to be taken. Bomylchar after many wordes beganne to counsell and warne hym/ praynge/ and obtestyng hym pyteously wepyng and wayling: and requyring that at last he wolde make some prouysion for the sauegarde and socours of hymselfe/ of his chyldren and frendes: and for the peple of Numidy which well had deseruedde agaynst hym to be prouydedde for and better sene to. Bomylchar also obiected to Iugurth how he and his menne were ouercome in euery batayle/ and his people also dyminysshedde or alyenate frome hym/ his feldes and townes wasted and distroyd or els in possession of his ennemies/ his men some taken and in prison. Some | slayne: and many wounded and maymed/ the richesse of his f. 52[v]

20 dysceyt[2]] a dysceyuer B; a deceyuer C 21 Iugurth:] *colon from* B 36 vnto] to C other] either C 45 doutfull/] *virgule suppl.* 46 fortunes] fortune C

realme dyminysshed and wasted. Bomylchar alleged also to hym that he had proued the strength of his soudyours and fauour of fortune sufficyently ynough/ wherfore it were better for hym to se some remedy and prouision for all these ylles and other mo/ and to beware lest whyle he prolonged the tyme and douted: the people of the countrey shuld prouyde for themselfe without his aduyse or counsell. With these wordes and other lyke Bomylchar induced the kynges mynde to make some composicyon or els to yelde hymself/ and all other thynges to mercy and grace of the Romayns. Anone embassadours were sende to Metellus to certify hym that Iugurth was redy to do what euer he wolde desyre or commaunde hym: and that he wolde commyt and yelde bothe hymselfe and his kyngdome to the fayth and grace of Metellus: and of the Romayns without any pactyon/ couenaunt/ or exception: sauyng onely as it pleasedde them to deale with hym. Metellus herynge of this mynde of Iugurth was very glad: and commaunded all the moost wyse/ noble/ and worthy men of his army anon to be called togyder vnto hym from their wyntring places. Whan they were come/ than toke he counsell of them and of other suche as he knewe wysest and moost dyscrete touchyng the embassade of Iugurth. Anone it was concluded and decreed among the counsell and declared to the embassadours (acordynge to the olde custome of Rome) that they shuld commaunde Iugurth to sende to Metellus and the Romayns two hundred thousand pound weyght of syluer: all his elyphantes which he ocupyed in warre: and a certayne quantite of armour and a nombre of his chiefe horse. All these thinges were fulfylled and done of Iugurth without any tary or delay. Wherfore anone after Metellus commaunded agayne that all they which had betrayed his hoost/ forsaken him and fled to Iugurth shuld be bounden and so brought to hym agayne. The moost part of them were brought as he commaunded: but a fewe of them whan they harde first of this composicyon (feryng the same mater) fled vnto the kyng Bocchus which was the kyng of the Moryens.

¶Whan Iugurth after this maner was bereft of his armour/ of his horse/ of his men and also of his treasour. Anone after he was called by Metellus to come to a towne called Tysidium there to here what farthermore shuld be commaunded to hym: and to yeld himselfe to

62 and] *om.* C douted:] *colon from* B 71 couenaunt] conuenaunt B C 73 wyse/] *virgule from* B 75 come/] *virgule suppl.* (*end of line* A) 82 horse] horses C 88–9 the kyng Bocchus . . . Moryens] Bocchus kyng of the moryens B; Bocchus kynge of the Moryens C

thempyre of Rome acordyng to his embassade. But he began than to change and to turne his mynd agayn dreding for the knoleging of his cruel dedes | that he shulde neuer escape worthy punysshment if he f. 53[r] were ones in the Romayns handes. Thus he contynued many dayes in doutyng what was best to be done. Somtyme he volued in his mynde rather to subdue himself to any dyfficulte and to byde all paynes than to begyn warre agayne: consydring the aduers and vnhappy fortune which he had before. Somtyme agayn he called to mynde how greuous a fall it shulde be to descende from a kyngdome into subiectyon and bondage. But at conclusion whan in vayne and to none effect he had lost such great ordynaunce and helpe of warre as he had lately delyuered to Metellus: as a volage brayned man/ he fully determyned agayne to begyn and contynue the warre with Metellus: rather than to yelde hymselfe to deth or captiuyte.

¶But duryng this season at Rome was a counsell among the senatours concernyng thassignement of rule and gouernaunce of the pro[u]ynces belongyng to thempyre: in which counsell it was decreed that the contrey and warre of Numidy shuld be commytted to Metellus/ by prorogation of his authorite for an other yere more.

¶But here wyll I leue a whyle to speke of Metellus: and write of the ambytion of Marius: and how he behaued hymselfe in supplantyng the same Metellus for his rowme and dygnite.

¶How Marius by ambytion laboured to be consull and to prosecute the warre of Numidy: and how he detracted and supplanted the consull Metellus. ¶The .xxxix. chapyter.

[**63**] In the same season the sayd Marius was in a towne named Vtica/ and there made supplycation and oblacyon to the ydolles with moche sacrifice to the intent that it might be his fortune (by his helpe) to haue the place of Metellus. A custome damnable was among the people at those dayes: whan they slewe any beest in sacrifice: to loke within the intrayles and bowelles of the same beest so sacrifised. Where was shewed vnto them dyuers tokens whyther they shuld haue any hope to bring that mater to effect: for which they sacrificed or els nat. And often tymes the wycked spyrites to cause them perseuer in their ydolatry: and to gyue credence to that blynde errour shewed many tokens to them in such maner sacrifice: which | tokens they often f. 53[v] founde true. But nowe to my purpose. The preest of the ydolles which

96 worthy] condigne B C 98 his] *om.* B C 110 prouynces] B C; pronynces A

Ch. 39 4 In] At B C 6 his[2]] *om.* B C

sacrifysed for Marius shewed great and marueylous tokens vnto hym: wherby he myght greatly trust to come to his intent and purpose/ byddyng hym prosecute that thyng on which he had sette his mynde: and haue sure confydence in his goddes. Sayng that yf he wolde proue the extremyte of fortune dyligently and often: than doutlesse euery thyng prosperously shulde happen to hym. But Marius afore that tyme: long season wonderously desyredde in his mynde the dygnite of the consull. And to say trueth he wanted nothyng which longed to hym/ which shulde haue suche a dygnite saue onely antiquite of his progeny and auncient noblenesse of byrthe. For though he were but a gen[t]ylman of the first heed: neuerthelesse his condycions were worthy and exellent. In hym was great experience of wysdome/ moch probyte/ honestie/ and sadnesse. He had great policy and connyng in chyualry: in batayle his mynde was exellent and bolde. But in peace it was lowe and moderate. He ouercame ryches and sensualyte of his body. He desyred nor coueyted nothyng erthly saue glorie/ laude/ and worshyp. This Marius was borne and brought vp by all his chyldhode in the contrey of Champayne beyond France in a towne named Arpyne. But assone as he was encreased/ so that he myght bere harnesse and byde the hardnesse of warfare: he concluded to lyue on the wages of chyualrie. And in that study he exercysed hymselfe: and nat in eloquence of Greke langage or in other study or science: nor yet in the superfluous aparayle nor carnall lustes of citezyns vnto which he neuer subdued his body. And thus was he indued with good maners: and exercysed among honest ocupations and so contynued that his hole and vndefyled wyt shortly encreased and exalted hymself growyng to honour and vertu. First whan this Marius desyred of the comenty of Rome to haue an office: that is to say/ to be ordayned protectour of the soudyours: many of the citezyns knewe nat his person: bycause he was alway from the cyte in warre and batayle: but his actes made his name well knowen. Wherfore after that the commenty vnderstode that he was Marius of whose nobles all Italy moch communed and talked: anon they graunted his peticion/ and proclamed hym protectour of the soudyors ouer all the prouinces and tribes of Italy. In that maistership and office he behaued himself so well and wysely that after that he obtaynd an other office of more worship and authorite: and after that agayne an other of hyer dygnite.

22 long] a long C 25 though] thought B; thoughe C 26 gentylman] B C; genylman A 30 ryches] couetyse B; couetise C 32 glorie/] *virgule from* B 41 wyt] wytte C; with B

And shortly to speke: | in euery office and dygnite he so behaued hymselfe that euery man thought and counted hym worthyer of more dygnite and honour than he had. How beit for all these condycions: as honorable as he was: he durst neuer before desyre thoffice of consull of Rome tyll this tyme whan he had suche confort by his sacryfice. But whan he was thus warnedde and put in hope and confort/ euer after he was hedelyng enclyned to ambytion and couetyse of that dygnite. f. 54r

¶At this season the commenty of Rome had all other offices among them or at their gyft and dystribucyon. But the estates and noble men kept among them and in their handes the consulshypp yerely one succedyng another by electyon. So that of the commenty was none so noble nor exellent of dedes/ but that he was reputed vnworthy of that dygnite/ and as who sayth vyle and polluted.

[64] But whan Marius sawe and considredde that the wordes and counsell of the enchauntour and preest whiche behelde his sacrifyce pretended to the same poynt and conclusion as the desyre of his mynde moued hym longe before. Anone he came to his capytayne Metellus/ beseching hym to be dyscharged of the batayle tyll he might go to Rome to thintent to desyre the consulshyppe of the senatours. But howbeit that in this Metellus was vertu/ glorie/ worshyppe/ and all other thynges longynge to a good man plentifully ynoughe. Neuertheles of his courage and mynde was he somwhat proude/ despysing/ and dysdayning other: which were nat come of so hy lynage as he was. But specially he was stately and proude of mynde: which is a commen vyce and myschefe among estates and gentylmen. Wherfore Metellus heryng this enterprise of Marius/ first of all was moued with the newelty of his peticyon. For at that tyme were none wont to speke for that dygnite/ but yf they were come of a noble stocke. And so was nat Marius. And thus Metellus marueyled moche at his enterprise: and who myght counsell hym therto: warnyng hym as vnder colour of amyte and frendshyppe/ nat to presume vpon so contrary and vnlikely a thyng: nor to exalt his mynde so hy aboue fortune conuenyent for his state and condycion. Sayng also to hym that euery thing was nat to be coueyted nor desyred of euery man. And that it became him well by reason to be contented/ pleased/ and satysfied with that honour which he had and that was his owne/ and nat to desyre thinges vnmete for his degre. And finally he exhorted and counselled hym to beware to desire that thing of the Romayns

63 another] other B C 64 he] *om.* B C 79 newelty] nouelty C 86 nor] or C

f. 54v which laufully might be denyed vnto hym: | consydring and hauyng regarde to his lynage and auncetry.

¶After Metellus had counselled Marius with these wordes and otherlyke: and that he coude nat tourne nor apease his mynde/ he answered hym at last that assone as he coude conuenyently (nat lettyng the besynesse of the commen wele) he wold graunt his desyre and peticyon. But after this whan Maryus desyredde the same dyscharge importunely and often: he made hym answere sayng that he shulde nat make so great hast to Rome for that purpose/ for he shulde come tymely ynough to demaunde that dygnite acompanyed with the sonne of the same Metellus/ which sonne shulde also go to Rome in tyme to come/ to demaunde of the senatours the same dygnite with Marius. This sonne of Metellus was at that tyme in the army of his father Metellus contynually exercysing the feates of warre nat withstandyng that he was but .xx. yere of age. This answere of Metellus styredde Marius agaynst hym with greuous yre and wrath/ what for the honour which he desyred: and what for the lycence to depart/ which he coude nat obtayne of him by no prayer nor request at his pleasure. Insomoch that he enraged agaynst Metellus moued by desyre of that office and prouokedde by yre/ which two vyces ambysion and yre counselled and impelled this Marius to moche yll agaynst the sayd Metellus/ sparyng nouther worde nor dede which myght endamage or hynder hym/ his honour and name. And that myght helpe or auaunce hymselfe by ambysion to come to the dygnite which he desyred. He gouerned the soudyours which passed forthe the wynter vnder his gouernaunce nat as he ought to do: but suffred them to haue their pleasure to thintent therby to obtayne their fauour and goodwyll in his enterprise. Also he spake often in blamyng Metellus/ and proudly commendyng and exaltyng hymselfe vnto the marchantes of Rome: of whom was great resort and concours to the sayd cite of Vtica where Marius soiourned. And often tymes he boosted sayeng to them that if the one halfe of the army were graunted and commytted to hym within fewe dayes he wolde behaue hymselfe that he wold haue Iugurth in bondes and subiection. Farthermore he sayed to them in auancynge hymselfe that Metellus prolonged the batayle for the nonest/ for a craft bycause he was a man pompous and

99 purpose/] *virgule suppl.* 102 come/] *virgule suppl.* 104 Metellus] *om.* C
105 .xx. yere] twenty yeres C 110 vyces] B C; vyces and A 111 yll] euyll C
112 nouther] neyther C 119 vnto] to C 123 behaue] so behaue C
124 Farthermore] Furthermore C 126 nonest] nonce C

desyrous of glorie and worshyppe/ vtterly reioysing in authorite and gyuen to pride and affection of dygnite: and bycause he knewe well that whyle the batell contynued he shulde be reputed in maner as a kyng/ therfore he dyd his deuoyre the | more to prolong the warre to f. 55r thende that in the mean tyme he myght exalt and magnify hymselfe. These wordes of Marius semed to the sayd marchantes certayne and true/ and also as they thought (by suche informacion) moost expedyent to the commen wayle that some newe capytayne were chosen/ which shortely wold finysshe that warre. For by long contynuance of the same warre: many of the sayd marchantes had wasted and spent moche of their substance and richesse. And also to suche desyrefull myndes as they had/ nothyng coude to fast be hasted or brought to ende.

[65] ¶Moreouer at this season was in company of the Romayne army a certayne Numidyan named Gauda/ whiche was sonne of Manastaball: and neuewe vnto Massinissa. Micipsa in his testament ordayned that this Gauda shulde be seconde heyre of Numidy/ after the deth of his two sonnes and of Iugurth. This Gauda was sore enfebledde with dyseases and syckenesse: and for that cause his mynde was a lytell endulled and priuate of reason and memorie. Whyle this Gauda (as sayed is) was in the Romayns army: he requyred of Metellus to suffre hym to haue his seat and siege next vnto hym after the vse of kynges of Numidy. Also after that bycause of defence and garde of his body: he desyred that a company of soudyours of the Romayns myght be graunted and assigned to hym. But Metellus extremely denyed bothe his peticyons sayng for the first: that suche honour longed onely to them whom the Romayns toke and named for kynges. And also for the seconde peticyon he sayd that it were an vnauysed and iniuryous ordynance if the Romayne soudyours were gyuen or assigned to the garde and seruyce of a Numidyan/ whiche was no kyng but a soudyour lyke many mo hyred for stypend. Whyle Gauda was dyspleased and angry with Metellus for denyeng of these his peticyons: Marius came to hym and prouoked hym [to reuenge] the dyspleasure and iniury whiche the captayne had done to hym with his helpe and [a]uauncement. This Gauda (as I haue sayd before) was of a feble and vnstable mynde: and the mannes wytte was of lytell valoure by meanes of dyseases which long had holden hym. Wherfore Marius with his elegant/ fayre/ and flatering wordes at his owne

137 their] their sayde C 154 an] *om.* C 159 to reuenge] B C; he wolde reneng A 161 auauncement] B C; euauncement A 162 of a] of B; *om.* C

pleasure induced hym and exalted his mynde sayng that he was a kynge/ an exellent and great man. And also neuewe to the worthy and noble kyng Massinissa. Wherfore (sayd he) yf Iugurth were outher slayne or taken prisoner it was lickely to come to that poynt: that the f. 55v kingdome of Numidy shuld be | assigned and commytted to hym of the senatours without any tary or resystence: which thinge shulde shortely be brought to passe yf Marius hymselfe were creat consull in place of Metellus and than assigned to execute and finysshe the warre with Iugurth.

Under this maner Maryus counselled and induced bothe the sayd Gauda/ the Romayne knyghtes/ the commen soudyours/ and also the marchauntes and occupyers whiche were in the towne at that season with many other whom he impelled with his wordes so: that some of them for loue whiche they had to Marius: And other some for great hope and desyre which they had to haue peace and concorde wrote to Rome to their kynsmen and frendes of the batayle of Numidy and that very sharpely agaynst Metellus desyring and besechyng them to labour at Rome with all their myght that Marius myght be elect consull and assigned to execute the warre of Numidy. And thus at Rome was the consulshyppe desyredde by many men with great fauour and very honest peticyons for Marius. Also at that tyme had the sayd Marius this auauntage. For the commentie at that season deposed many of thestates: and exalted such as were newe gentylmen after the lawe of one named Manlius which before had ben protectour of the commentie. This Manlyus ordayned and inactedde a lawe/ that if any thyng were vngoodly done and agaynst right of thestates beyng in any office or dygnite: than he which so had done shulde be deposed of his office: and in his place some newe gentyll or actyue man of the commentie sette and deputed and so exalted. This lawe at those dayes was kept in effect and executed at Rome: wherfore euery thyng proceded prosperously to the purpose and profet of Marius. For (as I haue sayd before) in hym was no noblenesse of auncyent lynage nor byrthe.

¶But here wyll I leaue to speke of the ambytion of Maryus and retourne to wryte of Iugurth: and howe he behaued hymselfe agaynst Metellus.

166 kynge/] *virgule suppl.* an] and an C 167 outher] eyther C 168 was] were B C 178 Marius:] *colon* B C; *punctus* A 183 execute] erecte C

¶Howe Iugurth renewed the warre agaynst Metellus/ and how the Numidyans inhabyters of the towne of Vacca by treason murdred the garnyson of Romayns which Metellus had set in the same towne. ¶The .xl. chap.

[**66**] In the meane tyme whan Iugurth had broken the composicyon f. 56r which he had before made with Metellus by counsell of Bomylchar/ and had concluded agayne to begyn the warre: than anone he preparedde all thynges necessary to batayle with great dilygence. And with great hast he assembled an army. Moreouer he dayly troubled with thretnynges/ or feare/ or els with great rewardes: suche cytees and townes as before had forsaken hym and yelded themselfe to Metellus. So that he sparedde no polycie to make them to render themselfe agayne to hym. In suche holdes and townes as were in his possession/ he sette garnyson and defence of men of warre. He renewed and bought agayne armour and wepyn/ and all other thynges which he had lost before: or delyuerd to Metellus in hope of peace. He attysedde vnto hym many of the Romayns subgettes and bondmen: by promysing to them theyr lybertie. Iugurth also proued and attempted with rewardes them: whome Metellus had sette and assigned in garnyson/ garde/ and defence of suche places as he had wonne in Numidy: so that vtterly he suffred nothyng to be left quyet nor vnassayed: but by all maner meanes made prouysion for hymselfe/ mouynge and puttyng in profe euery thynge. But among all other/ thinhabytantes of the cyte called Vacca (in which Metellus at begynnyng had sette his garnyso[n]: whan Iugurth first sought his peace of Metellus) were desyred often of Iugurth and with great and importune instance excited to treason. In somoch that at last they assented to hym to conspyre agaynst the Romayns. Thinhabytantes of the cyte dyd nat yelde themselfe from Iugurth with their owne goodwyll: and namely thestates and rulers therof dyd neuer yelde them to Metellus saue faynedly. Wherfore specially they were the first that conspyred agaynst hym secretely amonge themselfe. For why as it often happeneth the commentie and specially of the Numidyans were vnstable of mynde/ vtterly enclyned to sedycion and dyscorde/ couetous of newe thynges and changes: and contrary to rest and

Ch. 40 3 of] of the C 8 batayle] warre B C 12 to^{3}] *om.* C 15 and all] and set al C 17 vnto] to C 18 Iugurth] He B C 21 nor] or C 22 hymselfe/] *virgule suppl.* 23 other/] *virgule suppl.* 24–6 (in which . . . Metellus)] *brackets* B C; *colons* A 25 garnyson] B C; garnysou A 33 happeneth] happened B C 34 dyscorde/] *virgule suppl.* 35 and changes] *om.* C

quyetnesse. But (as I haue sayd before) whan the chyfe of the cyte had secretly concluded and apoynted their mater and treason among themselfe: agaynst the thyrde day they ordayned that the same thyrde day next after shulde be commaunded solem/ holy/ and worshypped ouer all the countrey of Affrike: and Numidy. Which day shewed and pretended by all symilytude myrth/ game/ and sport: f. 56v rather than any drede to the Ro|mayns which were in garde and garnyson of the cyte. But the Numidyans full of prodycion and treason whan they sawe their tyme called vnto their houses all the chefe captayns and maister soudyours of the Romayns which were in the towne. And also one named Turpylius: whom Metellus had ordayned to be his lyeutenant/ prouost/ and chefe captayne of the towne: they enuyted and called as yf it had ben to chere and feest them/ one to one house/ an other to an other. But this chere was suche as the Scorpyon is wont to make: which whyle she maketh gladde semblant with her mouth mortally styngeth with the tayle: so this feest was a cloke to mortall treason. For whyle the Romayns were in myddes of their daynties vnarmed suspectyng no paryll. All the Numydians at a token gyuen and one houre apoynted before/ slewe eche one his geest which dyned with hym without fauoure: so that among them all escaped nat one/ except the sayd Turpylius heed captayne or lyeutenant of the towne. This done: all the Numydians togyder sette vpon the remenant of the commen soudyours which wandred and strayed abrode in the towne and in the stretes/ dyspersedde abrode without any armour: as is wont on suche a day/ without order/ feryng nor doutyng no daunger. Some of the commens whan thestates had made them pryue of this treason came also to helpe them/ and some other ignorant of the mater sauyng that/ that they had desyre and pleasure in suche murder inuadedde the Romayns also. For though they were ignorant of the counsell of this dede: yet the noyse or skirmysshe and newelty of the mater pleased them ynough.

[67] The Romayn soudyou[r]s were ignorant and incertayne of this vnprouyded feare and cruell murder doutyng what was best to be done. Their ennemies compasynge them on euery syde lette them to go to the castell of the towne where their armoure and wepyn was: and the gates of the towne were shet on euery syde before this skyrmisshe

36 the[2]] this B C 42 garde and] *om.* C 45 the[2]] *om.* C 53 token] tokens B 54 and] and at B C 60 day/] *virgule suppl.* 65 newelty] nouelty C 67 soudyours] B; souldyours C; soudyous A this] the C 69 lette] letted B C 71 shet] shut C

began/ wherby they were prohibyted and letted to escape or auoyde the towne. Moreouer women and chyldren thrue downe vpon them stones/ and other thynges that came next to hande from the wyndowes and hyest partes of their houses: stryuing who myght throwe first and moost. Thus this doutfull and vnprouyded myschefe coude nat be eschued: nor they which were ryght worthy and stronge soudyours were nat able to resyst the very cowardyse and feblenes of women and chyldren/ which thrue downe vpon them. Thus many of them: both good and yll/ worthy/ and vnworthy/ strong/ and | feble: were all slayne after one maner without dyfference. f. 57r

In this so great ieopardy: the Numidyans beyng madde and cruell in murdre/ and the gates shette on euery syde: of all the Romayns/ or Italyans: onely Turpylius the captayne escaped without hurt of his body. Whyther it so happened by the fauour of his hoost which called hym to banket: or by some apoyntment of treason: or els by fortune or chance: it was nat knowen for certayn. But this was knowen that euer after as long as he lyued he was reputed for a vyle and a wretched cowarde and without credence: bycause that in so great losse and myschefe he counted it better to escape: and after to lyue/ and dye in shame/ and rebuke: than manly to haue dyed in defence of the towne. And euer after to haue had a parfet and immortall name of a worthy capytayne.

¶How Metellus destroyed the towne of Vacca and murdredde all the inhabytauntes/ in reuengyng their treason. And how Turpylius lyeutenaunt or captayne of the towne/ was beheded at commaundement of Metellus. ¶The .xli. chap.

[68] Whan Metellus vnderstode of this lamentable chance/ and treason done at the towne of Vacca: his mynde was meruaylously greued/ abasshed/ and sadde withall. But to thyntent that none shulde parceyue his heuynesse/ he withdrue hymselfe from company a lytell tyme: and after whan he had satysfyed his mynde with teares/ and secrete lamentacyon. And whan his dolour was myxed with wrathe and dyspleasure agaynst that cruell dede: than hasted he hymself with great cure and dilygence to go to reuenge this iniuryous

72 and letted] *om.* B C escape or] *om.* B C 79–80 many of them:] *om.* B C 81 after one maner] *om.* B C 83 shette] shutte C 85 happened] happed B C 86–7 fortune or chance] some other chance B C 92 a parfet and immortall] an honorable B C

Ch. 41 1 murdredde] slewe B; slew C 3 the] *om.* B 6 done] downe B; doone C 9 and] but B C 12 to[2]] *om.* B

and cruell treason. Anone he called forthe a legion of soudyours which passed forthe the wynter with hym: and with them also as many horsmen of the Numidyans as he myght assemble which had forsaken Iugurth and fledde to hym: whom he thought most trusty. His legyon he arayed in lyght harnesse and easy armour to thintent to [spede] the way more redely. And bycause he entended to go about this mater secretly: therfore secretly euyn with the sonne goyng downe/ he toke his iournay and proceded forwarde towarde Vacca: and laboured so f. 57v that on the next day | after about the thyrde houre he came with his company into a certayne playne a lytell closed or compased about with small hylles nat moche hyer than the extremytees of the valey. There called he togyder his soudiours which were wery for the great labour of their iournay: and long way which they had gone. In somoch that they denyed to procede any farther. But Metellus conforted them sayeng that the towne of Vacca was no more but one myle thens. Wherfore he desyred them to suffre and endure the remenant of their labour with pacyent myndes/ but onely tyll he reuenge the deth of his cytezins and their felawes which were stronge and worthy men: and very myserably murdred. Moreouer he shewed to them benyngely the great pray which was redy for them/ if they wolde manly procede. Thus were their myndes exalted/ conforted/ and enbolded with his wordes. Metellus seyng that: was gladde and anone commaunded the horsmen to go forth in the forward: these horsmen were Numidyans. And the fotemen he commaunded to kepe secrete their standerdes/ conysances/ and badges: and to go behynde vnder the shadowe of the horsmen as nere togyder as they myght: and so proceded he to the towne.

[69] ¶Whanne the citezyns sawe an army approche and moue towarde them: at the begynnyng they thought it had ben Metellus (as it was in dede) and anone they shytte the gates of the towne agaynst him. But afterwarde whan they aduysed them well: and sawe that the company which approched made no deuastacyon nor dystruction by the feldes nor co[u]ntrey as they went. And also whan they parceyued that the horsmen which were in the forwarde were Numidyans: agayne they thought that it was Iugurth with his company. Wherfore

17 spede] B; rydde A; speede C 19 secretly[2]] priuely B; pryuely C 23 hylles] downys B; downes C 26 denyed] refusyd B; refused C 27 of Vacca] *om.* C no more] *om.* C 29 tyll he reuenge] tyll reuenged B; to reuenge C his] the B C 34 seyng] seynst B and] *om.* C 35 go forth] procede B C forward:] *colon from* C; *no punct.* A B 38 to] towarde B C 42 they] *om.* B C shytte] shut C 45 countrey] B C; conntrey A 47 they] the C

with great ioy they issued forthe of the towne to mete hym. Metellus anone parceyued their ignorance and gaue a token to his people to assayle them. The horsmen and fotemen knowynge the wyll of their captayne by blast of the trumpettes assayled and ouerthrue the commentie which came out of the cyte agaynst them: which were dyspersed ouer all the feldes. Some of the Romayns ranne to the gates of the towne and entredde without resystence: and some toke and inuaded the towres of the walles maugre the kepars. Thus the dyspleasure and yre which the Romayns had for deth of their felawes: and the hope of prayes of the towne ouercame and excluded their werynes which they had in their iournay thyderwarde.

Thus the inhabytantes of Vacca enioyed their treason but onely two dayes. | For onely the space of two dayes contynued their falshode f. 58r and crueltie vnreuenged. For the great and riche cyte was all gyuen to hauocke and murdre and vtterly dystroyed of the Romayns: so that no creature escaped alyue to boost of their treason before commytted agaynst the Romayns whom they had so trayterously slayne within their cyte. Turpylius lyeutenant or captayne of the towne which (as I haue sayd before) escaped onely with his lyfe: was called before Metellus and commaunded to answere for hymselfe by what way or meanes he escaped/ whyther by treason done to the towne/ or by any other policy. But bycause he coude but simply excuse nor pourge himselfe of that which was layed agaynst hym/ he first was scourged and beaten: and after that his heed stryken of from his sholders/ for that it was thought that yf he had nat betrayed the cyte he coude nat escape more than any other. Farthermore that great dystruction of the Romayns was ascrybed to his neglygence or treason. If this Turpylius had ben a Romayn he shulde nat haue ben put to deth. For the lawe of Porcius prohibyted any cytezyne of Rome to be slayne: but if they commytted any great offence the extreme punysshment by the lawe was to commyt them to exyle. But this Turpylius inioyed nat the priuyleges of this lawe: for asmoch as he was no citezyne of Rome/ but an Italyan of the towne of Collace.

48 the] that C 52 them: which were] them B C 53 all] *om.* B C 59 their] *om.* C 61 the] that B C 62 and²] *om.* B C 73 escape] haue escaped B C 75 ben] *om.* B 79 priuyleges] priuylege C

¶Howe Bomylchar conspyred treason agaynst Iugurth and by what meanes this treason was dyscouered and Bomylchar with certayn other put to deth for the same. ¶The .xlii. chapyter.

[70] Bi the same tyme Bomylchar (by whose counsell and mocyon Iugurth before had begon the composicion with Metellus/ which he omitted and brake agayn for feare) was conuersant with Iugurth/ which a lytell suspected this Bomylchare of treason. Wherfore he suspectyng hym agayne ymagenedde newe polycie agaynst Iugurth dayly sekynge and deuysing some gyle to his dystructyon and dethe/ so that in dyuerse deuyses there about his mynde wandredde and was f. 58v weryed bothe day and nyght. But whan he had assayed | many wayes and that nothing came to purpose: he adioyned vnto hym an other companyon named Nabdalsa/ a noble man exalted and enhaunced with great rychesse: and moche beloued of his commentie and people of whom he had rule. This Nabdalsa was so well beloued with Iugurth/ that often tymes he commytted to hym an army and power by hymselfe to execute all other thynges which longed to meane besynesses whyle Iugurth hymselfe was weryed or lette with other gretter thynges: wherby the sayd Nabdalsa had obtaynedde great honour and gathered great richesse. Thus at conclusyon: by apoyntment and counsell bothe of Bomylchar and of Nabdalsa a day was prefixed bytwene them to execute their treason agaynst Iugurth. And in the meane tyme they prouyded euery thynge to that purpose as the matter and case requyredde. This apoyntment made: they both departed in sonder. Nabdalsa went to the army which Iugurth had commytted to hym for to tary with the same nere to those places where the Romayns wyntredde: to thyntent that if the Romayns wasted or dystroyed the countrey. Nabdalsa with his company shulde other prohybet them: or els so dystourbe them that they shulde nat escape vnreuenged. But whanne the tyme apoynted drewe nere: than was Nabdalsa so abasshedde for the greatnesse of the dede that he mette nat with Bomylchar at the day and tyme assigned. This his great feare letted all the matter. But whan Bomylchar was thus dysapoynted of his partynge felowe he was greatly abasshed: neuerthelesse his mynde was moche desyrous to parfourme his enterprise. But agayne he was doutfull for this cowardouse fere of his companyon: lest he wolde omytte their first apoyntment and counsell/ and begyn some other newe apoyntment. Wherfore he sent letters vnto hym by trusty

Ch. 42 4 Bi] At B C 18 besynesses] besynesse B C 19 obtaynedde] obtayneddde A; optayned B C 38 vnto] to C

frendes/ and partyners of the same treason. In which letters he sharpely blamed the pacyence/ delayeng/ and cowardyse of Nabdalsa/ and vnstablenesse of his mynde/ obtestyng and callyng vnto wytnes the goddes by whome he had sworne to perfourme the sayd treason. Moreouer he warned hym that he [sh]olde nat tourne to their dystruction and confusyon: the great rewardes which they bothe myght haue of Metellus. Which thyng truly shuld fortune if Metellus hymselfe shulde bring Iugurth into captiuyte. Farthermore Bomylchar in the same letters gaue monycion to Nabdalsa that thende of Iugurth was nere come: and that it was nat possyble that he myght longe contynewe all thynges consydredde. | But than was the mater in f. 59r
hand whyther he shuld be destroyed by them or els by Metellus. Wherfore he exhorted hym well to consyder in his mynde whyther he had leuer betray hym/ and therby optayne great fauour and rewardes: or els to leaue of tyll Metellus ouercame hym: and than to be put to deth also with hym.

[71] ¶These exhortacions with other lyke were contayned in the letters of Bomylchar dyrected vnto Nabdalsa. But whan these letters were delyuerd: as chaunce was: Nabdalsa lay in his bedde to recreate and refresshe his body weryed with labour and besynesse/ which he had taken before. Whan Nabdalsa had redde these letters and vnderstode the mynde of Bomylchar: first many deuyses entred his mynde and moche cure he had in musynge what was moost expedyent to be done in the cause. But whyle he was in this study: sodenly he fell in a slombre and his wery membres desyringe rest moued hym to fall in slepe. This Nabdalsa had a seruant longynge to hym whom he moche loued and trusted: in somoch that no besynesse nor counsell he hydde nor kept secret from hym: this counsell of betrayng of Iugurth onely except. Whan this seruant vnderstode that the sayd letters were brought to his lorde he thought that he had nede of his counsell as he was wont and acustomed to haue in other maters: and anone entred in to the tabernacle or tent where his maister lay. And seyng hym fast in slepe: he toke the letters which Nabdalsa had v[n]wysely layd aboue his heed vpon the pyllowe: and seyng by the superscripcyon that the letter came from Bomylchar he redde it to thende. But whan he vnderstode the treason: in all hast he addressed hym with the same

41 mynde/] *virgule suppl.*; *comma* C vnto] to C 43 sholde] B; wolde A; shulde C 50 whyther] whether C 51 his] *om.* B C whyther] whether C 57 in] on B C 65–6 he hydde] B C; that he hydde A 69 and²] *om.* C 70 tabernacle or] *om.* B C 74 hym] *om.* C

letter to Iugurth. Nabdalsa nat long after awoke of sleape and myssed the letter/ wherfore anone he enquyred who had ben there in his tent. But in shorte season came dyuers of his louers from Iugurth/ which certyfyed hym of all the mater as it was done. Nabdalsa first of all entended to pursue his accuser: but whan he perceyued that it was but in vayne so to do/ consydring that he was all redy in the company of Iugurth: he went vnto Iugurth hymselfe to thentent to pacify and mytigate his dyspleasure and wrath. And sayd vnto hym that whan the sayd letters were first delyuerd vnto hym he had fully purposed nat to kepe them secret: but hymselfe to haue dysclosed them to Iugurth. But whyle he was slepyng his false seruant (in hope to be aduansed therby) had preuented hym and done the same thyng which he himself had fully purposed to do. Farthermore in wepynge he
f. 59v obtested and requyred | hym by all amyte and loue which had ben bytwene them and for all the faythfull seruyce which he had done to hym in foretyme nat to haue hym suspected in so cruell a dede.

[72] Iugurth answered to these requestes of Nabdalsa myldly and soberly lest any gretter varyaunce myght ryse therof: but moche contrary to the dysposicyon of his mynde. For he thought otherwyse than he answeredde: howbeit he had well refrayned and alayed his wrath before with the deth of Bomylchar/ and of many other whom he knewe first deuysours and partyng felowes of that treason/ whome he had caused to be put to dethe before the cummynge of Nabdalsa: lest some by batayle or other insurrectyon shulde haue procededde of that besynesse if they had lyued any lengar.

¶From this day forwarde Iugurth was neuer quyet day nor nyght: so that he trusted nouther place/ nother man/ nor tyme: but suspected and mystrusted euery thynge. His ennemies and his owne subgettes he dreded and suspectedde bothe in lyke and after one maner. He sherched and espyedde euery place for drede of treason doutyng and suspectynge euery sounde or noyse that he harde. He rested and lay some nyght in one place and some nyght in an other/ and that in abiect and secrete places agaynst the honoure of his estate royall. Somtyme he rose from his bedde in his slepe in myddes of the nyght and armed hymselfe cryeng/ arragyng/ and vyolently smyting agaynst the walles of the chambre: as if he had ben

75 awoke of sleape] awakenyd B; awaked C 86 hym] hym his purpose B; him his purpose C 87 in] *om.* B C 88 obtested] besought B C by] for B C 96 treason/] *virgule suppl.* 98 by] *om.* B C 101 nouther] neyther C nother] neither C 106 and²] *om.* C 109 arragyng] enragyng B; enraging C

in batayle. So that for the great drede of treason which he had/ he toke no rest nother sleping nor waking: but was vyolently vexed and fered lyke a mad man without reson or dyscression.

¶How Metellus renued the warre agaynst Iugurth: and howe Marius was creat consull and assigned to execute the warre of Numidy at pleasure of the commens agaynst the wyll of all the noble men of Rome. ¶The.xliii. chapyter.

[73] Whan Metellus by suche as fledde bytwene the two parties vnderstode of the chaunce of Bomylchar and of this treason dysclosed/ he began than agayne to contende with Iugurth: with open warre and therto hasted all thyng necessary and expedyent. And consydring that Marius was contynually cryeng on hym for the sayd lycence and congy to depart to Rome | and also greuous/ hatefull/ f. 60r
and contrary to hym: aduysynge hym nat moche necessary but lytell mete in so sharpe a besynes. And seyng hym yll wyllyng to euery thyng/ he graunted hym lycence at last: to depart towarde Rome as he before had often requyred and demaunded by peticyon.

¶But as I haue sayd long before/ the letters which were sende to Rome to the commens by fauourers of Marius were well accepted. For whan the commentie had ouersene them/ and by them vnderstode the praysing of Marius: and the dyspraysing of Metellus. They were all enclyned vtterly to the auauncement of Marius and detractyon of the other. The noblenes of Metellus the captayne which was before to his great worshyp and honour tourned nowe toward enuy and hatered agaynst hym. But the lownes and vnnoblenes of Marius encreased to him fauour specially of the commentie which were come of vnnoble blode/ as he was. But the dilygence and fauour of bothe the parties (that is to say of thestates which helde with Metellus: and of the commens that helde with Marius) dyd measure and gyde euery thynge rather than the good or yll dysposycions of the two aduersaryes Metellus or Marius. For the commens to dy for it/ concludedde to exalt Marius. And the estates in the same maner laboured to kepe hym vnder bycause he was vnnoble borne/ and to exalt none saue them which were come of noble progeny. Farthermore the maisters and heed offycers of the commentie which loued debate/ on euery assemble and congregation of the commens sore blamed Metellus and

Ch. 43 2 at] at the C 6 this] his C 13 thyng/] *virgule suppl.* 21 toward] to B C 24 dilygence and fauour] diligente fauour C 32 debate/] *virgule suppl.* on] at B C dyspised his dedes desyring of the commens that Metellus might be put to the punysshe of his heed/ sayng that he was so worthy: for that he prolonged the warre in Numidy agaynst Iugurth more than nede was. But in dyspisyng and accusyng Metellus they forgat nat to commende Marius/ and exalt hym with wordes somwhat to moche: and more than he was worthy in many poyntes. In somoche that the people were so greatly enclyned to hym with their fauoure: that all the crafty men and labourers of the cyt[e: a]nd also of the countrey which had no lyuynge saue in the labour of their handes left their warke and besynesse and folowed Maryus/ frequentyng and resortyng to his company. And sette more by his auauncement and honour than by their owne profet or aduauntage/ trustyng that after yf he obtayned the sayd honoure: they shulde haue their lyuenge by hym. And thus shortly to speke the estates and noble men of Rome beynge sore f. 60v astonyed/ the consulshyppe was | commytted to Marius a newe gentylman whose predecessours before hym to such dygnite coude neuer attayne and were counted vnworthy. Thus that thynge which many yeres before that tyme coude neuer be done nor brought about: was nowe brought to effect: that is to say the consulshyp which was the moost exellent dygnite of Rome was nowe in handes of the commentie and commytted to a man of basse byrth. Shortly after this: the protectour of the commente named Lucius Manlius enquyred and demaunded of the people whom it wolde please them to send into Numidy to finysshe the warre with Iugurth. The moost part of the commenty answered that Marius shulde haue that office and besynesse: howbeit a lytell before that tyme the senatours had assigned by their ordynaunce the prouynce of Numidy to Metellus for his worthy dedes: wherfore nowe this ordynaunce was frustrate and voyde. For the commenty wolde haue their statutes executed and fulfylled.

¶Of the seconde batell foughten bytwene Metellus and Iugurth: and howe Iugurth lost the batayle and also one of his chiefe townes named Thala. ¶The .xliiii. chapyter.

[74] In the meane tyme whyle the interprise of Marius proceded thus forwarde at Rome: Iugurth was sore troubled in his mynde for many consyderations. First he consydredde the losse of many whome he reputed for his frendes tyll before he knewe their treason of whom he

34–5 be put to the punysshe of] lose C 41 crafty men] craftes men C cyte: and] cyte. And A; cite: and B; citie, and C 47 of Rome] *om.* C had many put to deth/ and many other had fledde from hym for feare/ some to the Romayns/ and other some to Bocchus kynge of the Mauryans. He called also to his mynde that without mynisters and men of warre he was nat able to execute the warre: and moreouer he thought it ieopardous after so great falshode and treason of his olde frendes to proue or assay [the] fydelite of newe. For these causes and mo lyke (as I haue sayd before) his mynde was driuen to and fro/ varyable and incertayne in dyuers opynyons. In somoch that there was no maner thyng/ no counsell nor no maner man: that coude sufficyently satisfy nor please his mynde. He changed his iournayes and wayes euery day into sondry places for feare of treson. Somtyme he addressed hym towarde his ennemies: and anone after returned into wo|des and f. 61r wyldernesses. Often tymes he had trust and confidence in flyght: and anone he put his trust in armour and batayle. He douted whyther he myght lesse trust to strength or trueth of his men which were with hym: so that what euer he purposed to do: or whyther so euer he intendedde/ euery thyng was contrary to hym.

But whyle Iugurth thus prolonged and taryed: sodenly Metellus with his army appered in his syght. Iugurth that parceyuing: set in order and array his Numidyans as well as he myght after the short tyme which he had therto. And immedyatly the armyes approched: and the batayle began. In that part of the batayle where Iugurth hymselfe was: they stroue and resysted a lytell space: but all the other Numidyans at the first brunt/ concourse or assaut were put to flight with vyolence: and driuen backwarde. The Romayns toke some of their standerdes and armour/ which they fleyng away left behynde them: but of their ennemies they toke but fewe. For the Numidyans in that batayle and almoost in all other defended themselfe better with their fete: than with their handes or armoure.

[75] Iugurth at this tyme: mystrustedde his case moche more than at any other tyme euer before/ for the cowarde withdrawyng of his peple. Wherfore he acompanyed hymselfe with the Romayns which had forsaken and betrayed Metellus: and fledde to hym. With them/ and with a part of his horsmen he fledde into the wyldernesses therby: and from thens vnto a towne named Thala/ which was a great towne and a riche: and moche of his treasour and of the aparell longyng to the yongth of his yong chyldren was in the same towne. But whan Metellus vnderstode that Iugurth was fledde to so ryche a towne/

Ch. 44 8 deth/] *virgule suppl.* (*end of line* A B) 13 the] their A 21 he] after B C 38 cowarde] cowardous B C 44 yongth] youthe C

howbeit he knewe that bytwene the towne and the next flod therto was .l. myle space of dry ground voyde and without habytacyon: neuerthelesse he toke in hande to ouercome all sharpnesse and dyfficultie of places[: a]nd also to ouercome nature/ though it semed impossyble to mannes mynde. This thyng Metellus toke in hande in hope to finysshe the batayle moche soner yf he might wynne that towne.

¶Wherfore he comma[u]nded that all the beestes which serued for caryage/ shulde be vnladen of all suche baggage and burthens as they caryed longynge to the soudyours: saue onely whete and vitayle for the space of .x. dayes. Also he commaunded some of the beestes to be laded with bottels full of water/ and other vessels mete to be caryed with water. Moreouer: ouer all the contrey he gathered togyder as many tame beestes as | [f. 61v] he coude get and them laded with empty vessels of euery sort. Many of them were trene vessell which he had done to be gathered among the vyllages of the Numidyans. Farthermore he commaunded thinhabytantes of those marchesse which after the flyght of Iugurth had yelded them to Metellus that they shulde make them redy to folowe the hoost euery man with asmoche water as they myght beare. And assigned them a day and place/ where they shulde be redy vnder payne of dethe. Whan Metellus was come to the sayd flodde which was fyftie myle from the towne of Thala and nerest water therto (as I haue sayd before): he dyd all the beestes to be laded of the same water. And so went towarde Thala/ his hoost set in order and aray: so that yf any ieopardy apered he was euer redy at defence[. B]ut afterward whan he was come to that place where he had apoynted the Numidyans to mete hym with the water wherwith they were laded and folowed the hoost. And whan his tentes were pytched/ sette/ and defended about with trenches: cutte trees/ bowes/ and stakes after the polycie of warre: sodenly from the heuen dyscended great vyolence and plenty of rayne water that is more than sufficyent to all the army as well to men as beestes. Moreouer their vytels were more plentyfull than they trusted or lokedde after. For the Numydians which newly were yelded were somoche the more seruysable/ and redy to mynistre euery thynge necessary vnto the army. And no maruell: for euery thyng is quycke at

49 places: and] B C; places. And A nature/] *virgule from* B 54 burthens] burthen C 60 trene] treen B; treene C 63 Metellus] hym B; him C 68 (as . . . before)] *brackets om.* A 71 defence. But] *virgule* A B; *no punct.* C 76 is] it was B C 77 sufficyent] sufficiently B; sufficient C

the begynnyng which often fadeth at the ende. But the soudiours and men of warre: were more gladde to ocupy the rayne water for deuocyon/ than suche water which was brought vnto them in vessels by caryage. For they supposedde that their goddes loued and fauoured them which in so drie a contrey/ and in suche a chaunce sent to them so great plenty of water besyde prouisyon of their captayne. This thyng greatly conforted the myndes of them all : and incouraged them with boldnesse/ strength/ and dilygence: to ouercome all dyfficulties which remaynedde. This confort kyndlyng their myndes: they spedde themselfe so forwarde that on the next day after they came vnto the towne of Thala: contrary vnto the opynion or knoledge of Iugurth. Thinhabytantes which thought themselfe surely defended by the sharpnesse and dyfficultie of the place/ were sodenly abasshed and astonyed for that great vnwont and unprouyded case. Neuerthelesse they made prouysion to batayle as quickely as they might by sufferaunce of the tyme. The Romayns addres| sed them in the f. 62^{r} same maner.

[76] But the kyng Iugurth anone cast in his mynde that to Metellus was nothyng vnprouydedde nor vnable to be done: as he that by his craft/ dilygence/ and polycie: had ouercome both wepen/ armour/ place/ and tyme. And also nature itselfe which ruleth other thynges longynge vnto men. Iugurth this aduysing and reuoluing in his mynde fledde priuely by night forth of the towne with his children and a great part of his treasour. Nor after this tyme he neuer taryed in one place past the space of a day or of one nyght/ faynyng that he fledde so from one place to an other bycause of his present besynesse: but the ryght cause of his remouynge was for that he feared treason which he thought best to auoyd and eschue by contynuall changyng of places. For suche counsels of treason can nat be taken without delyberation and processe of tyme/ and conuenyens or oportunyte of places where princes dothe long soiourne and contynue.

¶But whan Metellus sawe that thinhabytantes were redy to batayle/ and also that the towne was strongly defended bothe by craft of mannes handes and by nature of the place. Anone he compased about the towne [on] euery syde with profounde dychesse/ trenches/ and herdels: of sharpe stakes the poyntes upwarde to thentent that none of thinhabytantes shuld breke out nor escape by night/ as Iugurth had done before: nor that no vytels shulde be

84 vnto] to C 91 vnto] to C 92 vnto] to C 99 the] *om.* C 106 one] a C nyght/] *virgule suppl.* 116 on] one A

conuayed in to them/ wherby they might the lengar resyst agaynst hym and indure the sege. Afterwarde he commaunded scaffoldes to be made about the walles specially in [two] suche places as were moost conuenyent: and pentyses of sheldes conioyned in maner of vynes to be driuen to the walles vpon wheles. And aboue the sayd scaffoldes to be cast a hepe of grauell and stones: and toures of tymbre and bulwarkes set vpon them: and other soudyours he assigned to defende the warke/ and them also that laboured therevpon. These scaffoldes/ pentyses/ and pauases: were made to thentent that vnder them the Romayns might vndermyne the walles without great paryll or dammage. On the other syde/ the garnyson and inhabytantes hastely laboured to resyst the Romayns and to defende themselfe and their towne manfully. So that on both parties was nothing forgoten which was able to be done touchyng their defence. But brefely to speke the Romayns weryed with moche labour and batayle .xl. dayes after they were come thyder: at last wanne the towne. But all the pray and ryches of the towne was distroyed by them which were within the
f. 62v towne | in garnyson of the Romayns/ which had fledde from Metellus to Iugurth: which specially had assigned them to defende the towne. These traytours whan they sawe the walles vndermined and brused with dyuerse ingens of batayle: and their fortune was brought to extremyte: and no socours nor hope remaynedde. Than they assembled and caryed togyder all the treasour and riches of the towne/ as golde/ syluer/ with other precious ornamentes or iewels into the palays of Iugurth/ and there fylled themselfe with wyne and other delycate meates. And at conclusion whan they were full saturate and ingorged: they sette fyre on the palays and wylfully brent and distroyed the richesse/ the palays: and themselfe withall. So that suche punysshement as they dreded to suffre of their ennemies they voluntarily suffredde the same with their owne handes to auoyde the subiectyon and daunger of their ennemies: by desperate folly and presumptuous madnesse.

120 agaynst] *om.* B C 122 in two] into A; in B C 124 aboue] about C
132–3 which was] *om.* B C

¶How Metellus fortified the cite of Leptis and at request of the embassadours of the same cytie sende thyder garnyson to defende the cyte agaynst Iugurth: and of the sytuacion of the same cyte and behauour of thinhabytantes therof. The .xlv. cha.

[77] At the same tyme whan Thala was wonne of the Romayns/ embassadours came from a towne of Numidy named Leptis vnto Metellus/ requiryng hym to send thyder socours of garnyson and a capytayne to defend them from the oppression and iniury of a certayne noble and debatefull man which was within that cyte named Amylchar which (as they sayd) contynually laboured for newe changes/ excityng and mouyng the commen people to forsake the Romayns agayne. In somoch that agaynst the sayd Amylchar no man was able to resyst nor to preuayle: for he set nought by commaundement of their officers and rulers/ nor yet by the auncient lawes of their cyte. At conclusion these imbassadours sayd to Metellus for a surete that except he graunted their petycion that both their owne helthe/ and also the frendes and louers of thempyre which were within that cite shuld be in great danger and paryll.

¶These Leptitans at begynning of this warre of Iugurth required frend| shyppe with the Romayns of Calphurnius of whom is made f. 63r
mencion in begynning of this hystorie. And after that they sende to Rome vnto all the senatours requirynge the same amyte and peace of them: which thyng was graunted to them gladly. Therfore from thensforth they euer contynued good and faithfull to the Romayns: and worthely and substancially dyde euery thyng which was commaunded vnto them by Calphurnius/ by Albynus/ or by Metellus. For this consyderation they lightly obtayned all their desyre of Metellus/ which at their request sent forth with them vnto the sayd towne of Leptis: four cohortes of Lombardes chosen out of all his army with whome he sent to be captayne ouer them a noble knyght of his army named Caius Annius/ whom he also assigned to be lyeutenant of the towne.

[78] ¶This towne of Leptis was bylded first of all by the Sidonians which (as we rede) fledde from their owne contrey for dyscorde and varyance which fell among their cyties at home. Which Sidonyans came in shyppes into these coostes of Affrike: where at last they bylded this cyte of Leptes/ which is situate bytwene two quickesandes of whom the cyte hath his name.

Ch. 45 6 vnto] to C 11 changes/] *virgule suppl.* 22–3 of them] to be confermed of them B; ~ confirmed ~ C 36 these] the B C

¶For about thextreme partes of Affrike be .ii. breekes of the see nere togyder nat lyke of quanti[t]e: but lyke of nature. Of which two breekes those partes which be nerest vnto the lande ar very profounde and depe with hye bankes of sande on euery syde. But the other places natte nere vnto the lande be somtyme depe: somtyme shalowe after the dysposytion of the wether. For whan the see begynneth in ragyng to be great and tempestyous by mouyng of the wynde/ than the wawes of the see draweth forth of the same places the slyme/ grauell/ and great stones: which in cawme wether were gathared togyder before in the same places. And thus the facyon/ aspect/ and regarde of the same places is mutable and changed at euery tempest and great wynde.

¶The langage of the cite of Leptis is nowe chaunged from the langage of Sydoni into Numidyan langag by maryages of the Numidyans. But their lawes/ their apparell/ and maners (for the moost part) styll foloweth the custome of Sydoni/ which they mentayned and kept styll: somoch the more easely: bycause they dwelled seperat in the extreme and vtter partes of the countrey farre from the court and frequentation of kynges of Numidy. For bytwene this cyte of Leptis and the well inhabyted partes of Numidy be many places desert and wyde wyldernesses vnhabyted for drienes of the contrey.

f. 63v ¶The dyscripcion of that place of Affrike which is named the Phylen auters: and for what cause the same place was first so named. The .xlvi. chap.

[79] But for asmoche as by occasyon of this besynes of the cyte of Leptis and their embassodours/ I haue made mencyon of their cyte and partly discrybed the sytuacion of the same. Nowe me thynketh it thing conuenyent/ and nat vnworthy to recount an exellent and meruaylous dede done in the same coostes by two brethern borne of the cyte of Carthage/ and namely bycause the place is called the Phylene auters me thynketh it requisyte to declare the cause of that denomynation. For this place of our hystorie so requireth.

¶What tyme the Carthaginenses had in possession and were lordes ouer the moost part of Affrike: at the same season the Cyrenenses also

40 quantite] quantie A; quantitie C 43 somtyme] and somtyme C 45 wynde/] *virgule suppl.* 46 wawes] waues B C 47 cawme] calme C 59 desert] deserte B; deserted C

Ch. 46 6 thynketh it] thynke it a C 8 of] at C 9 Carthage/] *virgule suppl.*

were great and famous of name: and abundant of welth and richesse. Than bytwene the coostes of thes two cyties was a great and large felde all ouerspredde with sande without deuysion/ particyon/ or dyfference. But bytwen them was neyther flodde nor mountayne/ which might dyscerne the bo[u]ndes and marchies of bothe their coostes: which thing caused contynuall and long warre often and great batayls bytwene both the parties. But after that many armies on both sydes were ouercome/ slayne/ or put to flight bothe by lande and by see. And whan both peoples had somwhat wasted the one the other by spoyling and murdre: than began they to perceyue their owne folly on both partes feryng lest some other natyon anon after shulde assayle them both/ the ouercomers and them that were ouercome whan they were wasted and weryed with batayls and brought to extremite. Wherfore this consydred: they toke truys bytwene them both and to auoyed that long variance which had ben bytwene them: they made agrement and couenant that messangers or embassadours of bothe parties shulde depart out of their cyties at a certayne day and houre assigned. And that same place where the messangers of both the cyties shulde mete togyder: shulde be for euer after taken for the boundes and marchesse of the countrey/ of both the natyons and cyties without more contencyon or varyance. To bringe this apoyntment to effect and conclusyon forth of the | cyte of Cyren were chosen two f. 64r
for their part and sende forthe at the day and hour apoynted. And in lykewyse out of Carthage were sende two brethern/ eche of them named Phylene which swiftly sped them in their iourney. But the Cyrnenses went moche more slowly whether it so fortuned by neglygence or chaunce I knowe but lytell the trueth. But this is knowen for certayne that about those coostes tempest of wynde and weder is wont to let men and prolong their iournay in likewyse as vpon the see: and that for this cause. For whan by those euyn places wyde/ and bare without any thing growynge on them: the wynde ryseth and styreth the small sande from the ground: the same sande moued by great vyolence of the wynde is wont to fyll the faces/ mouthes/ and eyen of which passeth that way with dust and sande. And thus often by lettyng of their sight: their iournay is prolonged and hyndred. But after whan the Cyrenenses sawe themselfe somwhat

18 boundes] B C; bondes A 20 the] *om.* B C 22 peoples] people C 25 both/] *virgule suppl.* 27 truys] truce C 28 which had ben] *om.* B C 30 a] one B C 37 eche of them] *om.* C 47 eyen] eyes C which passeth] such as passeth B; such as passe C

ouerslowe and late in their iournay: they fered punysshment at their retournyng home for their neglygence. And blamyng they accused the Carthagynenses obiectyng and sayeng that they had come forth of their cyte before the tyme assigned: and thus they troubled all the mater and brake the ordynance. But shortly to speke these Cirenenses concluded rather to suffre deth and to do any thyng possyble than to retourne home agayn ouercome. Wherfore the Carthagynenses desyred some other condycion or apoyntment to be made indyfferent and equall bytwene both the parties. The Cyrenenses consented therto and put the Carthagynenses in choyse whyther they wolde be quicke buryed in that same place which they desyred for their marches and boundes: or els that the Cyrenenses vnder the same condycion shulde procede forwarde to that place which they desyred for their marches and there to be quicke buryed vnder the same maner. The .ii. brethern both named Phylene alowed and graunted the condycion subduyng and abandonyng their bodyes to deth for the profet and wele of their contrey and cyte of Carthage: and so were they buried quicke. Wherfore the Carthaginenses in the same place where they were buryed raysed and halowed .ii. auters in worshyp and remembrance of these two brethern which set more by encrese of their contrey: than by their owne lyues. These auters to this present day be called the Phylen auters after the name of the .ii. brethern named Phylenis therunder buried/ as said is for wele of their contrey: also besyde this memoriall within the cite of Carthage were many other thinges ordayned to the f. 64v gret honour of them | and remembrance of their worthy dede.

¶But nowe wyll I leaue this mater and retourne to my purpose.

¶How Iugurth assembled a newe army of the rude Getulyans agaynst the Romayns: and how he associat[e]d vnto hym Bocchus king of the Mauryens to strength hym in batayle agaynst Metellus. ¶The .xlvii. chapyter.

[**80**] Whan Iugurth had lost the cytie of Thala/ one of the strongest cyties of his lande (as sayd is before) than he consydred well that in all his kyngdome was no place stronge ynough to resyst the might of Metellus. Wherfore he hasted hym with a small company through desertes and great wyldernesses fleyng from his owne countrey. And at last he came to the lande of Getulyans which is a maner of people

75 wyll I] I wyll C

Ch. 47 2 associated] B C; associatd A vnto] to C 9 wyldernesses] wyldernesse B fleyng] flying C

rude/ wylde/ and without order or maners: and at that season nought knowyng of the preemynent honour and fame of the Romayne empyre. Of this people Iugurth assembled a multitude togyder and by lytell and lytell enduced and taught them by custome and exercyse to folowe the order of chyualry: to kepe array/ to insue their standerdes/ to obey the commaundementes of their capytayns/ to dyscerne and haue knowlege of the signyfiaunce of soundes of trumpettes: and to obserue all other poyntes belongyng to warfare and chyualry. These thynges with otherlyke necessary to batayle/ Iugurth ceassed nat to prepare and ordayn with all dilygence.

¶Moreouer he prouoked vnto his fauour and felashyp by great rewardes and moch gretter promises suche as were moost nere frendes to Bocchus kyng of the Mauryens: by whose helpe he hymselfe went to the kyng Bocchus. And moche desyredde hym in his quarell with hym to warre agaynst the Romayns. To this request of Iugurth Bocchus agreed somoch the more for asmoch as at first begynnyng of the same warre: this Bocchus sent vnto Rome embassadours to desyre of the Romayns amyte and a bonde of contynuall peace bytwene hym and them. But nat withstandyng that this peticyon and peace was moche expedyent and necessary to the Romayns for dyuerse consideratyons and namely bycause of this warre. Nat the lesse it was nat graunted by mean of a fewe such as at Rome blynded with auaryce: were wont to sell for money | euery thyng both honest and dyshonest. Also before this f. 65r
tyme the doughter of Iugurth was spoused to the sayed Bocchus. But this bonde of frendshyppe or affinite amonge the Numidyans/ and Mauryens: is reputed but of small valour or effect: bycause they ar wont euery man to haue dyuerse and many wyues acordyng to their substance and richesse. Some .x. and some mo: after as they ar of abylite or power to mentayne. But the kynges bycause they ar of moost power and substance: therfore haue they mo thanne an other. Thus is their mynde and fauoure dystract and dyuersly deuyded from all their wyues for the multytude of them: and bycause they haue so many so that they reserue none for their speciall bedfelawe. Wherfore they all ar reputed vyle/ and lytell sette by: after one maner. Thus the affinite bytwene these two kynges Iugurth and Bocchus/ was lytell sette by and small thyng auayled in this besynesse.

11 rude/] *virgule suppl.*; *comma* C 17 signyfiaunce of] signifiaunce of B; signifiyng of the C 21 vnto] to C 24 the] *om.* C moche] *om.* C 25 this] which C 26 at] at the C 36 but of small valour or effect] but of effect B; but of lytel or none effecte C 40 haue they] they haue C 42 so] *om.* C 46 thyng] *om.* C

[81] Nat withstandyng bothe they and their hoostes came togyder in a place apoynted therto: where after that they had gyuen and taken fayth and trueth one to [an] other of fydelite/ to be obserued bytwene them. Iugurth greatly inhauncedde and lyfted vp the mynde of Bocchus with his wordes sayeng that the Romayns were iniust grounded in auaryce without suffisance or measure. And commen ennemies to euery man and to euery contrey: and that they had asmoche quarell agaynst Bocchus/ as agaynst hym. And one selfe cause to warre agaynst them bothe. And also agaynst many other natyons whiche cause was but onely the pleasure of great lordshyppe and ryches. So that for the same cause all kyngdoms to them were aduers and contrary/ and that he hymselfe to them was ennemy for the same cause. And nat long before that tyme the Carthaginenses: and afterwarde Perses kyng of Macedony were subdued and vndone by the Romayns without any iust tytle or cause of batayle: saue onely ambytion and enuy which the Romayns had agaynst them. And that in tyme to come euery natyon whiche shulde haue welth and richesse shulde become ennemies to the Romayns for their inordynat pride/ and insaciable couetyse.

¶With these wordes and otherlyke Iugurth moued the mynde of Bocchus agaynst the Romayns. Insomoch that anone a day was apoynted bytwene bothe the kynges to procede forth togyder to the towne of Cyrtha/ and to assayle the same with both their powers conioynedde. This towne they purposed first of all to besige: bycause Metellus had left within the same towne his prayes and prisoners
f. 65v which he had taken of Iugurth. | And also moche of his owne ordynaunce had he left there to auoyde impedyment in his voyage. Thus Iugurth thought it moost expedyent to do. For if he myght wynne the towne by assaut before the rescous of Metellus: he thought that shuld be moost to his honoure and profette. Or els yf the Romayne captayne Metellus/ and his army shulde come to socours of the towne: than thought he that there both hymselfe and Bocchus shuld gyue batayle to Metellus. Iugurth for craft and subtylte hasted hereto somoch the more to tangle Bocchus in the warre before any peace shulde be mouedde bytwene hym and the Romayns. And lest the same Bocchus by prolongyng of the tyme myght rather enclyne to peace than to warre after he at leasour shuld haue taken better

48 a] one C that] *om.* C 49 an] ua A; *om.* B C 50 greatly] *om.* C 51 iniust] vniust C 71 his] *om.* C 74 it] *om.* B C 77–8 to socours of] to succour C 80 hereto] thereto C 81 peace] place B C

counsell and aduysment. For Iugurth suspected at beginnynge that Metellus in processe of tyme wold desyre thus Bocchus nat to medyll in this warre assistyng the part of Iugurth nor mentayning his cause.

¶Howe Metellus vsed hymselfe herynge that these two kynges were confederat agaynst hym and how after he was certifyed that the prouynce of Numidy was assigned to Marius the new consull: he ceassed the warre for the nones. ¶The .xlviii. chapyter.

[82] Whanne Metellus knewe that the two kynges were assocyate togyder: he thought nat to fyght with them rasshely without prouisyon: nor in euery place for his aduantage or nat/ as he was wont to do often tymes before after the first tyme that he had ouercome Iugurthe. But within his felde well and surely defended he kept hymselfe abydinge the commynge of the two kynges: and that nat farre from the towne of Cyrtha. This dyd he thynking it best to knowe the myght/ maners/ and condycions of the Mauryens first or he wolde fight with them/ bycause they were but newe ennemies and therfore their maners vnknowen to hym. And whan he sawe his best auantage than thought he to gyue them batayle.

¶In the meane tyme whyle Metellus taryed the commyng of the two kynges: letters were brought vnto hym from Rome: which certyfied hym that the prouynce of Numidy/ was | committed and gyuen to Marius the newe consull. For he had harde long before this tyme that the sayd Marius was creat consull: but this was the first tyme that he vnderstode the prouince of Numidy commytted to hym. For this cause was Metellus mouedde and dyspleased moche more than longed to measure or honesty. In somoche that he coude neyther refrayne his eyen from wepyng nor measure his tong from spekyng yll by Marius. This Metellus was a synguler noble and worthy man in all other condycions: but the dyspleasure of his mynde he toke ouer womanly and tenderly to his hert/ and namely in this cause. Which condycion: some reputed to procede of a proude hert of Metellus. And other some thought it no meruayle though his noble hert were moued and kyndled with anger/ for this iniury and wrong done to hym. And many sayd that Metellus toke so great sorowe and dyspleasure: bycause the vyctorie which he had almoost obtayned shulde be pulled out of his handes his selfe hauyng the labour and f. 66r

85 thus] this B C

Ch. 48 7 nat/] *virgule suppl.* 9 felde] feldes B C 12 myght/] *virgule from* B 20 creat] elect B C 24 eyen] eyes C

paryll. And another man the tryumphe and honour. But to be playne in the mater and indyfferently to write: it was nat vnknowen to the wysest Romayns/ but that the dygnite/ auauncement/ and honour of Marius greued Metellus: moch more than dyd his owne iniury. And that he wolde nat haue taken it so heuely if the prouynce of Numidy which was taken from hym had ben gyuen to any other noble m[a]n than to Marius.

[83] Wherfore Metellus was let from his first besynesse for the sayd dyspleasure so that he purposed nat to vexe hymselfe from thensforth without thanke or profette. And also he thought it folly to take in hande the charge of an other mannes mater to his owne paryll/ labour/ and payne. Wherfore he sende messangers to the kyng Bocchus/ desyring hym nat to become ennemy to the Romayns without occasion. And sayeng that he was as yet in suche case that he myght adioyne with the Romayns felawshyp/ loue/ and amyte: which shulde be moche better to hym and more profytable than batayle. And howbeit he trusted gretly in his power/ richesse/ and treasour: yet ought he nat to change certayne thynges/ for thynges incertayne. For euery batayle to begyn is easy and lyght: but it is a very harde thyng to ende the same whan it is ones begon. The begynning and endynge therof: is nat alway in the power of one same man. For batayle may be/ begon of a cowarde or of any other wretch: but it can nat be left of agayne/ nor ceassed but whan it pleaseth him which is strongest/ and
f. 66^{v} is maister hauyng the vpper hande. | And finally he badde hym better to prouyde for hymselfe and for his kyngdome than he beganne to do: and nat to adioyne nor myngle his goodes/ treasour/ and fortune: which were in estate royall florisshyng with the goodes and fortune of Iugurth: which were lost and dystroyed to the vttermoost. The imbassadours of Metellus came to kynge Bocchus and shewed hym their capytayns wyll: as is sayd before vnder suche sentence. To the which wordes of Metellus/ Bocchus answeredde agayne benignely and mekely ynough sayng that he desyred nothyng more than peace: saue that he had pyte and compassyon of the aduers and myserable fortune of Iugurth/ but yf the same Iugurth myght be suffred also to haue frendshyp and amyte with the Romayns and forgyuenesse: than sayd Bocchus that he wolde gladly agre to euery thynge desyredde of Metellus/ and euery thyng shulde be acorded bytwene them. The captayne Metellus heryng this answere of Bocchus: agayne sent

39 man] C; men A B   47 as] *om.* C   48 felawshyp/] *virgule suppl.* (*end of line* A B)   49 than batayle] *om.* C   52 a] *om.* B   54 batayle] warre B C

messangers to hym replyeng agaynst his requestes and sayeng that some of his petycions were agaynst iustyce and reason: also Metellus by these embassadours desyredde many other thynges of Bocchus/ of whom Bocchus graunted and alowed some: and other some of them he denyed. After this maner the tyme ouerpassedde and proceded forth/ messangers often goynge and commyng bytwene them bothe: so that by suche maner the warre and batayle remayned vntouched and depended nat medled with: as Metellus dyd greatly coueyt and desyre in mynde bycause he wolde kepe sure that laude which he had goten and wonne: and also for that to his owne paryll and dammage he wolde nat auantage nor auance Mari[u]s: in thyng which to hym belonged.

¶But here wyll I leaue to speke of Metellus/ and retourne to speke of Marius which contrary to the wyll of all the noble men of Rome was creat consull by fauour of the commens: lykewyse as I haue written before.

¶Of the great ordynaunce and preparatyon which Marius the newe consull made agaynst Iugurth/ and for the warre of Numidy. ¶The .xlix. chapter.

[84] But Maryus (as I haue sayd before) was create consull/ at f. 67r
synguler desyre and instaunce of the commen people: which also commytted to hym the prouynce of Numidy. Marius seyng himselfe thus auanced: where he was euer agaynst the noble men of Rome before. Nowe was he specially fiers of mynde/ and stately. And besy to dysplease and hurt thestates: som tyme one by one/ and other whyle altogyder. He often tymes boosted and sayd that he had goten the consulshyppe of them maugre their wyll/ as if it were a pray or spoylinges goten of his ennemies: and of men ouercome. Many other boostyng wordes spake he to his owne commendation/ and to great dyspleasure and anger vnto these estates of Rome. But in the meane space he forgat nat to prepare euery thing necessary to the warre: wherof the charge rested on hym to execute the same agaynst Iugurth from thensforth. He demaunded of the senatours and commens newe supplement of soudyours to repare and restore the army which was in Numidy with Metellus. For many of them were slayne/ and many deed of sickenesse: thus was the army sore deminisshed. He called

80–1 goten and] *om.* B C 82 in] in a C 85 all] *om.* C

Ch. 49 4 create] elect B C 5 synguler] great B C 14 these] the B C
15 space] tyme B C

also for socours of suche nations as marched to thempyre. And of kynges whiche were confederate and had conioyned felaweshyppe with the Romayns. Moreouer he raysed vp in Italy and nere about Rome/ as many as were strongest and bolde mennes bodyes. And namely such as he hymselfe had proued before in warre: and such as in warfare were proued by dedes: and nat suche as were boosted by fame. And namely olde soudiours which had long hau[n]ted the warre and were pardoned therof. So that it was in the power of no man to constrayn them to warre without their owne fre assent: bycause that they had contynued styll in batayle the season to them assigned of their captayns. These treated Marius with so fayre flateryng and paynted wordes/ that they were redy to go with hym in warfare. And howbeit that the senatours were contrary to hym: yet durst they nothyng deny vnto hym belongyng to his besynesse: but gladly and with good wyll they decreed that he shulde rayse and chuse soudyours to fulfyll the nombre of them which were lost in batayle in the contrey of Numidy. But this dyde they for no gret loue which they had to Marius: for they thought that he shuld lese outher the execution of the batayle which he intended with Iugurth: or els the fauour of the people which wolde refuse to go forth to warre. So that if Marius f. 67v constray| ned them: their olde loue might turne into newe malyce and hateredde agaynst hym. But this thyng was trusted but in vayne of the senatours: for the moost part of the commens had an inestymable desyre to go to batayle with Marius. For euery man cast in his mynde to be inryched by prayes and spoylynges of warre. And that more is: to retourne home agayn vyctours with moche honour and tryumphe. These thynges and otherlyke: they consydred in their myndes/ which caused them gladly to folowe Marius/ and also Marius dyd nat a lytell enbolde and confort their myndes with his exhortacyon. For whan euery thyng which he desyred of the senatours was confermed and decreed by them. And whanne Marius shulde assemble his soudyours: he thought to put them in comfort by exhortacion/ and also to trouble and dysplease thestates of Rome as he was wont to do: and to chafe their myndes. Wherfore he assembled and called togyder a great company of the commen people/ and spake to them by exhortacion and confortyng of them as herafter ensueth.

27 haunted] B C; hauuted A 30 batayle] warre B C 38 outher] eyther C
47 in their myndes/] *om.* B C; *virgule suppl.* 49 enbolde] enbolden C

¶The orison or exhortacion of the consull Marius: had to the commen people of Rome before his voyage into Numidy/ which exhortacion is demonstratyue contaynynge the laude and prayes of Marius: and dysprayse and blames of the noble men of Rome. ¶The .l. chapyter.

[85] Right worthy cytezins/ I knowe well that many of these estates of auncyent name haue nat themselfe behaued after one maner of condycion in desyring of you honorable dygnities and great offices: and in admynistracyon and gouernyng of them after they haue obtayned the same of you. For whyle they make their peticyons: at begynninge they be dyligent/ seruyable/ meke: and curtayse of behauoure. But whan they haue obtayned their desyre: than passe they their tyme in slouth/ ydelnes/ and pride. But it semeth to me in my mynde that they ought to do moche contrarely. For of howe moch more valour the hole commen wayle is: than is the consulshyp/ thoffice of the hy iudge/ or any other great office: with | somoch more f. 68r
dyligence and charge shulde the hole commen wele be gouerned/ than suche dygnities or offices desyred of you. Nor I am nat ignorant but knowe right well how great the benefite is that ye haue gyuen to me: and how great charge and besynesse therto belongyng is layed vpon me withall: whiche besynes I nedes must sustayne. That is to say: to prepare and make redy an army/ with all other thynges necessary to bat[ay]le and to execute the same: and neuertheles to spare the commen treasour. To compell to warfare and batayle: such as a man wolde nat greue nor dysplease/ that is you the commentie of Rome: whome I wolde nat dysplease by any meanes. To take charge and care for euery thyng within the cite and without. And to do such thynges among enuyous gentylmen obiectyng and layeng agaynst me in euery thynge which I go about/ as men full of dyscorde and varyance. Verily noble cytezins among such men to take in hande suche charges it is more harde and thynge of more dyfficultie/ thanne any man can thynke or deuyse. And moreouer: as for other consuls which haue ben before my tyme/ whan they haue done any thyng amysse: than their olde noblenesse/ the strong and valyant actes of their predecessours/ the riches and power of their frendes and kynsmen: and their many clyentes and seruantes of them retayned. All these haue supported and mentayned them in their mysdedes. But all my richesse and helpe/ and trust of confort which I haue/ is in my

Ch. 50 1 orison] oracion C 4 blames] blame C 10 dyligent/] *virgule from* B 22 batayle] B; bataile C; batyale A 28 I] *om.* C 29 such men to take in hande] *om.* C 30 thynge] a thinge C

selfe and nat in my kynsmen nor other fauourers: which ayde of myself I must of necessite defende with my vertue/ strength: and innocence. For all other thynges which these auncient noblemen haue to defende them be vnsure to me for I haue them nat.

Farthermore noble cytezins this I vnderstande that all ye haue good trust and confydence in me: and that all such as be equall/ iust/ and good: haue fauour vnto me. For I kno well that my good dedes hath profited the commen wayle. And neuerthelesse these noble men seke occasyons agaynst me/ inuadyng and assaylyng me with their malyce and enuy. Wherfore it standeth me in hande of necessyte to labour somoche the more besely and quickely: that neyther ye be disceyued in this great trust whiche ye haue in me: and also that all the purposes of myne ylwyllers and aduersares/ may be frustrate and nothyng auayle agaynst me. Forsoth I haue euer from my chyldhode vnto this age ben of such behauour that I haue ben acustomed and exercysed in
f. 68v all maner labour and paryls: which I suffred and | toke paciently for the commen wele without any rewarde before this your benefyte and honour which ye haue nowe gyuen to me. Wherfore worthy cytezins seyng that ye haue nowe rewarded me better than I am worthy: I haue nat purposed to desyst nor leue of myne olde goodwyll agaynst the commen wele: nor now I rewarded of you purpose nat to omyt my good dedes agaynst the comen wele which I dyd frely before vnrewarded. But touchyng these auncient gentylmen: it is very harde for them to tempar themselfe beyng in power or dygnite whiche onely dyd but fayne themself good and honest before they obtayned promocyon/ to thintent to come therby to honoure and dygnite. But where as I haue passed all my lyfe in right good occupatyons by contynuall custome it is roted in me to do well: and this custome is tourned with me into a nature. Trouth it is: that ye haue commaunded me to warre and do batayle with Iugurth: which thyng these noble men taketh very greuously. I require you consyder and dyscus in your myndes and in your inwarde consyderation/ ponder ye whyther it be better/ more necessary and expedyent to change the same your commaundement agayne: and to sende forth some other of that sort of auncyent gentylmen vnto this besynes with Iugurth or els to any other lyke. Send forth a noble man of old

38 nor] or B C 46 occasyons] occasion C 53 labour] labours B; laboures C 57 leue of] *colon* A; *om.* B C agaynst] anenst B; ageynste C 59 agaynst the comen wele] *om.* B C 66 a] *om.* B C 67 and do batayle with] agaynst B C 72 with] agaynst B C

auncetry: in honour and remembrance of whom many ymages may be made and erect or set vp on hy. But of polycie of chyualry or warfare is he vtterly ignorant and inexpert. Wyll ye change your purpose and sende forth suche one to warfare at pleasure of these gentylmen/ as who sayeth: that is best to be done for this cause. To thintent that in so great a mater and wighty besynesse: such a captayne more ignorant and ferefull than any of all his soudyours/ shalbe chosen of you which anone after shal chuse forth agayne some one of the commen people to be his maister: to informe and tech hym in such besynes as to his offyce and charge belongeth hymselfe beyng ignorant of euery thyng necessary to be done? By this meane it often fortuneth: that he whom ye ordayne to be captayne and commaunder of your army: dothe chose an other to be captayne and commaunder ouer hymselfe. In somoch that (if ye indyfferently iudge) he: whom is chose for capitayne is moche more mete to be made a symple soudyour/ than a captayne ouer other. And also worthy cytezins: I knowe some of these noble men so farre out of order that whan they haue ben made consuls: than haue they gyuen themselfe to redyng of the actes of | f. 69r
their elders and predecessours. And of the Grekes preceptes of chyualrie: which doutlesse may well be called men without order/ for this consyderation. For they shulde by due order first lerne to rule their office before they shulde take vpon them the charge therof. But they do contrary. First they take charge of office and than after lerne to rule it by way inordynate: howbeit euery wyseman wyll first lerne to gouerne an office before he desyre it or take vpon him the rule therof. But these estates contrarily demeane themselfe.

Thus worthy cytezins compare me a newe gentylman with their immoderate pride and take dyligent consyderation which is best: to be nat gentyll of byrth and lowly and gentyll of maners: or els to be gentyll of blode/ and proude and vngentyll of maners. Of suche thynges as they be wont to here and to rede: some haue I sene/ and some I my selfe haue done. I haue lernedde that by excercyse of chyualrie/ which they haue lerned by redyng. Nowe iuge and consyder ye: whyther is better of dedes or warkes: of redyng [or] doyng. They dispyce my neweltie of honour and vnnoble lynage: and I dispyce the vncraftynesse and slouth of them. My happy fortune is

84 done?] *punctus* A B C 87 is] ye B C 88 soudyour] soudyours B; souldyoure C 89 some] somewhat C 91 the] *om.* C 96 of] of the C 97 way] waies C 98 it] *om.* C 100 a] *om.* C 101 best:] *colon from* B 104 some] somewhat C 107 whyther] whether C 107 or] C; and A B 108 neweltie] noueltye C

obiected of them agaynst me as to rebuke: but shame and dyshonest behauour/ may be obiected and layed agaynst them in rebuke. Is nat trueth that euery man is come of one lyke nature? I consyder and knowe well that one man is nat better nor more noble than an other: but if it be by his wysdome/ good maners/ vertu/ and strength. And I consyder well that euery man the more that he is endued with vertue: the more exellent and noble is he. Thus is the strongest/ wysest/ and moost vertuous/ moost exellent in noblenesse.

¶But yf the fathers of Albynus/ and of Calphurnius: late consuls and captayns in Numidy/ to the great dyshonoure and damage of this empyre/ were nowe lyueng that it myght be inquyred of them whether that they had leuer that I had bene begotten of them: or els the sayd Albynus and Calphurnius? What thynke ye they wolde answere? Forsoth nought els (as I suppose) but that they wolde desyre and couet good chyldren and honorable lynage to procede of their stocke and generation. Thus syth it is so: that these estates dispyseth me: reasonably and of ryght lette them also dispyce their owne predecessours and forefathers/ of whose stocke and lynage they proceded: which came to noblenes and honour: nat by their auncetry: but by their owne strength/ wysdome/ and vertue: likewyse as I haue
f. 69v done. They haue enuy at this | myne honour. Than lette them also haue enuy at my labours taken for defence of the commen wayle: let them enuy myne innocentie and great peryls/ which I haue ouercome. For by these meanes I haue obtayned and also shall mentayne this honour which they so greatly enuy. But these men corrupt by pride: after ye haue promoted them to worshyppe: so pas forth their tyme as if they sette nought by your offices and honours by you obtayned: but vtterly dyspysed them. Thus they desyre such dygnities of duety: as if they were worthy and deserued to haue them by their honest lyueng and vertuous conuersacion. But certaynely they be greatly disceyued which loketh after two thinges contrary bothe togyder and at one season. So do these noble men. For they wold haue the voluptuous pleasure of slouth and ydelnesse/ and their rewardes due vnto vertue and laborious dilygence. But whan these gentylmen vtter their wordes before you or speke before the senatours: than in the moost part of their speche they exalt and commende their auncetry/ wenyng to be

111 Is] Is it B C 112 nature?] *punctus* A B C 115 that[2]] *om.* C is he] he is C 121 that[1]] *om.* B C 125 dispyseth] despise C 129 likewyse] lyke C 132 innocentie] innocence B; innocency C 140 loketh] looke C togyder] together C 142 their] the B C 145 auncetry/] *virgule suppl.*

counted more noble and exellent by recountyng and reducynge to remembrance the valyant dedes of their progenitours. But it is nothyng so. For how moche more exellent the fame and honour of their progenytours was: somoch more shamefull and reprouable is this cowarde ydelnesse of these gentylmen nowe lyueyng which so farre go out of kynde from the honorable conuersacyon of their progenytours: as if they had neuer dyscendedde of them. And verely this is certayne: the glorious dedes and honorable of forefathers be lyke an example or luminary vnto their offspringe or progeny. So that the same light suffreth neyther the good dedes nor badde of their progeny to be hydde. For yf the progeny varie from the glorious actes of their progenytours than the honour of both is distaynedde: but if they folowe them in vertue/ than the light and glorie of the progenitours shyneth more radiantly by vertu of their progeny. Of this laude and honoure of my progeny I can nat boost me for they were but of base degre. Their dedes can nat auaunce me nor make me noble. But it is laufull to me to speke of myne owne dedes/ whiche laude is moche more clere and exellent than to boost of other mennes actes. But nowe consyder ye how vnrightwyse these gentylmenne are to me: they wyll nat graunt me that laude and honoure by myne owne vertue and actes: whiche they vsurpe and proudely take vpon them by the vertue and dedes of other men. And wherfore thynke ye doo they this? | Playnely f. 70r
I suppose bycause I haue no ymages of my progenytours exaltedde in remembrance of them as these gentylmen haue: and bycause my noblenesse is but newe and springing. But theirs is auncient and by their dysorder decayng. But certenly I count it more better and honorable to be rote and begynner of noblenesse vnto all my progeny and to leue the same vnto my branches: than to corrupt and defyle noblenesse receyued of my progeny: as many of these gentylmen do.

Forsoth I am nat ignorant but that yf these estates were nowe present and shulde answere to my wordes their spech shulde be abundantly payntedde: ornate/ and elygant ynough. But syth they cease nat to blame and reuyle with their lewde wordes in euery place bothe you and me for this your great office which ye haue gyuen vnto me: it hath nat pleasedde me to be styll nor to kepe secrete their fautes: lest some might count me culpable and worthy of their rebukes: by reason of myne indyscrete pacyence and sylence. Neuerthelesse sothely their

149 progenytours] progenitour B; progenitours C 162 dedes/] *virgule suppl.* 164 are] be B C 166 the] *om.* B C 173 defyle] defele B 181 me] *om.* B of] *om.* B C

wordes can nat greaue nor hurte me: after the conscyence of myne owne mynde. For if they say trueth they can nought say but good and worshyp by me: but if they wyll nedes ly on me: my maners/ my lyueng/ and conuersacyon is such that I shall ouercome their wordes and proue their iniust accusementes fayned and false. But syth your counsell is blamed of these noblemen bycause ye haue commytted to me this great honoure and gretter besynes: consyder ye in your myndes dilygently and often whyther ye shall nede to repent you of this dede or nat. To say trueth I can nat boost my self of the ymages of my progenytours nor I can nat recount vnto you the tryumphes or consulshyps of myne auncetry. But yf the mater requyred: I coude well shewe vnto you speares/ standerdes/ horse trappers/ harnesse: with many other rewardes of chyualrie: some gyuen to me of themperour/ and some of other captayns for myne actes in batayle. And other some which with myne handes I haue won of thennemies of thempyre. I coude also if it neded shewe you in the fore part of my body manyfolde scarres of many and large woundes whiche I haue taken in good worth for defence of our countrey and commen wele. These be my ymages which I can shewe. This is my noblenes: nat lefte to me by heritage (as theirs is to them) but noblenes which I haue won and goten with great and sore labours of my body and peryll of my lyfe.

¶My wordes be nat ordred in ornate langage nor my spech paynted
f. 70v with rethorike like theirs/ for I set lytell therby. My | vertue sheweth it selfe playnelie ynough without glosedde or payntedde wordes. But these noble menne must of necessyte haue craft for to couer their shamefull and vngoodly dedes/ with their eloquent wordes/ their crafty and rethorike spech. Nor as for me: I neuer lerned the Greke letters nor langage which thing these estates obiect agaynst me: as a great faut. But to be playne: my pleasure was neuer moche to lerne suche thynges/ which haue lytell auayled vnto the techers of the same/ neyther to acquysityon of vertue nor expulsyon of vice. But I haue lerned and am taught in other thinges moch better: and more profitable to the commen wayle: as to assayle and stryke myne ennemies: to reaue away their ordynance and vytayls: to chafe their garnyson. Nothyng to drede nor feare saue an yll name: to endure and

190 whyther] whether C 194 horse trappers] horse/ trappers A B; horse, trappers C 206 theirs/] *no punct* A B; *comma* C 209 their[1]] this B; these C 211 letters nor] *om.* C 213 techers] techers or lerners B C 217 reaue away] dispoyle B C

take in good worth the pleasure of the somer and the hardnes of the wynter both in lyke: to ly vpon the grounde: to endure hunger and labour both togyder. Therfore I shall exhort and informe my soudiours with these preceptes: which I myself haue lerned/ vsed and assayed. Nor I shall nat handell or treat theym by crafte to thintent that they may auance me with richesse: nor vse them sharply and my selfe plesantly: but in euery dyfficulte I shall be their example of laboure: nor I shall nat put the labour to them and take the worshyp to me. This order is profytable. Thus ought a captayne demean hym among his soudiours and namely among worthy cytezins. For whan a man lyueth dilycately hymself/ and driueth his soudyours to the peryll of batayle by punisshment or other rygour: he is nat to be called a capytayne or ruler of an army: but rather a proude lorde or tyrannous oppresser of cytezins. Our elders worthely behauyng themselfe after this maner haue made noble and exellent and inryched this commen wayle: and themselfe also. But thes estates which nowe lyueth trustyng to be honouredde by the worthynesse of their progenytours/ they themselfe vnlyke of condycions despyce vs and haue vs in dysdayne which folowe the maners of their progenytours. And euery hye office and all honours they chalange and demaunde of you nat by their merytesse: but as it were of duetie and herytage.

But sothely the ouer proude men erre moche from the trueth. For though their progenitours and auncetry haue left vnto them euery thing which to them was possyble to leaue: as ryches/ patrymony/ and their ymages: for remembrance and example of them and of their worthy dedes. Neuertheles their vertu haue they nat left | vnto them: f. 71r
nor they coude nat kepe it: for that onely can neyther be gyuen unto them in rewarde nor receyued of any man. These gentylmen say that I am a man without maners and vnclenly of behauoure. And why? Forsoth bycause that I prepare and dresse nat curyously many delycious bankettes so superfluous and dentyous as they do: and bycause I haue no iougler nor dysare with me to moue sportes and dyssolute laughyng: nor no more curyouse coke than one of the vyllage longyng to rurall people/ which thynges to haue as these gentylmen haue: it pleaseth me nat to knowledge. For I neuer had pleasure in such thynges. For I haue harde of my father and of other incorrupt and well dysposed men: that such delyciousnesse and curyosite belongeth vnto women. And that labour and besynesse belongeth vnto men. Euery good man: thynketh it more conuenyent to haue plentie of worshyppe

223 treat] intreate C 224 that] *om.* C 235 lyueth] lyue C 241 vnto] to C

than of rychesse: And more honour it is to a good man to haue the walles of his house garnysshed and ouercoueredde with armour/ wherewith he may defende his countrey/ his frendes/ and hym[s]elf than with riche ornamentes of curyous warke of no profette saue onely the syght and vayne regarde therof. But sith thes gentylmen thus obiect such maters to me: let them contynue alway in suche vyces which lyketh them/ and that [t]hey haue euer reputed so dere. Let them inclyne to voluptuosyte as daunsing/ synging/ bankettyng/ playng/ to lechery/ to glotony/ and dronkenes. For in such vyces haue they spende their youth: in the same let them pas forth their age vtterly subdued to the bely/ to slepe/ to ydelnes/ and subiect to the lustes of the vylest part of the body. Let them leaue the swete of fyghting/ the peryll of deth/ the blyndyng of dust in batayle: and otherlyke paryls vnto vs/ to whom these be more acceptable than their feestes and voluptuous bankettes or other vyle pleasurs. But they do nat so/ they be nat so contented. For after that such vngoodly and vyle men haue dyshonested themselfe/ by their foule dedes: than be they redy to take away the rewardes of good men vnto them. Thus (agaynst all right) lechery and slouth moost cursedde vyces dothe no hurt to such as occupyeth them: but they be vtter dystruction to the commen wayle: and commens which be innocent and vnculpable.

¶But syth I haue made answere to these dysordred gentylmen: and that moderately after my custome and condycion and nat so largely as their cursednesse and vices ar worthy. I shall speke nowe a fewe
f. 71v thynges touchyng the commen wele. And first of all haue | ye good trust and asperance touchyng the besynes of Numidy. For ye haue nowe moued and auoyded euery thyng wherby Iugurth was defended from beginnynge of the warre vnto this tyme: that is to say the couetyse of Calphurnius/ and of Albynus: the vncraftynes and foly of Aulus: and the pride of Metellus. By these founde Iugurth socour hytherto: but all these be auoyded nowe. Moreouer ye haue there an army whiche knoweth the contrey/ but verily it is more noble and manly than fortunate or happy. For a great part therof is wasted and spent (and that wors is) infected and corrupted: what by the auaryce and by the vnbol[d]nesse and cowardyse of their captayns. Wherfore ye which be of lusty age and mete to endure the hardnesse of warre and batayle: nowe labour ye with me/ and take ye in hande the

260 hymself] B C; hymfelf A 264 they] B C; hey A 268 the[2]] *om.* C 275 them] themselfe B C 283 asperance] esperance B C 292 vnboldnesse] B; vnboldnes C; vnbolnesse A 294 batayle:] *colon from* B me/ and] B; me. And A the] *om.* C

defence of the commen wayle. Nor let none of you be afrayed nor abasshed for the mysfortune of the other soudyours which haue foughten there before this tyme nor of the pride of their captayns. For I myselfe as counsellour of your besynesse and felowe of your peryls shall be present with you in euery besinesse both in your iournays and in your batayls also. So that I shall gouerne you and my selfe without dyfference/ and vnder one forme in euery poynt. And verely by helpe of the goddes we shall within shorte season obtayne all auantages and commodyties which any man may wynne in batayle/ as prayes/ victory/ with immortall laude and worshyppe. And certaynlie if these pleasours [and] auantages were in dout or harde to obtayne (as they be nat). Neuerthelesse it were conuenyent to euery good man (as ye be) to socour and defende the commen wayle of their countrey fro dystruction and rebuke. For certaynlie there was neuer manne which obtayned immortall laude nor euerlasting name by cowardyse or sleuth. Nor there was neuer wyse father whiche wolde wysshe his chyldren or sonnes to lyue euer: but onely that they might lyue so long as they behauedde themselfe worthely in goo[d]nesse and honesty: and so to passe forth their lyfe as naturall course requireth.

¶Worthy Romayns: I wolde speke more vnto you if I vnderstode that strength coude be encreased to feble or fearfull men: by wordes: but it is nat so. Wherfore me semeth that I haue sayed ynough and abundantly to noble and bolde hartedde menne: as my trust is to proue you.

¶How Marius after his exhortacion endyd: anone ladedde shyppes with ordynance of warre and sende forwarde with the same one Manlyus his imbassadour: and how he hymselfe anone after folowed with all his company. And howe he behauedde hymselfe in Numidy at firste begynnynge. ¶The .li. chapyter. f. 72r

[86] Whan Marius had vttred and ended his wordes vnder this forme: and whan he sawe all the myndes of the commens enclyned to the warre in trust of vyctorie and prayes. Than anone without more delay he caused shyppes to be charged with vitayls/ and treasour for the soudyours wages with armour/ wepyn/ and all other thynges necessary to warre. And commaunded one named Aulus Manlyus/ which was assigned embassadoure to hym: to depart forwarde with

296 the[1]] *om.* B C 300 batayls] batayle C 305 and] B C; *om.* A
308 rebuke] dyshonour B C 312 goodnesse] B; goodnes C; goonesse A

Ch. 51 4 at] at the C 12 embassadoure] embassadours B; embassadour C

the same shyppes so charged. In the meane season Marius hymselfe remayned at Rome a lytell tyme: and chose forth soudyours suche as hym thought moost expedyent: and nat after the custome of the olde Romayns his predecessours nor after instytucion of the auncyent captayns/ which had ordred certayne maner of peple of whom soudyours shulde be chosen for warfare in tyme conuenyent. But contrariwyse Marius admytted euery man indyfferently whiche was any thynge lickely and had pleasure to go with hym. And many such he admytted also which were poore and nat suffredde to go to warfare before: lest their pouertie myght haue constrayned them rather to fall to robbery than to dedes of chiualry. Howbeit/ it was inacted of the olde Romayns that suche excused of warre for cause aboue sayd: shulde pay a certayne somme of money pretaxed towarde the wages of such as laufully were admytted to warre. Marius suffred none of these to pay any thyng at all: but elect many of them for his soudyours. Many of the Romayns surmysedde that Marius elected vnto warre these abiect persons: for want of other good soudyours. Some other demed that he so dyde for fa[u]oure/ ambytion/ and parcialyte: bycause this sort of people assistedde and honouredde hym by auauncement at begynninge of his promocyon. | f. 72v And also men consydred that vnto a man desyrous of dygnite and powere: the moost nedy men be moost mete and behouable. For such nedy wretches be moost auenturous: for they haue nought to lose and alway trust in auauncement by auenturyng themselfe. And therfore they iudge euery thynge which they do: good/ honest/ and laudable: if any auantage be therto appendant. Thus dout they no paryll so that they may come therby to promocyon. At last Maryus departed from Rome with somwhat gretter nombre than was graunted and decreed to hym of the senatours. Within fewe dayes after that: he toke shypping and aryued in the prouynce next vnto Affrike vnder the Romayns at a towne named Vtica. The army whiche was there with Metellus/ was delyuered to hym by one Publyus Rutilyus/ which was embassadour with the sayed Metellus. For Metellus hymselfe fledde the sight of Maryus bycause he wolde nat se that with his eyen/ which his mynde coude nat endure to here.

[87] But whan Marius had restored and fulfylled the legions of his soudyours/ and the cohortes for the subsidyes and rescous. Thanne went he into a plentyfull plagge of Numidy whiche was full of prayes.

17 certayne] cartayne B; a certayne C 21 to[2]] *om.* B C 30 fauoure] B C; fanoure A 46 eyen] eyes C 47 his mynde] he B C 50 plagge] place B C

All that he toke there: he gaue frely in rewarde to his soudyours. This done: he assayled suche castels and townes which were but febly defended with men and walles. He had many batayls and light skyrmisshes: and many other thynges he dyd in other places nat with moch dyfficultie. In the meane tyme the newe soudyours were redy/ manly fightyng without fere: and seyng that they which fledde were other taken or slayne: therfore they aduysed them well that the strongest and boldest was most sure of all. They consydred well that it stode them in hande to defende with wepyn and armour their lybertie/ their countrey/ their frendes/ and all other thynges longyng to their helth and honour. Thus laboured they for glorie/ laude/ and riches whiche they obtayned: so that within short season the olde soudyours and the newe encreased togyder cherisshing and infourmynge one another tyll their vertue and boldnesse was lyke. But whan the two kynges Iugurth and Boccus vnderstode of the commyng of Marius: they deuyded their hoostes and went in sonder into dyuers places where no man coude attayne to them for dyfficultie of the places. This was done by counsell of Iugurth. For it pleased hym so to do trustyng that within short space the Romayns wolde be spredde abrode in spoyling and than thought he to assayle them in euery place whan they | were moost without fere at lybertie/ at large/ and f. 73r
vnprouyded: as men ar wont to be specially whan their ennemies behaueth them as if they were affrayed. Than often be the vyctours inprouydent and lesse circumspect.

¶Howe Metellus the olde consull retourned to Rome: and of the worthy and valiant behauour of Marius agaynst Iugurth: and of his great actes at his beginnyng. ¶The .lii. chapyter.

[88] In the meane tyme Metellus went vnto Rome: which contrary to his opynion was receyued with gladde myndes of the Romayns: and after that the enuy which Marius had moued agaynst hym was aswaged and ouerpassedde: he was like dere and beloued both to the commens and senatours. ¶But Marius on his part applyed and toke hede to his owne besynesse and his ennemies also: without slouth but with great wysedome. He perceyued well and knewe what was good and yll for auantage on both sydes or agaynst. He caused the

54 places] place C 56 redy/] *virgule suppl.* 62 obtayned:] *colon from* B
73 vyctours] victour B; victours C

Ch. 52 4 went vnto] returned to B C 5 Romayns:] *punctus* A; *no punct.* B C
11 or agaynst] *om.* B C

wayes and iournayes of the two kynges to be daylie serched and espyed. He preuented and interrupted their counsels/ prouysions/ and gyles. He suffred nothyng to be vnprouyded and vnredy on his syde: but of the other syde and party of his ennemies: he suffred nothyng to be sure or prouyded: for alway he preuented their prouysions and pursued them. Often whyle Iugurth and the Getulyans spoyled the Numidyans which had yeldedde themselfe to the Romayns. Marius was redy in their way and valyantlie assayled them: and slewe and ouerthrue many of them/ whyle they were dyspersed abrode and fleyng away for feare. And also nat ferre from the towne of Cirtha/ he made Iugurth hymselfe so trust in his flyght that for hast to ren away: he laft his armour behynde hym. But whan Marius consydred that his actes were onely glorious and exellent without any auantage: and that he might nat execute batayle with Iugurth for his vnstedfastnes and mouyng from place to place: he concluded in mynde and ordayned hym redy to besyege the cyties of the contrey one after an other. And namely suche as outher of men or of place were necessary and behouable to his ennemies/ and contrary or hurt[full] to hym. This dyd he thynkyng: that if Iugurth without
f. 73v dystourbance suf| fred hym so to do/ he shulde other be spoyled and bereft of his cyties/ ordynance/ socours/ and refuge: or els he must abyde the fortune of batell and stryue for the maistry in playne feld. Bocchus the kyng of the Mauryens had often sende messangers before vnto Marius: sayeng that he wolde gladly come into fauour/ amyte/ and frendshyp of the Romayns: and byddyng Marius nat to dout hym as an ennemy nor to fear any thyng longynge to a[n] ennemy to be commytted of hym agaynst the Romayns. It is but lytell knowen for trueth whether Bocchus fayned this thyng to the intent that his commyng to batayle vnknowen and vnprouedde myght be to Marius more greuous: or els whether he was wont by vnstablenes of mynde to change peace somtyme for warre: and somtyme warre for peace.

[89] But Marius the consull (as he had purposedde before) drue hym vnto the castels and townes which were walled and defended: and fiersly assayled them. Anone he tourned many of them from his ennemies to hym/ some by strength and vyolence/ some by feare: and other some by promysinge and gyueng of rewardes and prodycion of

15 of] on C 20 slewe and] *om.* B C 21 fleyng] flying C 26 concluded] consydred B; considered C 27 contrey] countrey B; contreys C 28 outher] eyther C 30 hurtfull] B; hurt A; hurtefull C 31 other] eyther C 37 an] B C; a A

their capitayns. But at first begynning he medled but with mean castels and townes thynking that Iugurth shuld come to defende and socour his people and townes: and so come into danger of the Romayns. But whan Marius harde that Iugurth was farre thens and ocupyed in other besynesses: than thought he nat to lose his tyme: but to auenture on gretter thynges wherin was more harde besynesse and gretter labour and honour. Wherfore he entendedde to besiege the cyte of Capsa/ which was a great cytie/ stronge/ and riche.

¶How Marius wanne the great and rych cytie named Capsa: and how he vtterly distroyed the same and gaue all the rychesse therof to hauocke among his soudyours. ¶The .liii. chapyter.

[89. 4] Among the moost wydest and thickest wyldernesses of Numidy was this great and ryche cytie named Capsa: which (as men say) was first bylded by that Hercules whiche was borne in the lande of Libya: and nat by Hercules the sonne of Iupyter and Alcumena. Thinhabytours of this cyte were | ruled by Iugurth f. 74r peasably and easely/ put to no charges nor besynesse/ and therfore were they moost true and faythfull to hym. They were defendedde agaynst all ennemies: nat onely with walles/ armour/ and men: but also with moch stronger defence of the dyfficulte and hardnesse of the place and contrey nere about them. So that it was in maner impossyble that any army coude come nere them for want of water: and scarsyte of vytels. For except the feldes and places nere to the cite/ all the other be voyde and wast grounde and desart without habytacyon/ vneared/ barayne: and drie without water. All full of serpentes: which were somoch more vyolent and fiers for lacke of meat and sustenance/ as all other wylde beestes be wont to inrage for hunger. And moreouer the myscheuous and perylous nature of serpentes is more kyndled to ragyng and vexed with thyrst/ than with any other thyng. Which thyrst they coude nat quench there: for want of water. Wherfore neyther man nor beest might surely passe by them. Whan Marius cast all these dyfficulties in his mynde: his hert was persed with a merueylous desyre to wynne this cyte/ both for that it was moche hurtfull to hym: and profytable to Iugurth/ and also bycause it was harde to do and moche honour myght be gotten in wynning therof. And moreouer bycause Metellus the other consull before hym had wonne the cyte of Thala/ with great honour and

54 gretter] *om.* C

Ch. 53 9 easely/] *virgule suppl.* 15 places] place C

glorie: which of sytuation was nat vnlyke to this cyte: nouther vnlyke in defence. Saue that nat farre from the walles of Thala were a fewe fountayns: but about this cyte of Capsa was no water/ well/ nor fontayne: saue one and that was within the walles of the cytie alway full of water. All other which dwelled without the walles/ as in the suburbes: occupyed but rayne water. The inhabytantes of that countrey and of all the remenant of Affrike/ which were farre fro the see and rude people coude moche the better endure this scarsyte of water and thirst: for this cause. For the moost part of them were fedde with mylke and venyson nat lokyng after salt/ sauces/ nor other suche thynges as be norisshynges or prouocatyues to glotony. They toke meate and drinke onely to slake their hunger/ and to quench their thyrst: and nat without measure to prouoke themselfe to pleasure of the flesshe/ as many Christen men do nowe in our dayes: which make of their bely their god. And eate nat to lyue: but they lyue to eate contrary to mannes lyfe/ and vtterly enclyned to bestialyte. O cursed glotony let vs Christen men lerne here of panyms to eschewe | [f. 74v] the: which wastest the body and goodes: damnest the soule: and art mother and norice of all vyces.

[**90**] But to retourne to my purpose: this Marius after that he had serched euery thyng by his espyes/ he proceded in his interprise and purpose (as men thought) holpen of the goddes. For agaynst so many and harde dyfficulties he coude nat haue made sure prouysion by counsell of man nor by his owne priuate wyt: as he which had impedyment was letted nat onely by sharpnesse of the contrey: but also by lacke and scarcyte of wheat and of all other corne. For the Numidyans intendeth more to norisshe pasture for beastes than to labour or ere the grounde for corne. And also they had brought togyder all the seed and corne of the yere before into strongholdes as their kyng Iugurth had commaunded them and moreouer at that season the feldes on euery syde were dry and bare without corne: and [no] maruayle. For it was about the extremyte or later ende of somer. Nat withstandyng all these dyfficulties and sharpnesses Marius made prouysion ynough as the mater required. First he commytted all the beests which he had taken in pray in foretyme vnto the horsemen/ which of their owne wyll folowed hym to warre: or were sende to hym for helpe by frendes of thempyre. Marius commaunded them to take charge to driue forth these beestes. Than sent he Aulus Manlyus

30 nouther] neyther C 36 fro] from B C 45 enclyned] enclined B; encline C
47 wastest] wasted B 54 was] and was B C 61 no] B C; *om.* A

which was embassadour of the hoost to a towne named Laris/ and all the cohortes of his soudyours with hym which were fotemen and light harnysed for to kepe the treasour of the soudyours wages and vitayls: which he had lefte in the same towne. Marius kept his counsell of this interprise so secrete that none of all his company hye nor lowe knewe of his purpose or what he intendedde. But whan Manlius and his company shulde depart towarde Laris: Marius dyssemuled with them sayeng that he wolde stray abrode in Numydy in rouyng/ and afterwarde within fewe dayes: he and his company wolde come also to the same towne of Laris/ laded with prayes of his ennemies. This done: he departed towarde a flode named Tana: no creature liuely knowyng of his purpose.

[91] And euery day he dystribued in his iournayes among his hoost .xlii. heed of oxen for vitayle/ which he commaunded to be deuyded by euyn porcion amonge them by hunders and halfe hunders togyder: deuidyng vitayls to euery company after their nombre. And in the meane season he charged bottels and bowges to be made of the hydes of the same beestes and of other leddar in great nombre. Moreouer he eased their | scarcyte of wheate and other corne: by wyse prouisyon. f. 75r
And without knowledge of all his company he made good prouisyon of euery thing/ which might be necessary vnto his army in tyme of nede. At conclusyon the sixt day after whanne they were come to the sayd flodde of Tana: thyder was brought a myghtie multytude of bottels and bowges made of ladder. The[re] pytchedde they their tentes with easy labour and small defence. Than refresshed they themselfe with meate and drinke: and easedde themselfe a certayne space. This done: Marius their capytayne commaunded them that euery man shulde be redy to procede forwarde euyn with the sonne goyng downe and that euery man shulde onely lade hymselfe and his beastes with water in the sayd bowges and bottels leauynge all other caryage/ burthens/ and baggage: there behynde them in their tentes/ vnder the custody of other soudyours therto assignedde. After this whan he sawe his tyme: he departedde forth from his tentes with his company: and laboured all the nyght longe in his iournay. The day after folowynge he rested in a secrete and couert place. In the same wyse behauedde he hymselfe the nyght next insuynge: and in the thyrde night moche before the day light/ he came and entredde into a

68 which was] *om.* B C 73 or what] nor whan B; nor what C 75 rouyng/] *virgule suppl.* 84 be made of] *om.* C 85 beestes] beastes B; beaste C 91 There] B C; Their A 94 their capytayne] *om.* B C 104 came and] *om.* B C

fayre and large felde full of small hylles and downes/ no more but two myle space from Capsa. And there he taryed with all his hoost in the moost priuest maner abydinge the day lyght. But assone as the day beganne to appere: many Numidyans yssued forth of the towne: some to dysport themselfe: and some about their besynes/ nought fearyng nor suspectyng of their ennemies. Whan Marius sawe that: anone with all haste he sent all his horsmen to the towne and with them as many fotemen in lyght harnesse as were moost swyft and spedy. Whome he commaunded to renne with all hast and boldely and valyantly to assayle the towne: and to besiege the gates. Than after he hymselfe folowed spedely: but with good hede and aduysement: nat sufferyng his soudiours in the assaut nor in the way thyderwarde to fall to robynge nor prayes by spoylynge of their ennemies. Whan thinhabytantes of the towne knewe herof: their case was vnsure/ their feare great and horryble: for the sodayne chaunce of them was nothyng suspectedde before/ nor prouyded. Many of the cytezins which were without the towne/ and were taken and in power and captiuyte of the Romayns their ennemies/ sent vnto them within the towne desyring them for saue garde of their lyues to yelde themselfe
f. 75v and the cyte to | Marius. So was it done at conclusion. Howbeit this nat withstandyng Marius brent the cyte. All the Numidyans inhabytantes therof which were of full age and able to bere wepen were slayne: and the remanent as women/ chyldren/ and aged men were taken prisoners and solde for their raunsome. The pray and rychesse was deuydedde amonge the soudyours. This dede agaynst the lawe of armes was nat thus done by Marius: by couetyse nor any outher crueltie of hym: but bycause the towne and place was profitable/ behouable/ and necessare to Iugurth/ and to the Romayns harde to come to. And the maner of the people proued mouable and vnfaythfull euer of nature before: and neyther refrayned from their yll apetyte by benefite or good dede: nor yet with awe or feare of punysshment.

105 downes/] *virgule from* B   107 priuest] priueest B; priuiest C   day^{2}] daye light C   109 nought] nothinge C   111 all] *om.* C   121 towne/] *virgule suppl.* 122 ennemies/] *virgule suppl.*   132 behouable] *om.* B C   134 vnfaythfull] vnlauful B C

¶How Marius by fortune more than by strength wanne the strongest castell of all Numidy/ wherin were the tresours of Iugurth. ¶The .liiii. cha.

[92] After that Marius had brought to ende so great and harde an interprise without any losse or dammage to hym or any of his peple. Though he were reputed noble/ great/ and exellent before: than began he to be counted more famous and exellent. Euery noble dede which was done: was reputed to be don by strength and wysedom of Marius: and ascribed to his strength and polycie. And that such thynges as were done by good counsell and prouysion/ and also suche as hapened by fortune or chance: and by neglygence of their ennemies. The soudyours were so manerly treated without cruelty or fiersnesse of their captayne/ and also made riche and abundant of tresour and iewels: that they exalted and praysed his name to the heuen. And loued hym as themselfe. But in contrari wyse the Numidyans feared hym more than any man lyueyng. Shortly to speke: both the frendes of thempyre and ennemies also/ thought verily that outher Marius had a godly mynde and was a god hymselfe: or els that he was priue with the goddes: and dyd all his dedes and besynesse by their ad| uyse/ counsell/ and prouysion: which shewed f. 76r hym before what shulde fortune after.

But whan this chaunce had fortuned so well at Capsa: anone Marius drue hyme to other townes/ and toke as many as he besieged. In some townes the Numidyans resysted hym to their power: but it coude nat auayle. In many other townes the dwellars gaue them ouer and left them voyde and ran away feryng so to be treated and delt withall as they of Capsa were: bycause their townes were lyke behouable to Iugurth/ and hurtfull to Marius. Whan Marius cam to any such towne: destitute and voyde of dwellars he set fyre in them and brent them grounde smothe. The aged men/ women and chyldren: toke them to wodes and caues to hyde them. The yong men and lusty which were taken were slayne downe right. Thus was euery place fylled with wepyng and waylyng/ brennynge and slaughter: one mengled with another. Finally after that Marius had won into his handes/ many townes and castels: and some without resystence or blodeshedyng of his men. He went in hande with an other maistry and dyfficultie nat so sharpe nor harde to come to as was Capsa/ but to be won or besiged it was nat les harde nor of les dyfficulte.

Ch. 54 8 which was done] *om.* B C 11 their] *om.* C 13 of[2]] in B C 18 outher] eyther C 31 them[2]] themselfe B C 34 another] other B

¶Nat farre from the flodde of Mulucha (which water deuydeth the kyngdome of Iugurth: from the kyngdome of Bocchus) was a great rocke or mountayne of stone in myddes of a playne: open ynough to be sene hauynge thervpon bylded a meane castell of quantite: but of a meruaylous altytude and onely one strayet passage and narowe/ lefte to come therto. But on euery other syde the rocke of naturall growynge was downeright lyke a wall: as if it had ben made for the nones with mannes handes. Marius purposed with all his might to take this castell: and namely bycause the tresours of Iugurth were within the same. But this his purpose at last came to effect/ rather by chaunce of fortune/ than by prouision or counsell. For this castell was garnysshed and plentuously instored with men/ wepen/ vytels/ and with all other ordynance requisyte and necessary to defence of such a forteres. Moreouer within the same was a fountayne plentyfull of clere water. And bysyde this the sytuacion therof was such that without maruelous dyfficulte and vnmesurable labour none ennemies myght attayne or approche nere therto their ingens of batell to frusshe the walles or any other part therof. Besyde all these defences the double walles of this castell were garnysshed with towres/ bulwarkes/ and all
f. 76v other defences and ingens which coude be ymagined by man| nes mynde: and that rownde about in compasse as well within/ as without. The way therto: by whiche the inhabytantes and garnyson vsedde to go and come/ was very strayet and narowe. In somoche that the Romayns entrynge by the same way with their ingens of batayle: were constrayned to cutte their pauases on both sydes and to make them more narowe for strayetnesse of the passage. And in suche maner they proceded forwarde vnder the same in great paryll and with moche dyfficultie: and at conclusyon all in vayne. For whan they were come nere to the walles and wolde haue sette vp and adioynedde the same pauases to the walles to haue vndermyned vnder them: all their labour was frustrate. For what with stones and what with fyre the defenders of the castell brake and brent them agayne downe to the grounde. Thus cowde nat the soudyours whiche vndermynedde the walles: contynue togyder at their worke and besynesse: for strayetnes and dyfficultie of the place and importune vyolence of them within the castell. Nor other soudyours coude nat serue them whiche made and repared the pauases without great paryll and daunger. For contynually as fast as they raysedde the pauases to couer and defende themselfe: they were broken and brent bytwene their handes. In the

41 in] in the C 59 in] *om.* C

meane tyme no soudioure was so good/ stronge/ nor bolde: but that he was outher wounded or beatten downe to dethe. Than was feare encreasedde to other that were feble and faynt hertedde.

[93] ¶But after that many dayes and great labours in this manere were ouerpassed and spent in vayne. Marius was sore angred and vexedde in his hert/ reuoluyng many thynges in mynde: but specially whyther he myght gyue ouer his purpose (seyng his labour frustrate) or els abyde the chaunce of fortune whiche at many tymes before he hadde founde fauorable and frendly to hym. Whyle Marius chafedde and brennyng in desyre tourned and reuoluedde suche thynges in his mynde both day and night: it hapened by chaunce of fortune that a certayne Lumbard a symple soudyour/ one of the company which was last sende from Rome to Numidy to supply the army: strayedde abrode frome his company a lytell way: whiche Lumbarde as he wandredde founde among the stones many small snayles crepynge on the grounde: nat farre from that syde of the castell which was ouer agaynst the syde which the Romayns besyged and assayled. Bycause this Lumbard in his countrey was acustomed lyke other of his countrey men | to eate suche snayles preparedde after their manere: f. 77r
therfore he gathered first one and than an other/ and after that many: assendyng vp by lytell and lytell: somtyme crepyng somtyme clymyng/ for non other intent or purpose saue to gather such snayles: and so farre he proceded by lytell and lytell tyll at last he came almoost to the toppe of the mountayne. But whan he sawe all that syde of the castell desolat and no person steryng: anone he beganne to haue a pleasure and desyre in his mynde for to worke some maistry/ as the propertie and condycion is of euery man couetyng to wyn a name/ laude and riches: and to be spoken of. B[y] chance of fortune in the same place where the Lumbard stode in this aduysement/ among the stones grue a great and olde oke tre hauyng the myddes a [l]ytell bowyng downe towarde the grounde: and the remanent crokyng vpwarde agayne with mighty armes and branches ascendyng to the hyest of the walles with the toppe erect and lyfted vp as euery herbe and tre of nature is wont to growe vpwarde at the toppe. This Lumbard well aduysed the same and aduentured to clyme vpwarde takyng his holde somtyme by the branches and bowes of this oke: and

79 outher] eyther C 83 hert/] *virgule suppl.*; *no punct.* A B; *comma* C
87 tourned and] *om.* B C 91 way:] *colon suppl.* 94 which] that C
99 non other] no other B C; no nother A or] and C 103 for] *om.* C 105 By] B C; But A 107 lytell] tytell A; lytel B; lytle C

somtyme takyng holde and leanynge by the stones which apperedde forth in the wall/ tyll at the last he attaynedde vnto the very toppe of the wall. And whan he sawe no man styring on that part/ there stode he styll espyed of no man and notedde and consydred well at his pleasure all the inwarde part of the castell and the playne within the walles about the towre. This Lumbard had somoche the more leasour to take so longe aduysement vnespyedde for all the Numidyans defenders of the castell were on the other syde attendyng and gyueng hede to the assaut and defendyng themselfe and the castell agaynst the Romayns. Whan the Lumbard had espyed and consydred euery thing which he though[t] might be auantage to his after purpose: than he descended agayne downewarde by the same way which he ascended: but nat without hede nor with so lytell aduysement as he ascended vpwarde: but prouyng euery way/ and lokyng about yf it were possyble to bringe into the castell any company of men by that syde or nat. This well consydredde: assone as he descended: anone he went to Marius and inform[ed] [hym] of euery thyng as he had done/ exhorting and requiryng hym to put in profe whether the castell might be won on that syde where he had ben. Farthermor he promysed himself to be gyde vnto such as wold vndertake that interprise sayeng that in the mater was no danger.

f. 77v Marius hering | these wordes of the Lumbard/ sende forth with hym certayne of his men of them which were there present to vnderstande and knowe the trueth of the mater. Whan they had ben there and retourned to Marius agayne: some brought hym word that the mater was easy to do: and some other sayd that it was very harde and perylous. The sentence of euery man was after as their mynde gaue them. The cowardes thought it harde/ but suche as were of bolde hertes and desyrous of worshyppe thought it easy and without moche peryll. Neuerthelesse the mynde of Marius was somwhat exalted to confort/ and good hope. Wherfore of all the company of trumpettes/ and of other such mynstrelles as be wont to be in batayle to gyue courage and signes to the fighters/ he chose forth fyue which were moost swyft and moost lyght and delyuer: and .iiii. hundred men he assigned to assyst and defende the sayd trumpettes. And all them he commaunded to obey to the Lumbard and to be ruled

116 part/] *virgule suppl.* 124 thought] B C; though A 129 consydredde:] *colon from* B 130 informed hym] B C; informyng A 131 done/] *virgule suppl.* 140 mynde] mindes C 141 harde/] *virgule from* B 144 Wherfore] and therfore B C 147 and delyuer] *om.* C

and ordred by hym in euery thynge. The day next folowyng was assigned to them to procede forth in their besynesse.

[94] Whan the tyme assigned and prefixed by Marius was come the Lumbard with his company had made redy and ordred euery thyng: and so went to the place where he had ben before. But whan they were come thyder: the Lumbard their gyde caused them to change their armour/ and to make bare their heedes and their fete: to thintent that they so bare heded the better might se aboue them and on euery syde of them: and that they beyng bare fote myght labour somoche the better and take better holde in clyming vp by the stones. Their swerdes were fastned behynde at their backes and their buckelers withall/ which were made after the fassion of the Numidyans buckelers of lether: bycause of lyghter weyght and burthen. And also to thintent that they shuld gyue lesse sounde or noyse/ if it hapned any stone to smyte agaynst them. This done: the Lumbard went vp before them/ and bounde small cordes to the stones and to the olde rotes which apered aboue the stones where he coude espy any suche wherby the soudyours sustayning themselfe and takyng holde might more lightly and with more ease mount and clyme vpwarde. And somtyme he went before and helped them vp with his handes/ specially such [as] for that vncustomed way were somwhat ferefull. Somtyme whan thassendyng or goyng vp was ouerharde and sharpe: he put ech of them vp before hym without armour: and than he hymselfe folowed with the armour and wepyn. Suche places where moost dout was in: he spe| cially prouede and assayd them moost of f. 78r
all: and in goyng and comyng often tymes vp and downe by the same moost dangerous passages: he encreased audacyte and boldnesse to the remenant. Thus after they had ben sore weryed/ and with long and great labour endeuored themselfe: at last they came into the castell/ which on that syde they founde desolate and without defence. For (as sayd is before) all they which were within the castell were ocupyed in fightyng/ or redy to fight agaynst the Romayns: as they were on other dayes before.

But whan Marius vnderstode by messangers how the Lumbard had done: howbeit that all the day before his men had ben sore besied and occupyed in fightynge: and assaylinge the castell. Neuertheles specially at this tyme he exhorted and enbolded them: and he hymselfe departyng forth from vnder his pauases caused his soudyours to

169 handes/] *virgule suppl.* 170 as] B C; and A 171 thassendyng] thascendyng B; thascending C 173 the] their B C

adioyne themselfe nere togyder/ and to holde vp their sheldes aboue their heedes/ so that the conioyning of them semed as it were the frame of a volt. Marius kept hym vnder the same for his defence/ and so approched to the walles. And both he and his company which were nere about hym valyantly assayled the castell: and also other of his company which stode a farre of and coude nat come nere the walles for prease: assayledde the castell fiersly from a farre and sore vexed and put in feare their ennemies within the castell throwyng agaynst them plumettes of leed with slynges/ arowes/ dartes/ and all other maner engyns of batell: wherwith any thynge coude strongely be throwen into the castell. But the Numidyans within the castell had often before this tyme ouertourned and brent the tentes and pauases of the Romayns and toke therby so great audacyte and boldnesse that they defended nat themselfe within the castell walles: but walked vp and downe without the castell walles bothe day and nyght reuilyng and reprouynge the Romayns and obiectyng cowardyse agaynst Marius. And thretnyng that his soudyours shulde be made subgettes and bonde men to Iugurth in tyme to come/ whom they purposed at that tyme to make bonde to them. Thus whyle they thought themselfe sure and their mater in good case: they were harde and egar ynough reuyling and thretynyng the Romayns.

In the mean space whyle the Romayns and their ennemies were besyest fightyng with all their might: the Romayns for laude/ glorie/ and lordshyp: and the Numidyans for their helth and sauyng of their lyues. Anon sodenly the Lumbard with his company which were f. 78v within the ca| stell on the backsyde blewe their trumpettes. First of all the women and chyldren which went to the walles to se the bykering were all abasshed and fledde inwarde to the castell: and after them all the soudyours which were without and nerest to the walles and coude escape in. And finally they all both armed and vnarmed fledde inwarde. Whan the Romayns sawe this they assayled the castell more fiersly: some they slewe and ouerthrue: some they wounded ouerpassyng or standyng vpon the bodyes of them which were slayne. All their desyre was with their handes to wynne glorie and worshyppe. They stryued to ascende vnto the walles euery man couetyng to be before other. None of them all taryed nor was let with spoylinges nor prayes. Their great courage suffred them nat to loke there after/ tyll by manhode and strength they had won the castell. Thus was fortune fauorable to Marius: so that his first neglygence and vnwyse boldnesse to assayle a castell inexpugnable/ was tourned by chance from rebuke to glorie and laude/ such was his fortune. But whan Marius had wonne this castell after estimacion of man nat able to be wonne: than was he lorde of the moost part of all the treasour of Iugurth: the castell was gyuen all to murdre and hauocke. And the soudyou[r]s of Marius richely rewarded euery man after his desert.

¶How in the mene tyme whyle this castell was in wynnyng/ a noble man of Rome named Lucius Sylla: came from Rome to Marius with a great bende of horsmen: and of the maners and behauour of this Sylla. ¶The .lv. chapyter.

[95] In mean tyme whyle this fiers assaut and vyctorie was concluded at this castell: a famous lorde of Rome named Lucius Sylla/ tresourer of the army came from Rome to Marius with a great bende of horsmen. Whom the same Marius at his departyng from Rome had lefte the[re] to rayse and assemble socours vnto the warre among the Italians and other nations frendes and louers of thempyre of Rome.

¶But forasmoche as the matter moueth vs to make mencyon of so worthy a man and of his dysposition and maners: therfore it semeth vnto me conuenyent in this part somwhat to write | of his behauour f. 79r and conuersacyon: and that as brefely as I may conuenyently: namely for two causes. The first for that I intende nat to make relacion of his behauour and maners in any other place of this cronycle saue here. Secondly for asmoch as non other authour hath written sufficyently of hym. For how beit that one hystoriagraph named Lucius Sysenna: wrote moost dyligent[ly] and best of his actes of any other before/ neuertheles me semeth that he spake lytell acordyng to trueth nor indyfferently. For his tong nor penne were nat at lyberte for asmoch as he was somwhat in danger to the sayd Sylla: wherby he was prohibyted to say or to write/ acordyng to the trueth. For what by fauour and what by fere he durst nat touche playnlie the vyces which were in hym. But here I purpose (all fauour and fere layd apart) indyfferently to write of him.

¶This Sylla of progeny: was descended of moost noble stocke of the Romayns. Howbeit the name of his auncetry was almoost lost and decayed by dulnesse/ neglygence/ and slouth of some of his lynage. In Greke and in Latten he was of lyke connyng: and exellently seen in bothe the langages. His mynde was great/ and bolde of courage. Of

228 this] his C 231 soudyours] B; souldiours C; soudyous A

Ch. 55 9 there] their A socours vnto] socour to C 13 vnto] *om.* B C 16 maners] maner C 19 dyligently] B C; dyligent A before/] *virgule suppl.* 30 in[1]] *om.* C

voluptuous pleasours he was desyrous: but moch more desyrous of glorie and laude. In vacant leser he was moch enclyned to the lustes of his body. But suche pleasure or voluptuousnes dyd neuer let nor withholde hym from any besynesse or ocupation necessary: howbeit such pleasure so blynded hym that he toke no wyfe of byrth/ maners/ and honestie conuenyent for his estate. He was moch eloquent of spech crafty and subtyll ynough. He had the wayes easely to get frendshyp/ and it was also no maistry to get frendshyppe of hym: in fayning/ dyssimulyng/ and counterfayting of besynesses: his wytte was very hye and exellent. He was a maruelous and incredyble gyuer of many thynges/ but specially of money: and before the warre and vyctorie which the noble men of Rome had agaynst the commen people. He was so noble and worthy reputed that it is in maner incredyble: nor his good fortune neuer passed the polycie of his wyt: in somoche that many men were in dout whyther he was more fortunate than strong. But after the vyctorie of this warre: so vngoodly was his demeanour and so cruell/ that verily I knowe nat whyther I may more be asshamed or greued to write it or to speke therof. For after that this warre of Numidy was ended: and both Marius and this Sylla were retournedde to Rome: a
f. 79v great dyscorde fell bytwene the lordes and commens. | Marius toke part with the commons: but Sylla toke part with the lordes and at last droue Marius forth of the cytie. After that: an other man of great power called Cynna which had ben fyue tymes consull of Rome gathered an hoost of men and toke part with Marius agaynst this Sylla. But at conclusion Sylla ouercame hym in batell: and slewe hym. After this: Sylla cruelly murdred an other noble man of Rome named Cayus Carbo: and with hym yonge Marius/ sonne of this Marius which warred in Numidy. Last of all whan this Sylla had won vyctorie ouer Mari[u]s and all his fauourers: than became he moost cruell of all other: in somoch that he fylled all the cytie with blode of the cytezins. But here wyll I leaue to speke farther of this Sylla/ or of his behauour in cruelte: and returne to write of his behauour in this warre of Numidy vnder Marius.

[96] ¶After that this Sylla (as I haue sayd before) was come to Affrike and to the hoost of Marius with his company of horsmen: within short season he became moost expert in chiualry and crafty aboue all other: howbeit before this tyme he was but rude and ignorant of dedes of chyualrie. And moreouer he treted and gouerned his soudiours with maners and mekenes. And gaue rewardes to many:

36 so] *om.* C 43 Rome] Rome: A B C 49 it] *om.* C 52 part] *om.* C
59 Marius] B C; Maris A all] *om.* B C 68 of[1]] in C

to some which desyred hym: and to some other of his owne pleasure non desyring hym therto. But he wolde take no rewardes nor gyftes agayne/ without it were agaynst his wyll. And if he so dyd at any tyme agaynst his wyll: than was he more redy to gyue againe that which was gyuen to hym: than to pay that money which he had borowed of other. He demaunded nothyng agayne of any man though it were due and dette to hym: but rather he laboured and endeuored hymselfe that many myght be in his dette/ and by suche meanes to haue them bounde to hym. And howbeit that he was one of the grettest of Rome: yet disdayned he nat the company of the moost symple soudyours of the hoost: but communed and acompanyed with them both in sportes and in sadnes. In labours he was alway redy. In batell and in watchynges with other besynes of warre he suffred no man to be before him. Nor in the meane season he neyther hurt the good name of the consull nor of none other good man: which thing men desyrous of worshyp and honour be often wont to do/ for in dispraysing of other they thinke to obtayne great laude to themselfe. He onely laboured that none might passe hym neyther in counsell nor in myght/ or manhode of his handes. But he passed many. By whiche maners and condycions in short | tyme he became very dere and well f. 80r
beloued/ nat onely to Marius: but also to all the hoost.

¶How Marius preuayled in batayle agaynst both the two kynges/ Iugurth and Bocchus. ¶The .lvi. chapyter.

[97] But whan Iugurth had lost the towne of Capsa/ as is sayd before: and dyuerse other fortresses and other places defensyues which to hym were profitable. And also a great quantite of his treasour/ wherin he moost trusted. Anone he sent messangers to kyng Bocchus requiryng hym in all hast to come to Numidy and to bryng his army with hym: sayng that it was hye tyme to make batayle with Marius. But whan he vnderstode that Bocchus prolonged the tyme in ouerlong taryeng/ hauyng dyuers consyderations of peace and warre/ as he that was in dout of the chaunce and fortune of the ende therof. Iugurth agayne corrupted the next of his counsell with gyftes in lykewyse as he had done before: and promysed vnto the kyng Bocchus hymselfe/ the thyrde part of the kyngdome [o]f Numidy: if the Romayns were dryuen out of Affrike/ or if the warre shulde be

71 non desyring hym] non desyred B; not desired C 81–2 in watchynges] watching C 85 do/] *virgule suppl.*

Ch. 56 1 both] *om.* C 10 of peace] *om.* C 14 of] B C; af A

brought to ende without losse or deminisshyng of his kyngdome and marches therof. The kyng Bocchus induced with hope of this reward: with a great multytude of people came to Iugurth/ and adioyned bothe their armies togyder in one.

¶At this tyme Marius with his company was in his iournay towarde the prouynce which was in the coost of Affrike and apartayned to thempyre: where the sayd Marius purposed to rest with his company/ tyll the wynter were past. But whan he was in his iournay and in leest dout: Iugurth and Bocchus bothe togyder inuaded and set vpon hym and his men whan the tenth part of the day scarsly remayned. This dyd they: thynkinge that the nyght which was nere come shulde to them be great socour and defence if they were ouercome. And if they dyd ouercome the Romayns: it shulde be to them no damage nor impedyment bycause they knewe the contrey and place better than the Romayns. But on the other syde both these chaunces: in darkenesse
f. 80v were harde and contrary to the Romayns: for they knewe nat | the coostes of that countrey. Marius anone had vnderstandyng of the commyng of his ennemies by many of his espyes: but it was ouer late. For assone as he had worde: his ennemies were euyn at hande. In somoch that before the army coude be set in order or aray: and or they coude remoue or gather togyder their baggage which at that tyme was abrode: and before they coude take any commaundeme[n]t of their captayne by worde or sounde of trumpettes. The horsemen of the Morians and of the Getulyans ranne togyder vpon them nat in order nor aray of batayle: but by companyes and bendes togyder/ as it fortuned them to come togyder in heapes and clusters. The Romayns for the moost part: were all amased and greuously abasshed for that sodayne and vnprouyded feare. Neuerthelesse they forgate nat their olde manhode and strength: some drue them to their armour: and other some which were armed alredy defended their felawes tyll they armed themself. Other some mounted on horsebacke and boldly rode agaynst their ennemies: and encountredde and met them valyantly. The fight on both parties was more lyke a skirmysshe among brigandes and rouers than to any apoynted or ordred batell. For the horsmen and fotemen were mengled togyder without standerdes/ cognysances/ or any ordynaunce: aray/ or order. The Mauryans and Numidyans were fierse on their syde. Some of the Romayns they beate downe and ouerthrewe. Some they wounded mortally: And many they bereft

21 the[I]] a C 37 commaundement] B C; commaundemeut A 40 nor] or C
44 strength:] *colon suppl.* 47 and met] *om.* B C

vtterly of their lyues/ and slewe them in that place. The remenant which sharpely and manly resysted and withstode: they compased them [a]bout [on] euery syde: and as well behynde as before assayled them: so that neyther manhode/ strength/ nor armour: was able sufficiently to defende them. And no maruell for their ennemies were mo in nombre than they: and compased them about on euery syde of them. But finally the Romayne soudyours which were bothe of olde and newe: and therfore both stronge/ bolde/ and craftie in batayle: gathered them as nere togyder as they might. And where it fortuned any nombre of them to mete togyder: they tourned backe to backe. And ioyned them rounde one with an other in maner of a compasse or cercle: and so they saued and defended themselfe togyder so that on the backehalfe no man coude assayle them: but yf he brake in thro[u]gh the myddes of them which was in maner impossyble. By this maner they sustayned and abode the might of their ennemies: and also saued themself.

[98] Nor their captayne | Marius in this ieopardous and sharpe f. 81r besynes was nat affrayed at all/ nor of lesse corage and boldnesse than he was before: but styred about euery where in the batell. And his men of garde about hym whome he had ordayned and chosen rather of the strongest and boldest men of the hoost/ than of such as were moost familyer with hym. For he set more by the audacyte of them/ than by the familyarite of the other: and namely in suche a ieopardous case. Somtyme he socoured his soudyours in their nede/ or suche as he sawe in paryll. And somtyme he ranne in among his ennemies: where they were thyckest. And nat withstandyng their resystence he assayled them valyantly: and wounded/ slewe/ and ouerthrue them: on euery side he dyed his weapen in the reed blode of the blacke Mauryans and Getulyans. And bycause that in so harde a case: and in so great and troublous noyse and rumour: he coude nat counsell nor confort his soudyours with his tong: therfore he thought to counsell/ incorage/ and confort them with his hande: gyueing them example surely to bestowe their horious strokes. Many of his ennemies send he to hell cryeng in vayne vpon their ydolles for helpe. The dartes/ iauelyns/ pykes/ plummettes of leed/ stones: with other such instrumentes of batell/ were cast so thicke on both parties: that the ayre therwith was indymmed. The strokes were so coursly charged on

55 and withstode:] *om.* B C 56 about on] B C; obout one A 65 so] *om.* B C 67 and abode] *om.* B C 72 ordayned and] *om.* B C 79 them:] *colon suppl.* 80 he dyed] *om.* C 85 horious] *om.* B C 86 for] of C 87 iauelyns/] *virgule suppl.* 89 indymmed] indymed B; dimmed C

the bright helmes and harnesse/ that the fyre sprange out on euery syde: so that it semed to be the lightnyng: the cry of the men dyeng: the neyeng of horses: and the dyn of the strokes/ with the sounde of the trumpettes: was horrible and tedyous to here. Thus contynued they tyll the daylight was passed/ and the nyght was come. The Numidyans/ Getulyans/ and Mauryans desysted nor ceassed nothing for that. But as both Iugurth and Bocchus before had warned and commaunded them: they contynued more sharpely than before/ thinkyng that the darkenesse of the night shulde be for their auantage. Marius this vnderstandyng toke counsell and made best pro[u]ysion for hymselfe and his men: which he might in such case: and as the mater required. And to thentent that his people might haue some place to resort vnto/ for refuge and socours: he prouyded before and ocupyed two hylles nere togyder of whom the one was ouer narowe/ and of lytell grounde to receyue his hole army and tentes: but in the top therof was a fayre fountayne of pure water moch necessarie. The other hyll was sufficiently large to receyue his hole hoost and tentes: f. 81v and also very defensyue: for it was of a great alty| tude and downe right on euery side. In somoch that they whiche shulde take that hyll were sure ynough without great defence of themselfe: for nature had it sufficiently defended. This well consydred: Marius commaunded Sylla his vndercapten to take with hym all the horsmen: and to tary that night about the smaller hyll where the fountayne was. This done: he hymselfe gathered togider by lytell and lytell the remanent of his soudyours which were dyspersed abrode: their ennemies being nat lesse troubled than were they. Whan Marius had thus assembled agayne his men togyder he led them all with full cours vp vnto the larger hyll. Thus the two kynges Iugurth and Bocchus seyng it vayne to fyght with them which were on the hyer ground/ and also on so sure a place: were constrayned to leaue the fight: for dyfficulte of the place which the Romayns had taken. But neuertheles in the mean tyme they suffred nat their men to depart farre thens: but compased both the hylles rounde about with their hole multytude and there taryed and rested/ shed abrode vpon the ground. Whan they had taken their place in this maner: thei made great fiers here and there in many places of their hoost: and the barbarians after their custome passed forth the moost part of the night in myrth/ pleasure/ and gladnes/ reioysing/ daunsyng: and makyng great noyse and dynne

92 horses] the horses B C 94 was[2]] *om.* B C 106 was] *om.* C 114 which were] *om.* B C 117 vayne] in vayne B C

with their fete: rennyng and goynge from place to place: and loudly crieng/ synging and reuellyng. The kynges themselfe were also nat a lyttell proude and fearse: bycause they had nat fledde from the batell: and counted themselfe as ouercomers seyng that they helde the Romayns so besieged which as they thought durst nat abyde them. On the other partie the Romayns intentyfly gaue aduertens to the demeanour of their ennemies. And for that the Romayns were on the hight of the hyll and without light: therfore more easely from darknesse of hyer places they parceyued all the dedes and behauour of their ennemies which were beneth them: and moch more euydently by light of the fyers. This vnwyse behauour of the Numidyans put the Romayns in great confort and was great courage to them.

[**99**] And specially Marius was greatly confermed in hope seyng their neglygence/ their folly/ and vncraftynese: wherfore he commaunded his folke to kepe sylence as styll as myght be possyble without any noyse. In somoch that he suffred nat the trumpets to sounde the watch: as warryou[r]s ar wont agaynst night. Afterwarde whan the day began to apere: the Numidyans were al weryed with their cryeng/ ouerlate watchyng | and reuell: and had gyuen themselfe to rest a lytell before as f. 82r
men without fere or dout of the Romayns. But certenly it is a true prouerbe which is often sayd: that after fayre wether succedeth tempestious cloudes: and after myrth and ioye often cometh sadnes and sorowe. So it hapened to the Numidyans. For whyle they ingorged and fylled with wynes lay slepyng on the grounde as beestes without fere and without prouision: Marius commaunded sodenly all his trumpets and clarionystes with other mynstrels to sound their instrumentes as shyrle as they coude altogyder and that all his soudyours shulde set vp a shout or cry as horribly as they might: and with that inuade and breke into the tentes of the Numidyans. This was shortly done: wherfore the Numidyans/ Mauryans/ and Getulyans astonyed and abasshed with that vnknowen and horryble noyse: were sodenly awakened of sleape: and seyng them thus compased with their ennemies: what for feare of deth and of the noyse they were so amased that they had no power neyther to fle nor to drawe to them their armour/ nor vtterly to do or prouyde any maner socour for themselfe. Thus they stode astonyed for this horryble noyse and cry as yf madnesse had entred them: none able to socour hymselfe nor other.

128 with their fete] *om.* B C 133 partie] part B C 135 easely] easy B C 144 warryours] B; warriours C; warryous A 153 and] *om.* C 160 of^{2}] *om.* C 161 nor to] nor C

The Romayns alway increased to them their noyse and feare assaylyng/ murdring/ and woundyng them without any resystence. Finally all they were outher ouerthrowen/ slayne/ or wounded: or els fledde/ their armour/ standerdes and weapen left behynde them: and mo were in this batayle slayne: than in all the batels before. For amonge them all none was taken prisoner: for with feare and sleape so amased were they/ that fewe escaped by flight.

¶Of the great prouysion and wysdome of Marius after his victory: and of the seconde batayle which he had agaynst the two kynges/ in which also he had great vyctorie with great laude and honour. ¶The .lvii. chapyter.

[**100**] Whan Marius had gloriously thus ouercome the moost part of his ennemies except the two kynges: he drue hym than towarde his wyntring places as he had purposed before. And ordred hymselfe and his men specially in hauen townes by| cause of more easy prouysion of vytels: but neuertheles: in his iournay thiderwarde: for all his vyctorie: he became nat neglygent/ vnware/ nor proude (as captayns often ar wont after vyctorie goten of their ennemies) but he prouyded and went forwarde with his army quadrat and deuyded into four partes ordred and apoynted as if his ennemies had ben in his sight. Sylla was assigned to take charge of the right wyng of the army and all the spear men with hym. And Aulus Manlius of the lyft wyng. And with hym the slyngars/ archars/ and the cohortes of Lumbardes. The peticapytayns with fotemen of light harnesse: were dystributed and dyuided in the vantgarde and rerewarde. Of the treatours whiche had forsaken Iugurth and came to the Romayns: such as were best laboured and knewe best the contrey/ were chosen forth and sent out to espy the contrey and wayes of Iugurth and Bocchus. But nat withstandyng Marius hymselfe was as prouydent/ circumspect/ and dilygent withall: as if he had commytted the charg to none other. He was mouyng continually from place to place ouer all the army: laudyng/ commendyng/ and rewardyng the good soudyours: and blamyng and rebuking the bad: he himselfe armed/ and dyligently prouidyng and minystring vnto them euery thing necessary and expedyent: and compelled them that were frowarde and ylwillyng to labour. In euery place where he set his tentes in his iournay: he ordred defence

f. 82v

167 fledde/] *no punct.* A B; *comma* C; *virgule suppl.*

Ch. 57 3 great[2]] *om.* B C 7 places] place C 11 ennemies)] *colon in place of closing bracket* A B C 13 sight.] *punctus suppl.* 26 bad:] *no punct.* A B; *colon* C

with depe dychesse/ and trenchesse rounde about his hoost. And in the entres of the tentes he assigned soudyours elect therto to kepe watch and some to kepe scoutwatch about the tentes in compasse. Moreouer some other he ordred on the castynge of the dyches and on outwarde bulwarkes to defende the remanent if any sodayne peryll apered. He hymselfe armed nightly went about and serched the watch. Nat specially for any feare nor mystruste of any paryll to come nor for feare that his soudyours wolde nat obey his commaundement. But specially to thentent that the soudyours seyng their captayne nat refusing labour nor paryll: shuld be also more wylling to folowe the same and to take payne vpon themself and ashamed if they dyd nat as moch as their capten. And certenly at this tyme and at many other during this warre (as I rede) Marius constrayned his soudyours to labour rather with shame than with sharpnes or punisshment. For shame it is to the seruant to be ydle whan the maister sore laboreth. Howbeit some sayd that Marius toke this labour vpon hym for the desyre of commendation and worshyp: bycause | that from his youth he was euer wont with hardnesse/ hunger/ f. 83^{r} thyrst/ and labour: and many other thynges whiche the delycate gentylmen of our tyme cownt for myseries. But to Marius were these hardnesses moche pleasure and delyte for affectyon which he had agaynst the commen wayle/ as equall persones supposed. But to what euer intent Marius treated his army in this wyse: it was knowen that his dedes dyd asmoche profet and worshyppe to the commen wayle of Rome: as if he had more rigorously and sharpely treated his soudyours. For all thynges were ordred well and worthely for the honour and profet of the commen wayle: as if he had more rigorously treated his army.

[101] ¶But to retourne to my purpose: whan Marius with suche dyligence as sayd is: was come nat farre from the towne of Cyrtha/ at the last the fourth day after the forsayd batayle: the espyes of their ennemies appered on euery syde. The Romains vnderstode anone therby that their ennemies were at hande. The espyes of the Romayns also which were sende forth: brought the same tidynges from euery coost of the countrey. Marius parceyued that his ennemies were in dyuerse companyes and deuyded: wherfore he was vncertayne how he myght best order his hoost to receyue them. And therfore parceyuinge it vnsure: how to order the forfront of his batayle as it ought: he abode

35 nightly] nyghtly B; myghtely C 38 specially] chiefely C 40 to[2]] *om.* C and] as B C 43 with[1]] for B C 56 if] *om.* C

his ennemies in the same place no order chaunged/ with his hoost deuyded in .iiii. partes (as sayd is) as he whiche was redy and prouyded for euery chaunce. Thus was Iugurth disceyued and frustrate of his purpose. For he had deuyded his hoost into four partes trustynge to inuade some of the Romayns on the backehalfe with parte of his army: and with an other part to encounter with them/ and with the other two partes to enclose them on both the sydes: and so to enuyron them rounde about. In the meantyme Sylla which first encountred with Iugurth exhorted and conforted his men as well as he might for breuyte of the tyme. That done: anone he proceded with his company by bendes and clustres togyder/ their horses conioyned in the moost thyckest maner: and so fiersly assayled the Mauryans. The remanent of the fotemen which were vnder Sylla: remayned and kept themselfe styll in their first place: and defended their bodyes from the dartes which their ennemies thrue agaynst them from farre of. But yf it chaunsed any of their ennemies to come bytwene their handes: they hewed them downe to decrease and inlesse their nombre.

f. 83v ¶Whyle Sylla and his horsmen thus fiersly were fightyng on the right wyng of the batell. The kyng Bocchus assembled togyder the fotemen whom his son named Volux/ had brought thyder with hym. These fotemen had such impedyment in their iournay thyderward that they came ouerlate to the other batell which was last foughten before this. Wherfore Bocchus: whan he had assembled and inbolded with his wordes these fresshe fotemen: with them he assayled fiersly the rerewarde o[f] the Romayns.

¶In the meane tyme Marius hymselfe was ocupyed in the forwarde of his hoost and there imployed his wysdom and strength/ as a valyant and worthy captayne: and so stode it hym in hande. For in the forwarde Iugurth hymselfe with his grettest power and strongest company of men inbatayled with hym. ¶But after that Iugurth knewe of the commyng of Bocchus to the felde: anone he turned hym with a small company about hym priuely vnto the fotemen of the Romayns: and there with an hye voyse he cryed vnto them with a lowde exclamation/ sayng that they fought but in vayne. For a lytell before (as he sayd) he had slayne Marius with his owne handes. And in cryeng these wordes he lyfted vp withall/ and shewed his

68 chaunged/] *virgule suppl.* (*end of line* A B) 83 of] *om.* B C 84–5 and inlesse their] the B C 93 of] B C; or A 101–2 with a lowde exclamation] *om.* B C 103 (as he sayd)] *om.* B C

swerde all ouersprincled and dyed with blode: which he had so couloured in the batell fiersly ynough in murdring the fotemen of the Romayns. These wordes Iugurth cryed in Latyn tong. For he had lerned to speke Latyn longe before in the batayle of Numance. Whan the Romayns harde these wordes they were affrayed/ but more for crueltie of the noyse: than for any confidence or trust which they had to the messanger. But on the other syde the myndes of the barbaryans were bolded and exalted by these wordes: by reason wherof more sharpely they inuaded the Romayns/ seyng them abasshed and astonyed. And nowe were the Romayns of the forwarde at that poynt that they were redy to gyue themselfe to flyght: as men dyscouraged for the sayd tydynges.

¶Whanne they were at this poynt: it fortuned so at the same tyme that Sylla had beaten and ouerthrowen the Mauryans which inuaded and assayled hym on the right wyng of the batayle: wherfore he retourned to his company and fiersy assayled the fresshe fotemen which were with Bocchus/ and at one syde brake in among the thyckest of them. But Bocchus anone tourned his backe: and gaue hymselfe to flyght.

¶On the other syde Iugurth whiche in his part of the batell almoost had obtayned vyctorie/ dyde his dilygence to incou|rage and support f. 84r his company: and to mentayne that auantage which he had goten. And at conclusion all in vay[n]e. For whyle he laboured there about as a worthy captayne: the spear men of the Romayns so compased hym and his company about both on the right syde and on the lyft: that all his garde and other which were about hym at conclusion were slayne. But he hymselfe gladde to saue his lyfe/ brake forth alone from among the myddes of his ennemies: and from wepyns and dartes with great dyfficulty.

¶But in the mean tyme Marius had ouercome and driuen away the horsmen which assayled hym. Wherfore anone he returned fiersly to helpe and socours of his company whom he vnderstode somwhat put backe by vyolence of their ennemies. But he by his polycie and valyant dedes anone so reconforted his men that none of his ennemies were able to withstande their vyolence in any part of that batayle.

¶Thus finally the Romayns after great laboure and many greuous woundes dysconfited their ennemies on euery syde. But whan the batayle was ended and the Romayns began to pursue the chase: than verily it was a pytefull and horryble syght to beholde in the open

126 goten] won B C 127 vayne] B C; vayue A 136 socours of] socour C

feldes and to consyder the cruell spectacle of batayle. How some fledde. Some pursued/ some inraged murdring/ some rored dyeng/ some slayne/ some taken prisoners. The horse and men mengled togyder: labouring in the panges of deth. The ground ouerspred with deed corpses mangled/ mutulate/ and horrible hewyn: inuolued in blode congeled. The horse wounded: as madde drewe after them the deed carcases of their maisters/ their legges hangyng in the styropes/ and their speares halfe thorowe their bodyes trayling after in the dust. The coursers wounded and fleyng cast vp with their fete the dust tempered with blode/ rennyng ouer the deed bodyes of their lordes. Many of the Numidyans which were sore wounded coude neyther fle: nor be suffred to take rest on the grounde. Somtyme they laboured to ryse and auoyde: and anone after for feblenesse fell downe to the grounde agayne: eche rowlyng and turnyng in others blode. And finally: as farre as any mannes syght myght extende/ all the grounde was ouerspred and coueredde with armour/ we[ap]en/ and deed caryons the rennyng of blode. And all the grounde infect with the same: thyng horryble to beholde.

f. 84v ¶How Bocchus after that he was twyse ouercom in batell/ purposed to make peace with the Romayns: and how at his request Marius sende vnto hym Sylla and Manlyus to knowe his mynde in that behalfe. ¶The .lviii. chap.

[**102**] After that this batell was thus ended to the vtter dammage and dystruction of the Numidyans: and to the laude and honour of the Romayns. Marius was nowe without dout ouercomer and vyctour and went vnto the towne of Cirtha as his iournay and purpose was at first begynnyng/ before these two batayls. Whan Marius had soiourned there fyue dayes after this batayle: there came vnto hym imbassadours from kynge Bocchus. Which in their kynges behalfe desyred of Marius to sende vnto hym two of the moost trusty men which he had: sayng that he wolde commen and treate with them of dyuers besynesses both for his owne profet/ and for profet and auantage of the Romayns also. Marius without tary sende forth Sylla for one: and Aulus Manlius for an other. Whan they were come to kyng Bocchus: howbeit he had sende for them to commen with them in his maters. Neuertheles it was concluded bytwene them to speke to hym first to

148 horrible] horribly B C 149 horse] horses C 157 others] other B
159 weapen] wepaen A; wepen B C 160 the[1]] *om.* B C 161 thyng] *om.* B C

Ch. 58 1 was] was thus B C

thentent to kyndell and inflame his mynde the more agaynst Iugurth: or els seyng hym somwhat desyrous and wyllynge to haue peace to prouoke hym with more desyre therto. Wherfore Sylla (to whom Manlyus gaue place nat for his age/ but for his eloquence) began and spake to Bocchus in maner: as foloweth.

¶Of the wordes of Sylla tresourer of the Romayne army had before kyng Bocchus. The .lix. cha.

[**102. 5**] King Bocchus we haue great gladnes and ioye syth it is so that the goddes haue thus admonysshed and [enspired] you so noble a man that at last ye haue reputed peace beter and more acceptable than warre: lest ye myght dyshonest and defyle your worthynesse by associatyng your selfe to the | moost vnhappy tyran Iugurth. And f. 85r
also we ar glad that ye haue auoyded the occasion and necessite: wherby we were moued to pursue in batayle: you: beyng ignorant of our quarell: and in the company of the sayd moost cursed Iugurth: tyran and ennemy to thempyre of Rome. And certenly the people of Rome euer syth their poore/ symple/ and small begynning haue thought it better to wyn frendes than seruantes or bondmen/ and also they haue thought it a moch surer thyng to haue vnder their empyre such as wyllingly and of their owne mocyon wolde yelde themselfe: than such as they haue constrayned therto agaynst their wyll. But verily no frendshyp is more necessary to you than our amyte or frendshyppe. And first of all: bycause we and ye be farre in sonder: wherby we shall haue les power to greue you/ or to put you to any charge: by reason of our frendshyp. But our fauour and thankes may be as redy to you: as if we were nere togyder: consydering the many and great frendes which we haue nat farre from your marchesse. And also vnto thempyre of Rome be obeyers/ subgettes/ and seruantes abundantly. But as touchyng louers and frendes we nor none other can haue sufficyently ynough. For this consyderation kyng Bocchus your frendshyp shalbe the more acceptable vnto vs. And wolde God it had pleased you thus to haue done at the begynning of this warre. Forsoth if ye had so done: than shulde ye before this tyme haue receyued of the Romayns mo commodyties/ auantages/ and good dedes than ye haue nowe suffred losse/ damages/ or hurtes. But whyle it is so that mannes dedes and besynesses (for the moost part)

19 the] *om.* C

Ch. 59 4 enspired] B C; ensprired A 13 bondmen/] *virgule suppl.* (*end of line* A B) 18 And] At B C 26 the] *om.* B C 27 of] to C

be ruled by fortune: to which fortune it hath pleased that ye shulde both proue and assay our myght and vyolence in batayle: and also our loue and fauour in peace: Therfore nowe syth amyte is proferred to you by suffraunce of fort[u]ne: and syth it is laufull to you to take it: be nat slowe from hensforwarde/ but hastely procede as ye haue begon: that ye may proue the Romayns frendes to you lyke as ye haue proued them ennemies before this tyme. Ye haue many expedyent oportunites and necesary commodytes by whome ye may make amendes with your good dedes for that which ye haue offended agaynst the Romains/ and ouerpasse your olde fautes with newe kyndnesses and benefites. [A]nd finally fix this in your hert that ye or any other shall neuer ouercome the people of Rome with kyndnes or good dedes. And as touchyng their hatered/ and of what myght the[y] ar in batell: ye yourselfe knowe that by profe and experience. f. 85v Wherfore | procede in acquiryng of their frendshyppe: which gladly shalbe graunted vnto you/ if your merytes shall so deserue.

¶Of the answere of Bocchus made to Sylla: and of the vnstablenesse of mynde of the same Bocchus. ¶The .lx. chapyter.

[**102. 12**] To these wordes of Sylla answered Bocchus myldely and sobarly: and a fewe wordes he spake in excusing his offence done agayne the Romayns/ sayeng that he had nat taken armour nor begon batell agaynst the Romayns in purpose as ennemy to do iniury or wrong vnto them: but to defende his owne kyngdome. And that the thyrde part of Numidy belonged vnto hym by lawe of armes: of the which the Romayns laboured to expell Iugurth. And in that doyng they distroyed his part of the contrey: which he coude nat suffer vnreuenged. Moreouer Bocchus sayd for hymselfe that he had sende vnto Rome before to require amyte and frendshyppe of the Romayns: which thyng vnto hym was denyed. But at conclusyon he sayd: that he wolde omyt and lay apart all olde malyce and that althyng shuld be done and agreed bytwene them: yf Marius wolde graunt hym that his embassadours might be sende to Rome for the sayd frendshyppe to be confederate with the Romayns. Upon this answere Sylla and his felawe retourned to Marius: which anone agreed that the same embassadours shulde be sent to Rome. But shortly after: what tyme Iugurth vnderstode of the commynge of Sylla and Manlyus he feared

34 peace:] *colon from* B; *punctus* A 40 which] *om.* B C 41 Romains/] *virgule suppl.* 42 And] and A B C 44 they] B C; the A

Ch. 60 6 batell] warre B C the Romayns in purpose] them B C

the same thyng/ whiche was ordende and in hande. And anone with rewardes so he corrupted the frendes of Bocchus: that agayne they chaunged his mynde with their counsell: so mutable and varyable was he of mynde.

¶How Bocchus chaunged his purpose yet ones agayne: and sende newe embassadours to Marius to treat of the peace: and howe Sylla receyued and treated them in absence of Marius. ¶The .lxi. chapyter.

[103] In the meane tyme Marius set and ordred his hoost in their wyntring places and toke with hym suche men as were of light harnesse: and also a part of his horsemen: and with them went into a desart nat farre thens/ to besyge a certayne towre belongyng to Iugurth: into which towre the sayd Iugurth had put for garnyson and defence: all the treatours which had forsaken and fledde from the Romayns/ and ranne to Iugurth. But in the meane whyle Bocchus of newe agayne consydred in mynde/ the mysfortune whiche had hapened to hym in the two batayls before. Or els by counsell of some other of his frendes: whom Iugurth had nat corrupted with rewardes: he chose forth among all his frendes .v. men whose fydelyte and trueth he had well knowen and often proued before: and whose wysdome was moost expert and redy. Them sende he to Marius: and commaunded them afterwarde yf the mater required as imbassadours to take their way to Rome. And commytted to them his full authorite in euery thynge which was to be done: and to conclude the batayle by what euer maner shulde seme best/ and moost expedyent to their dyscresion. These imbassadours toke leaue and spedely toke their iournay to the places where the Romayns soiourned the wynter season. But whyle they were in their iournay thyderwarde: they were assayled of theues of the Getulyans/ and robbed and spoyled of all that they had about them. Thus at last without worshyp or apparell: all affrayed and abasshed they fledde vnto Sylla for refuge. This Sylla was left by Marius in the wyntering places: to be ruler of the Romayne army in his absence. What tyme these imbassadours: thus spoyled were come to Sylla for refuge/ he receyued them nat fayntly as vayne and vnstable ennemies as they deserued: but curteyslie with moch gentylnes and lyberalite/ treatyng them in all poyntes honorably. By this meanes these barbaryan and rude peple f. 86r

Ch. 61 2 the] *om.* C 3 receyued] receyued them C 10 and ranne] *om.* B C 14 his frendes] *om.* B C 19 batayle] war B C 30 vayne and vnstable] *om.* C 32 barbaryan] barbarians B C

counted and supposed that the name of couetyse/ whiche was imputed vnto the Romayns by commen fame was but false and fayned of their ennemies/ to distayne their honoure. And also for the moch lyberalite of Sylla: they counted hym as their specyall frende. For yet vnto that tyme: the accloyeng of gyftes whiche be gyuen for rewardes and of polycie and falshode to ouercome couetous or symple myndes/ was vnknowen vnto many. No man was lyberall in f. 86v gyftes: but that he was thought | and counted to be faythfull of hert withall. Thus the barbarians reputed the lyberte and rewardes of Sylla to be a great and euydent token of loue which he had to them: as they demed. But to our purpose: the imbassadours anone opened and declared to Sylla the wyll and commaundement of Bocchus their kyng: gyuen to them to be executed: And also they required hym to be vnto them a frendly fauourer and counsellour in their besynesse. Farthermore with their wordes and spech they commended and exalted the army/ the trueth/ the greatnes and exellence of their kyng: and all other thynges which they thought might auayle them to obtayne benyuolence of the Romayns. After they remayned with Sylla about the space of .xl. dayes: which graunted them all his helpe and socour: and also in the meane space enfourmed them in what maner they shulde order their wordes whan they shulde speke with Marius/ and also before the senatours at Rome.

¶How Marius harde thembassadours of Bocchus and sende them to Rome: and how they were answered of the senatours. ¶The .lxii. chapyter.

[**104**] In the mean tyme Marius whiche was in assaut of the kynges towre coude nat fulfyll his desyre nor parfour[m]e his enterprise. Wherfore he retourned againe to Cirtha: anone was he certified of commyng of the imbassadours of Bocchus. Wherfore he commaunded them and Sylla also to come before hym: and also he called togyder all the moost worthy men of his hole hoost from euery place. Before them all presently he commaunded the imbassadours of Bocchus to reherse the petycion of their kyng (which rehersed and harde) it was graunted vnto them to go to Rome for the same poyntes. And of Marius was truesse required in the meane tyme bytwene Bocchus and hym. Sylla with many other noble men were pleased withall. A fewe

37 whiche be] *om.* B C 38 and of] for B C 46 vnto] to C

Ch. 62 5 fulfyll his desyre nor] *om.* B C parfourme] parfourne A; perfourme B; performe C 12 to[2]] *om.* B

other fiersly and sharply counselled otherwyse: as men without pyte and ignorant of others harde fortune which whan it begynneth to be frowarde with men and contrary: it tourneth euery thyng to aduersyte.

¶But whan the Mauryens had obtayned of Marius [a]ll their desyre: thre of them went to Rome with one named Octauy| us Rufo: whom [f. 87r] Marius had assigned to conuey them thyder. This Octauyus Rufo was sende before from Rome into Affrike to Marius with wages for the soudyours. The other two imbassadours of Bocchus returned home agayne to their kyng: which of them gladly harde of the good report whiche they made of the Romayns in euery poynt: and specially of the goodwyll/ lyberalite/ and courtesy of Sylla.

¶But whan the other thre imbassadours were come to Rome they apered before the senatours and in the humblest wyse that they coude deuyse/ dyd their message excusyng their kyng: and confessyng that he had offended agaynst the impyre nat by his owne sekyng: but by the cursed faut/ prouocation/ and instygation of Iugurth: wherof their kyng sore repented. Wherfore in his behalfe at conclusyon they besought the Romayns of pardon/ amyte/ and a bonde of peace. Than was it brefely answered to them in this maner.

¶The senatours and people of Rome: is wont to remembre both the kyndnesse and benifytes of their frendes: and also the iniuryes of their ennemies. But syth it repenteth and forthynketh Bocchus of his trespas: grace and pardon of his offence is graunted vnto hym. Peace and amyte shalbe also graunted vnto hym herafter/ whan he shall so deserue.

¶How Marius sent Sylla agayne to Bocchus at his desyre: and what danger the same Sylla escaped by helpe of Volux/ sonne of kyng Bocchus. ¶The .lxiii. cha.

[**105**] Whan Bocchus vnderstode and knewe all these thynges: he desyred Marius by his letters to send vnto hym Sylla: to thentent that after his aduyse and dyscression counsell might be had of the commen besynesses to both parties belongyng. Sylla anone was send forth with a great retynue of fotemen and horsmen: with dyuerse weapen and strong socours or defence as archars/ slyngars/ with otherlike. And to

17 with men] *om.* B C 19 all] al B C; oll A 29 deuyse/] *virgule from* B 33 a bonde of] *om.* B C

Ch. 63 4 and knewe] *om.* B C 7 besynesses] besynesse B; busynes C 9 socours or] *om.* B C

thyntent to spede their iournay more hastely: they were all armed with lightest harnes which coude be prouided: but for all the lightnes of their armour it was defensife ynough agaynst the weapyns of the Mauryans: for their wepyns be light in likewyse. But finally whan f. 87v Sylla had passed fyue dayes of his iournay: sodenly Volux | the sonne of Bocchus apered and shewed hymselfe to the Romayns in the open feldes: with no mo but .M. men which went scatered and dyspersed abrode neglygently: so that they semed to Sylla: and all other a greatter nombre than they were in dede. Sylla and all his company feared them/ thinkyng them as ennemies: wherfore the Romayns made them redy with armour and weapen: to defende themselfe/ and to resyst their ennemies: if nede shulde so requyre. A lytell feare was amonge them: but their hope and confort ouerpassed their feare. For why? they had the vpper hande before: and consydredde that they shulde bycker with them/ whom they had often ouerthrowen and ouercome before. In the meane tyme the horsemen which were sent before of both parties to espy the trueth of the mater/ certifyed eche of them that all thyng was quyet and sure ynough: as it was in dede: without treason or paryll.

[**106**] Volux in his metyng called Sylla by name: and welcomed hym benyngely/ sayeng that he was sent from his father Bocchus to mete the sayd Sylla for his honour/ socour/ and defence. And so proceded they forthwarde all this day and the next day after in company togyder without feare or daunger. But after that it was night and their tentes pytched: sodenly the Mauryan Volux came rennyng to Sylla all pale and quakynge: and sayd that he was infourmed of the espyes/ that Iugurth was nat farre thens. And with that prayed and exhorted hym to fle away with hym priuely by night. Sylla denyed that vtterly as fierse and bolde of courage/ sayeng that he feared nat a cowarde Numidyan: which so often had ben ouercome before. And that he trusted well ynough to the strength and courage of his men: and finally he gaue Volux this answere.

¶If I knewe without dout that our sure dystruction were instant: and that I and myne shuld b[e] slayne in the felde/ yet wolde I nat fle for any drede. But rather abyde and dye manfully: than cowardely to flee and shame my people of whome I haue charge in sparyng our lyues/ which be so incertayne and v[n]sure: and parauenture shortly after this shall fynisshe with some sickenes or dysease. Is it nat better to dye in a noble quarell manly/ than to lyue in shame cowardly?

19 as] *om.* B C 32 this] that C 43 be] B C; by A 48 to[I]] *om.* C

Whan Sylla had thus answered: than Volux counselled hym to depart from that place and to remoue forward by night. Therto Sylla consented: and anone commaunded his soudyours to refresshe them in their tentes with such vytels as they had/ and to make plenty of [fiers] ouer all the place to the intent that yf | their ennemies were f. 88r nere: in beholdyng the fiers they shulde thynke that they wolde nat remoue thens that night. But in the first hour of the night Sylla commaunded all his soudyours to leaue their fiers brennynge and so to depart forwarde in their iournay with scilence: so they dyd. And went all the night long: and euyn with the sonne rysing they all beyng weryed: Sylla pytched his tentes agayne. With that certayne horsemen of the Mauryans brought worde that Iugurth had taken place to his tentes: and rested about the dystance of two myle before them. Whan these tidynges were harde amonge the Romayns: a maruelous and great feare entred the myndes of them all. For they thought themselfe betrayed of Volux. And so enuyrounde and compased about with falshode/ gyle and treason. Many of them were which aduysed to take punisshment of Volux: sayeng that it was a thyng vnworthy to suffre hym to escape vnpunysshed for so great a myschefe and treason agaynst them commytted.

[**107**] But howbeit that Sylla was inwardly of the same opynion: neuerthelesse he defended the Maurian from damage. And exhorted his men to be of strong and bolde myndes: sayeng that often tyme before that tyme it had ben sene that a fewe worthy men had won vyctorie of a moche multytude of cowardes. And how moch the lesse that they spared their bodyes in batayle fro fightyng: somoch the surer shulde they be: and that it semed no man to whome God and nature had gyuen handes to defende his body withall: to seke defence in his fete vnarmed by rennyng away. And that in suche a ieopardy/ a noble soudyour ought nat to tourne away his body from his ennemy/ though he were naked and vnarmed.

¶Whanne Sylla had exhorted his men with suche wordes: he called vnto hym Volux: and called into wytnesse Iupyter and all his ydols to recorde the falshode and treason of Bocchus/ father of Volux: which had so betrayed hym. Than for asmoch as Sylla supposed that Volux had brought hym by treason into handes of Iugurth/ by counsell and commaundement of his father Bocchus: therfore he commaunded

53 fiers] B C; fierse A 64 and compased about] *om.* B C 65 gyle] *om.* B C of them were which] *om.* B C 71 tyme] *om.* B C 76 withall] *om.* B C seke] sicke B; seeke C 84 into] into the C 85 therfore] *om.* B C

Volux anone to depart from his company/ and from his tentes and felde. Volux pytuously wepyng: besought Sylla nat to byleue suche thynges in hym: and sayd that certenly by gyle nor by treason was nothyng done of hym nor of his father: but rather by Iugurth which by his subtylte had espyed and sherched their iournay and wayes by f. 88v his espyes and so knowen the same. But at conclu| sion said Volux: syth it is so that Iugurth hath no great company: and that his hope/ his trust/ and confort for the moost part dependeth on my father: I thinke that he shall nat be so bolde to do any damage to you openly whyle I am in your company: which may recorde his dedes to my father. Wherfore Sylla to thentent that ye may parceyue that no treason is in me: I shall openly go with you alone by the myddes of the tentes of Iugurth and so sauely conuey you: and other sende my folke before: or els leaue them here with your company whyther of both shall please you best. This counsell was alowed of Sylla: and anone without tary he proceded forwarde with all his company through myddes of the tentes of Iugurth. And bycause this was sodenly done: Iugurth nat knowyng therof before/ he meruayled moch therat: and douted long what was to be done. But at last he suffred the Romayns to passe and to escape saufe and sounde for loue of Volux/ and drede of Bocchus his father. And within a fewe dayes after: Volux and Silla with their company came to Bocchus: whether they intended.

¶Of the metyng and secrete apoyntmentes bytwene Bocchus and Sylla: and howe bytwene them both they abused Asper/ the imbassadoure of Iugurth. ¶The .lxiiii. chapter.

[**108**] At the same season ther was with Bocchus a certayne Numidyan named Aspere/ which was sende before to Bocchus from Iugurth/ by craft and subtylte: to espy his counsell/ assone as it was harde that Bocchus had sende for Sylla. This Numidyan was moch and familyerly conuersant with Bocchus at that tyme. Moreouer there was an other named Dabar the sonne of Massagrade: which of his fathers syde was of the stocke of Massinissa. But of mothers syde he was vnlyke of byrth: for h[er] father was borne of a concubyne. This

86–7 and from his tentes and felde] syght B; and sighte C 90 sherched] serched B; searched C 98 other] either C 102 myddes] the middes C 107 whether] wher C

Ch. 64 2 they] *om.* C 4 ther] *om.* B C 5 which was] *om.* B C to] *om.* B C 10 of] of his B C 10–11 he was] *om.* B C 11 her father] his father A; his mother B C

Dabar (as I haue sayd) was at this season also in the company of Bocchus: and to hym dere and welbeloued for his subtell wyt and great actes which he had done before: and namely bycause that Bocchus had founde and proued him trusty and faithfull many tymes before. Anone Bocchus sende this Dabar to Sylla commaundyng Dabar to shewe hym that he was redy to do | euery thyng [f. 89r] whiche the Romayns to hym wolde commaunde or assigne. And that Sylla hymselfe shuld apoynt/ assigne and chose a tyme and place where they myght commen togyder of their maters: and that he shulde nat fere nor dout though the embassadoure of Iugurth were there with hym. For he had reserued all thynges touchyng their counsell hole tyll commyng of Sylla: and of nothyng had apoynted/ communed/ nor concluded with the same imbassadoure of Iugurth. Whiche imbassadour was called thyder to thyntent that their commen besynesses might be done more at lybertie and with lesse suspectyon of Iugurth: for by other meanes they coude nat resyst nor make prouysion agaynst his gyles. Such wordes sende Bocchus to Sylla: by his trusty seruant Dabar. But nat withstandyng all these fayre promysses of Bocchus it was vnderstande that he prolonged the Romayns and the Numidyans in hope of peace/ rather for falshode and treason after the credence of Affrycans: than for profet to the Romayns or trouth of such thynges as he promysed to Sylla. And often tymes he cast in his mynde and douted whether he might betray Iugurth to the Romayns: or els Sylla to Iugurth: the pleasour and desyre of his mynde aduysed/ moued/ and counselled hym agaynst the Romayns: but the drede whiche he had of punysshment in tyme to come: moued hym with the Romayns.

[**109**] But to our purpose: Sylla answered vnto Dabar the messanger of Bocchus that he wolde come thyder/ and first speke a lytell of the peace and of suche other thynges in presence of Aspere the imbassadour of Iugurth: but concernyng the remanent of the besynesse: he wolde dyffer that to commen secretly with Bocchus/ fewe or none called to counsell. And also he taught Dabar what words Bocchus shulde answere vnto hym agayne/ whan they shulde come to communycation: and so departed Dabar. But whan Sylla sawe his tyme he went to Bocchus/ and sayd that he was sent from Marius the consull to enquire if he wold leuer peace or warre: and wheron he wolde conclude. Than Bocchus (as Dabar had warned hym before)

13 his] *om.* B C   19 assigne] *om.* B C   31 peace/] *virgule from* B   39 vnto] to B C

commaunded Sylla to retourne agayne after .x. dayes: and than shulde an answere be gyuen vnto hym. For at that tyme nothyng was concluded. That answere well noted and harde: Aspere the imbassadour of Iugurth/ which was sent to espy the intreatement: and so thought he that nothyng shulde be treated nor concluded without his knowlege. And thus after this answere Bocchus and Sylla departed: eche to their tentes.

f. 89v ¶Of the seconde commyng togyder of Bocchus and of Sylla: and of the wordes of Bocchus had to Sylla: and replycation and answere of Sylla agayne to hym. And how Bocchus graunted and concluded to betray Iugurth to the Romayns. ¶The .lxv. chapyter.

[109. 4] But after that moche of the night was ouerpassede: Bocchus priuely sende for Sylla/ none beyng in their company saue such as on both parties might truely interprit and declare the sentence and vnderstandyng of their wordes. And also Dabar the sayd messanger was present/ whiche solemly swore and promysed to be faythfull interpretoure of both their sayenges/ and sentences. Than Bocchus anone began his wordes in this sentence.

[110] ¶I haue thought forsoth: that it shulde neuer haue fortuned that I the greattest kyng of all them in these landes: and rychest of all them that I knowe: shulde haue ben bonde a meane and priuate person. And forsoth Sylla or euer I hard of you: I haue gyuen helpe and socours to many other men. To some of myne owne voluntary and frewyll. And to some other: required of them: my selfe nat nedyng helpe of any man. But now syth I haue knowen you: I haue nede of your helpe and frendshyppe of which I am glad: nat withstandyng other men ar wont to be sory of such fortune. And certenly this nede whiche I haue of your frendshyppe is nat of me counted damage nor losse: but moch profet and pleasure. For inwardly in my mynde nothyng is derer/ nor more acceptable: whiche ye may conuenyently proue if it please you: demaunde and take of me armour/ men/ treasour: and finally what euer it pleaseth you in your mynde: and vse and occupy the same as your owne. And thinke ye for certayne that whyle ye lyue and I togyder: I can neuer render worthy thankes vnto your kyndnes: nor condygnely recompence your great humanyte: but euer my good wyll and mynd shalbe

Ch. 65 1 of[2]] *om.* C of[3]] *om.* C 9 present/] *virgule after* messanger A B be] be a C 14 bonde] bounde B; bound to C 25–6 and finally . . . mynde:] *om.* C 28 vnto] to C

hole and newe agaynst you. And certenly if I may knowe your mynde and wyll: ye shall nought nede to desyre of me: I shall preuent your requestes with my benefytes: so that ye shall coueyt nothynge in vayne. Verely | as I thynke it is lesse reprouable and lesse dyshonour a kyng to be ouercome with armour: than with lyberalite. Wherfore I haue concluded in my mynde that a man shall rather ouercome me in batell with weapen and force of armes: than with lyberalite. f. 90r

¶But touchyng your commen wayle (for whose besynes ye be sende hyther as procuratour of the same) this is my sentens and mynde in fewe wordes. Agaynst the Romayns/ nor agaynst their empyre: I neuer mouedde nor made warre: nor to make batell agaynst them: it was neuer in my mynde by my wyll. But the endes of my marchesse haue I endeuoured me to defend agaynst the vyolence of your armed men. But this I leaue and set asyde: syth I se that it pleaseth you to do the same: execute and contynue [th]e batell with Iugurth as ye wyll. And as touchyng me: I shall nat ouerpasse the water of Mulucha/ which was boundes bytwene my marches and Micipsa whyle he lyued. Nor into my countrey I shall nat suffre Iugurth frome hens forthe: to entre for socours/ as he hath done in tymes passed. Farthermore if ye desyre any thyng of me conueniently: which I may worthely graunt/ my royalte nat dystayned: it shall nat be denyed vnto you. Thus concluded Bocchus his wordes.

[111] ¶Unto these wordes Sylla answered for his owne part but moderately and with fewe wordes. But towchyng the peace and besynesse concernyng the commen wayle: he spake many wordes/ wherof the conclusion was such.

¶Kyng Bocchus I insure and promesse you: that the Romayns shall nat be vnkynde to you if ye do some pleasure to them: which may rather long to them all holy in comen: than to me alone. And thynke ye for certayne: that they which haue ouercome you in batayle: shall likewyse ouercome you with lyberalyte/ kyndnesse/ and good dedes: if ye so contende with them: which thyng is nowe redy in your power to do: consyderyng that ye haue Iugurth redy at your wyll and pleasure. Therfore among all benefites or pleasurs: ye can do none more acceptable vnto the Romayns: than to delyuer vnto theym Iugurth. By this meanes shall they be moche beholden to you: and thynke ye stedfastly: it shall nat be vnrewarded on our behalfe. For

31 nought] not C 32 my] *om.* B C 41 endes] boundys B; boundes C 43 it] *om.* C 44 the] ye A B C 48 tymes] time C 50 vnto] to C 58 to[2]] in B C 62 ye] I B 66 stedfastly:] *colon from* B

than shall the Senate graunt vnto you amyte and peace: and also a part of Numidy whiche ye do nowe clayme: shall than be graunted vnto you vnrequired.

f. 90^{v} ¶Bocchus heryng these wordes of Sylla: first excused hym| selfe by the affinyte which was bytwene hym and Iugurth: and by the long familyarite and aquayntance which they had togyder: sayeng also that a bonde of peace was confyderate and sworne bytwene them. And also that he fered and suspected that if he so dyd: his owne subgettes shulde hate hym therfore/ which moch loued Iugurth: and greatly hated the Romayns. But nat withstandyng these wordes of Bocchus: Sylla desysted nat to attyse and counsell hym: tyll at last he agreed and consented to his desyre/ promysing to do euery thyng as Sylla requyred hym. But to thyntent to fayne a treaty of peace (of whiche Iugurth weryed in warre was moche desyrous) they ordayned such craft: as to their purpose semed moost expedyent. But whan they had ymagined and deuysed all thynges after their myndes: than both they departed in sonder: and retourned agayne to their rest.

¶Howe Bocchus betrayed Iugurth and delyuered hym bounde vnto Sylla. ¶The .lxvi. cha.

[**112**] On the morowe after/ Bocchus called to hym Aspere the imbassadour of Iugurth/ and sayd to hym that he vnderstode of Sylla by the interpretacion of Dabar that the warre might be finysshed vpon certayne condycions. Wherfore he bad hym go and inquire the mynde and pleasure of his kyng in that behalfe. Aspere of these tydynges was glad and toke his leaue of Bocchus: and departed to the tentes of Iugurth: and certyfied hym of the same. Iugurth shewed to Aspere: all his mynde and pleasure concernyng the premisses. And within .viii. dayes after: sende hym agayne to Bocchus. Whan Aspere was retourned agayne to Bocchus: he shewed to him the wyll of Iugurth/ sayeng that Iugurth coueyted to do althyng which shulde be commaunded to hym of Bocchus: but he had but small trust or confydence in Marius. For asmoch as the peace which often before had ben conuented and apoynted of the Romayne captayns had anon after ben frustrate: and broken of them agayne. But if ye wyll (sayd Aspere to Bocchus) that peace shalbe confermed of the Romayns with Iugurth and you also: Iugurth desyreth and requireth you to labour

67 vnto] to C 68 vnto] to C 75 therfore/] *virgule suppl.*

Ch. 66 1 vnto] to B C 3 after/] *virgule suppl.* 13 Iugurth^{2}] he B C 14 trust or] *om.* B C

so: that Sylla/ Iugurth/ and ye: may | come togyder to communycation: as if it were to treat of peace and that ye wyll there betray and delyuer Sylla to hym. For yf ye may ones bring such a man into power and handes of Iugurth: anone after it shall fortune without dowte that peace shalbe made and graunted to him by commen assent of the senatours: and commens of Rome also. And that: to thyntent to recouer Sylla agayne out of the handes of Iugurth. For without dout the Romayns wyll nat suffre so noble a man to be left in handes and danger of their ennemies. And namely: whan they shall vnderstande hym taken/ nat by his owne folly nor cowardyse: but in besynesse belongyng to the commen wayle. f. 91r

[113] ¶Bocchus heryng these wordes: reuolued and cast long in mynde what he might answere to them: but at last he graunted therto. But whether he douted so long before he graunted: for subtylte or very trouth/ it is harde to dyscerne. But this is playnly knowen: that for the moost part in likewyse as the wylles and myndes of kynges be vehement/ immoderat/ and hasty: right so be they mouyng/ vnstedfast/ and varyable. And often aduers and contrary to their owne selfe: and with themselfe repugnyng. But to our mater: Bocchus assigned to Aspere a place and tyme: where Sylla and they shulde commen togyder of the peace. And in the meane whyle somtyme he communed secretly with Sylla: somtyme with Aspere imbassadour of Iugurth/ treatyng them both mekely and courtesly: and promysing one self thyng vnto them both. Wherfore they both were gladde: and also eche of them both had good hope in the promysses of Bocchus.

¶But the night before that day: which was assigned to intreatment of the peace: Bocchus called vnto hym dyuerse of his frendes/ as yf he wolde haue taken counsell of them: and than immedyatly he chaunged that mynde/ commaundyng them agayne to auoyde from hym. And so (none of his counsell about hym) he stode all alone reuoluyng and tournyng in mynde many thynges by hymselfe alone/ chaungyng oftentymes in countenaunce/ and colour varyable and dyuerse: aperynge forthwarde by tokens of feare conceyued in his mynde and expressed by outwarde tokens of his body. In so moche: that all yf he expressed nat his mynde by wordes: neuertheles this often changing of countenance/ declared the secretes of his hert. But at conclusyon: after long conflyct had within hymselfe: at last he commaunded Sylla to be called vnto hym. And than after his

31–2 long in mynde] long in minde B; in his mynd C 35 in likewyse] lyke C 38 repugnyng] repugnant B C 48 mynde/] *virgule from* B 50 alone] *om.* B C

aduyse and counsell/ he deuysed and prepared al thynges | con- f. 91v cernyng the prodycion of Iugurth.

¶After this counsell concluded: assone as the day light apered: tidynges were brought to Bocchus/ that Iugurth was nat farre thens: and commyng towarde hym. Bocchus thys herynge: anone prepared hymselfe and proceded forth agaynst hym accompanyed with a fewe of his frendes/ and also with Sylla: fayninge that he went so forth to mete with Iugurth and to receyue hym/ bycause of honour. And thus they proceded forwarde: tyll at last they came to an opyn heyth/ where they might easely se the commynge of Iugurth: whiche place was apoynted before to their treason. For in dyuerse valeys of the same heyth: were armed men lyenge in wayt redy and apoynted before by Bocchus: for to assayle Iugurth and his company/ whan signes shulde be gyuen to them: to yssue forth of their lurkyng places. Anon Iugurth with many of his men about hym came to the same place all vnarmed: as apoyntement was made before. For it was ordayned that Bocchus/ Iugurth/ and Sylla: shulde come togyder to communycation: eche one with a small company/ and all vnarmed.

¶Anon as Iugurth was come thyder: kyng Bocchus gaue a token to his men/ which lay in wayt for Iugurth. Anone as they harde the token: sodaynlie they brake forth and inuaded Iugurth and his company: compasyng them about on euery syde. Without great labour: all the company of Iugurth were murdred: and he hymselfe taken and bounde hande and fote/ and so delyuerd vnto Sylla. Which without tary ledde hym forth and delyuerd hym vnto Marius: whose hert was replenysshed and inuyroned/ with ioye inestymable.

¶How Marius was receyued into Rome with triumphe: and howe Iugurth was cast into prison: where he contynued in myserable captiuyte tyll he dyed. ¶The .lxvii. chapyter.

f. 92r [114] After that Iugurth thus bounde was delyuered by Bocchus vnto Sylla: and than to Marius. Anone all the Numydyans/ submytted and yelded themselfe to the Romayns. Marius with great wysedome sette an ordre among the people/ and garnysshed and fortyfied the townes: and than with the remanent of his army toke his iournay agayne to Rome: leadyng Iugurth and his two sonnes bounde with hym: with innumerable other prisoners/ great treasour/ olyphantes/ and armoure: whiche he had wonne in the warre of Iugurth. But after that tidynges were brought to Rome: howe the warre was ended in

Ch. 67 4 vnto] to C 8 than] *om.* C

Numidy: and howe Iugurth was led thyderwarde bounde and prisoner. Anone the Senate and commens assembled to consyle: and Marius was create consull agayne for the next yere: in his absence. And by decre and ordynaunce: the prouynce of Fraunce was decreed and commytted vnto hym to be recouered.

¶For the same tyme whyle Marius warred in Numidy: and toke Iugurth prisoner. This countrey of France (whose peple that tyme were named Cymbrians) rebelled agaynst the empyre of Rome. Agaynst whom the Romayns sende forth to represse their rebellyon: a great army with two captayns: the one named Quyntus Scipyo/ the other Marcus Manlyus: which at last with frowarde fortune had a great and greuous batell with the same Frenchmen Cymbrians. In which both these Romayne capytains were ouercome: and twyse lost the felde. Of the Romayns men of warre: were slayne .lxxx. thousande: of tylmen/ and pages .xl. thousande. Thus was this batayle foughten with so yll fortune vnto the Romayns: that the cytie of Rome/ and all the countrey of Italy trymbled for fere therof. In somoch that both the Romayns which lyued at that tyme: and all their progeny which succeded after them: counted all other nacyons redy to their obesance: and to wynne honoure by them: but they thought neuer to contende in batayle with this nacyon of Frenchmen: to wynne glorie or honour by them: but rather to defende themselfe and their lybertie: which thyng if they might do/ they counted themselfe fortunate. Wherfore (as I haue before recounted) the Senate: and commens of Rome/ decreed this prouynce of [France] to Marius for to reueng the deth of their men: and to recouer the countrey.

¶But (to our purpose) whan Marius shuld entre into Rome he was f. 92v
ioyfully receyued with great glorie and tryumphe: wherof the order was suche. Marius hymselfe was sette on hye in a golden chayre: which was drawen of foure whyte palfrayes. Iugurth and his two sonnes/ with many other noblemen: whome he brought captyue frome Numidy/ proceded before his charyot: their handes and armes bounde as prisoners. Farthermore for more ample ostentation of his glorie/ and to declare howe moche he had inryched the commen wayle of Rome: all the elyphantes/ armour/ iewels/ treasure/ and

14 consyle] counsel B C 17 decreed and] *om.* B C vnto] to C 19 This] That B C 26 Romayns] Romaine C 27 thousande: of tylmen/] *punct. from* B 28 vnto] to C 29 trymbled] trembled B C 31 after] *om.* B C 34 or] and C 37 France] B; Fraunce C; Frõance A 46 Farthermore] Farther C

rychesse whiche he had wonne in Numidy of Iugurth: were ledde and borne before him. Than all the senatours. All the offycers and noble men of Rome/ with an vnnumerable multytude of commens receyued hym with all honoure and ioye: and conuayed hym vnto the princypall palayes of Rome/ named the Capytoll: where he made sacrifyce with a bull vnto Iupyter: for his vyctorie: after the custome of that tyme. His sacrifyce ended: than was he conuayed into the Senate house/ in his robe triumphall: as neuer consull was brought before his tyme. Marius was receyued at Rome with suche triumphe at the kalendes of Ianuary. From thens forth all the hope of confort/ helth/ socours: and welth of the cyte of Rome resysted on Marius.

¶Iugurth was casten into prison: where he ended his wretched lyfe in myserable captiuyte/ and manyfolde calamytees/ as to such a murderer vnnaturall: and tyran inhumayne was conuenyent.

Finis.

f. 93r ¶Thus endeth the famous cronycle of the war which the Romayns had agaynst Iugurth vsurper of the kyngdome of Numidy. which cronycle is compyled in Laten by the renowmed Romayn Salust. And translated into Englysshe by sir Alexander Barclay preest: at commaundement of the right hye and mighty prince/ Thomas duke of Northfolke. And imprented at London by Rycharde Pynson/ printer vnto the kynges noble grace: with priuylege vnto hym graunted by our sayd souerayne lorde the kyng.

51 vnnumerable] vnmesurable C 52 vnto] to C 54 vnto] to C 55 into] to C 58 socours] socoure C 59 of the cyte] *om.* C resysted on] resisted in B; rested in C 60 casten] cast C

Colophon 6–8 And imprented . . .] And imprinted at London in Foster lane by Ihon Waley. C

APPENDIX I

PREFACE TO THOMAS PAYNELL'S EDITION OF 1557

To the ryghte honorable Lorde Antonye Vycounte Mountegue, knyghte of the ryghte honorable order of the garter, and one of the Kynge and Queenes magesties pryuie counsayle: Thomas Paynel with honoure and perfecte felicitie.

A friend of myne (most honorable Lord) beinge muche desirous to haue the Conspiracie of Catiline, that noble and learned Citizen of Rome, and the historie of Iugurth kynge of Numidie, most valiaunt and politike in feates of warre, in one volume comprised, instantlie desired me: for as much as I had already translated the one, to peruse the other. Whose translator was nowe departed, but yet not out of freshe memorie: suche are his diuers workes very ingeniouslie inuented, and ryght eloquentlie translated. But yet here and there (thorough vnlearned correctors) somewhat mangled and corrupted.

I, to do my friend a pleasure, and the gentle readers of these two excellente histories no disprofite, haue accomplyshed my friendes requeste: trusting the matters of these histories to be so cherefull and pleasaunt, the oracions so ingenious and wyttie, the stratagemes so close and craftie, the inuencions of things so diuers and subtile, the answers of the prudent and polytike Romaines so ingenious and readie, the feates of Iugurth with his Numidians so worthy and manlie, the Romains resistence and enterprises so warlyke and coragious, the actes of the whole warre betwene them so variable and diuers, and Ladye Fortune (whiche in these thinges hathe rule and dominion) nowe smylinge vpon the one and the other most flatteringly and clokedlie, that no man (except enuie do rule hym) can myslyke the historie or the translacion of the same: The whiche because the reader shulde most redelie and plainely vnderstande and perceiue the thinge, dothe paraphrasticallie so open the hole matter, that no scruple remaineth to be douted vpon. For Saluste the noble historiographe, doth in the Laten tonge so compendiouslie and briefely, but yet moste eloquentlie and truely, knyt vp the whole historie of Iugurth, that the reader in diuers places (excepte he be very rype and perfecte in the eloquence and figures of the Laten tonge, and phrases of the same) shal stumble and stagger in the conueyaunce and vnderstandinge of the true meanyng and sence therof.

But nowe to turne my pen somewhat vnto your lordeshyp: What thinge is there so obscure or intricate in sence, be it in Laten, Italian, Frenche, or Englyshe, that your fine and subtile wytte can not perce and perceiue? What politike feat of war, what instrument or warlyke engine is ther that ye mooste finelye and exactlye can not handle? Yea what tytle or poynte of nobilitie, or of any other thynge perteinynge to a noble man, is unknowen to your lordshyp, or yet to manie other of this moste noble realme? But I at this presente wyll not speake of your knoweledge and litterature, of your comely and decent ciuilitie and maners, nor howe ye fauoure and maintaine learnynge and learned men, nor yet howe your lordeshyp to your great renowme and eternall fame, hathe at all tymes, and against all the rablemente of heretykes sustained, and moste constantly and christianly auaunced the catholyke fayth of our Sauiour and redemer Jesus Christ. And truely to saye, suche a nother was that excellente and noble man your father, faithfull I mean to his liege lorde and kynge, and to our lorde his God, most faithfull. But of hys constante faythe, and other his famouse actes, prudent counselles, and wyttye inuencions, at more leasure.

In the meane season I mooste humblye desire your good Lordeshyp fauourablye to accepte thys hystorie wyth my rude preamble, and mutually wyth fauoure to loue me, for to my slender power I am youres to commaunde.

APPENDIX II

SOLDUS'S SUMMARY OF THE *BELLUM IUGURTHUNUM*, AS REPRODUCED BY ASCENSIUS

The version provided here is taken from Ascensius's first edition (**1504.1**), with variant readings from the first edition of Soldus's commentary (**1495.1**) and from the parallel text in the first edition of Barclay's translation (A).

Bellum. Huius historiæ narrationem ne inaniter noua queram aut superbe inuenta contemnam sic ex Iohanne Chrisostomo Soldo habeto. Exordio præmisso rem ipsam aggreditur. Dicit se scripturum esse bellum quod populus Romanus gessit cum Iugurtha rege Numidarum. Numidia est pars Affricæ in qua regnauit Massinissa rex socius et amicus populi Romani. Hic Massinissa tres habuit filios: Micipsam: Manastabalem: et Gulussam. Sed mortuo Manastabale et Galussa: Micipsa solus regnum obtinuit: qui Aderbalem et Hiempsalem filios ex se genuit. Iugurtham autem filium fratris sui Manastabalis educauit vt filium quem Massinissa auus priuatum reliquerat: quia ex concubina natus erat. Sed Iugurtha virtute et virtutibus multum valebat: ingenio maxime excellens: maior natu Aderbale et Hiempsale. Micipsa igitur timens ne post mortem suam Iugurtha paruis liberis Aderbale et Hiempsale existentibus regnum sibi vsurparet: statuit eum obiectare periculis et eo modo tentare: si quo modo Iugurtha perire posset. Cum igitur populus Romanus Numantiam ciuitatem Hispaniæ duce Scipione obsideret Micipsa auxilia peditum et equitum ad id bellum populo Romano misit: quibus Iugurtham præfecit: sperans illum in eo bello posse interire: sed longe aliter

1–3 Huius historiæ . . . habeto] *added to* 1504, *and in* A   3 Dicit se . . . Numidarum] *om.* A   9 ex se] 1504, A; ex sese 1495   fratris sui] fratris A   11 Sed Iugurtha] Sed Iugurtha et corporis A   11–12 virtute & virtutibus multum valebat] uirtute & uiribus multum ualebat 1495; viribus ac virtute animi plurimum valebat A   15–16 statuit eum . . . perire posset] 1495, 1504; multum eo negocio permotus est: multaque in animo voluebat quibus modis regni inuasorem (vt ipse timebat) tollere possit e medio. Tandem hæc in animo herebat sentencia: se velle Iugurtham belli periculis obiectare et eo modo fortunam tentare si quo modo perire posset A (*taking phrases from* **6. 2, 7. 1**)   17 ciuitatem hispaniæ] 1495, 1504; Hispanie ciuitatem A   19–20 sed longe aliter euenit.] 1495, 1504; Sed ea res longe aliter ac ratus erat euenit. A

euenit. Nam virtus Iugurthæ in eo bello plurimum enituit: ac multa præclara facinora gessit: ob quæ Scipio Iugurtham in concione laudatum: ac donis militaribus insigne donatum finito bello et capta ac deleta Numantia ad Micipsam remisit cum litteris in quibus virtutem Iugurthæ miris laudibus extollebat. Quo factum est vt Micipsa mutato consilio atque animo quem antea interire cupiebat: hunc maxime incolumem esse vellet. Micipsa igitur Iugurtham sibi in filium adoptat: et paulo post moriens fortunas suas omnes ac regnum ipsum cum liberis commune relinquit. Mortuo Micipsa cum tres reguli Adherbal Hiempsal et Iugurtha regnum inter se diuidere constituissent: loco et tempore ad id faciendum constituto: Iugurtha Hiempsalem natu minorem per insidias interfecit. Quo extincto cum ad occupandum vniuersum regnum iecisset animum contra Adherbalem exercitum parat: et prælio facto illum victum fundit fugatque. Adherbal victus ac regno spoliatus Romam venit expositaque nefanda crudelitate Iugurthæ in se fratremque suum Hiempsalem extinctum a senatu petit auxilium contra illum. Senatus decreto fit vt mittantur decem legati qui regnum inter Aderbalem et Iugurtham diuiderent. Diuiso itaque regno cum legati Romani ex Affrica discessissent: rursus Iugurtha animum intendit ad occupandum regnum Aderbalis. Igitur exercitu comparato regnum eius inuadit. Aderbal necessitate coactus et ipse copias parat et Iugurthæ obuiam proficiscitur: mox prælio commisso Iugurtha Aderbalis exercitum fundit: atque ipsum Aderbalem cum paucis equitibus in Cirtham oppidum fugere compellit. Iugurtha oppidum obsidet. Interea Aderbal per litteras senatum monet: quo in statu fortunæ suæ sint positæ: regno se spoliatum a Iugurtha esse: fame ac ferro ad extrema esse deductum: nec amplius obsidionem posse sustinere. Iugurtham decreta senatus paruifacere: petere vt sibi auxilium mittat. His litteris in senatu recitatis fuerunt qui censerent statim Aderbali subueniendum esse et exercitum in Africam contra Iugurtham esse mittendum. Sed resistentibus amicis Iugurthæ quos sibi pecuniis parauerat ne quid tale fieret. Legati ad Iugurtham mittuntur qui verbis senatus eum ab incepto desistere cogerent. Iugurtha legatis verba dedit quoadusque discessere. Quo facto illi qui cum Aderbale intra oppidum obsidebantur persuadent ei:

22 insigne] magnifice A 23 cum] eum A 26 incolumem esse] incolumen esse 1495; incolumem A 27 adoptat] adoptauit A 28 cum] ei cum 1495 relinquit] reliquit A 28–9 tres reguli] reguli A 32 iecisset] iecissent 1495 35–6 a senatu] 1495, A; .i. a senatu 1504 36 decreto] decretum 1495 39 regnum] imperium A 45 positæ] possite A se] *om.* 1495 54 illi qui cum Adherbale] illi qui Iugurtham contra cum Adherbale A

vt oppidum Iugurthæ tradat: tantum ab eo vitam petat. Deditione igitur facta Iugurtha statim contra fidem datam Aberbalem excruciatum interficit. Quæ cum Romæ nunciata essent: grauiter a senatu sunt habita. Igitur Lucius Calphurnius Bestia consul cum exercitu contra Iugurtham mittitur: a quo consul pecunia corruptus turpiter cum eo fœdus fecit: quam rem senatus populusque Romanus grauiter tulit. Post Calphurnium Albinus consul mittitur contra Iugurtham: a quo diu ludificationibus tractus cum ei rex spem deditionis faceret: tandem re infecta quia tempus comitiorum instabat Romam rediit: Aulo fratre suo pro prætore relicto: qui exercitui et prouinciæ præesset. Hic seu belli conficiendi cupidus seu vt a [r]ege pecuniam acciperet: mense Ianuario aspera hyeme exercitum ex tabernaculis in expeditionem vocat. Iugurtha cognita imperitia eius velut pauidus ad eum supplices legatos mittit. Ipse exercitum per loca saltuosa velut fugiens ducit. Aulus hoc magis insequitur. Vbi Iugurtha videt se traxisse Romanos in locum sibi commodum ad pugnandum: prælium committit: in quo Romanos fundit ac fugat. Postero die cum Aulus et Iugurtha in colloquium venissent fœdus inter eos ita factum est: vt omnes Romani incolumes sub iugum mitterentur: et post vt decem diebus extra Numidiam decederent. Quæ cum Romæ nunciata essent dolor ac timor omnes inuasit. Post Auli fœdus et Romani exercitus fugam: Metello consuli prouincia Numidia per sortem euenit. Hic optimi imperatoris artibus vsus cum exercitum vicio superiorum ducum licentia solutum accipisset: ad normam veteris disciplinæ reduxit. Atque ita Iugurtham aggressus aliquot grauibus præliis opes eius attriuit. Postremo Caius Marius post Metellum consul creatus cum ei Numidia prouincia decreta esset Iugurtham bello persequens tandem illum ad extrema compulit: et per proditionem sibi traditum in triumphum duxit. Hoc est totius operis argumentum.

62 tractus] tractatus A 63 re infecta] in facta A 65 rege] lege 1504 68 velut] veluti A 71 Postero] Postera A 72 ita factum est] factum est ita A 74 Romæ] Romane A Hic incipit praefatio huius operis per Caiium Crispum Salustium hystoriographum clarissimum] *added in* A

APPENDIX III

SELECTED PASSAGES FROM THE COMMENTARIES OF SOLDUS AND ASCENSIUS

For purposes of comparison, the following presents the sections of commentary covering Sallust **48. 2–49. 3** in Soldus, and **48.2–49.2** in Ascensius (where at **49.2** a new chapter division is made in the latter). The transcriptions are largely diplomatic, except for the correction of some obvious errors and the normalization of capitals for proper nouns. As in citations provided in the Explanatory Notes, the common abbreviations .i. 'id est' and .s. 'scilicet' are not expanded; all other abbreviations are silently expanded.

Soldus

sig. l.2r ¶Ex opportunitate loci: Iugurtha sperabat uincere propter opportunitatem loci. Ipsum autem locum infra describit. ¶Anteuenit .i. preoccupauit. Iugurtha cum cognouisset quo tendebat Metellus cum exercitu: eo ipse prior uenit. ¶A quo aberat: a quo fluuio procul erat mons fere uiginti millia passuum. ¶Tractu pari .i. pari longitudine. Nam mons tantæ longitudinis erat quantum a fluuio distabat. ¶Vastus ab natura et humano cultu .i. desertus: et quia a natura asper erat: et quia ab hominibus non colebatur. ¶Sed ex eo medio. Ex medio huius montis: collis nascens longissimus et transuerso ducebatur plenus oleastro et myrtetis atque aliis arboribus: quæ nascuntur in terra arida et arenosa. ¶Vestitus .i. plenus. Vestire enim significat implere. Virgil in Georgicis. Iuuat Hismara Baccho conserere: atque olea magnum vestire taburnum. .i. implere. ¶Oleaster. Oleaster arbor agrestis oliuæ. ¶Ac myrtetis. Myrtetum est locus plenus arboribus myrtetis. Myrtus est arbor Veneri consecrata. ¶Media autem planities. Inter montem et flumen planicies erat deserta propter penuriam aquæ: praeter loca quæ sunt flumini uicina: nam ea loca habitantur et pecore atque cultoribus sunt plena. ¶Ea .s. loca propinqua flumini. ¶Igitur in eo colle. Locum descripsit: in quo Iugurtha in insidiis latens exercitum Metelli de monte descendentem aggressus est. ¶Porrectum .i. in longitudinem extensum. ¶Extenuata .i. rarefacta: quia non conferti nec densi: sed

rari consederant Iugurthini milites. ¶Elephantis. Antiqui in praelio elephantis utebantur: et maxime Affri. Sunt enim belluæ mire magnitudinis. ¶Quæ ageret .i. quæ agere deberet. ¶Turmas. Turmæ proprie sunt equitum. Nam turma triginta equites continet: dicta quasi ter una eo quod ter deni equites ex tribus tribubus Ticiensium Ramnium Lucerum fiebant. Nam singulæ tribus singulas decurias equitum mittebant. unde et decuriones dicti: qui decem equitibus .i.viii. decuriæ præerant. ¶Manipulos. Manipulus ut antea dixi ducentos milites continebat .i. duas centurias. Nam antiquis hic mos fuit cum adhuc reges Romæ regnarent: ut manipulos miscerant ex Romanis et Latinis: ita una centuria Romanorum et una Latinorum unum manipulum conficerent: et unum sequirentur signum. Manipulus autem dictus est: quia dum Romani adhuc pauperes essent: manipulos fœni perticis alligabant: et eos pro signis sequebantur: ut Lucanus pertica suspensos portabat longa manipulos. ¶ Obtestatur: rogat. ¶Pristinæ. Pristinus dicitur antiquus: cuius deriuatio dubia est: etiam apud peritos. ¶Cum his certamen fore: et dicebat. ¶Quos antea uictos sub iugum miserint. hoc supra uisum est. Nam Iugurtha Romanos uictos sub iugum misit. ¶Ducem illis non animum mutatum: subauditur dicebat: per omnia. ¶Non animum: quia quamuis nouum acceperint ducem: tamen pristinum animum retinent: uidelicet ignauum et timidum. ¶A bono imperatore .s. prouideri. ¶Locum superiorem .s. esse prouisum. Ecce quo modo omnia prouisa sunt a Iugurtha suis militibus prouidit ut haberent locum superiorem .s. collem montis. et prouidit ut periti cum imperitis: nec pauciores cum pluribus nec rudes cum bello melioribus certarent. ¶Nec pauciores cum pluribus: quia Iugurthini non erant pauciores numero quam Romani. ¶Aut rudes .i. ignari: quia Iugurthini milites peritia belli non cedebant Romanis. ¶Magnum consererent .i. pugnarent. ¶Proinde .i. ideo: et dicebat: ut ideo essentparati et intenti inuadere Romanos: dato signo. ¶Illum diem: Iugurtha suos ad proelium exhortans dicebat O milites: hic dies aut omnes labores praeteritos et uictorias: aut erit initium magnarum calamitatum. Omnes labores et uictorias confirmaturum: uidelicet ne labores frustra suscepimus et frustra uicerimus.
¶Confirmaturum | scilicet si uicerimus. ¶Maximum erumnarum .i. sig. l.2v
miseriarum calamitatum. ¶Initium fore .s. si uicti erimus.

Ascensius

Igitur explorato itinere. Commemorat quomodo Iugurtha se ad f. 69r
prelium accinxit et quam orationem ad suos habuit dicens. Igitur

quia Iugurtha decreuerat certare armis ipse explorato itinere hostium .i. cognito quod hostes irent per loca apta insidiis et in quibus circumueniri possent: adductus in spem victoriæ ex opportunitate loci parat quam .i. quantum potest: maximas copias .s. militum omnium generum ac anteuenit .i. preuenit exercitum Metelli per tramites occultos .i. vias transuersas et occultas. Flumen oriens a meridie .i. a meridionali plaga Muthul .s. nomine: erat in ea parte Numidiæ quam Adherbal possederat in diuisione .s. regni cum Iugurtha per legatos Romanos facta: a quo flumine: mons .s. quidam: aberat .i. distabat ferme .i. quasi viginti milia passuum: tractu .i. protensione eius: pari .i. æquali in distantia existens vastus .i. vacuo situ non habitatus nec consitus: natura .i. per naturam quae illic nihil nasci sinebat: et alienatus .i. desertus cultu humano: quia a nemine habitabatur. Sed quasi collis .i. humilior mons et vt dicunt costa montis seu cliuus: oriebatur ex eo medio .i. ex medio eius montis: pertingens .i. porrectus in altum: in inmensum .i. sine mensura facili. vestitus .i. coopertus: oleastro .i. oleis siluestribus: ac myrtetis .i. copia myrtorum arborum illic nascentium et aliis generibus arborum: quae gignuntur .i. nascuntur: humo .i. terra arida .i. sicca atque arenosa. At .i. sed planities media inter montem et flumen erat deserta .i. inhabitata et inculta: pœnuria .i. ob defectum aquæ. praeter loca propinqua flumini: quia ea .i. loca ad flumen: consita .i. vndique sata et vestita arbustis .i. arbusculis frequentabantur pecore .i. ouino et caprino et cultoribus .i. hominibus. Igitur Iugurtha consedit .i. locum cepit in eo colle quem docuimus porrectum .i. extensum a monte: intinere transuerso: quia ex medio eius sumpto: et hoc acie suorum .i. militum: extenuata .i. deducta et sparsa vel rarefacta: et præfecit Bomilcharem amicum et propinquum suum: elephantis .i. bellicis. (Notum est enim a genitiuo huius elephantos fieri nominatiuum hic elephantus huius elephanti: notumque vt illis impositis machinis vtantur in bello Numidæ Æthiopes et ceteri eius regionis in qua nascuntur). et parti copiarum pedestrium. Et edocet eum .s. Bomilcharem: quae ageret .i. facere deberet inito aut in ineundo prelio: ipse existens propior .i. magis prope montem collocat .i. instruit suos .s. milites .i. quibus ipse præesse volebat. Deinde ipse circuiens .i. obambulans singulas turmas .i. classes equitum: triginta equites continentes et manipulos: qui ducentos continebant .i. duas centurias (Nam antiquis hic mos fuit adhuc sub regibus Romanis vt milites misceret ex vna centuria Romanorum et vna Latinorum manipulum conficientes: cui signum vnum dabant: id autem manipulum vocabant. quod dum Romani adhuc pauperes essent manipulos fœni perticis alligabant: et eos pro signis sequebantur vnde est illud Lucani. Pertica suspensos portabat longa maniplos.) monet dico Iugurtha more Romanorum atque obtestatur supple eos: vti .i. vt: ipsi memores pristinæ .i. prius ab ipsis habitæ virtutis: et victoriæ .s. quam paulo ante ex hoste retulerant: cum eum sub iugum miserant: defendant sese .i. se ipsos. vnde ostendit necessitatem pugnandi. et regnum. scilicet Numidiæ ab auaritia Romanorum: quasi dicat si victi fuerint eos immania pensuros Romanis tributa. vt quos ipse iam sæpe auarissimos expertus fuerit.

EXPLANATORY NOTES

Latin citations are taken from the Oxford Classical Texts edition of Sallust by L. D. Reynolds (with a few adaptations of spelling: e.g. *cum* not *quom*), checked against the editions of Rolfe, Kurfess, and Comber and Balmaceda. Badius Ascensius's text and commentary (*AscT*, *Asc*) are cited from the first edition (Paris, **1504.1**), with notice of any variation in the Barclay/Pynson Latin text of *c.*1522 (*BarcT*), which is based on one of the reprints of *AscT*. The text of Sallust edited by Pomponius Laetus and Johannes Britannicus, with commentary by Johannes Chrysostomus Soldus (*Laet–BritT*, *Sold*) is cited from the first edition (Brescia, **1495.1**). Variant readings from later editions of Laetus–Britannicus and Badius Ascensius are cited by date (see Introduction, §3, for a checklist of these texts). In passages cited from these texts and commentaries, original spelling and punctuation are retained, but capitalization of proper names is normalized. Abbreviations are silently expanded except for the frequent abbreviations .i. 'id est' and .s. 'scilicet', which are retained. Bracketed bold numerals at the beginnings of chapters or paragraphs in the text provide the standard chapter numeration for modern editions of Sallust.

Title and Contents

48 **polycie.** See Glossary for other examples of usage. Here Barclay's *inexpert: and without polycie* is an expansion of Sallust's *adulescentes.*

129 **speremen.** Cavalry soldiers (*equites*). See Glossary for other examples of this usage within the text. Barclay translates *equitatus* (*pl.*) variously by *speremen* or *horsemen.*

English Preface

2 **Thomas duke of Northfolke.** Thomas Howard (1443–1524), second duke of Norfolk from 1514, and victor at Flodden in 1513. See Introduction, pp. xv–xviii.

23 **stodyng.** 'Studying'; disyllabic forms such as this are attested elsewhere in the sixteenth century.

35–6 **Which shal nat be to tedyous . . . vnderstande Latyn.** The sense perhaps requires a punctus after *Latyn. BarcB* improves the reading by omitting the punctus after *perfetly*. A further improvement might have been the placement of a colon rather than a punctus after *this my translation*. The Latin version of this passage presents its own difficulties (see below).

61 **Job.** Job 7: 1: 'Militia est uita hominis super terram et sicut dies mercenarii dies eius.' The second half of Barclay's sentence is not from Job, but rather echoes Virgil (see note on the corresponding sentence in the Latin preface, ll. 59–60).

77 **An hystore.** Cicero, *De Oratore* 2. 9. 36: 'Historia uero testis temporum, lux ueritatis, uita memoriae, magistra uitae, nuntia uetustatis, qua uoce alia nisi oratoris immortalitati commendatur?' Barclay takes this and other quotations from Badius Ascensius's *De Utilitate Historiae*, prefaced to the **1504.1** and later editions of Sallust's *Opera* (see note to Latin preface, ll. 75 ff. below).

79 **Tytus Lyuius.** Livy, *Ab urbe condita* 1, praef. 10–11: 'Hoc illud est praecipue in cognitione rerum salubre ac frugiferum, omnis te exempli documenta in inlustri posita monumento intueri; inde tibi tuaeque rei publicae quod imitere capias, inde foedum inceptu foedum exitu quod uites.'

87 **Cicero.** *Orator ad M. Brutum* 34. 120: 'Nescire autem quid ante quam natus sis acciderit, id est semper esse puerum.'

88–9 **as who sayth.** 'as if to say'.

93–8 **For in likewyse . . . of the worlde.** Cf. Ascensius's *De Utilitate*: 'et in primis utile est ut enim senibus multarum rerum experientia maior est cognitio et auctoritas quam iuuenibus: sic legenti historiam non unius uitae, sed omnium seculorum gesta patere possunt.' Like the following citation, Ascensius appears to have taken this idea from Diodorus Siculus's *History* 1. 1. 4 (possibly via the translation into Latin by Poggio Bracciolini).

98 **Dyoderus.** cf. Ascensius's *De Utilitate*: 'Unde pulchrum est, inquit Diodorus, ex aliorum erratis in melius instituere vitam nostram.' Diod. Sic. *Hist.* 1. 1. 4.

101 **Demotreus.** Demetrius Phalereus was the Athenian orator who influenced Ptolemy I of Egypt to begin building the collection of scrolls that eventually became the Royal Library of Alexandria, tragically destroyed by fire in 48–47 BC during Julius Caesar's attack. Cf. Ascensius's *De Utilitate*: 'Quamobrem Demetrius Phalereus Ptholemeum regem subinde admonebat ut libros lectitaret, quoniam quae amici non audent principibus demonstrare, ea omnia in libris scripta reperiuntur.'

108 **Quintylian.** *Inst.* 10. 1. 31: 'Historia quoque alere oratorem quodam uberi iucundoque suco potest. Verum et ipsa sic est legenda ut sciamus plerasque eius uirtutes oratori esse uitandas.' Cf. Ascensius's *De Utilitate*: 'historia alere potest orationem molli quodam ac iucundo succo.'

127–30 **What els . . . pardycion.** The sentence should be construed as a rhetorical question.

131–5 **valyaunt mennes bodyes . . . the men cryeng.** This scene echoes Barclay's expansion of *Sal* **101. 11** in 57/147–61.

136 **the tentes and townes brennynge.** Cf. Barclay's parallel in Latin: 'flammam ac fumum castrorum vrbium templorumque ardentium.' On the habitual translation of *castra* by *tentes* see note to 13/73.

142 **These manyfolde and holsome examples . . .** Cf. Aldus Manutius's prefatory letter in his edition of Sallust (**1509.3**), addressed to Venetian general Bartolomeo Liviano d'Alviano (1455–1515), who distinguished himself in the defence of the Venetian Republic against the Holy Roman Emperor Maximilian: 'Est enim sensus. Imperium in initio uirtute ab optimis partum, eadem uirtute facile retinetur. Prauis autem rectoribus factis, immutatur fortuna cum moribus, et imperium rursus ad optimos redit. Hos libros Liuiane tibi dicauimus, tum quia te ducibus iis, quorum his libris gesta traduntur, fortitudine, et rei militaris scientia iam adæquasti, tum etiam, quod paucis admodum datur, et legis facta, et facis legenda. Deinde quia sæpe me hortatus es, ut encheiridii forma, libros, quibus clarorum uirorum gesta continentur, excudendos curarem, quo belli eos tecum commodius habere posses.'

Latin Preface

The Latin Preface is set in columns parallel with the English Preface. Apart from the opening dedications to different persons, the two texts are loosely parallel in content.

1 **domino Ioanni Veysy.** John Veysey (born John Harman) *c.*1464–1554, Bishop of Exeter 1519–51. Under John Arundell's patronage he became bishop's chancellor and vicar-general at Exeter in 1502, and further received a canonry and prebend in 1503. He was appointed precentor of the cathedral in 1508.

4 **sacelli regii presul.** Veysey was dean of the Chapel Royal by 1514, and was made a canon and prebendary of St Stephen's Chapel, Westminster. Henry presented him with a number of other benefices before securing his appointment as Bishop of Exeter.

15 **Thome: borialis gentis ducis.** See note to English Preface, l. 2.

58 **Iob attestante.** See note to English Preface, l. 61.

59–60 **ac vere miseriarum . . . domus ambigua.** Cf. Virgil, *Aeneid* 1. 661: 'domum timet ambiguam Tyriosque bilinguis'; *Aeneid* 6. 27: 'hic labor ille domus et inextricabilis error' (of the Minotaur's Labyrinth). Cf. also Sidonius Apollinaris, *Epistulae* 2. 5: 'inextricabilem labyrinthum negotii multiplicis'. (Sidonius's *Epistolae et carmina* were first printed in Utrecht by 1474, and again in Milan in 1498.)

75 **Beroaldus.** Philippus Beroaldus the Elder (1453–1505) produced an edition of Sallust's *Opera* for Ulrich Gering (Paris, **1478**; reprinted **1483**). The introduction to this edition is reprinted in Ascensius's editions of **1504.1**

and later. Parts of what follows, beginning with the citation of Cicero, come from Ascensius's own introductory section, *De Utilitate Historiae*: 'Vtilitas autem historiae ex hac eiusdem descriptione haberi potest. Historia testis est temporum: lux veritatis: vitae magistra: memoriae preses: et vetustatis nuntia [Cicero, *De orat.* 2. 9. 36]. Ceterum vt Livius in praefatione prima dicit [*Ab urbe condita* 1, praef. 10–11] Hoc illud est praecipue in cognitione rerum salubre ac frugiferum. Omnis te exempli documenta in illustri posita monumento intueri vnde tibi tuæque rei publicae quod imitere capias: unde fedum inceptu fedumque exitu quod vites. Quocirca et Cicero nihil inquit earum rerum scire que antequam nascereris facte sint: id est semper esse puerum. Cognoscere vero res gestas memorie veteris ordinem tenere antiquitatis exemplorumque omniumque habere notitiam decorum et in primis vtile est, vt enim senibus multarum rerum experientia maior est cognitio et auctoritas quam iuuenibus: sic legenti historiam non vnius vite: sed omnium seculorum gesta patere possunt. Vnde pulchrum est inquit Diodorus ex aliorum erratis in melius instituere: vitam nostram. Quamobrem Demetrius Phalereus [Cicero, *De Orat.* 2. 9. 95] Ptholemeum regem subinde admonebat vt libros lectitaret: quoniam que amici non audent principibus demonstrare: ea omnia in libris scripta reperiuntur. Adde quod orator nullus euasit bonus historiarum ignarus. Nam vt Quintilianus ait [*Inst.* 10. 1. 31]. Historia alere potest orationem molli quodam ac iucundo succo. Sed hec hactenus. Nunc ad tertiam.'

78 **Cicero.** See note to English Preface, l. 87.

84 **Quintilianus.** See note to English Preface, l. 108.

87 **vt idem Beroaldus inquit.** He echoes Livy, Preface to *Ab Urbe Condita*.

89 **vt Diodorus inquit.** See note to English Preface, l. 98.

92 **Demetrius Phalereus.** See note to English Preface, l. 101.

146 **Ex cellula Hatfeldensis regii.** In the introduction to her edition of the *Eclogues* (p. xxxix), Beatrice White points out that this is not Hatfield in Hertfordshire, as earlier biographers claimed, following Warton, but rather King's Hatfield in Essex, where a Benedictine House existed at the time.

An Extract

2 **Here begynneth a compendyous extract.** Barclay's summary is taken directly from *Asc*, which reproduces a section of *Sold.* The acknowledgement of Soldus in the opening of the parallel Latin text in Barclay–Pynson is reproduced from Ascensius. The summary does not appear in *BarcC*. For Ascensius's version (and variant readings from Barclay–Pynson) see Appendix II.

7–9 **In this present . . . kyngdome of Numydy.** *Asc*: 'Dicit se scripturum esse bellum quod populus Romanus gessit cum Iugurtha rege Numidarum' (f. 40^{v}). The sentence is omitted (apparently accidentally) in the Latin side text in *BarcA B*. For the replacement of *rege* by *vsurper* cf. Barclay's rendering of the opening of ch. 1 and note.

7 **batayle.** *Asc*: bellum. Barclay's use of *batayle* to mean 'a continued state of hostilities, or war', rather than a single combat, is attested in *OED* from the 14th to 16th centuries. In many instances the word *batayle* is replaced by *warre* in *BarcB C* (see Introduction, p. lxviii).

14–17 **For after the custome . . . issuyth.** Barclay's addition.

21–3 **but left hym priuate . . . vnlaufully borne.** See note to 2/31–4.

31 **What tyme.** A conjunctive phrase equivalent to *when*, introducing a subordinate clause. Up to ch. 21 this phrase appears fifteen times, but only three times thereafter.

31–9 **What tyme . . . in batell.** A variant version not found in any surviving edition of Soldus or Ascensius's commentary appears in Pynson's Latin side-text (see Appendix II, ll. 13–16), and seems to be echoed in Barclay's phrasing.

37–8 **determyned to obiect . . . paryll of batayle.** *Sold*, *Asc*: 'statuit eum obiectare periculis' (f. 40^{v}) (= *Sal* 7. 1); *BarcT*: 'se velle Iugurtham belli periculis obiectare'.

38–9 **and by such menes . . . slayne in batell.** *BarcT*: 'et eo modo fortunam tentare si quo modo perire posset'.

39–42 **Therfore what tyme . . . fotemen.** *Sold*, *Asc*: 'Cum igitur populus Romanus Numanciam Hispaniæ ciuitatem duce Scipione obsideret Micipsa auxilia peditum et equitum ad id bellum populo Romano misit.'

40 **captayne.** Here and at many points, *captayne* renders *dux* and refers to a general or supreme commander.

55 **many and ryche gyftes of chyualry.** *Asc*: 'donis militaribus' (f. 40^{v}). Barclay often uses *chivalry* with reference to general military arts.

63 **two other naturall sonnes.** That is, sons born to him legitimately, and not adopted.

66–8 **And besyde this . . . the kyngdome.** This is Barclay's addition. Micipsa did not appoint Jugurtha regent or 'protector' of the younger siblings in any formal sense. As Sallust describes it, he merely appealed to Jugurtha to act fairly towards his adoptive brothers.

85 **shulde be sent embassadours.** Perhaps the noun is used quasi-adverbially here: 'as ambassadours'.

109 **many of them were.** 'there were many of them'.

115 **and that men auncyent.** 'and those were senior men'.

117 **in payne of their hye dyspleasure.** 'or suffer the consequences of their great displeasure'.

140 **dyrect.** 'directed'.

141–2 **But this Iugurth droue him forth vnder hope and coloure.** That is, Jugurtha played a delaying game with Albinus. *Sold*, *Asc*: 'Albinus . . . diu ludificationibus tractus' (f. 40^{v}).

154–8 **This dyde he: other bycause . . . bye his peace.** *Sal*: 'aut conficiundi belli aut terrore exercitus ab rege pecuniae capiundae' (37. 3). *Asc*: 'Hic seu belli conficiendi cupidus seu vt a rege' [**1513.1**, **1514.1**, **1519**; *Sold* **1495.1**, **1497/8** etc.; lege **1504.1** to **1511.2**, **1513.2**; Soldus **1514.2**] 'pecuniam acciperet . . . in expeditionem vocat' (f. 40^{v}).

165–6 **to fyght for his aduauntage.** 'to fight where he would have the advantage in battle'.

182 **And by faute . . . before.** In apposition with the preceding phrase *to moche lybertie*.

The Prologue

BarcC begins at this point and omits the preceding prefatory matter of *BarcA* and *B*.

4 **naturall dysposicyon.** *Sal*: 'natura' (1. 1).

5 **sayeng/ that his feble and frayle lyfe.** *Sal*: 'quod imbecilla atque aeui breuis' (1. 1) (the adjective *imbecilla* referring to *natura*). *Laet–BritT*, *AscT*, and *BarcT*: 'quod aetas imbecilla: atque aeui breuis'. Following Aldus Manutius's edition **1509.3**, and a good manuscript to which he had gained access, Ascensius removes *aetas* in his **1513.4** and later octavo editions (which do not contain the commentary). For the participle *sayeng*, cf. *Sold*: 'dicentes quod natura sua'. *Sold* continues: 'Imbecilla sit et uiribus infirma: et breui tempore duret: et quod fortuna potius quam consilio regatur. . . . ¶Quod imbecilla: id est uiribus infirma. Ecce causas quare homines conqueruntur de natura sua. Tres sunt cause. primam causam esse dicunt: quia natura hominis infirma sit uiribus. Nam multa sunt animalia fortiora hominibus quantum ad uires: ut bos: leo: et multa alia. Secundam causam esse dicunt: quia naturam hominis: breuis ætatis est. Nam ætas hominis breuis admodum est: pauci enim sunt qui centesimum annum attingant . . . Tertia causa quare conqueruntur de natura sua est: quia dicunt hominem magis regi et gubernari: a fortuna quam a consilio' (sig. e5^{r}).

6 **by chaunces of fortune.** *Sal*: 'forte' (1. 1). *Sold*: 'dicunt hominem multis casibus fortunæ esse subiectum . . . forte hoc est fortuna' (sig. e5^{r}); *Asc*: 'forte .i. fortuna aut fortuito eventu' (f. 38^{r}).

6–7 **by prouysion of strength or vertu.** *Sal*: 'uirtute' (1. 2). On Sallust's distinctive theory of *uirtus* 'intellectual and moral power' and his insistent use of the term, see D. C. Earl, *The Political Thought of Sallust* (Cambridge, 1961), 11, and Comber-Balmaceda 20–6. For Barclay's rendering here cf. *Asc*: 'virtute .s. prudentia et fortitudine' (f. 38^{r}).

10 **dylygence and exercyse.** *Sal*: 'industriam' (1. 2). *Sold*: '¶Industriam .i. exercitationem animi et ingenii' (sig. e5^{r}). *Asc*: '.i. gnauitatem et solertiam' (f. 38^{r}).

12–13 **But in this opynion to iuge indyfferently . . . lyfe.** *Sal*: 'Sed dux atque imperator uitae mortalium animus est' (1. 3). *Asc*: 'Sed vt recte reputent sciant quod dux . . . est' (f. 38^{r}).

15 **clere.** 'famous, illustrious'. *Sal*: 'clarus' (1. 3).

23 **by cowardous slouth.** *Sal*: 'per socordiam' (1. 4). The adjective perhaps echoes *Sold*: '¶Vbi per socordiam .i. ignauiam et negligentiam' (sig. e5^{v}).

32–3 **than shulde nat they be . . . sayd chaunces.** A statement, not a question. *Sal*: 'neque regerentur magis quam regerent casus' (1. 5).

34–5 **that where they be mortall . . . renowmed fame.** *Sal*: 'ubi pro mortalibus gloria aeterni fierent' (1. 5). *Sold*: '¶Gloria æterni: ubi sunt mortales: efficerentur immortales: non quia non morerentur: sed quia post mortem facta eorum uiuerent' (sig. e6^{r}). *Asc*: 'vbi .i. in quo: aut in qua magnitudine fierent pro mortalibus .i. vbi nunc sunt mortales: æterni .i. vt æther semper duraturi et ita immortales' (f. 38^{v}).

37–8 **all thynges/ all besynesses/ and exercyses/ to mankynde belongyng.** *Sal*: 'res cunctae studiaque omnia nostra corporis alia' (2. 1). *AscT, BarcA B*: 'res cunctae studiaque omnia: alia corporis'. *Sold*: '¶Studiaque omnia .i. omnia exercitia: omnia quæ facimus et exercemus' (sig. e6^{r}).

41–2 **the goodly beauty of the vysage/ and shape of mankynde.** *Sal*: 'præclara facies' (2. 2). *Sold*: 'pulchritudo corporis' (sig. e6^{r}). *Asc*: 'facies .i. figura oris: praeclara .i. valde formosa et quasi resplendens' (f. 38^{v}).

61–2 **that suffre thei to slomber.** 'they allow that [wit] to slumber'.

68–9 **great offyces/ lordshyppes/ rowmes to commaunde and rule.** *Sal*: 'magistratus et imperia' (3. 1). Sallust uses contrasting terms: 'civil offices' and 'military commands'.

70–1 **All maner cure . . . commen wayle.** *Sal*: 'omnis cura rerum publicarum' (3. 1). Barclay regularly renders *res publica* as *common weal.* Thomas Elyot criticized this type of usage: 'Hit semeth that men haue ben longe abused in calling *Rempublicam* a commune weale. There may appere lyke diuersitie to be in Englisshe betwene a publike weale and a commune weale, as shulde be in Latin, betwene *Res publica*, *et Res plebeia*' (*The Governour* (1531), i. i).

72–3 **For neyther . . . nother suche.** Barclay's *neyther* and *nother* are a coordinate pair, as are *neque . . . neque* in the Latin. *Sal*: 'quoniam neque uirtuti honos datur, neque illi quibus per fraudem [iis] fuit [uti], tuti aut eo magis honesti sunt' [*AscT*, *BarcT*: ius fuit vtique eo magis tuti aut honesti sunt] 'since honour/authority is not allotted according to merit, nor are those who have gained it dishonestly safe or any more honourable because of it' (3. 1). Thus Barclay's passage should be read: 'For neither is honour given for virtue, as a fitting and worthy reward belonging thereto, nor do those who have obtained jurisdiction and honour dishonestly', etc.

77 **kynred.** *Sal*: 'parentes' (3. 2). Modern editors are divided on Sallust's meaning, which may be 'parents' or 'subjects' (from *pareo* 'obey'). Barclay seems to prefer the former, which is the interpretation found in *Sold* (sig. e6^{v}), and was that adopted by Aldus Manutius. Nevertheless, the sense 'subjects' is attested at *Sal* 102. 7, where Barclay renders *parentes* as *subgettes*, following *Sold*: '¶Parentes: id est obedientes: et subditos: sicuti sunt qui bello subiguntur' (sig. p5^{r}). Cf. *Asc*: 'parentes .i. obedientes nobis. quasi dicat coactos: vt Carthaginenses: Macedones et alios' (f. 100^{v}).

77 **myght and vyolence.** *Sal*: 'ui' [*BarcT*: si] (3. 2). As at many points, Barclay's translation reflects the correct Latin reading, not that of Pynson's erroneous side-text.

81–2 **all mutacions of thynges/ and chaunges of gouernours.** *Sal*: 'omnes rerum mutationes' (3. 2). *Asc*: 'omnes imitationes' [thus all edns. 1504–1519; recte *mutationes* as in *AscT*] 'rerum .i. regiminum et rectorum' (f. 39^{r}).

83–5 **slaughter of some . . . defenders of the same.** *Sal*: 'caedem, fugam aliaque hostilia' (3. 2). *Sold*: '¶Fugam. id est exilium. ¶Aliaque hostilia: alia mala quæ hostes facere solent: ut est dirreptio bonorum' (sig. f1^{r}). *Asc*: 'cædem .i. occisionem. fugam et alia hostilia .s. bonorum publicationem. exulationem. incarcerationem' (f. 39^{r}).

84–5 **and in weryeng**: The conjunctions *and . . . and*, substituted in *BarcB* for *BarcA nor . . . or*, improve the sense of the passage considerably. *Sal*: 'Frustra autem niti neque aliud se fatigando nisi odium quaerere, extremae dementiae est, nisi forte quem inhonesta et perniciosa lubido tenet potentiae paucorum decus atque libertatem suam gratificari' (3. 3).

90–1 **for pleasure of a fewe myghty men vsurpers of dominion and lordshyp.** *Sal*: 'potentiae paucorum' (3. 3). In Sallust 'the few' usually refers to the ruling clique, but here it probably refers to the members of the Second Triumvirate of 43 BC, Octavian (Augustus), Antony, and Lepidus. *Sold*, however, names Caesar and Pompey as the principal objects of the reference (sig. f1^{r}) and *Asc* adds Augustus (f. 39^{r}).

93–4 **the redyng of hystories . . . memory**. *Sal*: 'memoria rerum gestarum' (4. 1). Barclay's expansion of this phrase may be compared with *Asc*: 'memoria rerum gestarum id est lectio historiæ' (f. 39^{v}).

94–5 **to all degrees . . . vnto princes.** Barclay's addition to his source, perhaps for the benefit of his patron, the Duke of Norfolk. On the tenuousness of the relationship between Barclay and Norfolk, however, see *St George*, ed. Nelson, pp. xiii–xiv, and Introduction above, pp. xvii–xviii. Ascensius's prefatory *De utilitate historiae* includes a section that may have influenced Barclay: 'Quamobrem Demetrius Phalereus . . . in libris scripta reperiuntur' (cited in note to Latin Preface, l. 75 above). Nevertheless, the sentiment reflects more generally evocations of the practical applications of historical works that Roman historians added to justify their efforts: cf. Livy *Praef.* 10, Tacitus *Annales* 3. 65. 1.

109 **festyng.** 'feasting'. *Sal*: 'conuiuiis gratiam quaerere' (4. 3).

110–21 **Whiche enuyous maligners . . . the commen wele.** To be taken as a single sentence, in which three *if* clauses precede the coordinate main clauses *than shall they thinke . . . and they shall fynde . . .*

114 **wyllers.** Perhaps emend to *yll-wyllers.*

124–5 **the famous princes Quintus Maximus/ and Publius Scipio.** Q. Fabius Maximus Cunctator and P. Cornelius Scipio Africanus Maior (or perhaps the younger Scipio). Barclay does not expand, as he might have done, following *Sold*: 'Quin. Maximum. hic est qui Hannibalem iuueniliter exultantem patientia sua uicit: cuius non dimicare uincere fuit. ¶P. Scipionem. hic est qui Hannibalem prælio fudit atque fugauit: et Carthaginem tributariam populo Romano fecit' (sig. f2r). Sallust's selection of two men renowned for their successes in the Carthaginian wars implies that the protagonists of the Jugurthine war are inferior by comparison, and affairs in Africa now corrupt and debased.

127–9 **the ymages of their forefathers . . . commen wele**: *Sal*: 'maiorum imagines' (4. 5). Sallust refers to the wax masks of ancestors who had held a curule office. These were displayed in the atrium, and worn at funerals or exhibited ceremonially. Perhaps following the glossators, Barclay generalizes the reference to statues and other memorial images. The expansion of *ceram* 'wax' into *of stone, of waxe, or of metall* appears to be his own. *Sold*: '¶Imagines uel statuas: uel picturas' (sig. f2r). *Sold* observes that Sallust echoes Cicero: 'An statuas et imagines, non animorum simulacra sed corporum, studiose multi summi homines reliquerunt; consiliorum relinquere ac virtutum nostrarum effigiem nonne multo malle debemus, summis ingeniis expressam et politam?' (*Or. pro Licinio Archia* 30). *Asc*: 'imagines .i. stemmata maiorum dicere ita: videlicet animum accendi sibi vehementissime ad virtutem: scilicet .i. scire licet vnde id eueniat: quia non cæram illam stemmata fiebant: vt in Iuuvenalem ibi [Juvenal, *Sat.* 8. 1] stemmata quid faciunt: late scriptum est. neque figuram .i. faciem aut imaginem maiorum: habere in sese tantam vim .s. vt accendat animos intuentium: quia sic cuiuslibet animum incendissent: sed eam flammam .i.

illud incendium crescere egregiis viris in pectore: memoria .i. per memoriam rerum gestarum a maioribus suis: vnde dici solet quod picturæ et celaturæ sint illiteratorum libri' (f. 40^{r}).

141–3 **Than how moch more . . . redyng of the same.** Barclay's addition, following *Sold*: 'quia in ipsa imagine quodammodo cernant facta illius: cuius effigiem intuentur: quanto magis hoc facit historia: que multo clarius multoque expressius quam statua uel pictura non solum facta sed etiam dicta et consilia et animos uirorum excellentium ante oculos ponat' (sig. f1^{v}) [*Sold* **1497/8**: non solum egregie gesta et facta . . . animos clarorum atque excellentium uirorum].

147–8 **in couetyse . . . wastfull expences.** *Sal*: 'diuitiis et sumptibus' (**4. 7**). *Sold*: '¶Diuitiis et sumptibus: per hoc duo uitia notat contraria: auariciam et prodigalitatem. Auariciam in accumulandis diuitiis: prodigalitatem in expendendis. ¶Sumptibus: id est expensis' (sig. f2^{r}).

149–50 **gentylmen of the first heed.** *Sal*: 'homines noui' 'new men' (**4. 7**). By this Sallust means honoured men whose ancestors had held no curule office (curule aedile, praetor, or consul). Barclay's metaphor relates to venery: 'of the first head' describes a deer at the age when antlers are first developed, and the phrase was also used figuratively of a man newly ennobled or raised in rank (see *OED s.v.* **head** n. 1, 7.b.). *Sold*: '¶Homines noui. Homines noui dicuntur qui nulla maiorum suorum nobilitate aut gloria sed propria uirtute ad honores accedunt: sicuti fuit Marius et Cicero: qui cum maiores sui nulla gloria aut fama rerum gestarum claruissent: facti sunt consules: alter septies: alter semel. Hi nobilitatem non acceperunt: sed uirtute sibi pepererunt. Ergo noui homines dicuntur ignobiles genere: qui uirtute sibi nobilitatem et gloriam acquirunt' (sig. f2^{r}). *Asc*: 'homines noui (qui nunquam et quorum maiores nunquam fuerunt in eo magistratu in quo noui homines dicuntur)' (f. 40^{r}).

154–5 **offyce of a hye Iuge . . . other great offyces.** *Sal*: 'praetura et consulatus atque alia omnia huiuscemodi' (**4. 8**).

156–8 **And nat in maner . . . hy rowmes.** *Sal*: 'ac non perinde habeantur ut eorum qui ea sustinet uirtus est' 'as though possession of these [offices] did not depend on the character [*uirtus*] of those who hold them' *or* 'and not to be estimated according to the worth of those who fill them' (**4. 8**).

158–9 **But playnly . . . nor worshypfull.** Barclay's addition, amplifying the substance of the preceding sentence.

Chapter 1

3 **In this warke I purpose to wryte.** *Sal*: 'scripturus sum' (**4. 9**). *Asc*: 'Ego scripturus sum. scilicet in hoc opere' (f. 41^{r}).

4–5 **agaynst the tyranne Iugurth . . . lande of Numydy.** *Sal*: 'cum Iugurtha rege Numidarum' (5. 1). *Asc*: 'cum Iugurtha rege Numidarum: non qui verus rex esse debebat: sed qui pro rege institutus erat et sese regem gesserat. Sicut in euangelio [Luke 1: 5]: In diebus Herodis regis Iudæ: qui tamen non ex successione legitima erat rex: sed a Romanis institutus' (f. 41^{r}).

7–9 **First for that . . . victory.** *Sal*: 'primum quia magnum et atrox uariaque uictoria fuit' (5. 1). *Asc*: 'magnum: quia multis copiis gestum: et atrox: quia multis trucidatis: et varia victoria .i. habens variam victoriam nunc Romanorum nunc Iugurthinorum' (f. 41^{r}).

10 **the Iugurthyns.** 'the followers of Jugurtha, the Numidians' *Asc*: 'Iugurthinorum' (f. 41^{r}).

12 **the princes/ and states.** *Sal*: 'nobilitatis' (5. 1). Barclay frequently renders *nobilitas* as *estates* (see Glossary), and perhaps *states* should be emended here. But cf. *OED s.v.* **state** n., sense 24. *BarcB* omits *and states.*

12–24 **For where as . . . commen wayle.** Barclay's addition, which draws upon the explanations of both *Sold* and *Asc*, outlining the *cyuyle batayle* (*Asc*: 'ciuilia bella' (f. 41^{r})) between Marius, *a man of basse byrth* (*Sold*: 'nouum hominem et ignobilem' (sig. f3^{r})), and Sylla (88–82 BC). Sallust may also have had in mind the elder Lepidus's uprising in 77 BC, Catiline's conspiracy of 63 BC, and the civil war between Caesar and Pompey (49–45 BC).

25–6 **Which contencion . . . dysordred.** *Sal*: 'Quae contentio diuina et humana cuncta permiscuit' (5. 2). For Barclay's phrase *the lawes of God and man* cf. *Sold*: 'quo bello omnia iura diuina et humana uiolata sunt: nec enim leges humanæ aut diuinæ in eo bello ualuerunt: sed prout libido uictoris erat: ita fiebat' (sig. f3^{r}).

37–8 **may be more euydent/ open/ and clere/ to the reders.** *Sal*: 'illustria magis magisque in aperto sint' (5. 3). *Sold*: '¶Illustriora: clariora' (sig. f3^{r}).

Chapter 2

4 **The Romayns had thre notable and famous batayls . . . theyr ennemyes.** Both *Sold* and *Asc* provide a fuller outline of the three Punic wars, but Barclay restricts himself to Sallust's brief account of the second Punic war (218–202 BC). Sallust's own silence about the third Punic war (149–146 BC) here and at other points is noteworthy.

7–8 **duke and captayne of the Carthaginences.** *Sal*: 'dux Carthaginiensium' (5. 4).

17 **many noble and famous actes of chyualry.** *Sal*: 'multa et praeclara rei militaris facinora' (5. 4). Cf. note to Extract, l. 55.

20 **Sciphar.** Syphax, king of the Masaesyli in Western Numidia, was

captured by C. Laelius and Masinissa in 203 BC (Livy, *Ab Urbe Condita* 30. 11–12). His was one of a number of tribes and kingdoms absorbed into Masinissa's domain.

25–6 **but at last . . . decayed also with hym.** *Sal*: 'Sed imperi uitaeque eius finis idem fuit' (**5. 5**). Sallust may mean simply that Masinissa's reign extended until his death (thereby confirming that he was a successful client king), or perhaps that following his death the extended regions under his sovereignty reverted to Rome, and that his son Micipsa only inherited his father's former kingdom.

31–4 **But Manastaball . . . without lande or lyuelode.** *Sal*: 'quem Masinissa, quod ortus ex concubina erat, priuatum dereliquerat' [*Laet-BritT*, *AscT*, *BarcT*: reliquerat] (**5. 7**). Barclay apparently makes Mastanabal the subject of the last clause rather than Masinissa, although he does attribute the action to the grandfather Masinissa in the preliminary *compendyous extract* of events (see Extract, l. 21). Sallust's *priuatum dereliquerat* probably means that Iugurth's grandfather left him with the status of commoner rather than princely status, and not that he deprived Iugurth entirely of inheritance, as Barclay suggests. *Sold*: '¶Priuatum: uidelicet sine regno non dedit ei partem aliquam regni' (sig. f4^{r}). *Asc*: 'priuatum .i. sine regno' (f. 42^{v}).

39 **This Iugurth.** Cf. *Sold*, *Asc*: 'Qui: scilicet Iugurtha' (sig. f4, f. 42^{v}).

43–5 **he exercysed . . . in ronnynge and wrestlynge**. *Sal*: 'cursu . . . certare' (**6. 1**). Sallust refers only to running; Barclay's addition of wrestling is not taken from *Sold* or *Asc*.

46 **in laude and prayse.** *Sal*: 'gloria' (**6. 1**). *Sold*: '¶Gloria .i. fama et laude' (sig. f4^{r}).

46 **yet none inuyed hym.** *Sal*: 'omnibus tamen carus esse' (**6. 1**). *Sold*: 'tamen nemo ei inuidebat: sed omnibus carus erat: et ab omnibus amabatur' (sig. f4^{r}).

58–9 **he reuolued many thynges in mynde.** *Sal*: 'multa cum animo suo uoluebat' (**6. 2**) [*AscT*, *Laet–BritT*: multa in animo suo uoluebat; *BarcT*: in animo multa voluebat].

59 **solycitude and besynesse.** *Sal*: 'negotio' (**6. 2**). Cf. *Asc*: 'negocio .i. sollicitudine ex ea re sumpta' (f. 42^{v}).

60–2 **Forthermore he consydred . . . subiect.** *Sal*: 'Terrebat eum natura mortalium auida imperi' (**6. 3**). Take *desyre* as a noun, and *to rule/ and commaunde* as infinitives.

60 **of kynde.** 'by nature'.

62–3 **prone and hedlynge inclyned.** *Sal*: 'praeceps' (**6. 3**). *Sold*: '¶Et praeceps: id est prona procliuis et inclinata' (sig. f4^{v}).

65–70 **Moreouer aduysing . . . pray and promocyons.** *Sal*: 'praeterea opportunitas suae liberorumque aetatis, quae etiam mediocris uiros spe praedae transuorsos agit' (**6. 3**). Barclay's expansion is in part attributable to *Sold*: '¶Etiam mediocres: non solum malos set etiam moderatos et modestos. ¶Spe praedæ .i. spe lucri et commodi' (sig. f4^{v}).

70–1 **Such consyderatyons feared sore the mynde of Micipsa.** 'such considerations put great fear into Micipsa's mind'. This is to be taken as the concluding main clause of the preceding sentence, and might better be terminated with a punctus.

73 **kyndled agaynst Iugurth.** *Sal*: 'in Iugurtham accensa' (**6. 3**). *Sold*: '¶In Iugurtham .i. erga' (sig. f4^{v}). The ambiguous phrase is changed in *BarcB* to *inclyned to Iugurth*.

79 **begyle**. Perhaps to be taken as preposition and noun: 'by guile'. *Gyle* occurs frequently in the text, but *begyle* may appear as a noun at 38/8 (see note).

82 **redy of hande to stryke.** *Sal*: 'manu promptus' 'physically active, energetic' (**7. 1**). Barclay's phrase, more suggestive of threat to Micipsa, was perhaps suggested by *Asc*: 'promptus manu .i. ad percutiendum' (f. 43^{r}).

86–7 **a cyte of Hispayne named Numance.** *Sal*: 'bello Numantino' (**7. 2**). *Sold*: '¶Numantino: Numantia ciuitas est Hispaniæ: quam Scipio Africanus minor diu obsessam tandem cœpit atque deleuit' (sig. f4^{v}). The Romans besieged Numantia for nine years from 141 to 133 BC. In 134 Scipio Aemilianus took command, improved discipline, and captured the town the following year.

87–8 **vnto which warre . . . the same cyte.** *Sal*, *Sold*, and *Asc* mention no kings other than Micipsa here. *Sold*'s gloss on *socios* in **8. 1** might account for Barclay's version: '¶Apud socios: socii populi Romani dicebantur qui erant cum populo Romano confœderati: sicuti erant Latini: sicuti fuit Massinissa: et Micipsa. Nam quotiens populus Romanus bellum gerebat: socii auxilia mittebant: et uicissim si sociis bellum ab aliquo populo illatum esset populus Romanus eis auxilia mittebat et eos tuebatur' (sig. f5^{v}). On other possible sources see Introduction, p. l.

100–1 **and often tymes countryng his ennemyes without drede of peryll.** *Sal*: 'et saepe obuiam eundo periculis' 'and frequently placing himself in danger' (**7. 4**).

102 **to so great fame and worshyppe.** *Sal*: 'in tantam claritudinem' (**7. 4**). *Asc*: 'in tantam claritudinem .i. splendorem nominis et gloriae' (f. 43^{r}). *Sold*: '¶Claritatem .i. famam gloriam' (sig. f5^{r}). *Laet–BritT* has *claritudinem* at this point, but *Sold* glosses the alternative reading *claritatem*.

110–11 **But his wysdome . . . obedyent to wysdome.** Barclay's addition.

120–1 **newe gentylmen: and also auncyent gentylmen**. *Sal*: 'noui atque nobiles' (**8. 1**). See note to the Prologue, ll. 149–50.

122–3 **sowers of dyscorde and debatefull.** *Sal*: 'factiosi' (8. 1). Sallust's meaning is that the noblemen constituted a clique (*factio*) united in intrigue, seeking to keep power in their own hands, and out of the hands of the common people. *Sold*: '¶Factiosi: factio: dicitur malorum hominum conspiratio' (sig. f5^{v}).

123–5 **myghty of fame . . . by honest conuersatyon.** *Sal*: 'potentes apud socios, clari magis quam honesti' 'having influence over our allies, but notorious rather than respected' (8. 1). *Sold*: '¶Clari hoc est fama insignes. ¶Quam honesti .i. quam uirtute præditi. Clarus autem et nobilis in bonam et in malam partem accipitur' (sig. f5^{v}).

125–6 **nat a lytell.** The phrase *nat a lytell* as placed suggests that Barclay misread *non mediocrem* as adverbial rather than adjectival (perhaps seeing it as *non mediocre*: most *Asc* edns. including **1514.1, 1517** read *non mediocrē*; **1519** spells out the suffix *-em*). *Sal*: 'Iugurthae non mediocrem animum' (8. 1) should be rendered 'Jugurtha's not unambitious mind'.

129–33 **For in hym . . . noble men.** The sentence expands considerably upon the dependent clause of reported speech in *Sal*: 'in ipso maxumam uirtutem, Romae omnia uenalia esse' (8. 1). Concerning this passage, Comber-Balmaceda observes that 'the corrupt continue to exploit the language of virtue' (p. 195). On Sallust's use of the term *uirtus*, see note to Prologue, ll. 6–7.

Chapter 3

7 **to congye and lycence suche socours.** *Sal*: 'dimittere auxilia' 'to dismiss or release the auxiliary troops from service' (8. 2). *Sold*: '¶Dimittere: uulgo dicitur licentiare' (sig. f5^{v}).

8–9 **and before the multytude of all the army assembled.** *Sal*: 'pro contione' (8. 2). *Sold*: 'Contio est multitudo populi uel exercitus conuocata' (sig. f5^{v}).

13–17 **that he shulde contynu. . . than to a hole commente.** *Sal*: 'ut potius publice quam priuatim amicitiam populi Romani coleret neu quibus largiri insuesceret' (8. 2).

20–1 **shortly . . . more than he wolde desyre.** One or both of these phrases seems to translate *ultro*, which in context actually means 'spontaneously; without his having to make any effort'. *Sal*: 'ultro illi et gloriam et regnum uenturum' (8. 2). *Asc*: 'vltro .i. vltra quam peteret' (f. 43^{v}). *Sold*: '¶Vltro .i. etiam si non quæsiueris' (sig. f5^{v}).

23 **both he and his ryches fall heedlyng to ruyne and decay.** *Sal*: 'suamet ipsum pecunia praecipitem casurum' (8. 2) 'hasten his own ruin by

means of his money'. *Laet–BritT*, *AscT*: 'suam pecuniam et ipsum precipitem casurum' (sig. f5^{v}, f. 44^{r}).

Chapter 4

4–6 **Publius Scipio captayne . . . Rome.** Barclay adds this sentence. Observing that Sallust omits the opening formula of the letter for the sake of brevity, *Asc* supplies a form of words that appears to be Barclay's source (as Nelson notes in the introduction to the *Lyfe of Saynt George*, p. xvii, without identifying the commentator). *Asc*: 'Iugurthæ tui. Breuitatis gratia omittit salutationem quæ esse potuit huiuscemodi. Publius Scipio imperator Romanus Micipsæ Numidarum regi et socio Romani imperij Salutem dicit. deinde breuiter addit' (f. 44^{r}). There is no similar passage in *Sold*.

13–15 **I am surely . . . your commodyte.** *Sal*: 'Tibi quidem pro nostra amicitia gratulor' 'as a friend I congratulate you' (**9. 2**). *Asc*: 'Quidem .i. certe ego gratulor .i. pro bono tuo hilarem me significo tibi: pro nostra amicitia .i. iuxta nostram amicitiam qua tibi plurimum benevolo' (f. 44^{r}).

Chapter 5

3–5 **With these letters . . . commentie.** Barclay adds this sentence.

8 **had harde.** *Sal*: 'acceperat' (**9. 3**). *Sold*: '¶Acceperat .i. audiuerat: intellexerat' (sig. f6^{r}).

8–9 **than what for the nobles . . . commendatyon of Scipio.** *Sal*: 'cum uirtute tum gratia uiri' (**9. 3**). *Laet–BritT*, *AscT*, *BarcT*: 'tum uirtute tum gratia uiri'. The referent of *uiri* might be Jugurtha, as *Asc* argues (and modern editors agree), or Scipio, as *Sold* asserts. Barclay seems to embrace both options simultaneously in his translation. *Sold*: '¶Gratia uiri .s. Scipionis: et uirtus Iugurthæ mouit eum: et gratia Scipionis: qui ad eum scripserat' (sig. f6^{r}). *Asc*: 'tum .i. simul: virtute viri .s. Iugurthæ. tum .i. simul: gratia .i. complacentia: eiusdem potius quam Scipionis: quia dictum est quod Iugurthæ inerat quædam gratia ad captandam beniuolentiam' (f. 44^{r}).

12–14 **to thentent: . . . nor his heyres.** Barclay's addition. 'With the purpose in mind that Jugurtha thus influenced, out of a sense of pity, would not find it in his heart to harm Micipsa or his heirs.' The phrasing seems awkward.

21 **consumed by age and dysease.** *consumed* only in *BarcA*; *by age and dysease* supplied from *B C*. *Sal*: 'morbo atque aetate confectus' (**9. 4**). *Sold*: '¶Confectus: consumptus: maceratus' (sig. f6^{r}).

Chapter 6

6 **kyngdome.** *Sal*: 'regnum' (**10. 1**). Sallust here means 'royal household'.

13–15 **ye commynge . . . to honoure and glory.** *Sal*: 'gloria honorauisti 'by means of your glory you have conferred honour' (**10. 2**). *Laet–BritT*, *AscT*, *BarcT*: 'gloria decorasti'. Perhaps emend *to honoure* to *the honoure*.

18–20 **So that in Hispayne . . . renouate and renewed.** Barclay makes this a result clause dependent on the preceding, which may be implicit in Sallust's independent clause. *Sal*: 'in Hispania nomen familiae renouatum est' 'your actions have renewed the family's good name in Spain' (which Masinissa established by his exploits) (**10. 2**). *Sold*: 'Sicuti supra monstrauimus: Massinissa amicitiam cum Scipione contraxit' (sig. f6^{r}).

43–4 **if ye wyll contynue . . . bytwene yourselfe.** *Sal*: 'si boni eritis' (**10. 6**). *Sold*: '¶Boni eritis: id est concordes: et unanimes' (sig. f6^{v}). *Asc*: 'si eritis boni id est fideles et concordes' (f. 44^{v}).

55–8 **For in euery stryffe . . . his feble aduersary.** *Sal*: 'Nam in omni certamine qui opulentior est, etiam si accipit iniuriam, tamen, quia plus potest, facere uidetur' (**10. 7**).

59–60 **this Iugurth your worthy vncle.** *Sal*: 'talem hunc uirum' (**10. 8**). Unless Barclay here wishes to emphasize Jugurtha's seniority, *vncle* is a mistake for cousin.

64 **chyldren.** *Sal*: 'liberos' (**10. 8**). Sallust's use of the plural is rhetorical. Micipsa has adopted only Jugurtha.

66–70 **Than howbeit . . . answere.** Barclay may be paraphrased as: 'Then although Jugurtha well perceived that the king's words were feigned and spoken contrary to his heart (for he could think of no other remedy), nevertheless Jugurtha answered benignly for the occasion, even if he had quite another course of action in mind which was contrary to this humble reply.' The phrase that Barclay has added to his source (*spoken agaynst . . . ben founde*) may derive from *Asc*: 'locutum ficta .i. excogitata per dolum contra mentem suam' (f. 45^{r}).

Chapter 7

4–7 **whose dethe . . . afterwarde declare.** Barclay's addition.

8 **funerall exequyes.** *Sal*: 'Postquam illi more regio iusta magnifice fecerant' (**11. 2**). *Sold*: ¶Postquam: mortuo inquit rege: cum exequias magnifice celebrassent. . . . ¶More regio: secundum regiam consuetudinem: magna enim ambitione et pompa exequie regum celebrantur. Iusta: id est exequias funebres' (sig. f6^{v}).

9–10 **that is to say Adherball/ Hiempsall/ and Iugurthe.** *Sold*: '¶Reguli. scilicet Iugurtha Adherbal et Hiempsal' (sig. f6v).

11–12 **concernynge partycion and separatyon of the same.** Barclay's addition. Sallust states only that they met to discuss various matters (*Sal*: 'de cunctis negotiis' (11. 2)).

14–15 **somwhat fyers of nature/ and dysposed to statelynesse.** *Sal*: 'natura ferox' (11. 3). The *OED* first citation for *stateliness* is from Barclay's 1509 *Shyp of Folys*, and carries the same negative sense as here of 'haughtiness, arrogance': 'Suche as foloweth shamefull wantonnes, Ungoodly luste, and statelynes of mynde' (sig. q6r; Jamieson, 217).

15 **Also in mynde long before this tyme.** *Sal*: 'et iam antea' (11. 3). *BarcA* reflects *Laet–BritT*, *AscT*: 'etiam iam antea'. *BarcB C* change *also* to *and*, reflecting the reading now preferred.

17–18 **and a bastarde borne: as is sayde before.** Barclay's addition. Cf. *Sold*: 'nam ex concubina natus erat: ut dictum est ante' (sig. f6v).

25–6 **vnnethes coude he with moche payne.** Cf. *Sold*: '¶Vix: id est cum labore difficulter' (sig. f6v).

26–7 **by requestes of his brother and of other noble menne of the realme.** Neither Sallust nor the commentators state that others joined Adherbal in his urging.

33 **Iugurth sayde.** *Sal*: 'iacit' (11. 5). Many MSS, *Laet–BritT*, *AscT*, *BarcT*: 'ait'.

34 **statutes and ordynaunces.** *Sal*: 'consulta et decreta' (11. 5). *Sold*: '¶Consulta: id est statuta' (sig. f6v).

36–47 **For within the same . . . for the remenant.** Barclay partially converts into direct speech the indirect speeches which Sallust attributes to Jugurtha and Hiempsal, probably to emphasize the latter's sarcasm. He expands his source with the section *whiche was the worst . . . the remenant*. The commentators do not put this into direct speech as in some other cases that Barclay follows.

50–1 **for drede of losse of his porcyon of the kyndome.** *Sal*: 'metu' (11. 8). *Asc*: 'metu ne ab hæreditate penitus excluderetur' (f. 45v).

55–6 **frowarde desyre and vnrefrenable appetyte of his mynde.** *Sal*: 'animus ferox' (11. 9). *Sold*: '¶Animus ferox .i. indomitus animus .s. Iugurthæ' (sig. g1r).

56–7 **mytigated nor pacyfied.** *Sal*: 'neque lenitur' (11. 9). *Sold*: '¶Neque lenitur .i. mitigatur' (sig. g1r).

58–9 **other by preuy treason . . . force of armes.** Barclay adds these phrases. Cf. *Sold*: '¶Quouis modo .i. quoquomodo : quolibetmodo. uidelicet ut si non posset per insidias interficere Hiempsalem: ui aperta eum occideret' (sig. g1^{r}). *Asc*: 'quouis modo: siue per dolum et clam: siue per vim et manifeste' (f. 45^{v}).

67–70 **than to deuyde . . . auenge hym.** Barclay's addition.

Chapter 8

3 **Whan the thre prynces.** The first seven lines are inset for the insertion of a large capital W, but it is absent. See Introduction, pp. lxii–lxiii.

5–17 **Hiempsall drewe hym . . . brynge them vnto hym.** Barclay's translation of this passage is somewhat freer than usual, and not without error, as the following notes indicate.

6–9 **In which towne . . . greatly in fauoure.** Barclay follows Soldus in making Hiempsal the owner of the house, where Sallust intends that the owner is the servant of Jugurtha. Both *BarcA* and *B* punctuate the passage as given, but would have done better to put the punctus after *place* and the colon after *dystant*. *Sal*: 'Sed Hiempsal in oppido [*AscT* and *mod edns.*; *Laet–BritT*: oppidum] Thirmida forte eius domo utebatur qui, proxumus lictor Iugurthae, carus acceptusque ei semper fuerat' (12. 3). *Sold*: '¶Eius domo .s. Hiempsalis . . . ¶Vtebatur: quia hic lictor familiariter uersabatur in domo Hiempsalis' (sig. g1^{r}). *Asc* (f. 45^{v}) disagrees with *Sold*'s text and interpretation.

7 **a man of the garde.** *Sal*: 'proxumus lictor' (12. 3). Sallust uses the specific Roman term *proxumus lictor* loosely to mean 'trusted attendant'. It is doubtful that any such office existed in Numidian society. In Roman society, the lictor nearest to the magistrate or consul is the chief of the twelve lictors, or attendants who march in front of him. Cf. *Asc*: 'lictor id est satelles et custos corporis Iugurthæ' (f. 45^{v}).

9–11 **This seruaunt . . . remembredde this oportunyte.** *Sal*: 'Quem ille casu ministrum oblatum' (12. 3) 'this man, whom chance threw in [Iugurtha's] way'.

13–14 **induced and made hym.** *Sal*: 'impellitque' (12. 3). *Sold*: '¶Impellit .i. inducit' (sig. g1^{r}).

17 **nyghly.** *Sal*: 'nam ueræ [*Laet–BritT*, *AscT*, *BarcT*: veræ claues] ad Hiempsalem referebantur' (12. 3). Taken in the sense that the keys were delivered to Hiempsall personally, *nyghly* is an acceptable reading. Barclay might have intended *nyghtly* (as in *BarcC*), if he were following *Asc*: 'Nam veræ claues referebantur scilicet singulis noctibus postquam portæ erant clausæ: ad Hiemsalem' (f. 45^{v}).

32 **treatoure Satellyte.** Here Barclay echoes *Asc*'s earlier gloss on the Numidian servant: 'proximus lictor id est satelles et custos corporis Iugurthæ' (f. 45^{v}).

40–1 **euery hydde corner and secret.** *Sal*: 'loca abdita' (12. 5). *Sold*: '¶Abdita .i. secreta' (sig. g1[r]).

59–60 **Insomoche that finally . . . lande of Numydy.** *Sal*: 'omni Numidiae imperare parat' 'he prepared to make himself ruler of all Numidia' (13. 3). *Laet–BritT*, *AscT* and *BarcT* omit the verb *parat*, which explains Barclay's reading.

61–2 **to certyfy.** *Sal*: 'docerent' (13. 3). *Asc*: 'docerent .i. certiorem facerent' (f. 46[r]).

Chapter 9

10 **strypes.** Changed to *strokes* in *BarcB*, *C*. Barclay uses *stripe* elsewhere: *Myrrour of Good Maners* 3163: 'Lest both fall to braulyng / or some strypes among'; *Shyp of Folys* (sig. s6[r]; Jamieson, 248): 'Rebuke out-braydynge / and strypes whan they fall.'

12 **a prouynce marchynge on the lande of Numydy.** *Sal*: 'prouinciam' (13. 4). Sallust takes it as known that this is the Roman province of Africa, consisting of the territory formerly possessed by Carthage. *Sold*: '¶Profugit in prouinciam. Romani partes terrarum quas bello subiugabant: prouincias appellabant: ad quas uel prætores uel proconsules cum officio mittebant qui eas regerent' (sig. g1[v]).

17–18 **whan he consydred . . . out of his kyngdome.** Barclay adds these clauses. Cf. *Sold*: 'uidelicet cum Hiempsalem interfecisset: et alterum fratrem Aderbalem regno expulisset' (sig. g1[v]).

18–20 **whan he was ydle and at rest.** *Sal*: 'in otio' (13. 5). *Sold*: '¶In ocio: in quiete et pace' (sig. g1[v]).

36–7 **maruelous enuy/ hatred and euylwyll.** *Sal*: 'maxuma inuidia' (13. 7); *Laet–BritT*, *AscT*, *BarcT*: 'maxima inuidia et maliuolentia'. *Sold*: 'maxima inuidia .i. odio' (sig. g1[v]).

Chapter 10

1–2 **Here insueth . . . in forme delyberatyue.** Barclay's use of the term *forme delyberatyue* is the earliest known in English. Cf. *Sold*: 'Hæc autem oratio in genere deliberatiuo posita est. Est autem genus deliberatiuum quod positum in consultatione habet in se suasionem et dissuasionem' (sig. g2[r]). *Asc*: 'Hec oratio in genere deliberatiuo versatur. Suadet enim senatui vt sibi suppetias ferre iubeant ostendens id vtile et honestum ac facile factu Romanis fore. vtile vt socius Romani imperii permaneret: honestum quia id pater et auus meriti erant: facile quia dicturus est.' (f. 46[v]).

8 **Moost dyscrete chosen fathers: and noble senatours.** *Sal*: 'patres

conscripti' (**14. 1**): the form of words normally used to address the Senate. *Sold*: 'Patres conscripti. Romulus qui primus Romæ regnauit: centum senatores elegit: quos a similitudine curæ patres appellauit. Postea centum alii ut refert Liuius additi sunt: qui quia simul cum primis in senatu scripti sunt: simul omnes patres conscripti sunt appellati: quasi simul scripti' (sig. g2^{r}). *Asc*: 'O patres conscripti .i. vos senatores Romani' (f. 46^{v})

11 **rule and admynystratyon.** *Sal*: 'procurationem' (**14. 1**). *Sold*: '¶Procurationem .i. administrationem' (sig. g2).

14–15 **bothe in peace and in warre.** *Sal*: 'domi militiaeque' (**14. 1**). *Asc*: 'domi et militiæ. id est tam in pace quam in bello' (f. 46^{v}). *BarcB C* read *bothe in place and in warre*, but this does not seem to be an improvement, even if one takes *place* in *OED* sense 9 'a dwelling, a house; a person's home . . .'.

15–16 **in place and stede of kynsmen: and nerest frendes of alyaunce.** By *alyaunce* Barclay means marriage, following *Asc* rather than *Sold*. *Sal*: 'uos mihi cognatorum, uos adfinium loco' (**14. 1**) [*Laet–BritT*, *AscT*, *BarcT*: vos mihi cognatorum et affinium loco]. *Sold*: '¶Vos mihi cognatorum: uos affinium: cognati genus paternum respiciunt: affines genus maternum' (sig. g2). *Asc*: 'cognatorum id est consanguineorum: et necessariorum: et loco affinium. id est adquisitorum per legem' (f. 46^{v}).

24 **neuewe.** 'grandson'. *Sal*: 'nepotem' (**14. 2**). This usage is attested elsewhere in the text, and is common in the 16th c. (see Glossary).

33 **and vse your socours of duety.** 'avail myself of your aid which is due to me'.

35 **probyte/ honest lyfe/ and innocence.** *Sal*: 'probitas' (**14. 4**). *Sold*: '¶Ipsa probitas .i. ipsa bonitas ac si diceret: quoniam bonitas mea et innocentia per se tuta esse non potest' (sig. g2^{v}). *Asc*: 'probitas .i. proba et honesta vita' (f. 47^{r}).

36–8 **Moreouer syth it was nat . . . iniury of Iugurth.** *Sal*: 'neque mihi in manu fuit Iugurtha qualis foret' 'since it was not in my power to form Jugurtha's character' (**14. 4**). *Asc*: 'quasi dicat: licet sedulo cauerim ne merito mihi ab illo iniuria fieret: tamen non potui cauere quin immerenti iniurius [**1504.1–1509.1**; intutius **1511.2**; iniustius **1514.1, 1517, 1519**] esset' (f. 47^{r}).

39–41 **coarted of necessyte . . . profet vnto you.** *Sal*: 'cogor prius oneri quam usui esse' (**14. 5**). *Sold*: 'quod prius uobis sum oneri quam utilitati: quia a uobis beneficium peto antequam aliquid utilitatis uobis attulerim' (sig. g2^{v}).

48–9 **our forefathers and rote of our lynage Massinissa confeterated hymselfe.** The plural subject with singular reflexive is awkward. *Sal*: 'familia nostra . . . amicitiam instituit' (**14. 5**). *Sold*: '¶Familia nostra: uidelicet Massinissa' (sig. g2^{v}).

49–50 **in the seconde batayle of Affryke/ or Cartage.** *Sal*: 'bello

Carthaginiensi' (14. 5). *Sold*: '¶Bello Carthaginensi .s. bello Punico secundo. hoc supra monstrauimus' (sig. g2^{v}).

50–3 **what tyme . . . often batayles.** *Sal*: 'quo tempore magis fides eius quam fortuna petunda erat' (14. 5). *Sold*: 'Ergo fides eius magis quam fortuna erat petenda: quia potentia eius erat parua: utpote qui spoliatus erat a Carthaginensibus: et cum his postea fœdus fecerat' (sig. g2^{v}). *Asc*: 'quia tunc maxime attrita erat res Romana' (f. 47^{r}).

53–7 **Thus is it euydent . . . your empyre.** Barclay's addition, effectively a repetition and clarification of the preceding sentence.

61–73 **But prudent fathers . . . from their true herytage.** This passage must be taken as a single complex sentence. Barclay constructs two *yf* clauses where *Sal* has one, preceding the main *Neuerthelesse* clause. *Sal*: 'Si [*Laet–BritT*, *AscT*: Sed si] ad impetrandum nihil causae haberem praeter miserandam fortunam, quod paulo ante rex genere, fama atque copiis potens, nunc deformatus aerumnis, inops, alienas [*Laet–BritT*: alias; *Sold*: alienas] opes expecto' [*Laet–BritT* 1497/8, *AscT* 1513.2, 1514.1: expecto; *Laet–BritT* 1495.1 etc., *AscT* 1504.1–1511.2: expeto], tamen erat maiestatis populi Romani prohibere iniuriam neque pati cuiusquam regnum per scelus crescere' (14. 7).

77 **Siphar.** See note to 2/20.

77–8 **bothe moost vyolent . . . Rome.** Cf. *Asc*: 'Syphacem .s. regem potentem in Aphrica: et Carthaginenses: Romani nominis perpetuos hostes' (f. 47^{v})

84 **our stocke and housolde.** *Sal*: 'familia nostra' (14. 9). *BarcB*, *C* correct the error in *BarcA*, which reads *your*.

87 **whyle the Carthagynences raygned in prosperite.** *Sal*: 'Dum Carthaginienses incolumes fuere' (14. 10). *Sold*: 'dum Carthaginenses in imperio fuerunt' (sig. g3^{r}).

87–8 **we suffred . . . and vexacion.** *Sal*: 'iure omnia saeua patiebamur' 'as is to be expected, we suffered all kinds of hardship' (14. 10).

91–2 **Thus al our hope . . . strength and armour.** Here, as elsewhere in his text, Barclay uses *armour* to mean 'arms, weaponry'. *Sal*: 'spes omnis in armis erat' (14. 10).

98–9 **this cruell Iugurth . . . by cruelte/ and pride.** *Sal*: 'Iugurtha, intoleranda audacia, scelere atque superbia sese ecferens' (14. 11). *BarcB*, *C* omit *cruell*; the emphasis on cruelty in *BarcA*, not found in *Sal*, may derive from *Sold*:' ¶Intolleranda audacia: Iugurtham in odium adducit: superbiam eius ar[ro]gantiam et crudelitatem exponens' (sig. g3^{r}).

103–5 **what tyme I douted . . . which I holde of you.** *Sal*: 'nihil minus quam uim aut bellum expectantem in imperio uostro' 'when under your rule I expected anything rather than violence or war' (14. 11).

108–10 Insomoche that . . . which I holde of you. *Sal*: 'ut ubiuis tutius quam in meo regno essem' (**14. 11**).

111–12 **as I haue oftentymes . . . report with sadnesse.** *Sal*: 'uti praedicantem audiueram patrem meum' (**14. 12**). *Asc*: 'prædicantem .i. serio afferentem' (f. 48^{r}).

116–18 **And sothely . . . to assyst you.** *Sal*: 'Quod in familia nostra fuit, praestitit uti in omnibus bellis adesset uobis' 'Whatever our family was able to do for you, it has done; it has aided you in all your wars' (**14. 12**).

118–123 **Wherfore if ye folowe . . . in this enterprise.** An expansion of *Sal*: 'nos uti per otium tuti simus, in uostra manu est' (**14. 13**).

119–20 **it is bothe right and honesty.** Barclay uses *right* in the sense of 'justice'. Cf. *Sold*: 'Arguit a partibus iustitiæ: uidelicet a gratia. Nam partes iusticiæ sunt: religio: pietas: gratia: uindicatio: obseruantia: et ueritas' (sig. g3^{r}). (Citing Cicero, *De Inv.* 2. 161.)

135–8 **All the socours . . . trybute of nature.** *Sal*: 'Generis praesidia omnia extincta sunt. Pater, uti necesse erat, naturae concessit' (**14. 15**).

142 **withall myne other frendes.** Perhaps to be taken as '(along) with all my other friends'. If *withall* is the adverb 'moreover', its positioning is awkward.

147 **in dongyons and darknes.** *Sal*: 'in tenebris' (**14. 15**). *Sold*: '¶In tenebris .i. in carcere' (sig. g3^{v}).

150–3 **But if it were so . . . my best estate.** *Sal*: 'Si omnia quae aut amisi aut ex necessariis aduorsa facta sunt incolumnia manerent' (**14. 16**); *Laet–BritT*: 'Etiam si quae aut amisi . . .' (but *Sold* gloss begins: 'Sed si omnia' (sig. g3^{v})); *AscT*: 'Sed si omnia mihi quae aut amisi . . .'; *BarcT*: 'Sed si omnia mihi que aut amisi . . . *Asc*: amisi: per violentiam Iugurthae' (f. 48^{r}).

165–73 **Shall I resort . . . oure extremyte.** Expanding a series of questions in Sallust, and to be taken as questions in construction.

167 **for your amyte ioyned with you.** *Sal*: 'ob uostram amicitiam' 'because of our friendship with you' (**14. 17**).

171 **Whyther shall any of them.** *Whyther* stands in place of Latin *Aut*, introducing the second of two direct questions.

171–2 **which haue ben our olde ennemis.** *Sal*, *Laet–BritT*: 'qui aliquando uobis hostis' 'who was ever your enemy' (**14. 17–18**); *AscT*, *BarcT*: 'nobis'.

173–4 **my father Micipsa thus ordred.** *Sal*: 'Masinissa . . . instituit' (**14. 18**); *Laet–BritT*, *AscT*, *BarcT*: 'Micipsa . . . instituit'.

184–5 **all thyng to you is prosperous/ and to your commaudement obeyng.** *Sal*: 'omnia secunda et oboedientia sunt' (**14. 19**). *Sold*: '¶Omnia secunda .i. prospera' (sig. g4^{r}).

188–91 **I am onely in drede and dout . . . Iustice and right.** *Sal*: 'Tantum illud uereor, ne quos priuata amicitia Iugurthae parum cognita transuorsos agat' (**14. 20**). By *as he is worthy* Barclay means 'as he deserves [to be known]'. Cf. *Asc*: 'parum cognita: quia si cognesceretur non foueretur neque coleretur a quoquam: et ita nititur odium aduersarii inducere agat quos. id est aliquos vestrum transuersos .i. extra tramitem equitatis et iustitie' (f. 48[v]).

200 **That wold God.** 'If only'. *Sal*: 'utinam' (**14. 21**).

218–19 **And that by cruelte of hym whom it semed nat of all men so to haue done.** *Sal*: 'et unde minume decuit' 'and by the person who least of all might be expected to have done so' (**14. 22**).

220 **this chaunce of thy deth** *Sal*: 'casum tuum' (**14. 22**). *Sold*: '¶Casum tuum .i. propter mortem tuam' (sig. g4[r]).

230–1 **or els whether I may prouyde and seke socours . . . Numidy.** *Sal*: 'an regno consulam' (**14. 23**). *Sold*: '¶Aut regno consulam .i. prouidebo.' (sig. g4[v]).

241–4 **I obtest . . . chyldren and parentes.** *Sal*: 'Patres conscripti, per uos, per liberos atque parentes uostros' (**14. 25**). *Laet–BritT*, *AscT*: 'Patres conscripti obtestor vos per liberos atque parentes vestros.'

Chapter 11

8 **they replyed in effect.** *Sal*: 'paucis respondent' 'they replied briefly' (**15. 1**).

15–18 **of Iugurth: where as . . . warre of Numance.** *Sal*: 'Iugurtham ab senatu petere ne se alium putarent ac Numantiae cognitus esset' 'Jugurtha [they said] asks the senate not to think otherwise of him than they knew of him from his time at Numantia' (**15. 1**). As punctuated in *BarcA*, Barclay's added statement *of Iugurth all the faute . . . party of Iugurth* (which has no model in the commentaries) involves an awkward repetition of the phrase *of Iugurth*. The punctuation in *BarcB*, placing the colon after the first *Iugurth*, rather than after *senatours*, provides an acceptable reading ('to complain to the senators about Jugurtha'). However, in view of the larger structure, the punctuation of *BarcA* seems possible, although the pronoun *himselfe* referring to Adherbal is somewhat awkward. The ambassadours speak first about Adherbal's alleged motives, and then speak about Jugurtha, beginning with an emphatic *of Iugurth* ('with regard to Jugurtha, on the other hand'), which mirrors the Latin structure commencing with an emphatic *Iugurtham*. The modification in *BarcB* would work better if there were a punctus after *none other*, so that a new sentence began with *concernyng*.

26–7 **with laude/ fauour/ countenaunce/ voyce: and all other signes.**

Barclay's rendering follows the punctuation of *AscT*: 'Iugurthe virtutem extollere: laudibus: gratia: voce. Denique omnibus modis pro alieno scelere et flagitio sua quasi pro gloria nitebantur.' Modern editors place the clause break after *laudibus*, so that it modifies the previous *extollere* (*exalting et commendyng*), and the remaining ablatives modify *nitebantur* (*laboured*). In referring to *countenaunce* Barclay seems to follow *Asc*: 'laudibus .i. plausibus manuum. gratia .i. beneuolentia vultus: et voce .i. sermone' (f. 49^{v}). However, I can find no evidence that *fauour* might denote applause (*plausibus manuum*).

28 **for an others myscheuous vyce and cruell cryme.** *Sal*: 'pro alieno scelere et flagitio' (15. 2). Sallust perhaps uses *alienus* more emphatically to mean a foreigner.

34–7 **a man of noble byrth . . . these his fautes.** *Sal*: 'homo nobilis, impiger, factiosus, auidus potentiae, honoris, diuitiarum, ceterum uitia sua callide [*AscT*: callide sua] occultans' (15. 4). Barclay seemingly pairs *debateful* and *besy* as synonyms. However, as is apparent from his practice elsewhere, the former really translates *factiosus* (also rendered as *redy to dysturbe euery besynes*) while *besy* renders *impiger*.

37–8 **After this Emilius Scaurus sawe his gyueng of brybes of Iugurth.** 'After E. S. saw Jugurtha's bribery'.

50 **shuld be sent into Numidy.** *Asc*: 'legati missi .s. in Numidiam' (f. 50^{r}).

51–60 **The principall . . . chefe oppressers of them.** To be taken as a single sentence. *Sal*: 'Cuius legationis princeps fuit L. Opimius, homo clarus et tum in senatu potens, quia consul [*Laet–BritT*, *AscT*, *BarcT*: qui consulibus] C. Graccho et M. Fuluio Flacco interfectis acerrume uictoriam nobilitatis in plebem exercuerat' (16. 2). The use of *what tyme* as a conjunction is perhaps sufficient to convey the sense, but *bycause what tyme* would make the connection clearer. Lucius Opimius' favour with the senate resulted from his brutal elimination of Gracchus and his followers. Barclay's expansions derive from the explanations in *Sold* and *Asc* of the historical background to the deaths of Gracchus and Fulvius.

62 **one of his ennemis at Rome.** Most MSS and *Laet–BritT* have *amicis*; modern edns. and *AscT*, following Beroaldus (1478), emend to *inimicis*.

63 **worshypfully and with great diligence.** *Sal*: 'accuratissume' (16. 3). *Asc*: 'accuratissime: hoc est cum summa cura' (f. 50^{r}).

65–7 **this Lucius at conclusyon . . . belongyng to himselfe.** *Sal*: 'uti fama, fide, postremo omnibus suis rebus commodum regis anteferret' (16. 3).

75 **Mauritany/ or the lande of the Maurians.** *Sal*: 'Mauretaniam' (16. 5). *Sold*: '¶Mauritaniam: in qua habitant Mauri' (sig. g5^{v}).

77–8 **with hauyn townes and fayre edyfices.** *Sal*: 'quae portuosior et aedificiis magis exornata erat' (16. 5). According to Sallust, the eastern part of the kingdom allotted to Adherbal was superficially more attractive than Jugurtha's western region because of its harbours and towns, but actually less fertile and less extensive. The erroneous *without* appears to be Barclay's mistake, and does not derive from the commentaries. Modern commentators observe that Sallust himself seems to have been in error claiming that Adherbal's portion was inferior to Jugurtha's (see Paul, 70–1).

Chapter 12

4 **In dyuision.** To Sallust's geographical excursus Barclay adds some details from *Sold* and others from *Asc*: see notes following.

4–6 **the opynion of moost writers . . . Affrike.** *Sal*: 'plerique in parte tertia Africam posuere' (17. 3). *Sold*: 'Dicit communem esse opinionem scriptorum: quod orbis terrarum in tres partes diuisus sit: scilicet Asiam Europam et Aphricam' (sig. g6^{r}).

10–11 **on the see of Italy . . . and on the occean see.** *Sal*: 'fretum nostri maris et Oceani' (17. 4). Barclay's apparent failure to understand this reference to the Straits of Gibraltar indicates that he follows *Sold* and *Asc*, who both explain *fretum* as a reference to the Mediterranean only. *Sold*: '¶Fretum nostri maris .i. aquam nostri maris. Nam fretum licet mare significet: proprie tamen dicitur aqua maris mobilis ab undarum feruore nominatum' (sig. g6^{r}). *Asc*: 'fretum .i. feruorem aquarum. nostri .i. Italici seu Tyrrheni maris' (f. 50^{v}).

11–14 **on the Est part . . . a dependant valey.** Sallust refers to the broad sloping plateau between Cyrenaica in Libya and Egypt, and this indicates that he considered Egypt to be part of Asia. *Sal*: 'ab ortu solis decliuem latitudinem quem locum Catabathmon incolae appellant' (17. 4). *Sold*: 'decliuem .i. pendentem. ¶Quem locum Cahtabathmon [*sic*] incole appellant: habitatores eum locum lingua punica appellant Cahtabathmon [*sic*]' (sig. g6^{r}). *Asc*: 'latitudinem decliuem .i. in conuallem descendentem' (f. 50^{v}). For Barclay's reference to a valley, taken from *Asc*, cf. Pliny, *Nat*. 5. 11(38): 'finis Cyrenaicus Catabathmos appellatur, oppidum et uallis repente conuexa'; and Pomponius Mela, *De Chorographia* 1. 36: 'Catabathmos uallis deuexa in Aegyptum finit Africam'. In view of *Asc*'s wording, it may be that Barclay's *dependant* is an error for *descendent*, which is the reading in all editions of *Asc*.

22–3 **corruption of humours ingendring any infyrmite.** *Sal*: 'morbus' (17. 6).

29–30 **Howbeit that which . . . of many men.** *Sal*: 'quamquam ab ea fama quae plerosque optinet diuorsum est' (17. 7).

30–2 **I shall folowe the bokes . . . Hiempsall: whom Iugurth murdred.** Sallust says that his information was translated for him from certain Punic Books of King Hiempsal. This is not *the yonge prince*, but Hiempsal II (106–

60 BC), father of Pompey's ally Juba, and son of Jugurtha's half-brother, Gauda.

34–5 **But towchyng . . . to the authours.** *Sal*: 'Ceterum fides eius rei penes auctores erit' (17. 7).

37 **Getulyans/ and Lybeans.** *Sal*: 'Gaetuli et Libyes' (18. 1). *AscT* omits *et Libyes*. Barclay has restored the reference in the translation and in his Latin side-text, probably taking it from *Laet–BritT*.

38–9 **These lyued . . . beestes vnreasonable.** Barclay may mean that they ate their food upon the ground, or he may use *fedde vpon the grounde* to mean 'fed upon the fruits of the earth' as Sallust intended. *Sal*: 'quis [*Laet–BritT*, *AscT*, *BarcT*: quibus] cibus erat caro ferina atque humi pabulum uti pecoribus' [*AscT omits* humi; *present in Laet–BritT*, *BarcT*] (18. 1). Cf. *Asc*: 'quibus cibus erat caro ferina .i. ferarum. et pabulum .i. forma vescendi aut nutrimentum herbidum: erat humi .i. super terram: vti .i. quemadmodum supplendum est pecoribus' (f. 51^{r}).

55 **bye nor borowe.** *Sal*: 'emundi aut mutandi' (18. 5). Barclay seemingly takes *mutandi* as from *mutuor*, rather than *muto*. Sallust means 'buy or barter'.

62–3 **they named themselfe Numidyans/ that is to say herdmen deuyded.** *Sal*: 'semet ipsi Nomadas appellauere' (18. 7). As *Sold* points out, *nomades* is from the Greek (and was afterwards altered by the Romans into *Numidae*). His etymology, however, is not that now generally accepted. He derives the name from Gk. *νωμάω* 'distribute, divide'. The name is now connected with Gk. *νομόσ* 'pasture'. *Sold*: '¶Et quia sæpe temptantes agros: dicit quare hi Persæ cum Getulis adiuncti Numidæ sunt appellati: hi ab initio qualitatem agrorum temptantes sæpius: ut terram fertilem: et fecundam inuenirent: multa loca diuiserunt: et a diuidendo semetipsos Numidas appellauerunt: a Græco uocabulos. Nam *νωμαω* significat diuido. ¶Partiuerant: antiqui partio et partior dicebant. ut hoc loco partiuerant: dixit. Nos autem tantum partior dicimus' (sig. $g6^{v}$). *Asc*: 'Numidas .i. diuisos [diuersos **1519**] lege aut pastores. Nam nomao *νωμαω* dicitur diuido: sed quia numida primam corripit forte dicitur a nomos .i. lex et yduo .i. diuido: aut quia nomos dicitur regio pascua et nomas -ados. numida pastor' (f. 51^{r}).

64 **the cotages or tylmens houses.** Barclay omits Sallust's statement that the Numidians call the huts *mapalia*. *Sal*: 'aedificia Numidarum agrestium, quae mapalia [*Laet–BritT*, *AscT*, *BarcT*: quæ agrestium mapalia] illi uocant' (18. 8).

69–70 **The Getulyans inhabyted . . . countrey of Inde.** *Sal*: 'Gaetuli sub sole magis [agitabant], haud procul ab ardoribus' (18. 9). Sallust means further south, near the Torrid Zone. Barclay's reference to *Inde*, and seemingly an easterly direction, is not taken from *Sold*: 'Sub sole magis: in plagam australem magis descendentes' (sig. $h1^{r}$); nor from *Asc*: 'magis sub sole: haud procul ab ardoribus .s. Æthiopum' (f. 51^{r}).

76–7 **But the welth and riches of the Persiens.** *Sal*: 'Sed res Persarum' (18. 11) seems to refer to the mixed race of Persians and Gaetulians. Both *Sold* (sig. h1^r^) and *Asc* (f. 51^v^) gloss *res* as *imperium*.

93 **all the inwarde part of Affrike.** *Sal*: 'Africae pars inferior' (18. 12). Sallust means the lower or coastal Mediterranean regions of Africa, not the interior. Barclay follows *Sold*: 'Pars inferior: uidelicet pars illa quæ magis in plagam australem descendens meridiem respicit' (sig. h1^r^).

104–6 **Some bycause . . . And other some.** *Sal*: 'alii . . . pars' (19. 1). Sallust uses this construction for 'sometimes . . . sometimes', rather than 'some . . . others'.

119–23 **Neuertheles somwhat shall I touche . . . The quene Dydo.** *Sold* (sig. h1^v^) provides a similar excursus, but Barclay adds further details not found there, and does not include all of the detail that *Sold* provides. Barclay mentions Belus, *Sold* does not; he states that Sycheus was king of Phoenicia, where *Sold* does not; following Servius, he explains that Hiarba desired Dido, but she refused to marry him, where *Sold* says only that she greatly desired land. On the other hand Barclay omits details contained in *Sold*. He has consulted Virgil and Servius, as he claims in the side-note explaining his sources: '¶Hec tum ex Marone tum ex Seruio reliquisque probis auctoribus sunt excerpta.' *Asc* follows Sallust's lead in passing over the topic.

136–8 **which first was named Byrsa . . . called Carthage.** *Sold*: 'Atque ita urbem condidit: quæ primo Byrsa appellata est a corio bouis: nam *Βυρσι* significat bouis corium: postea Tyros dicta est: postremo Carthago uocata' (sig. h1^v^). Cf. Servius, *Comm. in Verg. Æn.* 4. 670: 'Antiqua Tyros vel nobilem dicit: vel illud ostendit, quia Carthago ante Byrsa, post Tyros dicta est, post Carthago a Cartha oppido, unde fuit Dido, inter Tyron et Beryton.'

148–9 **saue that an arme . . . called Cyrene.** Barclay's confusing syntax in the first edition is corrected in the second, but the reference to *an arme of the see* is in any case incorrect. *Sal*: 'Igitur ad Catabathmon, qui locus Aegyptum ab Africa diuidit, secundo mari prima Cyrene est' 'Thus, adjacent to Catabathmos, the area which divides Egypt from Africa, the first city as one follows the coast [westward] is Cyrene' (19. 3). Barclay's misapprension apparently arises from the punctuation of *Asc*: 'Igitur ad Catabathmon (qui locus Egyptum ab Affrica diuidit secundo mari) prima habitatio Cyrene est.' This parenthesis remains in all the editions to **1519**, except for **1513.2** (Venice).

150–1 **two cites/ the one named Tolonia: the other Thercon.** *Sal*: 'Cyrene . . . colonia Theraeon' 'Cyrene, which is a colony of Theræans' (19. 3). Sallust's brevity, perhaps, and certainly later textual corruption and the errors of the commentators have led Barclay astray here. *BarcT* reads: 'Cyrene est: Tolonia: Thercon'. *Laet–BritT* is better: 'Cirene est: colonia Thereorum'; but *Sold* gloss reads 'Tolonia: Tercon: nomina ciuitatum sunt' (sig. h1[v]). *AscT* reads 'Cirene est. tolonia. Thercon'; *Asc* gloss is 'tolonia. thercon .i. urbes ille sic dictæ' (f. 52[r]). Barclay appears not to have seen the 1511 *Annotationes centum in varios authores* by Jacobus à Cruce Bononiensis (printed by Johannes Parvus and Ascensius at Paris). Included among his notes on cruces is an explanation of the passage, correcting the corrupt readings and explaining the Greek genitive plural of Theraeon. These notes on Sallust frequently appear in editions of the *Opera*, usually at the beginning, first being incorporated in the **1517** Lyon quarto edition with Ascensius's commentary. The corrected reading also occurs in the octavo and quarto reprints of Ascensius's text which are without commentary (**1509.2** and later).

151–2 **beyond these thre cytees . . . a cyte named Leptis.** *Sal*: 'ac deinceps duae Syrtes interque eas Leptis' (**19. 3**). *SoldT*, *AscT*, *BarcT*: 'ac deinde duæ sunt Syrtes: inter quas Leptis'. *Sold*: '¶Duæ Syrtes. Ipse Salustius inferius describit has Syrtes. Sunt autem loca in mari periculosa: quia sunt arenosa' (sig. h1[v]). *Asc*: 'duæ Syrtes .i. loca arenosa in mari habentia breuia vada .i. nunc aquam nunc arenam vbi nauigantibus summum est periculum' (f. 52[r]).

153 **Phylenorum are.** *Sal*: 'Philaenon arae' [*Laet–BritT*, *AscT*, *BarcT*: Philenorum aræ, -e] (**19. 3**). The lack of punctuation in the English perhaps results from a compositor's confusion of the Latin *are* 'altars' with the English *are*.

158–9 **After this place on the syde costes . . . domynion of Punyke.** *Sal*: 'post aliae Punicae urbes' (**19. 4**). By *syde costes* Barclay may mean the tracts of land (as *coste* is used elsewhere in the text: see Glossary), or the Mediterranean coast, or perhaps more specifically the Gulfs of Tunis, Hammamet, and Gabes, and the eastern coast of Tunisia.

162–3 **beyond the Numidyans.** *Sal*: 'Super Numidiam' (**19. 5**) 'south of Numidia'.

163–4 **And some other more vylely without habytacion.** *Sal*: 'alios incultius' (**19. 5**). Take *more* as a modifier of *vylely* rather than as forming a phrase with *other* (see Glossary s.v. *mo*).

165 **the lande of Ethyope.** That part of Africa nearest the Torrid Zone and equator, from Atlantic coast to Red Sea.

168–9 **and moche of the costes of thempyre of Carthage.** *Sal*: 'et finis Carthaginiensium quos nouissume habuerant' 'and the territory of the Carthaginians which they held in later times [between the second and third Punic wars]' (**19. 7**). Barclay omits the relative clause.

Chapter 13

7–10 **how he escaped vnpunysshed . . . lande of Numidy.** *Sal*: 'praemia sceleris adeptum sese uidet' 'he saw how he had profited from his crime' (**20. 1**). *Asc*: 'praemia sceleris .i. ex scelere: quia partem regni maiorem quam habiturus fuisset si ille superuixisset' (f. 52^{v}).

23 **a meke man and oportune to take iniury.** *Sal*: 'quietus, inbellis, placido ingenio, opportunus iniuriae' (**20. 2**). Barclay's rendering is uncharacteristically terse, and something may have been lost here. All three editions read *mete*, which might be taken as a synonym with *oportune*. Emendation to *meke* supplies at least one synonym for Sallust's three earlier descriptors. Alternately, *mete* may be a form of the adjective *mate*, which, extended from chess usage, was used in ME and early Modern English to mean 'exhausted, weak', if not 'defeated'.

26–7 **with a great power and multytude of men of armes.** *Sal*: 'cum magna manu' (**20. 3**). *Sold*: '¶Magna manu .i. multitudo' (sig. h2^{r}).

27 **many of thinhabytauntes he murdred.** *Sal* does not say this; only that Jugurtha took many prisoners: 'multos mortalis cum pecore atque alia praeda capit' (**20. 3**).

70–1 **and the starre lyght somwhat dymmed with obscurite of clowdes.** *Sal*: 'obscuro etiam tum [*Laet–BritT*, *AscT*, *BarcT*: tunc] lumine' 'the sun had not risen' (**21. 2**). For Barclay's elaboration cf. *Asc*: 'lumine .s. naturali: vtpote stellarum aut lunæ: etiam tunc obscuro: alii legunt cum lumine: quasi lumen modicum secum adduxerint: milites Iugurthini' (f. 53^{r}).

72 **raysid by the sounde of trumpets.** *Sal*: 'signo dato' (**21. 2**). *Sold* '¶Signo dato: uidelicet cum bucina: tuba' (sig. h2^{v}). *Asc*: 'signo .s. ineundi belli per tubam aut aliud quoduis instrumentum' (f. 53^{r}).

73 **the tentes and felde of Adherball.** *Sal*: 'castra hostium' (**21. 2**). Barclay regularly translates *castra* 'fortified camp' with *tentes*, and occasionally *tentes and felde*.

73–7 **some they murdredde . . . Iugurth and his company.** Barclay embellishes Sallust's terse description. *Sal*: 'semisomnos partim, alios arma sumentis fugant funduntque' (**21. 2**). Cf. *Asc*: 'fugant et fundunt .i. prosternunt' (f. 53^{r}).

79–80 **that if the inhabytauntes of the town of Cirtha.** *Sal*: 'ni multitudo togatorum fuisset' (**21. 2**). By wearers of the toga Sallust probably means Roman or Italian traders. *Asc*, however, says: 'ni .i. nisi multitudo togatorum .i. ciuium non armatorum sed in togis existentium. Sane togati sunt proprie Romani: sed potuit et illis toga esse. nam non est verosimile Romanis illic tunc fuisse' (f. 53^{r}).

88 **large pauases.** *Sal*: 'uineis' (21. 3). The term *pavis* is normally used in late ME and early Modern English to describe a large, curved shield employed in siege warfare. Barclay, however, uses it here and elsewhere for the Latin *uinea*, denoting a shed-like structure (built like an arbour) employed for protection against missiles in siege assaults.

Chapter 14

7 **they send into Affrike thre yong gentylmen.** Barclay does not bring out Sallust's implication that the Senate were treating Adherbal with contempt by sending *legati* of low status.

20–1 **But this rumour . . . of Iugurth.** This clause belongs with the preceding statement, and should terminate with a punctus. *Sal*: 'sed is rumor clemens erat' (22. 1). Sallust means that although the report of the siege had reached Rome, the full extent of Jugurtha's depredations was not realized there: 'the rumour was short of the truth [not telling the whole of the atrocity]'. *Laet–BritT* retains the old and erroneous reading *demens* for *clemens*, but *Sold* has *clemens*: '¶Sed is rumor clemens erat .i. hæc fama mitis erat: quia non ualde asper nunciabantur: nec ea res ualde diuulgabatur' (sig. h3^r^). *Asc*: 'Sed is rumor .s. de oppugnatione erat clemens .i. mitis et modicus. Ita Soldus legit. Alii legunt demens .i. ab effectu: quia dementes faciebat' (f. 53^v^).

29–32 **for his vertu and manhode . . . nor for disordred maners.** *Sal*: 'uirtute, non malitia' (22. 2). This adverbial phrase is punctuated in *Laet–BritT* and *AscT* (1504–1519) so as to modify the preceding *probaretur*; modern editors, and *BarcT*, place it with the following clause to modify *placuisse*. Barclay effectively restates the phrase so that both translation possibilities are fulfilled.

34–5 **and nat for faute of chyldren naturall.** *Sal*: 'non penuria liberorum' (22. 2). That is, not because he lacked any children of his own.

53–4 **all onely . . . court of Rome.** *Sal*: 'Adherbalis appellandi copia non fuit' 'the ambassadours had no opportunity of addressing Adherbal' (22. 5). *Laet–BritT*: 'Adherbali non fuit appellandi copia.' *AscT*, *BarcT*: 'Adherbali modo fuit appellandi copia.' Cf. *Asc*: 'Et ita copia .i. facultas appellandi .s. ad Romanum senatum: supple erat modo .i. solummodo Adherbali: quia non potuit ius ab legatis obtinere' (f. 53^v^).

61–3 **with sharpe stakes . . . sharpe pykes on their vpper endes.** *Sal*: 'uallo' (23. 1). Cf. *Sold*: '¶Vallo: ualli dicuntur fustes fossarum genere masculino. Nam munitio ipsa uallum dicitur neutro genere. Nam uallum est munitio ex fustibus facta .i. ex palis' (sig. h3^r^).

63–71 **This dyde Iugurth . . . their garnyson.** Barclay's added explanation largely follows *Sold*: 'Vnde qui obsident urbes uallo et fossa solent eas cingere: ne oppida ni subita eruptione exercitum inuadere possint: et ne commeatus ex aliqua parte introduci possint: neue multitudo possit exire: atque ita ad famem ciuitatis deducatur: ut ea necessitate deditionem facere compellatur' (sig. h3^{r}).

73–4 **with garnyson of wyght and bolde men of armes.** *Sal*: 'praesidiis' (**23. 1**). *Asc*: 'præsidio .i. custodia militum impositorum (nam præsidium dicimus esse quod Galli guarnison [garnison **1519**] vocant') (f. 54^{r}).

75 **to attempt euery thyng.** *Sal*: 'temptare' (**23. 1**). Sallust here uses the verb absolutely to mean 'made attacks'. *Sold*: '¶Temptare: pro temptabat: more suo' (sig. h3^{r}). *Asc*: 'tentare .i. attentabat dies et noctes .i. sine intermissione' (f. 54^{r}).

81–6 **nothyng he omytted . . . within the same.** Barclay's addition.

89 **vyolent agaynst hym.** *Sal*: 'infestum' (**23. 2**). *Asc*: 'infestum .i. violentum' (f. 54^{r}).

Chapter 15

4 **Most worthy fathers.** Barclay's rendering of Adherbal's letter incorporates considerable rhetorical expansion. Some of this apparently is his own, while some may be traced to the expansive glossing and commentary of *Sold* and *Asc* (see following notes for examples).

6 **the vyolence and rygour of Iugurth.** *Sal*: 'uis Iugurthae' (**24. 2**). *Sold*: '¶Vis: uiolentia' (sig. h3^{v}). *Asc*: 'vis .i. violentia Iugurthæ' (f. 54^{r}).

8–9 **that neyther hath he . . . fear of your dysplesure.** *Sal*: 'ut neque uos neque deos immortalis in animo habeat' (**24. 2**). *Asc*: 'id est neque cogitet vltores fore: aut neque formidet vos: neque deos immortalis: quorum interdum vltio lenta quidem est sed tanto grauior: Valerio Maximo auctore' (f. 54^{r}) [paraphrasing Valerius Maximus *Facta* 1. 1. ext. 3: 'lento enim gradu ad uindictam sui diuina procedit ira, tarditatemque supplicii grauitate pensat'; cf. Juvenal, *Sat.* 13. 100: 'tamen certe lenta ira deorum est'].

13–15 **Neyther can preuayle . . . ordynaunces or decrees.** *Sal*: 'neque mihi Micipsae patris mei beneficia neque uostra decreta auxiliantur' (**24. 3**). *Sold*: '¶Beneficia .s. in Iugurtham: quia Iugurtha a patre meo in filium adoptatus et assumptus est' (sig. h3^{v}).

18–19 **my miserable fortune moueth me contrary.** *Sal*: 'dehortatur me fortuna mea' (**24. 4**). *Sold*: '¶Dehortatur fortuna mea .s. infœlix et aduersa fortuna dehortatur me' (sig. h3^{v}). *Asc*: 'Fortuna mea .i. miserabilis calamitas mea dehortatur me' (f. 54^{v}).

24–7 **at last he shall ryse . . . vsurper of your empyre.** Barclay's addition. Cf. *Sold*: 'Quare si mihi auxilio esse non uultis: saltem rebus uestris prouidere' (sig. h3^{v}). *Asc*: 'quod supra me est videlicet imperium Romanum. quod inuasurus sit si Numidia potiretur' (f. 54^{v}).

40 **But nowe he conspyreth hyer.** Barclay's addition, but a reiteration of what was said earlier (*Sal*: 'Nisi tamen intellego illum supra quam ego sum petere' (**24. 5**)). The use of the verb *conspire* to refer to a person plotting alone is attested elsewhere within the text and outside it (see *OED s.v.* **conspire** 1.b). Given the collocation with the adverb *hyer*, it may be that Barclay intended *aspireth*, but he nowhere else employs the latter verb.

43–5 **This Iugurth . . . and inward famyn.** Barlay's expansion of *Sal*: 'clausum obsidet' (**24. 7**).

48–9 **your power and vyolence.** *Sal*: 'uis uostra' (**24. 9**). *Sold*: 'uis uestra .i. potentia uestra' (sig. h4^{r}). *Asc*: 'vis .i. violenta iussio vestra' (f. 54^{v}).

52–3 **rather than this . . . credyble vnto you.** *Sal*: 'quam miseria mea fidem uerbis faceret' (**24. 9**). *Laet–BritT*, *BarcT*, *AscT*: 'uobis faceret'. *Sold*: 'uerbis' (sig. h4^{r}); *Asc*: 'uobis' (f. 54^{v}).

53–4 **But sith I was borne . . . cruelte by me.** It may be that *moost* should be read as 'must' (cf. 13/61), but an adverbial 'mostly' is possible. *Sal*: 'Sed quoniam eo natus sum, ut Iugurthae scelerum ostentui essem' (**24. 10**).

Chapter 16

12 **the commen wayle.** *Sal*: 'bonum publicum' 'the public good' (**25. 3**).

16–17 **nat yong men and inexpert as before.** Not in *Sal*. Cf. *Sold*: '¶Maiores natu .i. senes non sicuti paulo ante adolescentes' (sig. h4^{v}).

21–2 **was a man . . . counsellour of Rome.** *Sal*: 'consularis' (**25. 4**). Sallust means that he was formerly a consul. This is what *Sold* gives: 'qui et consul fuerat' (sig. h4^{v}). Barclay seems to follow *Asc*: 'existens homo consularis' (f. 55^{r}).

23 **and in maner ruler of them all.** *Sal*: 'et tum senatus princeps' [*AscT*, *BarcT*: et tum in senatu potens princeps; *Laet–BritT*: ~ potentes princeps] (**25. 4**).

27 **the messangers of Adherbal.** Paraphrases *Sal*: 'ab Numidis obsecrati' (**25. 5**). *BarcA*, *B*, *C* read *Iugurth*, where *Adherbal* is meant. Cf. *Asc*: a Numidis .s. legatis Adherbalis (f. 55^{r}).

30–1 **in Affrike . . . to the Romayns.** *Sal*: 'Vticam' (**25. 5**). *Sold*: '¶Vticam est ciuitas Affrice: quam Romani tenebant' (sig. h4^{v}). *Asc*: 'Vticam .i. ad ciuitatem illam Aphricæ (quam Romani tenebant et vbi Cato Minor sibi mortem conciuit: vnde postea Vticensis dictus est)' (f. 55^{r}).

32 **all the hast.** For this idiom instead of the more common *all haste* cf. cits. from *OED*: ?*c.*1500 *Mary Magdalene* (Digby) 1878 'Rere vp the seyll In all

the hast, as well as thou can.' 1540 *Acolastus* II. i. Hiijb, 'Take me hardely in all the hast to be bounde prentyse to thy felowshyp or craftes men of scoffars.' 1577 Hanmer, *Anc. Eccl. Hist.* (1619) 376: 'He got him in all the haste to Constantinople, and sued out a commandement from the Lieutenant of that province' [etc.].

34–5 **Whan Iugurth.** *Sal*: 'Ille ubi' (**25. 6**). *Sold*, *Asc*: 'ille .s. Iugurtha' (sig. h4^{v}; f. 55^{r}).

38–9 **to wyn the towne . . . into his handes.** *Sold*: 'uidelicet ut urbem Cirtham expugnaret et Adherbalem caperet' (sig. h4^{v}). *Asc*: 'contra inceptum suum .i. ad impediendum expugnationem Cirthæ et necem Adherbalis' (f. 55^{r}).

48–50 **This thyng determyned . . . towne rounde about.** *Sal*, *Laet–BritT*, *AscT*: 'Igitur exercitu circumdato' (**25. 9**). *BarcT*: 'Igitur exercitu comparato'. The **1517** and **1519** edns. of *Asc* have a chapter break here, where the earlier editions have a paragraph marker (¶).

54 **by such meanes.** *Sal*: 'aut ui aut dolis' 'either by force or by stratagem' (**25. 9**).

56–7 **to haue his pleasure of the towne of Adherball.** *Sal*: 'Adherbalis potiretur' (**25. 10**). *Sold*: 'Adherbalis potiretur .i. Adherbalem caperet: et eum in potestate suam redigeret' (sig. h4^{v}). *Asc*: 'potiretur Adherbalis supple copia (Aut potior etiam genitiuim regit . . .' (f. 55^{v}).

62 **many greuous manaces and wordes.** *of displeasour* added to the end of the phrase in *BarcB C*. *Sal*: 'uerbis graues minae' (**25. 11**).

67–8 **such as defended . . . of all.** Barclay's addition.

73–4 **For asmoch as . . . in such dyuises.** Barclay's addition. Cf. *Sold*: 'quia erant Italici sub imperio Romano constituti' (sig. h5^{r}).

75–6 **vpon apoynment and condycion . . . onely wold promyse.** *Sal*: 'tantum ab eo' (**26. 1**). *Sold*: 'hoc pacto . . . solum ex pacto' (sig. h5^{r}).

77–9 **and as touching . . . prouysion and remedy.** *Sal*: 'de ceteris senatui curae [*AscT*, *BarcT*: curam] fore' (**26. 1**).

85–6 **contrary to his promes.** Barclay's addition. *Sold*: 'contra fidem' (sig. h5^{r}).

88 **bothe Numidyans and Italyan marchauntes indyfferently.** *Sal*: 'Numidas atque negotiatores promiscue' (**26. 3**). Barclay's *indyfferently* seems to echo *Sold*: '¶Promiscue .i. mixtim pariter *sine differentia*: quia sic peregrinos sicuti incolas necauit' (sig. h5^{r}). Yet *Sold* also states that the Italians were the exception in the general slaughter: 'Dicit quid fecerit Iugurtha postquam Adherbal ei urbem tradidi. Primo ipsum Adherbalem interfecit: deinde omnes Numidas adultos et negociatores qui armati defenderant urbem. Italicos seruauit: quia timebat Romanos' (sig. h5^{r}). *Asc*

is less certain: 'armatus .i. in armis ergo per legem a contrario sensu inermibus pepercit. An tamen Italicis ex hoc loco non constat' (f. 55^{v}).

Chapter 17

7 **suche whose fauour Iugurth had bought before.** *Sal*: 'idem illi [*Laet–BritT*, *AscT*, *BarcT*: iidem] ministri regis' (**27. 1**). Cf. *Sold*: '¶Ministri .i. fautores: qui corrupti erant pecunia' (sig. h5^{r}).

23 **debatefull.** *Sal*: 'factiosos' (**27. 2**). Sallust seems to use the adjective here to mean 'of a faction, partisan', but it is used elsewhere in the text with the implication 'factious, turbulent' which Barclay's term here suggests (see Glossary and note to 11/34–7).

27–8 **therfore they dradde . . . insurrection agaynst them.** Cf. *Asc*: 'senatus timet populum id est tumultum et seditionem populi' (f. 56^{r}).

30–1 **a noble man of Rome named Sempronius.** Gaius Sempronius Gracchus. Despite the earlier reference to Gracchus in *Sal* **16**, Barclay does not indicate that it is the same Consul here. *Sold*: '¶Sed ubi: ordo est Numidia atque Italia prouinciæ decretæ sunt futuris consulibus lege Sempronia . . . Sempronius Gracchus consul legem tulerat' (sig. h5^{v}). For Barclay's idiosyncratic explanation of the Law cf. *Asc*: 'lege Sempronia .i. per legem quam Sempronius tulerat: vt si quando bellum timeretur consules futuri in prouincias destinaretur: ideo autem futuri: vt interea apparatum bellicum instrueret' (f. 56^{r}). Enacted during C. Gracchus' first tribunate (123 BC), the so-called Lex Sempronia stipulated that the consular provinces were to be determined and assigned by the Senate in advance of the consular elections.

42–3 **The prouynce of Italy . . . Numidy to be recouerd.** Cf. *Asc*: 'prouinciæ videlicet Italia quae erat conseruanda et Numidia quae erat in potestatem Romanam redigenda' (f. 56^{v}).

53–4 **the mater went froward . . . it shulde haue done.** *Sal*: 'contra spem' (**28. 1**). *Asc*: 'contra spem .i. contra id quod sperauerat' (sig. h5^{v}). For this adverbial use of *froward* cf. *OED* cit. 1580 Lyly *Euphues* (Arb.) 465: 'Thou knowest howe frowarde matters went, when thou tookest shippe.'

61–4 **For in his great treasour . . . to yls innumerable.** Barclay's addition. The first sentence is perhaps influenced by *Sold*: '¶Iugurtha totam suam spem habebat in pecunia sua: [et] in auaritia Romanorum nobilium' (sig. h5^{v}).

71–3 **Calphurnius commaunded . . . by one named Decius.** *Sal*: 'Consul Numidis ex senatus decreto nuntiari iubet' (**28. 3**). Barclay here conflates the text of *AscT*, which is that of modern editions, and that which appears in *BarcT*, with the incorrect reading found in *Laet–BritT* (edns.

from **1495.1**, except 1497/8): 'Consul Numidis ex Scipione Decio nunciari iubet.' *Sold* gives the better reading in his commentary: '¶Ex senatus decreto nunciari iubet. consul iubet: ut legatis nuncietur quemadmodum decreuisset senatus' (sig. h5^v^). *Asc* makes no mention of this alternative reading.

75–7 **and chose vnto hym . . . retayned with them.** *Sal*: 'legat sibi homines nobilis, factiosos' (**28. 4**). Barclay's rendering of *factiosus* as *debatefull* is characteristic (see Glossary and note to 11/34–7). For the phrase *and hauynge many clyentes and seruantes retayned with them* he follows *Sold*: '¶Factiosos .i. potentes: factiosi dicuntur qui multos habent sui studiosos et complices ac sibi adherentes' (sig. h6^r^). Sallust means that these noblemen were partisan supporters of Calphurnius, not that their own partisans accompanied them.

81 **propertis and vertues condycions.** The change from *vertues* in *BarcA* to *vertuous* in *B* and *C* repairs the syntax, yet *BarcA* seems to echo *Sold*: 'Artes .i. uirtutes' (sig. h6^r^).

89–90 **he deuyded . . . .vi.M.vi.C.lx. and six men.** Barclay adds this explanation of a legion's size, which increased from around 3,000 in earlier Roman times, to over 6,000 in the late Empire. It seems doubtful that legions were so large at the time of the Jugurthine war.

97–8 **as a hardy captayne . . . the first brunt.** Barclay's addition.

99–100 **suche as . . . their neighbours.** Barclay's addition. Sallust states only that Calphurnius took some towns by conquest (**28. 7**).

103 **hardnes and difficulte.** *Sal*: 'asperitatem' (**29. 1**). *Asc*: 'asperitatem .i. difficultatem' (f. 56^v^).

104–6 **Whan Calphurnius . . . receiue the money.** *Sal*: 'animus æger auaritia' (**29. 1**). Barclay's rhetorical expansion goes beyond the glossators' explanations (cf. *Asc*: 'talem magnitudine pecuniæ' (f. 56^v^)). In expanding Sallust's plain *auaritia* here, Barclay appears to use *valour* in the sense of material value (see *OED s.v.* **valour**, senses 2, 3), in which case the term fits a synonymous pairing with *weyght*. In *BarcB* and *C*, *wyght* might be taken simply as a spelling variant of *weyght*; alternatively, an editor or compositor may have read *valour* in a metaphorical sense 'forcefulness' and modified *weyght* to *wyght*, a reduced form (?) of *wyghtness* 'vigour, forcefulness'.

115–16 **But at first . . . of the warre.** That is: initially Jugurtha tried merely to purchase from Calpurnius a delay of the war.

124–5 **Howbeit he trusted . . . to his army.** Somewhat obliquely, Sallust states only that Calpurnius sent the quaestor *fidei causa* 'as a sign of good faith' (**29. 4**). For Barclay's fuller explanation cf. *Sold*: 'Nam Iugurtha non uenisset ad consulem: nisi data ei fides esset a consule: per quam tutus ad eum iret. Hac igitur causa consul sextum quæstorem in urbem Vaccam misit:

uidelicet ut fidem Iugurthæ daret: sed tamen simulauit se alia de causa consul mittere quæstorem' (sig. h6[v]).

130 **treasourer.** *Sal*: 'quaestor' (**29. 4**).

133–5 **And the same commaundement . . . openly in commen audyence.** Barclay omits *Sal*'s following clause: 'quoniam deditionis mora indutiae agitabantur' 'because, owing to the delay of the surrender, a truce was being observed' (**29. 4**). The phrase is present in *AscT* (all edns.), *Laet–BritT* and *BarcT*.

143 **of his purgation.** 'in justification of himself'.

145–6 **sayeng that . . . to resyst vyolence.** Barclay's addition.

154–9 **Now was it . . . the common wele.** Barclay's explanation of the *Satyre lawe* here is erroneous, despite the more reliable information in *Sold* and *Asc*, consistent with Festus, Isidore, and other sources, indicating that *per saturam* means that several propositions were voted upon in a bundle, with no opportunity to vote one way or the other upon motions individually. *Satura* was a dish with a variety of fruits, and later any mixture of ingredients. *Sold*: '¶Quasi per legem satiram. Dicendo quasi ostendit: consulem hæc omnia simulasse. Nam consul simulabat se nihil facere nelle: nisi de consensu consilii: cum Lex satiria est: quæ uno rogatu plura continet' (sig. h6[v]). *Asc*: 'quasi per Satyram legem: quæ vno rogatu priusquam respondeatur multa simul et varia comprehendit vt vultisne: iubetisne' (f. 57[r]).

156 **the Satyre lawe.** *Sal*: 'per saturam' (**29. 5**); *BarcT*, *AscT*: 'per satyram legem'; *Laet–BritT*: 'per Saritiam legem' [**1495.1**; Satiriam **1495.2**, **1497/8**, etc.].

169 **with a great somme of golde.** *Sal*: 'cum paruo argenti pondere' (**29. 6**). *Laet–BritT*, *AscT*, *BarcT*: 'non cum paruo argenti pondere'. The *non* of the Renaissance editions explains Barclay's translation *great*, rather than *little*, but not his substitution of *golde* for *silver*.

172–4 **to requyre the senatours . . . with Iugurth.** *Sal*: 'ad magistratus rogandos' 'to preside at the elections' (**29. 7**). Barclay's apparent misunderstanding of this phrase echoes *Asc*: 'ad rogandos magistratus .s. an consensu eorum et auctoritate confirmanda esset deditio facta' (f. 57[r]). *Sold* correctly explains: '¶Ad magistratus rogandos. Rogare legem uel rogare magistratum est: cum quis populum rogat: et a populo petit: ut eam legem quam fert: populus accipiat et sciscat ac sanciat. Sic et rogare magistratum est: cum quis populum rogat et a populo petit: ut hunc uel illum magistratum creet: siue consul siue prætor. siue alius magistratus sit creandus' (sig. h6[v]).

Chapter 18

12–13 **In this prolexite . . . longe tyme vncertayne.** The sentence is Barclay's addition, although it loosely anticipates his reiteration of the point (*But whyle . . . dubytacion*) which directly renders *Sal*: 'Ac . . . inter dubitationem et moras senatus' (**30. 2**). Accordingly, *prolexite* in *BarcA* echoes Sallust's *moras*, while the revised reading *perplexite* in *BarcB* and *C* echoes *dubitationem*.

15 **let them frome dyscussing of the ryght.** 'Hindered them from choosing the just course of action'. *Sal*: 'a uero bonoque impediebat' (**30. 2**).

17–18 **of whose condycions . . . estates and noblemen.** *Sal*: 'cuius de libertate ingeni et odio potentiae nobilitatis' 'about whose independence of character and hatred of the nobles' power' (**30. 3**). Barclay's rendering might be attributed to a conflation of glosses from *Asc*, who at separate points gives: (1) 'instigante praesertim Caio Memmio cuius concionem [**1504.1–1517**; conditionem **1519**] subiuncturus est; . . .' (2) 'Caius Memmius de cuius libertate .i. audentia loquendi et faciendi libere vel liberi ciues possunt sine alicuius timore ingenii .i. naturalis indolis' (f. 57^{v}).

22 **their commen wayle and lybertie of their cytie.** *Sal*: 'ne rem publicam ne libertatem suam' [MSS vary in readings] (**30. 3**). *AscT*, *BarcT*: 'populum Romanum ne libertatem suam' (f. 57^{v}); *Laet–BritT*: 'populum Romanum ne rem publicam ne libertatem suam' (sig. i1^{r}). Barclay is closer to the latter.

Chapter 19

1–3 **In which orison . . . the noble men of Rome.** Cf. *Asc*: 'In hac oratione deliberatiua Memmius callide inducit populum ad libertatis suæ defensionem: et ad nobilitatis potentiam odio prosequendam' (f. 58^{r}).

5–6 **from defence . . . your besynesses.** *Sal*: 'a uobis' (**31. 1**). *Sold*: '¶Multa me dehortantur a uobis .i. multa me dehortantur o Quirites a defensione uestri' (sig. i1^{r}). *Asc*: 'a vobis .i. a negociis vestris curandis' (f. 58^{r}).

11–16 **First the power . . . from oure cytye.** Barclay's expansion incorporates several clarifications taken from the glossators. *Asc*: 'Opes .i. facultates et potentiæ factionis .i. factiosorum videlicet Calphurnii et Scauri. Patientia vestra: qua suffertis tantam dominationem cum summo dedecore vestro' (f. 58^{r}).

13–14 **Secondly your pacience . . . this wronge.** *Sal*: 'uostra patientia' 'your submissiveness' (**31. 1**). For the latter added clause cf. *Sold*: 'uos patientes estis ad tantam iniuriam tollerandam' (sig. i1^{v}).

16–20 **And princypally . . . auantage/ and worshyppe.** *Sal*: 'ac maxume quod innocentiae plus periculi quam honoris est' (**31. 1**). Barclay's rhetorical expansion relates Sallust's generalized observation more directly to the participants in question. In this he follows *Sold*: '¶Ac maxime quod innocentiæ plus periculi quam honoris est. Ecce probat: quomodo ius nullum est: quia boni et innocentes plus periculi habent quam honoris. Hoc autem dicit. Plebs bona et innocens pericula quidem et labores sustinet: sed nobilitas honores habet: quia magistratus et imperia et prouinciæ per nobilitatem gubernantur' (sig. i1[v]). *Asc*: 'ac maxime quod plus periculi quam honoris est innocentiæ .i. volentibus innocenter et continenter viuere' (f. 58[r]).

22 **power and pride.** *Sal*: 'superbiae' (**31. 2**). *Asc*: 'superbiæ paucorum .s. potentum' (f. 58[r]).

23–5 **how vngoodly . . . for your sake.** *Sal*: 'quam foede quamque inulti perierint uostri defensores' (**31. 2**). *BarcB* and *C* omit *vngoodly and*. Barclay's addition *many of* can perhaps be accounted for by the erroneous reading *multi* for *inulti* in various editions, including those of *AscT* from **1508.1** (perhaps from the error *multi* in the gloss from **1504.1** or **1506.2**) and in *BarcT*. Yet, *vnreuenged* renders *inulti*. Cf. *Sold*: 'et piget dicere quam pro quantum fede multi uestri defensores perierint inulti . . . ¶Multi uestri defensores perierint .s. Tiberius Gracchus primo' (sig. i1[v]). Cf. *Asc*: 'Et quam fœde .i. turpiter: et quam .i. quantum multi [inulti?] .i. non vindicati a vobis perierunt' (f. 58[r]).

28–9 **wyll ye styl be subgette vnto these estates your ennemyes?** *Sal*: 'obnoxiis inimicis' (**31. 3**). Modern editors take Sallust to mean 'when your enemies are in your power'. Barclay's translation reflects the reading of *Laet–BritT*, *AscT*, *BarcT*: *obnoxii inimicis* 'you are subject to your enemies'. Cf. *Sold*: '¶Obnoxii inimicis .i. obligati inimicis: quia timetis eos qui uos timere deberent' (sig. i1[v]). *Asc*: 'obnoxii .i. obligati et quasi noxii obstricti: inimicis vestris .i. potentibus: sed timetis etiam nunc quum tam iustam habetis querelam' (f. 58[r]).

30–1 **whom it semeth to dout and to drede you.** 'who ought to fear and dread you'.

35 **to resyst.** *Sal*: 'obuiam ire' (**31. 4**). *Sold*: '¶Obuiam ire .i. resistere' (sig. i1[v]).

39 **in your handes and power.** *Sal*: 'in uostra manu' (**31. 5**). *Sold*: '¶In uestra manu .i. uestra potestate' (sig. i1[v]).

41 **our forefathers.** *Sal*: 'maiores uostri' (**31. 6**); *Laet–BritT*, *Asc*, *AscT*, *BarcT*: 'vestri maiores'. *Sold* has *nostri maiores* twice in his commentary (sig. i1[v]).

42–3 **from the senatours as ye haue done before tyme** [*BarcB*, *C*: your elders haue done]. Barclay's addition echoes *Sold*, and *BarcB* more closely still. *Sold*: 'Non est opus ui aut secessione: uidelicet ut secedatis et recedatis a patribus quemadmodum bis nostri maiores fecerunt' (sig. i2[r]).

43–5 **It must nedes be . . . condycions insolent and behauour.** *Sal*: 'Necesse est suomet ipsi more praecipites eant' (31. 6). The change in *BarcB*, *C* to *and insolent behauour* is more prosaic, if not more grammatical. For another example of a post-posited adjective see *pride incredeble*, below, l. 91.

49 **vsurper of a kyngdome ouer the commen people.** That is: aspiring to royal power. *Sal*. 'quem regnum parare' (31. 7). Cf. above, 19/56–7 **vsurpatyon of a kyngdome.** *Sal*: 'regni paratio' (31. 8). *Laet–BritT*, *AscT*, *BarcT*: 'regni reparatio'.

53–5 **And at both the seasons . . . immoderate pleasure.** *Sal*: 'Utriusque cladis non lex uerum lubido eorum finem fecit' (31. 7). On both occasions the bloodshed was ended not according to law, but according to the whims of the nobles.

62 **secretely and styll.** Paired adverbs. *Sal*: 'taciti' (31.9).

65–6 **and nat generall to the vnyuersall cyte in commen.** The phrase is Barclay's addition, meaning 'and not to the people of the republic as a whole'. If *generall* here is to be taken as an adverb, it is a usage unrecorded by *OED*.

72 **with all other thynges bothe humayne and dyuine.** *Sal*: 'diuina et humana omnia' (31. 9). The following sentence (*So that in pardonyng* . . .) enlarges upon the preceding, and connects better without the interpolation of the phrase *to your libertie belongynge*, added in *BarcB*, *C*.

79 **as who sayeth.** 'as if to say'.

83–4 **ye gentlemen: freborne cytezyns.** *Sal*: 'uos, Quirites, in imperio nati' (31. 11).

92–3 **their worshyppe/ their deuotyon/ and good name.** 'their reputation, fidelity, and good name'. *Sal*: 'fides, decus, pietas' (31. 12). *Laet–BritT*, *AscT*, *BarcT*: 'decus: fides: pietas'.

105–8 **whiche are conioyened . . . fere of your auauncement.** *Sal*: 'quos omnis eadem cupere, eadem odisse, eadem metuere in unum coegit' (31. 14).

108–11 **But amonge good men . . . and debate.** *Sal*: 'Sed haec inter bonos amicitia, inter malos factio est' (31. 15). *Laet–BritT* and *AscT* set a colon before *sed*.

115–16 **the offices / maistershyppes . . . where lyketh you).** *Sal*: 'beneficia uostra' (31. 16). *Sold*: '¶Beneficia uestra: id est honores et magistratus. Nam populi Romani beneficium est: dare honores et magistratus quibuscunque uoluerit' (sig. i4[r]).

121–2 **onely bycause . . . inacted for them.** *Sal*: 'parandi iuris et maiestatis constituendae gratia' (31. 17) 'to assert their rights and establish their sovereignty'.

122–5 **And maisters . . . other lyberties also.** Barclay's addition. Cf. *Sold*: '¶Parandi iuris gratia: id est causa acquirendi iuris sui: ut plæbs ius suum haberet ex quo concessum est: plæbi: ut suos magistratus haberet sacrosanctos: qui eam defenderent' (sig. i4r).

136 **I wyll forsothe and counsel.** 'Indeed, I desire and advise'.

153–61 **without ye thynke . . . if ye be dysposed.** 'unless you think that these great men do not yet have sufficient power, or unless you show outwardly that you were more content with the time when a few nobles controlled everything, than now when you can maintain your liberty if you so wish'. *Sal*: 'Nisi forte nondum etiam uos dominationis eorum satietas tenet et illa quam haec tempora magis placent, cum regna, prouinciae, leges, iura, iudicia, bella atque paces, postremo diuina et humana omnia penes paucos erant' (31. 20).

161–4 **But in that season . . . fewe mighty men.** *Sal*: 'uos autem, hoc est populus Romanus, inuicti ab hostibus, imperatores omnium gentium, satis habebatis animam retinere' (31. 20). *Laet–BritT* and *AscT* omit *hoc est populus*, although *Sold* has it in the gloss.

169–71 **But as for me . . . is suffred vnpunysshed.** *Sal*: 'Atque ego, tametsi uiro flagitiosissumum existumo impune iniuriam accepisse' 'As for me, although I consider it most shameful for any man to suffer wrong without taking vengeance' (31. 21). Only a few MSS read *uiro*; most, like *AscT*, *Laet–BritT*, *BarcT*, read *uirum*, which Barclay's translation follows. *Asc* explains: 'At ego tametsi existimo virum flagitiosissimum: scilicet Iugurtham accepisse impune id est sibi condonatam sine punitione' (f. 59v).

172 **the wicked doers of this dede.** Bestia and Scaurus, who made peace with Jugurtha.

174–81 **For ye may se . . . of your hands.** *Sal*: 'Nam et illis, quantum importunitatis habent, parum est impune male fecisse, nisi deinde faciundi licentia eripitur, et uobis aeterna sollicitudo remanebit, cum intellegetis aut seruiundum esse aut per manus libertatem retinendam' (31. 22). Barclay seems to have misread *importunitatis* as *opportunitatis*. No extant edition has this error. The phrase *to do vnhappely* renders *male fecisse* 'to have acted evilly'.

199–203 **For the authorite . . . by Calphurnius the consull.** *Sal*: 'Hosti acerrumo prodita senatus auctoritas, proditum imperium uostrum est; domi militiaeque res publica uenalis fuit' (31. 25). Cf. *Sold* and in particular *Asc*: 'proditum .i. porro datum et in manus alterius: et res publica supple vestra venalis: domi id est cum de Iugurtha ageretur in senatu: et militiæ .i. cum res ageretur in expeditione militari in Aphrica' (f. 60r).

212–13 **Nor certes worthy cytesyns . . . yll than well.** *Sal*: 'Neque ego uos, Quirites, hortor ut malitis ciuis uostros perperam quam recte fecisse' 'Nevertheless, Romans, I do not wish to encourage you to prefer finding your fellow-citizens guilty rather than innocent' (31. 27).

221–4 **And moreouer if suche . . . to call for socoure nor helpe.** *Sal*: 'Ad hoc si iniuriae non sint, haud saepe auxili egeas' (31. 29).

224–5 **Thus it is better . . . vnpunysshed.** For Barclay's added summation cf. *Sold*: 'Alia etiam est ratio: quare melius est obliuisci beneficium quam iniuriam obliuisci: id est punire nocentes quam non remunerare bene meritos: quia si nocentes puniuntur: non sunt qui faciant iniuriam. Et si inuriæ non sunt: nunquam indigebis auxilio' (sig. i5^{v}).

Chapter 20

4 **Memmius counsellyng and inducynge often tymes.** *Sal*: 'saepe dicundo' (32. 1); MSS, *Laet–BritT*, *AscT*, *BarcT*: 'saepe indicendo' (*or* 'in dicendo').

6 **one of the chefe .x. iuges of Rome.** *Sal*: 'qui tum praetor erat' (32. 1). Cf. *Sold*: '¶Prætor erat: decem prætores Romæ creabantur qui ius populo dicerentur' (sig. i5^{v}). In fact there were only six praetors at this time, the number being increased later by Sulla and then Caesar.

11–12 **which had ben corrupted by hym before by money and rewardes.** *Sal*: 'quos pecuniae captae arcessebat' (32. 1); *Laet–BritT*, *AscT*, *BarcT*: 'arcessebant'. 'Whom he [Memmius] (or they) arraigned for the taking of bribes'.

Chapter 21

4 **the chefe of the soudyours.** i.e. 'the leaders of the army' *Sal*: 'qui . . . exercitui praeerant' (32. 2).

8–9 **which he had gyuen . . . bytwene them.** Barclay's addition. Cf. *Sold*: '¶Elephantes quos Iugurtha tradiderat Romanis in conditionibus pacis' (sig. i6^{r}). *Asc*: 'quos per simulatam deditionem quaestori dederat' (f. 60^{v}).

10–11 **the traytours . . . vnto the Romayns army.** *Sal*: 'perfugas' (32. 3). *Asc*: 'perfugas .i. qui defecerant a Numidis ad Romanos' (f. 60^{v}).

Chapter 22

6–8 **Whan the estates . . . marueylusly abasshed.** Barclay has shifted the sequence of events and the sense a little. *Sal*: 'At Cassius praetor, perlata rogatione a C. Memmio ac perculsa omni nobilitate, ad Iugurtham proficiscitur' (32. 5). That is to say, once the Senate passed the bill, Cassius set off to meet Jugurtha whilst the nobles were still in shock at the result, and presumably not sufficiently organized to prevent his departure.

10–13 **yet Cassius . . . mercy and pyte.** *without* is used as a conjunction 'unless' introducing a clause dependent upon the main clause (*yet Cassius aduysed hym and induced hym . . . to come vnto Rome*). The sense is: Cassius advised and induced Jugurtha to come to Rome, since he had surrendered, adding that he would do better to test the mercy of the Romans than their force.

14–15 **Cassius promysed also his owne fayth and trouth.** *Sal*: 'Priuatim praeterea fidem suam interponit' (32. 5).

17–18 **Cassius had so good a name at Rome** [*BarcB*, *C*: Rome that tyme]. Cf. *Sal*: 'ea tempestate' (32. 5).

24–31 **And nat withstandyng . . . among the other mo.** *Sal*: 'Ac tametsi in ipso magna uis animi erat, confirmatus ab omnibus', etc. (33. 2). Sallust may be paraphrased as follows: although Jugurtha was confident, nevertheless, urged and advised (*confirmatus*) by his partners in crime, he bribed and corrupted Gaius Bebius. Barclay may intend a different point: that although Jugurtha was confident, considering all the support he was receiving from his partners in crime, nevertheless he bribed Gaius Bebius. In the former, it is the friends who desire more assurance, in the latter, Jugurtha himself. *Laet–BritT* reads *confirmatus*. *Sold*: '¶Confirmatus: id est cohortatus' (sig. i6^{r}). *AscT*, however, reads *confirmato*. *Asc*: 'Ac tametsi magna vis animi .i. summa animositas erat in ipso confirmato ab omnibus .s. corruptis auro: quorum potentia aut scelere gesserat ea cuncta quæ diximus supra. (Quidam legunt confirmatus: vt sit ordo: tamen confirmatus ab omnibus etc. Sed non procedit: non enim quia confirmatus erat Bebium parat: sed quia in eo vis animi erat)' (ff. 60^{v}–61^{r}).

30 **one of the protectours of the commenty.** *Sal*: 'tribunum plebis' (33. 2).

31 **among the other mo.** Barclay's addition. *Other mo* may refer to Jugurtha's other corrupt supporters, but more likely to the other tribunes, whom Bebius would be able to influence or even veto. Cf. *Sold*: 'Tanta autem erat auctoritas unius tribuni plebis: ut unus prohibere posset ne fieret id quod reliqui omnes tribuni uellent' (sig. i6^{r}).

31–2 **By whose dyshonest and vnmesurable couetise.** *Sal*: 'cuius impudentia' (33. 2). *Asc*: 'impudentia: id est impudenti cupiditate' (f. 61^{r}).

34–40 **But the commenty . . . called togyder the commenty.** Barclay fails to indicate that the hostility of the commons is expressed at a meeting convened by Memmius, and that then, within the same meeting, he calms them. *Sal*: 'At C. Memmius aduocata contione' (30. 3) is displaced chronologically in Barclay's translation.

35–6 **to haue hym to prison and there to kepe hym in bandes.** *Sal*: 'in uincula duci' (33. 3). *Sold*: '¶In uincula: id est in carcerem' (sig. i6^{r}). *Asc* does not provide this gloss.

36–8 **acordyng to the lawe . . . their mortall ennemy.** *Sal*: 'more maiorum de hoste supplicium sumi' (33. 3). *More maiorum* means 'according to the customary practice' (of scourging and beheading).

43–6 **Thus dyde Memmius . . . rude commens.** One of several sentences in this chapter which essentially rephrase the previous, and repeat Sallust's sentence in an alternative form of words.

52–3 **as slayne Adherball . . . dysceyued . . . and wasted.** 'such as having slain . . . deceived . . . and wasted', etc.

56–8 **Wherfore . . . cruell dedes.** Barclay's recapitulation of what has already been stated.

63–4 **And also . . . of his ryches also.** *Sal*: 'sed se suasque spes corrupturum' (33. 4); *Laet–BritT*, *AscT*, *BarcT* (and early edns., e.g. 1473): 'sese et suas opes corrupturum'.

71 **with angry countenances.** *Sal*: 'uoltu' (34. 1). *Sold*: '¶Vultu .s. iracundo' (sig. i6^{v}); *Asc*: 'vultu: scilicet minaci parato ad vltionem præsentem' (f. 61^{r}).

75 **had in derysion and abused.** 'being held in derision and abused'. *Sal*: 'ludibrio habitus' (34. 2).

Chapter 23

1 **¶How Iugurth encreased his crueltie.** The chapter head echoes *Asc*: 'Commemorat quomodo nouo facinore Iugurtha discedere coactus sit innouata belli causa dicens' (f. 61^{v}).

7 **neuewe.** 'grandson' (see Glossary and note to 10/24). *Sal*: 'nepos' (35. 1).

14–16 **and counsayled hym . . . and cruelty.** 'Envy and fear' should be the subject of *greve*, rather than Massiva. Sallust says that Albinus advised Massiva to ask the Senate for the Numidian throne first because he was descended from Masinissa, and secondly because hatred and fear hung over Jugurtha for his crimes. *Sal*: 'Iugurthamque ob scelera inuidia cum metu urgeat' (35. 2). *Sold* and *Asc* gloss in accordance with the correct translation. *Sold*: 'Secunda ratio: quia Iugurtha eo tempore erat in summis angustiis propter scelera eius . . . ¶Vrgeat .i. premebat' (sig. k1^{r})

31–2 **by gyftes and rewardes.** *Sal*: 'pretio, sicuti multa confecerat' 'by the use of money, through which the king had already accomplished so much' (**35. 4**).

42 **vnware.** Probably parallel with *rasshely: with small prouysion or auysement*, and referring to the assassin, but possibly to be construed as referring to Massiva, who was taken by surprise.

48 **And nat withstandynge . . . good conscience.** That is to say, because Bomilchar enjoyed a form of diplomatic immunity as one of Jugurtha's protected retinue, the Romans had no legal right to try him. Yet given that Jugurtha could not be trusted to impose a penalty upon him, natural justice demanded that they take action. *Sal*: 'Fit reus magis ex aequo bonoque quam ex iure gentium Bomilcar, comes eius qui Romam fide publica uenerat' (**35. 7**). Cf. *Asc*: 'ex æquo et bono .i. quia æquum et bonum visum est: hoc est in foro conscientiæ visum est iustum' (f. 62^{r})

59–60 **he had brought in and layd .l. suerties of his frendes.** Jugurtha had given fifty of his friends as sureties for the attendance of Bomilchar at trial.

69 **after him commaunded of the senatours.** 'after he had been commanded by the senators to leave Italy'.

74–77 **O noble and famous cytie . . . gyue money for the.** *Sal*: 'urbem uenalem et mature perituram, si emptorem inuenerit' (**35. 10**). This famous taunt was cited by other classical writers, and begins *O urbem* in some MSS and edns. (but not *Laet–BritT*, *AscT*, *BarcT*) and in, for example, Livy *Perioch.* 64; Aug. *Ep.* 138. 16; Orosius *Hist.* 5. 15. 5; Flor. *Epit.* 1. 36. 18.

Chapter 24

5 **the warre agaynst Iugurth.** *Sal*: 'bello' (**36. 1**). *Sold*: 'bello .s. contra Iugurtham' (sig. $k1^{v}$).

6 **vytayls.** *Sal*: 'commeatum' (**36. 1**). *Sold*: '¶Commeatum: quem nunc uulgo uictualia uocant' (sig. $k1^{v}$).

13 **before the tyme of electyon of newe consuls.** *Sal*: 'ante comitia' (**36. 1**). *Asc*: 'ante comitia id est antequam noui eligerentur magistratus' (f. 62^{v}).

20 **he boldely withstode and defended hymselfe manly.** *Sal*: 'instare' (**36. 2**): perhaps even 'attacked'.

22 **he abused and mocked the consull.** *Sal*: 'consulem ludificare' (**36. 2**).

26–7 **rather by falshode and gyle than by cowardyse.** *Sal*: 'neque . . . socordia magis quam dolo' (**36. 3**). For Barclay's rendering of *socordia* as 'cowardice' rather than 'sloth, incompetence, weak-mindedness' or similar, cf. *Asc*: 'secordia .i. pusillanimitate et ignauia' (f. 62v); on the other hand, *Sold*: '¶Secordia .i. negligentia' (sig. k2r).

Chapter 25

7 **protectours of the commentie.** 'tribunes'.

17 **of their tentes.** *Sal*, MSS: 'ex hibernis' (**37. 3**); *Laet–BritT*, *AscT*, *BarcT*: 'ex tabernaculis'.

18–21 **Outher dyde he . . . with great treasoure.** This sentence is misplaced. Sallust orders his narrative as follows: Aulus, hearing of Albinus' delay, hoped that he could either end the war or force payment from Jugurtha by threat of his army ('aut conficiundi belli aut terrore exercitus ab rege pecuniae capiundae'), and accordingly called out the troops from winter quarters. *Asc*: 'ab rege .s. Iugurtha' (f. 63r).

26 **of nature.** 'by natural features': the town was defended well by the landscape around it.

32–6 **Yet this nat withstandyng . . . damage or paryll.** *Sal*: 'tamen aut simulandi gratia, quo regi formidinem adderet, aut cupidine caecus ob thesauros [*Laet–BritT*, *AscT*, *BarcT omit* ob thesauros] oppidi potiundi, uineas agere', etc. (**37. 4**). That is, despite the improbability of succeeding, Aulus began a siege, either because he wished to frighten Jugurtha by feigning an attack, or because he was blinded by avarice.

35–41 **pauayses about the walles . . . besygyng of a cyte or towne.** For Barclay's explanation of the procedures of siege warfare here compare his explanations in ch. 13 (*Sal* **21**), derived in part from the commentaries at that point (see note to l. 88). At this later point see *Asc*: 'vineas id est protectiones militum ex consertis scutis in morem vinearum quibus vtuntur in expugnatione murorum' (f. 63r). This may lie behind Barclay's odd *sheldes conioyned lyke vynes*.

40 **he made redy.** Barclay's translation reflects the variant reading *preparare* (*BarcT*, *AscT*, *Laet–BritT* **1497/8**) instead of *properare* 'hasten' (*mod. edns.*, all other *Laet–BritT* edns.).

44 **in derysion.** Barclay must mean Jugurtha's private derision or toying with his attacker, since publically he was feigning supplication and fear of defeat by Aulus. *Sal*: Iugurtha . . . subdole eius augere amentiam, missitare supplicantis legatos (**38. 1**).

53 **Aulus gaue vp the sygyng of the town of Suthull.** *Sal*: 'relicto Suthule' (**38. 2**). *Laet–BritT*, *AscT*, *BarcT*: 'Suthule relicto'. *Sold*: '¶Relicto Suthule .i. omissa obsidione et oppugnatione Suthulis' (sig. k2v).

54 **Iugurth as fleyng from him for drede.** Jugurtha, who acted as if fleeing in fear from him.

54–5 **places vnknowen to hym and his men.** *Sal*: 'abditas regiones' (38. 2). Perhaps *BarcA* was intended to read *places vnknowen and hid*. The reading in *B* may have been an authorized revision, however.

55–7 **Thus was the treason . . . lesse prouysion therfore**. *Sal*: 'ita delicta occultiora fore' (*or* 'fuere') (38. 2). *Asc*: 'ita id est per hoc delicta Auli fuere occultiora. hoc est magis latentia. vel dicebat ita delicta Auli fore occultiora quia exercitus nesciret quid ageretur' (f. 63r). Sallust's phrase has puzzled editors and commentators. Dietsch rejected it as a gloss. Paul, 113, notes: 'grammar forbids the ascription of these words to Jugurtha, and they do not make sense, if a comment by S[allust], for no *delicta* occurred. *Fore* (recentiores) does not help greatly, since even in the *abditae regiones* Aulus would be accompanied by the army. Whose observation would they escape? Excise as an interpolation.' Rolfe, however, retains the construction (with *fore*) and translates: 'thus, he [Iugurtha] suggested, any misconduct of the Roman's would be less obvious'.

57–65 **In the mean season . . . on one syde or other.** As punctuated in *BarcA B C*, the text makes poor sense. A punctus or a colon after *felawes* is necessary. In effect this whole passage forms one sentence. *Sal*, *Laet–BritT*: Interea per homines [*AscT*, *BarcT*: Interea Iugurtha per homines] . . . desererent' 'Meanwhile through cunning emissaries Jugurtha was working his tactics upon the Roman army day and night, bribing the officers of both infantry and cavalry either to desert immediately or to abandon their posts at a given signal' (38. 3).

63–4 **whan the trumpettes shulde blowe to batayle.** *Sal*: 'signo dato' (38. 3). *Sold*: '¶Signo dato .s. pugnæ per tubam. Nam tuba canitur cum milites in pugnam uadunt' (sig. k2v).

67 **Than about mydnight.** *Sal*: 'intempesta nocte' 'in the dead of night' (38. 4). *Sold*: '¶Intempesta nocte .i. media nocte' (sig. k2v).

69–72 **The Romayne soudyours . . . feare of this treason.** *Sal*: 'Milites Romani perculsi tumultu insolito' (38. 5). *Laet–BritT*, *AscT*, *BarcT*: 'Milites Romani perculsi insolito metu.' *Asc*: 'perculsi .i. stupefacti et attoniti: insolito metu: cum diu in ocio fuissent' (f. 63v). Barclay's *feare* renders *metu*. Although modern editors reject the reading *metu*, it does echo an idiosyncratic Sallustian usage. Sallust's use of *metus* to mean 'peril' (that which causes 'fear') is attested in his works, but outside them more commonly found in poetry than prose. (cf. note to 40/67–9 for an example.)

79–81 **Howbeit . . . drede and danger.** Barclay's expansion of *Sal*: 'trepidare omnibus locis' (38. 5). Modern editors of Sallust take the phrase as the end of the preceding sentence, but the punctuation in *Laet–BritT* and *AscT* places the phrase at the head of the following sentence (*vis magna hostium*). Barclay's translation reflects the latter patterning.

85–9 **For deth was instant . . . abyde to their auenture.** Barclay's addition.

90–1 **one bende or cohort of Lomberdes.** *Sal*: 'cohors una Ligurum' (38. 6). *Asc*: 'vna cohors Ligurum: qui Longobardi dicuntur' (f. 63v). The geographical correspondence is approximate: Liguria is south and west of the main region of Lombardy, as part of northern Italy later came to be named.

100–1 **insomoch that they trusted . . . handes or armour.** This phrase is Barclay's addition. It echoes a turn of phrase that Sallust uses later in the speech attributed to Sulla (107. 1): 'nec quemquam decere, qui manus armauerit, ab inermis pedibus auxilium petere' 'it was not seemly for anyone with weapons in hand to seek help from unarmed feet' (i.e. flee).

111–12 **Neuertheles he remembred . . . mannes besynesse.** *Sal*: 'tamen se [*Laet–BritT*, *AscT*, *BarcT*: tamen dicit se] memorem humanarum rerum' (38. 9). It is possible that *BarcA* should read *incertayn cases*. The reading of *BarcB* and *C* (*incertayn chances*) is an improvement, if Sallust's somewhat vague phrase is taken to refer to the vicissitudes of human affairs, as it is usually. Cf. *Asc*: 'tamen se memorem humanarum rerum quia dubiæ sunt: quia rerum vicissitudo est et fors omnia versat' (f. 63v).

120–1 **Neuertheless their myndes so wauered for drede of deth.** *Sal*: 'tamen quia mortis metu mutabantur' [*Laet–BritT*, *AscT*, *BarcT*: metu nutabant] (38. 10). Barclay's translation follows the latter reading. The phrase has puzzled editors and commentators, and the MSS and edns. give several different readings. That now generally preferred (with *mutabant* or *mutabantur*) is taken to mean that the Romans accepted the terms as the only alternative to death, which they feared.

Chapter 26

5–7 **Some bewayled . . . shamefull composicyon.** *Sal*: 'Pars dolere pro gloria imperi' (39. 1). *Sold*: '¶Pro gloria imperii: nam gloria imperii Romani in tam turpi fœdere maculata et uiolata esse uidebatur' (sig. k3r).

7–10 **And other vncustomed . . . of all their empyre.** *Sal*: 'pars insolita rerum bellicarum timere libertati' (39. 1). *Asc*: 'pars insolita .i. inconsueta rerum bellicarum .i. nesciens varias esse vicissitudines victoriarum in bello: timere .i. timebat. libertati .s. suæ aut ciuitatis .i. pro libertate ne amitteretur' (f. 64r).

23–8 **Wherfore (these thynges . . . nat conferme the same.** *Sal*: 'senatum de foedere consulebat' (39. 2). For Barclay's additions cf. *Asc*: 'consulebat senatum .i. rogabat senatum consilium de fœdere .i. an fœdus ratum haberet: et tamen .i. nihilominus quia satis sciebat senatum non probaturum' (f. 64r).

32–3 **of suche as were . . . other nacyons.** *Sal*: 'ab sociis et nomine Latino' (**39. 2**). Cf. note to ll. 89–95 below, and Sallust's use of similar formulae in **40. 2** and **42 1**. 'The Latin name' was used for Latin cities not incorporated into the Roman state (notably Praeneste and Tibus) and also for 'colonies' founded by Romans and Latins in various localities. The Latins possessed certain privileges not held by other *socii* or allies of Rome. *Sold*: '¶Homines Latini nominis .i. pro homines Latinos: quibus ciuitas Romana data erat .i. qui ciues Romani facti erant' (sig. $k4^r$).

43 **the protectours of the commenty.** *Sal*: 'tribunis plebis' (**39. 4**).

56–7 **of whom some were fled tretourously to Iugurth.** *Sal*: 'quos praeter fugam' (**39. 5**). Barclay has misunderstood Sallust, who is saying that the Roman army was demoralized by lack of discipline, not to mention their defeat and flight (*fugam*) from Numidia. *Sold* and *Asc* do not comment on the phrase, but seem to understand that it refers to the retreat.

64 **¶In the mean season whyle.** *Sal*: 'Interim Romae C. Mamilius Limetanus', etc. (**40. 1**). It is possible that *whyle* functions as a noun here, but more likely it is a conjunction, and the opening is subordinate to the main clause beginning *At Rome*, etc.

66–7 **Caius Manlius elect and lymited protectour of the commen people.** *Sal*: 'C. Mamilius Limetanus tribunus plebis' (**40. 1**). It appears that Barclay has apprehended *Limetanus* as the past participle *limitatus* 'appointed' which he renders with the participles *elect and limited*. The cognomen derives from the law Mamilius had passed to regulate boundaries (cf. Cicero, *Leg*. 1. 55). Barclay's error does not seem to result from editions of *Laet–BritT* or *AscT*, where the name is capitalized. In *BarcT* (*A* and *B*), however, *limitanus* is not capitalized. Cf. *Asc*: 'Caius Manlius: aut vt alii textus habent Caius Marullus Limitanus: seu Limetanus: tribunus plebis' (f. 64^v).

67–9 **assembled the commens . . . inquisicyon myght be made.** *Sal*: 'rogationem ad populum promulgat, uti quaereretur' (**40. 1**) 'proposed to the people a bill instituting an inquiry'. *Sold*: '¶Rogationem ad populum promulgat .i. petitionem uel legem populo proponit . . . populum conuocatum ita interrogat' (sig. $k3^v$).

71–6 **And against them which . . . armies ayenst hym.** *Sal*: 'quique ab eo in legationibus aut imperiis pecunias accepissent, qui elephantos quique perfugas tradidissent' (**40. 1**). *Laet–BritT*, *AscT*, *BarcT*: 'et qui tradidissent elephantos et perfugas: quique ab eo in legationibus aut imperiis pecunias accepissent'. Barclay omits mention of the deserters (*perfugas*) returned to Jugurtha, although the meaning is made clear by *Sold*: 'Nam qui in castris relicti sunt: elephantas et transfugas uendiderunt' (sig. $k3^v$). Cf. *Asc*: 'perfugas: qui ad fidem Romanorum perfugerant deserto Iugurtha' (f. 64^v).

89–95 **The princes . . . noble men and commens.** This is Barclay's addition. The Latins (cf. note to ll. 32–3 above) and other Italian allies could do little directly to hinder the bill, as they were not franchised until 89 BC. Cf. *Sold*: 'qui erant ciues Romani. Sed tamen nihil facere potuerunt. Nam rogatio perlata est et iussa' (sig. k3[v]). Barclay seems to suggest in his explanatory expansion that they took a conciliatory role. Sallust implies, rather, that those with commercial interests at stake in Numidia were coopted by the nobles to disrupt the proceedings by whatever covert means they could.

99 **agaynst whom the sayd inquisycion was ordayned.** *Sal*: 'cui mala illa parabantur' 'for whom it boded trouble' (Rolfe); 'against whom these severe measures were aimed' (Comber–Balmaceda) (**40. 3**).

101–19 **Wherfore whyle the remenant . . . thre pointes rehersed.** *Sal*: 'Igitur, ceteris metu perculsis, M. Scaurus, quem legatum Bestiae fuisse supra docuimus, inter laetitiam plebis et suorum fugam, trepida etiam tum ciuitate, cum ex Mamilia rogatione tres quaesitores rogarentur, effecerat uti ipse in eo numero crearetur' (**40. 4**). [*Laet–BritT*, *AscT*, *BarcT*: perculsis metu; fuisse *om.*; memoravimus *for* docuimus; *BarcT A*: trepidam etiam tunc ciuitatem.] On Barclay's additions see the next note. As a result of his insertion outlining the nature of the three articles, the syntax is confused. In effect, Sallust's sentence, already complex, has been split apart.

109–15 **to examyne the thre artycles . . . as was Iugurth.** Barclay's added explanation, suggesting that each of the three commissioners heard cases relating to one of the three articles, derives from *Sold* and *Asc*. Actually the setting up of three separate courts probably indicates merely that the number of cases needing to be heard was very large. *Sold*: '¶Tres quæstiones: prima questio erat: de his quorum consilio Iugurtha senatus decreta contempserant: et qui pecuniam ab eo acceperant. Secunda erat de his qui elephantos et transfugas uendiderant. Tertia de his qui pactiones de pace aut bello cum hostibus fecissent. ¶In eo numero .i. numero quæsitorum: obtinuerat: ut ex tribus quæsitoribus unus esset: nam opus erat: ut singuli quæsitores singulis inquisitionibus preessent. Nam quæsitores dicuntur qui de criminibus suspectis inquisitionem faciunt' (sig. k4[r]). *Asc*: 'rogarentur tres quæsitores .i. tres inquisitores de tribus inquisitionibus: quarum prima erat de his quorum consilio accepta pecunia Iugurtha decreta senatus contempserat. Secunda . . . Tertia . . .' (f. 64[v]).

115–16 **But nat withstandyng . . . noble men.** Barclay's addition. He errs in naming Calphurnius Bestia rather than Scaurus as one of the commissioners, or at the very least confuses the reader with the pronoun *he* which follows, if its reference is indeed Scaurus.

121–2 **after the commen rumour and pleasure of the commenty.** *Sal*: 'ex rumore et lubidine plebis' 'according to hearsay evidence and the commoners' caprice' (**40. 5**).

Chapter 27

3–5 **This maner of deuisyon . . . all other inconuenyences.** *Sal*: 'Ceterum mos partium et factionum ac deinde omnium malarum artium' (**41. 1**). *Laet–BritT*, *AscT*, *BarcT*, most MSS: 'Ceterum mos partium popularium et senatus factionum: ac deinde omnium malarum artium.'

7–8 **by superfluous habundance of richesse/ voluptuosyte/ and of other worldely delectacyons.** *Sal*: 'atque abundantia earum rerum' (**41. 1**). *Asc*: 'et abundantia earum rerum .s. diuitiarum et voluptatum' (f. 65^{r}).

8–9 **which many count and repute for moost chiefe pleasures of this lyfe.** *Sal*: 'quae prima mortales ducunt' (**41. 1**).

20–4 **So that they desyred . . . the warre was before.** *Sal*: 'Ita quod in aduorsis rebus optauerant otium, postquam adepti sunt, asperius acerbiusque fuit' [*AscT*, *BarcT*: acerbius asperiusque tulere] (**41. 4**). Even with re-punctuation, Barclay's construction is awkward. I take the initial *So* as emphatic 'thus', and the first *that* as introducing a noun clause, loosely coordinate with a second *that* noun clause, both preceding the main clause after the colon.

34–5 **For all the estates were all togyder assembled/ conioyned/ and unyed.** For this addition cf. *Sold*: 'quia magis erant uniti et coniuncti' (sig. $k4^{v}$).

37–8 **gettyng their lyueng . . . their bodyes.** *Sal*: 'plebis uis soluta atque dispersa in multitudine' (**41. 6**). Cf. *Sold*: '¶Soluta .i. disiuncta: quia pauperes ciues quærebant quotidie quomodo uictum sibi pararent: non quomodo diuitibus et nobilitati resisterent' (sig. $k4^{v}$).

56–65 **But at last . . . tempestyous wynde.** *Sal.* 'Nam ubi . . . oriri coepit' (**41. 10**). The sentence appears in *AscT*, *Laet–BritT*, but is omitted from *BarcT*.

59–60 **And were moued in myndes . . . socour their misery.** For this addition cf. *Sold*: 'uera gloria erat: dare operam: ut plæbs quæ pro rem publicam semper bella gerebat: non opprimeretur a nobilitate' (sig. $k4^{v}$).

63–5 **as it were drye dust . . . wynde.** *Sal*: 'quasi permixtio terrae oriri coepit' (**41. 10**). Modern editors take this as a comparison with an earth-quake, rather than a dust storm. For the latter cf. *Sold*: 'quemadmodum puluis turbari et suscitari solet turbine uenti commotus' (sig. $k5^{r}$). *Asc* explains: 'quasi permixtio terræ .i. quasi ex puluere concitato turbo fieret: aut quasi terræ motu orto omnia permiscerentur' (f. 65^{v}).

67 **progenytours.** *Sal*: 'maiores' (**42. 1**). *Asc*: 'maiores .i. progenitores' (f. 65^{v}).

68–9 **began to restore . . . olde lyberty.** *Sal*: 'uindicare plebem in libertatem . . . coepere' (42. 1). *Sold*: '¶Vindicare .i. trahere . . . sed ipsam plæbem seruitute oppressam in pristinam libertatem reuocare cupiebant' (sig. k5r). *Asc*: 'in libertatem .s. pristinam' (f. 65v).

69 **detect.** *Sal*: 'patefacere' 'expose, reveal' (42. 1).

69–70 **of the fewe iniuryous estates.** *Sal*: 'paucorum' (42. 1). Barclay seems to have conflated *paucorum* with *nobilitas noxia*, which belongs with the next clause, meaning 'the noblemen who were guilty', rather than 'the harmful noblemen'.

71 **chafedde with yre.** *Sal*: 'perculsa' 'daunted, terrified' (42. 1). *Sold*: '¶Perculsa: id est perterrita' (sig. k5r). *Asc*: 'perculsa .i. attonita' (f. 65v).

72 **in hope of promocion.** *Sal*: 'spes societatis' 'hope of an alliance' (42. 1). Cf. *Sold*: '¶Spes societatis: et quia equites sperabant se socios fore senatus in administratione totius rei publici. Nam senatus totam rem publicam in sua potestate habebat' (sig. k5r).

77–80 **whyle he was protectour . . . their ennemies.** Sallust states that one brother was a tribune and the other a commissioner for founding colonies. Both had held each office at one time or another, but if Sallust means the offices they held at the time of death, then he means that Tiberius died when Tribune, and Gaius when Commissioner. Barclay seemingly overlooks Tiberius and attributes both offices to Gaius, but omits to translate 'alterum triumuirum coloniis deducundis' (42. 1). For the explanatory addition (*such landes . . . ennemies*) cf. *Sold*: '¶Triumuirum coloniis deducendis: Quando agri publici ex hostibus capti pauperibus ciuibus Romanis diuidendi erant: tres uiri creabantur a populo: qui eos agros diuiderent' (sig. k5r).

85–9 **Neuerthelesse . . . hasty and besy.** *Sal*: 'Sed bono uinci satius est quam malo more iniuriam uincere' 'but a good man would prefer to be defeated rather than to triumph over injustice by establishing a bad precedent' (Rolfe) (42. 3). Sallust's highly compressed construction has been variously interpreted as a negative comment upon the Gracchi, who pursued their case immoderately; or upon the nobles, who should have shown restraint in the face of the Gracchi's righteous excesses. Barclay takes the latter interpretation, following *Sold*: 'Quamuis Gracchi immoderatum animum haberent: tamen melius erat ut nobilitas eos uincere permitteret: quam ut eos interficeret: et exemplum malum introduceret' (sig. k5v). *Asc* provides a similar explanation.

94 **cytees.** *Sal*: 'ciuitatis' 'states' (42. 4).

94–6 **whyle . . . And whyle.** To be taken as coordinate.

Chapter 28

12–13 **he was of fame . . . on both parties.** *Sal*: 'fama tamen aequabili et inuiolata' 'uniformly or consistently irreproachable of character' (43. 2). Barclay's expansion follows the glossators' interpretation of *aequabili*. *Sold*: 'tamen erat æquabili fama: quia Metellus æqualiter et similiter probatus erat apud populum: sicuti apud senatum' (sig. k5ᵛ). *Asc*: 'habenti famam equabilem .i. æqualiter ab vtriusque partibus' (f. 66ʳ).

27–30 **And shortly to speke . . . chargeable.** *Sal*: 'ad hoc commeatum affatim, denique omnia, quae in bello uario et multarum rerum egenti usui esse solent' 'and in short every thing which was likely to be of use in a war varied in its character, and demanding great resources' (43. 3).

30–6 **But suche as were . . . Metellus in his besynesse.** *Sal*: 'Ceterum ad ea patranda senatus auctoritate, socii nomenque Latinum et reges ultro auxilia mittundo, postremo omnis ciuitas summo studio adnitebatur' 'Furthermore, to assist in these preparations, the allies and Latins, by the appointment of the senate, and certain kings of their own accord, sent troops and supplies; and in short the whole state exerted itself with the greatest zeal' (43. 4). Some modern editors take *senatus* as nominative rather than genitive, placing it in apposition with *socii*, *nomen Latinum*, *reges*, and *omnis civitas*. *Laet–BritT*, *AscT*, *BarcT* (ed. *A*) read *ultro auxilia mittere*, where *mittere* stands for *mittebant*, and terminates a main clause (the phrase is omitted in *BarcB*). Barclay's rendering is perhaps improved with the removal of *and by* from the phrase *and by the Latynians*, but difficulties with the syntax remain.

33 **strange kynges.** 'foreign kings'. Cf. *Sold*: '¶Et reges: qui erant socii populi Romani: sicuti sunt: Eumenes: Ariobarzanes rex et multi alii' (sig. k6ʳ). *Asc*: 'et reges .s. externi et socii atque amici Romano imperio' (66ᵛ).

41–4 **For before his departynge . . . wasted and demynisshedde.** *Sal*: 'et auaritia magistratuum ante id tempus in Numidia nostrae opes contusae hostiumque auctae erant' (43. 5).

46 **by Albynus.** *Sal*: 'a Sp. Albino proconsule' (44. 1).

46–7 **vncrafty/ sluggysshe/ and feble.** *Sal*: 'iners, inbellis' (44. 1); *Laet–BritT*, *AscT*, *BarcT*: 'iners, imbecillis'.

52 **without authorite or maners.** *Sal*: 'sine imperio et modestia' (44. 1).

53–4 **for suche corrupt and vycious maners.** *Sal*: 'ex malis moribus' (44. 2). *BarcT* (*A*, *B*) and editions of *AscT* from 1514.1 read 'ex malis maioribus', but Barclay is aware of the correct reading here, from *Asc* gloss and *Laet–BritT*. The virgule after *besynesse* should not be taken as a clause separator. The sense is: Metellus had more anxiety about the indiscipline of the troops than he had comfort from their increased numbers.

60–1 **with besynesse and labour . . . before his tyme.** *Sal*: 'maiorum disciplina' (44. 3). Cf. *Sold*: 'ad normam ueteris discipline reuocasset' (sig. k6^{r}). *Asc*: 'disciplina .i. ex disciplina et institutis maiorum .i. veterum imperatorum' (f. 67^{r}).

61–8 **For why . . . to remoue.** *Sal*: 'Nam Albinus Auli fratris exercitusque clade perculsus, postquam decreuerat non egredi prouincia, quantum temporis aestiuorum in imperio fuit, plerumque milites statiuis castris habebat, nisi' etc. [*Laet–BritT*, *AscT*, *BarcT*: (in) statutis castris]. 'For Albinus, shocked by the disaster of his brother Aulus and his army, and having resolved not to leave the province during the part of summer that he was in command, had kept the soldiers, for the most part, in a permanent camp' (44. 4). Barclay's structure mirrors that of the Latin. He regularly translates *castra* 'fortified camp' with *tentes* (cf. note to 13/73).

68–9 **Nor accordynge . . . was no watche.** *Sal*: 'Sed neque muniebantur ea neque more militari uigiliae deducebantur' (44. 5). Most MSS, *Laet–BritT*, *AscT*, and *BarcT* omit *neque muniebantur ea*, which accounts for Barclay's omission of the observation that no fortifications were constructed around the camp.

71 **from their standardes.** *Sal*: 'ab signis' 'from duty' (44. 5). *Sold* (sig. k6^{v}) and *Asc* point out the origin of the figure of speech: 'a signis .i. vexillis' (f. 67^{r}). *ab signis* is omitted in the early edns. of *AscT* (1504.1–1513.1), although it appears in the gloss; it is restored in the 1514.1 edition and appears in *BarcT*.

71–2 **scolyons/ and pages.** *Sal*: 'lixae' (44. 5). The sutlers, cooks, servants, and other camp followers. *Asc*: 'Lixæ .i. baiuli aquarum qui a veteribus lixæ dicebantur vnde elixum dicitur quicquid aqua mollitur et decoquitur: vnde et lixiuium et elixas .i. in aqua decoctas carnes dicimus: erant autem vilissimi vt nunc quoque sunt' (f. 67^{r}). Cf. note to 28/99 below.

72–3 **among the horsemen and chiefe of the soudyours.** *Sal*: 'cum militibus' (44. 5). *Laet–BritT*, *AscT*, *BarcT*: 'cum equitibus'.

74–5 **fyghtynge agaynst . . . cytees nor townes.** *Sal*: 'uillas expugnare' (44. 5). *Asc*: 'et expugnare .i. expugnabant: non castella aut oppida: sed villas .i. domos rusticas' (f. 67^{r}).

82–3 **the whete . . . amonge them in commen.** *Sal*: 'frumentum publice datum' 'grain allotted to them by the state' (44. 5). *Asc*: 'frumentum datum publice .s. ab imperatore in menses singulos' (f. 67^{r}).

90–3 **he whiche in myddes . . . fautes.** *Sal*: 'comperior; [*Laet–BritT*, *AscT*, *BarcT*: comperio:] tanta temperantia inter ambitionem saeuitiamque moderatum' (45. 1). Barclay apparently takes *ambitionem* and *saeuitiam* to refer to the soldiers of Metellus' army. Sallust means that Metellus steered a middle course between 'ambition' (hoping to win popularity with the soldiers by relaxing discipline) and 'severity' (treating them too harshly). *Moderatum* (from *moderor*): supply *esse* (all clauses down to *modum statiusse* being governed by the opening archaic deponent *comperior* 'I find' (or by the more common active form *comperio*). *Sold* correctly explicates, and cf. *Asc*: 'tanta .i. tam insigni et præstanti temperantia inter ambitionem .i. cupiditatem dignitatis et magistratuum: ad quos fere ambientes .i. populo supplicantes et obsequentes perueniunt. et sæuitia .i. rigorem nimis seuerum' (f. 67^{r}).

98–9 **saue the commen prouicyon.** Barclay's addition, presumably referring to the statutary ration of *frumentum*.

99 **pages/ waterlaggers/ and scolyons.** *Sal*: 'lixae' (**45. 2**). *Asc*: 'lixæ .i. aquarum baiuli et in cæteris etiam militum ministri' (f. 67^{v}). Cf. note to 28/71 above.

100–2 **That none of the commen . . . place to place.** *Sal*: 'ne miles gregarius in castris neue in agmine seruum aut iumentum haberet' (**45. 2**). For *tentes* cf. note to 13/73. The omission of *or army* in *BarcB C* perhaps indicates the obsolescence of the sense 'armed expedition' for *army*, as Barclay apparently uses it.

104–5 **all other fautes he mesured by his wysdome/ craft/ and policy.** *Sal*: 'ceteris arte modum statuisse' 'and he set strict controls on other abuses' (Comber–Balmaceda); 'and he set a strict limit on other practices of the kind' (Rolfe) (**45. 2**). Most modern editors read *arte* as the adverb 'strictly', but some have taken it as ablative of means from *ars*, here meaning 'skilfully'. This is Barclay's reading. *Asc* only glosses *modum*: 'modum .i. mensuram et moderationem' (f. 67^{v}).

106–7 **and that nat in wayes . . . vnoccupyed wayes.** *Sal*: 'transuorsis itineribus' 'with cross-country marches' (**45. 2**). *Sold*: '¶Transuersis itineribus: quia exercitum ducebat: non per uias publicas et rectas: sed ex transuerso per loca insueta: et uias ignotas' (sig.k.6^{v}). *Asc*: 'itineribus transuersis .i. non per vias stratas: sed ex transuerso per agros et arua' (f. 67^{v}).

108–10 **He caused them daylie . . . rest and ydlenesse.** The latter explanatory clause is Barclay's own. *Laet–BritT*, *AscT*, *BarcT* omit Sallust's preceding clause: 'iuxta ac si hostes adessent' 'just as if the enemy were close by' (**45. 2**). It does appear in *Sold* gloss, however.

110 **often watch.** 'frequent watch': changed in *BarcC* to *ouermuche watch*. *Sal*: 'uigilias crebras' 'numerous guards, set at short intervals' (**45. 2**).

113 **compasynge about the army on euery syde.** Barclay's construction is ambiguous. The participle *compasynge* may be read with *he* (Metellus) as its antecedent, or *the watches*. The latter seems more natural for the English, but *Sal* indicates the former: 'et eas [uigilias] ipse cum legatis circumire' (**45. 2**).

120–4 **he confermed and sette . . . offences with crueltie.** *Sal*: 'Ita prohibendo a delictis magis quam uindicando exercitum breui confirmauit' 'thus by keeping them from wrong-doing, rather than by punishing them, he soon restored the army's effectiveness' (**45. 3**). Barclay's construction seems mixed and awkward. Perhaps *or* is to be read as meaning 'over, rather than, before' (see Glossary), if not emended to *than*. Douglas Gray suggests reading 'nor' for 'or' (personal comment).

Chapter 29

7–10 **and also whan . . . lyke other before.** *Sal*: 'simul de innocentia eius certior Roma factus' (**46. 1**). For Barclay's expansion cf. *Sold*: '¶Innocentia .i. integritate: quia Metellus pecuniis corrumpi non poterat' (sig. l1^{r}). *Asc*: 'factus certior id est edoctus Romæ: hoc est cum Rome ageret: de innocentia id est de integritate et incorruptione eius .s. Metelli' (f. 67^{v}).

13–14 **a true composytion . . . gyle/ or dysceyt.** *Sal*: 'ueram deditionem' (**46. 2**). *Asc*: 'deditionem veram .i. non fictam nec simulatam' (f. 67^{v}).

19–20 **by often experyence and profe.** *Sal*: 'experimentis' (**46. 3**). *Asc*: 'experimentis .i. per experientiam' (f. 67^{v}).

25 **And whan he knewe . . . his mynde.** *Sal*: 'postquam opportunos sibi cognouit' 'when he found that they could be used for his plan' (**46. 4**).

33 **as his pleasure was.** *Sal*: 'ex uoluntate' (**46. 4**). Barclay's construction seems to apply the phrase to Metellus, whereas Sallust intends it to refer to Jugurtha: 'he directed that they take back a reply that would satisfy the king's wishes'.

35–6 **his hoost moost redy and contrary to Iugurth.** *Sal*: 'intento atque infesto exercitu' (**46. 5**). *Sold*: '¶Intento .i. parato atque infesto .i. aduerso' (sig. l1^{r}).

38 **vyllages and cotages.** *Sal*: 'tuguria' (**46. 5**). *Asc*: 'tuguria .i. villae ac domus rurales' (f. 68^{r}).

39–42 **and euery where . . . defence nor socoure.** Barclay's addition, somewhat awkwardly grafted into the sentence. Perhaps a punctus should follow *fere*. Both *AscT* and *Laet–BritT* punctuate Sallust rather misleadingly, with a stop before *ubi* rather than before *ex oppidis* in **46. 5**. Cf. *Asc*: 'contra faciem .i. speciem belli quia a facie belli in aduentu inimici omnes aufugere solent. et pecora et cultores erant in agris' (f. 68^{r}).

43–4 **townes/ vyllages/ and lodges.** *Sal*: 'oppidis et mapalibus' (**46. 5**). *Sold*: '¶Mapalibus .i. domibus pastoralibus. Nam ut supra dixit ædificia agrestium mappalia dicebantur' (sig. l1^{r}).

55–65 **Wherfore Metellus . . . their ennemies.** Although *Sold* and *Asc* provide quite extensive explanations of the Roman hollow square formation, and the equipment belonging to the different kinds of soldiers that Sallust mentions, Barclay adds little to Sallust's account. He omits translation of 'tribunis legionum et praefectis cohortium' 'to the tribunes of the legions and the prefects of the cohorts', which describes the officers to whom command of the flanking troops was assigned (**46. 7**).

55–6 **Wherfore Metellus thus mysdemyng kept hymselfe in the forwarde of the batayle.** *Sal*: 'Itaque ipse . . . apud primos erat' (**46. 7**). *Sold*: '¶Itaque: quia timebat insidias Metellus' (sig. l1r). The *forwarde of the batayle* is the vanguard: see Glossary *s.v.* **batayle**.

57–8 **soudyours apoynted in lyght harnes.** *Sal*: 'expeditis cohortibus' (**46. 7**). *Sold*: '¶Expeditis .i. cum cohortibus leuis armaturæ. Nam cohortes expeditæ dicebantur cohortes leuis armaturæ quæ grauibus armis non erant impeditæ: ut clipeo et galea: sed expeditæ et leues ad cursum tela missilia gerebant' (sig. l1r). *Asc*: 'cohortibus expeditis hoc est leuis armaturæ quæ hastilia hoc est iacula gerentes: et aggredi et regredi celeriter poterant' (f. 68r).

63–4 **were mengled bowmen . . . pykes/ and iauelyns.** *Sal*: 'permixti uelites' (**46. 7**). *Laet–BritT*, *AscT*, *BarcT*: 'uelites permixti'. *Sold* (citing Festus):' ¶Permixti uelites. Velites: Rorarii: et Ferentarii idem sunt' (sig. l1r). *Asc*: 'velites .s. rorarii et ferentarii .i. leuis armaturæ milites ab helistein .i. circumflectendo dicti' (f. 68r).

71–2 **moche acustomed . . . strange countreis.** *Sal*: 'ubi et incolere et mercari [*Laet–BritT*, *AscT*, *BarcT*: mercari res] consueuerant Italici generis multi mortales' (**47. 1**). Perhaps *acustomed* renders *mercari* 'to trade', and means 'visited or used for commercial purposes'. See Glossary.

74–85 **Metellus drewe hym . . . in peace.** *Sal* **47. 2** has puzzled editors and commentators. Various manuscript readings have been preferred, or emendations suggested; and Sallust's meaning has been disputed. With some repunctuation (removal of the punctus after *resortyng thyder*), Barclay's translation selects from the possible interpretations set out by *Sold* and *Asc*. *BarcT* follows *AscT*: 'Huic consul simul tentandi gratia et capiundi [*Laet–BritT omits* et capiundi] (si paterentur oportunitates loci) presidium imposuit. Præterea imperauit frumentum et alia quæ bello vsui forent comportare: ratus (id quod res monebat) frequentiam negociatorum et commeatum et iam paratis rebus munimento fore.' The translation incorporates the phrase *iuuaturum exercitum* (after *commeatu*), which *Laet–BritT*, *AscT*, *BarcT* omit, but which *Asc* mentions in his commentary (f. 68v), and which modern editors retain.

75–80 **This dyd he . . . the same garnyson.** For this expansion cf. *Asc*: 'quia si presidium recusassent: declarassent se hostes: et supple simul gratia capiundi: si presidium admittere nollent (Est autem vt sæpe dixi: presidium guarnyson vulgo dictum)' (f. 68v).

85–9 **But whan the citezins . . . garnyson and retynue.** Barclay's addition, in which he makes more explicit what is implied in the sentence preceding. Cf. *Asc*: 'ad mandata suscipienda dispositis .i. putans quod propter commeatum comportatum negociatores et Vaccenses ciues facilius reciperent presidium: quod forte ob penuriam victus recusare potuissent' (f. 68ᵛ).

95–100 **to the other embassadours . . . graunted and agreed.** *Sal*: 'priores' (47. 4). *Sold*: '¶Vti priores: sicut priores legatos. Nam supra dixit: Metellum cum legatis Iugurthæ tractuisse de proditione. ¶Promissa legatorum expectare: expectabat id quod promiserant legati: uidelicet ut sibi tradaretur Iugurtham uel uiuam uel mortuum' (sig. l1ᵛ).

100 **pardicyon.** Possibly a misspelling of *prodicyon* 'betrayal', but perhaps to be read as a variant spelling of *perdicyon* 'destruction'. The latter part of the sentence is Barclay's addition, but echoes the reference to *prodycion* (L. perditionem) two sentences earlier.

103 **with his owne craftes of subtylte.** *Sal*: 'suis artibus' (48. 1). *Sold*: '¶Artibus .s. dolis et fraudibus' (sig. l1ᵛ).

107–8 **his greattest towne . . . lost from hym.** *Sal*: 'urbs maxuma alienata' (48. 1). *Sold*: 'maximam urbem .s. Vaccam . . . ¶Alienata .i. amissa' (sig. l1ᵛ). *Asc*: 'Urbs maxima .s. Vacca: alienata a se hoc est ab Iugurtha' (f. 68ᵛ).

108–9 **his ennemyes . . . countrey of Numidy.** *Sal*: 'ager hostibus cognitus' (48. 1). *Asc*: 'ager cognitus hostibus per frequentationem' (f. 68ᵛ). By *coostes* Barclay means regions (see Glossary).

109–10 **The myndes of his lordes . . . agaynst hym.** *Sal*: 'animi popularium temptati' (48. 1). Barclay's expansion of *popularium* to *lordes and commens* seems to conflate the explanations offered in the commentaries. *Sold*: '¶Animi popularium .i. animi hominum uulgarium et infimorum. Nam popularis est: qui a populo amatus est: popularis ciuis est: popularis humilis: popularis uilis. ¶Tentati: id est sollicitati' (sig. l1ᵛ). *Asc*: 'et animi popularium .i. fautorum vtpote legatorum tentati .s. ad proditionem' (f. 68ᵛ).

114 **to submytte hymselfe.** Why *BarcB* incorporates the change to 'to meke nor submitte hymselfe' is unclear. The last clause is Barclay's addition.

Chapter 30

5–7 **hauyng hope of vyctorie . . . place and countrey.** The repetition of *place* is awkward, and possibly in need of emendation. The punctuation of *BarcA* is wrong, and *B* corrects it by replacing the punctus after *some place* with a colon, thereby making *where . . . countrey* a modifier of *some place*; but the repetition of *place* is still awkward. If *intended* is taken to mean 'made his way, directed his course', then it seems possible to omit either *of some place* or alternatively *of place and countrey*.

8–9 **by hylles/ narowe passages and bypathes.** *Sal*: 'per tramites occultos' (48. 2). *BarcA*, *B* read *by pathes* (i.e. with word separation); *BarcC* reads *bypaths*. Either to be construed as the noun *path* with repetition of the preposition *by*, or as the compound form *by-path*.

9 **preuented and ouerpassed.** That is, overtook. *Sal*: 'anteuenit' (48. 2). *Asc*: 'anteuenit .i. preuenit' (f. 69r).

15–16 **of equall dystance in length.** *Sal*: 'tractu pari' (48. 3). That is to say, the hill-range and river ran parallel, with about twenty Roman miles between them. *Sold*: '¶Tractu pari .i. pari longitudine' (sig. l2r).

16–18 **The grounde . . . but desert.** *Sal*: 'uastus ab natura et humano cultu' (48. 3); *Laet–BritT*, *AscT*, *BarcT*: 'et humano cultu alienatus'.

18–21 **About the myddes . . . grounde.** *Sal*: 'Sed ex eo medio quasi collis oriebatur in immensum pertingens, uestitus oleastro ac murtetis aliisque generibus arborum quae humi arido atque harenoso [*Laet–BritT*, *AscT*, *BarcT*: humo arida atque arenosa] gignuntur' 'from about the middle of this range an elevation branched off and extended for a long distance [that is, a spur extended at right angles from the main range, towards the river], clothed with wild olive, myrtles, and other varieties of trees which grow in a dry and sandy soil' (Rolfe) (48. 3). Barclay seems to be saying that the hill was of great height (*of an vnmesurable heght*, translating *immensum*?), but his sentence should probably be interpreted as saying that the tree-cover was high, or extended high up the side of the hill. *Sold* seems correctly to understand that *Sal* describes a long spur; but *Asc* differs, and his explanation seems to lie behind Barclay's version: 'ex eo medio .i. ex medio eius montis: pertingens .i. porrectus in altum: in immensum .i. sine mensura facili vestitus .i. coopertus' (f. 69r). Barclay may be using *pendant* as a noun 'slope' (cf. 12/11–14, and 29/27, 67), or as a participle 'hanging, attached, arising out of' (cf. *Sal*: 'oriebatur').

27 **ouerthwart the valey.** *Sal*: 'transuorso itinere' (49. 1). Some editors take the phrase to mean across the Romans' line of march; others as at right angles to the river and mountain, as Barclay does. *Asc*: 'porrectum .i. extensum a monte: itinere transuerso: quia ex medio eius sumpto' (f. 69r).

29–30 **he made his frende Bomylchar capytayne and gouernour.** *Sal*: 'Bomilcarem praefecit' (49. 1). *Asc*: 'et praefecit Bomilcharem amicum et propinquum suum' (f. 69r).

31–2 **infourmed . . . shulde behaue hymselfe.** *Sal*: 'edocet quae ageret' '[Jugurtha] told him what his [Jugurtha's] plan was' (Rolfe); 'gave him instructions as to what he [Bomilcar] had to do' (Comber–Balmaceda) (49. 1). *Sold*: '¶Quæ ageret .i. quæ agere deberet' (sig. l2r).

32–4 **them whom he had commytted . . . to the poynt.** Barclay's addition. Cf. *Asc*: 'inito aut ineundo prælio' (f. 69^r).

37–8 **euery company/ cohort/ and bende syngulerly.** *Sal*: 'singulas turmas et manipulos' (**49. 2**). Both *Sold* and *Asc* (f. 69^r) explain the nature of *turma* (cavalry unit) and *manipulus* (company of foot soldiers). Barclay blurs the distinction.

43–4 **with such as they before had ouercome and subdued.** *Sal*: 'quos antea uictos sub iugum miserint' 'those [Romans] who had been defeated previously and sent under the yoke' (**49. 2**).

44–6 **And howbeit . . . was nat chaunged.** The new *captayne* is Metellus. *Sal*: 'ducem illis, non animum mutatum' (**49. 2**). *Sold*: '¶Non animum: quia quamuis nouum acceperint ducem: tamen pristinum animum retinent: uidelicet ignauum et timidum' (sig. l2^r). *Asc*: 'non animum: quia iterum fugituri essent' (f. 69^v).

48–50 **He declared . . . vncrafty cowardys.** Barclay's rendering is rather loose. *Sal*: '[dicit] locum superiorem, ut prudentes cum imperitis, ne pauciores cum pluribus aut rudes cum belli [MSS, *Laet–BritT*, *AscT*, *BarcT*: bello] melioribus manum consererent' '[he said] they would fight on higher ground and having the element of surprise as advantage over men taken unawares [*or* having knowledge of the terrain as advantage over men unfamiliar with it]; and they would not be fighting as a smaller force against a larger, nor as men inexperienced in war against those better trained' (**49. 2**).

53 **establysshe.** *Sal*: 'confirmaturum' (**49. 3**). *Asc*: 'confirmaturum: supple esse .i. stabiliturum omnes labores .s. inceptos et victorias .s. obtentas' (f. 69^v). Here Barclay uses *establysshe* to mean 'crown, cap, fix permanently, secure for all time'.

65–7 **Metellus nought knowyng . . . the great hyll.** *Sal*: 'Metellus, ignarus hostium, monte degrediens cum exercitu conspicatur' [MSS, *Laet–BritT*, *AscT*, *BarcT*: conspicitur] (**49. 4**). Barclay is right to translate *conspicitur* as *aperyd*. Cf. *Sold*: 'Ecce Metellus cum exercitu apparere incepit' (sig. l2^v). *Asc*: 'conspicitur .s. a Iugurtha cum exercitu' (f. 69^v). However, following Havercamp, Kritzius, and Dietsch (on the authority of Donatus *Ad Ter. Eun.* 2. 3), many editors read the deponent *conspicatur*, meaning 'Metellus saw the enemy'.

67 **which seyng.** The subject antecedent is Metellus. *BarcB*, *C* rightly shift the place of *at first* (*Sal*: 'primo' (**49. 4**)).

80 **he ordayned as it were a forwarde.** He deployed [the wing] as if it were a vanguard. That is, because expecting it to bear the brunt of an attack.

80–2 **enforced with a threfolde subsidy . . . whan nede shuld be.** *Sal*: 'triplicibus subsidiis aciem instruxit' (**49. 6**). Sallust probably means that three lines of reserves were placed behind the front line, although some editors argue that he describes how the right wing was placed in an array of three lines.

86–8 **where as after . . . so requyred.** Barclay's explanatory comment here condenses information from *Sold*, including: 'Nunc dicit Metellum in ea parte quæ hostibus erat uicina subsidia triplicia collocasse. Funditoresque et sagitarios: qui in prima acie locari consueuerant: inter manipulos diuisisse' (sig. l2^v^).

89–90 **in the extremytees . . . of the batayle.** *Sal*: 'in cornibus' 'on the wings' (**49. 6**). *Asc*: 'in cornibus .i. angulis aciei' (f. 70^r^).

92–7 **but bycause Iugurth . . . and the flodde.** *Sal*: 'transuorsis principiis in planum deducit' 'he led the army down onto the plain, with the front changed into a flank' (**49. 6**). *Sold*: '¶Aciem. Exercitus ad pugnam instructus dicitur acies. ¶Transuersis principiis. Vide quid dicat. Metellus de monte descendebat: Iugurtha autem in colle consederat: qui ex transuerso montis nascebat. Metellus igitur de monte descendens aciem instructam dirigebat non contra collem et contra Iugurtham: sed per transuersum: uersus flumen quod distabat a monte uiginti millibus passuum. ¶Principiis: dixi iam ante quod principia dicuntur milites qui in secunda acie locantur' (sig. l2^v^). *Asc*: 'deducit aciem in planum .s. locum sicuti instruxerat supple eam .i. saluis ordinibus iam instructis: et hoc principiis .s. aciei supple incedentibus transuersis .i. ex transuerso: ad insultum hostium deprimendum. nam a latere erant dextro' (f. 70^r^).

99–100 **he consydred the hete and faruentnes of the somer season.** *Sal*: 'ueritus ex anni tempore' [*Laet–BritT*, *AscT*, *BarcT*: ex anni tempore veritus] (**50. 1**) *Sold*: '¶Veritus ex anni tempore: quia erat estas: quo tempore rarius pluit' (sig. l3^r^). *Asc*: 'ex tempore anni (quia in æstate erat)' (f. 70^r^).

115 **which alway remoued forward first of all his army.** That is, the army moved towards the river with Metellus and his horsemen in the lead, but could halt and face right towards the Numidians, with the right flank then forming the van, and Metellus' cavalry the left flank. Marius, effectively in the centre of the formation, would then be in a position to command the front line once the formation faced to the right.

Chapter 31

8 **he dyd the trumpettes to be blowen.** *Sal*: 'signo dato' (**50. 3**).

15–17 **The Romayns . . . the vncertayne batell.** *Sal*: 'quorum etiam qui firmioribus animis obuii hostibus fuerant, ludificati incerto proelio' (**50. 4**). That is, even those of the Romans who most firmly stood their ground were baffled by the unfamiliar method of fighting.

23–5 **they shulde nat kepe . . . another there.** *Sal* does not specify that the Numidians were instructed to attack in this manner, merely that they should disperse and withdraw when under counterattack. Barclay's expansion seems a reasonable inference, nevertheless.

25–9 **And where . . . from their company.** *Sal*: 'Ita numero priores [*Laet–BritT*: plures], si ab persequendo hostis deterrere nequiuerant, disiectos ab tergo aut lateribus circumueniebant' (**50. 6**). *Bycause* and *therfore* form a causal construction: even if the Numidians could not withstand the Romans' pursuit of them, nevertheless, because they outnumbered the Romans, they were able to cut off and surround stragglers, in the rear or on the flanks, who had been separated from their formation.

29–30 **any of them to fle.** That is, the Numidians.

40–1 **the batayle on both sydes.** *Sal*: 'facies totius negoti' 'the aspect of the whole business' (**51. 1**). Sallust refers to the Romans' point of view here, not that of both sides, and proceeds to describe the confusion specifically within the Roman ranks. Barclay follows *Sold*: '¶Dispersi .s. tam Romani quam Iugurthini: nam nec Romani nec Iugurthini ordines seruabant' (sig. l3^{v}).

42–6 **for the best men . . . sonest ouerthrowen.** Barclay's addition; cf. *Asc*: 'miserabilis: quia etiam boni cadebant' (f. 70^{v}).

46–50 **Some which were deuyded . . . eyther partie manly.** *Sal*: 'Dispersi [*Laet–BritT*, *AscT*, *BarcT*: diuersi] a suis pars cedere [*BarcT1*, *2*: sedere], alii insequi' 'removed from their comrades, some gave way, others attacked' (**51. 1**). Barclay appears to say that some surrendered. He may be using *yelde* reflexively to mean 'remove oneself' (see Glossary), but this would be the only example of such usage in the text, and the more familiar sense 'give up, surrender' is frequently employed. The commentators make no mention of surrender. *Sold*: 'cedere significat cedebat .i. retrocedebat: et retrahebat se' (sig. l3^{v}). *Asc*: 'cedere .i. cedebant: hoc est locum dabant' (f. 70^{v}). Accordingly there may be two *parties* of Romans. That is, whether they withdrew or attacked, the scattered Romans regrouped to continue fighting. It could be that *they* refers to those on both sides, and that when they take a stand, *eyther partie*, that is, both Numidians and Romans, fought bravely. In the following sentence, however (*None of both parties kept vnder their standerdes* . . . 'neque signa neque ordines observare'), Sallust is certainly referring to the Romans only, but Barclay's account is less clear. The picture of general confusion that he draws can reasonably be inferred from what Sallust says in the remainder of the sentence.

54–6 **And so the armour . . . mengledde togyder.** *Sal*: 'arma tela, equi uiri, hostes atque ciues permixti' (**51. 1**). Sallust makes a series of paired contrasts, the first of which is, presumably, arms used at close quarters and those thrown from a distance. Barclay echoes *Asc*: 'Et ita arma .s. defensiua: tela quæ de longe iaciuntur et sunt inuasiua' (f. 70^{v}). Here as elsewhere he employs the word *armour* with the sense of 'arms, weapons'. There seems little doubt that by *hostes atque cives* Sallust meant Numidians and Romans. Barclay's addition *of soudyours / and pages* may derive from the gloss of *Asc* which is confusingly rendered in later printings: 'hostes .s. Romanis atque ciues .s. Romani' (**1504.1**, **1506.2**); 'hostes scilicet Romanos' (**1511.2**); 'hostes .s. Romani' (**1519**), perhaps taking this to mean Roman combatants and non-combatants; or perhaps it is simply his own addition. *Sold*: '¶Arma: tela: equi uiri: hostes ciues permixti .s. erant. ostendit omnia fuisse confusa' (sig. l3^{v}).

63 **At last both parties.** *Sal*: 'Denique, omnibus' (**51. 3**). Sallust means all of the Romans, not both sides in the battle.

69–73 **But before Metellus . . . rest themselfe.** *Sal*: 'Eorum magna pars superioribus locis fessa consederat' (**51. 3**). The antecedant of *eorum* is *hostium*: Sallust means that a great part of the enemy (the Numidians) through fatigue had taken refuge on the higher ground. Barclay follows *Asc* in taking the sentence to refer to the Romans: 'Eorum magna pars etc. Commemorat in quo statu suos ostenderat Metellus et quam orationem ad eos habuerit dicens. Magna pars .s. militum Romanorum fessa [fasso **1504.1**, **1506.2**] .i. fatigata diuturno prælio consederat' (f. 71^{r}).

76–88 **¶O worthy . . . dye in prison.** *Sal*: 'Simul orare et hortari milites, ne deficerent neu paterentur hostis fugientis uincere . . .' (**51. 4**). Sallust renders Metellus' exhortation in *oratio obliqua*, Barclay in direct speech, following the model of *Sold*: 'O milites nolite a pugna deficere: et nolite pati ut hostes uincant: fugientibus uobis non habetis castra . . .' (sig. l3^{v}). Barclay more or less captures the sense of Sallust: because the Romans lack any fortified camp to take respite within, they must pursue their retreating enemy and finish them off. Here *Asc* is more certain than *Sold*, who suggests that the passage is ambiguous: '¶Fugientes .s. Romani: ordo est et Metellus hortabatur ne Romani fugientes paterentur hostes uincere: uel ne Romani paterentur hostes uincere fugientes .s. Romanos' (sig. l3^{v}).

80–1 **no tentes/ no cyties/ no townes/ no castels.** *Sal*: 'neque illis castra esse neque munimentum ullum' (**51. 4**). For *tentes* see note to 13/73.

84–9 **Wherfore dere frendes . . . his soudyours.** This final exhortation appears to be Barclay's own addition.

93–5 **he fought and proued . . . myght be wonne.** *Sal*: 'ipse . . . temptare omnia' 'he tried every strategem' (**51. 5**).

97–100 **and such as he knewe . . . socoured of them.** *Sal*: 'quos firmos cognouerat eminus pugnando retinere' (**51. 5**). Cf. *Asc*: 'retinere retinebat .i. immorabatur ne ad suos accederent: pugnando eminus .i. de longe quasi e manumissis telis' (f. 71^{r}).

102–3 **lyke in strength/ courage/ wysedome/ and policy.** *Sal*: 'pares'

(**52. 1**). *Sold*: '¶Ipsi pares .s. erant. Ipsi imperatores uirtute et scientia militari pares erant' (sig. l3^{v}). *Asc*: 'pares .i. æquali virtute praediti' (f. 71^{r}).

103–4 **but of thynges longyng to chyualry vnlyke of prouysion.** *Sal*: 'ceterum opibus disparibus' (**52. 1**). *Asc*: 'cæterum .i. sed opibus .i. facultatibus ad prælium disparibus .i. habentes opes dispares' (f. 71^{r}).

111–12 **they ascended . . . ouer agaynst them.** *Sal*: 'aduorso colle . . . euadunt' (**52. 3**). *Sold*: '¶Euadunt .i. ascendunt: aduerso colle: euadere est: de ima parte sursum uersus ascendere' (sig. l4^{r}). That is, the Romans charged up the hill occupied by the Numidians.

117–19 **and so by flyght . . . nor auantage.** Barclay's addition.

Chapter 32

15 **Wherfore after he vnderstode by his esypyes.** *Sal*: 'Postquam . . . accepit' (**52. 6**). *Sold*: 'Bomilcar diligenter inuestigabat per exploratores quid agent Rutilius' (sig. l4^{r}). *Asc*: '¶Postquam .s. Bomilchar accepit .i. intellexit ab exploratoribus aut oculis suis' (f. 71^{v}).

27–8 **if they prepared towarde rescous of Metellus.** Barclay's addition (echoing Sallust's earlier statement). Cf. *Asc*: 'officeret .i. noceret: itineri hostium videlicet Romanorum: si redire vellent' (f. 71^{v}).

29 **Rutilyus and his company.** *Sal*: 'Romani' (**53. 1**). *Sold*: '¶Romani: uidelicet: qui erant cum Rutilio legato non cum Metello' (sig. l4^{r}).

44–6 **The Numydians . . . al their trust.** *Sal*, *Laet–BritT*: 'Numidae tantum modo remorati [*AscT*, *BarcT*: sunt remorati], dum in elephantis auxilium putant' (**53. 3**). That is, the Numidians only stood their ground so long as they believed they could look to (*abydynge and lokyng after*) the support of their elephants.

48 **by the compasing of the Romayns.** *Sal*: 'circumueniri' (**53. 3**). *Sold*: 'circumueniri .s. a Romanis' (sig. l4^{r}).

56–7 **the company of Rutilyus.** *Sal*: 'Romani' (**53. 5**). *Sold*: '¶At Romani Rutilius ad flumen praemissus' (sig. l4^{v}).

57 **they were fatygate and weryed.** *Sal*: 'fessi erant' (**53. 5**); MSS: 'fessi laetique'; later MSS, *Laet–BritT*, *AscT*, *BarcT*: 'fessi lassique'.

58–9 **with moche labour in orderyng of their tentes.** *Sal*: 'opere castrorum' (**53. 5**). Here, as elsewhere, Barclay apparently presents the *castra* as little more than a collection of tents. *Sold* makes it clear that the real labour was in the construction of the ditch and rampart surrounding the tents: '¶Opere castrorum .i. munitione. Nam castra muniuerant fossa: et uallo' (sig. l4^{v}).

63–6 **For the falshode . . . with delayeng.** *Sal*: 'Nam dolus Numidarum nihil languidi neque remissi patiebatur' (**53. 6**). *Asc*: 'remissi .i. minus intente facti: quia omni accuratione et vigilantia opus esse sciebant' (f. 71^{v}).

73 **had almost ben made.** [*BarcB C*: ben committed] *Sal*: 'paene . . . admissum' (**53. 7**). *Sold*: '¶Admissum .i. perpetratum et commissum' (sig. l4^{v}).

77–8 **in stede of their sadnes . . . ioye and gladnesse.** *Sal*: 'Igitur pro metu repente gaudium exortum' [*AscT*: exortum est; *BarcT A B*: exhortum est] (**53. 8**). The revision in *BarcB* ('their sadnes and feare tourned to great ioye and gladnesse') seems to echo the textual emendation suggested by Priscian 3. 297. 6–7, emending *exortum* of the MSS to *mutatur*. Neither *Sold* nor *Asc* mentions this emendation.

82–91 **And that as well . . . skirmysshes of batell.** *Sal*: 'Quippe res humanae ita sese habent: in uictoria uel [*Laet–BritT*, *AscT*, *BarcT*: etiam] ignauis gloriari licet, aduorsae res etiam bonos detrectant' [*Laet–BritT*, *AscT*, *BarcT*: detractant bonos] (**53. 8**). Barclay characteristically expands Sallust's moralizing observation on human nature and human affairs, taking ninety-six words to express what Sallust does in seventeen.

82–3 **And that as well . . . vnworthy cowardesse.** Both worthy men and unworthy cowards.

85–6 **suche as be but cowardes/ rude and vncrafty.** Cf. *Sold*: '¶Vel ignauis [*sic*; etiam ignauis *in Laet–BritT*] .i. etiam ignauis. In rebus humanis ita euenire solet: ut ab ea parte ubi est uictoria: etiam ignaui et rudes glorientur: et econtra' (sig. l4^{v}).

93–6 **Metellus hasted hym . . . foure dayes.** The sentence in *BarcA* is acceptable, but the separation of the verb *taryed* from its adverbial phrase (*the space of foure dayes*) is awkward. The change of *ordayned* to *seiourned* in the second edition is an improvement.

94–5 **in the places and tentes which Rutilyus preparedde and ordayned.** *Sal*: 'in isdem castris' (**54. 1**). *Sold*: '¶In iisdem castris: uidelicet in castris Rutilii' (sig. l4^{v}).

103–20 **¶O worthy soudyours . . . by ignomynious cowardyse.** *Sal* provides only a short summary, in reported speech, of Metellus' exhortation: 'hortatur ad cetera, quae leuia sunt, parem animum gerant; pro uictoria satis iam pugnatum, reliquos labores pro praeda fore' (**54. 1**). Soldus's rendering in direct speech is partial and brief, compared to Barclay's: '¶Reliquos labores: dicebat Metellus. Amplius laborare non oportet pro uictoria: quia iam uictoriam sumus assecuti. Sed si laborabimus: pro præda laborabimus' (sig. l4^{v}).

123–4 **But in the mean season . . . and therfore.** *Sal*: 'Tamen interim'. *AscT* **1514.1**, **1517**: 'Tn̄ interim'; *AscT* **1519** and *BarcT*: 'Tum interim'.

125–8 **certayne of the Numidyans . . . to such besynesse.** *Sal*:

'transfugas et alios opportunos' 'deserters and other suitable agents' (54. 2). *Asc*: 'transfugas .i. eos qui ad se ab Iugurtha fugerant: et alios oportunos .i. idoneos ad hoc: exploratum' (f. 72^r^).

133–5 **suche places . . . defended of nature.** *Sal*: 'loca saltuosa et natura munita' [*Laet–BritT*, *AscT*, *BarcT*: munita natura] (54. 3). *Asc*: 'in loca saltuosa .i. saltuum et fossarum plena: et munita natura .i. per naturam' (f. 72^r^).

137 **vncraftie/ inexpert/ and dull to batell.** *Sal*: 'hebetem infirmumque' (54. 3). *Asc*: 'hebetem .i. obtusum' (f. 72^r^).

137–8 **coude better tyll . . . dedes of chiualry.** *Sal*: 'agri ac pecoris magis quam belli cultorem' (54. 3). *Sold*: 'homines quos congregabat Iugurtha erant assueti magis ad agros colendos et ad curanda pecora quam ad bella gerenda' (sig. l4^v^).

Chapter 33

21–2 **He toke . . . nor garnyson.** *Sal*: 'multa castella [*Laet–BritT*, *AscT*, *BarcT*: castella multa] et oppida temere munita aut sine praesidio capit' (54. 6). *Sold*: '¶Temere munita: id est male munita. Nam temere multa significat . . . aliquando male: ut hoc loco. Aliquando improuide. ¶Temere munita: male munita: scilicet mœnibus et fossa et agere. ¶Sine præsidio sine custodia militum' (sig. l5^r^). *Asc*: 'multa castella et oppida munita: temere .i. inconsulte: aut supple existentia: sine præsidio .i. custodia et defensione militum' (f. 72^v^).

23–5 **All suche as came . . . apt to batayle.** *Sal*: 'puberes' (54. 6). *Sold*: '¶Puberes interficit: ætatem bello et armis opportunam et idoneam' (sig. l5^r^). *Asc*: 'puberes .i. omnes bellipotentes' (f. 72^v^).

35–6 **For he loost . . . other meanesse before.** Cf. *Sold*: 'quia multo plures populi defecerunt a rege propter uastationem hostilem quam propter prœlium . . . quia per huiusmodi uastationem multos populos a se deficere uidebat' (sig. l5^r^).

42 **Neuertheles of suche poore shyft and counsell as he had.** *Sal*: 'Tamen ex copia' (54. 9). Most MSS, *Laet–BritT*, *AscT*: 'tamen ex inopia'. As *Sold* observes (sig. l5^r^), the usual Sallustian turn of phrase is *ex copia (rerum)* 'under the circumstances' (cf. 39. 5, etc.), the reading modern editors adopt.

49–50 **in foragyng and spoylinge.** *Sal* only describes the victims of the raid as *palantis* 'stragglers' (54. 9) who are *inermes* 'unarmed' (54. 10). Cf. *Asc*: 'inermes .i. quia sine armis contra pecus non contra milites exierant' (f. 72^v^).

Chapter 34

5–7 **Whyle Metellus . . . and gyle.** *Sal*: 'Interim' (55.1). *Asc*: 'Interim .i. interea dum supra dicta fierent in Numidia' (f. 73r).

8–9 **for that Metellus behaued hymselfe and gyded his army.** *Sal*: 'ut seque [*Laet–BritT*, *AscT*, *BarcT*: se] et exercitum . . . gereret' (55. 1). *Sold*: '¶Se et exercitum gereret: id est regeret et gubernaret' (sig. I5v).

9–11 **acordyng to the maner . . . before his days.** *Sal*: 'more maiorum' (55. 1). *Asc*: 'more maiorum .i. priscorum imperatorum' (f. 73r).

11 **in place aduers and contrary to hym.** *Sal*: 'in aduorso loco' (55. 1). *Sold*: '¶In aduerso loco: id est in loco iniquo et sibi ad pugnandum incommodo: atque contrario' (sig. I5v).

18–19 **by the fear and cowardyse of Aulus.** *Sal*: 'ex Albini [*Laet–BritT*, *AscT*, *BarcT*: ex Auli] socordia (55. 1). Some modern editors think that here Sallust refers to the slackness of the Consul Spurius Postumius Albinus, rather than the weakness of his brother Aulus Postumius Albinus (whose military failure occurred when authority had been delegated to him by his brother). *Laet–BritT* and *AscT*, with the reading *Auli*, and glosses, account for Barclay's rendering. *Sold*: '¶Auli socordia: id est ignauia Auli: quem prœlio uicerat' (sig. I5v). *Asc*: 'ex secordia .i. pusillanimitate et ignauia: auli scilicet fratris Albini' (f. 73r).

21 **their ydolles.** *Sal*: 'dis immortalibus' (55. 2).

34–5 **the more besy and dyligent.** *Sal*: 'eo magis anxius' (55. 4). *Sold*: '¶Anxius .i. sollicitus' (sig. I5v).

37–8 **his hoost . . . one from an other.** *Sal*: 'effuso exercitu' (55. 4). *Sold*: '¶Effuso .i. sine ordine sparso' (sig. I5v).

40 **mannes meate or horsemeat.** *Sal*: 'frumento aut pabulo' (55. 4). *Sold*: '¶Frumento: ad usum hominum. ¶Pabulo: ad usum equorum' (sig. I5v). *Asc*: 'pabulo .s. equorum et iumentorum' (f. 73r).

57–60 **(that is to say) . . . hylles vpon them.** *Sal*: 'qua uenturum hostem audierat, pabulum et [*Laet–BritT*, *AscT*, *BarcT*: aut] aquarum fontis, quorum penuria erat, corrumpere' 'he ruined the feed and contaminated the springs, which were very few, in the places towards which he had report that the enemy were marching' (55. 8). Barclay's translation here is uncharacteristically loose. Perhaps he misread *corrumpere* as *corripere*. *Sold* and *Asc* make the correct sense clear enough.

61–4 **Somtyme he shewed . . . vnto the mountaynes.** *Sal*: 'modo se Metello, interdum Mario ostendere, postremos in agmine temptare ac statim in collis regredi' 'he showed himself sometimes to Metellus, and sometimes to Marius; he would attack those in the rear of the line, and at once retreat to the hills' (**55. 8**). Barclay may have been misled to some degree by *Laet–BritT* and *AscT*, which read *postremo* instead of *postremos*. Nevertheless, *Asc* makes it clear enough that *agmine* refers to the Roman formation, not the Numidian: 'postremo tentare .i. tentabat .i. lacessebat: eos in agmine' (f. 73ʳ).

68–9 **from their begynnyng . . . whiche they intended.** *Sal*: 'ab incepto' (**55. 8**). *Sold*: '¶Ab incepto retinere: ut prohiberet Romanos a uastatione agri' (sig. I6ʳ).

Chapter 35

4 **Metellus the Romayne captayn.** *Sal*: 'Romanus imperator' (**56. 1**). *Asc*: 'Imperator Romanus .s. Metellus' (f. 73ᵛ).

5 **with the gyles and craftes of Iugurth.** *Sal*: 'dolis' (**56. 1**). *Asc*: 'dolis .s. Iurgurthæ' (f. 73ᵛ).

11 **thynkyng (as the mater requyred).** That is: thinking that as a consequence Jugurtha would come. *Sal*: 'ratus, id quod negotium poscebat' (**56. 1**).

17 **gret iourneis.** *Sal*: 'magnis itineribus' 'forced marches' (**56. 2**). *Asc*: 'magnis itineribus .i. faciendo magna itinera: hoc est quod vulgo dicunt magnas dietas' (f. 73ᵛ).

22–5 **For they coude nat dysceyue . . . to them to do.** *Sal*: 'quia fallere nequibat' 'for they dared not be treacherous' (**56. 2**). Barclay's expansion suggests that they faced an uncertain fate if they returned to the Roman side. Sallust implies that they knew full well they faced crucifixion or some equally severe punishment, should they fall into the hands of the Romans. *Sold*: '¶Quia fallere nequibat: ne in manus eorum ueniet a quibus fugerat' (sig. I6ʳ). *Asc*: 'nequibat fallere .i. decipere regem: eo quod apud Romanos summo odio habebantur propter defectionem et perfugium' (f. 73ᵛ).

31–2 **he sende Marius.** *Sal*: 'Marium ex itinere [*Laet–BritT*, *AscT*, *BarcT*: ex itinere Marium] frumentatum cum paucis cohortibus Siccam missum' (**56. 3**).

33–4 **the first towne . . . yelded to Marius.** *Sal*: 'quod oppidum primum omnium post malam pugnam ab rege defecerat' (**56. 3**). Barclay surely means 'yielded to Metellus'. Cf. *Sold*: '¶Siccam est ciuitas: quæ prima a rege ad Metellum defecerat' (sig. I6ʳ).

35 **to his great damage.** That is, to the damage of Iugurth, who lost the battle at the river Muthul.

45–7 **And certaynely if Marius . . . men of armes.** *Sal*: 'Ac [*Laet–BritT*, *AscT*, *BarcT*: At] ni Marius signa inferre atque euadere oppido properauisset' 'and if Marius had not hastened to advance and escape the town' (**56. 5**). *Signa inferre* is a set phrase for 'advance'.

48 **All they of the towne or the moost part.** *Sal*: 'profecto cuncti aut magna pars Siccensium' (**56. 5**).

55 **some were slayne.** *Sal*: 'paucis amissis' (**56. 6**). *Asc*: 'paucis amissis .i. occisis' (f. 74^{r}).

60–2 **in the playne ground . . . nature of the place.** *Sal*: 'in campo situm magis opere quam natura munitum erat' (**57. 1**). *Sold*: '¶In campo .i. in plano: non in monte. ¶ Quam natura: quia nec monte nec flumine nec aliqua re naturali munitum est oppidum illud' (sig. 16^{v}). *Asc*: 'opere .s. manuali aut humano' (f. 74^{r}).

64 **Anone whan Marius was come.** *Sal*: 'Igitur' (**57. 2**). Cf. *Asc*: 'Igitur (hic continuatiua est vox. aut quia iam Marius aduenerat)' (f. 74^{r}).

67–8 **assignyng to euery one . . . shewe his manhode.** *Sal*: 'legatis imperat ubi quisque curaret' (**57. 3**). *Asc*: 'curaret .s. rem bene gerere in oppugnationem oppidi' (f. 74^{r}).

69–70 **Metellus commaunded . . . trumpettes and claryons.** *Sal*: 'signo dato (**57. 3**). See note to 13/72, and cf. 25/63–4 and 31/8.

72–5 **but abode styll . . . to him assigned.** *Sal*: 'sine tumultu' (**57. 3**).

78–9 **some with slynges . . . into the cyte.** *Sal*: 'pars eminus glande aut lapidibus' (**57. 4**). *Sold*: '¶Glande: uidelicet fundis: glandis est plumbum in modicum formatum: quod funda iacit.' *Asc*: 'eminus hoc est de longe: glande .s. plumbea e funda proiecta' (f. 74^{r}).

82 **escaled.** *BarcA*: 'escaped'; *B* 'escaled'; *C* 'scaled'. *Sal*: 'scalis adgredi' 'approached/attacked with scaling ladders' (**57. 4**). *OED* cites only one instance of this verb, from 1579.

85 **gret and weyghty stones.** *Sal*: 'saxa' (**57. 5**). *Asc*: 'saxa .i. magnos lapides' (f. 74^{r}).

86–9 **Some pytched downe . . . ardently flamyng**. *Sal*: 'sudes, pila, praeterea picem sulphure mixtam et taeda ardentia mittere' (Rolfe) (**57. 5**); '. . . et taeda mixtam ardentia mittere' (Reynolds, Comber-Balmaceda); *Laet–BritT*, *AscT*, *BarcT*: 'sudes: pila præterea pice et sulphure tædam mixtam ardenti mittere'. *brennynge polles*: probably 'burning poles' (L. *taęda ardentia*), although possibly 'burning polls', i.e. either lumps of inflammable material, or perhaps torches: a length of stick with a 'poll' or lump on the end. *Asc*: 'tædam .i. facem resinosam: qua plurimi pro candelis ac lucernis etiam hodie vtuntur: vnde tædæ arbores pro facibus ac flammis nuptualibus ponuntur: vt Enei.iiii. *Si non pertæsum thalami tædæque fuisset* [*Aeneid* 4. 17] mixtam .i. illitam pice et sulphure ardenti' (f. 74^{r}).

89–97 **Some boldly ouertourned . . . defenders of the walles.** The coordinate construction is clumsy, in that 'some' refers to the Numidians, and 'some other' to their opponents, where one might expect the construction to refer to varieties of activity by combatants on the one side. Both sentences are Barclay's addition, but the second echoes both Sallust's previous reference to the Roman slingers hurling plummets and stones from a distance, and his subsequent reference to the missiles shot by the Numidians either from engines or by hand ('iacula tormentis aut manu emissa' **57. 6**). Sallust, however, only states that such missiles harmed Romans who stayed at a distance and feared to attack the walls. The claim that the Romans wounded many Numidians by means of missiles is Barclay's. It would appear that he overlooked revision and correction of this section.

97–9 **The dartes and crosbowes . . . nat yet inuent.** *Sal*: 'iacula tormentis aut manu [*Laet–BritT*, *AscT*, *BarcT*: manibus] emissa' (**57. 6**). *Sold*: '¶Tormentis: omnis machinæ qua aliquid ui emittitur dicebantur tormentæ: sicut nunc uulgo Balistæ et Bombarde uocantur: sed balista apud antiquos aliud erat. Bombarda nec nomine nec re erat apud antiquos' (sig. l6^{v}). *Asc*: 'Bombardæ autem quæ nunc dicuntur quod cum bombo .i. sonitu et ardore globos emittant tunc non erant inuentæ' (f. 74^{r}).

Chapter 36

7 **tentes.** *Sal*: 'castra' (**58. 1**). See notes to 13/73and 32/58–9.

9 **at their rest.** *Sal*: 'remissis' (**58. 1**). Many editors take *remissus* to mean 'careless, remiss, negligent' rather than merely 'at rest' here. *Asc*: 'remissis .i. remisse agentibus et quietis ac minime sollicitis' (74^{v}).

9–10 **and suspecting nothing lesse than any such assaut.** That is, expecting anything but such an atttack. *Sal*: 'et omnia magis quam proelium expectantibus' (**58. 1**).

11 **The Romayns.** *Sal*: 'nostri' (**58. 2**). *Sold*: '¶Nostri .s. Romani' (sig. l6^{v}).

13–15 **Some which were cowardes . . . their ennemis.** *Sal*: 'alii fugere, alii arma capere' (**58. 2**). *Sold*: 'Nam qui strenui erant arma capiebant: et pugnabant: qui uero ignaui: fugiebant' (sig. l6^{v}).

18–19 **remembring the worshyp of the empyre of Rome.** *Sal*: 'memores nominis Romani' (**58. 3**). *Asc*: 'memores nominis .i. fame: et laudis ac decoris Romani' (f. 74^{v}).

29–32 **these .xl. valyant Romayns . . . force and strength.** *Sal*: 'uirtutem ostendere' (**58. 3**). If Barclay is using *bestow* as a synonym of *shew*, the sense is otherwise unattested.

34 **in the forsayd assaut of Zamam.** *Sal*: 'rem gereret' (**58. 4**). *Sold*: '¶Rem gereret .s. apud Zamam' (sig. l6^{v}). *Asc*: gereret rem .i. oppugnationem oppidi' (f. 74^{v}).

35 **a great clamour and noyse of people.** *Sal*: 'clamorem hostilem' (some MSS, Reynolds, Comber–Balmaceda, etc.); 'clamorem ut tumultem hosti-

lem' (Rolfe and others); 'clamorem uel tumultum' (some MSS); *Laet–BritT*, *AscT*, *BarcT*: 'clamorem' (58. 4). Sallust says that Metellus heard a noise that sounded like an enemy attack.

41 **with his retynue and company.** *Sal*: 'cum cohortibus sociorum' 'with cohorts of the allies' (58. 5). *Asc*: 'cum cohortibus sociorum .s. equitum quos socii populi Romani miserunt in auxilium' (f. 74^{v}). (*Sold* similarly.)

44–6 **that he wold nat suffre . . . laude and honour.** *Sal*: 'nequam contumeliam remanere in exercitu uictore' (58. 5). *Asc*: 'in exercitu victore .s. prius' (f. 74^{v}).

49–56 **But in the meane season . . . mortally wounded.** *Sal*: 'At Iugurtha munimento castrorum impeditus, cum alii super uallum praecipitarentur, alii in angustiis ipsi sibi properantes officerent, multis amissis in loca munita sese recepit' (58. 6). Barclay has misunderstood Sallust and seemingly overlooked the gloss in *Asc*. Sallust says that Jugurtha's men, not the Roman defenders, were impeded by the fortifications of the camp and suffered considerable losses, on account of which Jugurtha withdrew them.

58 **without any thyng brought to ende at Zamam.** *Sal*, *Laet–BritT*, *AscT* (1504.1–1511.2, 1513.2): 'infecto negotio' (58. 7); *AscT* (1513.1–1519), *BarcT*: 'incepto negotio' [changed to *infecto* in *BarcT B*]. *Asc*: 'negocio .s. incepto: infecto .i. non perfecto: hoc est expugnatione non obtenta' (f. 75^{r}).

61–2 **to course up and downe before their tentes.** *Sal*: 'pro castris agitare' (59. 1). Sallust may mean 'ride up and down' or perhaps simply 'take up their post'. *Asc*: 'agitare .i. curare res suas: aut more eorum qui feras agitant obequitare: pro castris .i. ante castra sua' (f. 75^{r}).

62–3 **where they supposed Iugurth wolde come to socour his people.** *Sal*: 'qua regis aduentus erat' 'where the king was likely to attack' (59. 1). *Asc*: 'qua aduentus regis erat .i. qua putabat regem aduenturum auxilio suorum' (f. 75^{r}). It is not clear whether *Asc* and Barclay mean that Jugurtha's attack was intended to aid the defenders of the town, or perhaps the remnants of his troops who attacked the Roman camp the previous day.

68–9 **the Romayns . . . before the tentes**. *Sal*: 'nostros' (59. 2). *Asc*: 'nostros .s. milites Romanos et potissimum equites pro castris agitantes' (f. 75^{r}).

74–5 **if their fotemen . . . myschefe and dystruction.** *Sal*: 'ni pedites cum equitibus permixti magnam cladem in congressu facerent' (59. 3). Sallust here describes how the Numidian attackers consisted of a mixture of infantry and cavalry. Barclay is mistaken, and has overlooked the commentaries, which correctly explain the passage.

75–82 **For the horsemen of Iugurth . . . the Romayne hoost.** *Sal*: 'Quibus illi freti non, uti equestri [*Laet–BritT*, *AscT*, *BarcT*: uti in equestri fieri] proelio solet, sequi, dein cedere, sed aduorsis equis concurrere, implicare ac perturbare aciem' (59. 3). Sallust says that the cavalry, confident in the support of their infantry, did not advance and retreat, using conventional tactics, but charged head on ('aduorsis equis' (59. 3)) to break the Roman lines. Barclay's 'ouerthwart and sydelinges: infoldyng et dowblyng' makes the tactic seem more complex.

83–4 **it lacked but lytell . . . ouercome.** That is: the Romans came close to being defeated.

87 **speremen.** At several points Barclay uses this term to denote cavalry (see Glossary).

Chapter 37

8–9 **with moche strength/ vyolence/ and murder.** *Sal*: 'magna ui' (60. 1). *Asc*: 'magna vi id est violentia ac virtute' (f. 75^{v}).

18–20 **The clamoure . . . quelled and murdredde.** *Sal*: 'clamor permixtus hortatione laetitia gemitu' (60. 2). *Asc*: 'lætitia vincentium: gemitu occubantium' [occupantium 1519] (f. 75^{v}).

20–1 **The sounde of the armour/ horrious/ and strokes mounted to the ayre.** *Sal*: 'item strepitus armorum ad caelum ferri' (60. 2). Barclay's punctuation and syntax here suggest that a noun should be present, rather than the adjective *horrious*. Perhaps the text should be emended to read *harness* (cf. the collocations of *armour* and *harness* at 25/102, 28/25, and 41/17), although *armour* is here used in the sense of weapons, as it as at 31/83, 38/19, etc. *OED* includes this passage as the only example of the adjective *horrious*, citing the reading from *BarcC* (*and horrious strokes*). The adjective occurs again in the text at 56/85.

22–4 **And the walles and dychesse . . . pytefull to se.** Barclay's addition.

30–1 **And as well as they coude be sene . . . kyng Iugurth.** *Sal*: 'ac sicuti audiri a suis aut cerni possent' (60. 4).

35–9 **If they sawe . . . cast it themself.** *Sal*: 'quasi uitabundi aut iacientes tela' (60. 4). As commentators have often observed of this picturesque account, Sallust is imitating Thucydides' description of the battle in the harbour of Syracuse (7. 71. 3), where those of both sides on the shore observe the naval battle at sea. For Barclay's expansion cf. *Sold*: 'Et si uidebant Romanum iacientem telum in Numidam: corpore uitare illud uidebantur: tanquam si in se iactum fuisset. Similiter si uidebant Numidam telu iacientem in Romanos: ita corpus mouebant: tamquam si ipsi iacerent' (sig. m1^{v}). *Asc*: 'agitare .i. agitabant supple se huc et illuc quasi vitabundi .i. vitantes tela inimicorum: aut quasi iacientes tela. Non enim reuera vitabant pro se aut iaciebant: sed affectione suorum afficiebantur et agitabantur' (f. 75^{v}).

44 **he abated his fiersnes for policy.** *Sal*: 'consulto lenius agere' 'he deliberately slackened his efforts' (**60. 5**).

51 **with ladders and other ingens.** *Sal*: 'scalis' (**60. 6**).

58 **They which abode last.** *Sal*: 'qui supersteterant' (**60. 7**). That is, those who stood upon the scaling ladders. Barclay has overlooked *Asc*: 'illi qui superstiterant .s. super scalas' (f. 75^{v}).

60 **a fewe or non hole.** That is, few if any unharmed. *Sal*: 'pauci integri' (**60. 7**).

Chapter 38

7–9 **and also that Iugurth . . . and great auantage.** *Sal*: 'neque Iugurtham nisi [*Laet–BritT*, *AscT*, *BarcT*: niti: nisi] ex insidiis aut suo loco pugnam facere' 'and that Jugurtha would not fight except by means of surprise attack or on his own ground' (**61. 1**). *Asc*: 'niti .i. obseruare' (f. 76^{r}). *Sold*: '¶Niti .i. contendere pugnare' (sig. m1^{v}).

8 **begyle and falshode.** *Sal*: 'ex insidiis' (**61. 1**). *BarcB* and *C* change the phrase to *by gyle and falshode*, which may well be what Barclay intended; but for another possible instance of the noun *beguile* see 2/79 and note.

10–11 **in such townes as he had won of Iugurth.** *Sal*: 'in iis [*Laet–BritT*, *AscT*, *BarcT*: his] urbibus quae ad se defecerant' 'in those towns which had defected to him [Metellus]' (**61. 1**). Barclay's version seems to derive from *Laet–BritT*, which reads *quae a rege*. *Asc* discusses the textual variant *ab se* for *ad se*, but has the latter in his text. In considering how to read *ab se*, *Asc* raises the possibility (only to reject it) that the towns defected from Metellus, only to be won back by him.

11–12 **strongly defended with walles and water.** *Sal*: 'satisque munitae loco aut moenibus' 'strongly enough fortified by their position or by walls' (**60. 1**).

19–21 **he began to proue . . . gyle of Iugurth.** *Sal*: 'insidias regi per amicos tendere et eorum perfidia pro armis uti parat' (**61. 3**). The change of *dysceyt* to *a dysceuer* in *BarcB C* may be an improvement, but the reading in *BarcA* is acceptable as it stands.

37–9 **what for his treaterous . . . what for that he douted.** *Sal*: 'cum ingenio infido [*BarcT*, *Laet–BritT*, *AscT* (**1504.1**): infido; *AscT edns. from* **1506.2**: fido] tum metuenti ne . . . traderetur' 'who was not only treacherous by nature but was also afraid that he would be handed over to the Romans' (**61. 5**). Cf. *Asc*'s note on *ingenio*: 'Et persuadet facile Numidæ non dicit Bomilchari: sed Numidæ quasi dicat vt Numidæ: quia Numidis varium est ingenium et perfidiæ commodum' (f. 76^{r}).

40–1 **by condycion.** *Sal*: 'per condiciones' (**61. 5**). That is, according to the terms of any peace settlement made between Jugurtha and the Romans.

51–2 **and for the peple of Numidy . . . better sene to.** *Sal*: 'et genti Numidarum optume meritae' 'and for the people of Numidia who had served him so faithfully' or perhaps 'who had so much claim upon him' (**62. 1**). *Asc*: 'et genti Numidarum meritæ .s. de se in fide conseruanda: optime .i. summe bene' (f. 76^{v}).

58–60 **Bomylchar alleged . . . sufficyently ynough.** *Sal*: 'satis saepe iam et uirtutem militum et fortunam temptatam' 'that the valour of his soldiers, and the decree of fortune, had been sufficiently tested already' (**62. 1**).

70–1 **without any pactyon/ couenaunt/ or exception.** *Sal*: 'sine ulla pactione' 'unconditionally' (**62. 3**). *Asc*: 'sine vlla pactione .i. exceptione per pactum' (f. 76^{v}).

73–4 **all the moost wyse noble/ and worthy men of his army.** *Sal*: 'cunctos senatorii ordinis' 'all the men of senatorial rank' (**62. 4**).

79 **acordynge to the olde custome of Rome.** *Sal*: 'more maiorum' (**62. 5**). *Asc*: 'more maiorum .i. sicut prisci Romani consueuerant mandare' (f. 76^{v}). The correct procedure is in marked contrast with the private negotiations conducted with Jugurtha earlier (**29. 5**).

95–6 **dreding for the knoleging . . . worthy punysshment.** *Sal*: 'et ex mala conscientia digna timere' 'and, out of guilty conscience, he feared punishment worthy of his crimes' (**62. 8**). The change of *worthy* in *BarcA* to *condigne* in *BarcB C* is unsurprising, but Barclay's use of *worthy* in this sense occurs elsewhere: 'condyng and worthy punysshement' 23/65, 'worthy to be punysshed' 25/119.

101–7 **Somtyme agayn . . . deth or captiuyte.** *Sal*: 'interdum secum ipse reputaret quam grauis casus in seruitium ex regno foret, multis magnisque praesidiis nequiquam perditis, de integro bellum sumit' (**62. 9**). The description of Jugurtha as *volage brayned* is Barclay's own. Cf. *Asc*: 'ne quicquam .i. frustra' (f. 77^{r}).

Chapter 39

4–7 **In the same season . . . Metellus.** *Sal*: 'Per idem tempus Vticae forte C. Mario per hostias dis supplicanti magna atque mirabilia portendi haruspex dixerat' (**63. 1**). Sallust is not so explicit about Marius' intention in making the sacrifice. Furthermore, Barclay's parenthesized phrase *by his helpe* sits awkwardly, and is changed to *by helpe* in *BarcB*, *C*. By Marius' own help? By the help of the haruspex or seer? Or perhaps to be emended to *by their helpe* meaning the *ydolles*.

7–15 **A custome damnable . . . founde true.** Barclay's own aside. Both

Sold and *Asc* provide notes on the process of divination by examining entrails, but neither engages in Christian moralizing as Barclay does. *Asc* does, however, state: 'vt cætera superstitiosa: calliditate spirituum malignorum putatur inuenta' (f. 77^{r}).

25–7 **For though he were . . . worthy and exellent.** Barclay's own expansion on the preceding. For the phrase *gentylmen of the first heed* see note to Prologue, ll. 149–50.

27–8 **In hym was great experience of wysdomc/ moch probyte/ honestie/ and sadnesse.** *Sal*: 'industria, probitas' (**63. 2**). *Asc*: '¶Industria .i. exercitata uis ingenii' (f. 77^{r}). Cf. *Sold* (sig. $m2^{v}$).

29–30 **But in peace it was lowe and moderate.** *Sal*: 'domi modicus' (**63. 2**). *Sold*: 'In pace moderatum et temperatum. . . . ¶Domi .i. in pace' (sig. $m2^{v}$).

30–1 **He ouercame ryches and sensualyte of his body.** *BarcA* (*ryches*) translates Sallust literally: 'lubidinis et diuitiarum uictor' (**63. 2**); *BarcB* and *C* (*couetyse*) provide a more balanced English construction, reflecting Sallust's intended meaning.

33–4 **in the contrey . . . towne named Arpyne.** *Sal*: 'Arpini' (**63. 3**). Arpinum in Campania. Barclay follows the glossators: *Sold*: 'sed erat ex Arpino: quæ est ciuitas Campaniæ' (sig. $m2^{v}$). *Asc*: 'Arpini. id est Arpino oppido Campaniæ' (f. 77^{r}). They refer to the Campania of central Italy, not Champagne in France. Perhaps this potential confusion is what Barclay intends to clarify by using the phrase *beyond France*.

35–6 **he concluded to lyue on the wages of chyualrie.** *Sal*: 'stipendiis faciundis' 'by going on active service' (**63. 3**). *Stipendium* is the pay of a soldier, or, by transference, a tour of service. Sallust probably refers to Marius' experience at Numantia.

37–9 **and nat in eloquence . . . subdued his body.** *Sal*: 'non Graeca facundia neque urbanis munditiis sese exercuit' (**63. 3**). Cf. *Asc*: 'Ubi palam docet quod Iuuenalis Satyra sexta manifeste fatetur Græcas litteras ad lasciuiam plurimum conferre: vnde etiam Romanæ mulieres libidinibus expositæ Græcas litteras didicerunt: vnde ait. Nam quid rancidius [etc.: Juvenal, *Satire* 6. 185–95] (f. 77^{r}).

39–42 **And thus was he indued . . . honour and vertu.** 'and taken up with wholesome pursuits, he continued so that his unspoiled mind/nature increased and raised itself, growing to honour and virtue'. *Sal*: 'ita inter artis bonas integrum ingenium breui adoleuit' (**63. 3**).

44 **protectour of the soudyours.** *Sal*: 'tribunatum militarem' (**63. 4**).

44–6 **many of the citezyns . . . name well knowen.** *Sal*: 'plerisque faciem eius ignorantibus, factis facile notus per omnis tribus declaratur' 'although most people did not know him by sight, being famous through his deeds, he was elected by vote of all the tribes' (**63. 4**). There were thirty-five electoral divisions (*tribus*) in Italy. All MSS, *Laet–BritT*, *AscT*, *BarcT* read *facile notus*. Following Palmer many modern editors emend to *factis notus*, or *factis facile notus*. Hellwig's emendation, to *fama facile notus*, is foreshadowed in *Sold*: 'Sed postquam dictum est eum esse Caium Marium cuius fama in bello clara erat: omnes tribus eum tribunum declarauerunt' (sig. m3^{r}). Cf. *Asc*: 'cum plurimi eum nunquam cognouissent nisi ex fama' (f. 77^{v}).

57–9 **But whan he was thus warnedde . . . of that dygnite.** *Sal*: 'nam postea ambitione praeceps datus est' 'for afterwards he was driven headlong by ambition' (**63. 6**). *Sold*: '¶Præceps datus est .i. præcipitauit se ambitione: quia supra modum procliuus fuit ad honores' (sig. m3^{r}).

62–3 **yerely one succedyng another by electyon.** *Sal*: 'Etiam tum alios magistratus plebs, consulatum nobilitas inter se per manus tradebat' (**63. 6**). Cf. *Sold*: '¶Per manus .i. per successionem: quia cum aliquis nobilis deponebat consulatum. alii nobili tradebant ipsum consulatum' (sig. m3^{r}).

63–5 **So that of the commenty . . . vyle and polluted.** *Sal*: 'Nouus nemo tam clarus [*Laet–BritT*, *AscT*, *BarcT*: præclarus] neque tam egregiis factis erat, quin indignus illo honore et is quasi pollutus haberetur' [*is* before *indignus* in most MSS; changed by Eussner; omitted by Reynolds] 'No "new man" was so famous or so illustrious for his deeds, that he was not considered unworthy of that honour, and the office, so to speak, sullied by such an incumbency' (**63. 7**). Rolfe's translation reflects some modern editors' shift of *is*, so that its referent is the *office*, rather than the *man*, as in Barclay's translation. Barclay passes over the term *nouus* 'new man' here although he recognizes it elsewhere: see note to Prologue, ll. 149–50.

74–6 **Neuertheles of his courage . . . hy lynage as he was.** *Sal*: 'tamen inerat contemptor animus et superbia' (**64. 1**). *Asc*: 'tamen inerat animus contemptor .i. despector plæbeiorum' (f. 77^{v}).

79–81 **For at that tyme . . . Marius.** Barclay's addition, following *Sold* and *Asc*: 'quod nouus homo et municipalis vellet consulatum petere' (f. 77^{v}).

81–2 **And thus Metellus . . . counsell hym therto.** *Sal*: 'mirari eius consilium' (**64. 2**). The second clause is Barclay's addition.

84–5 **aboue fortune conuenyent for his state and condycion.** *Sal*: 'super fortunam' (**64. 2**); *AscT*, *BarcT*: 'supra fortunam'. Sallust means the position or rank assigned to him at birth by Fortune. *Sold*: '¶Super fortunam .i. super statum' (sig. m3^{r}).

95–6 **nat lettyng the besynesse of the commen wele.** *Sal*: 'per negotia publica' 'the business of state allowing' (**64. 3**).

98–105 **he made hym answere . . . .xx. yere of age.** Sallust begins 'fertur dixisse' 'Metellus is reputed to have said', because the reply is extremely dismissive and insulting (**64. 4**). If the son were only twenty years old, he would not be eligible to seek the office of consul for another twenty-three years. Hence, Metellus is telling Marius to wait indefinitely.

103–4 **in the army of his father Metellus.** *Sal*: 'contubernio patris' 'in his father's tent' (**64. 4**). That is to say, he was a trainee staff officer, and in Metellus' personal retinue.

105–12 **This answere of Metellus . . . the sayd Metellus.** The omission of the extraneous *and* (after *two vyces*) in *BarcB* and *C* corrects an obvious grammatical error, but the passage remains somewhat awkward, and obscures Sallust's balanced *cum . . . tum* construction. This is not Barclay's fault, however. *AscT* introduces an additional clause (see Introduction, p. xl). *Sal*: 'Quae res Marium cum pro honore quem affectabat tum contra Metellum uehementer accenderat. Ita cupidine atque ira, pessumis consultoribus . . .' 'This answer inflamed Marius even more, not only with desire for the honour to which he aspired, but also with hatred for Metellus. So, influenced by ambition and resentful anger, the worst of counsellors . . .' (**64. 4**). *AscT* and *BarcT* read: 'Quæ res Marium tum pro honore quem affectabat: tum pro licentia redeundi quam ab eo impetrare nequibat contra Metellum vehementer accenderat.' The additional clause does not appear in *Laet–BritT* (except for the Paris edn. **1497/8**). Barclay omits to translate *pessumis consultoribus* 'the worst of counsellors', which Sallust then uses to refer to the vices of ambition and ire.

117–18 **to thintent therby . . . in his enterprise.** Barclay's addition. Cf. *Sold*: '¶Milites. Ecce factum ambitiosum. Marius: ut fauorem militum sibi conciliaret' (sig. m3^{v}).

118–20 **Also he spake . . . marchantes of Rome.** *Sal*: 'apud negotiatores . . . criminose simul et magnifice de bello loqui' (**64. 5**). Cf. *Sold*: '¶Criminose: contra Metellum: magnifice pro se: et in laudem sui ipsius' (sig. m3^{v}).

125–6 **that Metellus prolonged . . . for a craft.** *Sal*: 'ab imperatore consulto trahi [*Laet–BritT*, *AscT*, *BarcT*: consulto bellum trahi] 'the war was deliberately prolonged by the commander' (**64. 5**). *Sold*: '¶Trahi .s. bellum .i. prolongari' (sig. m3^{v}). *Asc*: 'consulto .i. ex consilio et deliberatione preuia' (f. 78^{r}).

126 **a man pompous.** *Sal*: 'homo inanis' (**64. 5**).

128–31 **and bycause he knewe . . . magnify hymselfe.** Barclay's addition, essentially restating the previous sentence.

135–7 **For by long contynuance . . . substance and richesse.** *Sal*: 'quia diuturnitate belli res familiaris corruperant' 'because prolongation of the war, had ruined their businesses' (**64. 6**).

142 **neuewe.** grandson. Cf. note to 10/24.

143 **seconde heyre.** Heir in the second degree, who should succeed if there

were no issue of the first heir or heirs (in this case Adherbal, Hiempsal, and Jugurtha). *Sold*: 'Nam primos heredes reliquit filios Adherbalem et Hiemsalem et Iugurtham filium adoptiuum: qui si morerentur: secundum reliquit heredem Gaudam filium fratris sui Manastabalis' (sig. m3^{v}).

145–6 **his mynde . . . reason and memorie.** *Sal*: 'mente paulum [*LaetBritT*, *AscT*, *BarcT*: paululum] imminuta (**65. 1**). Cf. *Asc*: 'mente .i. ratione aut memoria: imminuta paululum' (f. 78^{v}).

150–1 **a company of soudyours of the Romayns.** *Sal*: 'turmam equitum Romanorum' (**65. 2**). Barclay does not make it clear here that Gauda is requesting 'Roman Knights' for a bodyguard, and that these members of the landed class would only form the bodyguard of a Roman general. His request is tantamount to claiming the kingship of Numidia.

156–7 **whiche was no kyng . . . for stypend.** Barclay adds this clause, which seems to refer to Gauda. But it is unlikely that Gauda was an ordinary mercenary soldier, given his poor health. *Sold* and *Asc* point out that it would be an insult to the *equites*, should they be assigned, like mercenaries, to guarding a Numidian. *Sold*: 'Satelliti Numidae: satellites proprie dicebantur milites mercede conducti' (sig. m4^{r}). *Asc*: 'esset contumeliosum: si equites Romani traderentur .s. ad custodiam et ita in famulatum Numidæ satelliti .i. militi mercede conducto' (f. 78^{v}).

178 **for loue whiche they had to Marius.** *Sal*: 'alios ipse, plerosque pacis spes impellit' (**65. 4**). *Asc*: 'ipse .i. fauore sui' (f. 78^{v}).

184–5 **with great fauour and very honest peticyons.** *Sal*: 'honestissuma suffragatione' (**65. 5**). Sallust makes the point that Marius gains support through his merits, not through bribery.

189–94 **This Manlyus . . . executed at Rome.** *Sal*: 'Simul ea tempestate plebs, nobilitate fusa per legem Mamiliam, nouos extollebat' (**65. 5**). Barclay here supplements Sallust, who has already explained Mamilius' legislation setting in motion proceedings against those Romans who had colluded with Jugurtha (**40**; Barclay's ch. 39). As Sallust points out, the commons took advantage of the situation and attempted to advance 'new men'. It was not legislated that a 'new man' must replace any convicted nobleman, as Barclay seems to suggest. For his interpretation cf. *Asc*: 'per legem Manliam .i. quam Manlius seu Manilius tribunus plebis constituit vt re male gesta a nobilibus: noui ad magistratum admitterentur' (f. 78^{v}).

198–200 **¶But here wyll I leaue . . . agaynst Metellus**. Cf. *Asc*: 'Postquam finiuit digressionem factam de ambitione Mariana: redit ad gesta Iugurthina dicens' (f. 79^{r}).

Chapter 40

9–10 **Moreouer he dayly . . . with great rewardes.** *Sal*: 'formidine aut ostentando praemia affectare' (**66.** 1). Barclay's use of *troubled* is awkward in its conjunction with *great rewardes*, if it is used transitively with *cytees and townes* as the direct object. Perhaps an infinitive should be supplied: *troubled to obtain*; that is, 'exerted himself to win (back)'.

16–18 **He attysedde . . . theyr lybertie.** *Sal*: 'seruitia Romanorum allicere' 'he tempted the Roman slaves (to revolt)' (**66.** 1). *Sold*: '¶Seruitia .i. seruos' (sig. m4ᵛ). *Asc*: 'allicere: .i. alliciebat ad se seruitia .i. seruos Romanorum pollicendo eis libertatem' (f. 79ʳ).

22–3 **but by all maner meanes . . . euery thynge.** *Sal*: 'cuncta agitare' 'he kept everything in motion' (**66.** 1).

32–3 **For why as it often happeneth.** *Sal*: 'Nam uolgus, uti plerumque solet' (**66.** 1). The precise force of *nam* is unclear. Perhaps it should be translated as 'moreover' rather than 'for' or 'because'.

38–40 **agaynst the thyrde day . . . and Numidy.** *Sal*: 'in diem tertium constituunt, quod is festus celebratusque per omnem Africam' 'they decided upon the third day from that time, because it was celebrated as a holiday throughout all Africa' (**66.** 2).

41 **shewed and pretended by all symilytude.** *Sal*: 'ostentabat' (**66.** 2); *Laet–BritT*, *AscT*, *BarcT*: 'ostendebat'.

47 **lyeutenant/ prouost/ and chefe captayne of the towne.** *Sal*: 'praefectum oppidi' (**66.** 3). Modern commentators debate Turpilius' status (Roman or Latin) and official function. He may have been *praefectus fabrum* (cf. Plutarch, *Marius* 8) or *praefectus cohortis*. He probably commanded the town garrison.

49–51 **But this chere . . . with the tayle.** The comparison with the scorpion is Barclay's addition, and proverbial. Cf. *Ancrene Riwle* 206: 'þe scorpiun is ones cunnes wurm þet haueð neb, ase me seið, sumdel iliche ase wummon, ant is neddre bihinden, makeð feir semblaunt, ant fikeð mid te heaued, ant stingeð mid te teile.' Chaucer, *Merchant's Tale* IV. 2058–60: 'Lyk to the scorpion so deceyvable, / That flaterest with thyn heed whan thou wolt stynge; / Thy tayl is deeth, thurgh thyn envenymynge'; and see B. J. Whiting, *Proverbs, Sentences and Proverbial Phrases* (Cambridge, Mass., 1968), S96.

64–5 **For though they were ignorant of the counsell of this dede.** *Sal*: 'quis acta consiliumque ignorantibus' 'for although they knew nothing of what had been done or of the plan behind it' (**66.** 4).

67–9 **The Romayn soudyours . . . best to be done.** Barclay's rendering is loose. *Sal*: 'Romani milites, improuiso metu incerti ignarique quid potissumum facerent, trepidare' 'the Roman soldiers, perplexed by the unforeseen peril, and not knowing what to do, were in a state of trepidation' (**67. 1**). Sallust's use of *metus* to mean 'peril' (that which causes 'fear') is more commonly found in poetry than prose (cf. note to 25/69–72).

70 **armoure and wepyn.** *Sal*: 'signa et scuta' 'standards and shields' (**67. 1**).

75–6 **stryuing who myght throwe first and moost.** *Sal*: 'certatim' (**67. 2**).

76 **this doutfull and vnprouyded myschefe.** *Sal*: 'anceps malum' 'twofold danger' (**67. 2**). Sallust means the danger from the armed force blocking the Romans' way on the one hand, and the missile-throwing women and children on the other.

78–9 **the very cowardyse and feblenes of women and chyldren.** *Sal*: 'infirmissumo' (**67. 2**). Sallust does not describe their actions as cowardly.

79–81 **Thus many of them: . . . without difference.** *BarcB*, *C* omit *many of them* and *after one maner*. A reviser appears to reject the reading *multi*, but does not insert an equivalent for *inulti*. *Sal*: 'iuxta boni malique, strenui et inbelles inulti obtruncari' (**67. 2**). *Laet–BritT*, *AscT*, *BarcT* read *imbecilles* for *inbelles*, and *multi* for *inulti* 'unavenged, without being able to strike back'. *Asc*: 'multi .i. magno numero (nisi sit legendum inulti)' (f. 79^v). Cf. 19/23–5 and note.

87–9 **But this was knowen . . . without credence.** *Sal*, *Laet–BritT*: 'improbus intestabilisque uidetur' (**67. 3**). Barclay's insertion of *as long as he lyued* is somewhat inapposite, for Metellus quickly executed Turpilius for his failure to die with his comrades (as the next chapter states). Sallust says that whatever the reason for Turpilius' survival (whether connivance or something more innocent), his choice to remain alive rendered him detestable. *BarcT* and *AscT* read *instabilisque* instead of *intestabilisque*; Barclay's rendering *without credence* reflects the latter reading. Sallust's phrase *improbus intestabilisque* echoes the Twelve Tables of the law. *Intestabilis* signified a person so infamous of character that he was not allowed to give evidence in a court of law.

Chapter 41

7–8 **But to thyntent that none shulde parceyue his heuynesse.** Barclay's addition. Cf. *Sold*: '¶Ex conspectu abiit .s. ne uideri posset a militibus latuit donec mesticia et dolor uersus est in iram' (sig. $m5^r$). *Asc*: 'e conspectu .s. nuntiantium et assistentium ne aut lacrimas aut aliud signum animo virili indignum ostenderet' (f. 79^v).

17–18 **to thintent to spede the way more redely.** The reading in *BarcA* (*rydde*) might be accepted if understood as a misspelling of *ryde*; but it is clear that the passage refers to the legionary footsoldiers.

30–1 **and very myserably murdred.** *Sal*: 'miserrumis' (**68. 3**). *Asc*: 'miserrimis .i. miserrime occisis' (f. 80^{r}).

31–2 **Moreouer he shewed . . . redy for them.** Barclay's rendering is awkward. *Sal*: 'Praeterea praedam benigne ostentat' 'Moreover he generously promised them all of the plunder' (**68. 3**).

34–5 **the horsmen to go forth in the forward.** *Sal*: 'equites in primo late' 'the cavalry to take the lead in open order' (**68. 4**). Most MSS, *Laet–BritT*, *AscT*, *BarcT*: 'equites in primo latere'.

43 **whan they aduysed them well.** The object pronoun *them* is not reflexive; it refers to the members of the approaching army.

47 **agayne they thought that it was Iugurth.** *Sal*: 'rursum Iugurtham arbitrati' 'conversely they thought it was Jugurtha' (**69. 1**).

50–1 **knowynge the wyll of their captayne by blast of the trumpettes.** *Sal*: 'signo dato' (**69. 2**). Cf. notes to 13/72, 25/63–4.

55 **the towres of the walles.** *Sal*: 'turris' (**69. 2**). *Asc*: 'turres .s. murorum' (f. 80^{r}).

55–6 **Thus the dyspleasure . . . of their felawes.** *Sal*: 'ira' (**69. 2**). *Asc*: 'Et ita ira de occisis Romanis' (f. 80^{r}).

58 **which they had in their iournay thyderwarde.** Barclay adds this clause. Cf. *Sold*: 'Romani propter magnitudinem itineris lassi et fessi erant' (sig. m5^{r}). *Asc*: 'lassitudo .s. ex magnitudine itineris contracta' (f. 80^{r}).

61–5 **For the great . . . within their cyte.** *Sal*: 'ciuitas magna et opulens [*Laet–BritT*, *AscT*, *BarcT*: opulenta] cuncta poenae aut [*Laet–BritT*, *AscT*, *BarcT*: atque] praedae fuit' (**69. 3**). For Barclay's expansion cf. *Sold*: '¶Pœne aut præde fuit: quia urbs direpta est: et ciues interfecti sunt. ¶Prædæ: propter direptionem rerum omnium' (sig. m5^{r}). *Asc*: 'Quia ciuitas magna atque opulenta fuit cuncta .i. simul tota: pœnæ .i. ad pœnam exposita: quia omnes occidebantur ab iratis et sanguinem suorum vlciscentibus: et prædæ cuius fuerant cupidi. dicit autem ciuitas: quia oppidum quidem vastatum est: sed non dedit pœnas sanguinis: vt ciuitas: quae est ciuium collectio' (f. 80^{r}).

71–4 **for that it was thought . . . treason.** Barclay's addition.

75–80 **For the lawe of Porcius . . . towne of Collace.** Collatia was a town of Latium, which no longer exists. *Sal*: 'nam is ciuis ex Latio erat' (**69. 4**). As a Latin and not a Roman citizen, Turpilius was not protected from these punishments under Porcian Law. The reading *ex Latio* occurs in *Sold* commentary, Rome **1473**, *AscT*, *BarcT* and *Laet–BritT* **1497/8**. It is found in the good MSS, A1, K2, H1, D2, F2, but the other MSS read *ex collatia erat* and this appears in some early editions. Barclay's *Collace* probably comes from *Laet–BritT*: 'Nam is ciuis e Collatia erat' (in contradiction of the gloss). *Sold*: '¶Nam ciuis ex Latio erat: lex Portia uetabat ciuem Romanum interfici: sed in exilium mitti iubebat. Nunc ergo dicit. Ideo Turpilius damnatus interfectus est: quia non erat ciuis Romanus: sed ciuis ex Latio' (sig. m5[v]). *Asc*: 'capitis obtruncatione: quod ideo permittebatur. Nam is erat ciuis ex Latio non ex urbe quem lex portia vetabat ad supplicium posci: sed in exilium permittebat mitti' (sig. m5[v]). For a summary of the textual and interpretative difficulties of this passage see Paul, 179–85. See also Plutarch *Marius* 8.

Chapter 42

6 **was conuersant with Iugurth.** Barclay adds the phrase, and probably means that Bomilcar was in close and constant contact with Jugurtha.

7–8 **Wherfore he suspectyng hym agayne.** 'Wherefore Bomilcar, for his part, in return regarding Jugurtha with suspicion'. *Sal*: 'et ipse eum suspiciens' (**70. 1**).

8 **ymagenedde newe polycie agaynst Iugurth.** *Sal*: 'nouas res cupere' '[Bomilcar] desired a changed of government' (**70. 1**).

23–4 **And in the meane tyme . . . case requyredde.** *Sal*: 'cetera, uti res posceret, ex tempore [*Laet–BritT*, *AscT*, *BarcT*: pro tempore] parari placuit' (**70. 3**). Sallust indicates that having fixed the time, they decided to leave the details of the plot until the appointed time, and act then 'extempore' as circumstances should dictate. *Asc*: 'et placuit .s. vtrique: cætera quæ præter diem ad insidias facerent: parari .i. disponi: pro tempore .i. opportunitate: vti .i. quemadmodum res posceret .i. exigeret' (f. 80[v]).

40 **pacyence/ delayeng/ and cowardyse.** *Sal*: 'mollitiam socordiamque' (**70. 5**). Barclay's use of *pacyence* here is striking. *OED* does not record such a negative sense; but cf. Latin *patientia*. *OLD* includes under sense 3 'submissiveness, . . . apathy, passivity'.

43–5 **Moreouer he warned . . . of Metellus.** *Sal*: 'monere ne praemia Metelli in pestem conuorteret' (**70. 5**). That is to say, Bomilcar warns Nabdalsa not to remain apparently loyal to Jugurtha, when the rewards being offered by Metellus for the latter's destruction would lead to the destruction also of all those associated with Jugurtha.

60–4 **first many deuyses . . . to fall in slepe.** *Sal*: 'primo cura, deinde, uti aegrum animum solet, somnus cepit' [*BarcT*, some editions of *Laet–BritT* and *AscT*: coepit] (**71. 2**). *Asc*: 'cura cepit .i. inuasit et occupauit primo animum ægrum .i. affectum molestia. deinde somnus .i. dormitatio: cepit supple eum vti hoc est quemadmodum solet: quia somnus omnia domat tandem' (f. 81[r]).

66–7 **this counsell of betrayng of Iugurth onely except.** *Sal*: 'nisi nouissumi' (**71. 4**). *Sold*: '¶Nisi nouissimi .s. consilii coniurationis contra Iugurtham' (sig. m6[r]). *Asc*: 'nisi .i. præterquam nouissimi .s. de prodendo Iugurtha' (f. 81[r]).

72–3 **and seyng by the superscripcyon that the letter came from Bomylchar.** Barclay's addition.

75–8 **Nabdalsa nat long after . . . as it was done.** *Sal*: 'Nabdalsa paulo post experrectus ubi neque epistulam repperit et rem omnem uti acta erat, [ex perfugis] cognouit' (**71. 5**). The phrase *ex perfugis* 'by those fleeing' (which is the basis of Barclay's expanded explanation of how Nabdalsa realized what had happened) appears in *Laet–BritT*, *AscT*, *BarcT*, and most MSS (but *A*: ex servis, *N*: expertus), but has been rejected by Kritz and other modern editors. If the phrase is omitted, the Latin can be taken to mean that Nabdalsa deduced what had happened simply from the absence of the letter.

82 **And sayd vnto hym.** Barclay does not convert this reported speech into direct oration, although *Sold* provides a model for doing so.

94–9 **howbeit he had well refrayned . . . lyued any lengar.** *Sal*: 'Bomilcare aliisque multis, quos socios insidiarum cognouerat, interfectis iram oppresserat, ne qua ex eo negotio seditio oreretur' (**72. 1**). *AscT*, *BarcT*: 'Bomilchare interfecto aliisque multis quos socios insidiarum cognouit iram oppresserat [*Laet–BritT*: oppressit] ne qua seditio aut bellum ex eo negotio oriretur.' Sallust says that Jugurtha, having slain Bomilcar and many others involved in the plot, restrained himself from further anger and retribution for fear that the matter might cause a rebellion. He does not say that the execution of Bomilcar and his associates was the means by which he assuaged his anger, as Barclay appears to do (unless we take *with* to mean 'following'). Barclay's used of the verb *refrayned* seems to echo *Asc*'s use of the verb *frenauerat* in his gloss. *Asc*: 'Et causa est quia oppresserat id est frenauerat iram: Bomilchare interfecto: et aliis multis supple interfectis quos cognouit socios insidiarum: et id supple fecerat: nequa .i. ne aliqua seditio aut bellum supple. aliquod oritetur ex eo negocio hoc est ex criminatione Nabdalsæ' (f. 81[r]). *Sold*:' ¶Iram oppresserat hoc est extinxerat: uel potius clauserat' (sig. m6[r]). The last two clauses are odd syntactically and the omission of *by* in *BarcB* and *C* does not go far enough to restore the substance of Sallust.

98 **batayle or other insurrectyon.** *Sal*: 'seditio' (**72. 2**). *Laet–BritT*, *AscT*, *BarcT*: 'seditio aut bellum'.

107–8 **in abiect and secrete . . . estate royall.** *Sal*: 'loco saepe contra decus regium' (**72. 2**). *Sold*: '¶Contra decus regium: quia in loco humili et abiecto iacebat' (sig. m6[r]).

109–11 **and vyolently smyting . . . in batayle.** This is Barclay's picturesque addition.

Chapter 43

7–8 **he began than . . . with open warre.** *Sal*: 'rursus tamquam ad integrum bellum cuncta parat festinatque' 'he again hastened to make preparations, as if for an entirely new war' (73. 1).

8–14 **And consydring . . . demaunded by peticyon.** To be taken as one sentence. The first participial structure is more or less impersonal, although Metellus might be considered the subject. He is the subject of the second one: '[Metellus] aduysynge hym [Marius] nat moche necessary . . .'; and of the third, which is parallel with the second ('seyng hym yll wyllyng . . .'), after which comes the main clause ('he graunted him . . .').

10–11 **greuous/ hatefull/ and contrary to hym.** *Sal*: 'simul et inuitum et offensum sibi' (73. 2). For *inuitum* 'reluctant, discontented' *Laet–BritT*, *AscT*, *BarcT* read *inuisum* 'hostile'.

15–16 **the letters . . . fauourers of Marius.** *Sal*: 'litteris quae de Metello ac Mario missae erant' 'the letters which had been written about Metellus and Marius' (73. 3).

28–9 **For the commens to dy for it/ concludedde to exalt Marius.** This and the following sentence are Barclay's expansion upon Sallust's previous statement that party feeling had more influence than the good or bad qualities of either man. The phrase *to dy for it* does not occur elsewhere in Barclay's works or other writings of this era, as far as I have determined. Presumably it means that the commons were prepared to risk all to support Marius.

31–2 **the maisters and heed offycers of the commentie which loued debate.** *Sal*: 'seditiosi magistratus' (referring to the tribunes of the commons) (73. 5). *Sold*: '¶Seditiosi magistratus. Tribunos plebis maxime intelligimus' (sig. m6^{v}). *Asc*: 'magistratus seditiosi: videlicet tribuni plebis' (f. 81^{v}).

34–5 **that Metellus might be put to the punysshe of his heed.** *Sal*: 'Metellum . . . capitis arcessere' (73. 5). That is, they charged Metellus with a capital crime. Neither *MED* nor *OED* records a noun *punish*. Another example might be found in the damaged text of *Alterations of Kingdoms* composed *c.*1550 (*STC* 14999.5): 'Now do ye rega[. . .] / How God doth re[. . .] / The wicked world[. . .] / When punysh doth[. . .] / Uicious men truli[e] / He geueth to reign[. . .].'

40–1 **all the crafty men . . . also of the countrey.** *Sal*: 'opifices agrestesque omnes' (73. 6).

45–6 **trustyng that after . . . lyuenge by hym.** Barclay's addition.

46–54 **And thus shortly to speke . . . of basse byrth.** *Sal*: 'Ita perculsa nobilitate, post multas tempestates nouo homini consulatus mandatur' (73. 7). On *nouus homo* see note to Prologue, ll. 149–50.

55 **Lucius Manlius.** *Recte* Titus Manlius. *Sal*: 'T. Manlio Mancino' (73. 7). *Laet–BritT*, *AscT*, *BarcT* and other early edns. read *L.* or *Lucio*.

Chapter 44

9–10 **to Bocchus kynge of the Mauryans.** *Sal*: 'ad regem Bocchum' (74. 1). *Sold*: '¶Regem Boghum: Boghus rex Maurorum erat' (sig. m6ᵛ). *Asc*: 'ad Bocchum regem .s. Mauritaniæ' (f. 82ʳ).

10–11 **mynisters and men of warre.** *Sal*: 'administris' (74. 1). *Asc*: 'administris .i. auxiliariis' (f. 82ʳ).

13 **or assay their fidelite of newe.** *BarcA* makes sense: 'to test their fidelity anew' (*of new* is frequently used in this way), but *BarcB* follows *Sal* more accurately: 'et nouorum fidem in tanta perfidia ueterum experiri periculosum duceret' 'he considered it dangerous to trust in the fidelity of new friends in view of the treachery of old ones' (74. 1).

14 **his mynde was driuen to and fro.** *Sal*: 'agitabat' (74. 1); *Laet–BritT*, *AscT*, *BarcT*: 'agitabatur'. Sallust uses *agitare* intransitively. Barclay translates the reading of his source text.

17–18 **He changed . . . feare of treson.** *Sal*: 'Itinera praefectosque in dies mutare' 'he changed his routes and his officers from day to day' (74. 1). *Laet–BritT*, *AscT*, *BarcT*: 'Itinera profectusque' 'his routes and his advances'.

43–4 **and moche of his treasour . . . the same towne.** *Sal*: 'ubi [*Laet–BritT*, *AscT*, *BarcT*: ibi] plerique thesauri filiorumque eius multus pueritiae cultus erat' 'where much of his treasure was kept, and where there was lavish provision for the education of his children in royal manners' (75. 1). *Asc*: 'et multus cultus .i. ornatus pueritiæ filiorum eius erat ibi' (f. 82ᵛ). This gloss does not disambiguate *cultus* particularly well, for both *cultus* and *ornatus* may denote either 'preparation, education' or 'adornment, dress or apparel'. Barclay seems to take the latter meaning. Cf. note to 45/53.

54–5 **all suche baggage . . . the soudyours.** *Sal*: 'omnia iumenta sarcinis' (75. 3). *Asc*: 'sarcinis .i. oneribus rerum militarium' (f. 82ᵛ).

57–8 **bottels full of water/ and other vessels mete to be caryed with water.** That is, leather waterbags and other vessels to carry water. *Sal*: 'utris modo et alia aquae idonea portari' (75. 3). *Laet–BritT*, *AscT*, *BarcT*: 'alia vasa aquae'.

62 **thinhabytantes of those marchesse.** *Sal*: 'finitumis' 'the people nearby' (75. 5).

75–6 **sodenly from the heuen . . . rayne water.** *Sal*: 'tanta repente caelo missa uis aquae' (**75. 7**). *Asc*: 'vis .i. copia seu abundantia aquæ dicitur missa .s. per pluuiam quasi cælitus data sit' (f. 83^{r}).

79–82 **For the Numydians . . . often fadeth at the ende.** *Sal*: 'quia Numidae, sicuti plerique [*Laet–BritT*, *AscT*, *BarcT*: plerique faciunt] in noua deditione, officia intenderant' (**75. 8**). Compare Barclay's addition in his second sentence with *Asc*: 'quia vt dicitur: principium feruet: medium calet: et tepet imum' (f. 83^{r}). This proverb appears elsewhere as: 'Principium fervet, medium tepet, exitus alget'; or 'Principium fervet, medium tepet, ultima frigent.'

83–4 **for deuocyon.** *Sal*: 'religione' 'out of religious motivation' (**75. 9**). *Sold*: '¶Religione: id est propter religionem: hoc est propter honorem deorum' (sig. $n1^{r}$).

96–7 **by sufferaunce of the tyme.** 'As time allowed'.

99–100 **to Metellus was nothyng vnprouydedde nor vnable to be done.** *Sal*: 'nihil iam infectum Metello' (**76. 1**).

102–3 **And also nature itselfe which ruleth other thynges longynge vnto men.** *Sal*: 'denique naturam ipsam ceteris imperitantem' 'and even Nature herself, who rules all others' (**76. 1**).

110–12 **delyberation and processe . . . soiourne and contynue.** *Sal*: 'per otium et ex opportunitate' (**76. 1**). *Asc*: 'ex opportunitate .i. conuenientia temporis' (f. 83^{r}).

114–15 **defended bothe by craft of mannes handes and by nature of the place.** *Sal*: 'et operibus et loco munitum' (**76. 2**).

115–30 **Anone he compased . . . paryll or dammage.** Barclay expands upon Sallust's account of the siege with more detailed explanation of the stockade and moat, and of the siege engines. He has looked to *Sold* (who cites Vegetius *Mil.* I. 10) and *Asc*, but does not follow them closely. Verbal echoes of *Asc* include: *by craft of mannes handes and by nature of the place*; 'operibus .s. manualibus: opera humana perfectis: et loco .i. naturali situ'; *with profounde dychesse . . . escape by night*; 'vallo .i. sepimento ex vallis .i. stipitibus acutis: et fossa ante vallum facta contra eruptionem oppidanorum: simul ne perfugæ elaberentur' (f. 83^{v}).

122–3 **specially in two suche places as were moost conuenyent.** *Sal*: 'duobus locis ex copia maxume idoneis' (**76. 3**).

123 **pentyses of sheldes conioyned in maner of vynes.** *Sal*: 'uineas' (**76. 3**): sheds or mantlets, so called because they resemble an arbor or wooden frame for training vines. Cf. *Asc*: 'vineas .i. machinas bellicas figuram vinearum habentes' (f. 83^{v}).

124–5 **And aboue . . . grauell and stones.** The change of *aboue* to *about* in *BarcC* makes more sense, but Barclay literally translates *Laet–BritT*, *AscT* (and MSS): 'vineas agere superque eas aggerem iacere'. Editors since Korrte and Popma have deleted *superque eas*.

135–8 **But all the pray . . . fledde from Metellus to Iugurth.** *Sal*: 'praeda omnis ab perfugis corrupta' [*Laet–BritT, AscT, BarcT*: corrupta est] (76. 5).

140 **dyuerse ingens of batayle.** *Sal*: 'arietibus' 'rams' (76. 6). Both *Sold* and *Asc* explain the battering ram and the derivation of its name, but Barclay removes Sallust's specificity.

150–1 **by desperate folly and presumptuous madnesse.** Barclay's addition.

Chapter 45

1 **Leptis.** Leptis Minor.

10–12 **contynually laboured . . . the Romayns agayne.** *Sal*: 'nouis rebus studere' (77. 1).

16–18 **except he graunted . . . danger and paryll.** *Sal*: 'Ni id festinaret, in summo periculo suam salutem, illorum socios fore' (77. 1). Sallust's brevity makes his meaning obscure. Comber–Balmaceda translate: 'Unless Metellus moved quickly, they [the Leptitans] would be in extreme danger of losing their lives, and the Romans of losing their allies.' An alternative might be: 'their safety, allies of Rome as they were, would be in the greatest danger'. *Sold* does not discuss. *Asc* says: 'ni .i. nisi: festinaret id .s. mittere præsidium et præfectum: salutem suam .i. legatorum id dicentium: et socios illorum (aut legatur suam et sociorum) fore in summo periculo' (f. 84^{r}).

25 **worthely and substancially.** *Sal*: 'naue' (77. 3); *AscT, BarcT*: 'gnauiter'; *Laet–BritT*: 'grauiter'.

29 **four cohortes of Lombardes.** *Sal*: 'cohortes Ligurum quattuor' (77. 4). *Asc*: 'Ligurum qui sunt populi Italiæ iuxta Insubres' (f. 84^{r}). For *Lombardes* cf. note to 25/90–1.

34–5 **for dyscorde . . . cyties at home.** *Sal*: 'ob discordias ciuilis' (78. 1).

37–8 **which is situate . . . hath his name.** *Sal*: 'ceterum situm inter duas Syrtis, quibus nomen ex re inditum' 'it is situated between the two Syrtes [the gulf of Sidra and the gulf of Qabès], which take their name from their nature' (78. 1). Barclay is mistaken here, although the glossators correctly explain the construction and the etymology of Syrtes, which Sallust takes from the Greek geographers. *Sold*: '¶Quibus nomen ex re inditum est .i. impositum. Dicit quare uocatæ sunt Syrtes. Dicit nomen a tractu Syrtes esse uocatas. Nam σύραω sirao significat traho. Syrao est traho. unde Syrtes' (sig. n2^{r}). *Asc*: 'nomen est inditum .i. impositum: ex re .i. ex effectu quia *σύρω* syro significat traho: et *σύρμα* syrma tractus aut vestis longa quæ trahitur' (f. 84ʳ).

39–40 **For about thextreme . . . see nere togyder.** *Sal*: 'Nam duo sunt sinus prope in extrema Africa' (**78. 2**). Barclay has construed *prope* with *sinus*, where it should be taken to modify *in extrema Africa* 'almost at the extreme end of Africa' (that is, close to the frontier with Egypt). On the view that Egypt formed part of Asia, not Africa, see note to 12/11–14. Sallust apparently describes the situation of Leptis Major, rather than Leptis Minor, in placing it close to the frontier with Egypt. The Greater Syrtes is the modern Gulf of Sidra, the Lesser Syrtes, the Gulf of Qabès.

49–50 **great wynde.** Following this sentence there appears in *Sal*: 'Syrtes ab tractu nominatae' 'from this "sweeping" the Syrtes get their name' (cf. note to ll. 37–8 above) (**78. 3**). The clause is missing from *Laet–BritT*, *AscT*, *BarcT* (and from the translation), but it appears in some early edns. such as Adam Rot's (**1473**).

53 **their lawes/ their apparell/ and maners.** *Sal*: 'legum [*Laet–BritT*, *AscT*, *BarcT*: leges] cultusque' 'laws and customs' (**78. 4**). Cf. *Sold*: '¶Cultus: cultus pertinet ad uestitum et ad mores uiuendi' (sig. n2ᵛ).

Chapter 46

15–17 **Than bytwene the coostes . . . particyon/ or dyfference.** *Sal*: 'Ager in medio harenosus, una specie' (**79. 3**).

24–5 **feryng lest some . . . were ouercome.** Barclay passes over the opportunity to incorporate *Asc*'s comparison at this point with Æsop's fable of the mouse, the frog, and the hawk.

39–40 **whether it so fortuned by neglygence or chaunce.** *Sal*: 'Id socordiane an casu acciderit' (**79. 5**). *Sold*: '¶Socordia .i. negligentia' (sig. n3ʳ).

Chapter 47

5–6 **the cytie of Thala/ one of the strongest cyties of his lande.** *Sal*: 'Thala'. *Asc*: 'Thala .s. vrbe fortissima' (f. 85ʳ).

13 **Of this people Iugurth assembled a multitude togyder.** *Sal*: 'Eorum multitudinem in unum cogit' (**80. 2**). Barclay misses the force of *in unum* 'in one place', which follows from the notion that the Gaetulians were nomadic, scattered, and difficult to coordinate.

16–18 **to dyscerne . . . soundes of trumpettes.** Barclay's addition. For his interest in trumpets as signalling devices cf. 13/72, 25/63–4, 31/8, 35/70, 41/51.

21 **Moreouer he prouoked vnto his fauour and felashyp.** *Sal*: 'Praeterea . . . ad studium sui perducit' [*Laet–BritT*, *AscT*, *BarcT*: pellicit] (**80. 3**). Cf. *Asc*: 'Preterea .i. insuper. Iugurtha pellicit .i. perfecte allicit et attrahit ad studium .i. fauorem sui .s. ipsius Iugurthæ' (f. 85^{v}).

23–4 **by whose helpe he hymselfe went to the kyng Bocchus.** *Sal*: 'quis adiutoribus regem aggressus' (**80. 3**). Sallust probably does not mean that Jugurtha went to Bocchus, rather that he worked his influence upon the latter through Bocchus' friends. *Sold*: '¶Aggressus .i. ad regem accedens' (sig. $n3^{v}$). *Asc*: 'quis .i. quibus: adiutoribus: ipse agressus .i. insidiose accedens regem .s. Bocchus' (f. 85^{v}).

24–5 **And moche desyredde . . . agaynst the Romayns.** That is, Jugurtha wished Bocchus to join with him in his struggle and to wage war against the Romans. *Sal*: 'impellit uti aduorsus Romanos bellum incipiat' (**80. 3**).

34 **the doughter of Iugurth was spoused to the sayed Bocchus.** *Sal*: 'Etiam antea Iugurthae filia Boccho nupserat' (**80. 6**). *Laet–BritT*, *AscT*, *BarcT* and the best MSS read *Boccho*, but other MSS read *Bocchi*, which accords with the statements of Plutarch, *Marius* 10. 3; *Sulla* 3. 2; Florus 1. 36. 17; Joannes Antiochenus, fr. 64, that the daughter of Bocchus married Jugurtha. Accordingly, some modern editions (including Comber–Balmaceda) adopt the reading *Bocchi*.

34–5 **But this bonde of frendshyppe or affinite.** *Sal*: 'Verum ea necessitudo' (**80. 6**). *Asc*: 'verum ea necessitudo .i. necessitas coniunctionis ex affinitate' (f. 85^{v}).

40–2 **Thus is their mynde . . . multytude of them.** *Sal*: 'Ita animus multitudine distrahitur' (**80. 7**). *Asc*: 'ita animus .i. affectio et amor: distrahitur .i. in diuersa trahitur et dissipatur. multitudine .s. vxorum' (f. 85^{v}).

42–4 **and bycause they haue so many . . . after one maner.** *Sal*: 'nulla pro socia optinet, pariter omnes uiles sunt' (**80. 7**).

60 **Perses kyng of Macedony** *Sal*: 'regem Persen' (**81. 1**). *Sold*: '¶Item regem Persen: Perses rex Macedoniæ fuit' (sig. $n4^{r}$). *Asc*: 'Persen regem: scilicet Macedoniæ deuictum et in triumphum deductum a Paulo Æmilio Macedonico' (f. 85^{v}). Perseus, son of Phillip III, was the last king of Macedonia, defeated by Aemilius Paulus at the battle of Pydna (168 BC).

72–3 **And also moche of his owne ordynaunce . . . in his voyage.** *Sal*: 'ibi Q. Metellus . . . impedimenta locauerat' (**81. 2**). *Asc*: 'impedimenta .i. sarcinas militares vt sunt machinæ et arma militaria tam ad bellum quam ad victum necessaria quæ dicuntur impedimenta quod impediant militum properationem dum cum eis migrant' (f. 86^{r}).

Chapter 48

6–7 **rasshely without prouisyon.** *Sal*: 'temere' (**82. 1**). *Sold*: '¶Temere: inconsulte: improuide: incaute' (sig. n4[r]).

9 **within his felde well and surely defended.** *Sal*: 'castris munitis' (**82. 1**). Cf. 'tentes and felde' 13/73. On the habitual translation of *castra* 'military encampment' by *tentes* see note to 13/73 and Glossary.

23–5 **In somoche that . . . yll by Marius.** *Sal*: 'neque lacrumas tenere neque moderari linguam' (**82. 2**). *Sold*: '¶Neque moderari .i. non temperabat linguam: neque abstinebat a maledictis' (sig. n4[r]). *Asc*: 'neque tenere pro tenebat lachrymas. neque moderari: hoc est moderabatur: seu refrenabat linguam a conuitio seu maledicto' (f. 86[r]).

26–7 **but the dyspleasure . . . his hert.** *Sal*: 'nimis molliter aegritudinem pati' (**82. 2**). *Asc*: 'pati .i. patiebatur: ægritudinem .i. dolorem animi: nimis molliter .i. muliebriter' (f. 86[r]).

32–4 **bycause the vyctorie . . . labour and paryll.** *Sal*: 'quod iam parta uictoria ex manibus eriperetur' (**82. 3**). *Sold*: '¶Iam parta: id est prope acquisita'.

34–6 **But to be playne . . . wysest romayns.** *Sal*: 'Nobis satis cognitum est' 'but to me (Sallust) it is evident' (**82. 3**).

41–9 **Wherefore Metellus . . . than batayle.** *Sal*: 'Igitur eo dolore impeditus . . . pro certis mutare' (**83. 1**). Sallust's construction is punctuated as a single sentence in *AscT* and *BarcT*, hinging on the main verb *missit*. Barclay somewhat obscures the causal chain which Sallust has set up.

59–60 **his goodes/ treasour/ and fortune: which were in estate royall florisshyng.** *Sal*: 'florentis res suas' (**83. 1**). Barclay's construction in the relative clause is unusual. Perhaps *royall* and *florisshyng* are to be taken as post-posited adjectives in apposition, modifying the noun *estate*, or perhaps *royall* is to be taken as adverbial, modifying *florisshyng*. Cf. *Castle of Labour*: 'Some dethe tacheth in theyr estate prosperous / Whome he ouerthroweth with his mortall blast' (sig. A4); *Shyp of Folys*: 'All kyngdomes dekay and all estate mundayne / Example of Rome Cartago and Mycene' (sig. v3).

77–80 **so that by suche maner the warre . . . desyre in mynde.** *Sal*: 'tempus procedere, et ex Metelli uoluntate bellum intactum trahi' (**83. 3**).

80–3 **bycause he wolde . . . to hym belonged.** Barclay's addition. Cf. *Asc*: 'et bellum trahi: hoc est trahebatur intactum ex voluntate Metelli: hoc est sicut summopere cupiebat Metellus ne aut Mario profit aut famam perdat' (f. 86[v]).

Chapter 49

8 **Nowe was he specially fiers of mynde/ and stately.** *Sal*: 'tum uero multus atque ferox instare' (84. 1). *Sold*: '¶Multus .i. uehemens' (sig. n5^{r}). *Asc*: 'ipse multus .i. immodicus et vehemens ac immodestus: et ferox .s. per insolentiam et sæuitiam' (f. 87^{r}).

19–20 **For many of them were slayne/ and many deed of sickenesse.** Barclay's addition. Cf. *Asc*: 'supplementum legionibus .s. occisis et detritis seu imminutis cæde et morbo' (f. 87^{r}).

20–3 **He called also for socours . . . felaweshyppe with the Romayns.** Following Wirz, many modern editors shift *sociisque* to follow *ex Latio* in the next clause: 'auxilia a populis et regibus arcessere, praeterea ex Latio sociisque fortissumum quemque . . .' [MSS, *Laet–BritT*, *AscT*, *BarcT*: auxilia a populis et regibus sociisque accersere. Praeterea ex Latio fortissimum quemque . . .] (84. 2).

24–7 **And namely . . . boosted by fame.** *Sal*: 'plerosque militiae, paucos fama cognitos' (84. 2). Sallust says that Marius knew most of his troops from their previous service with him, but a few by reputation only.

27–32 **And namely olde soudiours . . . with hym in warfare.** Barclay expands considerably on *Sal*: 'et ambiundo cogere homines emeritis stipendiis secum proficisci' [*Laet–BritT*, *AscT*, *BarcT omit* secum] 'and by special appeals he induced veterans who had served their full time to enlist' (84. 2). Cf. *Sold*: '¶Cogere omnes emeritis stipendiis secum proficisci. Illi dicuntur emeritis stipendiis: qui debita tempora militiæ compleuerunt: et hi contra uoluntatem suam ad militiam compelli non possunt. Tamen hos Marius blandiendo cogebat secum proficisci' (sig. n5^{r}).

37–42 **But this dyde they . . . hateredde agaynst hym.** *Sal*: 'quia neque plebi militia uolenti putabatur et Marius aut belli usum aut studia uolgi amissurus' (84. 3). Sallust means that the senate thought Marius would either lose the war because the plebs were disinclined to military service, or he would lose the commoners' favour in his efforts to compel them to enlist.

Chapter 50

2–4 **which exhortacion . . . noble men of Rome.** For this chapter heading cf. *Sold*: 'hæc oratio posita est in genere demonstratiuo. Est autem genus demonstratiuum: quod attribuitur in alicuius certe persone laudem uel uituperationem: hæc autem oratio et laudem Marii et uituperationem continet nobilitatis' (sig. n5^{v}).

13–17 **For of howe moch more valour . . . offices desyred of you.** *Sal*: 'Nam quo pluris est uniuorsa res publica quam consulatus aut praetura, eo

[*AscT*, *BarcT omit* eo] maiore cura illam administrari quam haec peti debere' 'for just as the whole commonwealth is of greater consequence than a consulate or a praetorship, so its governance ought to be managed with greater care than that which is shown in seeking those offices' (**85. 2**).

17 **Nor I am nat ignorant.** 'Neither am I unaware.'

23–25 **To compell to warfare . . . nat dysplease by any meanes.** Take *a man* as the object of *greue nor dysplease*. *Sal*: 'cogere ad militiam eos quos nolis offendere' (**85. 3**).

42–3 **all ye haue good trust and confydence in me.** *Sal*: 'omnium ora in me conuorsa esse' (**85. 5**). *Asc*: 'ora omnium esse conuersa in me .i. habere spem in me' (f. 87[v]).

48–9 **that neyther ye be disceyued in this great trust whiche ye haue in me.** *Sal*: 'uti neque uos capiamini' (**85. 7**). *Asc*: 'vti .i. vt: neque vos capiamini .i. decipiamini per spem et expectationem vestram de me' (f. 87[v]).

55–60 **Wherfore worthy cytezins . . . dyd frely before vnrewarded.** *Sal*: 'quae ante uostra beneficia gratuito faciebam, ea uti accepta mercede deseram non est consilium, Quirites' (**85. 8**).

58 **nor now I rewarded of you purpose nat.** 'Nor do I, now thus rewarded by you, intend.'

73–5 **Send forth a noble man . . . set vp on hy.** *Sal*: 'hominem ueteris prosapiae ac multarum imaginum' 'a man of ancient lineage, possessing many ancestral portraits (death masks)' (**85. 10**).

76–84 **Wyll ye change . . . necessary to be done.** The whole construction may be considered interrogative, or perhaps the question terminates after *these gentylmen*.

89–93 **some of these noble men so farre out of order . . . men without order.** *Sal*: 'praeposteri homines' (**85. 12**). That is, those who put things in reverse of their proper order.

92–3 **And of the Grekes preceptes of chyualrie.** *Sal*: 'Graecorum militaria praecepta' (**85. 12**). For the following sentence, *For they shulde* . . . cf. *Sold*: 'Et ita faciunt posterius quod faciendum erat prius. Nam oportebat eos discere priusquam essent consules: id quod pertinet ad consulatum gerendum' (sig. o1[r]).

97–8 **howbeit euery wyseman . . . the rule therof.** *Sal*: 'nam gerere quam fieri tempore posterius, re atque usu prius est' (**85. 12**). *Asc*: 'Nam gerere .i. administrare decenter consulatum: est posterius tempore .i. quantum ad tempus: quam fieri .s. consulem: quia oportet prius fieri consulem quam gerat consulatum: sed est prius .i. potius re atque vsu .i. vtilitate. et ita deberent prius studere gerere .i. vt sciant bene regere consulatum: quam fieri consules: cum iam contra faciant. Sunt qui legant:

Nam gerere quam scire .s. rationem gerendi: est posterius: sed prior lectio placet' (f. 88^{r}).

106–8 **Nowe iuge and consyder . . . of redyng or doyng.** *Sal*: 'Nunc uos existumate facta an dicta pluris sint' 'Judge for yourselves now whether words or deeds are of greater value' (**85. 14**). The revised reading in *BarcC* only partially remedies the translation.

109–10 **My happy fortune is obiected of them agaynst me as to rebuke.** *Sal*: 'mihi fortuna, illis probra obiectantur' (**85. 14**). Sallust refers to Marius' fortune or fate of low birth. Perhaps Barclay uses *happy* merely to mean 'by hap, by chance', but cf. *Asc*, who sees *fortuna* as bearing a double sense: 'fortuna supple obiectantur .i. frequenter ad contumeliam obiicitur mihi: hoc est quod non sim sortitus nobiles progenitores: sicut mihi nobilem animum peperi: quod fortuitum est' (f. 88^{v}).

111–17 **Is nat trueth . . . moost exellent in noblenesse.** An expansion upon *Sal*: 'Quamquam ego naturam unam et communem omnium existumo, sed fortissumum quemque generosissumum' [*Laet–BritT*: generosum esse; *AscT*, *BarcT*: generosissimum esse] (**85. 15**).

180–2 **lest some might count me culpable . . . pacyence and sylence.** *Sal*: 'ne quis modestiam in conscientiam duceret' 'lest anyone interpret my reticence as consciousness of my unworthiness' (**85. 26**).

183–4 **after the conscyence of myne owne mynde.** *Sal*: 'ex animi mei sententia' 'I am quite sure' (**85. 27**). A common asseveration. *Laet–BritT*, *AscT*, *BarcT*: 'ex animi sententia' (*Sold*: 'ex animi mei').

184–7 **For if they say trueth . . . fayned and false.** *Sal*: 'Quippe uera necesse est bene praedicent, falsa uita moresque mei superant' 'Indeed, if they tell the truth, they must speak well of me, [and if they lie about me (*ly on me*)] my life and character will overcome any falsehood' (**85. 27**)

194 **speares/ standerdes/ horsetrappers/ harnesse.** [*BarcA B*: horse/ trappers; *BarcC*: horse, trappers] *Sal*: 'hastas, uexillum, phaleras' (**85. 29**). *Phalerae* (ornamented metal discs) were military honours worn by men as well as horses, but Barclay here probably follows *Sold* (sig. o2^{r}) and *Asc* (f. 89^{v}), who describe them only as 'ornamenta equorum'.

195–8 **some gyuen to me of themperour . . . of thempyre.** Largely Barclay's addition, but cf. *Asc*: 'alia dona militaria .i. quibus ob virtutem quod ea hostibus detraxerim ab imperatore donatus sum' (f. 89^{v}).

199–200 **whiche I haue taken in good worth.** 'Which I have received willingly.'

217–18 **to reaue away . . . chafe their garnyson.** *Sal*: 'praesidia agitare' 'to stand guard, or to mount a guard' (**85. 33**). For Barclay's interpretation and expansion cf. *Asc*: 'agitare .i. expellere oppidis præsidia .s. hostium' (f. 89^{v}).

223–6 **Nor I shall nat handell . . . take the worshyp to me.** *Sal*: 'neque illos arte colam, me opulenter, neque gloriam meam, laborem illorum faciam' (**85. 34**). *Laet–BritT*, *AscT*, *BarcT*: 'neque arte colam illos ut me opulentent . . .' Cf. *Sold*: '¶His igitur praeceptis milites cohortabor: neque illos arte colam: me opulenter' [opulenter **1495.1**; opulentet *in later printings*] (sig. o2^{v}). *Asc*: 'arcte .i. anxie: vt opulentent .i. opulentum faciant me' (f. 89^{v}). Soldus' commentary provides the correct reading adopted in modern editions (*me opulenter*) in contrast with the reading of *Laet–BritT*, *AscT* and other editions such as Rome **1490** (*ut me opulentent*). The preferred modern reading appeared in the earliest editions (e.g.Venice **1470.1**, Rome **1473**) and was taken up by Aldus Manutius **1509.3** and the reviser of the **1513.2** Venice edition of Ascensius's text. Barclay has provided both versions, first translating Ascensius's interpretation (taking *arte/anxie* to mean *by crafte*), then Soldus's in the next clause.

230–2 **he is nat to be called . . . oppresser of cytezins.** *Sal*: 'id est dominum, non imperatorem esse' (**85. 36**). *Asc*: 'id est esse dominum .i. tyrannum et superbum regem: non imperatorem liberi populi' (f. 89^{v}).

238–9 **And euery hye office . . . duetie and herytage.** *Sal*: 'et omnis honores non ex merito, sed quasi debitos a uobis repetit' (**85. 37**). *Asc*: 'sed quasi debitos hereditaria successione' (f. 89^{v}).

242–4 **as ryches/ patrymony . . . worthy dedes.** *Sal*: 'diuitias, imagines, memoriam sui praeclaram' 'riches, images and their own illustrious memory' (**85. 38**).

244–5 **Neuertheles their vertu . . . nat kepe it.** *Sal*: 'uirtutem non reliquere, neque poterant' 'their ancestors have not handed down their virtue, nor could they' (**85. 38**).

249–52 **and bycause I haue no iougler . . . rurall people.** *Sal*: 'neque histrionem ullum neque pluris preti cocum quam uilicum habeo' 'I keep no actor, nor give my cook higher wages than my steward' (**85. 39**). *Laet–BritT*, *AscT*, *BarcT* omit *preti*, which in part explains Barclay's version, although *Sold* and *Asc* include *preti* in their commentaries. *Asc* explains the term *vilicus*: 'villicum .i. curatorem villæ, hoc est hominem rusticum' (f. 90^{r}).

255–6 **such delyciousnesse and curyosite belongeth vnto women.** *Sal*: 'munditias mulieribus . . . conuenire' (**85. 40**). *Asc*: 'mundicias .i. curiosas exornationes' (f. 90^{r}).

256–7 **Euery good man: thynketh it.** Perhaps to be taken as an impersonal construction 'for every good man it seems . . .', which follows *Sal*: 'omnibusque bonis oportere' (**85. 40**), and appears to be what the punctuation indicates. Alternatively, the punctuation might be omitted in order to take the construction as simply subject-verb.

258–62 **And more honour . . . regarde therof.** *Sal*: 'arma, non supellectilem decori esse' 'arms and armour, not furnishings, are marks of honour' (**85. 40**).

264–6 **Let them inclyne . . . and dronkenes.** An expansion upon the understatement of *Sal*: 'ament, potent' (**85. 41**).

285–7 **that is to say the couetyse . . . pride of Metellus.** *Sal*: 'auaritiam, imperitiam atque superbiam' (**85. 45**). *Asc*: 'auariciam quæ in Bestia fuit et Albino: et imperitiam: in Aulo: et superbiam in Metello' (f. 90^{v}).

291–2 **by the auaryce and by the vnboldnesse and cowardyse of their captayns.** *Sal*: 'auaritia aut temeritate ducum' (**85. 46**). *Laet–BritT*, *AscT*, *BarcT*, and the commentaries all have *temeritate* 'rashness, overboldness'.

308–10 **For certaynlie . . . or sleuth.** *Sal*: 'Etenim nemo ignauia immortalis factus est' (**85. 49**). Barclay is not the only translator to have interpreted the clause in this way, but it is probably better rendered as 'certainly no one has gained immortal *life* through inaction'. *Asc* prefers the latter: 'Etenim .i. quia certe: nemo est factus immortalis ignauia .i. per ignauiam: quia tam ignaui quam strenui moriuntur' (f. 90^{v}).

Chapter 51

12 **which was assigned embassadoure to hym.** *Sal*: 'legatum' (**86. 1**). Here, as at l. 45 and 53/68, Barclay knowingly renders *legatus* as *embassadour* where it denotes a military lieutenant rather than a diplomatic functionary.

15–20 **and nat after the custome . . . to go with hym.** *Sold* (who cites Livy 1. 43 verbatim) and *Asc* provide explanations of the Servian Census, and the manner in which soldiers were traditionally recruited from the five higher classes, but not the sixth and lowest, the *capite censi*, who were entered on the censor's lists only for their persons, not for property tax. Barclay explains how Marius' recruitment from this lower class was a break with tradition. For his comment that they were 'nat suffrede to go to warfare before: lest their pouertie myght haue constrayned them rather to fall to robbery than to dedes of chiualry'; cf. *Sold*: 'Serui: capite censi et qui ex classes erant ad militiam non recipiebantur: utpote propter inopiam suspecti' (sig. o3^{v}). Neither *Sal*, *Sold*, nor *Asc* makes Barclay's point that Marius exempted the *capite censi* from the tax usually levied upon them to pay the wages of those eligible to go to war.

31–2 **bycause this sort of people . . . his promocyon.** *Sal*: 'quod ab eo genere celebratus auctusque erat' (**86. 3**). *BarcT*, *AscT*: 'adiutusque erat'; *Laet–BritT*: 'auctusque' (*Sold* has *adiutus* in commentary). *Sold*: '¶Celebratus .i. honoratus: ¶Adiutus .s. ad consulatum comparandum' (sig. o3^{v}).

42–3 **the prouynce next vnto Affrike vnder the Romayns at a towne named Vtica.** That is, the town of Utica in the Roman province of Africa.

45–7 **For Metellus . . . coude nat endure to here.** *Sal*: 'Nam Metellus conspectum Mari fugerat, ne uideret ea quae audita animus tolerare nequiuerat' (86. 5).

48–9 **But whan Marius . . . subsidyes and rescous.** *Sal*: 'Sed consul expletis legionibus cohortibusque auxiliariis' 'the consul, having restored to full strength his legions and cohorts of auxiliaries' (87. 1). Barclay does not quite make clear Sallust's meaning, despite *Sold*: '¶Cohortibus auxiliariis: cohortes auxiliariæ dicuntur cohortes quæ ab alienigenis populis in auxilium mittuntur' (sig. o4^{r}).

52–3 **but febly defended with men and walles.** *Sal*: 'natura et uiris parum munita' (87. 1); *Laet–BritT*, *AscT*, *BarcT*: 'parum munita natura et viris'.

59–60 **their lybertie/ their countrey/ their frendes.** *Sal*: 'libertatem patriam parentesque' (87. 2). On the meaning of *parentes* see note to Prologue, l. 77. Neither *Sold* nor *Asc* comments on the word here.

68–70 **For it pleased hym . . . in spoyling.** *Sal*: 'Ita Iugurthae placuerat speranti mox effusos hostis' (87. 4). *Asc*: 'hostes effusos per prædationem' (f. 91^{r}).

Chapter 52

10–11 **He perceyued well . . . on both sydes or agaynst.** *Sal*: 'cognoscere quid boni utrisque [*Laet–BritT*, *AscT*, *BarcT*: quid utrinque boni] aut contra esset' (88. 2). The removal of the redundant last phrase *or agaynst* in *BarcB C* is an improvement, but a change of *good and yll* to *good or yll* is also desirable.

17 **Often whyle.** Perhaps to be taken as a compound adverb 'many times' heading a main clause. Barclay's usual phrase, however, is *oftentymes*. Sallust's *saepe* refers to Marius, and *whyle* seems to head a subordinate clause: Marius often attacked Jugurtha and the Getulians when they were raiding the Numidians allied to the Romans.

18 **the Numidyans which had yeldedde themselfe to the Romayns.** *Sal*: 'sociis nostris' (88. 3). *Sold*: '¶Ex sociis nostris: uidelicet ex urbibus et ex agris populorum Numidiæ: qui se populo Romano dediderant' (sig. o4^{r}).

23–6 **But whan Marius consydred . . . mouyng from place to place.** *Sal*: 'Quae postquam gloriosa modo neque belli patrandi cognouit' (88. 4). *AscT*: 'Quæ postquam gloriosa modo facta sunt: neque belli copiam patrandi cognouit' [*Laet–BritT*: belli nec copiam]. Barclay appears to render the phrase *belli patrandi* as *without any auantage*.

47–8 **and prodycion of their capitayns.** Barclay adds this phrase.

48–9 **But at first begynning he medled but with mean castels and**

townes. *Sal*: 'Ac primo mediocria gerebat' (**89. 2**). *Sold*: 'Primo quidem Marius eas urbes capere cœpit: quae mediocres erant' (sig. o4[v]).

Chapter 53

5–8 **which (as men say) . . . Iupyter and Alcumena.** *Sal*: 'cuius conditor Hercules Libys memorabatur' (**89. 4**). *Sold*: '¶Cuius conditor Hercules Libys memorabatur. Hercules Libis dicebatur condidisse hanc urbem. Plures Hercules fuerant. Sed qui tot monstra superasse dicitur. Hercules filius Iouis et Alcumenæ fuit secundum fabulas. Non ergo hic Hercules Iouis filius: sed Hercules Libys Capsam condidit' (sig. o4[v]). *Asc* (f. 92[r]) provides a similar clarification.

20–2 **And moreouer the myscheuous . . . any other thyng.** *Sal*: 'Ad hoc natura serpentium ipsa perniciosa siti magis quam alia re accenditur' [*Laet–BritT*, *AscT*, *BarcT omit* ipsa] 'moreover, the venom of snakes, deadly in itself, is exacerbated by thirst more than anything' (**89. 5**). *Asc*: 'Ad hoc .i. insuper natura serpentium perniciosa .i. pernecans veneno: accenditur .s. ad iram: magis siti quam alia re' (f. 92[r]).

25–6 **both for that it was moche hurtfull to hym: and profytable to Iugurth.** *Sal*: 'cum propter usum belli' (**89. 6**).

34–5 **All other which dwelled . . . rayne water.** *Sal*: 'cetera pluuia utebantur' [*Laet–BritT*, *AscT*, *BarcT*: ceteri] (**89. 6**). *Asc*: 'cæteri .i. qui in suburbiis et agro erant: vtebantur pluuia .i. aqua pluuiali quam in cisternis conseruant' (f. 92[r]).

43–8 **as many Christen men . . . norice of all vyces.** Barclay's excursus derives only in part from *Asc*: 'Cibus et potus erat illis aduersus. id est contra famem atque sitim: et non erat libidini neque luxuriæ vt Epicureis et multis etiam nostratibus Christianis qui viuunt vt edant: nec edunt vt viuere possint. quod ne Socrati quidem placuit' (f. 92[r]).

49–50 **this Marius after that he had serched euery thyng by his espyes.** *Sal*: 'consul, omnibus exploratis' (**90. 1**). *Asc*: 'exploratis .i. per exploratores cognitis' (f. 92[v]).

51 **(as men thought) holpen of the goddes.** *Sal*: 'credo dis fretus' 'relying on the gods, I suppose' (**90. 1**).

53–5 **as he which had impedyment . . . all other corne.** *Sal*: 'quippe etiam frumenti inopia temptabatur' (**90. 1**). The readings of both *BarcA* and *B* present difficulties. *A* seems to mean: 'being the one who was impeded, he was hindered not only by the difficulty of the country, but also by the lack of grain.'

64–6 **horsemen . . . frendes of thempyre.** An expansion of *Sal*: 'equitibus auxiliariis' 'auxiliary cavalry' (**90. 2**).

68 **embassadour of the hoost.** *Sal*: 'legatum' 'lieutenant, second-in-command' (**90. 2**). Cf. note to 51/12.

80–3 **And euery day he dystribued . . . after their nombre.** *Sal*: 'Ceterum in itinere cotidie pecus exercitui per centurias, item turmas aequaliter distribuerat' (**91. 1**). *Laet–BritT*, *AscT*, *BarcT*: 'quotidie quadraginta duum [*Laet–BritT*: duo] pecus'. *Asc*: 'Cæterum: hoc est insuper: ipse distribuerat exercitui per centurias item per turmas æqualiter .i. æquali portione (sunt autem centuriæ peditum: turmæ equitum) in itinere. hoc est dum iter facerent: pecus scilicet agendum vt dicit commentarius [Soldus]: sed melius dices: comedendum: quin etiam additum inueni: quadraginta duum scilicet capitum: vt singulis diebus .xlii. duo assumpserint turmæ et centuriæ' (f. 92^{v}).

82 **by hunders and halfe hunders togyder.** *Sal*: 'per centurias, item turmas' (**91. 1**). *Laet–BritT*, *AscT*, *BarcT*: 'per centurias: item per turmas'. Probably to be understood as 'by hundreds' (that is centuries of foot soldiers) and 'by half-hundreds' (*turmas*, or groups of about thirty cavalrymen). The *centuria* was originally a division of one hundred soldiers, later reduced to sixty. It is possible that *hunder* and *half-hunder* refer to the centurians and cavalry commanders (cf. *OED* s.v. **hundreder**).

91–2 **There pytchedde they their tentes with easy labour and small defence.** *Sal*: 'Ibi castris leui munimento positis' (**91. 2**).

117–24 **Whan thinhabytantes . . . to Marius.** *Sal*: 'Quae postquam oppidani cognouere, res trepidae, metus ingens, malum improuisum, ad hoc pars ciuium extra moenia in hostium potestate coegere uti deditionem facerent' 'When the townspeople saw what was going on, their confusion, great panic, unexpected plight and also the fact that some of their fellow citizens were outside the walls and in the power of the enemy, forced them to surrender' (**91. 5**). Barclay's version is consistent with the text and punctuation of *Laet–BritT* and *AscT*, who begin a new sentence with *Ad hoc*, and who read *potestate deprehensa cogere*. *Asc* explains: 'Ad hoc .i. insuper: pars ciuium .s. Capsensium: depræhensa in potestate hostium: hoc est Marii et eius militum: coegere (Locutio congrua in re non in voce pars deprehensa coegere: hoc est ciues partim depræhensi: coegere reliquos) vti .i. vt facerent deditionem: hoc est vt se et oppidum dederent id est traderent fidei et potestati ipsius Marii verentes se aliter ad supplicium exposcendos si forte Marius male pugnasset' (f. 93^{r}).

125–8 **All the Numidyans . . . their raunsome.** *Sal*: 'Numidae puberes interfecti, alii omnes uenundati' (**91. 6**). *Sold* explains *puberes* as men and women of childrearing age (sig. o5^{v}); Barclay more or less follows *Asc*: 'Numidæ puberes et ita belli gerendi potentes: interfecti sunt: alii omnes .i. imbelles et inermes sunt venundati' (f. 93^{r}).

134–6 **and neyther refrayned . . . feare of punysshment.** *Sal*: 'neque beneficio neque metu coercitum' (**91. 7**). Barclay's placement of *neyther* is confusing. *neyther by benefite . . . nor yet with awe . . .* would be better. For the past participle *refrayned* (i.e. capable of being restrained) cf. *Sold*: '¶Coercitum refrenatum' (sig. o5ᵛ).

Chapter 54

7–12 **Euery noble dede . . . neglygence of their ennemies.** *Sal*: 'Omnia non bene consulta in uirtutem trahebantur' (**92. 2**). *Laet–BritT*: 'consulta: rerum etiam casu data in uirtutem'; *AscT*: 'consulta modo: verum etiam casu data in virtutem'. Sallust says that Marius' rash acts were regarded as proofs of his bravery, even if they were ill-advised. For the additional last phrase and Barclay's somewhat loose rendering of the whole structure cf. *Sold*: '¶Omnia non bene consulta in uirtute trahebantur. Vide quantam auctoritatem Marius apud omnes habebat. Si hostes non bene consulebant et non bene prouidebant: atque ob eam causam uincerentur a Mario: omnes dicebant hoc euenisse propter uirtutem Marii: non quia hostes male prouidissent' (sig. o5ᵛ).

15–16 **But in contrari wyse . . . man lyueyng.** *Sal*: 'Numidae magis quam mortalem timere' 'the Numidians feared him as a being more than mortal' [*Laet–BritT*, *AscT*, *BarcT*: quam ullum mortalem] (**92. 2**). Cf. *Sold*: 'hostes autem plusquam hominem timebant: ac si diceret: hostes Marium tanquam deum timebant' (sig. o5ᵛ). *Asc*: 'Numidæ timere .i. timebant Marium magis quam vllum mortalem .i. purum hominem' (f. 93ᵛ).

25–8 **In many other townes . . . hurtfull to Marius.** *Sal*: 'plura deserta propter Capsensium miserias igni corrumpit' [*Laet–BritT*, *AscT*, *BarcT*: plura propter] (**92. 3**). *deserta* is found only in a few later integri MSS. Nevertheless *Asc*'s gloss (f. 93ᵛ) has aided Barclay to grasp the implication that the towns were deserted.

30–2 **The aged men . . . slayne downe right.** Barclay's addition.

41–2 **open ynough to be sene . . . castell of quantite.** *Sal*: 'mediocri castello satis patens' 'wide enough to accommodate a fortress of moderate size' (**92. 5**). *Asc*: 'satis patens .i. perspicuus et apparens: castello .i. oppidulo mediocri .i. mediocris quantitatis. in eo posito' (f. 93ᵛ).

56–60 **Besyde all these defences . . . as without.** *Sal*: 'aggeribus turribusque et aliis machinationibus locus importunus' (**92. 7**). Sallust means that the location did not allow the Romans to construct earthworks, towers, or war engines. Barclay's reading, that the place was rendered *importunus* by such constructions on the Numidian side, perhaps derives from *Laet–BritT* punctuation. Nevertheless, the correct reading is indicated by *Asc*: 'importunus .i. inaccessibilis quasi nullum portum habens: aggeribus

.i. aggeres bellicos faciendos vt ante Thalam fecerat Metellus: et turribus .s. superædificandis: et aliis machinationibus. vt vineis. arietibus' (f. 94^{r}).

61–4 **In somoche that the Romayns . . . strayetnesse of the passage.** *Sal*: 'iter castellanorum angustum admodum, utrimque praecisum. Uineae cum ingenti periculo frustra agebantur' 'the path to the fortress was extremely narrow, with precipices on either side. Mantlets were moved forward with extreme danger and to no purpose' (**92. 7**). For Barclay's translation cf. the lack of a punctus before *vineæ*, and the variant reading of *AscT*, *Laet–BritT*: 'utrinque praecisæ vineæ'. *Sold*: '¶Vineae utrinque præcisæ cum ingenti periculo frustra agebantur: uia adeo erat angusta: ut uineas non caperet. itaque necesse erat: ut uineæ ab utraque parte preciderentur: ut ad castellum agi et appelli possent' (sig. $o6^{r}$). Cf. *Asc*: 'præcisæ .i. prius accisæ et arctiores factæ' (f. 94^{r}).

74–5 **Nor other soudyours . . . paryll and daunger.** *Sal*: 'neque inter uineas sine periculo administrare' 'nor operate within the mantlets without danger' (**92. 9**).

77–80 **In the meane tyme no soudioure . . . faynt hertedde.** *Sal*: 'optumus quisque cadere aut sauciari, ceteris metus augeri' 'the bravest of them were killed or wounded, and the rest grew more fearful' (**92. 9**).

81 **But after that many dayes.** The phrase *after that* functions as a compound conjunction 'after', subordinating the clause to the following one beginning *Marius*.

82–3 **Marius was sore angred and vexedde in his hert.** *Sal*: 'Marius . . . anxius' (**93. 1**).

85 **or els abyde the chaunce of fortune.** *Sal*: 'an fortunam opperiretur' (**93. 1**). *BarcT* reads *experiretur*, but his translation appears to follow *Laet–BritT* and *AscT*, which read *op(p)eriretur*.

86–7 **chafedde and brennyng in desyre.** *Sal*: 'aestuans' (**93. 2**). Cf. *Asc*: 'æstuans .i. feruens in desiderio' (f. 94^{r}).

89 **Lumbard.** *Sal*: 'Ligus' (**93. 2**). See note to 25/90–1.

89–91 **a symple soudyour . . . frome his company.** *Sal*: 'miles gregarius, castris aquatum egressus' 'having left the camp to fetch water' (**93. 2**). *Laet–BritT*: 'miles gregarius aliquantum egressus castris'. *AscT*: 'miles gregarius aliquantulum egressus castris'. *Sold* refers to the fetching of water, indicating that his text correctly had *aquatum*: 'Nam cum quidam miles gregarius de Liguria prouincia esset egressus ex castris ad aquam hauriendam' (sig. $o6^{r}$).

89–90 **one of the company . . . to supply the army.** *Sal*: 'ex cohortibus auxiliariis' (**93. 2**).

94–6 **Bycause this Lumbard . . . after their manere.** Barclay's addition. Cf. *Asc*: 'et deinde plures (vescuntur enim illis)' (f. 94^{r}).

102 **no person steryng.** Possibly 'steering, in command or control' but more likely 'stirring': cf. *no man styring* at l. 116.

104–5 **to wyn a name/ laude and riches: and to be spoken of.** Barclay's addition. Sallust merely says that the Ligurian was overcome by the natural desire to achieve an undertaking that appears difficult: 'more ingeni humani cupido difficilia faciundi animum inuadit' (**93. 3**). Neither *Sold* (sig. o6^{v}) nor *Asc* (f. 94^{r}) mentions desires beyond the one of attempting something difficult to achieve.

115–17 **tyll at last he attaynedde . . . notedde and consydred well.** *Sal*: 'Ligus in castelli planitiem peruenit . . . Exploratis omnibus' [*Laet–BritT*, *AscT*: Ligur castelli planiciem perscribit; *BarcT*: Ligur . . . perscripsit] (**93. 4**). *Asc*: 'ipse Ligur perscribit .i. intento animo ac sensibus notat planiciem castelli .i. in qua castellum situm erat' (f. 94^{v}). Some editors accept *perscribit*, taking it to mean that the Ligurian drew a plan of the fortress, but most adopt *pervenit* with the implication that he attained a sufficient height in the tree to be level with the fortress wall.

13–4 **Farthermor he promysed . . . no danger.** *Sal*: 'pollicetur sese itineris periculique ducem' 'offering himself as guide for the ascent and the perilous venture' (**93. 6**). *Laet–BritT* and *AscT*: 'pollicetur se ducem itineris: periculique nihil esse'.

135–43 **Marius hering . . . without moche peryll.** *Sal*: 'Marius cum Ligure promissa eius cognitum ex praesentibus misit, quorum uti cuiusque ingenium erat, ita rem difficilem aut facilem nuntiauere' [*AscT*, *BarcT*: nunciare] (**93. 7**).

144–6 **Wherfore of all the company of trumpettes . . . signes to the fighters.** *Sal*: 'Itaque ex copia tubicinum et cornicinum . . .' 'therefore from his collection of tuba and trumpet players . . .' (**93. 8**).

147–8 **and .iiii. hundred men . . . sayd trumpettes.** *Sal*: 'et cum iis praesidio qui forent quattuor centuriones' (**93. 8**). A passage in Sallust that has puzzled readers, and that in Barclay may be interpreted two ways: there were assigned either four *hundred-men* (centurions) or four-hundred *men*. It is clear from Sallust's subsequent account that some ordinary soldiers accompanied the four centurions, but the figure of four hundred which *Asc* suggests seems improbable: 'cum his .s. tubicinibus quattuor centuriones et ita quadringentos milites' (f. 94^{v}). *Soldus* might suggest this also: '¶Quattuor centuriones. Centurio dicebatur qui præerat uni centuriæ. Centuria centum homines continebat' (sig. p1^{r}). The commentators were no doubt influenced by the reading *illi qui centuriis præerant* (see note to ll. 154–6 below).

152 **Whan the tyme assigned and prefixed by Marius was come.** *Sal*: 'Sed ubi ex praecepto tempus uisum' [*Laet–BritT*: uisum est; *AscT*, *BarcT*:

præcepto ducis tempus uisum est] (94. 1). *Asc*: 'ex præcepto .s. Marii: aut potius vt alii textus habent: ducis videlicet ipsius Liguris' (f. 94^v^).

154–6 **But whan they were come thyder . . . their heedes and their fete.** Modern editors following Carrio, Kritzius, and Dietsch have adopted the reading of seven manuscripts: 'Ceterum illi, qui escensuri [*or* ascensuri] erant, praedocti ab duce arma ornatumque mutaverant'. Earlier editions, following other MSS, contained readings along the lines of that found in *Laet–BritT* and *AscT*: 'Ceterum illi qui centuriis præerant edocti a duce arma ornatumque mutaverant.'

163–4 **if it hapned any stone to smyte agaynst them.** *Sal*: 'offensa' (94. 1). Cf. *Asc*: 'offensa .i. contracta a lapide' (f. 94^v^).

173–5 **Suche places where moost dout . . . moost of all.** *Sal*: 'quae dubia nisui uidebantur potissumus temptare' (94. 2). That is, the Ligurian first personally tested the climbing points that appeared unsafe.

175–7 **and in goyng and comyng . . . the remenant.** Barclay omits the phrase *deinde statim digrediens* 'and then at once stepping aside', which should precede *he encreased*.

184–5 **howbeit that all the day . . . the castell.** *Sal*: 'Marius . . . quamquam toto die intentos proelio Numidas habuerat' 'Marius had kept the Numidians intent upon the fighting all day' (94. 3). Barclay's rendering arises from *Laet–BritT* and *AscT*: 'quamquam tota die intentos prælio suos habuerat' [*BarcT* and *AscT* 1519: prælios].

186–98 **and he hymselfe departyng forth . . . be throwen into the castell.** *Sal*: 'et ipse extra uineas egressus, testudine acta succedere et simul hostem tormentis sagittariisque et funditoribus eminus terrere' (94. 3).

188–90 **to holde vp their sheldes . . . the frame of a volt.** *Sal*: 'testudine acta' (94. 3). *Sold*: 'Testudo est scutorum connexio curuatam in testudinis modum. Nam milites scutati ita se inuicem connectunt atque condensant: ut nemo per eos irrumpere possit. Ita autem se scutati connectunt: ut curuaturam quandam faciant in modum testudinis' (sig. p1^r^).

203–4 **and obiectyng cowardyse agaynst Marius.** *Sal*: 'ac Mario uecordiam obiectare' (94. 4). For the translation of *uecordia* as 'cowardice', rather than 'madness', cf. *Asc*: 'vecordiam .i. pusillanimitatem et cordis exilitatem: aut dementiam' (f. 95^r^).

222 **They stryued to ascende vnto the walles.** *Sal*: 'certantes murum petere' (94. 6); *Laet–BritT*, *AscT*, *BarcT*: 'certantes murum ascendere'.

227 **was tourned by chance.** *Sal*: 'forte correcta' (94. 6); *Laet–BritT*, *AscT*, *BarcT*: 'forte correpta'.

Chapter 55

6–7 **tresourer of the army.** *Sal*: 'quaestor' (95. 1). *Asc*: 'quæstor .i. vt dicunt receptor vectigalium publicorum' (f. 95[v]).

8–10 **Whom the same . . . thempyre of Rome.** A dependent relative clause, with *Lucius Sylla* as the antecedent of *whom*. *Sal*: 'Ceterum dum ea res geritur, L. Sulla quaestor cum magno equitatu in castra uenit, quos uti ex Latio et a sociis cogeret Romae relictus erat' (95. 1). *Laet–BritT*, *AscT*, *BarcT*: 'qui uti ex Latio et sociis exercitum cogeret Romae relictus erat'.

14–15 **namely for two causes.** Cf. *Sold*: 'Duabus de causis scribam de moribus Syllæ: uidelicet: et quia alio loco non sum dicturus de rebus Syllæ: et quia nullus alius de eo satis diligenter et sincere scripsit' (sig. p1[v]).

21–6 **For his tong nor penne . . . to write of him.** This is Barclay's addition, which makes explicit Sallust's implication. Cf. *Asc*: 'videtur mihi locutus ore parum libero: et ita ficto et dissimulato: quia non ausus tanti viri scelera dicere' (f. 95[v]).

35–7 **howbeit such pleasure . . . his estate.** *Sal*: 'nisi quod de uxore potuit honestius consuli' 'except that his conduct towards his wife (wives?) might have been more creditable' (95. 3). To which of Sulla's wives Sallust refers is not clear. Plutarch, *Sulla* 35, states that he married five times. His divorces and possible infidelities would have been considered scandalous. The commentators' observations possibly link Sallust's observation with Sulla's frivolous and inappropriate fifth marriage to Valeria, as described by Plutarch. *Sold*: 'nisi quod uxorem honestiorem ducere potuit. Nam in hac parte uoluptas eum impediuit: ne pro dignitate sua uxorem duceret qualem oportebat. ¶Consuli: prouideri' (sig. p1[v]). *Asc*: 'nisi .i. hoc solo excepto: quod potuit .s. ab homine diligenti et negocioso: consuli .i. prospici et prouideri (sunt aut potuit et consuli impersonaliter posita) honestius .i. decentius de uxore quam per secordiam aut luxuriam minus honestam duxit' (f. 96[r]).

41–2 **He was a maruelous . . . specially of money.** *Sal*: 'ad simulanda negotia altitudo ingeni incredibilis; multarum rerum ac maxume pecuniae largitor' (95. 3). *Laet–BritT* and *AscT* punctuate so as to link *incredibilis* with *largitor*, which follows, rather than *ingeni* in the preceding clause.

42–4 **and before the warre . . . worthy reputed.** The punctuation in Barclay's first edition is misleading. The clause beginning *and before* is subordinate to the clause beginning *He was*. In *BarcB* a colon is substituted for a punctus before *He*, but the capital H remains.

44–6 **nor his good fortune . . . more fortunate than strong.** *Sal*: 'numquam super industriam fortuna fuit, multique dubitauere fortior an felicior esset' 'his fortune was never greater than his efforts deserved; and many have been undecided whether his fortitude or his luck was the greater' (95. 4).

46–61 **But after the vyctorie . . . with blode of the cytezins.** *Sal*: 'Nam postea quae fecerit, incertum habeo pudeat an pigeat magis disserere' 'As to his subsequent behaviour, I am not sure I should should speak of it with shame or more with sorrow' (Comber–Balmaceda, 95. 4). Barclay's expanded account of Sulla's later career is probably taken directly from *Sold* and *Asc*, although the general outline of the civil war between Marius and Sulla, and Sulla's reign of terror with his employment of the *proscriptio* would have been well known to Barclay. Following *Sold* and *Asc*, Barclay refers to Caius Carbo in error for Gnaeus Carbo. *Sold*: 'sed pristinam uirtutem amisit: et eam in impietatem crudelitatemque conuertit. Nam parta uictoria totam urbem ciuili sanguine repleuit. Sylla Caium Marium urbe pepulit. Deinde Cinnam quinquies consulem qui contracto exercitu Caio Mario fauebat uictum occidit .item. C. Carbonem et Marium iuniorem crudeliter necauit. Postremo parta ex omnibus uictoria crudelissimus omnium totam urbem sanguine repleuit' (sig. p1^{v}). *Asc*: 'quia infeliciter conuertit tam nobilem victoriam in tam turpem dominationem in qua Marium Priscum expulit: iuniorem et Cinnam quintum consulem et Caium Carbonem hominem adeo nobilem necauit' (f. 96^{r}). Caius Papirius Carbo Arvina was put to death by the Marian party in 82 BC. Gnaeus Papirius Carbo fought against Sulla, and having failed to relieve the Younger Marius, blockaded in Praeneste by the Sulla's forces, he fled to Africa, and then the island of Cossyra, where he was captured. Pompey Magnus executed him at Lilybaeum in 82 BC.

72 **without it were agaynst his wyll.** 'except unwillingly'.

77–8 **and by suche meanes to haue them bounde to hym.** Barclay's addition makes explicit Sallust's implication.

80–1 **in sportes and in sadnes.** *Sal*: 'ioca atque seria' (96. 3). Sallust states that Sulla could converse both in jest and in seriousness with the humblest of his men.

81–2 **In batell and in watchynges.** *Sal*: 'in agmine atque ad uigilias' (96. 3); *Laet–BritT*, *AscT*, *BarcT*: 'in acie atque ad vigilias'.

85–6 **for in dispraysing . . . to themselfe.** For Barclay's addition cf. *Sold*: 'Nam ambitiosi et laudis cupidi putant seipsos laudare: si alios uituperent et aliis detrahant' (sig. p2^{r}).

Chapter 56

16–17 **without losse or deminisshyng of his kyngdome and marches therof.** *Sal*: 'integris suis finibus' (97. 2). *Sold*: '¶Integris suis finibus: uidelicet si nihil de regno suo amisisset in conditionibus pacis' (sig. p2^{r}). *Asc*: 'finibus suis .i. regni sui. integris .i. non imminutis' (f. 96^{v}).

30 **both these chaunces.** That is, of victory or defeat.

33 **by many of his espyes.** *Sal*: 'ex multis' (97. 4). *Asc*: 'ex multis .s. speculatoribus aut exploratoribus' (f. 96^{v}). Sallust implies that the attackers were coming from several directions, and accordingly scouts from different positions were making the same report.

40–1 **but by companyes . . . heapes and clusters.** *Sal*: 'sed cateruatim, uti quosque fors conglobauerat' (97. 4).

42–3 **that sodayne and vnprouyded feare.** *Sal*: 'improuiso metu' (97. 5). See note to 40/67–9.

44–6 **some drue them . . . armed themself.** *Sal*: 'aut arma capiebant aut capientis alios ab hostibus defensabant' (97. 5). Barclay may be right in reading the text this way, or perhaps Sallust means that some fought without armour, enabling others meanwhile to arm. On Barclay's translation of L. *arma* (that is, arms and/or armour) by *armour* see notes 25/100–1, 31/54–6.

49–56 **For the horsmen and fotemen . . . assayled them.** Sallust's text (97. 5), as transmitted, is as confused as the battle. Most MSS, *Laet–BritT* and *AscT* read: 'sine signis, sine ordinibus equites peditesque permixti cædere alios, alios obtruncare: multos contra aduersos acerrime pugnantes ab tergo circumveniri'. Most mod. edns. emend. For example, Rolfe: 'alii, alii obtruncari, multi'; Reynolds, Comber–Balmaceda: 'alius, alius obtruncari, multi'.

60–1 **bothe of olde and newe . . . craftie in batayle.** MSS (except one), *Laet–BritT*, *AscT*, *BarcT*: 'veteres novique et ob ea scientes belli' (97. 5). Barclay's translation follows this order, and seems to imply that the combination possessed physical vigour from the new men, and wisdom from the old. Modern editors emend the order to *noui ueteresque* or omit *nouique*, on the assumption that the phrase *scientes belli* could only refer to the *ueteres*.

71–2 **And his men of garde about hym.** *Sal*: 'cum turma sua' (98. 1). That is, a bodyguard of cavalry.

76–7 **in their nede/ or suche as he sawe in paryll.** *Sal*: 'laborantibus' (98. 1). *Asc*: 'laborantibus .i. in periculo' (f. 97^{r}).

78–81 **And nat withstandyng . . . Getulyans.** Barclay's addition.

84–93 **gyueing them example . . . tedyous to here.** A further colourful addition by Barclay. Sallust relates that Marius had to resort to gestures to give commands because he could not be heard above the noise and confusion: 'manu consulere militibus, quoniam imperare conturbatis omnibus non poterat' (98. 1). *Asc* makes this clear: 'non poterat imperare supple eis: imperio .s. verbali' (f. 97^{r}). Barclay seems to link *manu* with the previous information that Marius joined in the fighting personally, rather than taking it to mean the hand-signalling of orders.

107–8 **downe right.** Steep, near-vertical. *Sal*: 'praeceps' (98. 3).

108–110 **In somoch . . . sufficiently defended.** *Sal* (emended): 'pauca munimenta quaerebat' (98. 3); *Laet–BritT*, *AscT*, *BarcT*: 'gerebat'; MSS: 'gerebat, gerebant, regebant, regebat'.

116 **with full cours.** At full speed: a literal rendering of *Sal*: 'pleno gradu' (98. 5). *Sold*: '¶Pleno gradu: id est pleno passu: hoc est celeriter' (sig. p2^{v}). *Asc*: 'pleno hoc est non impedito nec interrupto gradu: hoc est ingressu' (f. 97^{v}).

122–3 **and there taryed . . . ground**. *Sal*: 'effusi consedere' 'encamped in loose order' (98. 5). *Asc*: 'effusi: hoc est dispersi consedere. id est simul locum quietis ceperunt' (f. 97^{v}).

126–9 **in myrth/ pleasure . . . synging and reuellyng.** *Sal*: 'laetari, exultare, strepere uocibus' (98. 6). *Laet–BritT* and *AscT*: 'laetari: exultare: strepere pedibus: uocibus'. A variant not found in the important MSS. The phrase *with their fete* has been omitted in *BarcB* and *C*, perhaps on the basis of another edition, such as the Aldine. Nevertheless, *pedibus* stands in the Latin text in *BarcB*.

146–52 **as men without fere . . . without prouision.** Barclay's addition.

152–4 **all his trumpets . . . coude altogyder**. *Sal*: '[uigiles], item cohortium, turmarum, legionum tubicines simul omnis signa canere' [all MSS, *Laet–BritT*, *AscT*, *BarcT*: uectigales item cohortium] (99. 1). The emendation is Cortius's. Modern editors explain that Sallust refers to signallers from all quarters being ordered to sound their instruments: those in the watch (*uigiles*), cohorts (auxiliaries as distinct from the legions), cavalry, and regular legions. Barclay in any case sidesteps the difficulties of this passage. *Sold* explains *uectigales* as referring to troops from tributary nations: '¶Vectigales. Vectigal proprie dicitur tributum quod prouectura penditur: unde populi uectigales dicebantur qui populo Romano annuatim tributa soluebant. Vnde hoc loco fortasse tubicines uectigales dicit: qui missi erant ab alienigenis populis . . . sed hanc expositionem infirmam relinquo: non enim satis placet' (sig. p3^{r}). For Barclay's seemingly odd usage of *mynstrals* to refer to military musicians compare 54/145.

156 **and with that inuade . . . Numidyans.** *Sal*: 'atque portis erumpere iubet' 'he ordered them to burst forth from their camp' [*Laet–BritT*, *AscT*, *BarcT*: aut portis erumpere; *omit* iubet] (99.1). Barclay follows *Sold*: 'aut erumpere portis scilicet castrorum hostibus' (sig. p3^{r}); and *Asc*: 'aut erumpere portis .i. euadere vi in portas castrorum hostilium' (f. 98^{r}). On Barclay's use of *tentes* for a fortified encampment see note to 13/73.

Chapter 57

5–9 **Whan Marius . . . prouysion of vytels.** *Sal*: 'Dein Marius, uti coeperat, in hiberna proficiscitur, nam propter commeatum in oppidis maritumis agere decreuerat' [*Laet–BritT*: in hyberna proficiscitur: propter; *AscT*: in hiberna it [*sic*] propter] (**100. 1**). The MSS (except some *recentiores*) omit *proficiscitur*.

8 **in hauen townes.** *Sal*: 'in oppidis maritumis' 'in towns by the sea' (**100. 1**); that is, sea-ports.

13 **as if his ennemies had ben in his sight.** *Sal*: 'sed pariter atque in conspectu hostium' (**100. 1**).

14–15 **and all the spear men with hym.** *Sal*: 'cum equitatu' (**100. 2**). Barclay uses the term *spearman* to refer to a mounted soldier several times (see Glossary).

18–20 **Of the treatours . . . knewe best the contrey.** *Sal*: 'Perfugae, minume cari et regionum scientissumi' 'the deserters, least esteemed (and therefore expendable) and most knowledgeable about the region' (**100. 3**). *Laet–BritT*, *AscT*, *BarcT*: 'Perfugæ regionum scientissimi'. Although *Laet–BritT* omits *minume cari* (as does *AscT*), *Sold* glosses as if it were present (as, e.g., in Rot's edition, Rome **1473**). Neither version seems to account for Barclay's translation, in which *such as were best laboured* presumably means 'those most fitted to be put to work'.

26–8 **he himselfe armed . . . to labour.** Perhaps this should be a complete sentence, with a punctus before *he*, but the construction is awkward. *Sal*: 'Ipse armatus intentusque item milites cogebat' (**100. 4**). The passage is misleadingly punctuated in *AscT*, where there is a punctus after *intentusque* and the following clause is placed within the next sentence.

28–9 **In euery place . . . he ordred defence.** This seems approximately to render *Sal*: 'Neque secus atque iter facere, castra munire' (**100. 4**).

42–4 **Marius constrayned . . . or punisshment.** *Sal*: 'pudore magis quam malo exercitum coercebat' (**100. 5**). That is, Marius controlled his army by appealing to their sense of shame rather than by dealing out punishment.

45–51 **Howbeit some sayd . . . as equall persones supposed.** MSS: 'Quod multi per ambitionem fieri aiebant, quod a pueritia consuetam duritiam, et alia, quae ceteri miserias uocant, uoluptati habuisse [*or* habuisset]'. Editors have emended and interpreted in various ways. Reynolds, for example, following Wirtz, emends *quod a pueritia* to *alii a pueritia*; Rolfe simply omits *quod*. *Laet–BritT*: 'quod multi per ambitionem aiebant: quod a pueritia . . . habuisset'. *AscT* (also *Laet–BritT* **1497/8**) supplies *alii*: 'quod multi per ambitionem aiebant: alii quod a pueritia consuetam duritiam: et alia que cæteri miserias vocant: voluptati habuisset'. *Asc*: 'multi aiebant id est interpretabantur supple factum: per ambitionem . . . alii supple aiebant: hoc est dicebant factum: quod Marius habuisset voluptati: id est ad voluptatem: duriciam . . .' That is, some persons attributed Marius' leniency and personal example to the base motive of ambition and desire for popularity, while others attributed his actions to his lifelong experience of hardship, and his habitual effort and service. If Barclay were translating to express this, we might expect *others said* in the construction, but that appears to be the implication of *as equall persones supposed*. The Latin text in *BarcA B* reads *alii que cæteri* rather than *alia que cæteri* as in *AscT*, but this is more likely to be a compositor's error than any deliberate attempt to improve the Latin. Punctuation, orthography, and abbreviations indicate a close dependence upon Ascensius in other respects.

60–1 **the espyes of their ennemies appered on euery syde.** *Sal*: 'undique simul speculatores citi sese ostendunt' 'from all sides at once the scouts quickly appeared' (**101. 1**). This refers to Marius' scouts, who are also the referent of the following sentence. Barclay follows *Sold* and *Asc* in identifying two sets of scouts who appear: first those of Jugurtha, then those of Marius. *Sold*: 'speculatores hostium cito se ostendunt. Ex qua re Marius intellexit hostes adesse . . . ¶Speculatores .s. hostium' (sig. p4^{r}). *Asc*: 'speculatores: hoc est exploratores Iugurthæ: citi. hoc est properantes ostendunt sese' (f. 98^{v}).

66–9 **And therfore parceyuinge . . . .iiii. partes (as sayd is).** *Sal*: 'consul incertus quonam modo aciem instrueret, nullo ordine commutato' (**101. 2**). Cf. *Sold*: 'Ex quo Marius dubius et incertus quonam modo instrueret aciem: nullum ordinem commutauit. sed exercitum quadripartitum reliquit: et ita hostes expectauit' (sig. p4^{r}).

73–5 **and with an other part . . . rounde about.** Barclay's addition.

75–85 **In the meantyme . . . their nombre.** Barclay's expansions include *as well . . . tyme, the fotemen which were vnder Sylla*, and *to decrease . . . nombre*.

91–2 **Wherfore Bocchus . . . fresshe fotemen.** Another of Barclay's dramatic additions.

94–6 **In the meane tyme Marius . . . in hande.** *Sal*: 'Tum Marius apud primos agebat' (**101. 6**). In Barclay's expansion the last clause *and so stode it hym in hande* means 'and so he needed to be'.

99–100 **anone he turned hym . . . fotemen of the Romayns.** *Sal*: 'clam cum paucis ad pedites conuortit' (**101. 6**). Precisely which section of the Roman infantry (if not his own infantry) Jugurtha approaches is not clear, and modern commentators are divided. *Asc* specifies that it is the Roman infantry: 'pedites: scilicet Romanos' (f. 99^{r}).

105–7 **which he had so couloured . . . fotemen of the Romayns.** *Sal*: 'quem in pugna satis inpigre occiso pedite nostro cruentauerat' (**101. 6**).

Some take *pedite nostro* as a collective, as Barclay does, and see Sallust's reference to Jugurth's valour as positive. Others interpret *satis impigre* as a sarcastic remark, which would be more applicable to the slaying of a single Roman soldier. *Asc* observes: 'pedite nostro. id est Romano occiso satis impigre. id est strenue. in quo facto callide hostem laudat' (f. 99^{r}).

109–11 **they were affrayed . . . the messanger.** *Sal*: 'magis atrocitate rei quam fide nuntii terrentur' (**101. 7**). Sallust means that the Romans were shocked more by the horror of such an event than by their belief in the truth of the messenger. Barclay may use *noise* simply to mean 'outcry' here, but more likely he uses it in the sense of 'rumour, (false) report'.

114–15 **the Romayns of the forwarde at that poynt.** Barclay supplies the subject implied in Sallust's clause. He cannot mean the vanguard of the entire Roman army, because Jugurtha departed from there to play out his ruse. Sallust probably means those Romans in the front ranks close enough to see and hear Jugurtha, wherever he is now located. Nevertheless, *at that poynt* is here probably a temporal reference rather than one of position.

125–6 **dyde his dilygence to incourage and support his company.** *Sal*: 'sustentare suos' (**101. 9**). *Asc*: '.i. confirmare ne fugerent' (f. 99^{v}).

128–30 **the spear men of the Romayns . . . at conclusion were slayne.** *Sal*: 'circumuentus ab equitibus, dextra, sinistra [*AscT*, *BarcT* and some MSS: sinistraque] omnibus occisis' 'surrounded by the cavalry, and with all his men killed on left and right' (**101. 9**). *AscT* omits any punctuation after *equitibus*, and Barclay has linked *dextra sinistra* to the preceding phrase rather than the one following. For Barclay's use of the term *spear men* to denote cavalry see note to Title and Contents, l. 129.

131 **gladde to saue his lyfe.** *Sal*: 'uitabundus' 'taking evasive action' (**101. 10**). Perhaps Barclay understood the term as deriving from *uita* 'life' rather than *uitare* 'dodge, avoid'.

137–9 **But he by his polycie . . . that batayle.** Barclay's addition.

140–61 **Thus finally . . . horryble to beholde.** Both Orosius (5. 15. 18) and Diodorus (36. 1) relate that many tens of thousands of Libyans died in this battle. To Sallust's vivid account of the carnage Barclay adds a few details of his own, including ll. 148–51, with its anachronistic reference to stirrups: *deed corpses mangled . . . after in the dust*. On similar battleground descriptions in ancient historiography see Paul, 244.

154–5 **neyther fle: nor be suffred to take rest on the grounde.** *Sal*: 'neque fugere posse neque quietem pati' (**101. 11**). That is, many of the wounded could neither get up, nor remain quiet upon the ground.

Chapter 58

18–21 **Neuertheles it was concluded . . . more desyre therto.** *Sal*: 'tamen placuit uerba apud regem facere: ingenium [*Laet–BritT*, *AscT*, *BarcT*: quo ingenium] aut auorsum flecterent aut cupidum pacis uehementius accenderent' 'they decided to address the king, in order to change his mind if he should be hostile (to the Romans) or to make him more desirous of peace if he wished it' (**102. 3**). Barclay apparently overlooked the verb *flecterent*, and construes *auorsum* (*aduersum*) as referring to Jugurtha, rather than the Romans.

Chapter 59

7–11 **And also we ar glad . . . thempyre of Rome.** *Sal*: 'simul nobis demeres acerbam necessitudinem, pariter te errantem atque illum sceleratissumum persequi' [*Laet–BritT*, *AscT*, *BarcT*: et te errantem et illum] '[we are pleased that] at the same time you have spared us from the unpleasant necessity of inflicting punishment upon your errors as well as his crimes' (**102. 5**).

11–12 **the people of Rome euer syth their poore/ symple/ and small begynning.** *Sal*: 'populo Romano iam a principio imperi' (**102. 6**); MSS, *Laet–BritT*, *AscT*, *BarcT*: 'populo Romano iam a principio inopi'. Modern editions, after Selling, emend *inopi* to *imperi*.

38–40 **Ye haue many expedyent oportunites and necesary commodytes . . . good dedes.** *Sal*: 'Multa atque opportuna habes, quo facilius errata officiis superes' [*Laet–BritT*, *AscT*, *BarcT omit* atque] (**102. 10**). Cf. *Asc*: 'opportuna .i. accommoda' (f. 100v).

42–4 **ye or any other . . . good dedes.** *Sal*: 'numquam populum Romanum benificiis uictum esse' (**102. 11**). That is: no one has surpassed the people of Rome in acts of kindness.

Chapter 60

1–2 **of the vnstablenesse of mynde of the same Bocchus.** In this heading and in the concluding sentence of the chapter Barclay highlights the apparent fickleness of Bocchus, and perhaps the barbarians generally, which Sallust mentions elsewhere. See, for example, 52/41–2 (**88. 6**). Sallust places more emphasis on the skill of Jugurtha in bribing Bocchus' friends, and their power of persuasion.

7–11 **And that the thyrde part of Numidy . . . suffer vnreuenged.** *Sal*: 'Nam Numidiae partem unde ui Iugurtham expulerit iure belli suam factam'

[*Laet–BritT*, *AscT*, *BarcT omit* ui] (**102. 13**). The perfect subjunctive *expulerit* in this passage of reported speech is taken by modern editors to indicate Bocchus' assertion, not Sallust's; but it is not clear whether the subject of the verb is Marius (as Barclay takes it, supplying the subject *the Romayns*) or Bocchus himself. Bocchus might be asserting that he had at some time in the past aquired part of Numidia by conquest (a fact otherwise omitted by Sallust), but it would be more likely that he is now claiming the third part by right of conquest, even though this territory had in fact it had been promised to him for his part in attacking the Romans, thus making his claim all the more absurd. *Sold*: '¶Iure belli factam suam. Supradixit Iugurtham tertiam partem regni Numidiæ Bocho promisisse: si una secum bellum susciperet contra Romanos. Et ideo dicit partem Numidiæ iure belli factam suam' (sig. p5^r^). *Asc*: 'dicit se quoque habere partem Numidiæ iure belli prius acquisitam: non autem intelligo iure belli .i. promissione Iugurthæ facta in eo bello: licet enim dictum est quod Iugurtha promiserat illi tertiam partem Numidiæ: si voti compos euaderat sine regni imminutione: non tamen congrueret huic loco vt id Bocchus confiteatur: sic enim significaret se mercede conductum ad bellum alienum et ita pro excusatione afferret auariciam suam: odiosissimum malum quod non procedit. Intelligam itaque antequam Iugurtha illi filiam suam daret motam fuisse litem de confinibus regni: et partem a Boccho inuasam: illi pro dote ab Iugurtha concessam: propter bellum quod ab Romanis metuebat. Unde ordo est. Nam supradicit partem Numidiæ vnde expulerit Iugurtham factam supple esse suam: iure belli: quia in iusto bello capta cedunt captori: et dicit se nequisse pati .s. æquo animo: eam .s. partem vastari a Mario' (f. 101^{r}).

23–4 **so mutable and varyable was he of mynde.** Cf. Sallust's reference to Bocchus' mind as *animus barbari* (**102. 15**).

Chapter 61

10–16 **But in the meane whyle Bocchus . . . expert and redy.** *Sal*: 'Tum rursus Bocchus [*AscT*: Bocchus scilicet erga Romanos], seu reputando quae sibi duobus proeliis uenerant [*Laet–BritT*, *AscT*: evenerant] seu admonitus [*Laet–BritT*, *AscT*: monitus] ab aliis amicis, quos incorruptos Iugurtha reliquerat, ex omni copia necessariorum quinque delegit, quorum et fides cognita et ingenia ualidissuma erant' (**103. 2**). Barclay's construction is awkward in not subordinating the first clause.

25–6 **without worshyp or apparell.** *Sal*: 'sine decore' 'in a sorry plight' (**103. 4**). *Sold*: '¶Sine decore: id est sine ornatu' (sig. p5^{v}). *Asc*: 'sine decore .i. ornatu aut apparatu legatis debito' (f. 101^{v}).

30 **as vayne and vnstable ennemies.** *Sal*: 'pro uanis hostibus' (**103. 5**). Sallust may mean that Sulla would have reason to doubt their claim to be

envoys, given their sorry appearance, or, as Barclay takes it, following *Asc*, that they were untrustworthy in a more general sense. *Asc*: 'pro vanis .i. mendacibus: et inconstantibus hostibus' (f. 101^{v}).

34–5 **false and fayned of their ennemies/ to distayne their honoure.** That is, the Romans' reputation for avarice was falsely put about by the enemies of Rome.

37–9 **For yet vnto that tyme . . . vnknowen vnto many.** *Sal*: 'Nam etiam tum largitio multis ignota erat' (**103. 6**). Cf. *Asc*: 'Nam largitio .i. captiosa donatio sine amicitia ad captandum et inescandum facta. erat etiam .i. adhuc tum .i. tunc temporis: ignota multis .s. credentibus neminem largiri nisi idem amicus sit' (f. 101^{v}).

47–9 **they commended and exalted . . . their kyng.** *Sal*: 'copias, fidem, magnitudinem regis sui . . . oratione extollunt' (**103. 7**).

Chapter 62

4–5 **In the mean tyme . . . his enterprise.** *Sal*: 'Marius postquam confecto quo intenderat negotio' (**104. 1**). Modern editors favour the reading *confecto*, assuming that Marius must have succeeded in his task. Most MSS and many early editions read *infecto*, whence Barclay's translation. *Laet–BritT* adopts *confecto*, although Soldus' gloss assumes *infecto*: '¶Infecto negocio: quia turrim regiam capere non potuit' (sig. p5^{v}). *AscT* adopts *infecto*, and cf. *Asc*: 'Marius postquam infecto .i. non facto negotio: quo .i. in quod intenderat .s. animum et profectionem suam videlicet ad expugnandum turrim regiam' (f. 102^{r}).

7–9 **Wherefore he commanded . . . from euery place.** *Sal*: 'illosque et Sullam ab Vtica [*Laet–BritT omits* ab Vtica] uenire iubet, item L. Bellienum praetorem Vtica [*Laet–BritT*: ab utica; *AscT*, *some MSS omit* Vtica], praeterea omnis undique senatorii ordinis' (**104. 1**). Barclay is uncharacteristically periphrastic here, omitting the specific information that the camp was located at Utica, the name of the praetor of Utica, and the specific rank of those summoned from all parts of the province.

15–18 **as men . . . to aduersyte.** *Sal*: 'scilicet ignari humanarum rerum, quae fluxae et mobiles semper in aduorsa mutantur' [*Laet–BritT*, *AscT*, *BarcT omit* scilicet] (**104. 2**). Barclay's translation reflects a reading that many have accepted, taking Sallust to mean that things are constantly changing and always for the worse. Others see this as illogical, and favour a translation such as: 'namely men inexperienced in human affairs, which are unstable and fluctuating, and are always changing from one extreme of fortune to the other'.

Chapter 63

7–13 **Sylla anone . . . light in likewyse.** *Sal*: 'Is missus cum praesidio equitum atque [peditum] funditorum Balearum; praeterea iere sagittarii et cohors Paeligna cum uelitaribus armis, itineris properandi causa, neque his secus atque aliis armis aduorsum tela hostium, quod ea leuia sunt, muniti' (**105. 2**). *Laet–BritT* and *AscT*: 'Is missus cum præsidio equitum atque peditum: item [*Laet–BritT omit* item] funditorum et balistariorum [*Laet–BritT* (**1495.1**): balneatorum; (**1500**): balistariorum]. Præterea iere sagittarii: et cohors Peligna cum velitaribus armis itineris properandi causa: neque secus his atque aliis armis aduersum tela hostium quia ea leuia sunt muniti erant.' Both *Sold* and *Asc* explain that the Paelignians were a Latin people, but Barclay passes them over in silence.

9 **socours or defence.** Possibly this should read *socours of defence*.

22–3 **For why?** The text is punctuated thus in *BarcA B*. Perhaps *for why* was intended as a conjunction linking the clauses either side of it.

29–30 **Volux in his metyng . . . welcomed hym benyngely.** *Sal*: 'Volux adueniens quaestorem appellat' (**106. 1**). *Asc*: 'appellat .s. seorsum vocat et nominat questorem .s. Syllam' (f. 102^{v}).

30–1 **to mete the sayd Sylla for his honour/ socour/ and defence.** *Sal*: 'obuiam illis [*Laet–BritT*, *AscT*, *BarcT*: illi] simul et praesidio' (**106. 1**). *Asc*: 'obuiam illi: honorificentiæ videlicet gratia. et simul dicit se missum illi præsidio .i. ad præsidium et defensionem' (f. 102^{v}).

34–5 **all pale and quakynge.** *Sal*: 'incerto uoltu pauens' (**106. 2**). *Sold*: '¶Incerto .i. mobili et instabili uultu: quia in uultu colorem mutabat' (sig. p6^{r}).

37–8 **Sylla denyed that vtterly as fierse and bolde of courage.** Sylla absolutely refused, being a man of ferocity and courage. *Sal*: 'Ille animo feroci negat' (**106. 3**).

42–8 **¶If I knewe . . . lyue in shame cowardly.** Barclay converts Sallust's reported speech to direct address. *Sold* converts a few phrases also.

51–3 **to refresshe them . . . ouer all the place.** *Sal*: 'ac statim milites cenatos esse, in castris ignisque quam creberrumos fieri' (**106. 4**). Following punctuation in *AscT* (colon after *castris*), Barclay links *in castris* with *cenatos esse*, rather than with *ignis*. Sylla orders the soldiers to eat at once, and to build as many fires as possible within the camp.

59 **pytched his tentes.** *Sal*: 'castra metabatur' 'was laying out his fortified encampment' (**106. 5**).

60–1 **Iugurth had taken place to his tentes.** Jugurtha had encamped.

70 **neuerthelesse he defended the Maurian from damage.** *Sal*: 'tamen

ab iniuria Maurum prohibet' (**107. 1**). Cf. *Asc*: 'tamen prohibet .i. defendit Maurum .s. Volucem: ab iniuria' (f. 103ᵛ).

75–9 **and that it semed no man . . . naked and vnarmed.** *Sal*: 'nec [*Laet–BritT*, *AscT*, *BarcT*: neque] quemquam decere, qui manus armauerit, ab inermis [*Laet–BritT AscT*, *BarcT*: inermibus] pedibus auxilium petere, in maxumo metu nudum et caecum corpus ad hostis uortere' 'it was not fitting for any man bearing weapons in hand to seek aid from unarmed feet, or in time of great fear to turn the naked and blind part of his body towards the enemy' (**107. 1**). Barclay's last clause can perhaps be attributed to *Sold* paraphrase: 'O milites: non decet uirum armatum fugere: sed in maximo metu decet non solum armatum: sed etiam inerme corpus uertere contra hostes' (sig. p6ᵛ).

81 **and all his ydols.** Barclay's addition, where Sallust states that Sulla called upon Jupiter to witness. *Asc* explains that this is because Jupiter, as well as being the supreme god, is god of fidelity and hospitality: 'Deinde Sylla obtestatus .i. in testimonium vocans Iouem maximum .i. summum deorum: et qui fidelitatem et hospitalitatem curat' (f. 103ᵛ).

91–100 **But at conclusion said Volux . . . please you best.** A model for direct speech in place of Sallust's reported speech is found in *Sold*: 'O Sylla: Iugurtha magnam multitudinem non habet. Et totam spem suam habet in patre meo . . .' (sig. p6ᵛ).

Chapter 64

11 **for her father was borne of a concubyne.** *Sal*, *Laet–BritT*: 'nam pater eius ex concubina ortus erat' (**108. 1**); *AscT*, *BarcT*, *Laet–BritT* **1497/8**, Venice **1470.1** etc.: 'nam mater eius ex concubina orta erat'. *Sold*: 'mater' (sig. q1ʳ).

18–28 **And that Sylla . . . agaynst his gyles.** *Sal*: 'conloquio diem, locum, tempus ipse deligeret neu Iugurthae legatum pertimesceret; consulto sese omnia cum illo integra habere, quo res communis licentius gereretur; nam ab insidiis eius aliter caueri nequiuisse' (**108. 2**). *Laet–BritT*, *AscT*, *BarcT* (and MSS): '. . . deligeret: consulto sese omnia cum illo integra habere neu Iugurthæ legatum pertimesceret: quod eo aduocatus esset quo res communis licentius gereretur: nam ab insidiis eius aliter cauere nequiuisse'. Sallust's text and meaning are uncertain.

30 **it was vnderstande.** Sallust is more direct: 'ego comperior' (**108. 3**).

32 **after the credence of Affrycans.** *Sal*: 'Punica fide' (**108. 3**). Among the Romans 'Carthaginian faith' was a proverbial term for treachery. *Sold*: '¶Punica fide .i. ob Punicam fidem: uidelicet ut proderet uel Iugurtham Romanis: uel Syllam Iugurthæ. Nam fides Punica est: aliud promittere et aliud præstare. Nam Punici .i. Affri. ingenio mobiles sunt et infidi: raro uel

nunquam promissa seruantes. ¶Punica fide .i. mobili et fluxa [*later eds.*: ficta] fide: qualis est fides Afrorum' (sig. q1[r]).

52–5 **That answere . . . his knowlege.** Barclay's addition. The first clause is main, with inversion of subject *Aspere* and object *answere*.

Chapter 65

8–10 **And also Dabar . . . sayenges/ and sentences.** *Sal*: 'praeterea Dabar internuntius, sanctus uir et ex sententia ambobus' (**109. 4**). *Laet–BritT*, *AscT*, *BarcT*: 'sanctus vir iurat ex sententia ambobus' (MSS QD: iurat *for* uir et). Since interpreters have already been referred to, it seems more likely that Dabar's role is as intermediary or mediator, rather than translator. The phrase *ex sententia ambobus* means that both sides agreed to his role. Cf. *Sold*: '¶Dabar internuncius .i. interpres. ¶Sancte iurat ex sententia ambobus: iurat se fideliter interpretaturum' (sig. q1[v]). *Asc*: 'Præterea Dabar ille de genere Massinisse: vir sanctus .i. incorruptus: aut sanctus .i. sancitus et dictus ex sententia vtriusque: iurat ambobus ex sententia .i. quod eorum voluntas fideliter interpretaretur. vnde patet eum scisse Latine: forte quod in aula paterna cum pater esset socius Romani imperii etiam Latine loquebantur' (f. 104[v]).

13–14 **I the greattest kyng . . . them that I knowe.** *Sal*: 'ego . . . uti rex maxumus in hac terra et omnium, quos noui' (**110. 1**). Cf. *Asc*: 'ego rex maximus in hac terra et opulentissimus .i. ditissimus omnium quos noui' (f. 104[v]).

14–15 **shulde haue ben bonde . . . priuate person.** *Sal*: 'priuato homini gratiam deberem' (**110. 1**). 'That I should owe a debt of gratitude to a commoner.'

18–22 **But now syth . . . profet and pleasure.** *Sal*: 'Id imminutum, quod ceteri dolere solent, ego laetor; fuerit mihi eguisse aliquando pretium tuae amicitiae' (**110. 3**).

33–6 **Verely as I thynke . . . armes: than with lyberalite.** An emphatic repetition of the one statement. *Sal*: 'Nam, ut ego aestumo, regem armis quam munificentia uinci minus flagitiosum est' (**110. 5**). *Laet–BritT*, *AscT*, *BarcT*: 'Nam ut ego existimo, regem armis quam munificentia vinci minus flagitiosum.'

38 **procuratour.** Sal: 'curator' (**110.** 6). *Laet–BritT*, *AscT*, *BarcT*: 'curator'. Barclay echoes *Asc*, who (in error?) has *procurator* in his commentary: *Asc*: 'cuius procurator .i. vt dicam sollicitator et promotor' (f. 105[r]).

52–3 **but moderately and with fewe wordes.** 'Only a little.' *Sal*: 'breuiter et modice' (**111. 1**). *Sold*: '¶Modice: moderate' (sig. q2[r]).

53–4 **But towchyng the peace and besynesse concernyng the**

commen wayle. *Sal*: 'de pace et de communibus rebus' [*Laet–BritT*, *AscT*: de pace deque communibus rebus] (111. 1). Sallust means 'the common interests of Bocchus and the Romans' not 'the republic'. Barclay here follows *Sold*: '¶De pace et de omnibus .s. quæ ad rem publicam pertinebant' (sig. q2^r). *Laet–BritT* reads *communibus*, not *omnibus*.

56–69 **¶Kyng Bocchus . . . vnto you vnrequired.** Barclay's rendering of Sallust's indirect speech into direct speech follows *Sold* quite closely: 'O Bocche ego polliceor tibi quod senatus populusque Romanus non erunt ingrati: si tu eis aliquod beneficium præstiteris: quod magis ad illos pertinet quam ad me. Nam qui armis tecum certauerunt: et uicerunt: officio non uincentur. Hoc autem beneficium maximum eis præstare potes: si Iugurtham uidelicet eis tradideris. Hoc beneficio tibi plurimum debebunt. Et non erunt ingrati. Nam et amicitiam et fœdus et partem Numidiæ quam petis nunc: sponte tunc tibi concedunt' (sig. q2^r). *Sold* and Barclay do not fully render Sulla's point, that Bocchus must do more than end hostilities, which the Romans would have done by force anyway, and which only serves his own interests. To serve Roman interests he must go further, and deliver Jugurtha into Roman hands.

70–3 **¶Bocchus heryng . . . sworne bytwene them.** *Sal*: 'Rex primo negitare [*Laet–BritT*: agitare; *AscT*, *BarcT*: negare agitare]: cognationem, affinitatem, praeterea foedus interuenisse' (111. 2) 'At first the king refused, saying that ties of kinship and marriage were involved, and a treaty.' Jugurtha had married Bocchus' daughter (or as both Soldus and Ascensius have it, Bocchus had married Jugurtha's daughter; see note at 47/34). The nature of the blood ties between them is nowhere stated. Somewhat blurring Sallust's distinction between *affinitas* and *cognatio*, Barclay apparently takes *cognationem* to mean 'acquaintance' rather than 'kinship' despite *Asc*: 'cognationem quia ex eodem genere oriundi erant' (f. 105^v).

Chapter 66

5 **by the interpretacion of Dabar.** *Sal*: 'per Dabarem' (112. 1). *Asc*: 'per Dabarem .i. per interpretationem Dabaris' (f. 105^v).

34–8 **But this is playnly knowen . . . with themselfe repugnyng.** *Sal*: 'Sed plerumque regiae uoluntates ut uehementes sic mobiles, saepe ipsae sibi aduorsae' (113. 1). 'But commonly the desires of kings are as unstable as they are strong, and [the desires are] often contradictory.' Cf. *Asc*: 'sed voluntates regiæ .i. regum: vt .i. quemadmodum supple sunt vehementes plerumque .i. frequenter: sic supple sunt mobiles .i. inconstantes: et ipse .i. ipsemet voluntates regum sunt sæpe aduersæ .i. contrariæ sibi .s. ipsis: ita vt quod prius placuit postea displiceat' (f. 106^r).

50–5 **chaungyng oftentymes in countenaunce . . . secretes of his hert.**

The general sense is apparent, but the place of *aperynge forthwarde* in the syntax is problematic, and perhaps the passage requires emendation. Most modern editors give *Sal*: 'uoltu [corporis] et oculis pariter atque animo uarius; quae scilicet tacente ipso occulta pectoris patefecisse' (113. 3). However, *corporis* is probably a gloss, while Servius (*Aen.* 7. 251) proposed *uoltu et oculis*. Most early MSS read 'uultu corporis'; *Laet–BritT*: 'uultu colore ac metu'; *AscT*, *BarcT*: 'uultu colore ac motu corporis pariter atque animo uarius: quæ scilicet ipso tacente occulta pectoris oris immutatione patefecit'. *OED* provides one seemingly related citation: '?1504 W. Atkinson tr. *Ful Treat. Imytacyon Cryste* (Pynson) iii. lix, He wyll also apere forthwarde, and haue the syghte and experyens of many thynges by his outwarde senses.'

65–71 **And thus they proceded . . . their lurkyng places.** *Sal*: 'procedit in tumulum facillumum uisu insidiantibus' '[Bocchus and his party] proceeded to a mound in full sight of the ambushers' (113. 5).

72–5 **with many of his men . . . and all vnarmed.** *Sal*: 'cum plerisque necessariis suis inermis' (113. 6). *Sold*: '¶Eodem: in hunc tumulum Iugurtha cum paucis suis amicis uenit inermis: quia sic erat constitutum: ut omnes sine armis in colloquium uenirent' (sig. q3^{r}).

82–3 **whose hert was replenysshed and inuyroned/ with ioye inestymable.** Barclay's addition.

Chapter 67

4–11 **After that Iugurth . . . warre of Iugurth.** Barclay's addition.

22–3 **the one named Quyntus Scipyo/ the other Marcus Manlyus.** *Sal*: 'Q. Caepione et Cn. Manlio' (114. 1). *AscT*: 'Q. Cepione et C. Manlio'. *Laet–BritT*: 'P. Scipione et M. Manlio'. For the glosses on the names see note following. The early MSS are variously divided over *Caepione/ Scipione/Cipione* and *M[arco]/C[aio]*.

24–7 **In which both . . . .xl. thousande.** *Sal*: Per idem tempus aduorsum Gallos ab ducibus nostris Q. Caepione et Cn. Manlio male pugnatum (114. 1). *Sold*: 'Male pugnatum. hoc dicit quia. Qu. Seruilius Cepio consul et M. Manlius proconsul a Gallis Cimbris uicti prælio castrisque binis exuti sunt: militum millia octingenta occcisa: calonum et lixarum quadraginta millia' (sig. q3^{r}). *Asc*: 'Pugnatum autem fuerat male a Quinto Cepione: et Caio Manlio: vt in fine huius particulæ latius explicabo simulque de Iugurthæ exitu vitæ. Ordo autem est. Pugnatum est male .i.infœliciter et cum malo pugnantium per idem tempus .s. quo bellum Iugurthunum gerebatur in Numidia: ab ducibus nostris .i. Romanis .s. ab Quinto Cepione. et C. Manlio proconsulibus. Quidam autem legunt Publio Scipione: sed male. vnde Lucius Florus in Epitomatis Liuianis in lib. lxvij. Caius [*recte*

Marcus] Aurelius Scaurus fuso exercitu a Cimbris captus est: et cum in consilium ab iis vocatus deterreret eos ne alpes transirent Italiam petituri: eo quod diceret Romanos vinci minime posse: a Bolo rege [Boiorix] feroci iuuene occisus est. Ab iisdem hostibus Caius Manlius et Quintus Seruilius Cepio proconsules victi prelio: castrisque binis exuti sunt. Octoginta milia militum occisa calonum ac lixarum quadraginta milia. Secundum populi Romani iussionem Cepionis cuius temeritate clades accepta erat damnat bona publicata sunt. primoque post regem Tarquinium imperium ei abrogatum. In triumpho Caii Marij ductus ante currum eius Iugurtha cum duobus filiis: et in carcere necatus' (f. 106^{v}).

41–56 **great glorie and tryumphe . . . before his tyme.** There are various accounts of Marius' triumph, including that of Plutarch, *Marius* 12, which *Asc* cites. He summarizes Plutarch's account of Marius' entry into the Senate wearing his triumphal regalia, which caused great offence, and Barclay follows him in reporting this. *Asc* does not repeat Plutarch's account of how Jugurtha's gaolers roughly stripped him of his robes and gold earring (tearing off part of his ear lobe), prior to casting him into the pit of the Tullian prison, where he uttered his last words, 'Hercules! How cold this Roman bath is!' Plutarch does not mention captured elephants or other booty in his account. This detail, along with others following, including the reference to Marius' *golden chayre* (probably meaning chariot), the *foure whyte palfrayes*, and *sacrifyce with a bull vnto Iupyter* are commonplaces of the procedure in a triumph, and Barclay has perhaps included them from a source other than *Sal*, *Sold*, or *Asc*.

58–9 **From thens forth . . . resysted on Marius.** *Sal*: 'Et ea tempestate' 'and at that time' (**114. 4**). *Laet–BritT*: 'Ea tempestate'; *AscT*, *BarcT*: 'Ex ea tempestate'; *Sold*: 'Ex ea tempestate' (sig. q3^{r}). Although several early MSS have *ex* it makes no real sense.

Appendix III

13 **Virgil in Georgicis.** Virgil, *Georgics* 2. 37–8.

28–9 **dicta quasi . . . fiebant.** The fanciful etymology ('quod . . . fiebant') is taken from Varro *De lingua Latina* 5. 16. 3.

37–8 **ut Lucanus.** Cf. Lucan, *Pharsalia* 1. 295–6. The quotation 'Pertica . . . maniplos' is from Ovid, *Fasti* 3. 117.

GLOSSARY

The Glossary is designed for readers with some knowledge of late medieval or early Tudor English. It is selective, listing words no longer in use, words still in use whose spelling may provide difficulty, and words still in use whose sense in context is no longer current or is unusual in some way. Where a word may carry a current sense, in addition to a sense now obsolete, only examples of the latter are normally noted. Headwords are given according to the predominant text spelling, or that of particular citations, with some cross-referencing to or from modern or early-modern alternative forms where necessary. No attempt is made to gather all orthographic variants or complete inflexions. Chapter and line references are provided for three or four instances at least, where available. A complete Index of Proper Names follows the Glossary: references are by page number only.

Arrangement

Vocalic **i** and **y** are listed together (under **i** where initial, and alphabetically as **i** when medial or final); vocalic **u** and **v** are similarly treated as **u**. Consonantal **i** is treated as if **j**, consonantal **u** as v, and 'consonantal' **y** (as in 'yet') follows **w**.

Abbreviations

adj. (adjective), *adv.* (adverb), *comp.* (comparative), *conj.* (conjunction), *constr.* (construction), *fig.* (figurative), *gen.* (genitive), *impers.* (impersonal), *inf.* (infinitive), *interj.* (interjection), *intrans.* (intransitive), *lit.* (literal), *n.* (noun), *pa.* (past tense), *pa. p.* (past participle), *phr.* (phrase), *pl.* (plural), *ppl. adj.* (participial adjective), *prep.* (preposition), *pron.* (pronoun), *pr. p.* (present participle), *refl.* (reflexive), *sg.* (singular), *superl.* (superlative), *trans.* (transitive), *v.* (verb), *vbl. n.* (gerund or verbal noun)

Text sections coming before Barclay's numbered chapter one are indicated in Glossary references as follows: Cont (Table of Contents), Pref (Barclay's English Preface), LPref (Barclay's Latin Preface), Extr (Compendious Extract), Prol (Sallust's Prologue).

A

abasshed(de) *pa. p.* confused, confounded, discomfited 8/52, 16/68, 22/8, 25/71

abyde *v. intrans.* dwell, remain, stay 33/9; stand firm in defiance 63/44; **abode** *pa.* 35/73 dwelt, remained; *trans. inf.* face, encounter, withstand Extr/105; **abode** *pa.* endured 25/85, 56/67; **abyding** *pr. p.* awaiting 17/175, 48/10

abiect *adj.* worthless, of low status, cast out 10/106, 42/107; rejected, ineligible 51/29

abode *see* **abyde**

abrode *adv.* abroad, widely, at large 12/45, 27/36, 28/74

abrogate *v.* annul, cancel 18/12; **abrogate** *pa. p.* 26/40

abstinat *adj.* obstinate, determined, unrelenting(?) 13/76

abstract *pa. p.* drawn away, separated (from) 17/112, 27/29

abused *v. pa.* deceived, cheated; mocked, treated as a plaything Cont/222, 24/22, 64/2; *pa. p.* 22/75, 31/16

accept *pa. p. adj.* accepted, acceptable 14/32

ac(c)loyed *p. pa.* filled to satiety; overfilled; obstructed (by means of bribes) Cont/29, 9/3, 13/17, 17/4, 17/111

accloyeng v*bl. n.* filling up, overfilling 61/37

ac(c)ompanyed *v. pa.* accompanied, joined together (with), joined in (with) 10/76, 55/80; *reflex.* ~ **hymselfe with** united himself with 44/39; ~**ed themselfe togyder** gathered themselves together, formed a group 36/18

accusement *n.* accusation, the action of charging with an offence 23/59, 27/74, 50/187
acustomed *pa. p.* used habitually; frequented by customers 29/71
addressed *v. pa. refl.* ~ **hym(selfe)** directed his course (towards), set himself a course (of action) Cont/105, 29/36, 30/1, 42/74, 44/19; ~ **them** prepared themselves 44/97
admonest *v.* advise, exhort, counsel *pr.* 6/25; **admonysshed** *pa. p.* 59/4
adnexed v. *pa.* annexed 2/18
adnulled *pa. p.* annulled 7/35, 7/46
adradde *pa. p.* afraid, perturbed 25/49, 35/72
adv- *see also* **au-**, **av-**
aduert *v.* pay attention to, take note of, heed, consider Prol/143; **aduertyng** *pr. p.* 2/81, 17/101
aduertens *n.* notice, heed, attention, consideration Extr/201, 56/133
aduyse *v.* look at, view, observe, judge: **aduysing** *pr. p.* Prol/130, 2/65; **aduysedde** *pa.* 29/111, 32/30; **aduysed** *pa. p.* 26/24; *reflex.* consider, reflect 13/36, 33/10, 51/57
aduyse, auyse *n.* opinion, judgement 27/39, 33/43
a(d)uysement, aduisment *n.* the process of viewing or considering mentally; thought, consideration, reflection, deliberation Extr/34, Prol/116, 23/42, 53/115, 54/106; advice, counsel 16/84, 26/25
aferde *pa. p.* frightened Extr/160, 2/108
affection, -yon *n.* disposition, inclination ~ **vnto** Pref/4, ~ **agaynst** Pref/20, **cure and** ~ Prol/29 (*tr.* L. **cura**); affectation? 39/128
affinite, affinyte *n.* relationship by marriage Pref/160, 10/142, 47/35, 47/44, 65/71
affray *n.* attack, assault 8/45
af(f)rayed *pa. p.* (*adj.*) alarmed, afraid 24/17, 50/295, 51/73, 56/70, 57/109
after *prep.* according to, in accordance with 19/54, 31/14, 32/36; following (in time), consequent upon Cont/114, 38/39; behind Pref/135; ~ **that** as *conj. phr.* Cont/203
after *conj.* 2/18, 2/19, Extr/75
after *adv.* 34/63, 36/40, 44/91
after *adj.* next, following 54/124
agayn(e) *adv.* in return 37/15, 55/72, 55/75; again, once more 2/6, 7/60
agayne *prep.* against 60/5
agaynst *prep.* with respect to, in regard to Cont/38, Cont/103, Pref/21, Extr/24, 2/73, 10/29; against, in opposition to Cont/60, Cont/127, 6/67
alay *v.* 'allay', dilute, diminish, soften 17/29; **alayed** *pa.* 17/11; **alayd** *pa. p.* 14/20
alyenate *pa. p.* alienated, taken away, taken captive 29/107, 38/55
all *adv.* ~ **if, yf** although, even if Prol/77, 28/57, 33/12, 66/53
al(l)ow(e) *v.* approve, take as acceptable 26/25; **alowed** *pa.* praised, commended 14/29
a loufe *adv.* (*prep. phrase*) aloof, apart, at a distance 35/102
amased *ppl. adj.* confounded, thrown into confusion 25/71, 56/42, 56/161; distracted? overcome with wonder? 37/49
amasednes *n.* loss of self-possession through fear or distraction 37/53
ambassade *see* **embassade**
amyte, amite *n.* amity, friendship, friendly relations Cont/42, 4/14, 6/18, 10/17
amorous *adj.* loving, devoted (in non-physical sense) Pref/20
anenst *prep.* towards, as regards Extr/65, Pref/148 (B; **agaynst** A), 10/80 (B; **agaynst** A)
anon(e) *adv.* immediately after, as the next action or event Prol/24, 7/10; ~ **as** 66/76; ~ **after** 11/20, 12/45, 26/67; **somtyme . . . and** ~ 44/20, 57/156; **often tymes . . .** ~ 44/21
ap(p)arell, aparayle *n.* clothing, array 22/22; *abstract*: the work of fitly preparing for anything, preparation, array; *perhaps concrete*: objects provided for some purpose, material, requisites, apparatus 39/38, 44/43 (*tr.* L. **cultus**; *see note*); practices, customs (including dress?) 45/53 (*tr.* L. **cultus**); seemliness 61/26 (*tr.* L. **decor**)
aparelled *pa. p.* arrayed, clothed Pref/122
apartayne, apertayne *v.* ~ **to** belong to as a possession, right, or privilege 10/

10; **apertayneth** *pr. sg.* 15/60; **apartayned** *pa.* 56/21
apertenent *adj.* pertinent, appropriate Pref/53
apoynted *pa. p.* equipped, fitted out 26/14, 29/58; prepared 8/38
apoyn(t)ment *n.* agreement, pact 16/75, 17/123, 25/50, 26/49, 26/78
appelynge *vbl. n.* accusation 19/144 (A; **accusacion** in edns. B, C)
appendant *adj.* resultant, consequent 51/38
approbate *v.* formally approve 26/25
armour(e) *n.* armour; arms, weapons (*often tr.* L. *pl.* **arma**) 10/92, 25/102, 28/25, 31/55
army *n.* armed expedition 28/102
arragyng *pr. p.* raging, 42/109 (**arragyng** edn. A; **enragyng** edn. B, **enraging** edn. C); cf. **enrage, inrage** below, and *intrans.* **enrage** in *Saint George*
ascertayne *v.* inform, apprise, assure (someone) 19/10
asperance *see* **esperance**
assay *v.* put to the test Extr/39, 44/13; **assayed** *pa. p.* 42/11, 50/223
assemble *n.* assembly Extr/73
assystent *adj.* in attendance, present, accompanying 23/73
astonyed *pa. p.* astonished, astounded, stunned 43/48, 44/95, 56/158
attayne *n.* attainment Extr/201 (?, or *v.*)
attempt *v. trans.* tempt, try with temptations, entice 17/102; **attempted** *pa.* 25/57, 40/18; make an attempt on (by military force) *or* harass (*cf.* L. **temptare**) 34/63
attyse *v.* instigate, urge to a course of action 65/77; **attysed(de)** *pa.* allured, enticed Extr/165, 40/17; *pa. p.* 29/94; cf. *Saint George* 1762, *Ship of Fools* 240.20, etc.
auncetry *n.* ancestors, ancestry 10/24, 10/64, 39/92
auter *n.* altar Cont/162, Pref/65, 46/68
auenture *n.* that which happens, fate, fortune 25/89
auenture *v. trans.* take a chance with, risk 34/66; ~ **on** venture upon 52/53; **auentured** *pa.* 36/53; **auenturyng themselfe** *reflex.* 51/36
auenturous *adj.* willing to incur risk 51/35
auyse *see* **aduyse**
auysement *see* **aduysement**
auoyd(e), auoyed *v. trans.* repel, drive off(?) 31/26; remove 17/163, 28/94; **auoyded** *pa.* 50/284; disprove, refute 17/129; flee, depart 40/72; *intrans.* depart, leave, flee 34/53, 57/156, 66/48
auoyding *vbl. n.* avoidance, withdrawal, retreat 25/52
auowed *ppl. adj.* bound by a vow Pref/65

B

backway *n.* byway, roundabout route 25/48
banket(t) *n.* banquet, feast 40/86, 50/249, 50/272
bankettyng *vbl. n.* banqueting 50/265
barbarian, -yan *n.* barbarian, foreigner 56/125, 57/111, 61/32, 61/41
barbarike *adj.* barbaric (with reference to language) 12/75
barded *pa. p.* (*adj.*). armed or caparisoned with bards (plate armour, or protective or decorative studded leather or fabric) Pref/122
basse, base *adj.* low in the social scale 1/15, 43/54, 50/160
batayle, batell *n.* battle between forces (single encounter) Extr/97, 13/37; war, sustained period of conflict Extr/7, 1/3, 10/49, 17/103, 48/49 (*tr.* L. **bellum** *and synonyms*); an army or main division of an army 57/67; more specifically (usually called 'great' or 'main battle'), the main body of an army, as distinguished from the van, rear, or wings; **forwarde of the** ~ the van 29/56, 30/114
beedman *n. lit.* a man of prayer; petitioner; **your** ~: in 15th–16th c., the set term used to designate or subscribe oneself in addressing one's patron or superior Pref/158
before or *see* **or**
begyle *n.* guile, trickery 2/79? 38/8? (*see notes*; **gyle** in edns. B, C)
begynnyng *n.* a thing undertaken, enterprise (*cf.* L. **inceptum**) 34/68
behofe, behoue *n.* 'behoof', benefit, advantage 19/38, 27/47

behouable *adj.* useful, advantageous 51/34, 52/29, 54/27
bend(e) *n.* band, company Cont/195, 25/91, 30/29, 34/62
benynge *adj.* benign Pref/14
benyngely, benygnely *adv.* in a kindly manner, gently 6/68 (*tr.* L. **benigne**); generously 41/31 (*tr.* L. **benigne**)
beraue *v.* bereave, take away *inf.* 15/7, 15/23
besynes(se) *n.* anxiety, solicitude, distress, unease 2/59, 10/207, 19/179; diligence, industry, activity, eager devotion to a task 2/99, 14/81, 28/53; business, work, a task or duty (used both in *sg.* and *pl.*) Pref/12, Prol/27, 32/128, 50/283; more generally, affairs or matters (*tr.* L. **res**) 25/112, 26/7
bestowe *v.* give, bestow 56/85; **bestowed** *pa.* showed, manifested (? *see note*) 36/30
betyme *adv.* in good time 36/54
bycker *v.* fight 63/24
byckerynge, bykering *n.* fighting, exchange of blows 9/10, 54/214
bid *v.* offer: **bydde batayle agaynst** (set phrase) offer battle, challenge Pref/57; **badde** *pa.* asked? commanded? 48/57
byding place *n.* place of abode 12/41
bye *v.* buy Extr/158, 2/18
bylded *v. pa.* built 12/110; *pa. p.* 12/115, 45/33
blamyng *ppl. adj.* or *adv.* in an accusatory manner 46/51
blandyment *n. by-form of* **blandishment**; attractiveness, allure Pref/59
bondes *n. pl.* bounds, boundaries 12/10
bonde *adj.* slavish, servile 26/15
bonde *pa. p.* (*prob. of* **bind**) owing a debt (of gratitude) 65/14 (**bound** edn. B, **bound to** edn. C)
bondman *n.* slave 19/81
boost *v.* boast, brag 41/63; **boosted** *pa.* 39/122, 49/10; *refl.* ~ **me, myself, themselfe** 32/87, 50/160, 50/191
boostyng *ppl. adj.* boastful 49/13
bottel *n.* 'bottle'; leather vessel for carrying water 44/57, 53/84, 53/91
bowe *n.* bough, limb of a tree 32/47, 44/75, 54/113
bowge *n.* bag or bottle made of hide 53/84, 53/91, 53/97
braulyng *vbl. n.* noisy contention, quarrelling 17/10
breek *n.* 'break', gap, opening, bay 45/39, 45/41 (*tr.* L. **sinus**)
brefely *adv.* after a short space of time Prol/39
bremstone *n.* brimstone, sulphur 35/88
brent *v. pa.* burned 13/30, 44/146, 54/29; *pa. p.* burnt 12/165
brunt *n.* charge, attack, assault; **at the first** ~ 17/98 (perhaps literal, but tending to the *fig.* 'at first, in the beginning'); **first** ~ *lit.* 44/31, *fig.* 32/107
buckeler *n.* small shield 54/160
bulwark *n.* rampart, fortification 14/72, 44/126, 54/57, 57/34
burthen *n.* burden, load 44/54, 53/98, 54/162
but *conj.*, *adv.*, *prep.* **no more** ~ no more than 41/27; ~ **yf** unless 35/23, 39/80, 50/114; (strengthened by addition of **only**) 15/57, 17/116
by *prep.* (of extent of time) during, throughout 39/33; about, concerning 50/185
bypath *n.* side path, unfrequented back route 30/9

C

caduke *adj.* fleeting, transitory, perishable, corruptible Pref/128, Prol/48
cap(y)tayne *n.* usually refers to a general or supreme commander (*usu. tr.* L. **dux**) Extr/40, 1/16, 2/8, etc.; sometimes to a subordinate in command of a section of the army, centurion, cavalry officer 25/59, 32/41; *fig.* Prol/13
caryage *n.* transportation 44/54, 44/85; that which is carried, load, burden 53/98
cast *v.* cast Prol/89; *pa.* **kest in mynde** considered, pondered 10/20
cawme *adj.* calm 45/47
certes(se) *adv.* certes, assuredly 19/36, 19/140, 19/212
certify, certyfy *v.* inform reliably, make certain or sure (of a matter) 10/124, 14/49, 38/67
chafe *v.* vex, harass? 49/53 (*tr.* L. **exagitare**), 50/217 (*tr.* L. **agitare**, *see*

note); **chafedde** *pa. p.* vexed, inflamed, made hot of temper 27/71, 54/86 (*tr.* L. **aestuare**)
charged *pa. p.* aimed, directed 56/89; *pa.* ordered 53/83; *pa. p.* filled, loaded 51/10
chargeable *adj.* weighty, burdensome, troublesome 28/30
chaunce, chance *n.* chance, fortune, fate, that which befalls a person Extr/45, 10/220, 36/38, 41/5, 43/6 (*tr.* L. **casus**), 53/119, 54/85 (*tr.* L. **fortuna**); situation, turn of events 44/86
chefe *adj., n. elliptically for* the chief men, leaders 21/4 (*see note*)
chyualrie, chyualry *n.* soldiery, military art (*usu. tr.* L. **militia**) 2/17, 3/11, 29/67, 50/195; military resources, forces (*tr.* L. **opes**) 31/104
circumstaunce *n.* circumstantiality of detail, detailed or circuitous narration, circumlocution Prol/162
citezyn, citezin *n.* Roman citizen (L. **ciuis**) 34/22, 39/39, 41/79; inhabitant of any city or town 29/85, 41/40
clarionyst *n* player of clarion or trumpet 56/153
clemence *n.* clemency, mercy 17/148, 22/60
clere *adj.* distinguished, famous, illustrious Pref/34, Prol/15, Prol/65 (*tr.* L. **clarus**), 10/64
clymate *n.* a region of the earth (generally, rather than specifically as one of the belts of latitude) 12/7
cloke *n.* cloak, pretext, disguise 29/54, 40/51
cloking *n.* cloaking, concealment 11/36
coarted *v. pa.* constrained, pressed, urged 23/46; *pa. p.* 10/39; **coartynge** *pr. p.* restricting, repressing 28/92
cognysance, conysance *n.* 'cognizance', device or mark by which a person or company may be recognized; badge, crest, coat of arms; banner 41/37, 56/50
colour(e *n.* **vnder** ~ **(of)** under pretext (of) Extr/142, 39/83
combredde *ppl. adj.* obstructed 31/35
commen, commyn *v.* communicate, speak 64/43, 66/40; ~ **with** communicate, discuss, negotiate (with) 16/48, 58/17; ~ **of** speak about, discuss 18/7; **commyned** *pa. p.* 7/32
commen (common) wayle, -wele *n.* common weal, or common good 16/12, 17/159; commonwealth, body politic, state Pref/72, Pref/84, Prol/71, Prol/85 (*see note* Prol/70–1)
commenty, comment(i)e *n.* the plebeians, the body of the common people, commonalty, commons 5/5, 17/24, 18/27, 19/151, 22/30, 25/7
commodyte *n.* (esp. in *pl.*) advantage, benefit, profit Pref/52, Pref/76, 4/15, 50/303; valuable thing (or person) 4/15; suitability, usefulness 12/61; opportunity, convenient occasion 59/39
communed *v. pa.* talked about, discussed 39/48, 64/24; joined in common 55/80
commutacion *n.* change, exchange 12/62
compas(se) *n.* circumference, bound, circumscribed area; space, extent 12/140, 25/82, 34/54, 54/59
compasse *v.* go around, move about; **compasedde** *pa.* 30/37, (*tr.* L. **circumire**); **compased** *pa.* surrounded (*tr.* L. **circumvenire**) 35/66; ~ **about** surround 12/133; **compased about** *pa. p.* 2/77
compendyous *adj.* concise, succinct Cont/4, Extr/2
compendyouslie *adv.* briefly, concisely, comprehensively, summarily Pref/33
competent *adj.* fit, suitable 17/88
composicyon, composytion *n.* agreement, settlement, terms (of surrender) 25/118, 26/7, 38/4, 29/13
concours(e) *n.* coming together, assembling 39/120; running together, clash of hostile forces 44/31
condycion, -icyon *n.* provision, stipulation 46/57; *n. pl.* character, behaviour, morals 17/19, 19/45, 47/12, 50/236; *sg.* 50/7; position in life, rank Extr/199
condygne, condyng *adj.* deserved, merited Prol/73; *with reference to punishment* (the usual collocation in later usage) 23/65, 38/96 (edns. B, C)
condynglie, condygnely *adv.* worthily, fittingly, deservedly Pref/12, 19/58, 65/28
condyscended *v. pa.* ~ **to** acceded, agreed to Extr/124
confeterated *v. pa.* ~ **with** joined, allied (oneself) with 10/49 (**confederate** edns. B, C); cf. next

confyderate *pa. p.* **confyderate** confederated, joined 19/118, 65/73
confort *n.* aid, support, strengthening Extr/25, 2/68, 10/134
confort *v.* encourage, rally, embolden 49/49, 56/83; **conforted** *pa.* 44/88, 57/76
confortyng *vbl. n.* encouragement, exhortation 49/56
congruence *n.* **of** ~ by right or propriety, as is fitting or reasonable 7/35, 14/12
congruent *adj.* congruous, suitable, fitting Pref/25
congy *n.* authority, licence 43/11
congye *v.* release, give leave to go 3/7
conysance *see* **cognysance**
connyng *n.* knowledge, ability, skill, expertness 39/29, 55/30
conscience, -yence *n.* inward knowledge, inmost thought, internal conviction, conscience 22/10, 23/53, 50/183
conspyreth *v. pr. intrans.* (of one person) plots secretly, contrives 15/40 (*see note*); **conspyred treason** *pa. trans.* Cont/147, 42/1
consume *v. intrans.* be consumed, waste away, decay Prol/53
contemnyng *pr. p.* scorning, disdaining; 10/22; **contemned** *pa.* valued little 11/25; *pa. p.* Pref/40
contemplyng *vbl. n.* contemplation Prol/132
contrarely, -ily *adv.* on the contrary, in contrast Prol/45, 6/46, 10/48, 50/99
contumely *n.* insult, humiliation 36/44
contumelyous *adj.* (of words or actions) insulting, humiliating 13/43
conuenyent *adj.* suitable, fitting, consonant with the nature of Pref/7, Extr/110, 7/12, 16/7, 37/15; (of time) fit, proper 51/18
conuenyently *adv.* easily 33/9, 65/24; appropriately 55/14, 65/49
conuented *pa. p.* agreed, settled 66/16
conuersacyon, -tyon *n.* conduct, manner of living, manner of dealing with others Prol/160, 2/125, 14/32, 50/151
conuersant *adj.* ~ **with** constantly in company with (someone) 42/6, 64/8
coost, coste *n.* place, region 29/109, 33/40, 45/36, 56/32
corne *n.* grain, seed-crop 29/46, 53/55, 53/57, 53/86
corse *n.* corpse 37/23
counsel *n.* plan, purpose, intention 52/13, 53/53
counselhous *n.* house in which a council meets for deliberation; the senate-house (*tr.* L. **senatus**) 14/106, 15/51
counsellour *n.* consul, a consular (see *OED s.v.* **consular** *n.*) 16/22
course *v. intrans.* ride, gallop 36/62; **coursed** *pa.* 36/69
cours(e) *n.* running; **with full** ~ as fast as possible 56/116
courser *n.* war-horse, charger 57/152
coursly *adv.* quickly(?) 56/89
couenaunt *n.* covenant, agreement 17/167, 38/71
couerture *n.* covering, cladding 12/65
couetyse *n.* covetousness, greed, excessive desire Prol/147, 2/133, 12/126
cowarde *adj.* cowardly 31/86, 44/38, 50/150
cowardous(e) *adj.* cowardly Prol/23, 35/101, 42/36
craft *n.* trick, stratagem Prol/107, 17/56; plot, concealed plan 65/81; **for a** ~ on purpose; out of deceit, deceitfully(?) 39/126 (*tr.* L. **consulto**)
crafty *adj.* skilful, skilled 30/49, 55/66; skilfully constructed 50/210; cunning 11/36
crafty man *n.* craftsman, artisan 43/41
crakynge *pr. p.* ~ **of** boasting about 19/78
creat(e) *pa. p.* created, appointed Cont/97, 23/12, 24/4
credence *n.* belief: **give** ~ believe Pref/94, 15/20, 39/13; trustworthiness, credibility 12/35, 40/89, 64/32
crudelyte *n.* cruelty Pref/138
cure *n.* care, heed, concern Prol/29, Prol/70, 10/156, 41/12
curyosite *n.* delicacy, refinement of manners (carried to excess) 50/255
curyous *adj.* elaborate, intricate 50/261; (of a person) highly trained, elaborate in practice 50/251
curyously *adv.* carefully, elaborately, exquisitely 50/248

D

da(u)nger *n.* control, captivity 44/150, 66/28; reach, range (of an opponent) 7/

54, 52/50; **in ~ to** under the control of, under obligation to a lord or master 55/22
darkedde *pa. p.* darkened 37/22
dart *n.* light spear, javelin 2/44, 29/64, 31/99
debate *n.* strife, dissension, quarelling 1/27, 6/55, 11/40, 25/6
debateful *adj.* full of strife, contentious, factious 2/123 (*see note*), 11/35, 17/23, 45/9 (*tr.* L. **factiosus**); partisan?, influential? (*tr.* L. **factiosus**) 17/76 (*see note*)
defende *v.* forbid 10/181
defensyue *adj.* capable of being defended **places defensyues** 56/4 (*cf.* Fr. **places défensifs**)
degre(e) *n.* rank, class of society Pref/42, Extr/199, 39/89, 50/161
delate *v. trans.* dilate, expand, spread 2/10
delectacyon *n.* that which delights, a delight Pref/60, 27/8
delyberatyue *adj.* concerned with the discussion of a future course of action Cont/31, 10/1
delyciousnesse *n* delicacy, voluptuousness, fondness of delicacies 50/255 (~ **and curyosite** *tr.* L. **munditia**)
delyuer *adj.* nimble, agile 54/147
demeane, demene *v.* express, exhibit (sorrow or joy): **demened** *pa.* 24/34; **demeaned** *pa. p.* Cont/91; **demeanyng** *pr. p.* conducting, carrying out, employing 10/94, 13/56; *reflex.* **demeane themselfe** behave 30/60, **demeaned himselfe** *pa.* 14/37
demeanour(e) *n.* conduct, behaviour, way of living Extr/129, 2/52, 19/75, 55/47
demerites *n. pl.* deserts in a negative sense: qualities deserving blame or punishment; *or* sins, offences 22/34
demonstratyve *adj.* setting forth or describing with praise or censure (spec. rhetorical usage) Cont/176, 50/3
demurely *adv.* gravely 22/48
deny *v.* forbid 14/44; **denyed** *pa.* (*with following inf. v.*) refused (to do something) 41/26
dentyous *adj.* 'dainteous', dainty; costly, choice, excellent 50/249
departe *v. trans.* divide, partition, share out, distribute 7/66; **departed** *pa. p.* Extr/90; **departed company** 7/68; **depart themselfe** 34/37
departyng *vbl. n.* (act of) division, partition 23/23
dependant *adj.* descending, sloping (? *see note*) 12/14
depended *v. pa.* hung, remained 48/79; **depended** *pa. p.* suspended 25/86
deprauat *ppl. adj.* depraved, corrupted 11/24
derysion *n.* ridicule, mockery 19/22; deception? 25/44
desert *adj.* deserted, barren 30/18, 45/59
desyre *n.* request, petition 35/43, 39/96, 49/5
desire, desyre *v.* request, ask for 23/16, 39/90; ~ **hym** request of him 55/70, 55/71
desyrefull *adj.* full of desire, greedy 39/138
detect *v.* uncover, expose (something covered up or hidden); make known a person's guilt or crime; inform against, accuse 27/69 (*tr.* L. **patefacere**)
detracted *v. pa.* removed, deposed, supplanted (someone from authority) Cont/137, 39/2
detractyon *n.* deposition, removal, demotion 43/19
dette *n.* debt, obligation 55/77
dette *pa. p. adj.* due, owing 55/76
deuyse *n.* 'device'; inclination, desire; notion, thought, plan; something which preoccupies the mind 42/10, 42/60
devysour *n.* one who devises something 42/96
deuocyon, -tyon *n.* (in a secular sense) fidelity 19/93 (*tr.* L. **fides**); religious devotion 44/84
deuoyr(e) *n.* endeavour, effort; **do [one's]** ~ strive, do one's utmost 6/61, 10/14, 31/11, 35/68, 39/130
deuoyr *v. reflex.* ~ **vs** endeavour, attempt 4/11
dy *v.* die; **to ~ for it** wholeheartedly, as if one's life depended upon it 43/28 (*see note*)
dyffer *v. trans.* defer, put off 64/43
dygnite *n.* high status Pref/11, 3/21, 39/100

dilycately *adv.* 'delicately', sumptuously, luxuriously 50/229
dyrect *pa. p.* directed Extr/140, 4/1, 16/34
dyrection, dyreccion *n.* orderly arrangement or disposition of matters Cont/39, 11/2, 16/66, 16/79 (edns. B, C)
dysagreyng *ppl. adj.* not in agreement, out of harmony, incongruous Pref/48, 6/46
dysapoynted *pa. p.* thwarted in keeping an appointment 42/33; ~ **of** *pa. p.* frustrated in the expectation or desire of (some purpose) 26/47
dysare *n.* one who gambles with dice (with implication of dishonesty) 50/250
dyscerne *v.* mark out, show as distinct, divide 46/18
dyscessed *v. pa.* 'deceased', died 2/127
dysconfited *pa. p.* defeated 32/2
dysconfyture *n.* defeat Extr/176, 26/99
dysconfort *n.* discouragement, distress 24/19, 33/35
dyscourage *v. refl.* ~ **nat yourselfe** do not lose your courage 31/76
discouer, dyscouer *v.* expose, make known, reveal the identity of (someone) 22/38, 22/56
dyscression *n.* judgement, planning (*tr.* L. **consilium**] 31/58, 42/113, 63/6
dyscrete *adj.* judicious (with particular reference to speech or action), prudent 2/118, 10/8, 18/30, 38/76
dyscussing *pr. p.* ~ **of** settling, deciding 18/15
dysdayne *v.* think it beneath oneself (to do something) Pref/31; **ye dysdayned** *pa.* you were indignant, took offence 19/62
dysformed *pa. p.* marred, deformed, altered 10/65
dyshonest *v.* bring dishonour or disgrace upon 59/6; **dyshonested** *pa.* 50/274
dispyce, dyspise *v.* despise, scorn 50/108, 50/109; **dyspised** *pa.* 43/34; *pa. p.* **dyspised of** 13/44
dispraysing *vbl. n.* speaking ill of 55/85
dyssemuled *v. pa.* dissembled, feigned, pretended 53/74
dyssimulyng *vbl. n.* dissimulation 55/40
dyssimulate *adj.* false, feigned, pretended Prol/108
distayne *v.* stain, defile, dishonour 61/35; **distaynedde** *pa. p.* 50/157
dystincly *adv.* separately, one by one 27/99
dystract *pa. p.* distracted 16/39, 47/41
dystribued *v. pa.* distributed 53/80
dis-, dysworshyp *n.* dishonour 10/239, 18/25, 19/152, 31/85
dyuise *see* **deuyse**
dyuulgate *pa. p.* made public, divulged 8/50 (*tr.* L. **divulgare**)
do *v.* cause, instigate, command **dyd** *pa.* 31/8, 44/68; as *periphrastic aux.* 10/190, 19/30, 22/43, 43/26
dolour *n.* sorrow, distress 2/71, 37/29, 41/10
dolourous *adj.* distressing, causing grief 7/5
dougth *n.* doubt, suspicion 17/129
dout *n.* doubt, fear, apprehension 10/188, 56/11, 56/147
dout *v. trans.* fear, suspect, anticipate with apprehension 19/30, 40/60; **douted** *pa.* 26/82; be uncertain about 38/98, 40/68; *intrans.* be in doubt, waver, hesitate Pref//37, 38/62
doutfull *adj.* in fear, fearful 38/45; terrible, dreadful 40/76
downeryght *adj.* vertical 54/45, 56/107; outright, at once, without hesitation 54/32
drad *pa.* of **dread** 2/75; *pa. p.* **dradde** 2/104
draw *v. refl.* ~ **hym,** ~ **themselfe** go, proceed 8/5, 35/102; **drue hym** *pa.* 52/43, 54/23, 57/6
drede *n.* something to be dreaded, danger (*tr.* L. **formido**) 40/42; dread, fear 10/198, 16/37; (of something) 2/101, 64/37
dresse *v.* prepare, make ready 50/248; prepare, cook (food) 28/98
driue *v. intrans.* move quickly, hasten; *pa. refl.* **droue him forth** delayed, deferred, passed away time Extr/141; **droue forth the tyme** passed time, spent time 24/26
drue *see* **draw**
dubytacion *n.* state of doubt, uncertainty, hesitation 18/16
duety, duetie *n.* duty Pref/9; **of** ~ as of right, as of something owed 10/33, 50/137, 50/239

duke *n.* leader of an army, ruler of a people 1/7 (*tr.* L. **dux**)

E

edyfice *n.* room, apartment (*tr.* L. **ædis**) 8/33; building (*tr.* L. **aedificium**) 11/78, 13/30

effect *n.* with reference to a narrative: purport, drift, tenor, essential significance Cont/4, Extr/2, 14/22; outcome, conclusion Extr/113, 2/116, 7/58

egall *adj.* equal 33/12

elect *v. pa.* picked out, selected (in a general sense) 26/28; *pa. p.* 30/35; elected *pa.* 1/14; **elect** *pa. p.* Extr/139, 26/66

embassade, imbassade *n.* mission or function of an ambassador, statement or agreement delivered by an ambassadour 11/52, 14/7, 14/25, 29/34

embassadour(e) *n.* diplomatic officer, ambassadour 8/61, 10/26; military lieutenant (*tr.* L. **legatus**) 51/12, 51/45, 53/68

empareyled *v. pa.* equipped, arrayed 13/64

en- *prefix see also* **in-**

enbatayled *v. pa.* engaged in battle Extr/166

en-, inbold *v.* encourage, make bold Pref/17, 41/33, 50/49 (**enbolden** edn. C), 54/186, 57/91

encreased *pa. p.* grown (in bodily stature) Prol/52, 39/34

endamage, indammage *v.* damage, harm 5/14, 39/113

endeuo(y)red *v. pa. refl.* ~ **hymselfe** exerted himself 31/53; ~ **themselfe** 54/178

enduce *v.* (form of **induce**) induce, lead, persuade 22/21, 25/49; **enduced** *pa.* taught, instructed 47/14

endued *see* **indued**

endulled *pa. p.* made dull 39/146

engyn *see* **ingen**

en-, inrage *v. intrans.* fall into a rage, become or be angry or maddened; act in an enraged manner 53/19; **enraged** *pa.* 11/57, 39/109 (edns. B, C), 53/19, **inraged** 57/145

ensue *v. trans.* pursue, follow, accompany 33/46; *intrans.* **ensued by** *pa.* travelled in or near 34/55; *see also* **insue**

enuy *n.* hostility, enmity; displeasure, odium; envy (*often tr.* L. **inuidia**) 6/20, 9/36, 11/39, 17/143, 23/15, 34/33

enuyous *adj.* envious (in mod. sense), *or perh.* malicious Prol/110

enuyted *v. pa.* invited 40/48

enuyron *v.* surround, encircle 57/75; **inuyroned** *pa. p.* 10/149, 66/83, **enuyroned** 26/109

equall *adj.* equitable, just (*tr.* L. **æquus**) 50/43, 57/51

ere *v.* plough 53/57

escaled *v. pa.* scaled, climbed (by means of a ladder) 35/82 (*see note*)

eschue *v.* avoid, escape 44/109; **eschued** *pa. p.* 40/77

esperaunce, asperance *n.* hope, expectation 13/15, 25/87, 50/283

espy(e) *n.* the action of spying, reconnoitering; a spy, scout 29/7, 29/52, 32/13, 33/4, 53/50

espy *v.* watch for, spy out, look for 23/37; see, discover by spying, reconnoitre 34/56, **espyed** *pa.* 52/13, *pa. p.* 54/117

establysshe *v.* settle (something) finally or permanently 30/53 (*tr.* L. **confirmare**)

estate *n.* **the estates, thestates** the nobility (*tr.* L. **nobilitas**) 18/18, 27/3, 39/77, 43/25

euydently *adv.* with no possibility of mistake or misunderstanding, clearly, distinctly Extr/105, 20/12, 29/77

euylwyll *n.* ill will Prol/87, 9/37, 34/33

euylwyller *n.* one who wishes evil (of another) 19/48

exactour *n.* one who makes illegal or unjustifiable exactions; extortioner, oppressor Pref/68

exalted *pa. p.* raised, cheered (in mind, spirits) 41/33, 54/144

excecate *ppl. adj.* blind 1/28, 2/64

exchuyng *pr. p.* eschewing, avoiding 34/31

except *pa. p.* excepted 42/67

ex(c)ercyse *n.* state of being active, activity, exertion Prol/10, Prol/18, Prol/38

exercise, -cyse *v.* carry out, practise Prol/22, 32/138; *reflex.* exert oneself,

train oneself (mentally or physically) Pref/102, Pref/112
excourse *n.* the action of running out; an excursion or sally (for marauding) 13/32, 34/38
excusation *n.* condition of being excused Pref/53
expedycion *n.* speedy execution 14/16
expedyent *adj.* fit, proper, or suitable to the circumstances of the case Extr/110, 1/37, 24/7, 28/26
extremely *adv.* strongly, severely 18/28, 39/152
exulate *n.* exile 10/79, 10/134, 10/224
exulate *pa. p.* banished, exiled 10/160

F

facyon *n.* appearance, physical characteristics 45/48
fayne *v.* feign, pretend 10/197, 17/132, 24/17, 52/39
faynedly *adv.* under pretence, deceitfully 40/31
fayning *vbl. n.* feigning, pretending 55/39
fayntly *adv.* feignedly, by way of feint or pretence, deceitfully Prol/121; coldly, hesitantly 60/30
fayt *n.* feat Extr/202
fayth *n.* pledge, promise, assurance Extr/126, 20/8, 22/14, 38/69
fame *n.* public report, common talk, rumour 8/49, 23/29, 61/34
farforth *adv.* to a great extent, far 27/54
faruentnes *n.* fervour, heat 31/100
fatygate *ppl. adj.* wearied 7/26, 32/57, 35/4
faute *n.* lack, deficiency 14/34, 14/93; moral fault, failing Prol/26, 19/197
faute *v. intr.* be in need, be deprived 2/35
fautie, fauty *adj.* faulty, at fault, blameworthy 19/205, 22/10
fauour *n.* mercy, mitigation, lenience 40/55, 40/85
feared *v. pa.* frightened, put fear into 2/70; *pa. p.* **fered** 42/113
feare *n.* peril, terrifying situation (*tr.* L. **metus**) 25/72 (*see note*), 36/12, 40/68, 56/43
fearse *adj.* fierce 56/130
felde *n.* 'field' used of a military encampment 13/73, 48/9 (*see note*), 63/67
ferre *adv.* far Prol/104, 4/8, 8/6
festyng *pr. p.* inviting to a feast, or providing a feast for Prol/109
flod(de), flud(de) *n.* stream, river 12/171, 30/12, 30/96, 32/10
for that *conj.* because Prol/164, 28/39, 56/134
for why *conj.* for, because 6/11, 10/95, 28/61, 40/32, 63/23
forance *n.* (*pl.*) 'foreigns', foreigners 6/32
for asmoche as *conj. phr.* seeing that, because Extr/22, 2/36, 55/11
force *v.* **to ~ of** *intr.* to trouble oneself over, be concerned about, care about (something) Prol/16
foretyme *n.* former time; **in ~** 26/124, 29/41, 42/90, 53/64
forsoth(e) *adv.* truly, in truth Pref/137, 10/111, 15/49
forthynketh *v. pr. impers.* **it forthynketh** [someone] **of** [something]: (one) regrets 62/37
forthwarde *adv.* forward 63/32, publically, openly? 66/52 (*see note*)
forwarde *n.* van, body of soldiers in the forward formation 28/114, 29/56, 36/82, 41/46, 57/94
foteman *n.* foot-soldier Cont/128, 2/90, 29/64, 30/31
fountayn, fontayne *n.* naturally occurring spring of water 34/58, 53/32, 53/33, 54/52
frequentation *n.* the action of frequenting, visiting 45/57
froward *adv.* untowardly, badly 17/53
frowarde *adj.* perverse, bad, wicked Prol/21, Prol/57, 22/73, 57/28
frusshe *v.* batter, smash, break down 54/55
frustrate *pa. p.* frustrated, disappointed 54/69, 57/71, 66/17; useless, of no effect 2/116, 43/61
fulfyll *v.* refill, replenish, make good the gaps or what is lacking in something 26/29, 50/36, 51/48

G

garnyson *n.* garrison Cont/141, 14/71, 29/74, 35/26; guarding force 31/5
garnysshed *v. pa.* furnished, supplied,

equipped 67/7; *pa. p.* 50/259, 54/50, **garnisshedde** 35/63
generall *adv.* generally? 19/65 (*see note*)
gentyll *adj.* of noble birth or elevated rank; possessed of the qualities of one of noble birth 39/192, 50/102, 50/103
gest *see* **iest**
gyde *n.* guide Prol/13, 54/133, 54/155
gyle *n.* guile; plot, strategem, trick Extr/75, 2/74, 7/53, 10/103
glystering *pr. p.* glittering, shining Pref/126; **glystryng** *ppl. adj.* 17/105
glosedde *pa. p. adj.* glossed, polished 50/207
gostely *adj.* spiritual Pref/60
grauyte *n.* weight, influence, authority Pref/14, 16/17
grounde smothe *adj.* level with the ground 54/30

H

habounded *v. pa.* abounded, were plentiful 2/49
habunda(u)nce *n.* abundance, plenty 6/34, 17/114, 27/7
habundaunt *adj.* abundant 10/64
halfe hunder *n.* 'semi-century' (body of soldiers, originally fifty, later thirty) 53/82 (*tr.* L. **turma** 'body of thirty or thirty-two cavalrymen')
hand *n. in various phrases*: **at** ~ 57/62; **by** ~ 2/112; **in** ~ immediately(?), for the immediate purpose (covertly?) 11/68, 13/90, 17/56; in process, in the attempt, hastening? 13/75; in question, under consideration 42/50; **take in** ~ undertake, take up (a task) 44/48, 44/51; **out of** ~ immediately 10/232, 33/25; **redy of** ~ 2/82; **stode them in** ~ was needful for them 51/59; **stode it hym in hande** 57/96
happed *v. pa.* occurred by chance or accident 40/85 (~ edns. B, C; **happened** edn. A)
happy *adj.* blessed, fortunate 50/109, 50/290
harnes(se) *n.* armour, military equipment which is worn Pref/124, 16/89, 25/73, 28/25
haunted *v. pa.* practised or employed habitually 50/27
haut *adj.* 'haught', high, lofty, noble (in set phrase ~ **courage**) 2/110 (edns. B, C read **stout courage**)
haue *v.* perform, deliver (a speech-act) (cf. *OED* **have** sense 11); *pa. ppl.* **had** Cont/67, 19/1
hauen, hauyn towne *n.* town with a harbour, port 11/78, 14/100, 57/8
hauocke *n.* seizure of spoil, plunder Cont/189, 33/28, 41/62, 53/3
hede *n.* heed, care 37/39, 52/9, 53/115, 54/122
hede, heed *n.* head 8/27, 25/86; **of the first** ~ Prol/150 (*see note*), 39/26
hed(e)lynge, heedlyng *adv.* headlong 3/23; precipitately, impetuously 2/63, 39/59
hegth *n.* height Prol/52
herdel *n.* hurdle, fence, woven framework of rods or staves 44/117
here *v.* hear 10/191, 23/73, 32/80
hye *adj.* high, great Pref/1, Extr/117, Prol/128; ~ **voyce** loud voice 35/39, 57/101; ~ **tyme** due time 56/8
his *pron.* its Prol/4, Prol/57
hystore *n.* history, historical account Pref/77, Pref/118, Prol 141
hystoriagraph *n* historiographer, historian 55/18
holde *n.* stronghold, fortification 35/8, 35/11, 40/13
holden *pa. p.* held 19/85, 39/163
(w)hole *n.* **of (w)hole** wholly, fully Cont/82, 23/4
(w)hole *adj.* whole, entire 19/127, 65/30
(w)hole *adv.* wholly 19/39, 64/23
honest *adj* honoured, honourable, worthy Prol/75, 10/233
hor(r)ious *n.* horrible, horrifying? 37/21 (*see note*), 56/85
horsemeat *n.* food for horses, fodder (*tr.* L. **pabulum**) 34/40
horse trappers *n. pl.* defensive coverings for a horse made of metal or leather; decorative coverings with metal bosses 50/194 (*tr.* L. **phalerae** 'metal discs or bosses worn by horses, or soldiers; military prizes')
howbeit *adv.* however it may be, nevertheless, however 2/6, 17/146; *conj.* although 7/24, 12/28, 19/196, 22/70
hunder *n.* hundred, 'century' (body of

soldiers, originally one-hundred, later sixty) 53/82 (*see also* **halfe-hunder**)
hundred man *n.* centurion (? *see note*) 54/148

I

ylwyller *n.* one who wishes evil to another 6/21, 50/50
ylwillyng *ppl. adj.* unwilling, reluctant 57/28
ymagined *v. pa.* conceived in mind, planned, plotted, designed 14/84, 65/82; **ymagenedde** 42/8
imbassade *see* **embassade**
importune *adj.* pressing, persistent 40/27; troublesome, vexatious 54/73
importunely *adv.* persistently, pressingly 39/98
impossibylite *n.* impotence, inability Pref/10 (**impotence** in edns. B, C); (*cf.* med. L. **impossibilitas)**
inbatayled *v. pa.* joined battle 57/98
inbold *see* **enbold**
incommodyte *n.* disadvantage, difficulty 31/94
inconuenyence *n.* disagreement 26/94; that which is unfitting or improper 27/5, 28/103
inconuenyent *adj.* unsuitable, not fitting Pref/111
incorrupt *adj.* incapable of corruption, incorruptible Prol/54; *as prec. or perhaps* uncorrupted 50/254
incourse *n.* inrush, charge, assault 36/79
incrafty *adj.* unskilful, stupid 2/42
indammage *see* **endamage**
indyfferent *adj.* not different (in estimation) 25/85; equal 33/12, 46/57
indifferently, indyfferently *adv.* without bias or prejudice; impartially Prol/ 114, Extr/86, 28/13, 48/35, 50/87; on equal terms 31/110; without distinction 16/88
indyscrete *adj.* lacking sound judgement 19/216, 50/182
indued, endued *pa. p.* ~ **with** possessed of, endowed with 28/91, 39/40, 50/115
induryng *pr. p. intrans.* enduring, continuing 2/25; **induredde** *pa.* 37/8
inexpert *adj.* inexperienced 14/2, 16/16, 32/137, 50/76
inexpugnable *adj.* impregnable, unable to be captured or destroyed 54/227
infect *ppl. adj.* morally corrupt 23/74; stained, dyed, polluted (*tr.* L. **infectus**) 58/160
infected *pa. p.* corrupted morally 26/58
infectyon *n.* action of harming or injuring 19/15
infoldyng *pr. p.* surrounding? repeatedly turning or changing direction? 36/80 (*see note*)
ingen, engyn, ingynne *n.* engine; machine or device used in war 13/86, 14/82, 35/94, 44/140, 54/197
inhabytable *adj.* not habitable, uninhabitable 12/166
inhansed *v.* enhanced; magnified, increased 22/78
inioyned *pa. p.* 'enjoined'; specified, imposed Extr/88
iniust *adj.* unjust 2/131, 10/236, 13/13, 19/214
iniustly *adv.* unjustly Prol/121
inlesse *v.* decrease, lessen 57/84 (*om.* edns. B, C)
innocentie *n.* innocence 50/132
inquyet *adj.* restless, turbulent, troubled Prol/67
inquyeted *ppl. adj.* disturbed, disquieted 7/69
inrage *see* **enrage**
insomoche that *conj. or adv. phr.* to such an extent that, so that; accordingly Extr/51, Extr/152, 2/101, 7/52
instant *adj.* close at hand, impending, imminent 15/56, 25/75, 25/86, 63/42
insta(u)nce *n.* urgent request, urging, solicitation 28/31, 40/27, 49/5
institute *n.* purpose, design 12/144
instored *pa. p.* furnished, provided, filled 54/50
insue *v. trans.* follow, conform to 5/25, 47/15, **insuyng** *pr. p.* 12/178; **insuynge** *pr. p.* following (in time) 53/103; *intrans.* follow 14/108, 16/18
insufficyence *n.* (of a person) insufficiency, unfitness, incompetence Pref/17
insure *v.* assure 65/56
intendeth *v. pr.* ~ **to** aspires to, prefers Prol/14, 53/56
intentifely, -yfly *adv.* intently, with great attention 37/26, 56/133

intermell *v.* ~ **with** have to do with, concern oneself with, make contact with 25/47
intermyt *v.* 'entermete'; ~ **with** concern, occupy oneself with Pref/48
intermyxtion *n.* mixture, combination 32/141.
interprise *n.* enterprise, undertaking 35/16, 54/5, 54/134
intreat(e)ment *n.* discussion, negotiation 64/53, 66/45
inured *ppl. adj.* accustomed by habitual practice 13/21
inuade *v.* attack, assault 57/72; **inuaded** *pa.* 56/24, 66/78
inuasyue *adj.* pertaining to offensive or attack 13/86
inuasour *n.* invader Pref/151
inuent *pa. p.* invented 35/99
inuyron *see* **enuyron**
inuoulueth *v. pr.* surround, envelop, entangle 15/17; **inuolued** *pa. p.* 57/148
inuyed *v. pa.* envied 2/46
ieopardy *n.* danger 26/62, 27/44, 44/70, 63/77
ieopardous, ieoperdous *adj.* hazardous, fraught with danger Prol/22, Prol/111, 44/12
iest *n.* gesticulation, movement of the body or limbs 37/33 (edn. A; **iesture** edns. B, C)
iette *v.* strut, swagger, walk in an ostentatious manner; behave arrogantly 19/76 (*tr.* L. **incedere**)
iougler *n.* jester, buffoon, clown 50/250

K

kepar *n.* keeper, guardian 36/50, 41/55
kest *see* **cast**
kynde *n.* nature, natural disposition 2/60, 50/151
knyght *n.* knight, member of the equestrian order (originally Roman cavalrymen, but later wealthy landed gentry); the class between the Senators and the Plebeians 27/72, 39/175 (*tr.* L. **eques**)
knoleging *vbl. n.* recognition, calling to remembrance, acknowledgement 38/95
knowle(d)ge *v.* acknowledge Pref/9, 23/54, 26/86, 50/253

L

laboured *pa. p.* put to labour? 57/19 (*see note*)
ladder *n.* leather 53/91 (cf. **leddar**)
lade *v.* load (ship, beast of burden) 53/96; **laded** *pa.* Cont/179, *pa. p.* 12/124, 53/77; overloaded, oppressed 10/108
large *adj.* copious ~ **wordes** Prol/163; ~ **promesses** 13/16, ~ **promyses** 14/97
largely *adv.* (of speech, discourse) at length, fully 50/280
laud(e) *n.* praise Extr/49, 2/46, 11/26, 34/33; cause for praise(?) Pref/52, Pref/73, 58/6
laude *v.* praise Prol/99, 2/47, 3/9; *pa. p.* **lauded** 10/183
laudably *adv.* in a manner deserving praise Extr/146
leaned *v. pa.* ~ **to** inclined toward, supported 8/54, 13/40; **leanynge by** supporting oneself by means of (something) 54/114
leasour(e) *n.* leisure, freedom 17/150, 47/83, 54/119 (cf. **leser**)
leddar *n.* leather 53/85 (cf. **ladder**)
leed *n.* lead metal 35/79, 54/196, 56/87
leferre *comp. adj.* more agreeable, desirable 6/31 (cf. **leuer**)
lenger, -ar *comp. adv.* longer Extr/105, 42/99, 44/120
lese *v.* lose 19/129, 50/38
leser *n.* leisure 55/33 (cf. **leasour(e)**)
lessed *v. pa. trans.* lessened, decreased 13/51
let(te) *v.* prevent, hinder 19/16, 32/27, 39/96; *pa.* **letted** 32/34, 42/33; *pa.* **lette** 40/69; *pa. p.* **let** 36/53, 54/223, **lette** 32/47, 42/18, **letted** 12/58, 26/43, 40/72
lettyng *ppl. n.* hindrance 46/48
leuer *comp. adj. and adv.* **he/they had** ~, **wold** ~ he/they should prefer 42/52, 50/121, 64/48
ly *v.* ~ **on** tell lies about 50/185
lycence *n.* permission 14/51; *spec.* permission to depart 39/107, 43/13, ~ **and congy** 43/10
lycence *v.* give permission 3/7; **lycensed** *pa.* dismissed, gave leave to go (cf. Fr. **licencier**) 3/24
lycour *n.* liquid with medicinal or health-giving properties Pref/109

lyght *adj.* nimble, quick 54/147
lightly *adv.* swiftly 2/91, 36/72; easily 38/36, 54/168
lyke *n.* **in** ~ *adv.* alike 42/103, 50/220
lyke *v. impers.* suit, please **(it) lyketh you** *pr.* 15/60, 19/116; **it lykedde them** *pa.* 28/71
lymyte *v.* allot, apportion, delimit 7/67; **lymeted** *pa. p.* Extr/72; appointed to an office **lymited** *pa.* 26/22, 26/66
lymitacion *n.* allotment, apportioning, division 11/72
lyuelo(d)de *n.* livelihood, means of support Extr/22, 2/34
liuely *adj.* living, alive 53/78
long *v.* **it longeth . . . to** it belongs to, it is appropriate for or fitting that 10/68; ~ **to** belong to, pertain to 65/58; **longed to** *pa.* 15/40, 42/17; **longyng(e) to** *pr. p.* belonging to Prol/8, 27/41, 44/43
louer *n.* friend, well-wisher 42/77
loufe *see* **a loufe**
lucre *n.* monetary gain, profit 19/92, 25/59, 27/45
luminary *n.* source of illumination, guiding light 50/154

M

magnifycence *n.* sovereign bounty; greatness of reputation Pref/9, Pref/148
magnificent *adj.* noble, imposing, splendid Pref/3, Extr/53, 2/23; arrogant, proud, insolent 34/18
magnyficently *adv.* highly, in laudatory terms (*tr.* L. **magnifice**) 3/10, 7/8; well, manifestly? 11/19
mayntenar, -tayner *n.* one who aids, abets or supports (person or cause) Pref/71, 9/30, 22/31
maistres *n.* mistress, instructress Pref/78
maistry *n.* victory, upper hand 52/33; feat of strength or skill 26/61, 54/36, 54/103
manace *n.* 'menace', threat 16/62
manerly *adv.* decently, moderately 54/12
manhode *n.* manliness, courage, valour 2/14, 2/130, 6/19
mannes meate *n.* food for humans 34/40
marches(se), marchies *n. pl.* borders, frontier; 7/63, 13/26, 17/92, 46/18; adjacent place 44/62
march *v.* border upon: **marchynge on** *pr. p.* 9/12, **marched to** 50/21, **marched toward** 11/74; **marched nere** *pa. pl.* were situated near 12/88
marchandyse *n.* buying and selling of commodities for profit 12/58; commodities 12/73
marge *n.* margin Pref/31
marrayse *n.* or *adj.* marsh (if compounded with **grounde**) or marshy (if modifying **grounde**) 25/28
matched *v. pa.* ~ **with** opposed, fought 1/12
maugre *prep.* in spite of, notwithstanding 41/55, 49/11
mean(e) *adj* **in the** ~ **season** in the meantime 24/4, 25/57, 27/47; **in the** ~ **space** in the meantime 61/52
mean(e) *adj* small, unimportant 52/48, 54/42; **meane and priuate person** 65/14
mean(e) *n.* cf. present 'by means': **by** ~ **of** Prol/75, 12/59, 47/32; **by no** ~ 23/34
measure *n.* restraint, moderation, control 27/28, 47/52, 48/23
measure *v.* restrain, moderate, control 48/24; **mesured** *pa.* 28/104,
meke *v. reflex.* ~ **hymselfe** humble or abase himself 29/114 (added in edns. B, C)
men of garde *n. phr.* bodyguard 56/72
mercyall *adj.* martial, pertaining to warfare Pref/24, Pref/25
meridyonall *adj.* southern 30/13
mete *adj.* suitable, fitting 23/36, 43/12, 44/57
mynstrel *n.* musician 54/145, 56/153 (*see note*)
myr tree *n.* 'myrt-tree', myrtle 30/20
myschefe *n.* evil plight or condition (*tr.* L. **malum**): 39/77, 40/76, 40/90; affliction, calamity, ruin, defeat 30/55, 37/75; injurious action, crime 8/39, 10/100, 19/118, 63/67 (*tr.* L. **scelus**)
myscheuous *adj.* entailing mischief, harm or crime 8/11, 10/71, 21/6, 23/45
mysdemyng *pr. p. intrans.* mistrusting, being (justifiably) suspicious 29/56
mo *adj., n.* more 31/27, 32/136, 33/14;

other ~ others, more besides 17/112, 22/31, 29/111; ~ **lyke** similar 44/13
moch(e) *adv.* (qualifying a positive or uncompared *adj.*) very, greatly Pref/99, Prol/31, 1/8
moche *adj.* large, great 36/21, 39/5, 63/73
mocyon *n.* disturbance 22/40; proposal, prompting, suggestion 42/4; **of their owne** ~ 59/15
monycion, monicyon *n.* advice, warning Cont/20, Pref/82, Pref/85, 42/47
moost *v.* must 13/61, 15/54
mundayne *adj.* belonging to the mortal world Pref/59, Pref/120, 10/138
mutulate *pa. p. adj.* mutilated, hacked up 57/148

N

namely *adv.* especially Cont/42, Pref/67, Extr/201, Prol/63
natte *adv.* not 45/43
naturall *adj.* born in wedlock, legitimate (in contrast to present usage) Extr/67, 2/55, 5/18, 14/35
neded *v. pa. impers.* **hym neded** he needed 17/137
nedes *adv.* **wyll** ~ expressing insistence, determination 19/184, 50/185
nere hande *adv.* close, close by 24/18
nerely *adv.* closely 8/40, 8/43, 13/79
neuewe *n.* grandson 10/24, 10/59, 23/7, 39/142 (*tr.* L. **nepos**); nephew 4/7
newe *adj.* ~ **gentylman** (*tr.* L. **homo novus**) 2/120, 43/48, 50/100 (*see note* Prol/149–50)
newe *n.* **of** ~ newly, anew 13/18, 13/54, 14/60
neweltie, -y *n.* novelty, unusualness 29/22, 39/79, 50/108
newfangledde *adj.* over quick to take up new ideas, fickle 29/21
nyghly *adv.* closely 8/17 (*see note*)
nobles *n.* noblesse, nobility Prol/65, Prol/132, 39/47; strength, manly qualities? (*tr.* L. **virtus**) 5/8 (*see note*), 30/40
noyse *n.* report, rumour 56/82, 57/110
noysom *adj.* offensive, troublesome 19/90
none *adj. adv.* in place of **no** where following n. or adj. has initial vowel (e.g. *none ende*, *none other*) Extr/21, 7/36, 19/53, 25/75
nones, nonest *n.* **for the** ~ for the nonce, for the purpose, deliberately 39/126, 48/4, 54/46
norice *n.* nourice, nurse; *fig.* that which nourishes or encourages 53/48
norisshyng *vbl. n.* that which nourishes or nurtures 53/40
nother, nouther *conj.* neither 2/78, 12/174, 15/92, 28/47

O

obiect *v.* place in the way of, expose (to danger) Extr/38, 2/84; present or offer in discourse or argument, bring forward as a reason, ground, or instance, adduce 50/211; **obiectyng** *pr. p.* 10/196, **obiected** *pa.* 38/53, *pa. p.* 50/100,
oblacyon *n.* offering of a sacrifice 39/5
obscurely *adv.* **more** ~ **written** written in a style more difficult to understand Pref/33
obtest *v.* call upon (in the name of something sacred), beg earnestly, beseech, entreat (a person to do something) 6/27, 10/241, **obtested** *pa.* 36/42; call upon a deity as witness, invoke, appeal in confirmation of a statement **obtestyng** *pr. p.* 42/41
oc(c)upy *v.* make use of Prol/22, 44/83, 53/35, 65/26
of *prep.* by (expressing agency) Cont/87, 28/83, 38/83, 39/86
of *adv.* off 42/53
of newe *see* **newe**
often *adj.* frequent Pref/102, 10/53, 12/61; ~ **tymes** on many occasions, frequently Pref/5, 2/100, 20/4
onely *adv.* alone, as one person 41/66
ones *adv.* 'once', at some time in the future, one day 10/200, 10/204; **if . . .** ~ if ever 38/97
operatyon *n.* power to operate, force Prol/133
opynion *n.* expectation 2/94, 44/92, 52/5
oportune *adj.* fitted, suitable, serviceable 32/128; conveniently exposed; liable or open (*to* attack or injury) 13/23
optayne *v.* obtain 12/46; **optayneth** *pr. sg.* Prol/57; **optayned** *pa. p.* 6/37
or *adv.* in *conj. phrase* **before** ~ (i.e.

before ere) before, previous to the time when 10/41, 13/92, 16/48 (**or** omitted in edns. B and C); **first** ~ before 47/12

or *conj.* before 56/35; ~ **euer** before 65/15; *see also* **or** *adv.*

orbate *adj.* bereaved, destitute, without inheritance 2/34

ordayn(e), ordene *v.* ordain 9/21; set up, set in rows, put in order; furnish, equip **ordayned** *pa.* 32/95, 37/15; appoint (to an office) **ordayned** *pa. p.* 39/44, 40/46

ordyna(u)nce *n.* arrangement in ranks, battle array, army 31/14, 33/19, 56/51; preparation, provision, plan, strategy Cont/106, Extr/63, 34/10; decree, direction, order Extr/106, 17/53, 39/155; ordnance, military provision, equipment, or stores 28/26, 35/64, 38/104

orison *n.* speech, oration Cont/67, Cont/71, 19/1, 20/1 (**oracion** in edn. C), 50/1 (**oracion** in edn. C)

other *adv.* either (usually coordinate with **or**) Extr/154, 2/92, 7/58

otherlyke *adj.* similar Pref/110, Prol/84, 20/5, 26/90

ouer agaynst(e) *prep.* opposite 12/90–1, 31/112, 54/93–4

ouercome *v.* surpass, outdo 59/43 (*see note*)

ouercomer *n.* conqueror, victor 12/96, 46/25, 56/131, 58/7

ouerpasse *v.* pass over 6/12, 65/45; with reference to time or season (day, night, winter, summer) **ouerpassed** *pa. p.* Extr/150, 13/70; **ouerpassed** *pa.* overtook 30/9, 35/17

ouerthwart *prep.* across 30/27

ouerthwart *adv.* crosswise, across, transversely 36/80

P

pacyence *n.* timidity(?), hesitation(?) (*tr.* L. **mollitia**) 42/40, reticence (*tr.* L. **modestia**) 50/182

paction, -yon *n.* agreement, contract, settlement 26/77; **without any** ~ unconditionally 38/70

payne *n.* **in, vnder** ~ **of** cf. 'upon pain of'; i.e. followed by the penalty or consequence incurred in case of not fulfilling the command or condition stated Extr/117, 44/66

paynted *pa. p. adj.* coloured so as to make attractive, or to disguise or render false; feigned, false; ~ **wordes** 50/32, 50/207, **spech . . . payntedde (with rethoryke)** 50/177, 50/205

panym *n.* pagan, heathen 53/46

parauenture *adv.* peradventure, perhaps, possibly Pref/34, 63/46

parcell *n.* small group or party, detachment from a larger group (latter usually implied) 34/58

pardycion, -icyon *n.* perdition; destruction, damnation Pref/130, 29/100 (edn. A only)

pardon *v.* pardon, forgive 38/34; **pardoned** *pa. p.* granted, conceded by pardoning Extr/123; pardoned, released, exempted from duty or service 50/28

parforme *v.* complete, carry through Pref/12, 23/39; make up or supply (what is wanting) 26/29

parformyng *vbl. n.* fulfilment, satisfaction 22/45

paryll *n.* peril, danger Extr/38, 2/108, 17/86, 19/18

paryllous *adj.* dangerous 3/18

par-, perseuer *n.* persevere 3/19, 6/37, 39/12

partayninge *ppl. adj.* pertaining, associated 23/12 (edn. C; cf **appertayne**)

partie *n.* side in a battle 1/8, 9/8, 56/133

partyner *n.* partner Extr/14, 2/129; ~ **of** one who shares in (something) Extr/62, 10/83, 17/108

partyng(e) felawe *n.* partner 23/12, 25/10, 28/16, 42/96

pauase, pauayse *n.* pavise; large curved shield for covering the entire body, used for protection against missiles in siege warfare; Barclay uses the term for the larger mantlet or portable shed, used for a similar purpose 13/88, 25/35, 44/128, 54/63 (*tr.* L. **vinea** 'mantlet')

pendant *adj.* sloping 12/12 (*see note*); hanging from, attached to (something) 30/18 (*or another instance of n.* **pendent**? *see note*)

pendant, -ent *n.* slope (of a hill) 30/27, 30/67
pentyse *n.* canopy, shed, mantlet, protective structure 44/123, 44/128
penury *n.* lack, scarcity 14/91, 30/23, 34/59
performe *see* **parforme**
perplexite *see* **prolexite**
peticapytayn *n.* junior officer; tribune, one of the six senior officers in a legion (*tr.* L **tribunus**) 57/14
pyke *n.* sharp point 14/63; 'pike', spear 29/64, 35/87
pyll *v.* plunder, pillage, despoil 28/48; **pylled** *pa. p.* 27/32
plagge *n.* region, district 51/50
playne *adj.* level, flat 25/28, 35/60; ~ **feld** open battle 33/16, 52/33; ~ **batayle** 35/6
plummette *n.* lump of lead (or other metal) used as a missile 30/84, 35/79, 56/87
polycie, policy *n.* acumen, experience in a general sense Pref/149, 30/2; political acumen, experience Cont/48, 14/2; political cunning (often in a bad sense) 40/12, 61/38; trick, strategem, plot 25/43, 35/6, 42/8; system, method, practice 44/75; rational thought, reasonableness 32/90; **for** ~ deliberately, purposely 37/44
polle *n.* pole? 35/88 (*see note*)
ponder *v.* judge, appraise 50/70; **pondered togyder** *pa.* compared, weighed one thing against another 29/101
pourge *see* **purge**
pray *n.* prey, spoils, booty 2/70, 10/101, 44/135, *pl.* **praies, prayes** 13/29, 13/59, 27/46, 28/76; the action of taking spoils 32/113, 33/28, 34/47
prayes *n.* praise 50/3
prease *n.* press, crowd 35/91, 54/194
prease *v.* press 35/55
precessour *n.* predecessor 34/19 (**predecesso(u)r** in edns. B, C)
prefixed *pa. p.* (a time) fixed in advance 7/65, 42/22, 54/152; decided or determined ahead of time 25/74
pregna(u)nt *adj. fig.* full, loaded (of wit or intelligence) 2/106, 17/84
premysses *n. pl.* the premisses; the matters stated previously, the aforesaid Pref/110, Prol/114, 26/91
presydent *n.* one who presides, guardian Pref/78
pretaxed *pa. p.* (of money, payment) estimated, fixed beforehand 51/25
pretend *v.* portend, presage, foreshadow Prol/82 (*tr.* L. **portendere**), **pretended** *pa.* 40/41 (*tr.* L. **ostendere**); **pretended to** *pa.* (*tr.* L. **intendere**) pointed to, indicated 39/68; **pretendyng** *pr. p.* displaying, showing 17/97
preuent *v.* come before, outdo, surpass Prol/150; act before, in anticipation of, or in preparation for 15/26, 52/13, 65/31; **preuented** *pa.* arrived ahead of, came before (in time or place) 30/9, *pa. p.* 42/86
prince *n.* one of high status, leader, commander Pref/3, Prol/95, Prol/124, 16/22
priuate *ppl. adj.* deprived, dispossessed Extr/21, 39/146; not kingly, common, ordinary (citizen, individual) 65/14 (*tr.* L. **priuatus homo**)
priue *adj.* privy; intimate, familiar 54/19; **priuest** *superl.* most secret 53/107
probyte *n.* honesty, integrity 10/35, 39/28
proces(se) *n.* course of a narrative, treatise, or argument; drift, tenor, gist Cont/4, Extr/3, 1/1, 7/7; course, lapse (of time) 2/55, 12/109, 12/137
procuratour *n.* officer, agent (*tr.* L. **curator**) 65/38
prodycion *n.* treachery, treason 13/19, 40/43; betrayal 29/94, 52/47, 66/59
profe *n.* proof, trial 29/20, 59/45; **put in** ~ test, try, probe 40/23, 54/131
profound *adj.* deep (ditch, trench, channel) 14/61, 44/116, 45/41
prolexite *n.* prolixity, delay, slowness of action (**perplexite** in edns. B, C) 18/12 (*see note*)
prolonged *v. pa. intrans.* delayed, tarried 44/25; *trans.* delayed, kept waiting 24/14
prolonging *vbl. n.* action of delaying 16/59
prorogation *n.* extension in time (of authority) 38/112

protectour *n.* ~ **of the soudyours** military tribune 39/44 (*see note*), 39/49
proue *v.* try out, test 29/75; **proued** *pa.* 12/60, 31/93; tempted 14/76, 40/18
prouyde *v.* prepare 23/31; pay attention to, look to 10/230 (*see note*), 36/12; **prouyded** *pa.* took foresight, care 56/102; *pa. p.* foreseen 53/120
prouydence *n.* foresight, prudence, caution 2/108
prouydent *adj.* fore-sighted, prudent, cautious 17/85, 31/90, 57/22
prouyson, -sion, -cion *n.* (prudent) foresight, preparation, plan; action of preparing Cont/199, Extr/164, 35/16, 48/7, 52/13, 54/20
prouocatyue *n.* that which incites appetite or lust 53/40
prouoke *v.* invoke, incite, urge 53/42, 58/21; **prouokedde** *pa. p.* 29/110, **prouoked** *pa.* 47/21
prouost *n.* one who presides over or superintends something Prol/154 (*see note*), 40/47 (*see note*)
punysshe *n.* punishment, penalty 43/35
purgation *n.* the action of clearing oneself from the accusation or suspicion of crime or guilt 17/143
purge, pourge *v.* clear (oneself) from an accusation of crime 23/61, 41/69 (*tr.* L. **expurgare se**)
purpose *v.* propose, intend (to do something) Prol/96, 1/3, 55/25; *ppl. adj.* **mater purposed** Prol/166, **purposed mater** 12/177
purueyance *n.* provision, supply 29/85

Q

quadrat *adj.* in square formation, with a guard at front and rear, and on both sides (*tr.* L. **quadratus**) 57/12
quelled *pa. p.* slain, killed 37/20
quellar *n.* killer 37/19
quycke, quicke *adj.* alive, living 12/155, 29/30, 38/36, 46/59
quyet, quiet *adj.* quiet, at rest, inactive 30/98, 31/90; free from mental turmoil 10/85, 10/94, 32/17; (of things, or a state of affairs) undisturbed 40/21
quyetnes(se) *n.* stability, tranquillity 10/121, 40/36

R

radicate *adj.* rooted, firmly seated Pref/16
rapynous *adj.* given to rapine, rapacious 10/146
rathest *adv.* soonest, most readily 10/133
reaue *v.* ~ **away** take away 50/217; **reauynge** *pr. p.* robbing, plundering 27/28 (*intrans.*)
rebuke *n.* shame, disgrace 10/234, 19/129, 28/84
reconforteth *v. pr.* relieves, consoles Pref/17; **reconforted** *pa.* inspired, strengthened 31/89, 32/121, 57/138
recorde *v.* ~ . . . **to** (someone): tell, report 63/95
recounted *pa. p.* regarded, considered as possessing a certain character or quality 34/25
redeme *v.* ~ **of** buy, purchase (from) 25/21; **redemed of** *pa.* 17/115
refrayne *v.* restrain 48/24; **refrayned** *pa.* 11/42, 42/94; **refrayned** *pa.* reined back, reined in (a horse) 36/35
regression *n.* return to a subject 12/177
remytted *v. pa.* reduced, relaxed, ceased from 37/25; *pa. p.* sent back, released 17/128
ren *v.* run 25/101, 52/23; **renne** *inf.* 31/81, 53/113; **rennynge upon** *pr. p.* running at, attacking 22/72
renouate *pa. p.* renewed 6/20
renowmed *ppl. adj.* renowned Pref/29, Prol/35
reparacyon *n.* supply?, maintenance? 28/30
repent *v. impers.* **it repenteth them** 19/75, **it** ~ **of** 62/37; *reflex.* **to repent you** 50/190
replycation *n.* reply, answer Cont/225, 65/2
report *v.* refer to, *esp.* for information 12/35 (*OED* II.9.b); **reported by** *pa p.* reported about? 6/63
reprouable *adj.* blameworthy, reprehensible 50/149, 65/33
repugnant *adj.* opposed, contradictory 66/38 (edns. B, C)
repugnaunce *n.* resistance, opposition 17/15
repugnyng *ppl. adj.* contrary, opposed 66/38

requyre *v.* request 6/27, 9/14, 10/40; **requyred** *pa.* 11/16; ~ **(of) hym** ask, request one (for something) Extr/160, ~ **of me** 19/135
rereward(e) *n.* the part of an army stationed behind the main body; the third division in a force drawn up for battle (cf. **rear-guard**) 28/115, 29/59, 30/113
rescous *n. sg.* rescue, assistance 32/28, 33/54, 47/75
reserued *pa. p.* as *prep.* with the exception of, except, save 29/92
resysted *v. pa.* resided, rested 67/59
rethorike *adj.* rhetorical 50/210
reuolue *v.* turn over, search through, study, or read (a book, or the works of an author) **reuolued** *pa.* Pref/22; **reuloue in mynde** ponder, reflect upon Pref/6, **reuolued** ~ *pa.* 2/58, **reuoulued** ~ 9/19
rew *v. impers.* **it reweth . . . me** I am sorry, I regret Prol/164
richesse, rychesse *n. (pl.?)* 'richesse', or 'riches' Cont/188, 19/150, 27/7, 38/57
rydde *v. pa.* killed, destroyed 33/25
rightwyse *adj.* righteous Pref/71, Pref/114, 27/86
ryghtwysly *adv.* righteously Prol/78
roberies *n. pl.* plundered objects, booty 28/79
rote *n.* root 50/172, 54/166
roted *pa. p.* rooted 50/65
rouer *n.* robber, pirate 56/49
rouyng *vbl. n.* raiding, plundering, piracy 53/75
rowme *n.* 'realm' (*or poss.* 'room'): domain, office, sphere of influence Cont/85, Extr/152, Prol/69, 24/3; position 7/23; **rowmes and dwelling places** 12/71 (*tr.* L. **oppida**)
rumour *n.* outcry, noise, din 23/29, 26/122, 56/82

S

sacyate *pa. p.* satiated, satisfied Prol/139
sadnes(se) *n.* seriousness 55/81; seriousness of mind 10/112; steadfastness, constancy? (in phrase rendering L. **probitas**) 39/28
satellyte *n.* attendant upon a dignitary, forming part of his retinue and employed to execute his orders. Often with negative connotation, implying subserviency or unscrupulousness in the service 8/32
satyre *adj.* ~ **lawe** 17/156 (*see note*)
sauegard(e) *n.* (guarantee of) safety, safe-conduct 20/7, 23/49, 32/65
sauely *adv.* safely 17/128, 63/98
sauoure *n.* smell, aroma, odour 28/67
scolyon *n.* menial, kitchen-hand, servant 28/71, 28/99
scoutwatch *n.* action of keeping guard and watch 57/32
season *n.* non-specific period of time Extr/133, 6/47, 18/29; point in time 2/86, 9/41; *see also* **mean** ~
sect *n.* faction, party, body of followers 17/111 (*tr.* L. **factio**)
seen *ppl. adj.* versed (in some art or science) 55/30 (*tr.* L. **eruditus**)
self(e) *adj.* **one** ~ one and the same 47/54, 66/43
semblable *adj.* similar, of similar kind Prol/44
semblant *n.* appearance, demeanour, countenance (with implication that appearance is misleading) 40/50
seme *v.* beseem, be fitting for, be suitable to, befit; **me semeth** *pr.* 50/316; **it semeth you** *pr.* 6/52, 10/156; **whom it semeth** *pr.* 19/30, **whom it semed** *pa.* 10/219
send(e) *v. pa.* sent Cont/100, 13/41, *pa. p.* 13/94, 14/2
sentence, sentens *n.* way of thinking, opinion 54/140, 65/38; the thought or meaning expressed, as distinguished from the wording 65/7, 65/10; the sense, substance, or gist of a piece of writing Cont/15, 3/27, 14/107
seriatly *adv.* in succession, seriatim 27/98
seruyable *adj.* obedient, willing to serve 10/14, 50/10
shape *n.* (excellence of) form Prol/42
shed *pa. p.* scattered, dispersed 56/123
sherched *v. pa.* searched 42/104; *pa. p.* 63/90
shet(te) *pa. p.* shut 40/71, 40/83
shyft *n.* available means of effecting some end, option for acting 33/42
shyfted *v. pa.* ~ **so for himselfe** so provided for his interests 26/117

shyrle *adv.* shrilly 56/154
shytte *pa. tense* of **shut** 41/42
shortly *adv.* without delay, quickly, immediately 22/38, 36/49
sydelinges *adv.* sideways, obliquely 36/80
siege *n.* seat (*esp.* one used by a person of authority or distinction) 39/148
sygyng *vbl. n.* action of besieging, siege 25/53
signyfiaunce *n.* that which is signified or signalled, significance 47/17
symplenesse *n.* lowly condition, humble status Pref/7, Pref/10
syngular, -er *adj.* beyond the ordinary in amount, extent, or value; special, particular Prol/106, 10/189, 49/5; individual 3/15
syngulerly *adv.* individually, one by one 30/38
sith(e), syth *conj.* since, because Prol/63, 10, 26, 10/34, 50/187
syth *prep.* since Pref/98, 59/12
sleuth *n.* sloth, laziness 50/310
slyme *n.* soft mud, sediment (*tr.* L. **limus**) 45/46
socour *v.* aid, assist Extr/110, 11/32; **socoured** *pa.* 56/76; *pa. p.* 31/100
socour(s) *n. sg.* (*final* -**s** *apprehended as the plural suffix*) military assistance in men or supplies, reinforcements Pref/56, 2/88, 14/70; aid, assistance (more generally) Extr/83, 32/53, 35/12, 56/27; **socour(s)** refuge, shelter 31/6, 55/102
sonder *adj.*, *adv.* **in** ~ asunder, apart, separately 8/3, 14/51, 29/32
sore *adv.* sorely, seriously, gravely, intensely Extr/34, 2/71, 7/5
soudiour, -your *n.* soldier 13/71, 15/91, 25/114
space *n.* extent of time 44/30; **in the mean(e)** ~ 49/15, 54/209, 61/52
spearman, spereman *n.* cavalry soldier Cont/129, 36/79, 36/87, 57/128
spoyle *v.* plunder, rob 34/39; **spoyled** *pa.* 19/63; *pa. p.* Extr/80, 10/78
spoyling, -yng *vbl. n.* the action of plunder, theft 19/194, 33/50, 53/117; that which is taken as booty 49/12, 50/45, 54/223
spoused *pa. p.* joined in marriage, married 47/34
springing, sprynging *ppl. adj.* sprouting, growing Prol/50, 50/170
stale *v. pa.* 'stole', came or went stealthily 25/67, 36/6, 36/68
stand *v.* ~ **(someone) in hand** *see* **hand**
standerd *n.* military standard 28/118; *perhaps metonymy for* body of soldiers (cf. L. **signum**) 30/85, 35/47
state *n.* nobleman, person of standing (*cf.* **estate**) 1/12; status, condition, rank, position 7/9
stately *adj.* arrogant, haughty, proud 26/123, 39/76, 49/8
statelynesse *n.* haughtiness, arrogance 7/15
steryng *pr. p.* stirring 54/102
styll *adj.* silent; (hold oneself ~) **helde hym** ~ 22/66
styll *adv.* quietly 19/62
stypend *n.* the pay of a soldier 39/157
stocke *n.* family, kin group Cont/80, 4/17, 23/14, 50/125
strayet *adj.* narrow 54/43, 54/61
strayetnes(se) *n.* narrowness 54/64, 54/72
straytly *adv.* closely, narrowly, tightly 14/19
strange *adj.* foreign 28/33, 28/80, 29/72
streat *adj.* strait, narrow 25/48 (*cf.* **strayet**)
stryken *pa. p.* struck Extr/169, 31/19, 41/71; **stricked** 37/37
strype *n.* blow or stroke with a weapon 9/10
subget(te) *n.* subject 7/85, 42/103; bonded servant, slave, 40/17, 54/204
subget(te) *pa. p.* subjected, subjugated 19/28, 19/85, 26/51, 38/14
submyt *ppl. adj.* under a rule or control Pref/65
subsidy *n.* aid, assistance 29/61, 30/81, 51/49
subuercyon *n.* overthrow, ruin 1/24
suerty, surete *n.* surety, assurance of safety 10/108, 22/6, 45/16; person liable in the default of another 38/27
suff(e)raunce *n.* allowance, opportunity 19/175, 44/97, 59/35
suffisance *n.* satisfaction, contentment 47/52
suffrage *n.* prayer (usually for intercession) 34/21
superscripcyon *n.* heading (of a

document); address or direction on a letter 42/72

sure *adj.* safe, secure Prol/75, 10/115, 12/15

suspectyon *n.* suspicion 2/81, 64/26

sustayned *v. pa.* resisted, withstood 56/67

T

tabernacle *n.* tent (*tr.* L. **tabernaculum**) 42/70

tary *n.* tarrying, delay 31/67, 38/83, 39/170, 58/15

tary *v. intrans.* delay, wait, remain 9/29; **taryeng** *pr. p.* 24/6; **taryed** *pa.* 44/25, 56/21; *trans.* **taryed** *pa.* awaited, waited for 48/16

tastyng *pr. p.* trying, testing 29/23

tedyous *adj.* disagreeable, painful Pref/36, Prol/164, 56/93

temerous *n.* timorous, fearful 31/86

tempest(i)ous, -yous *adj.* tempestuous, stormy 12/56, 27/64, 45/45, 56/149

tent *n.* in the *pl.* freq. used to denote a Roman (or Numidian) military fortified camp 28/65, 31/80, 36/1; frame, protective cover for siege work 54/199

tenure *n.* tenor, meaning, substance 3/27

testify *v. trans.* attest, prove, demonstrate Pref/8

thentent *n.* the intent(ion) Extr/156, 1/36, 5/13, 42/81

therfore *adv.* for that reason, on that account 6/52, 8/38, 65/75

thiniures *n. pl.* the injuries 10/187

thynk *v. impers.* it seems to (me/him) **me thynketh** *pr.* 11/83, 46/6, **me thynke** 12/116; **hym thought** *pa.* 17/88, 51/15

thytherto *adv.* until then, until that time 36/45

thone *n.* the one 10/130

tylman *n.* farmer, peasant, tiller of soil 12/64, 29/39; soldier's servant (*tr.* L. **calo**) 67/27

tymely *adv.* quickly 14/15, 39/100

tyran(ne) *n.* tyrant, usurper of power, unjust ruler Pref/28, Pref/75, 15/27, 59/7

tytle, tytell *n.* entitlement, justification 47/61; *as prec.*, *or* assertion of right? claim? 27/86

token *n.* omen, portent 39/10, 39/14; sign, signal 40/53, 41/49

tong *n.* tongue, language Pref/37, 48/24, 57/107

trayne *n.* treachery, guile, deceit 10/103 (edns. B, C; **gyles** edn. A)

trayterously *adv.* treacherously 41/65

transpose *v.* transfer Prol/26, 19/104; **transposed** *pa. p.* turned upside down? used for a different purpose? 12/66 (edn. A; **transuerse** edns. B, C)

transuersed *pa. p.* turned upside down 12/66 (edns. B, C)

trapped *pa. p.* adorned (with **trappers**) Pref/123

trapper *see* **horse trapper**

treat *v.* ~ **of** discuss 7/11; negotiate, plan, arrange 17/122, 56/2, 66/21

treaterous *adj.* traitorous, treacherous 38/38

treatour(e) *n.* traitor 8/32, 35/22, 38/20

trenched *pa. p.* cut, sliced, severed 8/27

trene *adj.* wooden 44/60

treuth *see* **trueth**

trewes, truesse, truys *n.* truce Extr/169, Extr/176, 46/27, 62/13; **trues** 17/137 (treated as a plural)

trymbled *v. pa.* trembled 67/29

trowne *n.* throne, raised platform Prol/128 (**trone** edns. B, C)

trueth, treuth *n.* fidelity 11/70, 44/23, 60/15

trust *n.* hope, expectation 14/89, 19/182

trust *v. with inf. or noun clause* have confidence, hope 17/78, 39/17; **trusted** *pa.* Extr/155, 9/24

turme *n.* a troop of horsemen (usually thirty or thirty-two) 25/91 (*tr.* L. **turma**)

U

vnas(s)ayed *ppl. adj.* untried, untested 14/75, 40/22

vnauysed *ppl. adj.* ill-advised, thoughtless, irrational, unplanned 22/41, 31/59, 39/155

vnbehouefull *adj.* not profitable or useful, unnecessary ~ **and vnexpedyent** (*tr.* L. **importunum**) Prol/79

vnboldnesse *n.* cowardice 50/292 (*see note*)

vnclenly *adj.* impure, sordid 50/247

vncrafty *adj.* unskilled (with reference to military prowess) 28/46, 30/50, 32/86

vncraftynes(s)e *n.* lack of skill, inexperience, ineffectiveness 50/109, 50/286, 56/141
vnculpable *adj.* free from blame 50/278
vncustomed *ppl. adj.* unknown, unfamiliar 54/170; ~ **to** unaccustomed to 26/7
vndercaptayne, -capten *n.* captain, commander subordinate to another Cont/121, 25/59, 29/58
vnderstande *pa. p.* understood 64/30
vnderstandyng *vbl. n.* meaning, sense 65/8
vndyscrete *adj.* indiscreet, injudicious, without sound judgement Prol/123
vndyscretely *adv.* imprudently, with lack of judgement Extr/152
vneared *ppl. adj.* unploughed, untilled 53/17
vnexpedyent *adj.* not fitting, not proper Prol/80
vnexpert *adj.* inexperienced Extr/33, 2/55, 25/78
vnexpertnes *n.* inexperience Extr/159
vnfaynedly *adv.* Cont/101, 29/2, 29/13
vngentyll *adj.* not of noble birth; not possessed of the qualities associated with noble birth 50/103
vngoodly *adj.* wrongful, evil 19/31, 21/6, 50/209
vngoodly *adv.* badly, wrongly, wrongfully 19/23, 39/190
vnhappely *adv.* badly, evilly (*tr.* L. **male**) 19/176
vnhappy *adj.* luckless, ill-starred 10/134, 38/100, 59/7
vnkynde *adj.* severe, cruel; *or* unnatural, contrary to nature 1/23, 10/125, 19/189
vnmesurable *adj.* lacking in moderation, uncontrolled 22/32, 27/84; immense 30/19, 54/54
vnmete *adj.* improper 39/89
vnnoblenes *n.* state of not being noble or noble-born 43/22
vnouercome *ppl. adj.* not overcome, undefeated 19/161, 28/39
vnprouyded(de) *ppl. adj.* unprepared 51/72, 52/14; unforeseen 10/154, 36/11, 40/68, 44/100
vnquyet *adj.* restless, turbulent, troubled Prol/68 (*cf.* **inquyet**)
vnre(a)sonable *adj.* not possessed of human reason 12/39; irrational 1/28
vnrefrenable *adj.* unable to be curbed 7/56
vnrequired *ppl. adj.* without being demanded 65/69
vnreuenged *pa.p.* unavenged 19/24, unpunished 36/48, 41/61
vnrightwyse *adj.* wrong, wicked, dishonest 50/164
vnryghtwysly *adv.* wrongly, dishonestly Prol/76
vnstablenesse *n.* instability Cont/209, 42/41, 52/41, 60/1
vnstedfastnes *n.* tendency not to remain in one location 52/26
vnwardly *adv.* (*cf.* **unwarly**) 10/98 (edn. A; **vnwarely** edns. B, C), 25/70 (edn. A; **vnwarly** edns. B, C)
vnware *n.* **of** ~ unexpectedly, unawares 32/30, 36/6; **of vnwars** 33/48
vnware *adj.* unwary, incautious, negligent 57/10
vnware *adv.* incautiously 23/42 (*see note*)
vnwarly *adv.* unexpectedly 13/72
vnwont *ppl. adj.* unwonted, unusual, unexpected 25/71, 44/95
vnyed *pa. p.* united 27/35
vpset downe upside down 12/66
vsed *v. pa. refl.* ~ **hymselfe** conducted or comported himself Cont/168, 48/1
vtterly *adv.* in short (*tr.* L. **prorsus**) 18/25, 40/21

V

vayne *adj.* false, lying, dissimulating 61/30 (*tr.* L. **vanus**)
valyantyse *n.* bravery, valour Pref/150, 2/17, 17/97
valour *n.* material value 17/104; strength, (human or moral) value 39/163, 47/36, 50/14
vantgarde *n.* vanguard 57/18
varya(u)nce *n.* dissension, disagreement, discord, conflict 26/101, 26/126, 45/35
vehement *adj.* (of positive thoughts, feelings) extremely strong, ardent, eager, passionate Pref/4
venyson *n.* flesh of any beast taken in hunting 53/39
vertu(e) *n.* excellence, strength, courage

Prol/7 (*see note*), 39/72, 50/114, 51/64; merit 50/206; moral virtue Pref/55
vertues *adj.* virtuous 17/81
very *adj.* true Pref/62, Prol/153, 12/34, 23/52; sheer, neither more nor less than (something); exactly that specified 36/32; actual 29/106
viage, vyage, voyage *n.* 'voyage', expedition 21/16; military expedition or enterprise; a march against an enemy Extr/153, 17/78, 28/102
vysage *n.* the face, with reference to the form or proportions of the features Prol/42
vitel, vytell, vytayl *n.* (often *pl.*) victuals, provisions of food and necessaries of life 14/93, 17/49, 29/87
volage brayned *adj.* foolish, fickle, inconstant 38/105
volt *n.* vault 54/190
voluntary *n.* volition, free will 65/16
voluptuosyte *n.* voluptuosity, the state of being voluptous; love of sensual gratification 27/7, 28/91, 50/265
voluptuous *adj.* luxuriously sensual 26/59, 50/141, 50/272
voluptuousnes *n.* sensuality, inclination to luxury 55/34
volued *v. pa.* turned over (in the mind) 38/98

W

wayet *v.* 'wait'; watch out for (something) 23/38
wayle *n.* 'weal'; wealth, prosperity, well-being Pref/105 (*cf.* **commen wayle**)
warde *n.* guard, custody 17/127; duty of guarding, watch, defence 36/8, 36/65
ware *adj.* prudent, watchful, careful 17/85, 27/14, 34/30, 34/31
warke *n.* work, labour Pref/12, 35/61; written work, book 1/3
warnedde *pa. p.* informed, notified 39/58
watchyng *vbl. n.* watch, guard-duty 55/82; state of remaining awake 56/146
waterlagger *n.* one who carries water for sale 28/99
wawes *n. pl.* waves 45/46 (**waues** edns. B, C)
wayes *n. pl.* paths, routes, direction of a journey 23/37, 28/107, 30/5
weder *n.* adverse weather, storm 46/42
weyght *n. see* **wyght**
weldeth *v. pr.* wields, rules Prol/55
wenyng *pr. p.* 'weening'; expecting, thinking possible or likely 50/145
what *pron., n., conj.* ~ **by** *as coordinate pair*: by both . . . and 5/19–20, 12/86–7, 30/73; ~ **for** *as coord. pair* 25/30–1 (*tr.* **et . . . et**), 38/37–8, 39/107 (*tr.* **cum . . . tum** *constr.*); **what tyme** *conj. phrase* when Extr/31, 2/7, 8/21, 10/103–4
whether *interrog. adv.* 'whither', where to 10/133
whether *adv., conj. see* **whither**
which *pron.* who, whom 10/147, 10/208, 11/6
whyther *adj.* which of two (in indirect questions or clauses of similar meaning) 31/63, 50/107
whither, whyther, whether *adv. conj.* 'whether' (in indirect questions or clauses of similar meaning) 17/66; *as coord. pair* 10/228–30; as an interrogative particle introducing the second of two direct questions 10/171
whole *see* **hole**
whom *pron.* (*with inanimate antecedent*) which 12/146, 48/75, 56/103, 59/39
wyght *n.* (eds. B C; **weyght** A) *see note* 17/104
wyght *adj.* brave, bold, strong, vigorous 14/74
wighty *adj.* weighty 50/79
will, wyll *v.* wish, desire (*as main v. taking an object or introducing a subord. clause*); *pa.* **wold(e)** 22/36, 22/55, 64/48
wyntredde *v. pa.* encamped for the winter 42/27
wynt(e)ring place *n.* place where the winter is spent; winter camp 38/75, 57/7, 61/27
wyse *n.* way, manner, mode Prol/36, 1/18, 2/99
withall *adv.* moreover, in addition 10/142, 50/20, 61/41
without *conj.* unless 19/153, 19/155, 22/12, 55/72
womanly *adv.* like a woman 47/27
wont *pa. p. adj.* accustomed, customary Extr/15, Prol/130, 14/81; ~**with** accustomed to 57/47
worshypfull *adj.* worthy of honour, reputable Prol/159, Prol/161, 14/29

worshypfully *adv.* honourably, respectfully 11/63
worshyppe *n.* honour, reputation, high status Prol/90, 2/102, 19/20, 19/93
worshyppe *v.* treat with honour or respect 3/13, 6/59; **worshypped** *pa. p.* 40/40
worth *n.* **take in good** ~ take willingly, be content with 50/200
worthy *adj.* honourable, worthy Prol/45, 1/37, 2/105; deserved, merited by default or wrong-doing 23/65, 38/96

Y

yelde *v.* yield, give, surrender 16/3, 16/75; ~ **up** give up, surrender (something) Cont/101, Extr/122, 29/2; *refl.* retreat, give ground(?) 31/47
yerth *n.* earth Pref/62
yerth(e)ly *adj.* earthly Pref/128, Pref/139
yongh *n.* youth, young age 2/66 (poss. a misspelling of **yongth**)
yongth *n.* youth, state of being young (*tr.* L. **pueritia**) Extr/33, 44/44

INDEX OF PROPER NAMES

References to Proper Names are by page number.